DESIGNING FIT-FOR-PURPOSE ORGANISATIONS

A comprehensive, integrated route map

ENDORSEMENTS

What makes this book so significant is the elegant straddling of the science of organisation design with some examples of the application of the principles, as well as the provision of some very practical templates and process steps.

With all books of this nature, the question must be asked for whom is it really written? There are at least two specific users of this book, namely:

- senior executive grappling with the strategic challenge of enterprise architecture and organisation design to ensure they have a broad and deep enough "mental model"; and

- executive level consultants providing organisation design services to enterprises to ensure they have a broad and deep enough "mental model", as well as the toolsets to translate their thinking into actionable recommendations.

Over the decades I have had the privilege of knowing Theo and working with him, he has in my mind always been the one individual who could really be looked upon as a real "guru" with respect to organisation design. In this, his latest book, he again demonstrates his scientific (and academic) excellence in this very complex field of enterprise value generation.

Dr Anton Verwey, Executive Chair, inavit iQ (Pty) Ltd

This book is a gift; a jewel in the Organisational Design Landscape. It is relevant, timely, practical and grounded. In this extraordinary book, Theo Veldsman marshals his extensive experience, his profound passion and his wealth of rigorous research, and translates them into practical tools, tips, guidelines and templates on how to best design fit-for-purpose organisations that will unleash the potential of organisations to be fit-for purpose in the context of an emerging new order. He challenges us to radically rethink the shape, purpose, intent and impact of our organisations so that they deliver on their strategy, remain competitive, perform optimally and get the right people on the bus in the key seats, while remaining relevant and agile now and into the future. Organisational Design is a mission critical discipline and key executive leadership task. No business leader should miss this read if they want to be ahead of the curve on how to design fit-for-purpose organisations.

Professor Shirley Zinn, Non-Executive Director of Boards

A future-fit contribution to the design of large organisations. With his focus on purpose appropriacy, Veldsman emphasises systemic design consciousness in an elegant, expansive contribution to how organisations migrate themselves to a preferred future state. His circumspect approach embraces strategic, horizontal, vertical and lateral dimensions of design, and will enlighten the most senior of organisational architects.

Dr Morné Mostert, Director. Institute for Futures Research, Stellenbosch University

In this book, Veldsman masterfully deals with the topic of designing organisations that are not only fit-for-purpose, but because this innate organisational ability is deeply wired into the DNA of the social system, organisations in effect will be fit for the future and therefore sustainable. This book is an important contribution in a time when contextual intelligence and the adaptive ability of organisations is critical for survival; when employees need hope and purpose more than ever; and when leaders need to construct spaces where the true intent of the systems that they lead not only provide the glue for collective performance, but weave together human energy around a commonly shared purpose. Not only does the book makes a practical leadership contribution, but it also highlights the fact that organisational design is a discipline and an art, which is often diluted by the integration of this function into organisational effectiveness or Human Resources. This book is a must read for all leaders and practitioners.

Dr Rica Viljoen, Managing Director, Mandala Consulting

The changing world of work and talent necessitates a different way of organising a company. As a result, finding the right design for your company is one of the Executive team's most important tasks. And given the current global dynamics, it has become even more important to design companies to be agile and responsive to external factors. This book offers the reader a framework to guide organisational design that accounts for the evolving workplace and skills required.

Paul Norman, Group Chief Human Resources Officer, MTN

First published in 2019.

ISBN: 978-1-86922-770-8
eISBN: 978-1-86922-771-5

Published by KR Publishing
P O Box 3954
Randburg
2125

Republic of South Africa

Tel: (011) 706-6009
Fax: (011) 706-1127
E-mail: orders@knowres.co.za
Website: www.kr.co.za

Typesetting, layout and design: Cia Joubert, cia@knowres.co.za
Cover design: Cia Joubert, cia@knowres.co.za
Editing & proofreading: Jennifer Renton, jenniferrenton@live.co.za
Project management: Cia Joubert, cia@knowres.co.za
Index created with TExtract/www.Texyz.com

DESIGNING
FIT-FOR-PURPOSE
ORGANISATIONS

A comprehensive, integrated route map

by

THEO H. VELDSMAN

kr
publishing

2019

ACKNOWLEDGEMENTS

The book was conceived and written by one, but inspired, enabled, and supported by many:

- To my family for your unconditional love, patience, and encouragement during my physical and mental absence when I was grappling with the protracted birth of the book. Especially to Annie, my wife, who had to bear the full brunt of my absence in her every day presence. Also for the 'hundreds' of litres of tea and coffee she made to lubricate the painful birth of the book. But, also to Talita with Lawrence, and Dieter with Zani, our children, as well as our granddaughter, Arianna, and our grandson, Lawrence, who is still on the way. To my dearest Mother for her unbounded love, support and interest over so many years.

- Wilhelm Crous, the Managing Director of Knowres, for trusting that the book would eventually appear and that it would meet your expectations regarding what so glowingly was promised.

- Cia Joubert and your Technical Team for making the book a reality.

- Esthea Conradie, for your excellent research support and doing many of the figures in the book.

- My colleagues, Wynand Geldenhuys, Angela McKay, Clive Smit and the late Kent McNamara, for the mutual learning, fun, and joint achievement of great things, whilst working together to providing design solutions to clients.

- My clients, for the privilege of being of service to you in meeting your design needs over so many years, and gaining invaluable insights at the meeting point of concept and practice.

- Those professionals I had the privilege to train in Organisational Design, who helped me tremendously in making Organisational Design understandable to them and myself.

- To my esteemed colleagues, Anton Verwey and Andre Parker, for their invaluable comments on the manuscript.

- Praise to God, our Heavenly Father, in Jesus Christ, for all His grace and blessings.

SHORT TABLE OF CONTENTS

EXTENDED TABLE OF CONTENTS

ABOUT THE AUTHOR

Prof Theo H Veldsman

Theo, who is regarded as a thought leader in South Africa with respect to people management and the psychology of work, Over many years he has demonstrated his ability to proactively identify emerging people and leadership needs and arrive at fit-for-purpose, innovative solutions that are theoretically and practically sound.

Theo holds a PhD in Industrial Psychology and is a registered Industrial Psychologist and Research Psychologist and accredited HRM Practitioner. He prefers to call himself a Work Psychologist.

He has extensive research and development, as well as consulting experience gained over the past 35 years in strategy formulation and implementation; strategic organisational change; organisational (re) design; team building; leadership/management and strategic people/talent management. He consults with many leading South African companies as well as organisations overseas, in the roles of advisor, expert and coach/mentor.

In addition to being the author of nearly 200 technical/consulting reports/articles, he has done numerous management and professional presentations and attended seminars at a national and international level. He is the author of two books, and has contributed seventeen book chapters. He co-edited a book on leadership, *Leadership: Perspectives from the frontline* with Andrew Johnson.

Up to the end of 2016, when he retired, he was Professor and Head of the Department of Industrial Psychology and People Management, Faculty of Management, University of Johannesburg. Since the beginning of 2017 he is a Visiting Professor at the same Department. He is Extra-ordinary Professor at the University of Stellenbosch Business School. He has led the profession of Psychology and Industrial Psychology nationally as president on several occasions. He has been awarded fellowship status by the Society of Industrial and Organisational Psychology of South Africa (SIOPSA), and is the 2012 recipient of a Life-Long Achievement Award from the South African Board for People Practices (SABPP). In 2016 the Department of Industrial Psychology and People Management presented him with a Life Long Achievement Award.

1

SETTING THE SCENE

The journey we are embarking on

"Would you tell me please, which way I ought to go from here?"
"That depends a good deal where you want to get to," said the Cat.
"I don't much care where," said Alice.
"Then it doesn't matter which way you go," said the Cat.

(Lewis Carroll, Alice's Adventures in Wonderland)

"All organisations are perfectly designed to get the results they get."

(Arthur Jones)

The purpose of this chapter is to set the scene regarding the journey we are embarking upon in *Designing Fit-for-Purpose Organisations*. The following areas are covered: the purpose, unique value-add, foundations, themes covered, target audience and the conventions followed in the book.

Purpose

The purpose of *Designing Fit-for-Purpose Organisations* is to enable readers to gain in-depth insights into Organisational Design (OD) as a key executive leadership task: the Where, Why, Whereto, When, Who, What, and How of OD. *Designing Fit-for-Purpose Organisations* endeavours to capacitate readers with the necessary conceptual and action tools to architect Organisational Operating Models with fit-for-purpose delivery logics for the emerging new order. A fit-for-purpose Organisational Design refers to an organisation doing the right things right. The book offers a comprehensive, integrated route map for designing organisations as a systemic whole – covering the organisation in its entirety, as well as its functions, Work Teams, and Work Roles – in an all embracing, organic and systemic fashion. In the process, OD theory and practice are combined in a synergistic and complementary way.

Designing Fit-for-Purpose Organisations covers the total practice of OD as a mission-critical organisational discipline at all OD Levels and for all Dimensions. The contention is that Organisational Design is a formal organisational discipline of equivalent stature to that of Strategy, Marketing, Finance and People, for example, requiring the same attention by the leadership of the organisation.

Unique value-add

Designing Fit-for-Purpose Organisations aspires to be unique in the following important, interdependent ways:

- *First*, merging the *theory and practice of OD* seamlessly. Frequently either OD theory or OD practice is the primary focus of an author, consequently underplaying the other. *Designing Fit-for-Purpose Organisations* endeavours to give equal weight to both: theory-informed OD practice, and inversely, practice-informed OD theory. In the final instance, *Designing Fit-for-Purpose Organisations* deploys a pracademic vantage point: the seamless merging of theory and practice.[1]

- *Second*, extending OD to include not only the conventional technical and social organisational delivery modes, but also a virtuous (to be explicated later) mode. In this way OD is reconceived in terms of a *triple delivery mode: Technical-Social-Virtuous*. This view is more akin to the rise of the social enterprise against the backdrop of the snowballing pressure on organisations to be good citizens, serving the common good in a sustainable way.

- *Third*, presenting – for the first time in a single place – a *comprehensive, integrated OD approach and process* made up of all three Design Levels: Strategic, Tactical and Operational, each in terms of their Horizontal, Vertical and Lateral Design Dimensions. Currently the literature is fragmented by authors who exclusively address either Strategic Design (or portions thereof) (for example, Jay Galbraith, Michael Tushman, Dave Nadler, John Roberts, Naomi Stanford), or Operational (or Work or Job) Design (for example, Richard Hackman, Frederick Morgeson, Sharon Parker). Little, if any cross-referral occurs.

  Concurrently, Tactical Design receives little attention in the mainstream OD literature, whether Strategic or Operational. Since Tactical Design addresses the design of organisational functions like Finance, Supply Chain, and HRM, it is predominantly covered in discipline-specific literature dealing with the function. In this way, Tactical Design sits outside of the mainstream OD literature.

- *Fourth*, using a *comprehensive, integrated OD route map* as a primary, organising framework for *Designing Fit-for-Purpose Organisations*. This organising framework gives the book a strong 'How to' emphasis, but leveraged from a robust research base, addressing the 'What' and 'Why' of Organisational Design. The route map is based on a seamless combination of an in-depth literature review and cutting-edge practice.

  With a few rare exceptions, the overwhelming majority of OD books focus mostly on the building blocks of OD and/or possible OD solutions, that is the outcome of the OD process. Typically, the systematic process of architecting those building blocks and solutions in an integrated fashion is awarded a subsidiary position in the discussion, hovering implicitly in the background.

- *Firth*, incorporating the *latest contextual trends* – reflective of the emerging, new order – affecting architecting fit-for-purpose designs. Some of these trends are the qualities of the VICCAS (an extension of VUCA) world of increasing **V**ariety, **I**nterdependency, **C**omplexity, **C**hange, **A**mbiguity, and **S**eamlessness (that is boundarylessness); exponentially accelerating technological innovation,

---

1   The term 'Pracademic' was coined by my colleague, Andre Parker.

encapsulated in the term 'Fourth Industrial Revolution'; and the growing adoption of the core value orientation of sustainability through stewardship, which focuses on leaving the world a better place for upcoming generations.

My hope is that you, as the reader, will find that *Designing Fit-for-Purpose Organisations* adds unique value in the ways described above.

Foundations

Designing Fit-for-Purpose Organisations draws heavily on:

- the cutting edge thinking of OD thought leaders such as Andrew Campbell, Jay Galbraith, Michael Goold, Elliott Jacques, Henri Mintzberg, Dave Nadler, Andrew Pettigrew, John Roberts, Michael Tushman, Naomi Stanford (Strategic Design); Dave Ulrich (Tactical HR Design); Arnold Bakker, Evangelia Demerouti, Richard Hackman, Frederick Morgeson and Sharon Parker (Operational Design);

- the global sourcing of leading OD practices, the 'How' of doing OD;

- personal lessons learnt by myself from over 50 Organisational Design consulting assignments over about 20 years across multiple industries, nationally and internationally; and

- the opportunity to have trained close to 200 OD practitioners to date, who have assisted me greatly in gaining insight into how to convey the essence of OD.

Themes covered

Designing Fit-for-Purpose Organisations is made up of the following chapters:

- *Chapter 1* (this chapter) aims to set the scene regarding the journey we are embarking upon in *Designing Fit-for-Purpose Organisations.*

- *Chapter 2* enables the reader to engage, metaphorically speaking, with the right set of Lenses (or mental model) with OD as a mission-critical organisational discipline.

- *Chapter 3* provides the reader with the basic vocabulary and language when thinking, talking and doing OD.

- *Chapter 4* provides a high level overview of the OD process as an organisational intervention, that is the typical life cycle of OD interventions.

- *Chapters 5 to 10* respectively address doing Strategic (Horizontal, Vertical and Lateral Design consecutively), Tactical and Operational OD. More specifically, these chapters explicate architecting different designs as reflected in the accompanying shaded box.

DESIGN	DESIGN LEVEL	CHAPTER	DESIGN STEP IN CHAPTER EXPLICATING DESIGN
Total organisation (including Basic Organisational Shapes)	Strategic	5, 6, 7, 8 6	Step A.2.2.5
Board of Directors	Strategic	7	Step A.3.2
	Tactical	9	-
Corporate Centre	Strategic	7	Step A.3.2
	Tactical	9	-
Work Units	Tactical	9	-
Operating Units	Tactical	9	-
Delivery Enabling/Support Functions: Purchasing and Supply Chain; People; Finance; Information Technology; Corporate University (or Learning Academy); University Information Services	Tactical	9	-
Work Teams	Operational	10	-
Work Roles	Operational	10	-

- Chapter 11 elucidates imaging the organisation of the future for the future.
- Chapter 12 explores the critical success factors that are necessary to turn OD into a truly mission-critical organisational discipline.

Chapters 2, 3, 11, and 12 cover the *Where, Why, Whereto, When, Who, and What* of OD – the conceptual tools of OD as organisational discipline – whereas Chapters 4 to 10 cover the *How* of OD, that is the action tools of OD as an organisational discipline.

As the reader, you can take one of two possible approaches when engaging with *Designing Fit-for-Purpose Organisations:*

- work through the book cover-to-cover; or
- peruse Chapters 2 to 4, which give the essential, basic frame of reference for OD, and then depending on your interest, work through either Strategic OD (Chapters 5 to 8), Tactical Design (Chapter 9), or Operational Design (Chapter 10), finishing off with Chapters 11 and 12. However, a warning: Tactical Design is so intertwined with Strategic Design that the former can really only be understood if one has first worked through the chapters on Strategic Design.

Case studies are given throughout the book to demonstrate 'OD-in-action'. To make your journey through *Designing Fit-for-Purpose Organisations* more real for yourself, you may want to first identify an OD need in your organisation (or a client organisation). You can then address this need by progressively building an OD solution to satisfy it, as you work through the book.

Target audience

The target audience for *Designing Fit-for-Purpose Organisations* is organisational leadership who have to architect fit-for-purpose Organisational Designs, and OD Experts who have to advise them accordingly. The book can also be used at the post-graduate, masters level to teach OD in a module dedicated to OD as an organisational discipline.

Conventions followed

In *Designing Fit-for-Purpose Organisations* I use the term 'Organisational Design' (OD) interchangeably to refer to OD as: (i) an organisational discipline; (ii) the process of design; and (iii) the outcome of the design process, that is the actual design of the organisation. Sometimes the short hand term 'design' will also be used for brevity's sake. The context of the discussion should make it immediately clear every time in what sense the term is being used.

Two types of Endnotes are used, indicated by consecutive numbers in the test:

(i)   *Reference Endnotes.* References are referred to by numbers in normal font in the text: for example (1), (2). References are given in an abbreviated form in the Endnotes at the end of each chapter. Full references are listed in the Reference Section at the end of the book. I have tried to be as comprehensive as possible in my referencing in order to give due recognition. However given my involvement in OD from the early 1990s, combined with my evolving thoughts and insights, it is near impossible to recognise everyone who has influenced my OD thinking and practice, and what is ultimately presented in this book. My sincere apologies, therefore, where I have not given due recognition. It is not deliberate. However, I acknowledge that omissions do not expunge me of my personal debt to the parties concerned.

(ii)   *Explanatory Endnotes.* These notes are indicated in the text by numbers in italics, for example *(1)*, *(2)*. These Endnotes at the end of a chapter either extend a point made in the text, or provide additional or different views on the point elucidated in the text.

Templates as actions tools are provided throughout *Designing Fit-for-Purpose Organisations* as the discussion of the design process unfolds. Readers are free to use them as they see fit.

Conclusion

The purpose of this chapter was to set the scene regarding the journey we are embarking upon in *Designing Fit-for-Purpose Organisations*. The following areas were covered: the purpose, unique value-add, foundations, themes covered, and target audience of the book, as well as conventions followed in the book.

In the final instance, *Designing Fit-for-Purpose Organisations* is about offering a comprehensive, integrated route map to OD, covering all three Design Levels: Strategic, Tactical and Operational, each in terms of their Horizontal, Vertical and Lateral Design Dimensions. In the process, *Designing Fit-for-Purpose Organisations* sets out to capacitate organisational leadership and OD Experts with the necessary conceptual and action tools to architect organisational Operating Models informed by fit-for-purpose delivery logics matched to the emerging new order.

The promised, unique contributions of *Designing Fit-for-Purpose Organisations* are fivefold: merging seamlessly the theory and practice of OD; reconceiving OD in terms of a triple delivery mode: technical-social-virtuous, more akin to the rise of the social enterprise and the growing pressure on organisations to be good citizens; presenting – for the first time in a single place – a comprehensive, integrated OD approach and process; using a comprehensive, integrated OD route map as a primary, organising framework for *Designing Fit-for-Purpose Organisations*; and incorporating the latest contextual trends – reflective of the emerging new order – affecting architecting fit-for-purpose designs.

Enjoy the journey! May the journey truly provide the five-fold, unique contributions promised above for you as the reader.

2

ENGAGING WITH ORGANISATIONAL DESIGN

Putting on the right set of glasses

"If we want things to stay as they are, things will have to change."

(Giuseppe Tomasi di Lampedusa)

"It is not the answer that enlightens, but the question."

(Eugéne Ionescio)

The scene has been set regarding the journey we are embarking upon in *Designing Fit-for-Purpose Organisations*. The purpose of this chapter is to enable the reader to engage metaphorically with the right set of Lenses to position OD as a mission-critical organisational discipline. That is, to engage with OD from the right vantage point. This chapter addresses the 'Why' and 'Whereto' of Organisational Design.

To this end, the following themes are addressed:

- Why has OD become a mission-critical organisational discipline? In other words, why the growing, pressing need for OD?

- Defining OD.

- The overall purpose and objectives of OD.

- Dispelling common myths about OD.

- The expected benefits of a fit-for-purpose design.

Why has Organisational Design become a mission-critical organisational discipline?

OD has always been a mission-critical organisational discipline, but has become even more of a burning platform and will remain so for the foreseeable future, for at least five reasons:

- *Reason 1:* OD has always been a *key leadership task*.

- *Reason 2:* The *world is changing*, which requires a radical rethink of the design of organisations.

- *Reason 3:* Many *organisations are reconceiving their Identities* because of the emerging new order, in turn significantly affecting their designs.

- *Reason 4: People have moved to centre stage* in the future success of organisations, which demands a better design-people fit.

- *Reason 5:* OD significantly affects the *ability of the organisation to compete.*

Reason 1: Organisational Design is a key leadership task

OD equates to the Operating Model of an organisation, which expresses an organisation's delivery logic. Crafting the Operating Model of an organisation is one of the actions making up the portfolio of key tasks that has to be performed by the leadership in the organisation, as shown in Figure 2.1 by the arrow (1).

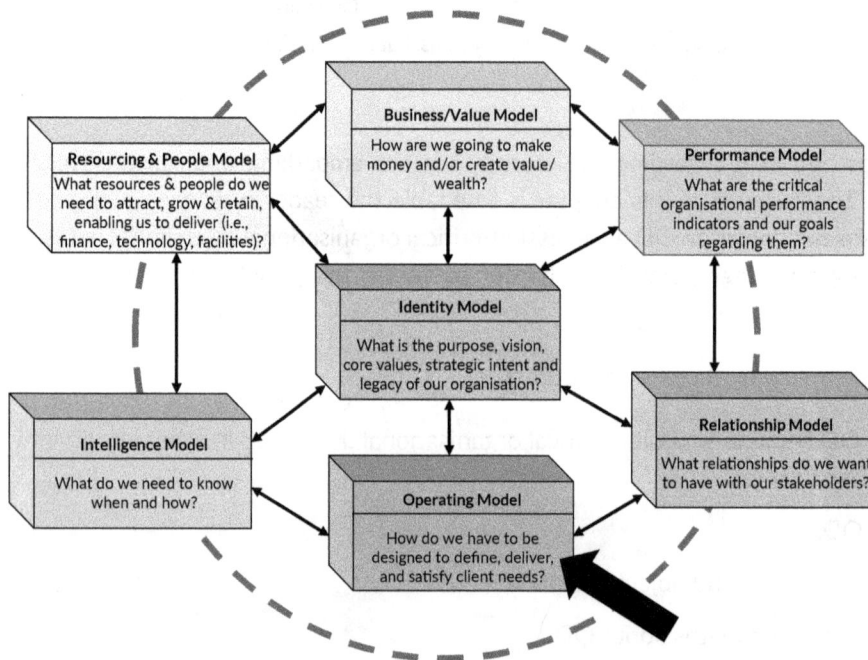

Figure 2.1: Organisational Design – the Operating Model of the organisation – as a key leadership task

The portfolio of leadership tasks shown in Figure 2.1 has to be viewed in a holistic, integrated and interconnected way. Congruence between the tasks making up the portfolio is a crucial requirement if an organisation wishes to be effective (that is doing the right things) and efficient (that is doing things right). In other words, all of the tasks in Figure 2.1 have to be aligned systemically.

By ignoring, underplaying, or misconstruing OD as an Operating Model through certain myths (see the discussion later in this chapter on OD myths), leadership severely compromises the ability of their organisation to deliver in a fit-for-purpose manner. In particular, the alignments between the Business/

Value, Identity (especially Strategic Intent) and Operating Models of the organisation are primary, which have to receive attention in the order given. The Operating Model is crucial in actualising the organisation's Identity successfully (2). The need to pay more explicit attention to the organisation's Operating Model will become even more apparent for the other four reasons discussed below.

Reason 2: The world is changing which requires a radical rethink of Organisational Designs

Organisations are facing a vastly different future in terms of substantive trends; contextual qualities represented by the VICCAS world; emerging success criteria; and 'competitive maths'. All of the aforesaid give rise to a 'recalibrated' competitive equation. Figure 2.2 provides an overview of the emerging new order (3).

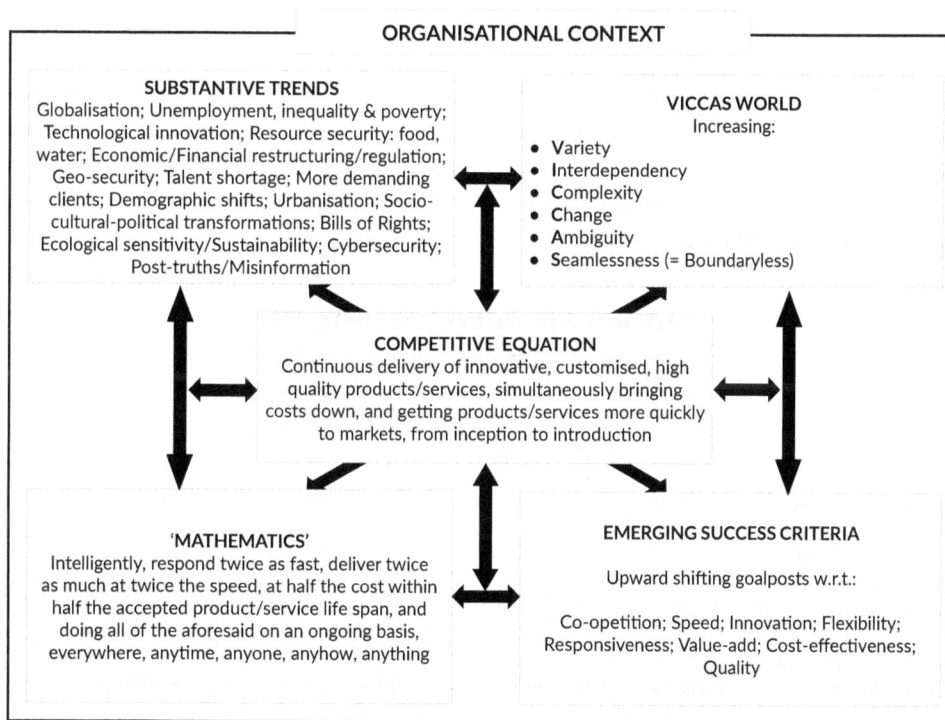

ORGANISATIONAL CONTEXT

SUBSTANTIVE TRENDS
Globalisation; Unemployment, inequality & poverty; Technological innovation; Resource security: food, water; Economic/Financial restructuring/regulation; Geo-security; Talent shortage; More demanding clients; Demographic shifts; Urbanisation; Socio-cultural-political transformations; Bills of Rights; Ecological sensitivity/Sustainability; Cybersecurity; Post-truths/Misinformation

VICCAS WORLD
Increasing:
- Variety
- Interdependency
- Complexity
- Change
- Ambiguity
- Seamlessness (= Boundaryless)

COMPETITIVE EQUATION
Continuous delivery of innovative, customised, high quality products/services, simultaneously bringing costs down, and getting products/services more quickly to markets, from inception to introduction

'MATHEMATICS'
Intelligently, respond twice as fast, deliver twice as much at twice the speed, at half the cost within half the accepted product/service life span, and doing all of the aforesaid on an ongoing basis, everywhere, anytime, anyone, anyhow, anything

EMERGING SUCCESS CRITERIA
Upward shifting goalposts w.r.t.:

Co-opetition; Speed; Innovation; Flexibility; Responsiveness; Value-add; Cost-effectiveness; Quality

Figure 2.2: The emerging new order

The emerging new order is permeated by 'wicked' challenges, issues and problems *(4)*. As depicted in Figure 2.2, the emerging new order therefore requires organisations to radically rethink the *Why?*, *What?*, *How?*, *Who?*, *Where?*, and *Where to?* the business of their business, not only in the present, but in particular whilst moving into the significantly different future. Organisations are facing a radically different context, resulting in a growing misfit between organisations and their contexts (5).

Playing fields, game plans, players and rules have to be fundamentally reconsidered, reframed and re-invented if organisations are to thrive sustainably in the future. All of the above forces and trends fundamentally impact on all of the leadership tasks given in Figure 2.1, *inter alia* the organisation's Operating Model: the way in which it wants and needs to deliver in the emerging new order. Organisations will have to apply 'wicked' thinking to re-invent their organisation designs relative to finding new identities for new times. With the emerging new order, Organisational Design has become a strategic, organisational imperative, not an arm chair luxury (6).

From 2016 to the present, 'organisation of the future' (read 'Organisational Design') has been the most important focus of Deloitte's annual Global Human Capital Trends survey amongst executives. The rated readiness of organisations to redesign themselves varied between 14% in 2016 and made a quantum jump to 46% in 2018 (7). "Business by Design" – the creation of compelling, memorable customer and employee experiences by adopting an outside-in design approach, commencing with re-imaging how customers and employees can be delighted beyond their expectations – has become/needs to become a core, strategic capability of organisations (8) *(9) (10)* within the emerging 'compelling, memorable experience-based' economy *(11)*.

The frequency of Organisational Design interventions is thus on the increase (12). Yet globally only 23% of executives say that their redesign efforts are a success. In 44% of cases, redesign gets bogged down in implementation and is never actually completed (13). The downfall of many leading organisations has been attributed directly to Organisational Design failures (14). The collapse of Nokia's mobile business is a recent, sobering example (15).

Reason 3: Many organisations are reconceiving their Identity because of the emerging new order, in turn affecting their designs

Because of the emerging new world order, organisations are reformulating their Identities. Organisational identity (we, us, and them) relates to organisational members' understandings of who and what their organisations are – what they stand for and do, who they belong to, and what they aspire to: How do we see ourselves? How are we seen? How do we wish to be seen? (16). Organisational Identity is made up of Purpose, Vision, Core Values, Strategic Intent, and Legacy. In the hyper-turbulent and hyper-fluid context described in the previous section, Identity becomes the organisation's only secure anchor and reference point in the stormy sea of change.

If an organisation's Identity changes, its Operating Model (= Organisational Design) also has to be reconsidered accordingly if overall coherence is to be attained within the portfolio of key leadership tasks (see Figure 2.1). By implication, all of the other key leadership tasks given in Figure 2.1 have to be re-aligned in order to achieve overall coherence and synergy across the total portfolio of leadership tasks.

Purpose-wise, the growing expectation is that organisations must demonstrate true, genuine citizenship within society by transforming themselves into social enterprises, driven by the core value orientation of sustainability through stewardship – leaving the world a better place for upcoming generations (17). Organisations have to question from first principles their very reasons for existence.

From an organisational (or institutional) vantage point, sustainability can be expressed in five, interdependent Ps (an extension of the triple bottom line of Profit, People, and Planet):

- *Productivity:* the effective and efficient use of resources.

- *Prosperity:* wealth creation by all, fairly and equitably distributed to all.

- *People:* engendering the well-being of and care for people.

- *Peace:* promoting harmony and co-operation between and within diverse communities and society.

- *Planet:* nurturing and protecting the ecological well-being of the universe; the environmental footprint of the organisation.

Sustainability with respect to the above 5 Ps can be described in terms of four actions: (i) *recover* what has been lost; (ii) *renew* what exists; (iii) *restore* to the necessary level/state; and (iv) *retain* at the desired level/state. Hence, the core value chain of the organisation can no longer be seen as a linear process of rampant consumption by exploiting/depleting the existing in the present, and thus compromising sustainability going into the future. The chain must rather be seen as a circular process of recovering, renewal, restoration and retention of existing value through zero waste *whilst* delivering value going into the future. Expressed as a Value Equation: Consumed/Delivered Value < Replaced Value through the core value chain (18).

Reason 4: People have moved to centre stage in the future success of organisations, which demands a better design-people fit (19)

Within today's knowledge society it is estimated that 85% and upwards of the assets of an organisation are intangible (for example, reputation, brand, patent rights, capabilities, people expertise and skills) rather than tangible (for example, facilities, technology, finance, products/services) (20). Probably at least 70% of the intangible assets are resident in people in the form of creativity, innovation, expertise, knowledge, skills, and experience.

In a knowledge society, people have become the predominant value unlockers of the potential contained in the assets of the organisation, by means of which sustainable wealth is created. People have moved centre stage in the future, sustainable success of organisations. The 21st century organisation will be an 'ideas business', driven by the creative thinking power of people who have, as core capabilities, an openness to new ideas, ingenuity and imagination, and the capacity to address the wicked challenges, issues and problems with wicked thinking. Organisations will need to match their designs to the people they hope to attract, engage, grow, and retain.

The shaded box below provides a high level profile of the worker of future.

HIGH LEVEL PROFILE OF THE WORKER OF FUTURE

- Growing proportion of independents/freelancers with certain specialist knowledge, expertise and experience, contracting individually with organisations to create and deliver products/services. Increasingly even full time employees will have the same mindset, values and attitudes of independents/freelancers.

- Much more diverse in terms of make-up, however profiled. For example, in terms of generation (up to at least four generations in the work setting), gender, ethnicity, nationality, and values.

- More demanding in terms of what they expect from organisations: reputable, purpose-driven organisations with credible, authentic, ethical leadership; work settings that are challenging, stimulating and meaningful; collaborative and team-based; offer ongoing learning and development opportunities, taken up at their own behest at times and places decided by them, built around their needs and aspirations relative to where they are in their self-navigated, chosen careers.

- The question, "What is in it for me?", will feature much more strongly on their personal radar screens, with the person putting him/herself at the centre of his/her self-crafted, individualised Work Role, career, and world of work.

- Engagement and identification with an organisation will occur according to the terms and objectives set by the individual within shorter time frames of commitment to any given cause, issue and/or organisation. Once achieved, they will move if new challenges are not set in their existing organisation.

- Seek out work settings that will allow them to satisfy their needs, actualise their potential, and apply their knowledge, skills and experience fully and in innovative ways in order to remain employable.

- Information/intelligence rich setting, (preferably self-generated) and highly technology enabled.

- Desire to be judged by what they can contribute and the results they (can) produce, not by the hours they spent at work and/or the number of activities they perform within a given period of work time.

- Be enabled and empowered as self-directed persons, in their own right, in their own spaces.

- Greater desire for optimal work/life integration because the boundaries between life and work have dissipated completely as a result of virtual connectivity, providing them the capability to work anywhere, anytime, anyhow with anyone on anything.

- Care for the total well-being of a person.

- The overall challenge will be to engage the heart, mind, soul and spirit of workers who will be much more inner-directed, assertive, calculative, independent, mobile, meaning and purpose seeking (that is 'why, and to what end am I doing this?').

The above-described profile of the worker of the future will fundamentally change the future employer-employee relationship. Future-fit organisations must be able to attract, engage, grow and retain the worker of the future through a good fit between their designs and their organisational members, in order to create and sustain compelling, memorable employee experiences. The challenge is how to architect 'humane' designs. These are designs that are able to satisfy the total range of the basic needs of people: their needs for meaning (or purpose); fulfilment; efficacy; belonging; and existence.

Reason 5: Organisational Design affects the ability of the organisation to compete

It is widely recognised that the way an organisation is designed has a profound effect not only on its ability to execute its strategy successfully, but also on its capability to:

- realise entrepreneurial opportunities timeously;

- create memorable client and employee experiences, resulting in their continued retention;

- operate efficiently;

- deploy and utilise resources expeditiously;

- enable the optimal flow of people energy and solicit a high level of people engagement; and

- nurture a constructive, healthy culture and dynamic.

These, in turn, affect the overall performance of the organisation, and ultimately its continued sustainability and success.

An organisation can indeed compete by design (21). Of course, this assumes the choice of the right Strategic Intent, and its correct conversion into a congruent Operating Model: the design of the organisation. For example, in a study by Bain of companies in eight industries and 21 countries, it was found that organisations with top quartile Operating Models — that is clear, robust, fit-for-purpose designs — had a five-year compound average revenue growth that was 120 basis point faster, together with operating margins that were 260 basis points higher, than those in the bottom quartile (22).

The case study of Hudson Bay Trading vs. Northwest Trading in the box illustrates how a fit-for-purpose design makes a real competitive difference (23).

CASE STUDY: ORGANISATIONAL DESIGN DOES MAKE A REAL DIFFERENCE	
Context: The trading industry in Northern Canada from 1670 until 1820, when Canada was still a British colony, with two trade companies competing in the same region: Hudson Bay Trading (established in 1670), the original company, and Northwest Trading, the intruding company (established approximately 100 years later).	
Hudson Bay Trading	**Northwest Trading**
Profile	**Profile**
• Long established, overwhelmingly dominant market player in Northern Canadian region for more than the first century of its existence with high profitability because of little/no competition. • Traded under a British Royal Charter in the region, hence trading legally in the region.	• Local immigrant leaders. • No Royal Charter to trade in the area. Their presence in the trading region was illegal. Hence they had to locate themselves in Montreal thousands of miles away from the centre of the trading region – Hudson Bay – which was a huge cost disadvantage. The company had to send traders into the region.

• Politically well-connected leadership, located in Britain. • Vastly superior technology with better access to finance. • Operating costs half that of its rival.	• No powerful political connections.
Organisational Design	**Organisational Design**
Inside-out, highly centralised, command-and-control, bureaucratised	**Outside-in, customer-centric, decentralised, responsive, empowering**
• Contacted traders located at forts only around Hudson Bay where ships off-loaded traded goods, and in turn uploaded furs. Customers had to come to forts to trade. Traders were instructed to stay at the forts. • Traders worked according to detailed job instructions, given straight from London, which governed all aspects of their work to the smallest detail. They were not able to use their discretion at all, for example, to set prices for furs. They were paid a fixed amount, and were punished physically for any infractions. • Passive, low self-motivated people with little initiative were selected as traders. They were merely doers, and were not expected to be thinkers. • Independent middlemen sourced furs from deep in the territory far away from Hudson Bay at their own risk, before trading with the Hudson Bay traders located at the forts. This resulted in mark-ups on mark-ups, and low trade volumes. • Slow, unresponsive, centralised decision-making in London by management who had never been to the territory and were thousands of miles away from the trading region about which they making decisions.	• Set up trading posts deep in the region where furs were collected by voyageurs (= traders) travelling by canoes/small boats deep into the region to bring goods to customers in exchange for high quality furs. • Trading posts headed up by wintering partners who were partners in/owners of company. Voyageurs could also become winter partners, that is partners in the company. • Entrepreneurial, participative culture: everyone had high autonomy to make independent decisions as they saw fit in their space. • Montreal-based partners handled the acquisition of trade goods, the sale of furs and financing. • An annual meeting of all partners was held to discuss and make decisions regarding business, for example, what goods to trade given shifts in customers' tastes and needs. • Highly responsive to changing market/customers' needs with information gathered directly from customers. • Simple supplier structure: no middlemen. • Transparency: information rich and sharing. • Minimum bureaucracy.
Outcomes	**Outcomes**
Once the dominant monopoly, now nearly bankrupt. Only 20% of market/customers.	Highly profitable. Eighty percent of market/customers.
Response	**Response**
Slow response to rival for over a decade. The past success recipe of 120 years was seen as good enough. When still unsuccessful, they adopted the rival's Organisational Design only after a change in leadership.	Made a failed attempt to take over Hudson Bay before the new leadership took over that company. Ultimately, Hudson Bay's huge cost advantage overwhelmed Northwest. A merger occurred in 1820.

At present organisations are forced to consider different permutations of strategic choices to execute their chosen Strategic Intent, given basic Strategic Intents such as product/service innovation, operational excellence and customer (or client) centricity. Given the wickedness of the challenges, issues and problems faced by organisations, as well as the need for continuous deep learning/teaching, organisations are adopting an action learning process to find and validate these choices. Figure 2.3 illustrates the array of strategic choices available to organisations regarding the five key organisational domains, embedded in the action learning process of explore, discover, act and learn/reflect.

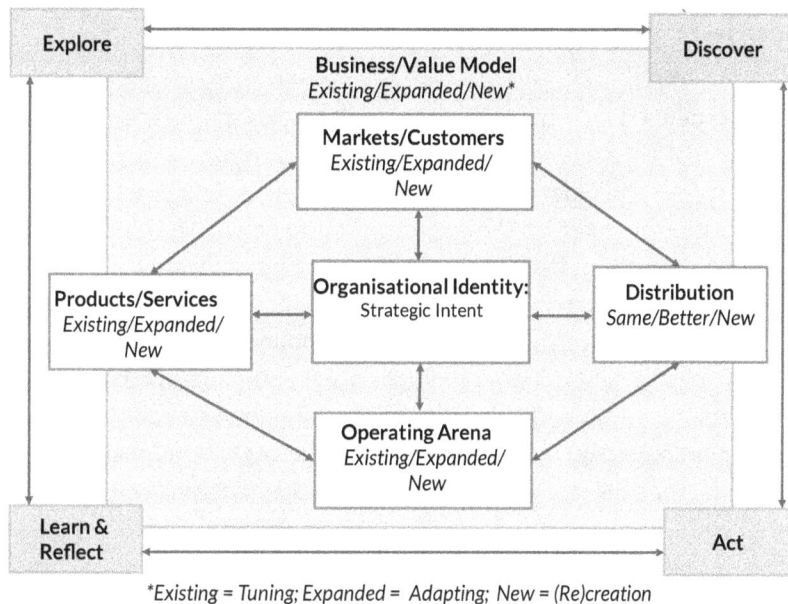

*Existing = Tuning; Expanded = Adapting; New = (Re)creation

Figure 2.3: Range of strategic domain choices relative to a chosen Organisational Identity, imbedded in an action learning process

According to Figure 2.3, an organisation can make strategic choices in five reciprocally interdependent domains: Business/Value Model; markets/customers; products/services; delivery; and Operating Arena. The domain choices can range from remain 'As-is' (low risk) to expand (medium risk) to new (high risk), relative to the organisation's chosen Strategic Intent. The highest risk position is where an organisation decide to move to 'New' in all choice domains simultaneously (24). Any of these choices affect the organisation's design to a greater or lesser extent.

The criticality of Organisational Design may be even truer in the emerging new order, which is characterised by discontinuous radical change, heightened complexity, snowballing chaos, deepening ambiguity, and widening seamlessness, as was explicated above under Reason 1 (25). This means that organisations are forced to reconsider their strategic choices in all five domains concurrently (see Figure 2.3). It is even argued that Organisational Design is *the* key to unlocking the opportunities of the 21st century (26). Organisational design can thus only be ignored at the risk of the effectiveness and efficiency of the organisation.

In summary: Given that the Operating Model of an organisation is a key leadership task to begin with, there is an increasing demand for OD to be fully acknowledged as a mission-critical organisational discipline. It has to move to centre stage in order to enable leadership to set up and roll out effective ODs, because their organisations will have to operate in a vastly different future and world. In this world, ODs will need to be closely matched to the people – central to value unlocking and wealth creation in the knowledge economy – occupying the design. All and all, leadership has to leverage OD as an indispensable means to compete sustainably in the emerging new order.

Defining Organisational Design

An organisation can be defined as a purpose-directed, consciously organised social entity operating within identifiable boundaries embedded within a certain context (27). Formally defined, OD (or organisational architecture) – the Operating Model of the organisation – pertains to the delivery logic required by an organisation (or part of the organisation, for example, Operations, Finance, People Management) to define, unlock and deliver ongoing value for stakeholders within its context (or Operating Arena). Put slightly differently, OD provides a formal map of how the required work of the organisation must be done effectively, as demarcated by boundaries of accountability, responsibility and authority, that is doing the right things in the right place at the right time by the right person, team and unit, with the necessary checks and balances (28). A distinction can be drawn between OD as the *process* of designing (or architecting) the delivery logic of the organisation, and Organisational Design as the *outcome* (or product) of the design process; the solution. *Designing Fit-for-Purpose Organisations* deals with both equally.

Like the strands of a rope, the delivery logic of the organisation is made up of three, interdependent modes (= strands) forming an indivisible, holistic whole (= rope) that have to be jointly optimised:

- *Technical:* the Core Operating Technology and Enablers with its people requirements, used by the organisation to satisfy customer needs.

- *Social:* how the work of the organisation must be done by its people by utilising the Core Operating Technology to deliver.

- *Virtuous:* delivering in a humane way, with stewardship, for the greater good. 'Humane' refers to ensuring people's dignity and well-being through the design; 'stewardship' to leaving the world, sustainably, a better place for future generations; and 'greater good' in considering the interests/needs of all stakeholders, and not only the self-serving, parochial interests of the organisation and its shareholders (29). In other words, the delivery logic of fit-for-purpose organisations going forward will need to be value-based and -referenced.

The first two strands are representative of the socio-technical perspective of OD that has been an inherent part of conventional OD for many years *(30)*. The third strand is a new, critical strand to be added to the delivery logic. I would like to argue that it is necessitated by the growing expectation that organisations must demonstrate true, genuine citizenship within society by transforming themselves in social enterprises, driven by the core value orientation of sustainability through stewardship. The

Operating Model of the organisation must support and be reflective of true, genuine citizenship in terms of real stewardship *(31)*. Going forward, it will be imperative to view the delivery logic of the organisation from a techno-socio-virtuous design logic perspective. This perspective will frame the explication in the book of the comprehensive, integrated OD route map, indicated as a TSV design logic in what follows.

In essence, OD entails architecting (or configuring) (32) (33):

- the grouping of the organisational work, contained in its core, enabling and support work processes, into Work Units (or Domains) (= Horizontal Design);

- awarding the requisite Levels of Work to Work Units, and identifying the critical Work Roles associated with the Work Units (= Vertical Design); and

- building the necessary integration and governance mechanisms necessary to ensure that all of the foresaid work together synergistically and accountably (= Lateral Design).

Horizontal and Vertical Design pertain to the differentiation of an organisation's work (its division of labour), while Lateral Design pertains to the integration of its work in order to create an overall, co-ordinated thrust (34).

Given the above description of OD as a critical organisational discipline, it should be apparent that OD:

- *does not equate to the organogram* (or organisational chart) of the organisation. The organogram only indicates jobs (or positions), functional areas (or departments, divisions, units) and reporting lines. It does not reflect the delivery logic of the organisation which is contained in the OD. As will be seen later, the organogram is virtually one of the last outputs of the OD process, not the first and/ or only output;

- *is not synonymous with re-engineering*. OD is aimed at doing the right things in the right places with the required responsibility, accountability, authority and autonomy. That is, OD deals with the effectiveness of the organisation. Re-engineering presupposes the design and aims to enhance the efficiency of doing the right things right – established through the design – in the organisation. That is, doing tasks and activities quicker, better, and even smarter;

- *is a separate exercise to the specific people who are necessary to staff up and operate the design*. OD looks at architecting the work to be done within the organisation. Only once the design has been architected does the question arise regarding the number and type of people required by the design, and who is available and suitable in the organisation to staff up the design. However, the design must be able to attract, engage and retain the worker of tomorrow as discussed above, but not list specific employees by name; and

- *is different to Organisational Development*, which aims to get the people of the organisation to work productively and constructively together within a given Organisational Design (35).

Overall purpose and objectives of Organisational Design

The *overall purpose of* OD is to architect fit-for-purpose organisations. Around the overall purpose, four *OD objectives can be* distinguished. Individually and severally, these objectives result in a total mandate for OD in the organisation in terms of the difference it must make. Figure 2.4 depicts the respective objectives which can be set for OD (36).

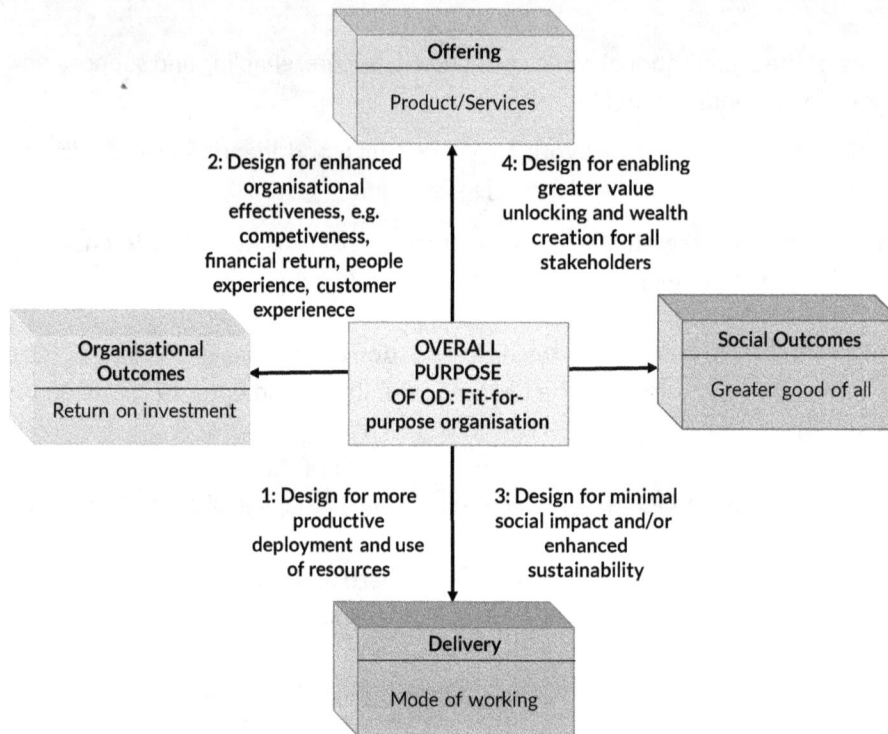

Figure 2.4: Different OD objectives relative to the overall purpose of OD

According to Figure 2.4, the four specific OD objectives relative to its overall OD purpose are:

- *Conventional OD* that focused primarily on Organisational Outcomes: Objectives 1 and 2. However, in recent times the relative weight has shifted to Objective 2, particularly with the significant growing emphasis on "Business by Design". That is, the creation of memorable customer and employee experiences through an outside-in design approach, as discussed above (37).

- *Emerging OD* that focuses in a complementary fashion on Social Outcomes: Objectives 3 and 4, because of the growing adoption of the core value orientation of sustainability through stewardship, that is leaving the world a better place for upcoming generations. This demands that organisations demonstrate true, genuine citizenship socially, as has been discussed in previous sections (38).

I would like to argue that going forward, the overall purpose of OD will have to include all four OD objectives given in Figure 2.4, although weighted differently depending on the Identity of the organisation. This position will inform the basis of the comprehensive, integrated route OD map explicated in *Designing Fit-for-Purpose Organisations*.

Dispelling the common myths about Organisational Design

An essential precondition to establishing OD as a proper organisational discipline demands debunking the prevalent myths regarding OD as a mission-critical organisational discipline. In other words, adopting the right frame of reference (or mindset) with respect to OD. One objective of *Designing Fit-for-Purpose Organisations* is to eradicate some of the more common myths, whilst elucidating the comprehensive, integrated route map. Ten of these myths are debunked below.

- *Myth 1:* OD design is common sense or a dark art of dubious reputation for which no, or at most a restricted, body of knowledge exists. *Reality:* A vast body of OD knowledge exists; one only need refer to the references given at the back of *Designing Fit-for-Purpose Organisations*. My book itself – with the OD literature reported on – also attests to the fallacy of this myth. However, in the final instance, OD remains both a science and an art. It requires both rational logical expert-based thinking and intuitive thinking, salted with solid practical wisdom (39).

- *Myth 2:* OD does not require the shifting of mindsets, frames of reference, attitudes and behaviours. Going through the motions of rehashing those that already exist is good enough. *Reality:* The emerging new world depicted in Figure 2.2, as well as the need for finding reformulated identities and strategic positions for organisations in that world, necessitate a fundamental rethink of an organisation's design. That is, how to deliver better and differently in this fundamentally different world (40).

- *Myth 3:* OD can be done on the back of a cigarette box or a serviette, preferably over a good bottle of wine, at the speed of lightning. *Reality:* A proper, well thought through and coherent OD requires an integrated, systematic design process that addresses all of the building blocks that make up a fit-for-purpose design (41). The purpose of *Designing Fit-for-Purpose Organisations* is to offer a comprehensive, integrated route map for designing organisations as a systemic whole.

- *Myth 4:* OD only involves rearranging boxes, titles, and reporting lines. That is, redrawing organograms. *Reality:* OD as the Operating Model of the organisation deals with its delivery logic. An organogram does not at all equate to a true, complete picture of an organisation's delivery logic; it is but one piece thereof. Additionally, the drafting of the organogram is just one of the very last steps in the OD process (42).

- *Myth 5:* OD (= structure) can be looked at in isolation. The greater Organisational Landscape, which is made up of ingredients like leadership, technology and culture, needs not be considered. *Reality:* The design of an organisation forms an inherent component of the overall Organisational Landscape, forming a systemic, holistic whole. In touching the OD of the Organisational Landscape, one touches the whole Landscape. A design therefore needs to be supported and reinforced by the other components of the Organisational Landscape (43).

- *Myth 6:* One must build one's design to fit around the people and the expertise they have, or to eliminate destructive interpersonal and team dynamics, however illogical that design may be. *Reality:* OD as the Operating Model of an organisation exists apart from the people who must staff up the design (44).

- *Myth 7:* By imitating what others are doing design-wise, one can be relieved from asking tough questions about the design of one's own organisation. *Reality:* One can learn from other designs, but in the end one has to go through the rigorous discipline imposed by the OD process in order to arrive at one's own fit-for-purpose design. Only then can the organisation use its design as a means of gaining a competitive edge (45).

- *Myth 8:* OD offers a quick fix solution if things are not going well. Restructure is the name of the game when the going gets tough. *Reality:* If done properly, an OD must have the same lifespan as the Identity of an organisation, including its Strategic Intent, because an OD solution provides one of the strongest ways to successfully roll out an organisation's Strategic Intent (46).

- *Myth 9:* A new OD can merely be announced and imposed. People will readily and willingly accept and adopt the new delivery logic. *Reality:* Any new design requires a carefully crafted change navigation strategy and plan to counter the insecurity, politics, turf wars, personal conflicts, and resistance invoked by an OD intervention, as well as to build buy-in and ownership of the new design. The more the new design is different from the existing design, the greater the need for sound change navigation (47).

- *Myth 10:* The aim of OD is to 'panel beat' the pains and wrongs out of the organisation; it is a band aid for the 'structural' pains torturing the organisation and putting it in distress. *Reality:* Proper OD is not about short term, quick fixes, but rather about thinking through in a systematic and fundamental way the organisation's delivery logic, aligned to its Identity relative to its Operating Arena (48).

Only by dispelling the myths regarding OD upfront, as well as by embracing the true nature of OD as a mission-critical organisational discipline and key leadership task, will an organisation be able to compete successfully through its design.

Expected benefits of a fit-for-purpose Design

One must have realistic expectations regarding what OD can deliver – nothing more, and nothing less. Given the overall purpose of OD and its associated objectives, a fit-for-purpose OD can capacitate an organisation to compete effectively through its design, because it would serve to (49):

- ensure a *best fit between the organisation and its context*, now and going into the future;

- mobilise the organisation in a focused manner to *meet market/customer needs* in a value-adding manner and more responsive way, thus creating memorable customer and employee experiences;

- *translate the organisation's Strategic Intent and business goals* into focused Work Units; day-to-day work flows and modes of working; and the requisite Levels of Work, with well-defined Work Roles with a clear distribution of responsibilities, accountabilities and authority;

- *integrate activities seamlessly* between organisational units, teams and individuals, resulting in an integrated strategic thrust and response by the organisation;

- mould the organisation's Identity, leadership, people, culture, resources and performance into a *coherent, synergetic whole*;

- create *greater economies of scale and cost efficiencies*;

- enable *optimal resource allocation and deployment*;

- build, enhance and protect *in-depth core competencies*, organisation- and people-wise, putting the organisation on a sustainable, strategic trajectory;

- direct and shape *people's efforts and performances* in the appropriate direction;

- retain *customers and employees;* and

- impact *sustainability* positively.

Given the above listed benefits of a fit-for-purpose OD, its pervasive impact on organisational functioning, performance and success can be readily seen.

Conclusion

The purpose of this chapter was to equip the reader with the right set of Lenses to engage with OD as a mission-critical organisational discipline. To this end, five reasons for the growing importance of OD as a critical organisational discipline were given; OD was defined as dealing with the delivery logic of the organisation, finding its concrete expression in its Operating Model; the overall purpose and objectives of OD were demarcated; ten common myths about OD were dispelled; and the need for understanding, and being realistic about, the expected benefits of OD was outlined.

The scene has now been properly set to formerly engage with OD as a mission-critical organisational discipline. The journey has commenced in the right place by providing you with the right set of Lenses for a 20/20 vision of OD.

The next chapter will deal with finding the right vocabulary and language to speak about OD.

Endnotes

(1) Ambroise, Prim-Allaz, Teyssier & Peillon (2018); Agarwal, Bersin, Lahiri, Schwartz & Volini (2018); Bersin, Geller, Wakefield & Walsh (2016); Bussin (2017a); (2017c); Fink (2019); Miles, Snow, Fjeldstad, Miles & Lettl (2010); Teece (2010); Santos, Pache & Birkholz (2015); Stanford (2015); Yeoman & O'Hara (2017).

(2) Bellerby (2017); Brickley, Smith & Zimmerman (2003); Bussin (2017a); (2017c); (2017d); Chandler (2018); Fenton & Pettigrew (2000); Hanna (1988); Hawryszkiewycz (2017); Galbraith (2014); Gruber, De Leon, George & Thompson (2015); Kates & Galbraith (2007); Kesler & Kates (2011); Kolko (2015); Levin (2005); MacKenzie (1986); Mohrman, Cohen & Mohrman (1995); Mosley & Matviuk (2010); Nadler & Tushman (1988); Price (2013); Stanford (2015); Pettigrew & Masini (2001); Worley & Lawler (2010).

(3) Adapted from Veldsman (2016a); and updated from Agarwal, Bersin, Lahiri, Schwartz & Volini (2018); Bhalla, Dyrchs & Strack (2017); Burton, Obel & Håkonsson (2015); Covin (2015); Friedman (2016); Harari (2018); Salas & Fiore (2012); Steinmetz, K. (2016); Verwey, Du Plessis & Haveman (2017).

(4) Hawryszkiewycz (2017). According to him wicked problems carry the following features: each is unique; is owned by many, diverse stakeholders with conflicting interests/needs; an unclear problem formulation exists; a range of possible solutions exist; solutions are better/worse, not true/false; no clear test exists whether a solution will work; every solution is unique to a specific situation; there is no clear termination point when the desired impact has been attained by the solution.

(5) McChrystal (2015).

(6) Verwey, Du Plessis & Haveman (2017).

(7) Agarwal, Bersin, Lahiri, Schwartz & Volini (2018); Bersin, McDowell, Rahnema & van Durme (2017); Pelster & Schwartz (2016).

(8) Brown (2019); Chandler (2018); Gruber, De Leon, George & Thompson (2015); Kolko (2015); Yoo, Boland & Lyytinen (2006).

(9) Based on especially Elsbach & Stigliani (2018), (but also Brown (2019); De Guerre, Se Guin, Pace & Burkeida (2013); Kolko (2010); (2015); and Kurtmollaiev, Pedersen, Fjuk & Kvale (2018)), design thinking can be typified in short as follows. Design thinking, coming out of product and architectural design, uses abductive reasoning – a combination of deductive and inductive reasoning – as well as intuition, to solve wicked problems (or puzzles), informed by reflective practices. Design is thinking by doing. According to abductive logic, there is no way to prove any new thought, concept, or idea in advance. New ideas can only be validated through the unfolding of future events. An intuitive-rational leap of the mind or an inference to the best explanation is required. This logic is located between reliability – to produce consistent, predictable outcomes, and validity – to produce outcomes that meet a desired objective.

Design thinking is about transforming existing conditions within a context into the preferred state by starting outside-in with the experiences of prospective beneficiaries – current or desired – viewed holistically and systematically. Because of its open-endedness and -mindedness, there is no upfront and/or imposed solution. Design thinking is imminently suited to craft plausible solutions, not correct solutions, under conditions of uncertainty, ambiguity, and instability.

Central to design thinking are the design thinking tools applied: (1) *Need finding tools*, that is tools such as ethnographic observations, in-depth contextual interviews, or customer journey mapping used to empathise with and understand the needs of end users; (2) *Idea-generation tools*, that is tools such as brainstorming, visualisation, and co-creation/co-design used to generate possible solutions to challenges, issues or problems; and (3) *Idea-testing tools*, that is tools such as rapid prototyping and experimentation applied to test ideas on a small scale to determine desirability, technical feasibility, and business viability.

Starting outside-in, design thinking essentially follows an action learning process (see Reason & Bradbury, 2002) of exploration, discovery, action (= design and apply), learning and reflection. Design thinking tools produce both physical artefacts (for example, prototypes, drawings, design spaces) and emotional experiences (for example, the experience of empathy or surprise/delight).

(10) De Guerre, Se Guin, Pace & Burkeida's (2013) discussion of their redesign journey at the School of Extended Learning at Concordia University, Montreal, demonstrates in practice their application of Design Thinking, called IDEA: Innovation, Design, Engagement, and Action.

(11)   Pine & Gilmore (2011) (quoted by Gruber, De Leon, George & Thompson, 2015) argued that the "experience economy" is the next economy following the agrarian, industrial and service economies. In an experience economy organisations must orchestrate memorable events for their customers and employees such that memory itself becomes the product: the experience invoked by the product/service.

(12)   According to the 2013 McKinsey Global Survey, reported by Keller & Meaney (2017).

(13)   Greenwood & Miller (2010)

(14)   For example, Burton, Obel & Håkonsson (2015); Nadler & Tushman (1988).

(15)   Doz (2018).

(16)   Ashforth & Schinoff (2016); Gibney, Zagenczyk, Fuller, Hester & Caner (2011); Gioia, Patvardhan, Hamilton & Corley (2013); Keiner & Murphy (2016); Pratt, Schultz, Ashforth & Ravashi (2016); Ravashi (2016); Schinoff, Rogers & Corley, (2016); Van Tonder (2004).

(17)   Agarwal, Bersin, Lahiri, Schwartz & Volini (2018); Ashton (2017); Bersin, O'Reilly, Magoulas & Loukides (2019); Brown (2019); Hawken (2010); Lankoski & Smith (2017); Lawler & Worley (2012); Lawler & Conger (2015); Mutuality Yeoman & O'Hara (2017); Nijhof, Schaveling & Zalesky (2019); Santos, Pache & Birkholz (2015); Veldsman (2015b).

(18)   In particular Hawken (2010), but also Brown (2019).

(19)   Based on a blog written by the author entitled "The People Professional of tomorrow: Challenges, demands and requirements: Part 1: Profiling tomorrow's world" published on 1 June 2018 at theohveldsman.com, supplemented by Agarwal, Bersin, Lahiri, Schwartz & Volini (2018); Bersin, McDowell, Rahnema & van Durme (2017); Bersin, O'Reilly, Magoulas & Loukides (2019); Friedman (2016); Garrett-Cox (2016); Gruber, De Leon, George & Thompson (2015); Hamel (2015); Lev (2001); (2004).

(21)   Ambroise, Prim-Allaz, Teyssier & Peillon (2018); Bellerby (2017); Brickely, Smith & Zimmerman (2003); Burton & Obel (2018); Capelle (2014); Capelle (2017); (2018); Foss, Lyngsie & Zahra (2015); Galbraith, Downey & Kates (2005); Greenwood & Miller (2010); Gruber, De Leon, George & Thompson (2015); Keller & Meaney (2017); Nadler & Tushman (1988); (1997); Nusem, Wrigley & Matthews (2017); Roghé, Toma, Scholz, Schudey & Koike (2017); Stanford (2015); Veldsman (2002); Worley & Lawler.

(22)   Davis-Pecoud & Moolman (2015).

(23)   Robertson (2004).

(24)   Cf. Hawryszkiewycz (2017), who also discusses similar creative, strategic design solution options that could be considered by organisations in the emerging new world.

(25)   Kelliher & Richardson (2012); Tofaya (2010).

(26)   Bryan & Joyce (2007), as quoted by Greenwood & Miller (2010).

(27)   Cf. Burton & Obel (2018); Burton, Obel & Håkonsson (2015); Huber (2011); Puranam, Alexy & Reitzig (2014).

(28)   Cf. Aubry & Lavoie-Tremblay (2018); Bellerby (2017); Burton & Obel (2004); (2018); Bussin (2017a); (2017c) (2017d); Capelle (2014); Goold & Campbell (2002b); Kates & Galbraith (2007); MacKenzie (1986); Miles, Snow, Fjeldstad, Miles & Lettl (2010); Mintzberg (1993); (1997); Stanford (2015); Nadler & Tushman (1988).

(29)   Garrett-Cox (2016); Sutcliffe & Allgrove (2018).

(30)   The socio-technical systems design perspective was propagated by E. Trist, K.W. Bamford and A.K. Rice at the Tavistock Institute, UK, during the 1950s (cf. Parker, 2014; Parker, Morgeson & Johns, 2017; Pasmore, 1988). A view of the virtuous organisation can be found in Williams, Haarhoff & Fox (2015), who make a strong case for organisations becoming virtuous, that is being directed and guided by virtues such as fun, compassion, self-awareness and worthiness.

(31)   The need for sustainability to become part of the very fibre of the organisation has been argued convincingly by Hawken (2010); Lawler & Worley (2012); and Lawler & Conger (2015). Also, the need for corporate social responsible organisations (Veldsman, 2015b). See also Adi (2018); Nijhof, Schaveling & Zalesky (2019).

(32)   Cf. Anand & Daft (227); Burton & Obel (2018); Burton, Obel & Håkonsson (2015); Huber (2011); Galbraith (2014); (1997); (2006); (2008); Galbraith, Downey & Kates (2005); Kesler & Kates (2011); Nadler & Tushman (1997); Roberts, (2004); Stanford (2007); Veldsman (2002).

(33)   To be discussed in greater detail in Chapter 2.

(34)   Lawrence & Lorsch (1967), as quoted by Burton & Obel (2018); and Puranam, Alexy & Reitzig (2014).

(35)   Bussin (2017a).

(36)   Adapted and expanded from Nusem, Wrigley & Matthews (2017).

(37)   Chandler (2018); Gruber, De Leon, George & Thompson (2015); Kolko (2015); Yoo, Boland & Lyytinen, K. (2006).

(38)   Agarwal, Bersin, Lahiri, Schwartz & Volini (2018); Ashton (2017); Lankoski & Smith (2017); Lawler & Worley (2012); Lawler & Conger (2015); Mutuality Yeoman & O'Hara (2017); Santos, Pache & Birkholz (2015); Veldsman (2015b).

(39)   Burton & Obel (2018); Burton, Obel & Håkonsson (2015); Capelle (2014); Fenton & Pettigrew (2000); Huber (2011); Keller & Meaney (2017); Kesler & Kates (2011); MacKenzie (1986); Meyer, A. (2013); Nadler & Tushman (1988); Puranam (2012); Snow, Miles & Miles (2006).

(40)   Laloux (2014); Liu, Sarala, Xing & Cooper (2017); Lee & Edmondson (2018); Miles, Snow, Fjeldstad, Miles & Lettl (2010); Mosley & Matviuk (2010); Keller & Meaney (2017); Thoren (2017); Yoo, Boland & Lyytinen (2006).

(41)   Brophy (2017); Stanford (2015).

(42)   Brophy (2017); Capelle (2014); Galbraith (2002); Keller & Meaney (2017); Stanford (2015).

(43)   Adler & Hiromoto (2012); Ambroise, Prim-Allaz, Teyssier & Peillon (2018); Birken (2000); Brophy (2017); Burton, Obel & Håkonsson (2015); Donaldson & Joffe (2015); Galbraith (2014); MacKenzie (1986); Mueller, Procter & Buchanan (2000); Ramos (2012); Stanford (2015).

(44)   Keller & Meaney (2017).

(45)   Kates & Galbraith (2007); Nadler & Tushman (1977).

(46)   Stanford (2015).

(47)   Goold & Campbell (2002a); (2002b); Keller & Meaney (2017); Pearce (2013), Tolchinsky & Wenzl (2014).

(48)   Keller & Meaney (2017); Stanford (2015).

(49)   Ambroise, Prim-Allaz, Teyssier & Peillon (2018); Bellerby (2017); Brickely, Smith & Zimmerman (2003); Burton & Obel (2018); Capelle (2014); Capelle (2017); (2018); Foss, Lyngsie & Zahra (2015); Galbraith, Downey & Kates (2005); Greenwood & Miller (2010); Gruber, De Leon, George & Thompson (2015); Keller & Meaney (2017); Lawler & Worley (2012); Lawler & Conger (2015); Nadler & Tushman (1988); (1997); Nusem, Wrigley & Matthews (2017); Stanford (2015); Veldsman (2002); Worley & Lawler (2010).

VOCABULARY AND LANGUAGE OF ORGANISATIONAL DESIGN

3

Basic concepts and frameworks informing Organisational Design

"What you look at, is what you see. What theory you use, determines what you look for."
(Marvin Weisbord)

"Principles come before methods. There are millions of methods, only a few principles. He who knows the principles, can select wisely amongst millions of methods."
(Adapted from Ralph Waldo Emerson)

Given what was covered in Chapter 2, we should now have the right set of Lenses on through which to look at OD as a mission-critical organisational discipline, hopefully giving us a 20/20 vision of OD. The purpose of this chapter is to address the basic vocabulary and language of OD, the 'What' of OD. The vocabulary and language provide the conceptual tools to inform and shape the OD discourse in the organisation. Without the proper and agreed upon OD language and vocabulary, confusion and misunderstandings will rule and undermine the organisation's OD narrative. The basic OD vocabulary and language need to be jargon free, user friendly, clear, distinct, simple, relevant, complete, and well-substantiated (1).

The following themes are covered in this chapter: Theoretical Lenses to frame the OD discourse; Positioning Design within the Organisational Landscape; Design Levels and Dimensions; Basic Building Blocks of Organisational Design; Generic Organisational Design Process; the Location of Organisational Design within the Organisation; and Key Questions to interrogate the fitness-of-purpose of a crafted Organisational Design.

A glossary of the key OD terms used throughout *Designing Fit-for-Purpose Organisations* is given in Appendix A for easy reference. The glossary also can assist in a clear discourse on OD.

Theoretical Lenses to frame the Organisational Design Discourse

The comprehensive, integrated OD route map elucidated in *Designing Fit-for-Purpose Organisations* is framed and informed by a number of Theoretical Lenses, which provide a rich, solid and robust conceptual foundation to the route map. Of course, the Theoretical Lenses provided below can and must also be used in an organisation as a foundation for its OD discourse. Generally such Lenses are used implicitly. However the contention is that they must be made explicit and be deliberately chosen.

Figure 3.1 provides a graphic illustration of the available Theoretical Lenses within the literature regarding OD. The typology is constructed around two dimensions, as viewed within the choice of an all embracing Foundational Lens as a vantage point:

- *Foundational Lens:* Complexity/Chaos as the Framing Lens through which all of the other Lenses can be viewed.

- *Dimension 1: Generalisability of Designs:* These Design Theoretical Lenses differentiate between *Ideal* (or Generic) and *Situation Specific* Designs. The former category applies to Lenses that propose that certain designs apply regardless of specific circumstances. Designs are ideal types that apply, in general, anywhere in the same way. The latter category relates to Lenses that portend that each design is unique. That is, each design is a function of situation-specific variables.

- *Dimension 2: Reality Lenses:* These Theoretical Design Lenses distinguish between *Objective* and *Subjective* Designs. According to the former category, designs have an independent existence from their stakeholders (for example, organisational members). That is, they exist separately from the views of stakeholders. The latter category argues that designs have a subjective existence; they exist through the shared understanding of, and enactment by, stakeholders regarding what the organisation is all about.

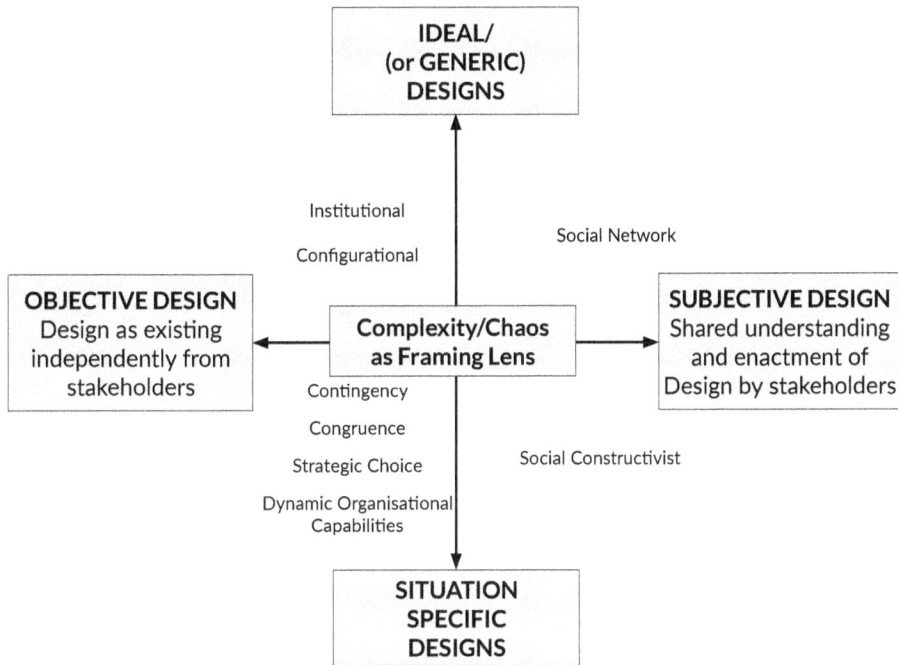

Figure 3.1: Typology of available Theoretical Lenses

Table 3.1 provides a description of the Theoretical Lenses, their major proponents within OD as an organisational discipline, and the application of the Lenses within the comprehensive, integrated route map espoused in *Designing Fit-for-Purpose Organisations* (2). Only examples of proponents of a Theoretical Lens within OD are given, althrough the lens may have originated outside of OD. As can be seen below, OD is informed by a rich theoretical heritage which has been used in my book to craft a theoretical, robust, comprehensive, integrated route map. Adopting a pluralist vantage point, multiple Theoretical Lenses are used in *Designing Fit-for-Purpose Organisations*.

Table 3.1: Descriptions of the available Theoretical Lenses within OD as an organisational discipline, major proponents, and the applications of Lenses within Designing Fit-for-Purpose Organisations

Theoretical Lens	Categori-sation of Lenses as per typology (See figure 3.1)	Description	Examples of major proponents	Application with regard to the comprehensive, integrated OD route map
Complexity/ Chaos	Framing Lens	Reality forms an interconnected whole of non-linearly, reciprocally influencing, interacting components. Everything affects everything else. Relationships between components are primary. Dynamically, relationships between components are characterised by the ongoing resolution of dynamic, opposing tensions (for example, in the case of an organisation, centralisation vs. decentralisation or control vs. autonomy). The resolution of tensions manifests in emergent, self-organising and self-destructing patterns that form virtuous or vicious cycles. The cycles are expressive of a limited number of underlying organising rules as the interconnected whole moves through successive states of chaos (tensions are unresolved) and order (the resolution of tensions).	J. Gharajedaghi; C. Kurtz; R. Marion; R. Stacey; D.J. Snowden, D.W. Tafoya; T.H. Veldsman; M. Wheatley	Used throughout, in particular: (i) as the basis of the construction of the comprehensive, integrated OD route map; and (ii) in my conception of the organisation overall, expressed in the concept "Organisational Landscape", that also informs the whole route map (see later discussion in this chapter).
Institutional	Ideal/ Objective Lens	Societal sectors often have typical Organisational Designs that are specific to them that are seen as the right way of doing things. For example, in the military, legal, medical, or manufacturing sectors (3).	P.J. DiMaggio; J. March; W.R. Scott; P. Selznik; W.W. Powell	Only touched on slightly, for example, Fordism vs. Lean manufacturing (see Chapter 6).
Configuration	Ideal/ Objective Lens	Ideal organisational types/shapes or archetypes that lay down certain prescribed, coherent ways of putting the total organisation and its components together. For example, generic Organisational Shapes like functional, process or divisional shapes. Alternatively, more Ideal types like Mintzberg's typology of Simple Structure, Machine Bureaucracy, Professional Bureaucracy, Divisionalised and Adhocracy.	R. Greenwood; C.R. Hinings; H. Mintzberg	Generic Organisational Shapes discussed under Strategic Horizontal Design (see Chapter 6).

Theoretical Lens	Categori-sation of Lenses as per typology (See figure 3.1)	Description	Examples of major proponents	Application with regard to the comprehensive, integrated OD route map
Contingency	Situation specific/ Objective Lens	Each Organisational Design is different depending on the state of exogenous factors such as context (stable vs. dynamic); Core Operating Technology with Enablers used; competitive forces and market conditions.	T. Burns; E.M. Fenton; P.R. Lawrence; J.W. Lorsch; A.M. Pettigrew; G. Stalker; J. Woodward	The use of a route map to arrive at fit-for-purpose organisations, depending on each organisation's unique contextual circumstances, lies at the heart of *Designing Fit-for-Purpose Organisations*.
Congruence (or Alignment)	Situation specific/ Objective Lens	Goodness-of-fit between all organisational components, internally and externally, regardless of whether a configurational or contingency design approach is followed.	J.R. Galbraith; D.A. Nadler; T. Peters; M. Tushman; R.H. Waterman	Informs the total OD route map as a grounding design principle.
Strategic (including socio-political) Choice	Situation specific/ Objective Lens	OD must operationalise the Strategic Intent (part of the organisation's Identity) chosen and pursued by the organisation's dominant coalition, directing and steering the organisation relative to its context. Designing the organisation is a socio-political process based on negotiation, directed and driven by the dominant coalition.	J. Child; S. Clegg; D.C. Hambrick; C.C. Snow	Designs based on different strategic choices are covered.
Dynamic Organisational Capabilities (including core competences/ resource management/ information processing)	Situation specific/ Objective Lens	OD must enable an organisation to attract the necessary resources through the external relationships it forms, and synergistically combine those into unique, inimitable, and valuable capabilities – for example, organisational routines/processes (= ways of doing things) and information processing capability – leveraged to give the organisation a competitive advantage.	J.B. Barney; S.G. Cohen; K.M. Eisenhardt; J.R. Galbraith; G. Hamel; J.A. Martin; A.M. Mohrman; S.A. Mohrman; D.A. Nadler; J. Pfeffer; C.K. Prahalad; G. Salancik; D.J. Teece; M. Tushman	The explicated route map's aim is, *inter alia*, to architect a design that is able to identify, establish and maintain the necessary dynamic capabilities, leveraged from the attraction and retention of the necessary resources, to provide organisations with a competitive advantage.

Theoretical Lens	Categori-sation of Lenses as per typology (See figure 3.1)	Description	Examples of major proponents	Application with regard to the comprehensive, integrated OD route map
Social Network	Ideal/ Subjective Lens	At its very essence, the organisation consists of internal and external social relationships, which are manifested in social, self-organising, emergent interactions and networks, typified, amongst others, by features like location, centrality, density and strength. The better the quality of social relationships, the more the available social capital to the organisation. This, in turn, affects access to stakeholders, people, opportunities and resources.	J.M. Molina	*Designing Fit-for-Purpose Organisations* is based on the premise that the organisation is a social entity made up of social relationships, which the design must enable, strengthen and extend, especially in the emerging new order.
Social constructivist	Situation specific/ Subjective Lens	The real organisation is brought to life through the daily interactions between stakeholders, in particular organisational members. Through their interactions, people ascribe shared meaning and purpose to the organisation. This shared meaning and purpose is expressed through beliefs, norms, values, language, symbols and artefacts, which are internalised by members firstly and then secondly externally enacted.	B. Czarniawska	Any OD can only be effective if organisational members buy into and take ownership of the proposed design. They must attach shared purpose and meaning to the organisation, which are nurtured through sound change navigation, forming an inherent part of the route map.

Positioning Design within the Organisational Landscape

Any OD process needs to be informed by an appropriate model of the organisation to direct and guide the process. Without such a model it is impossible to conceive and engage with the organisation because design forms part of it. The chosen model must be: based on sound assumptions, simple but complete, user friendly, relevant and jargon free (4).

However, before I proceed to present the chosen model of the organisation as a phenomenon informing the OD route map elucidated in *Designing Fit-for-Purpose Organisations*, the contrast between the conventional and new mindset when thinking about the organisation as a phenomenon must be explicated (see Table 3.2) *(5)*. As a model of the organisation presented below, the Organisational Landscape is an example of the new mindset.

Table 3.2: Conventional vs. new mindset in thinking about the organisation as a phenomenon

CONVENTIONAL MINDSET	NEW MINDSET
• Parts • Linear relationships • Either/Or • Sum total of parts • Homeostasis: seeking one best solution; preserving balance • Static	• Relationships • Patterns, reflective of virtuous or vicious cycles • And/Both • Integrated whole • Dynamic fusion of opposites, for example, centralisation *and* decentralisation • Dynamic/Evolving

The chosen model of the organisation informing the OD route map elucidated in *Designing Fit-for-Purpose Organisations* – of which design forms a building block – is entitled 'Organisational Landscape' (see Figure 3.2). In a certain sense, the Organisational Landscape is another way of depicting the key leadership tasks that were set out in Figure 2.1, Chapter 2.

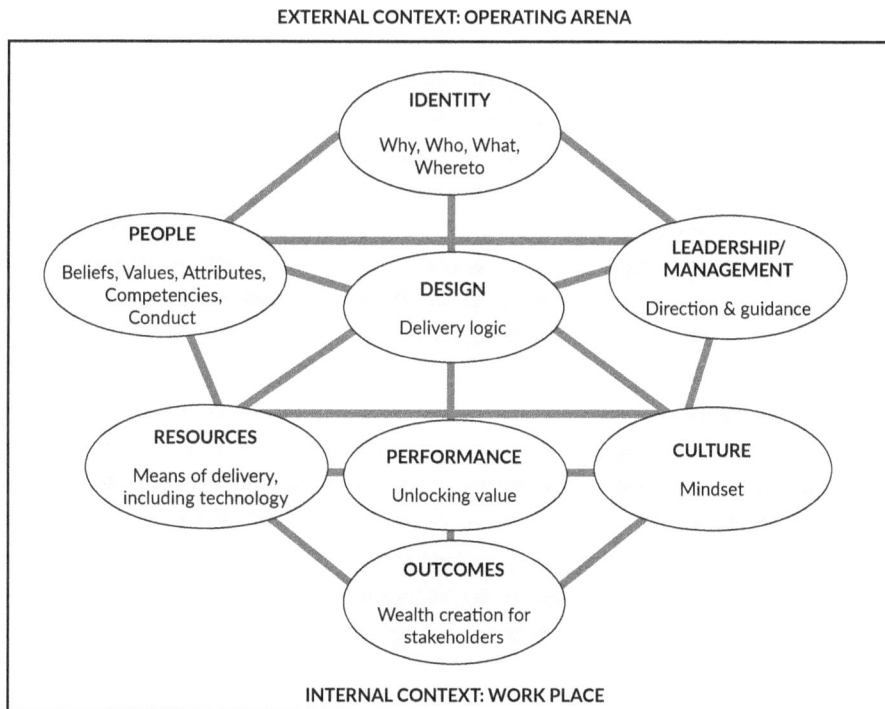

Figure 3.2: Design as part of the Organisational Landscape

According to Figure 3.2, the organisation is a dynamically interconnected, systemic whole: a living, social ecosystem. This view of the Organisational Landscape is based on the Complexity/Chaos Theoretical Lens (see Table 3.1) as framing world view (6) (7). According to this lens, the Organisational Landscape must be seen as an interconnected whole of reciprocally influencing, interacting components (for example, Identity, Design, Leadership in Figure 3.2.). Everything is related to, and affects, everything else.

The Landscape is characterised by the ongoing, emergent, non-linear resolution of dynamic opposing tensions through the 'And' fusions. These fusions manifest themselves in self-organising and self-designing patterns: overall ways in which the Organisational Landscape functions. A pattern is expressive of a limited number of underlying organising rules. Patterns can form constructive and virtuous or destructive and vicious cycles, as the interconnected whole moves through successive states of chaos (with no pattern in place) and order (with a pattern in place) (8).

The congruence (or alignment) of Design with the other components within the Organisational Landscape is thus of the utmost importance if overall organisational synergy is to be attained. This synergy is attained through the establishment and maintenance of a constructive, virtuous pattern, sustaining the chosen design in a re-enforcing manner by the other components making up the Organisational Landscape depicted in Figure 3.2. Importantly, the criticality of the crafted design fitting the context, as well as the design supporting and driving Identity, are recurrent themes that are heavily stressed in the literature (9). The Organisational Landscape presented in Figure 3.2 finally puts to rest OD Myth 5, that is that design can be done in isolation without considering its embeddedness in the Organisational Landscape.

Levels and dimensions of Organisational Design

OD as process and outcome is made up of certain Levels and Dimensions, within the framework of the TSV delivery logic, as illustrated in Figure 3.3 (10).

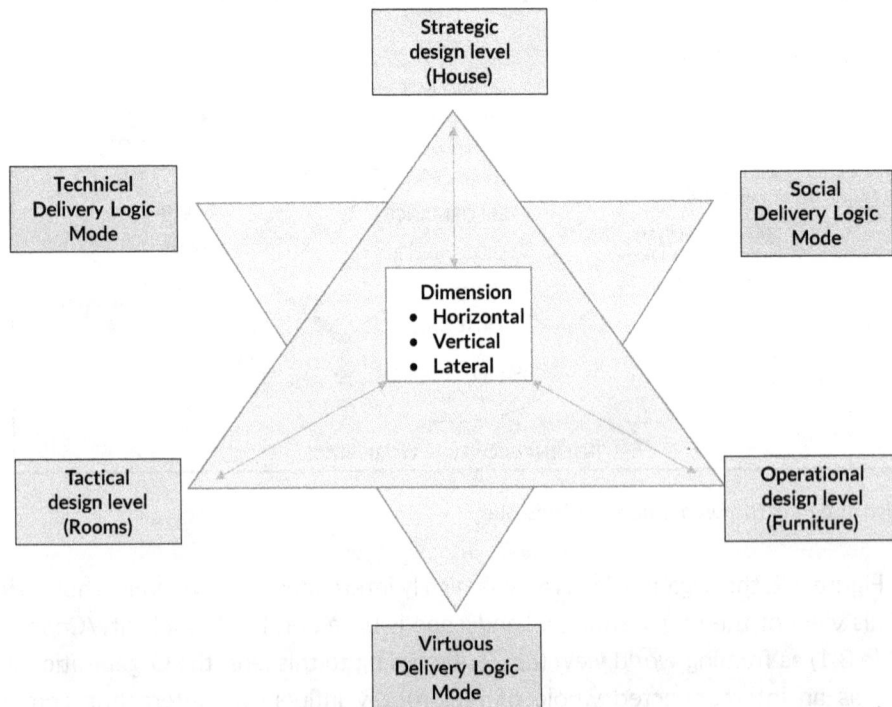

Figure 3.3: Levels and dimensions of Organisational Design within the framework of the TSV delivery logic

According to Figure 3.3, OD can be differentiated into Strategic, Tactical and Operational Design Levels, each framed by the TSV design logic:

- *Strategic Design* encompasses the design of the organisation as a total operating entity, with the Work Units making up the entity (that is operating, enabling and support units; and corporate centre), Levels of Work, Work Roles, integration mechanisms, as well as governance processes and structures.

- *Tactical Design* deals with the design of the different Work Units making up the Strategic Design.

- *Operational Design* addresses how the organisation will operate on a daily basis in terms of Work Teams and Work Roles.

To my mind, the metaphor of a 'House' best represents OD as the architecting of the organisation's delivery logic. For this reason, the terms 'Organisational Design' and 'organisational architecture' are used frequently as synonyms (11):

- The *House Plan* represents the overall design of the organisation, mapping the make-up of the House with its respective rooms, and their placement relative to one another (= its Strategic Design as contained in the basic delivery logic of the organisation, for example, a functional, process, or divisional Organisational Shape).

- The respective *Rooms* making up the House (= its Tactical Design as found in the design of its respective Work Units).

- The *Furniture* contained within each room, reflecting how people must live in the Rooms and House (= its Operational Design made up of the constituent elements of the Organisation and its Work Units, namely Work Teams and Roles).

By implication, a 'higher' Design Level serves as the framework for a 'lower' level of design. It is for this reason that it is critically important to have a comprehensive, integrated route map when designing a congruent delivery logic, as embodied in a total Organisational Design.

In my experience, organisations are strong at addressing the respective Design Levels in isolation, but poor at seeing their interdependencies. For this reason there is a need to translate the higher Design Level into the next lower Design Level(s). In terms of the 'House' analogy, given a new Strategic Design (= House Plan), the rooms in the House are not properly reconfigured, nor is the required furniture thought through that must populate the room.

In turn, each Design Level contains three Design Dimensions (12):

- *Horizontal Dimension:* this demarcates Work Units in terms of the work processes required by the organisation to deliver its work, and configures the demarcated Work Units into an overall Organisational Shape. As a differentiating process, Horizontal Design pertains to the division of labour in the organisation as expressed in its Work Units.

- *Vertical Dimension:* the allocation of the requisite Levels of Work and identifying the critical Work Roles with respect to the overall Organisational Shape and its Work Units.

- *Lateral Dimension:* the integration mechanisms that make all of the above work together in a synergistic manner to prevent silos from forming. In addition, it includes the commensurately required governance structures and processes, including decision-making rights/delegation and decision-making styles.

Figure 3.4 demonstrates the above discussion of the Design Dimensions graphically.

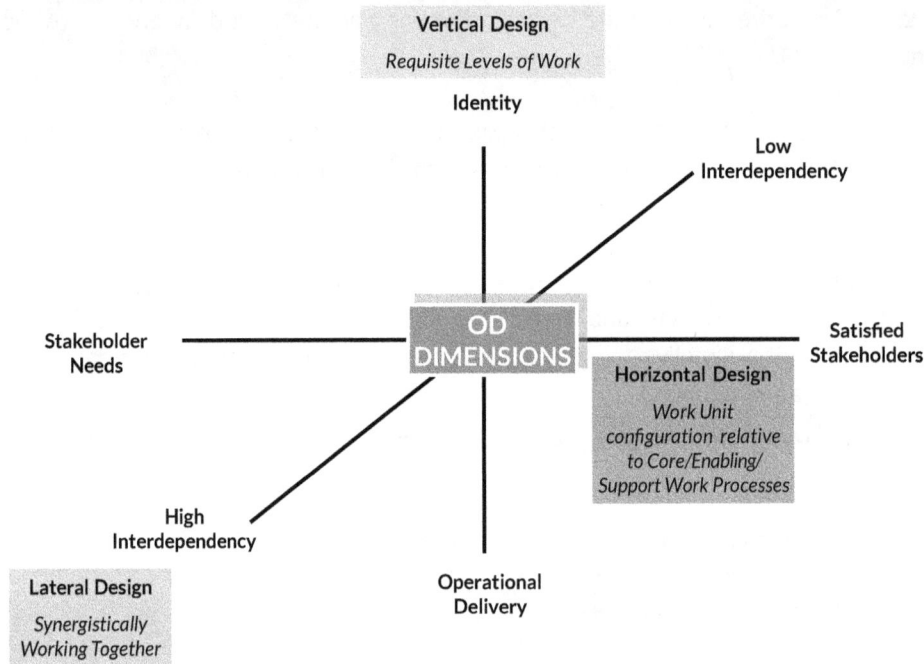

Figure 3.4: Organisational Design dimensions

Again, in my years of observation of OD in practice, organisations are relatively strong at addressing their Horizontal and Vertical Designs, which are the differentiating parts of a design. They are, however, particularly weak at deliberately thinking through their Lateral Design. That is, the integration of the differentiated dimensions, especially if they are merely re-arranging boxes and reporting relationships on an organogram. It is spontaneously assumed that the hierarchy (= reporting relationships) will ensure adequate organisational co-ordination and synergy. The more complex the organisation – for example, multiple Work Units distributed over wide and different geographical locations – the more critical the Lateral Design Dimension becomes.

Basic building blocks of Organisational Design

Certain building materials are required to architect the design of an organisation. Figure 3.5 depicts the basic OD building blocks needed for a complete OD process (13). If one of these building blocks is missing, the OD process is severely compromised in its ability to produce a completely fit-for-purpose design.

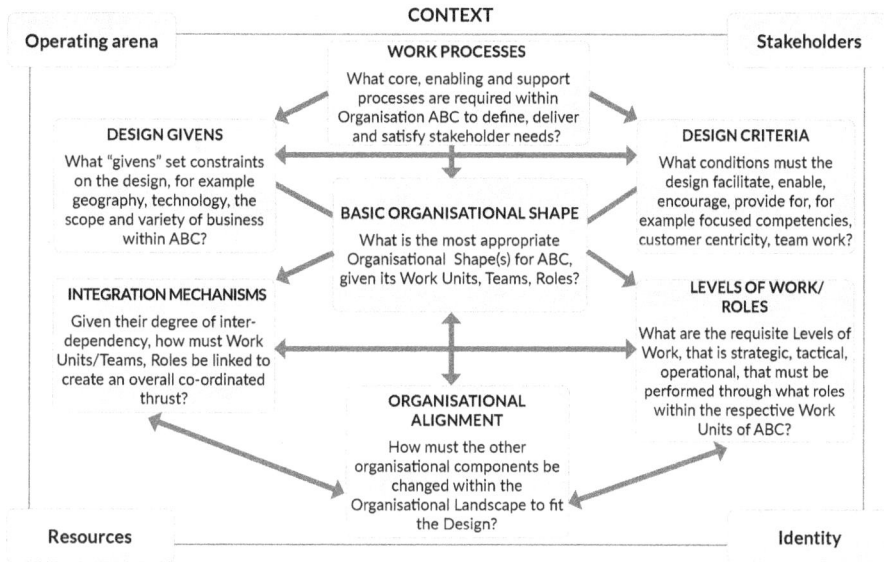

Figure 3.5: Basic building blocks of Organisational Design

According to Figure 3.5, a complete OD process is made up of the following basic building blocks:

- The *Context* in which the organisation has to function, that is matching the design to the characteristics of the organisation's Operating Arena; the Identity (including Strategic Intent) of the organisation; stakeholders; and available external resources.

- The *Design Givens*, which set constraints on the organisation's design, for example, geography, technology, legislation, and the scope of and variety within the organisation. These givens need to be incorporated into the design. In the case of a geographically dispersed organisation, for example, a regionalised design may have to be adopted.

- *Design Criteria*, which are the conditions that the organisation's design must facilitate, enable, encourage and provide for. For example, capacity to act, focused competencies, customer centricity and teamwork.

- The *core, enabling and support work processes* required by the organisation that represent the work of the organisation, all of which must be housed somewhere in the design.

- The *systemic grouping of work processes* into Work Units, Teams and Roles, and organising them into a basic Organisational Shape – the Horizontal Design.

- The requisite *Levels of Work per Work Unit* and their designated ownership as allocated to Work Units and Roles – the Vertical Design.

- Setting up the necessary *integration mechanisms* reflective of the interdependencies of Work Units and Work Roles with the *associated governance* in terms of decision-making rights and styles, in order to focus and direct people, resources, markets/clients, and products/services. In this way, the organisation as a totality is enabled to work synergistically together – the Lateral Design.

- The identification of all of the required *organisational alignments within the Organisational Landscape* which must be changed to support and reinforce the new design. For example, leadership, culture, people, and resources.

Generic Organisational Design process

Although already hinting at an OD process, given the sequence in which the building blocks have been mapped, the building blocks depicted in Figure 3.5 present a static picture. Figure 3.6 presents a full blown, generic OD process, incorporating the building blocks given in Figure 3.5 (14) *(15)*. The overall process depicted here is at a high level, but will be elucidated in more detail in Chapters 4 to 10.

The picture of the OD process reflected in Figure 3.6 instantaneously implodes a number of the OD myths described in Chapter 2. That is, Myth 3: OD can be done on the back of a cigarette box, or on a serviette over a good bottle of wine; Myth 4: OD is only about redrawing organograms; and Myth 9: OD needs no change navigation support.

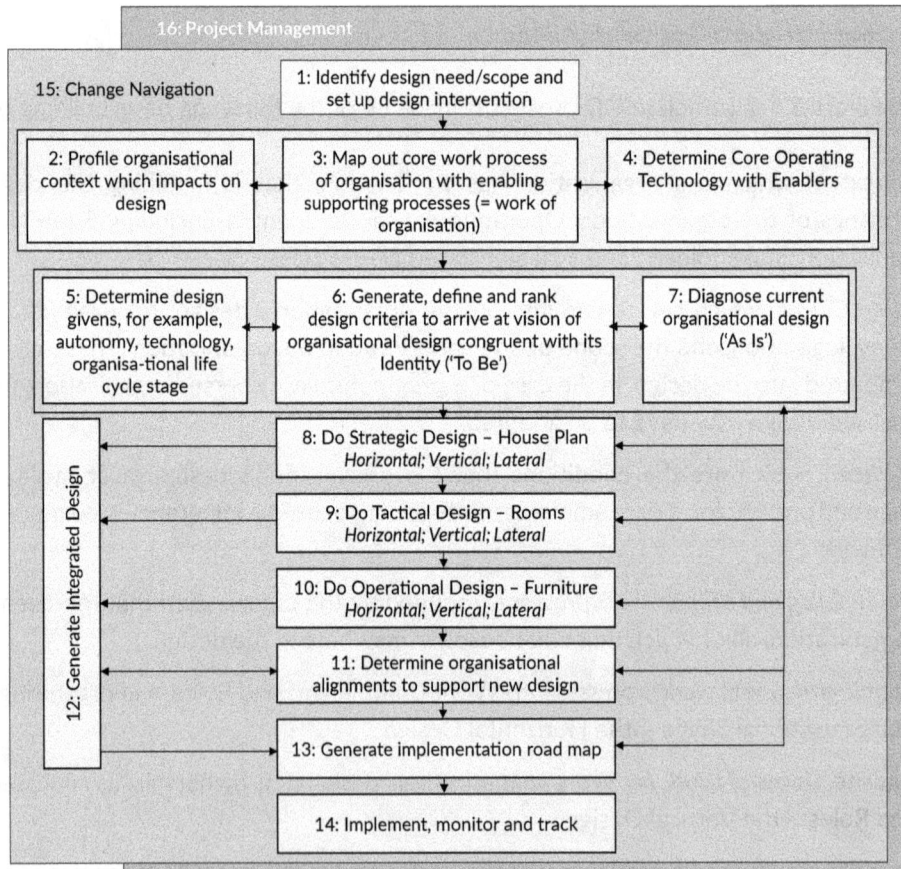

Figure 3.6: Generic, comprehensive, integrated Organisational Design process

Given what has already been discussed up to this point, it can be seen that the overall OD process presented in Figure 3.6 forms the backbone of the comprehensive, integrated route map for OD presented in *Designing Fit-for-Purpose Organisations*, covering Strategic, Vertical and Operational Designs – horizontally, vertically and laterally – in a seamless whole within the framework of a TSV design logic. As was stated in Chapter 1, such a comprehensive, integrated route map is at present missing in the existing OD literature and practice. This overall process will form the compass for the unfolding, in-depth discussion in the subsequent chapters of this book.

An easy way to present the overall OD process set out in Figure 3.6 is to depict it in terms of the Double Diamond Design Thinking Process proposed by the British Design Council as shown in Figure 3.7 (16). This process is reflective of Design Thinking as espoused in Chapter 2 (17).

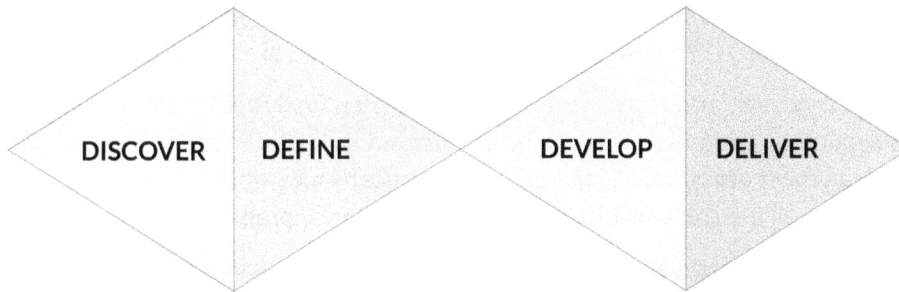

DISCOVER   DEFINE   DEVELOP   DELIVER

Figure 3.7: Double Diamond Design Thinking Process

The diamonds shown in Figure 3.7 refer to (with the related steps contained in Figure 3.6, given in brackets):

- *Discover:* Uncover the design need as the gap between the 'What Is' and 'To-Be' (or desired) Design, as derived from an outside-in understanding within the context of the desired experiences of actual/prospective beneficiaries (Steps 1 to 4).

- *Define:* Specify the Design Solution requirements (Steps 5, 6 and 7).

- *Develop:* Architect and test the preferred Design Solution (Strategic, Tactical and/or Operational; Horizontal, Vertical or Lateral) in detail, having considered different options and involving prospective beneficiaries (Steps 8 to 12).

- *Deliver:* Roll out the chosen Design Solution, followed by monitoring and tracking its outcomes in terms of the experiential impact on beneficiaries (Steps 13 and 14, with Steps 15 and 16 in support throughout).

The following points are important to highlight regarding the OD process given in Figure 3.6 and the Design Thinking Process presented in Figure 3.7:

- This process is *generic in nature and applicable to all types of organisations*, for example, public, private, for profit and non-profit, in all types of industries/sectors.

- *OD is a process*, not an event; it is a verb, not a noun (18). In the emerging new order sketched in Chapter 2, design becomes an everyday, ongoing organisational action, although more important and pertinent at certain times, such as when there is a change in the Business/Value Model or

Identity of the organisation. The recent significant emphasis on "Business by Design" as a core organisational capability to architect memorable experiences for customers and/or employees comes to mind here (discussed in Chapter 2).

- Proper OD necessitates an *integrated, comprehensive and systemic design process*, informed by leading OD practices like the process of building a House, to bring robustness, rigour and discipline to the creation of well-thought through, well-aligned OD solutions. The quality of the OD process directly affects the quality of the solutions architected, as well as the chances of architecting a fit-for-purpose design. Although one can move faster or slower through the process, depending on how pressing the OD need is, *all* steps must be followed at *all times*. The use of an explicit, well mapped, route map gives the security of a well thought through journey. It also minimises the risk of running after fads and fashions (19), as well as the politicisation of the process (see below).

- Although the process is made up of a series of set steps, it is firstly *open-ended in being content neutral*. Any fit-for-purpose design solution can be architected through the process. Secondly, although it appears linear, the process is *applied iteratively in practice* by moving forward and backward between respective steps as the creative juices flow in designing an appropriate solution (20).

- To make the 'To-Be' Design as work-in-progress real, it is most helpful to *visualise the solution being architected* in as many ways as possible visually as the process unfolds. This could be done through post-it notes, maps, flip charts, metaphors, simulated prototyping, industrial theatre, system diagrams, gamification, story-telling, and/or a picture of a 'House Plan' (21).

- The OD process must be enabled through *sound project management and change navigation processes*. The former is needed in particular if the OD intervention covers the total organisation and/or the organisation is complex. The latter process is necessary because without exception, OD triggers widespread insecurities, challenges empires, disrupts relationships, upsets career paths, invokes destructive organisational politics, sets off turf wars, causes personality conflicts, and raises the spectre of retrenchments (22) *(23)*.

- In terms of critical success factors (to be discussed in great detail in Chapter 4), firstly there must be a willingness to allocate the necessary resources (time, people and funds if outside expertise is bought in) in support of the OD intervention. A proper design process is resource intensive. A Strategic Design typically takes eight to twelve weeks; a Tactical Design per Work Unit about six to ten weeks, times the number of Work Units to be (re)designed; and a full-blown Operational Design covering all of the Work Units' Teams and/or Roles for the whole organisation, expressive of its daily mode of operation, can take up to a year.

  The appropriate OD expertise, at the requisite level of complexity of the OD need and intervention, must be available. There is a vast difference in the required OD expertise between redesigning a national, single product/service, uniform client/market organisation to that of a global, multiple product/service, diverse clients/markets organisation.

The box provides a case study of a major redesign done by the Technical Services of Cisco Services (24).

CASE STUDY: CISCO GLOBAL TECHNICAL SERVICES
CONTEXT
Cisco provides the 'plumbing' of the Internet, that is the hardware on which the Internet runs. Cisco Services, a Division of Cisco, provides after-sales customer care. Technical Services, part of Cisco Services, has the mandate to ensure that customers' networks operate efficiently. At the time of the redesign it had 2,500 employees and operated in 120 countries, being organised into five regions/theatres.
OD NEED
Although customer service was at a high level, margins were strong, and the business was exceeding revenue goals, customer satisfaction was starting to drop. So it was decided to proactively intervene through a redesign. The 'To-Be' design was defined as: a single point of client responsibility; a globally consistent client experience; autonomous decision-making at the coal face; a stronger long term strategic focus relative to operational delivery; the elimination of duplication; nurturing partnering/collaboration; and deepening leadership capabilities. The summarised design need statement read: "The organisational foundation is not in place to optimize customer experience and support the transformation of our business."
OD SCOPE
Executive ownership of the total customer experience in each geographical region; a new organisational shape, roles and accountabilities; redefined leadership teams; revised critical governance processes.
DESIGN CRITERIA
Enhanced customer experience; economies of scale; consistent processes/experiences.
ACTIVE OD LEVELS AND DIMENSIONS
Total redesign: Strategic-Tactical-Operational Levels; and Horizontal-Vertical-Lateral Dimensions.
CHOSEN OD PROCESS OPTION
Co-design
DESIGN GOVERNANCE AND PHASES
Phase 1Å: High level Design (= Strategic Design) by Executive Team of Technical Services *Phase 1B*: Tactical-Operational Design – Design teams working in four tracks: (i) design; (ii) transition – implementation; (iii) executive alignment; and (iv) change management. *Phase 2*: Optimising structure/alignment of leadership team – Four transformation areas: (i) vision and strategy (= To Be); (ii) executive dynamics (= shared model of trade-offs); (iii) governance (= mandates/charters); and (iv) mindsets (= behavioural commitments).

EXISTING VS. NEW DESIGN
Existing: Functional silos by regions: (i) Technical Assistance Centres (help desks); and (ii) Service Supply Chains, delivering a fragmented client experience, each reporting into a global Corporate Vice-President. Regionalised business support professionals. **New:** (i) One-stop, integrated, regionalised mini-businesses, containing a total customer value chain for each region (= theatres), delivering a seamless customer service; (ii) Corporate Centre: global service organisation; (iii) Global Business Services Group: roll out of strategic initiatives; and (iv) Business Support to regions, like Finance, HR.
ORGANISATIONAL ALIGNMENT
After the new design was rolled out, a two-day Leadership Alignment Workshop was held with the top 90 leaders to ensure an overall, integrated and co-ordinated business thrust.
CHANGE NAVIGATION
Change navigation supported the redesign throughout, operationalised into three levels of transformation which centred around communication and the adoption of a new design. Level 1: Solution buy-in; Level 2: Making it work; and Level 3: Building trust, creating a new mindset, and re-establishing relationships.
MEASUREMENT MODEL
Business impact; Adoption by organisational members; Project progress
OUTCOMES/BENEFITS
Immediate benefits: contract savings; consolidation of multiple functions; smaller growth in headcount; reduction in rework costs = US $9 million; won a top national US Quality Award *Longer term benefits:* Increased customer satisfaction (from 4.21 to 4.31); higher margins and revenues; increased leadership capacity; greater job satisfaction
CRITICAL SUCCESS FACTORS CONTRIBUTING TO THE SUCCESS OF THE REDESIGN
Executive sponsorship; business initiative; clear route map; adequate resourcing; sufficient time; multi-dimensional measurement; project management; change navigation; soft skills capacity building

Location of Organisational Design within the organisation

A typical burning question is where to locate Organisational Design as a critical organisational capability in the organisation. If OD is crucial in providing the organisation with a competitive edge, and is the critical means to implement the organisation's Identity and Business/Value Models, the short answer is, hierarchically, 'As high as possible'. Alternatively, as close to the executive fulcrum of the organisation. All in all, the short answer is that Organisational Design must form part of the executive core of the organisation.

Key questions to interrogate the fitness-of-purpose of a crafted Organisational Design

What are the 'Ten commandments' of a good design? The following questions – an overall stress test of one's design – can assist one to assess how fit-for-purpose one's design is in providing the requisite leverage from which to compete (25):

- Is the design aligned to the *Business/Value and Identity Models* of the organisation?

- How well is the chosen design aligned to the *organisational context* with its commensurate complexity in which the organisation has to function? For example, does the design match the characteristics of its context: organisational life cycle stage; stakeholders' interests and needs; Core Operating Technology with Enablers; as well as available resources?

- Does the design cover all of the *core, enabling and support work processes* required to define, deliver and satisfy stakeholder needs and the work of the organisation, even if they are not currently in place in the organisation?

- How well have the *Design Givens*, which set constraints on the design, been incorporated into the design, for example legislation, geography, technology, and the scope and variety within the organisation?

- Have the conditions the design must facilitate, enable, encourage and provide for, such as focused competencies, customer centricity and team work, been clearly spelt out, that is the *Design Criteria*? Has a *Design Vision* been formulated for the organisation, based on these Criteria? How well does the design comply with the Design Criteria and Vision?

- Has the best way of grouping the core, enabling and support work processes into Work Units, and hence the most appropriate overall *Organisational Shape* – for example a functional, process or front-back Shape – been selected in which to organise Work Units, given the organisation's context, work processes, Design Givens and Criteria?

- Have the requisite *Levels of Work* with the associated *Work Roles* been appropriately assigned, clearly defined and demarcated in the design with the right accountabilities, responsibilities and authority?

- Does the design make provision for the protection and enhancement of the *'crown jewels'* of the organisation – those capabilities that give the organisation an unassailable competitive edge, for example, its core competencies, brand, key technologies, and/or strategic suppliers/clients?

- Have effective *integration mechanisms* been set up to take account of the interdependencies between Work Units, Teams, and Roles in order to enable an overall co-ordinated thrust for the organisation?

- Does the design incorporate *sound corporate governance principles* in terms of the distribution of responsibility, accountability and authority with unambiguous decision rights and the accompanying decision-making style(s)?

- Has the *total Organisational Landscape* been re-aligned to support and reinforce the chosen design, for example required leadership, culture, people, resources?

- Has an explicit overall mode of working been generated – an Organisational Charter?

- Is the proposed design *implementable within the available window of opportunity*?

- Is the design not over-specified, but allows for *customisation in order to enable localisation*?

- All and all, is the design of the *requisite complexity*, that is not oversimplified or too complex?

- Is the design *affordable*? Do the expected benefits of the design outweigh its cost?

- In the final instance, will the design be *able to attract and retain customers and employees* because of the memorable experiences the organisation will create for them?

Conclusion

The purpose of this chapter was to establish the basic vocabulary and language of OD, which provides the conceptual tools to inform and shape a constructive and productive OD discourse in the organisation. This discourse in the organisation should centre around the following themes: clarity on the Theoretical Lenses underpinning and shaping the OD discourse; Design as an inherent part of the Organisational Landscape which must at all times be aligned; acknowledging the full portfolio of OD work consisting of the Strategic, Tactical and Operational Design Levels, and Horizontal, Vertical and Lateral Design Dimensions, all viewed within a TSV design logic; a complete set of basic building blocks of OD to be used in design; an overall systematic, integrated OD process exists and is followed; OD must be located in the right place in the organisation; and creating a set of key questions to interrogate the fitness-of-purpose of a crafted design.

Onto the next step in our OD journey: a high level, life cycle overview of the OD process as a large scale organisational intervention.

Endnotes

(1)   Cf. Stanford (2015).

(2)   Based on: Aubry & Lavoie-Tremblay (2018); Burton & Obel (2018); Burton, Obel & Håkonsson (2015); Czarniawska (2008); Galbraith, Lawler & Associates (1993); Gharajedaghi (2011); Goold & Campbell (2002b); Greenwood & Miller (2010); Hawryszkiewycz (2017); Huber (2011); Lehtimäki (2017); McChrystal (2015); Miterev, Mancini & Turner (2017b); Ramos (2012); Roh, Turkulainen, Whipple & Swink (2017); Snow, Miles & Miles (2006).

(3)   March's (1965) *Handbook of Organisations* has no fewer than nine chapters devoted to particular types of organisations, ranging from unions and political parties to military organisations, prisons, and business organisations.

(4)   Stanford (2015).

(5)   This mindset shift in thinking about the organisation as a phenomenon is reflected in the emergence of systems models, such as McKinsey's 7-S; Galbraith's Star; and the Fractual Design Models (cf. Stanford, 2015).

(6)   Cf. Cabrera, Cabrera, Powers, Solin & Kushner (2018); Cloete (2019); Gharajedaghi, 2011; Hanna (1988); Holman (2015); Kurtz & Snowden (2003); Laloux (2014); Marion (2008); Nedopil, Steger & Amann (2011); Preiser, Biggs, De Vos & Folke (2018); Snowden & Boone (2007); Stacey (2015); Stacey, Griffin & Shaw (2000); Tafoya (2010); Wheatley (2010).

(7)   The conceptualisation of the Organisational Landscape given in Figure 3.2 – developed by the author in conjunction with Wynand Geldenhuys, a colleague – is in the historical lineage of the widely known McKinsey 7-S and Galbraith's Star Design Models. Comprehensive overviews of organisational models can be found in Bergh (2017); Falletta (2008); Stanford (2015).

(8)   See also Edmondson (2012); Limnios, Mazzarol, Ghadouani & Scilizzi (2014); Meyer (2013); Preiser, Biggs, De Vos & Folke (2018); Silva & Guerrini (2018); Stodd (2016).

(9)   The organisational components making up the Organisational Landscape given in Figure 3.2, and the principle of their close alignment across the Organisational Landscape in bringing about congruence – especially regarding Context, identity and Design – draw on the following sources: Bellerby (2017); Brickley, Smith & Zimmerman (2003); Burton, Obel & Håkonsson (2015); Bussin (2017a); Capelle (2014); Fenton & Pettigrew (2000); Galbraith, Lawler & Associates (1993); Huber (2011); Laloux (2014); Lawrence and Lorsch (1967); MacKenzie (1986); Nadler & Tushman (1988); Pettigrew & Masini (2001); Stanford (2015).

(10)   Cf. Anand & Daft (227); Burton & Obel (2018); Burton, Obel & Håkonsson (2015); Huber (2011); Galbraith (2014); (1997); (2006); (2008); Galbraith, Downey & Kates (2005); Hackman (1987); Hackman & Oldman (1976); Kesler & Kates (2011); MacKenzie (1986); Mohrman, Cohen & Mohrman (1995); Morgeson & Humphrey (2008); Nadler & Tushman (1988); (1997); Parker, Morgeson & Johns (2017); Roberts, (2004); Stanford (2007); Veldsman (2002).

(11)   Cf. Nadler & Tushman (1997).

(12)   Cf. Anand & Daft (227); Burton & Obel (2018); Burton, Obel & Håkonsson (2015); Capelle (2014); Hackman (1987); Hackman & Oldman (1976); Huber (2011); Galbraith (2014); (1997); (2006); (2008); Galbraith, Downey & Kates (2005); Jaques (2006); Jaques & Clement (1994); Kesler & Kates (2011); MacKenzie (1986); Mohrman, Cohen & Mohrman (1995); Morgeson & Humphrey (2008); Nadler & Tushman (1988); (1997); Parker, Morgeson & Johns (2017); Roberts, (2004); Rowbottom & Billis (1987); Stanford (2007); Shephard, Gray, Hunt & McArthur (2007); Veldsman (2002).

(13)   Extracted from the references given under Endnote 9.

(14)   The OD process presented in Figure 3.6 has been progressively evolved, distilled and refined from personal lessons learnt from over 50 Organisational Design consulting assignments over about 20 years across multiple industries, nationally and internationally, but has been sourced, enriched and expanded from sources initially such as Galbraith (2014); (1997); Galbraith, Lawler & Associates (1993); Galbraith, Downey & Kates (2005); and Nadler & Tushman (1988); (1997); and in recent times by Bellerby (2017); Brickley, Smith & Zimmerman (2003); Burton, Obel & Håkonsson (2015); Goold, M. & Campbell, A. (2002b); Galbraith (2006); 2008); (2014); Hawryszkiewycz (2017); Keller & Meaney (2017); Kesler & Kates (2011); Mohrman, Cohen & Mohrman (1995); Shephard, Gray, Hunt & McArthur (2007); Stanford (2015); Visscher & Visscher-Voerman (2010).

(15)   Visscher & Visscher-Voerman (2010) distinguish three basic approaches to the OD process: (i) a rational-logical step-wise process; (ii) a political process of negotiations shaped by the dominant coalition in organisations; and (iii) a pragmatic learning, doing, experimenting, action learning process. My suggested OD process, as per Figure 3.6, is closer to (i) and (iii), although the participative execution of my suggested process contains some flavour of (ii).

(16)   Sourced from Hawryszkiewycz (2017).

(17)   See in particular endnote 9.

(18)   Aubry & Lavoie-Tremblay (2018); Burton, Obel & Håkonsson (2015): Hanna (1988); Hawryszkiewycz (2017); Huber (2011); Kates & Galbraith (2007); MacKenzie (1986); Pettigrew & Masini (2001); Yoo, Boland & Lyytinen (2006).

(19)   Bussin (2017a); Kates & Galbraith (2007); Keller & Meaney (2017); Nadler & Tushman (1988); Visscher & Visscher-Voerman (2010).

(20)   MacKenzie (1986); Tolchinsky & Wenzl (2014); Visscher & Visscher-Voerman (2010).

(21)   Hawryszkiewycz (2017).

(22)   Brickley, Smith & Zimmerman (2003); Goold & Campbell (2002a); Kates & Galbraith (2007); Kesler & Kates (2011); Keller & Meaney (2017); MacKenzie (1986); Nadler & Tushman (1988); Pearce (2013); Roh, Turkulainen Whipple & Swink (2017); Stanford (2015).

(23)   See De Guerre, Se Guin, Pace & Burkeida's (2013) discussion of their redesign journey at the School of Extended Learning at Concordia University, Montreal, which illustrates the criticality of change navigation – as an inherent part of the design process, phased as Connect, Innovate, Design, and Implement by them – and using a co-design process based on Design Thinking principles.

(24)   Novak (2008).

(25)   See also Anand & Daft (2007) and Goold & Campbell (2002a; 2002b) in this regard.

4

HIGH LEVEL OVERVIEW OF THE ORGANISATIONAL DESIGN PROCESS AS AN ORGANISATIONAL INTERVENTION

The Life cycle of Organisational Design interventions

"We tend to meet any new situation by reorganizing; and what a wonderful method it can be for creating the illusion of progress while producing confusion, inefficiency, and demoralization."

(Charlton Ogburn)

"It takes nine months to have a baby, no matter how many people you put on the job."
(American saying)

In the last chapter, the basic OD vocabulary and language to inform a constructive and productive OD discourse in the organisation were established. The purpose of this chapter is to walk through the critical life cycle phases of a typical OD intervention (1) (2), a high level overview of the 'How', 'Who', 'When' and 'Where' of OD. This chapter serves as a handy, high level tour guide, or 'Google map', to the OD process in its totality, as explicated further in the book. If you get lost in the detail of later chapters, you can always find your bearings and location by returning to this chapter to establish your exact 'Google co-ordinates' in the OD process.

The typical life cycle phases of an OD intervention are:

- Phase 1: Recognise the need for Organisational (re)Design

- Phase 2: Scope and set up the OD assignment

- Phase 3: Craft a fit-for-purpose OD solution

- Phase 4: Implement the signed off OD solution and assess its value-add

- Phase 5: Close out

Each phase will be discussed in turn.

Phase 1: Recognise the need for an Organisational (re)Design (3)

An OD intervention is triggered by a properly identified and well formulated need for a reconceived/new design for the organisation (or part thereof), and the clearly specified, expected benefits the new design must bring about. That is, the value-adding difference of the new design in making the organisation more efficient, effective, competitive, successful, and a better citizen. In short, a fit-for-purpose organisation. Without a clearly identified, compelling need with clearly specified expected benefits, the OD intervention starts at a significant disadvantage from the word 'Go'. A real likelihood exists that an inappropriate OD solution will be architected, not delivering any benefits, however much justified *post hoc*.

The expected benefits can (or even stronger, must) also be linked to the overall purpose and objectives of OD, as explicated in Chapter 2 (see Figure 2.4). In considering the OD purpose and objectives, new OD needs may be opened up, especially around the organisation demonstrating true, genuine citizenship as a social enterprise.

Normally, the need and the expected benefits will be identified by the leadership of the organisation. A proactive OD Expert, whether employed by the organisation or an external OD consultant, may also alert the organisation's leadership to an undetected OD need and the to-be-expected benefits if addressed properly.

In general, two types of OD needs exist: a *brownfield design need* that relates to the redesign of an existing organisation or a unit thereof. Or, a *greenfield design need* which pertains to a new design where nothing exists at present. An identified OD need translates into the type of change required, hence the nature of the change navigation strategy and plan required to enable and support the OD process. Table 4.1 provides examples of typical OD needs within the framework of the overall OD purpose and objectives.

Table 4.1: Examples of typical OD needs within the framework of the overall OD purpose and objectives

OVERALL OD PURPOSE Fit-for-purpose Design			
OD OBJECTIVES (See Figure 2.4)			
1: Design for more productive deployment and use of resources	2: Design for enhanced organisational effectiveness	3: Design for minimal social impact and/or enhanced sustainability	4: Design for enabling greater value, unlocking wealth creation for all stakeholders
EXAMPLES OF TYPICAL OD NEEDS			
BROWNFIELD	**The redesign of an existing Organisation or one or more of its Work Units**		
Context	• A shift in a key Contextual/Design Given, for example, deregulation, geographical expansion by organisation, technological innovation.		

Context (cont.)	• A changed stakeholder relationship engagement mode. For example, a new shareholder or a different relationship with an existing stakeholder.
Leadership	• Change in leadership.
Key Leadership Task(s) (4)	• Revised Business/Value Model. • A reformulated Identity, such as a revised Strategic Intent for the organisation or for a Work Unit, such as the People, IT or Finance Functions. • A different resourcing model, like partnering or outsourcing.
Organisation	• A changed/changing organisational success factor. For example, speed of responsiveness, cost effectiveness, or rapid organisational growth/expansion. • A merger/acquisition.
Organisational Design Requirements	• A changed/changing Design Criterion. For example, a greater client focus or an enhanced capacity to act. • A change in the Core Operating Technology and/or Enabler(s).
Organisational Functioning	A major weakness in the existing design, which negatively impacts organisational performance and success, such as: • poor organisational co-ordination, and consequently the proliferation of ad hoc organisational entities (for example task forces, working groups) to bridge co-ordination and planning gaps; • excessive, ongoing conflict between areas/units; • ambiguous roles, responsibilities and accountabilities; • the duplication of activities, task and/or responsibilities, resulting in poor economies of scale; • poorly deployed resources and/or inefficient resources utilisation; • fragmented work flows, causing poor delivery and low client satisfaction; • a low and/or slow responsiveness to client needs; • slow decision-making and communication; • compressed or missing Levels of Work and/or inflexibility; • a mismatch between information processing capabilities and requirements; • slow responsiveness; • slow/little innovation; and • an unexpected/unpredicted operational delivery crisis/failure for which a standard operating procedure does not exist.
People	• The need to attract, engage and retain different employees. • A shift in employee profile. • Enhanced employee engagement.
GREENFIELD	**A completely new design where nothing exists at present.**

The box below provides case study examples across a number of industries of OD needs; the design solutions architected; and the resultant benefits.

EXAMPLES OF OD NEEDS WITH DESIGN SOLUTIONS AND BENEFITS			
Organisation	**OD Need**	**OD Solution**	**Benefits**
Industrial Gases Division of BOC with 35,000 people working in 15 countries around the globe to produce and deliver a wide variety of industrial gases. (5)	First, Industrial Gases was slow to develop new technology and diffuse it from a region throughout the company globally. Competitors were copying Industrial Gases' breakthroughs to gain advantage over Industrial Gases' subsidiaries in other countries. Second, Industrial Gases' clients were globalising but Industrial Gases was still dealing with the same client in separate country silos. Global clients wanted a global, one stop, contact point with Industrial Gases.	Design Vision: To become the most customer-focused company in the industrial gases business through innovation and the service provided, by working together around the globe. Design Solution: The organisation crafted a global, lateral integrating Work Role. While retaining the existing design of separate, autonomous, country-based regions to address local needs, it architected Global Product Managers for each major sector of its business, such as food, steel, and chemicals, with accountabilities cutting across national boundaries. In this way it was able to deal with the unique demands of widely varying customers and markets, but the Global Product Managers also made it possible to meet the needs of large customers who demanded one-stop shopping for their worldwide needs. The managers were also accountable for meeting goals on developing, disseminating, and building new technology.	Within two years, the innovation rate drastically improved. Additionally, the organisation was once again winning major supply contracts from global customers.

Organisation	OD Need	OD Solution	Benefits
Cereal manufacturing and brewing companies. (6)	Operators controlled only one piece of equipment – one-task-one-job – and had little understanding of the what, when and who, up and down the core value chain. This triggered quality issues, absenteeism crises, and many narrow menial job descriptions and job grading levels.	Flexible, multi-tasked Work Roles with skills-based pay – Process Operators – across the whole value chain.	More meaningful work; more flexible work deployment; enhanced quality; higher pay; a richer skills pool.
ING, an Amsterdam-based global bank, the 28th largest in the world, with over 53,000 employees. (7)	The 2008 financial crisis adversely affected profitability, resulting in the selling off of product lines and the rethinking of the Business Model in the face of increasing regulation.	The redesign took place in the Dutch leg of ING. Apart from the cleaning up and simplification of internal processes, as well as a strategic push into digital banking, ING introduced an Adhocracy Organisational Design. This design is team-based, with people assigned to autonomous nine-person Squads. Each Squad focuses on servicing specific user needs – internal or external – with a high level of freedom to shape their own goals, KPIs, work flow, hours of work, and physical space. Work is broken down into short, successive sprints. The Squads were organised into 'Tribes' of linked, related customers' needs, and 'Chapters': like-minded colleagues, dealing more with people issues, and supported by 'agile coaches'.	Substantial improvements in customer service, cost efficiency, employee engagement, and innovation.

Organisation	OD Need	OD Solution	Benefits
Swiss watch industry. (8)	After dominating the worldwide watch industry for more than a century, the Swiss watch industry found themselves on the verge of disaster in the late 1970s. New technologies involving quartz, batteries, microelectronics, and digital timepieces had enabled low-cost manufacturers in Japan, Hong Kong and the United States to under-price their Swiss competitors and wrest control of both the low- and mid-range segments of the market. In 1983, the two giants of the Swiss industry, SSIH and ASUAG, faced insolvency. Swiss bankers stepped in and asked Nicholas Hayek to advise them on how to save the combined operation known as SMH. (He later purchased a controlling stake in SMH and became its CEO). The operation Hayek took over was an agglomeration of more than 100 different brands, including Omega, Longines, Rado, Tissot and Hamilton, each with its own research and development, manufacturing and marketing operations.	A Front-Back Organisational Shape was architected. Back Design: Both product development and manufacturing were centralised into single operating entities. The combination of more than 100 small, inefficient watch manufacturing and assembly operations into one immediately produced significant economies of scale. New, state-of-the-art technologies were introduced. For example, one of the SMH plants was turning out 35,000 Swatch watches and millions of components each day with virtually no people involved in the process. Together, mass production and new technology significantly lowered production costs. Front Design: Simultaneously, the marketing, sales, and distribution functions were completely decentralised and reorganised along product lines with Global Product Managers. Country managers were appointed everywhere to maintain and strengthen localised customer connections.	The result was an astounding success. In 1983 SMH suffered a loss of $124 million on sales of $1.1 billion. Ten years later, it was reporting $2.1 billion in sales and $286 million in profits. In ten years, the company was rescued from bankruptcy, having amassed a market value of $3.5 billion.

Organisation	OD Need	OD Solution	Benefits
Swiss watch industry. (8) (cont.)	His Strategic Intent was to win back the mass market for watches, by making the innovative, inexpensively priced, Swatch one of the most popular watch brands in the world. His Strategic Intent was to combine the Swiss reputation for excellence with technologically innovative production techniques and exciting, sharply delineated product lines to compete across the entire spectrum of the global watch business.	Making the Front-Back Design operate effectively required a cultural transformation within SMH, from a political minefield of fiercely defended, competing fiefdoms into a global operation completely dependent on the ability and willingness of managers to negotiate and cooperate across boundaries of function, product, and geography. In the course of reshaping the company and its culture, Hayek eventually replaced every member of the original executive team.	
Financial Services: Short term insurance. (9)	The organisation experienced a significant loss in market share due to new competitors entering the market, together with a significant decrease in sales and an increase in operational costs. This led to a need to not only rethink the organisation's strategy and product offering to address its competitive positioning, market share and profitability, but also to change the organisation's tactics, design, and operational conditions to improve efficiencies.	The OD solution was a Process Organisational Shape, configured around the core value chain of the organisation, with accountabilities assigned in accordance with value chain elements (Horizontal Design), as well as a Vertical Design in accordance with the requisite Levels of Work (to be discussed in Chapter 7).	The following resulted from the revised OD: Improved competitive advantage: the creation of a well-aligned, flexible, and productive organisation, able to meet the demands of the shifting market place. Improved financial performance: better alignment between organisational goals, processes and employees led to greater productivity and less waste. Improved talent management: a clearer understanding of the type of talent required to perform effectively at the different Levels of Work,

Organisation	OD Need	OD Solution	Benefits
Financial Services: short term insurance. (9) (cont.)			resulted in a significant improvement in talent allocation and development processes. Improved customer satisfaction: employees were better able to deliver high quality services and products to customers through shorter cycle times, meeting customer expectations better, resulting in improved overall customer satisfaction. Improved employee satisfaction: a culture of accountability was created where employees were well-managed, had clarity regarding their roles and what was expected of them; understood their responsibilities and authorities; and had greater insight into how they were contributing to the organisational goals.

Phase 2: Scope and set up the OD assignment

A properly identified need for an OD intervention with clearly specified expected benefits was demarcated in Phase 1. Phase 2 is about properly scoping and setting up the OD assignment. This has to occur between the leader(s) who identified the need with expected benefits, and whoever is going to conduct the OD assignment. That is, the leader(s) him/herself; a designated leader or leadership team requested to address the need; and/or an OD Expert(s). To simplify the ensuing discussion, the party who identified the need will be called the Client, and the party responsible for the execution of the OD assignment, the OD Expert.

Phase 2 consists of eight sub-phases, namely:

- demarcate the boundaries of the intervention;
- contract mutual expectations;
- assess the organisational readiness for the intervention;
- decide on the most appropriate OD process option;
- establish the ground rules to frame the intervention;
- set up a proper intervention governance structure and process;
- sign-off on a Client Memorandum of Understanding; and finally,
- prepare and distribute a communication brief, announcing the intervention.

Phase 2.1: Demarcate the boundaries of the OD intervention

The Client must clearly demarcate the boundaries of the OD intervention to the OD Expert. Typical boundaries include:

- The need (or business case) for the OD intervention: why is the OD intervention necessary?
- The desirable OD end state: what benefits must the OD solution bring about?
- The focus of the OD intervention. Either the total organisation or the organisational area concerned:
  - Vertically: which organisational levels are included?
  - Horizontally: from where to where in terms of the core/enabling/support work process(es) concerned?

A template that can used for a proper demarcation is given in Appendix A: Design Template 1.

Phase 2.2: Contract the mutual expectations between the Client and OD Expert

The mutual expectations between the parties involved must be contracted to avoid any possible misunderstandings. Table 4.2 lists the typical expectations to be agreed upon between the Client and OD Expert.

Table 4.2: Mutual expectations to be contracted between the Client and OD Expert

CLIENT EXPECTATIONS OF OD EXPERT	OD EXPERT EXPECTATIONS OF CLIENT
• Client is accountable for the OD intervention and agreed upon solution, as well as its implementation. • A thorough understanding of the client system to be (re)designed. • Keeping commitments and promises. • Straight talk. • Up-to-date OD expertise and leading practices befitting the OD assignment. • Co-responsibility for the success of the OD assignment. • Ability to deliver at the requisite level of complexity of the OD intervention. • Objectivity and impartiality.	• OD Expert is responsible for leading the OD intervention and for crafting a fit-for-purpose OD solution within the agreed upon time. • The Client taking full accountability for the signed-off OD solution and its implementation. • A clear brief and scope. • Client accessibility. • Acceptance of OD as a formal organisational discipline. • The necessary resources. • Open-mindedness. • Rapid turnaround on the signing-off on deliverables as the OD process proceeds. • Providing back up and support at all times and under all circumstances. • Trust in the expertise and advice of the OD Expert.

Phase 2.3: Assess the organisational readiness to undertake the OD intervention

An upfront assessment must be co-conducted by the Client and OD Expert to determine whether favourable readiness factors, the critical preconditions to a successful OD intervention, are in place (10) *(11)*:

- The *sponsorship* for the intended OD intervention must be at the right organisational level relative to the organisation or organisational area to be (re)designed – at least at the top organisational level of OD intervention's focus, or one level up.

- The Client, as the key leader of the organisation/organisational area affected and the final decision maker with regard to the proposed OD solution, must have a *permanent appointment*. In other words, this key role cannot be filled by an acting person. An acting person will not be able to give the required backing to the design process, solution and its implementation.

- A *well-articulated need and scope* with *clearly specified expected benefits* have been formulated and clearly communicated.

  The expected benefits of the new design must outweigh the costs of the OD intervention, including both the hard and soft benefits and costs. If the latter does not outweigh the former by a significant margin – I would argue by at least 30% – the OD intervention is not worth the effort.

- *Shared agreement must exist on the Strategic Intent* as an element of the Organisation's Identity amongst the senior leadership group of the affected area. The Strategic Intent forms the departure point for a fit-for-purpose design. Without such an Intent, the OD will occur in a vacuum and the chances of a fit-for-purpose design are slim.

- *A well-functioning leadership community/team with a healthy dynamic* must exist in the affected area. An effective design process and robust design need fierce, zero-based conversations with no holy cows. Only if the former is in place, that is a well-functioning leadership community/team, can the latter occur.

- *An integrated, comprehensive and systematic design process*, informed by leading OD practices, must be used. This process needs to be enabled by *sound project management and change navigation*. If leadership wants a superficial, quick fix job, the design assignment must not be undertaken.

- *The necessary resources* (for example, time, people, funds) should be allocated to the OD intervention.

- The OD Expert really must have *genuine OD expertise, at the requisite level of design complexity*, as necessitated by the OD need to be addressed. Design needs vary in complexity, hence the necessary OD expertise. For example, the complexity difference between a national and global organisation or a total vs. an organisational functional design.

A template that can used in assessing the organisational readiness for an intended OD intervention is given in Appendix A: Design Template 2.

If the above readiness preconditions are not in place, the likelihood of a successful OD intervention will be slim. The OD intervention will cause more harm than benefit; more organisational agony than a constructive organisational re-invention; more confusion and chaos than clarity and focus; more passive or active resistance and sabotage than support and ownership; and more bad than good organisational politics.

If one or more preconditions are unfavourable, actions must be taken to change them or the intervention must be delayed until preconditions become favourable. For example, the appointment of a permanent CEO to replace an acting CEO.

Phase 2.4: The Client and OD Expert jointly decide on the most appropriate OD intervention process option

The execution of the OD intervention process can be set up in different ways. The importance of deciding on the appropriate option cannot be overstressed. It must suit the preference of the Client; the typical decision-making culture of the organisation; the available resources; and the speed at which the intervention must move relative to the strategic window of opportunity for the roll out of the OD solution.

Table 4.3 gives four possible execution options, and when each would be most applicable (12).

Table 4.3: OD process execution options with their respective applicability

OPTION	DESCRIPTION	APPLICABILITY	DOMINANT STRENGTH(S)	DOMINANT WEAKNESS(ES)
1. Assurance	The Client has already generated a desired design. The OD Expert has merely to quality assure the Client's proposed design, independently and in an impartial, objective manner, against leading OD practice.	• The Client has already made up her/his mind. • The best OD solution(s) to consider is/are clear cut. • The sponsor has the power to implement. • Upfront buy-in by key stakeholders is of lesser importance.	• Speed	• Poor in-depth understanding of organisation: solution is only assessed on its pure technical merits.
2. Expert generated	The Client wants the OD Expert to craft a design and submit it to him/her for a decision.	• Little OD interest/expertise exists in the Client system. • The Client is unwilling to invest a significant amount of internal resources (time, people) in the OD intervention. • Speed is of the essence. • The sponsor has the power to implement. • Upfront buy-in by key stakeholders is of lesser importance.	• In-depth OD expertise can be mobilised. • Speed. • In-depth understanding of the organisation.	• High investment in obtaining buy-in and ownership of OD solution. • Organisational insecurity and uncertainty. • No internal OD capacity is built.
3. Straw Model	The OD Expert crafts a 'straw model' design which is workshopped with the relevant key decision makers in the client system for a final decision.	• The Client is unwilling to invest a significant amount of internal resources (time, people) in the OD intervention. • Speed is of the essence. • Some upfront buy-in by key decision makers in the client system is important.	• Opportunity to adapt/refine/enrich proposed OD solution.	• Organisational politics can wreck the workshop.

OPTION	DESCRIPTION	APPLICABILITY	DOMINANT STRENGTH(S)	DOMINANT WEAKNESS(ES)
4. Co-design *(13)*	The OD Expert facilitates an OD co-design process with the relevant stakeholders in the client system.	• Strong buy-in and ownership by key decision makers in the client system are crucial. • Co-determination is a typical decision-making style in the client organisation. • 'Wicked' design challenges, issues and problems. • The Client is willing to invest a significant amount of internal resources in the OD intervention. • There is a need to build and embed (a new) shared mental model(s), which is/are essential to enhance the likelihood of a fit-for-purpose OD solution, and strong buy-in into and ownership of the 'radical' solution is needed to make it work. • Fresh, out of the box, thinking is required regarding the existing design, arising out of multiple, diverse perspectives.	• Chances of more radically innovative, integrated OD solutions because multiple voices and disciplines are in the Room. • Information/ knowledge richness of process. • In-depth understanding of OD solution. • Higher levels of upfront buy-in and ownership is needed: 'our' solution. • Relatively quicker, more successful implementation, and faster realisation of benefits.	• Ample time and opportunity for organisational politics, turf wars, lobbying, and coalition formation to hijack the process. • Time consuming. • Resource demanding.

The different process execution options, given in Table 4.3, imply different levels of participation by organisational members. This has a direct implication for what change navigation strategy and plan must be crafted in support of the OD intervention. The less upfront participation during the generation of the OD solution, the more intense the consultation once the solution has been approved by the powers that be. And, vice versa.

For the sake of simplicity, Option 2 will be adopted in the discussion of the respective Strategic, Tactical and Operational Design processes in the to-come chapters. At the end of the discussion of each Design Level, for example, Strategic Design, the other process options will be briefly addressed.

Phase 2.5: Establish the ground rules to frame the OD intervention correctly

The ground rules to frame the OD intervention must established upfront, as these set the parameters for the kind of OD solution that can be considered by the OD Expert. Typical ground rules are:

- a zero-based look at the design to be reviewed: 'If we had to set up this business again...';
- no Holy Cows – everything is open for reconsideration;
- an attitude of, 'If this was my business, how would I do things?';
- think out of the box: consider radical, way out possibilities/options;
- the strategic timeframe applicable to the OD solution; and
- whether Designs used in other industries/sectors can be considered.

Phase 2.6: Set-up a proper intervention governance structure and process

Given the OD process execution option selected in Phase 2.4, a sound governance structure and process must be set up to oversee the OD intervention: who is to meet when to discuss, review and approve what. A clever way to set up OD governance meetings is to synchronise them with key milestone dates and delivery deadlines. This will expedite approvals, sign-offs, and moves ahead.

Phase 2.7: Sign-off on a Client Memorandum of Understanding

The Client must sign-off on a MOU with the OD Expert to ensure that a written, shared understanding exists on what the OD assignment entails within the agreed upon parameters. Typically the MOU (about two to three pages), drafted by the OD Expert, must cover at least the following: the OD need; the scope of the OD intervention; deliverable(s); the OD process execution option decided on; a high level work plan with milestones and dates; the expected value add/benefits of the OD intervention; the respective roles, responsibilities and expectations of the Client and OD Expert; and the OD assignment governance structure and process.

Phase 2.8: Prepare and distribute a communication brief

A communication brief under the Client's name – which can be drafted by the OD Expert on behalf of the Client – must be compiled and circulated throughout the affected organisational area and key stakeholders, even customers and suppliers.

In some cases, the community in which the organisation is located may also be informed. The importance of early communication to counter fears of retrenchments; stop speculation and rumours; and proactively minimise destructive personal and organisational dynamics, cannot be overstated. Change navigation commences the moment the OD intervention is announced.

This brief must cover at least the following: why the OD intervention is being undertaken, that is the need (or business case); the expected deliverables and benefits; how the intervention will proceed with key milestones and dates; the expected involvement of people in the exercise; how people will be kept informed at what frequency; and any assurances without overpromising on unknowns, like 'Nobody will lose their jobs'.

Phase 3: Craft a fit-for-purpose OD solution

Within the signed Client Memorandum of Understanding as the basic frame of reference for the OD intervention, the intervention can now proceed. Three steps make up this phase:

- Phase 3.1: the OD Expert obtains the relevant information on the client system from the Client and peruses it.

- Phase 3.2: In terms of the chosen OD process execution option (see Table 4.3), the OD Expert crafts a fit-for-purpose OD solution, following the relevant design route map(s):
    - Stage A: The Strategic Design route map;
    - Stage B: The Tactical Design route map; and/or
    - Stage C: The Operational Design route map.

    What form the roll out of the route map will take on the ground will be determined by the design process execution option selected. What will be previewed below and discussed in detail in subsequent chapters essentially follows Options 2 and 3, where the OD Expert conducts the OD assignment, following the relevant route map. As discussed above, in Option 4, the OD Expert facilitates a selected leadership group through the route map concerned. In Option 1, the OD Expert quality assures the OD solution generated by the Client by testing it against the required deliverables from the steps making up the route map.

- Phase 3.3: OD Expert submits his/her report to the Client who signs off on the complete, proposed OD solution.

Phase 3.1: The OD Expert obtains the relevant information on the client system from the Client

Obtaining and studying upfront relevant information on the client system is essential to the success of the OD intervention. Otherwise, the OD Expert will look at the client system uninformed and/or gather information that is already available. The information needed and available is, of course, a function, whether one is talking about a brownfield or greenfield OD situation. Table 4.4 lists the typical minimum necessary information to be supplied by the Client, predominantly assuming a brownfield OD need.

Table 4.4: Upfront minimum needed information for an OD intervention by the OD Expert

STRATEGIC DESIGN	TACTICAL-OPERATIONAL DESIGN
1. Identity of organisation: Purpose, Vision, Core Values, Strategic Intent, Legacy.	1. Identity of organisation: Purpose, Vision, Core Values, Strategic Intent, Legacy.
2. High level profile of the organisation: markets, clients, products/services, Core Operating Technology with Enablers, people,	2. High level profile of the organisation, including Organisational Unit: markets, clients, products/services, Core Operating Technology with Enablers, people.
3. Organisational Strategic Intent for the coming period.	3. Organisational and organisational entity Strategic Intents for coming period.
4. High level work processes: core, enabling and support.	4. Strategic Organisational Design, documented or otherwise.
5. Organogram/structure for top three to four levels of entity to be (re)designed.	5. High level Work Unit work processes: core, enabling and support.
6. Job/role profiles for the top three to four levels of the organisation.	6. Organogram/structure for top three to four levels of the Work Unit to be (re)designed.
7. One-on-one interviews (first prize) and/ or focus groups with the top three to four levels of the organisation to be (re) designed. Alternatively, but least preferred, an e-mail survey of the top three to four levels of the entity to be (re)designed, covering:	7. Job/role profiles for top three to four levels of the Work Unit concerned.
5. strengths and weaknesses of current design;	8. One-on-one interviews (first prize) and/or focus groups with the top three to four levels of the organisational entity to be (re)designed. Alternatively, but least preferred, an e-mail survey of the top three to four levels of the entity to be (re)designed, covering:
6. suggested Design Criteria for the to-be-redesigned entity; and	• strengths and weaknesses of current design;
7. suggested (revised) design with rationale and benefits.	• proposed Design Criteria for the to-be-redesigned entity; and
	• proposed (revised) design with rationale and benefits.

Phase 3.2: In terms of the chosen OD process execution option, the OD Expert crafts the appropriate design

Depending on the OD need, and given the three OD levels discussed in Chapter 3, the route map for one or more of the respective OD levels have to be covered. Each level-specific route map, from Strategic through to Tactical and Operational Design, is given here only for high level orientation and review purposes. In addition, in case a reader gets lost in subsequent chapters, he/she will be enable to pick up their 'Google co-ordinates' again in this chapter. Each route map will be discussed in greater detail in subsequent chapters.

At this point in time, only a few high level comments will be made with regard to the respective route maps. However, three general points are worth making, which are applicable to all of the route maps. First, the OD Expert must enlighten the Client at a high level of the major Design Steps – given a specific route map – that will be followed in architecting the Design Solution. An informed and capacitated Client is a great bonus to the success of the process.

Second, in order to take the Client along in terms of thinking as the OD Expert moves through the route map, regardless of the chosen OD process execution option followed, it is of critical importance to obtain progressive client sign-off at key points as one moves through the sequential steps of the route map. This progressive sign-off is similar to building a House. A client signs off with the architect, and later the builder, at key steps in the design and building of the House, given the sequential, interdependency of steps. In this way, progressive consensus and agreement are achieved. If a disagreement surfaces, the OD Expert and Client would know exactly what the issue is for *that* specific step in the design process, and can immediately address it on the spot before proceeding to the next step. The whole solution is not under contention. This would be the case if one only 'unveils' the complete solution to the client at the completion of the route map. In the case of progressive sign-offs, only that disputed portion of the solution being addressed at that point in the route map would be under debate.

This implies real time, constant interaction between the Client and OD Expert for the progressive sign-off of the OD solution to occur as the solution takes shapes. Phase 3.3 is merely the sign-off of the complete solution, similar to when a client signs off with the architect the final House Plan, and with the builder the completely built House. The typical sign-off points are upon the completion of a design step in a route map. As has been indicated above, synchronising the OD intervention governance meetings with key sign-off points would be a clever thing to do.

Third, though the route maps appear to only move in one direction, in practice the design process moves iteratively, backwards and forward as progressively deeper insights are gained.

What follows is a high level overview of the different design route maps in logical order from Strategic, though Tactical, to Operational Design. It is important to note that in order to keep the Strategic, Tactical and Operational route maps simple, the Change Navigation and Project Management Building Blocks of the OD process have been left out (see Figure 3.6), but are essential enabling elements to the design maps.

Stage A: The execution of the Strategic OD route map

Figure 4.1 gives an overview of the Strategic OD route map (14). The Strategic Design literature focuses virtually, exclusively on profit-driven organisations (that is business organisations). To complement this virtually exclusivity, I also pay some attention to Co-operatives (see Chapters 5 and 6) within the context of the increasing emphasis on social enterprises (raised in Chapter 2). The design of Boards of Directors also does not form part of the mainstream design literature. However, I include its design because Boards are crucial from a corporate governance perspective in the design of the total organisation.

The Strategic Design map will be discussed in greater detail in Chapters 5 to 8. As has been discussed before, the aim of Strategic OD is to generate and implement the House Plan of a total organisation. Hence, the use of the metaphor of the generation of a House Plan, followed by the building of the House. Myth 4, that is that OD is merely about drawing/changing organograms, is also exorcised in Figure 4.1. As can be seen, the generation of organograms only comes in Step A.5.2, the 20th step of the route map.

Generally, the need for Strategic (re)Design is triggered when there is a change in the executive leadership of the organisation; a change in the organisation's Business Model and/or Strategic Intent; or the current design as Operating Model is ineffective. At a minimum, a crafted Strategic Design must be in place for the same time period as the organisation's Strategic Intent.

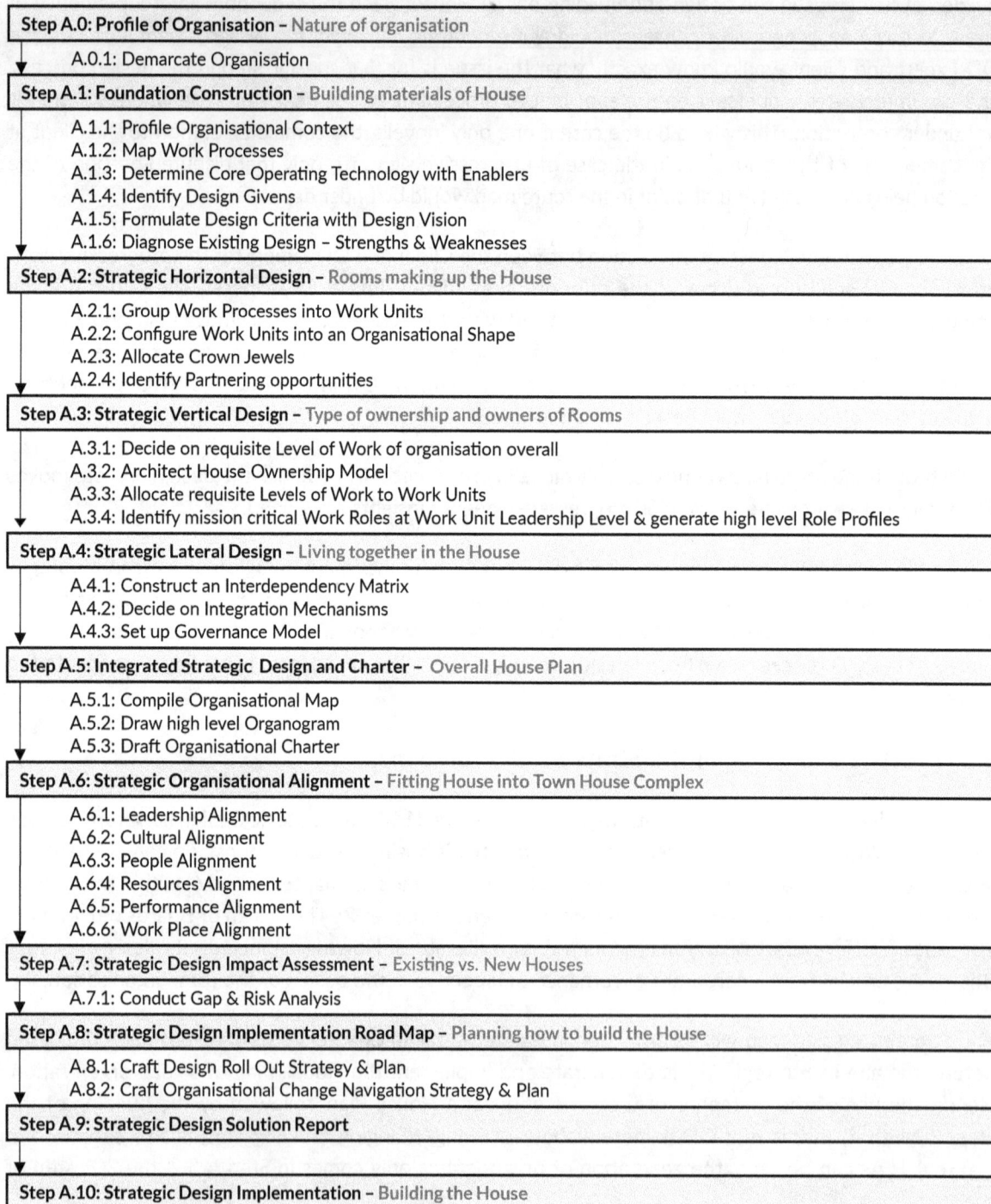

Step A.0: Profile of Organisation – Nature of organisation

    A.0.1: Demarcate Organisation

Step A.1: Foundation Construction – Building materials of House

    A.1.1: Profile Organisational Context
    A.1.2: Map Work Processes
    A.1.3: Determine Core Operating Technology with Enablers
    A.1.4: Identify Design Givens
    A.1.5: Formulate Design Criteria with Design Vision
    A.1.6: Diagnose Existing Design – Strengths & Weaknesses

Step A.2: Strategic Horizontal Design – Rooms making up the House

    A.2.1: Group Work Processes into Work Units
    A.2.2: Configure Work Units into an Organisational Shape
    A.2.3: Allocate Crown Jewels
    A.2.4: Identify Partnering opportunities

Step A.3: Strategic Vertical Design – Type of ownership and owners of Rooms

    A.3.1: Decide on requisite Level of Work of organisation overall
    A.3.2: Architect House Ownership Model
    A.3.3: Allocate requisite Levels of Work to Work Units
    A.3.4: Identify mission critical Work Roles at Work Unit Leadership Level & generate high level Role Profiles

Step A.4: Strategic Lateral Design – Living together in the House

    A.4.1: Construct an Interdependency Matrix
    A.4.2: Decide on Integration Mechanisms
    A.4.3: Set up Governance Model

Step A.5: Integrated Strategic Design and Charter – Overall House Plan

    A.5.1: Compile Organisational Map
    A.5.2: Draw high level Organogram
    A.5.3: Draft Organisational Charter

Step A.6: Strategic Organisational Alignment – Fitting House into Town House Complex

    A.6.1: Leadership Alignment
    A.6.2: Cultural Alignment
    A.6.3: People Alignment
    A.6.4: Resources Alignment
    A.6.5: Performance Alignment
    A.6.6: Work Place Alignment

Step A.7: Strategic Design Impact Assessment – Existing vs. New Houses

    A.7.1: Conduct Gap & Risk Analysis

Step A.8: Strategic Design Implementation Road Map – Planning how to build the House

    A.8.1: Craft Design Roll Out Strategy & Plan
    A.8.2: Craft Organisational Change Navigation Strategy & Plan

Step A.9: Strategic Design Solution Report

Step A.10: Strategic Design Implementation – Building the House

---

Figure 4.1: Overview of the Strategic OD route map

Stage B: The execution of the Tactical OD route map

Figure 4.2 gives an overview of the Tactical OD route map *(15)*, which will be discussed in greater detail in Chapter 9. As has been noted before, the aim of Tactical OD is to design one, more or all of the Rooms making up the total organisational House Plan, its Work Units, as per the Strategic Design. In other words, the Divisions/Departments of the organisation, for example Operations, Finance, People, Supply Chain. This assumes that in conducting a Tactical OD intervention, a thorough understanding of the organisation's current Strategic Design exists. The Work Unit design implications of this understanding is typically incorporated into Step B.1.1: Profile Work Unit Context.

Typically, the need for Tactical (re)Design arises when the Strategic Design changes significantly; the senior leadership of the Function changes; the Functional Strategic Intent is revised; or the Operating Model of the Function is ineffective. Generally speaking, the Tactical Design of a Function must be in force for the same period as its Strategic Intent.

As can be seen in Figure 4.2, the Tactical OD route map is, except for the first step, stepwise the same as the Strategic OD route map. The only difference between the two route maps lies in their respective foci, that is the latter deals with the total organisation (the whole House), while the former deals with a Work Unit of the organisation: a Room in the House such as People (or HR), Supply Chain, or Finance.

In my opinion, it is, because of this design process similarity that Tactical Design is treated in the mainstream Strategic OD literature most frequently as a step-child and does not get the attention it deserves in its own right. The criticality of following the Strategic Design with proper and thorough Tactical Designs for each Room making up the House is glossed over. This oversight creates major alignment issues at the Tactical Work Unit level once the Strategic Design has been implemented, as will become apparent in later discussions.

Step B.0: Profile of Work Unit – Nature of Room

> B.0.1: Demarcate Work Unit (WU)
> B.0.2: Align WUs

Step B.1: Foundation Construction – Building materials of Room

> B.1.1: Profile WU Context
> B.1.2: Map WU Processes
> B.1.3: Determine WU Core Operating Technology with Enablers
> B.1.4: Identify WU Design Givens
> B.1.5: Formulate WU Design Criteria with Design Vision
> B.1.6: Diagnose Existing WU Design – Strengths & Weaknesses

Step B.2: Tactical Horizontal Design – Work Domains making up the Room

> B.2.1: Group WU Work Processes into Work Domains (WDs)
> B.2.2: Configure WDs into WU Shape
> B.2.3: Allocate WU Crown Jewels
> B.2.4: Construct Partnering Relationships

Step B.3: Tactical Vertical Design – Type of ownership & owners of Work Domains

> B.3.1: Decide on requisite Level of Work of Work Unit
> B.3.2: Architect WU House Ownership Model
> B.3.3: Allocate requisite Level of Work to Work Domains
> B.3.4: Identify mission-critical WU Work Roles & generate high level Role Profiles

Step B.4: Tactical Lateral Design – Living together in the Room

> B.4.1: Construct WU Interdependency Matrix
> B.4.2: Decide on WU Integration Mechanisms
> B.4.3: Set up WU Governance Model

Step B.5: Integrated Tactical Design and Charter – Overall Room Plan

> B.5.1: Compile Work Unit Map
> B.5.2: Draw Work Unit Organogram
> B.5.3: Draft Work Unit Charter

Step B.6: Tactical Organisational Alignment – Fitting Room into House Plan

> B.6.1: Leadership Alignment
> B.6.2: Cultural Alignment
> B.6.3: People Alignment
> B.6.4: Resources Alignment
> B.6.5: Performance Alignment
> B.6.6: Work Place Alignment

Step B.7: Tactical Design Impact Assessment – Existing vs. new Rooms

> B.7.1: Conduct Gap & Risks analysis

Step B.8: Tactical Design Implementation Road Map – Planning how to build Room

> B.8.1: Craft Design Roll Out Strategy & Plan
> B.8.2: Craft Organisational Change Navigation Strategy & Plan

Step B.9: Tactical Design Solution Report

Step B.10: Tactical Design Implementation – Building the Room

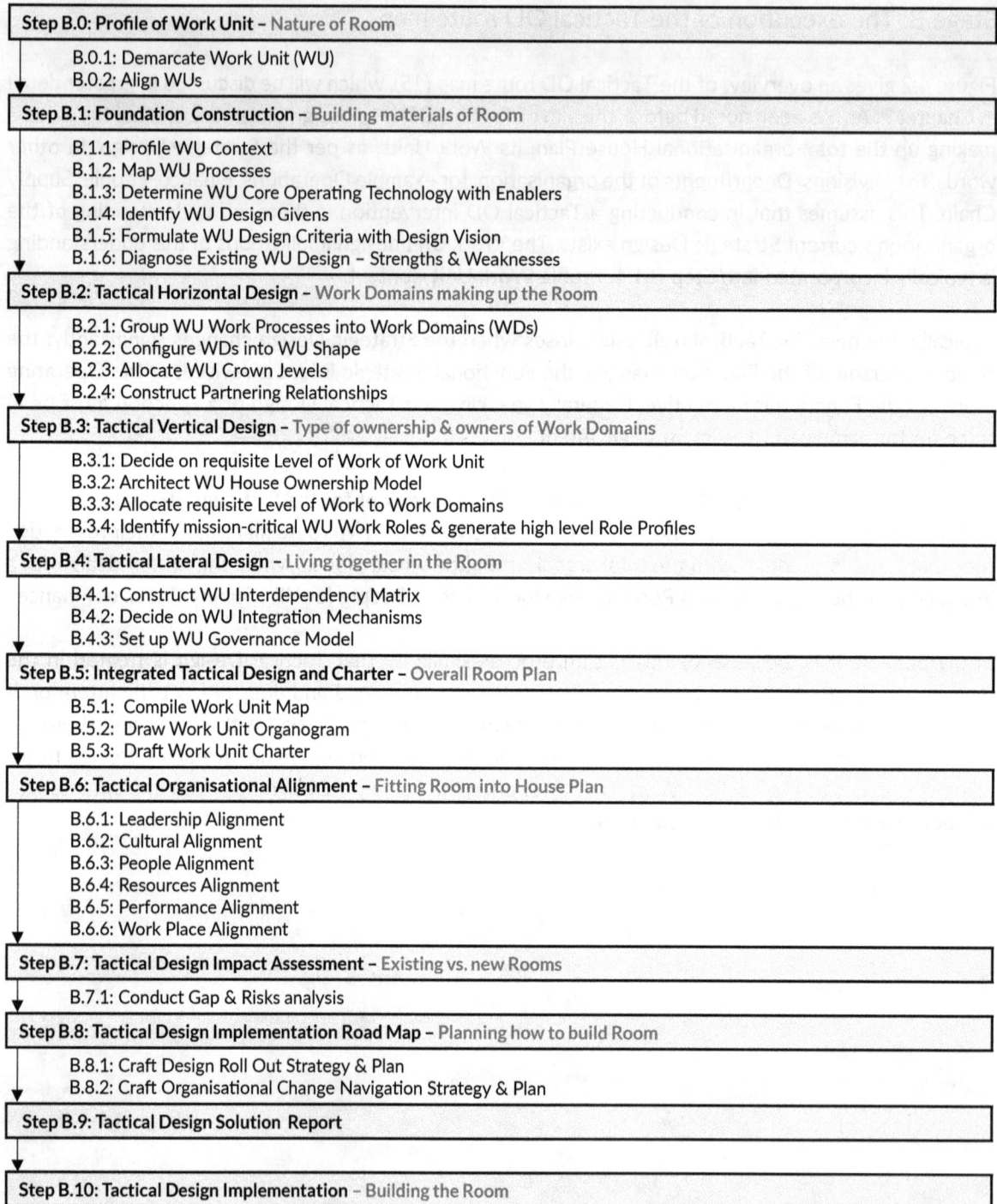

Figure 4.2: Overview of the Tactical OD route map

Stage C: The execution of the Operational OD route map

Figure 4.3 gives an overview of the Operational OD route map. Operational Design focuses on the daily living in the House with its Rooms as contained in its Work Teams and Work Roles. It is intriguing to note, particularly regarding the Work Role (job design or work system) literature, the overwhelming focus on desirable Work Role characteristics (in my OD vocabulary 'Design Criteria') and their interrelationships – the *content* – with little if any detailed explication of the *process* of designing Work Roles (16). Relative to Work Role design, Work Teams receive far less attention. This is ironic since Work Teams are widely propagated as the key building block of the organisation of the future (see Chapter 11).

Generally, the need for Operational (re)Design is triggered when the Strategic and/or Tactical Designs in force are revised; there is a change in leadership requiring a relook at Work Roles and Teams; a new Work Role or Team is created; and/or a critical operational delivery crisis/failure occurs.

The Operational OD route map will be discussed in greater detail in Chapter 10. As discussed above, the aim of Operational OD is to design the furniture required in the Rooms given by the Tactical Design. The furniture is essentially of two kinds: Work Teams and Work Roles. This assumes that in conducting an Operational OD intervention, a thorough understanding must exist of the Strategic and Tactical Designs for the Organisation and the Work Units concerned. The Work Unit design implications of this understanding are to be incorporated into Step C.1: Work Context Givens.

As reflected in Figure 4.3, after Step C.2.C, a key design decision has to be made whether a Room will be furnished with one or more Work Teams (each having Work Roles) or only Work Roles. In the latter case, the Room as a whole equates to a Work Team. It is important to note that for *each* Work Team and Work Role an Operational Design has to be done. This makes the execution of a comprehensive Operational Design most demanding in terms of design resources if many Rooms have to be covered.

```
┌─────────────────────────────────┐
│   Step C.1:  Design Givens      │
│       Work Unit Context         │
└─────────────────────────────────┘
                 │
                 ▼
┌─────────────────────────────────┐
│  Step C.2: Operational  Design  │
│          Framework              │
└─────────────────────────────────┘
                 │
                 ▼
┌─────────────────────────────────┐
│   Step C.2A: Operational        │
│        Design Vision            │
│  Mechanistic ◄──► Organic       │
└─────────────────────────────────┘
```

Step C.2B: Design Autonomy

| Step C.2C: Expected People Conduct | ◄──► | Step C.2D: Design Criteria |

Step C.2E: Desired Outcomes

Step C.3: Current Design Strengths and Weaknesses

| Step C.4: Work Team Design *(per Team)* | ◄──► | Step C.5: Work Role Design *(per Role)* |

Step C.6: Competency Profiles

Step C.7: Evolving phases of increasing Work Team/Work Role Autonomy

Step C.8 Integrated Operational Design

Step C.9: Operational Design Alignment

Step C10: Operational Design Impact Assessment

Step C.11: Operational Design Implementation Road Map

Step C.12: Operational Design Solution Report

Step C.13: Operational Design Implementation

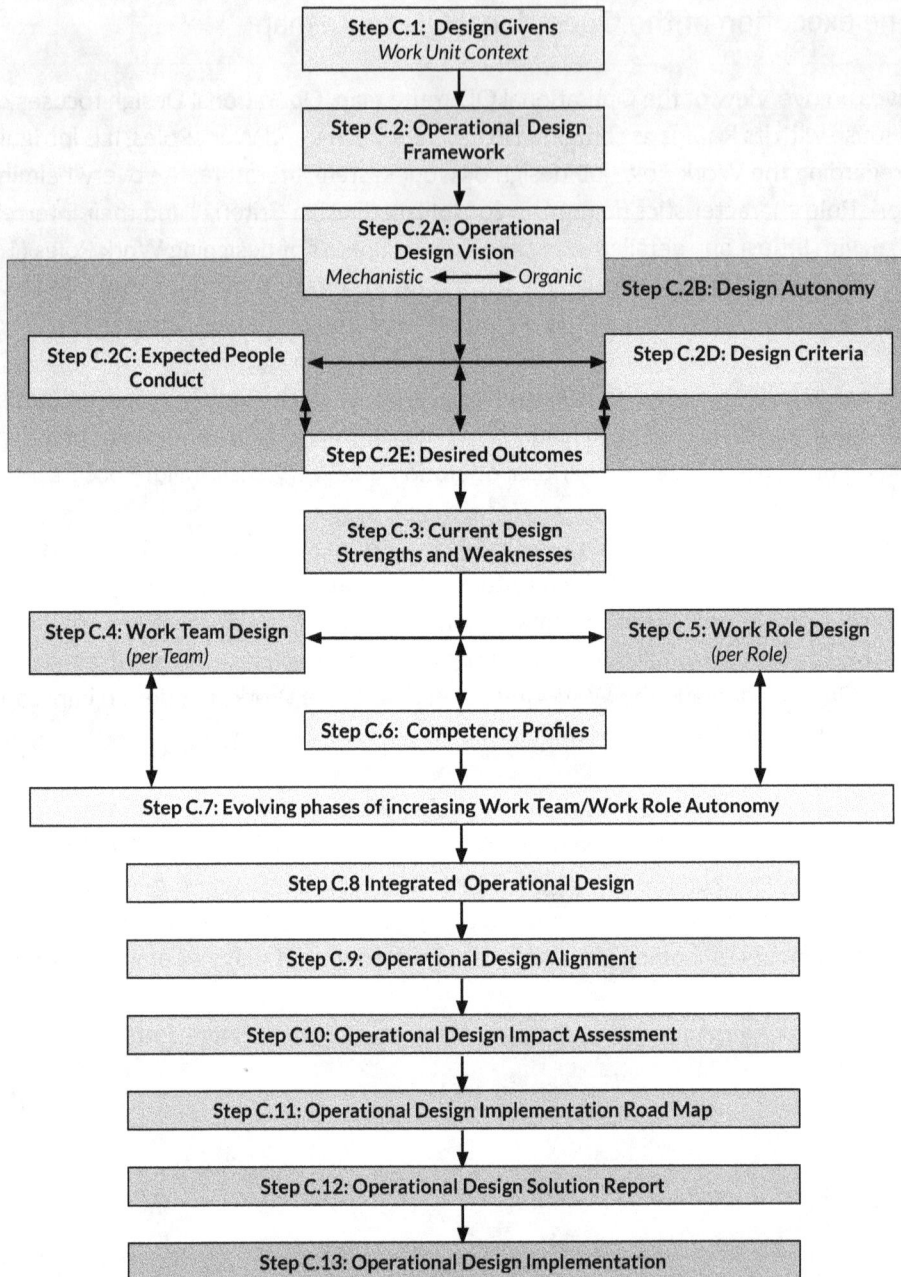

Figure 4.3: Overview of the Operational OD route map

Phase 3.3: OD Expert submits his/her report to the Client who signs off on the proposed, complete OD solution

Phase 3 concludes with the submission of a report to the client of the proposed, complete OD solution to consider. Given the comprehensiveness of the OD need, the report on the solution can contain a Strategic Design, one or more Tactical Design(s), and one or more Operational Design(s).

To reinforce an important point already made above with respect to the complete solution, a low risk approach is to have the client progressively sign-off each Design Level solution in sequence, apart from signing-off at critical points within a design route map as elucidated above. In other words, progressively also signing-off in sequence on the complete Strategic through Tactical to Operational Designs. In this way disagreements can be dealt with at the appropriate juncture, and not be affected by what comes later in terms of subsequent Level Designs. The chances of surprise at this step should be minimal.

The report produced by the OD Expert forms the basis of implementation, that is Phase 4. Without proper documentation, the implementation has a high likelihood of derailment given the intensity of the personal and organisational dynamics that OD invokes. Typical report templates will be provided where the respective Design Levels are discussed in later chapters. It is important to stress the proper documentation of the proposed, and finally Client approved, OD solution.

Phase 4: Implement the signed-off OD solution and assess its value-add

Although each of the design route maps describe the implementation of the final step for completeness (see Figures 4.1 to 4.3), implementation can only really commence once the proposed solution has been signed off. The accountability of the OD Expert concludes when he/she has delivered an approved solution.

Now the client has to take over in terms of full accountability for implementation. The OD Expert has no authority to do this, even if he/she is part of the formal leadership of the organisation concerned. However, the OD Expert can advise on the roll out of the OD solution, because he/she knows it intimately, having architected it.

If all Design Levels are covered, a low risk implementation strategy to avoid organisational chaos would be to progressively architect and roll out the approved designs by organisational level. In other words, first architect and implement the complete Strategic Design, followed by the Tactical and Operational Designs in parallel. The rationale for this implementation sequence will be discussed later.

Phase 5: Close out

This phase relates to the OD Expert exiting the client system at the end of Phase 3. Or, if requested, to provide advice during implementation after Phase 4.

Either way, a proper close out by the OD Expert at a minimum necessitates at least the following steps:

- Phase 5.1: Finalise the OD Intervention Project File and close.
- Phase 5.2: Meet with the Client to sign-off on the OD intervention against the Memorandum of Understanding.
- Phase 5.3: Reflect on the OD intervention, distil lessons learnt, and adapt/renew one's own OD insights, expertise and methodology, if and where necessary.
- Phase 5.4: Finally, and to be recommended, share the insights gained and lessons learnt from the intervention with fellow OD Experts, within the organisation and/or even beyond in the wider OD community.

Conclusion

At this point in our OD journey, the critical life cycle phases of a typical OD intervention should be clear as a handy high level guide to the total OD process. The life cycle phases of an OD intervention covered were: Phase 1: Recognise the need for Organisational (re)Design; Phase 2: Scope and set up the OD assignment; Phase 3: Craft a fit-for-purpose OD solution; Phase 4: Implement the signed-off OD solution and assess its value-add; and Phase 5: Close out. All that remains is to stress the importance of following the phases diligently in order to heighten the likelihood of a successful OD intervention.

Next comes an in-depth discussion of the respective design route maps in their logical sequence. In other words, Phase 3: Step 3.2 of the OD life cycle as discussed above.

Endnotes

(1) Based on my personal OD consulting experience over 20 years over more than 50 OD assignments, nationally and internationally, supplemented by sources listed in the chapter itself.

(2) The concept 'OD life cycle' is also used, for example by Capelle (2014).

(3) Bellerby (2017); Burton, Obel & Håkonsson (2015); Hanna (1988); Kates & Galbraith (2007); Keller & Meaney (2017); Kesler & Kates (2011); Nadler & Tushman (1988); Stanford (2015).

(4) See Table 2.1.

(5) Nadler & Tushman (1997).

(6) Christos (2017).

(7) Barton, Carey & Charan (2018); Birkinshaw & Ridderstråle (2017).

(8) Nadler & Tushman (1997).

(9) Case study kindly supplied by Anton Verwey of InavitIQ.

(10) For example, Laloux (2014); Stanford (2015); Kesler & Kates (2011); Kates & Galbraith (2007); Mosley & Meaney (2017).

(11) The organisational readiness factors discussed also relate to the Critical Success Factors of OD in general, to be discussed in-depth in Chapter 12.

(12) Dunbar & Starbuck (2006); Gruber, De Leon, George & Thompson (2015); Hawryszkiewycz (2017); Kesler & Kates (2011); Mosley & Meaney (2017); Nadler & Tushman (1988); Pearce (2013); Stanford (2015); Tolchinsky & Wenzl (2014).

(13) In De Guerre, Se Guin, Pace & Burkeida's (2013) discussion of their journey of redesign at the School of Extended Learning at Concordia University, Montreal, the use of the co-design option is well illustrated.

(14) Anand & Daft (2007); Burton & Obel (2018); Burton, Obel & Håkonsson (2015); Galbraith (1997); (2014); (1997); (2006); (2008); Galbraith, Downey & Kates (2005); Jaques (2006); Jaques & Clement (1994); Kesler & Kates (2011); MacKenzie (1986); Nadler & Tushman (1997); Roberts, (2004); Rowbottom & Billis (1987); Stanford (2007); Shephard, Gray, Hunt & McArthur (2007); Veldsman (2002).

(15) As was mentioned in Chapter 1, the literature on Tactical Design does not typically form part of mainstream OD. Because Tactical Design addresses the design of Organisational Functions like Board of Directors, Finance, Supply Chain and HRM, it is predominantly covered in discipline-specific literature related to the function. The Tactical OD route map presented here has been distilled from personal experience in doing Tactical Designs.

(16) Berg, Dutton & Wrzesniewski (2013); Campion (1988); Campion & Thayer (1985); Campion, Mumford, Morgeson & Nahrgang (2005); Campion, Mumford, Morgeson & Nahrgang (2005); Courtright, Thurgood, Stewart & Pierotti (2015); Cross (1990); Daniels, Le Blanc & Davis (2014); Demerouti & Bakker (2014); Edmondson (2012); Goodman & Associates (1986); Grant (2007); Grant & Parker (2009); Grant, Fried & Juillerat (2011); Hackman (1987); Hackman & Oldham (1976); (1980); Mohrman, Cohen & Mohrman (1995); Morgeson & Campion (2003); Morgeson & Humphrey (2006); Morgeson & Humphrey (2008); Mueller, Procter & Buchanan (2000); Parker (2014); Parker, Morgeson & Johns (2017); Parker & Wall (1998); Parker, Wall & Cordery (2001); Rφd & Fridjhon (2016); Veldsman (1995); West (2008).

STRATEGIC ORGANISATIONAL DESIGN

5

Architecting the overall Organisational Shape – Organisational Identity Demarcation and Foundation Construction

---

> *"If you want to build a ship, don't drum up people to collect wood and don't assign them tasks and work, but rather teach them to long for the endless immensity of the sea."*
>
> (Antoine de Saint-Exupery)

> *"...context is the key – from there comes the understanding of everything."*
>
> (Kenneth Noland)

> *"The power of the fish is in the water."*
>
> (Shona saying)

The purpose of this chapter – in combination with Chapters 6 to 8 – is to address Strategic Design as a complete and integrated process (1), the 'How' of this Design Level. As previously discussed in Chapter 3, Strategic Design aims to architect the complete House Plan of the organisation, reflected in an overall Organisational Design as the ultimate outcome of this process. It is directed at the design of the organisation as a total operating entity, specifying:

- the Work Units making up the entity (its Board, Operating, Enabling and Support Units, Corporate Centre): the Horizontal Design;

- the requisite Levels of Work and Work Roles: the Vertical Design; and

- the integrating and governance mechanisms binding the organisation together: the Lateral Design.

To re-iterate what was stated in Chapter 4, generally speaking, the need for Strategic (re)Design is triggered when there is a change in the executive leadership of the organisation; a change in the organisation's Business Model and/or Strategic Intent; or the current design as Operating Model is ineffective. At a minimum, a crafted Strategic Design must be in place for the same time period as the organisation's Strategic Intent, or broader, its Identity.

Strategic Design was 'triggered' in 1962 by the seminal work of Chandler, entitled *Strategy and Structure* (2). From this seminal work, the design mantra emerged: 'Structure follows Strategy'. Or, 'Form follows Function'. In the current Strategic Design literature, two distinct, separate bodies of knowledge exist that rarely even cross-reference each other:

(i)   *Strategic Horizontal* (with Lateral Design as a minor subset). Its major proponents are J. Galbraith, A. Campbell, M. Goold, H. Mintzberg, D. Nadler, M. Tushman, and N. Stanford (3); and

(ii) *Strategic Vertical Design*. Its major proponents are E. Jacques as 'founding father', as well as J.L. Gray, J.G. Hunt. S. McArthur and K. Shephard. All of them predominantly subscribe to Stratified Systems Theory, proposed by E. Jacques as their theoretical departure point (to be discussed in Chapter 7) (4).

In addressing Strategic Design, my intention is present a comprehensive, integrated Strategic Design process by merging the above separate literatures, as well as literature from other sources, in order to enrich the current thinking and practice of Strategic Design. Additionally, the rise of the social enterprise; the requirement for a TSV delivery logic; the emerging new order of the VICCAS world; the design implications of the Fourth Industrial Revolution, as well as the design of Co-operatives and Boards of Directors (usually not covered in the design literature) are incorporated in the discussion about architecting a Strategic Design.

This chapter uses the Strategic Design route map – introduced in the previous chapter on the OD life cycle – as its structure. For the sake of convenience, the map is reproduced here again in Figure 5.1. For the sake of easy reference and to avoid confusion, the chapter numbering will follow the numbering system used for the design steps given in Figure 5.1. May I remind the reader again, that in order to keep the Strategic Design route map given in Figure 5.1 simple, the Change Navigation and Project Management Building Blocks of the OD process have been left out (see Figure 3.6), but are essential, enabling elements to the design map.

This chapter, as well as the subsequent Chapters 6 to 8, proceed as follows: each step in the route map given in Figure 5.1 – with its associated OD concepts – is defined; the actions with respect to the steps concerned are discussed; and guidelines to inform these steps, based on OD thought leadership and leading practices, are provided to enhance the chances of a best-in-class, fit-for-purpose design solution. Quality assurance questions are given at the end of each major step in the design route map (for example, Step A.1) to allow for the progressive stress testing of the robustness of the design as it is being architected. Where it is helpful, Design Templates are given in Appendices B to D.

The specific purpose of this chapter is to address Steps A.0: Profile of Organisation – Nature of organisation, and A.1: Foundation Construction – The Building Materials of the House, indicated by arrows in Figure 5.1. The critical assumption throughout is that the organisation to be redesigned, and its people, have been readied for the Strategic OD intervention. Conditions are thus favourable for a successful intervention, or have been made favourable (see Phase 2.3 of the design intervention life cycle).

Step A.0: Profile of Organisation – Nature of organisation

    A.0.1: Demarcate Organisation

Step A.1: Foundation Construction – Building materials of House

    A.1.1: Profile Organisational Context
    A.1.2: Map Work Processes
    A.1.3: Determine Core Operating Technology with Enablers
    A.1.4: Identify Design Givens
    A.1.5: Formulate Design Criteria with Design Vision
    A.1.6: Diagnose Existing Design – Strengths & Weaknesses

Step A.2: Strategic Horizontal Design – Rooms making up the House

    A.2.1: Group Work Processes into Work Units
    A.2.2: Configure Work Units into an Organisational Shape
    A.2.3: Allocate Crown Jewels
    A.2.4: Identify Partnering opportunities

Step A.3: Strategic Vertical Design – Type of ownership and owners of Rooms

    A.3.1: Decide on requisite Level of Work of organisation overall
    A.3.2: Architect House Ownership Model
    A.3.3: Allocate requisite Levels of Work to Work Units
    A.3.4: Identify mission critical Work Roles at Work Unit Leadership Level & generate high level Role Profiles

Step A.4: Strategic Lateral Design – Living together in the House

    A.4.1: Construct an Interdependency Matrix
    A.4.2: Decide on Integration Mechanisms
    A.4.3: Set up Governance Model

Step A.5: Integrated Strategic Design and Charter – Overall House Plan

    A.5.1: Compile Organisational Map
    A.5.2: Draw high level Organogram
    A.5.3: Draft Organisational Charter

Step A.6: Strategic Organisational Alignment – Fitting House into Town House Complex

    A.6.1: Leadership Alignment
    A.6.2: Cultural Alignment
    A.6.3: People Alignment
    A.6.4: Resources Alignment
    A.6.5: Performance Alignment
    A.6.6: Work Place Alignment

Step A.7: Strategic Design Impact Assessment – Existing vs. New Houses

    A.7.1: Conduct Gap & Risk Analysis

Step A.8: Strategic Design Implementation Road Map – Planning how to build the House

    A.8.1: Craft Design Roll Out Strategy & Plan
    A.8.2: Craft Organisational Change Navigation Strategy & Plan

Step A.9: Strategic Design Solution Report

Step A.10: Strategic Design Implementation – Building the House

Figure 5.1: Strategic OD route map

Note: Part of Phase 3: Step 3.2 of the OD life cycle (see Chapter 4)

Step A.0: Profile of Organisation – Nature of the organisation

Step A.0.1: Demarcate the organisation

The objective of Step A.0: Profile of Organisation is to demarcate the essential nature of the organisation under consideration as contained in its Identity. This Profile forms the crucial starting point and foundation for the Strategic Design. The constituent elements of the organisation's Identity are depicted in Figure 5.2. The Operating Model of the organisation – its Design – must enable the actualisation of the organisation's Identity. Relevant to the discussion here is the Identity element, Purpose: Why do we exist, and for whose benefit? (5)

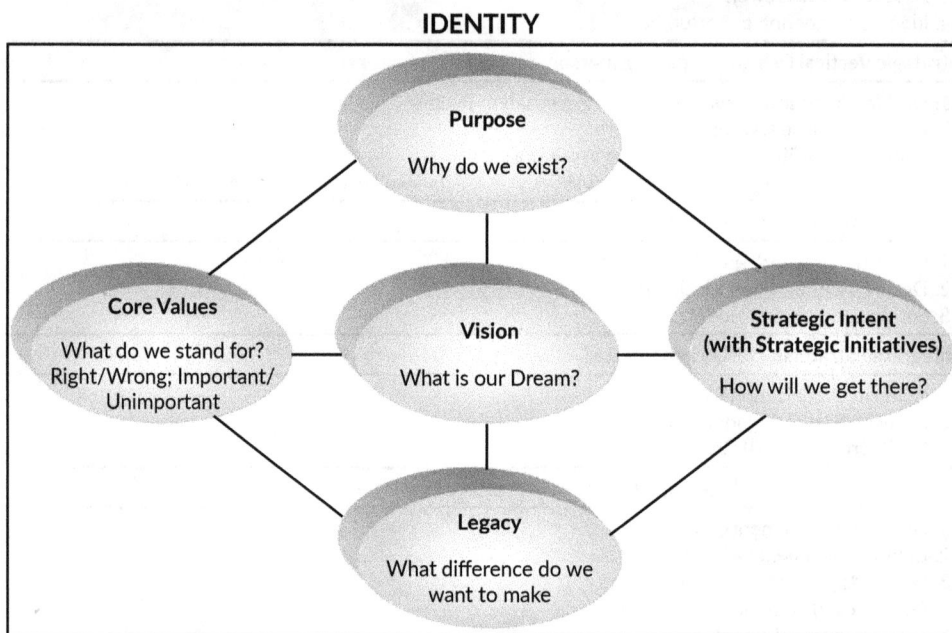

Figure 5.2: Make-up of organisation's Identity

The Purpose of organisations has a specific Driver: Profit maximisation and/or Social Benefit (or Welfare). The mix of the two types of Drivers can be depicted along a continuum in terms of their relative weighting (6). Figure 5.3 reflects this continuum.

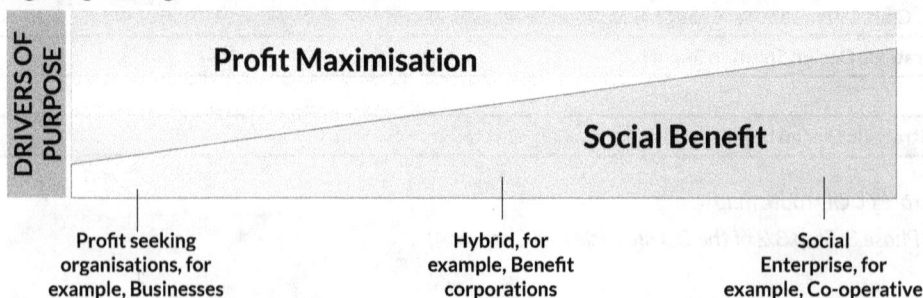

Figure 5.3: Relative weighting of the Drivers of the organisation's Purpose

Essentially, the relative weighting given in Figure 5.3 is reflective of for whom value is being created: Shareowners: Profit Maximisation, or Stakeholders: Social Benefit. The relationship between the two Drivers of Purpose can be mutually supportive or mutually conflicting. The two Drivers are mutually supportive when pursuing one also serves the achievement of the other. Or, at least does not harm it. In contrast, the two Drivers are mutually conflicting when the pursuit of one Driver demands a trade-off with the other. For example, the pursuit of Profit Maximisation can be beneficial for Social Benefit, but it can also be to the detriment of Social Benefit under many circumstances (7).

Table 5.1 provides a list of possible Purpose Driver combinations that organisations can have along the continuum given in Figure 5.3 (8).

Table 5.1: Alternative Purposes of Organisations

	PURPOSE	DESCRIPTION	SOME EXAMPLES
Profit Maximisation	1: Single profit maximisation	Maximise profit	
	2a: Enlightened profit maximisation	Maximise profit through contribution to social benefit	Nestlé: "…It is fundamental that… Nestlé plays a positive role in society…we believe that we will create long term value for shareholders only if we connect positively with society at large."
	2b: Constrained profit maximisation	Maximise profit so that social benefit outcomes stay in an acceptable range	
Multi-objectives: Hybrid	3a: Hierarchical goals with priority to profit	Maximise profit, then maximise social benefit contributions without adversely affecting profit	
	3b: Weighted combination of goals	Maximise a weighted combination of profit and social benefit contributions with weights that vary based on pre-set criteria	
	3c: Complementary goals with equal priority given to profit and social benefit	Maximise profit and social benefit contributions equally	Danone: "…dual project for business success and social progress."
Social benefit maximisation	4a: Constrained social benefit maximisation	Maximise social benefit contributions whilst profit outcomes stay within an acceptable range	

	PURPOSE	DESCRIPTION	SOME EXAMPLES
Social benefit maximisation (cont.)	4b: Enlightened social benefit maximisation	Maximise social benefit contributions through profit	Merck: "To discover, develop and provide innovative products and services that save and improve lives around the world."
	5: Simple social benefit maximisation	Maximise social benefit contributions	Patagonia: "Build the best product, cause no unnecessary harm, use business to inspire and implement solutions to the environmental crisis." Intel India Development Centre: "...we will create and extend computing technology to connect and enrich the lives of every person on earth."

Against the backdrop of the shift in thinking towards sustainability – expressed as the 5Ps in Chapter 2 – and the growing requirement by leading stock exchanges worldwide for integrated reporting by listed companies, organisations in a fundamental way have to re-consider their Purpose, and by implication their delivery logic, in terms of how to bring the different voices of their respective stakeholders into the organisation though opening up organisational boundaries. They have to demonstrably combine the Purpose of Social Benefit with the Purpose of Profit Maximisation as responsible corporate citizens. Organisations will have to master the art of building and nurturing deep, morally-based relationships with stakeholders through their delivery logic, informed by the values of legitimacy, fairness, meaning, mutuality, and equity. This implies regarding the design of organisations, *inter alia*, the adoption of 'Outside-In' design thinking and processes: commence with the needs, wants, and stakes of stakeholders, then deliberate and decide how the organisation is going to meet and satisfy their needs, wants and stakes through a sustainably referenced delivery logic (9). This is why a TSV delivery logic is adopted as the basis of the comprehensive, integrated design route map presented in the book.

The shaded box provides a description of Co-operatives as an example of a Social Enterprise with the dual purpose of primarily Social Benefit, and secondly Profit Maximisation.

AN EXAMPLE OF A SOCIAL ENTERPRISE: CO-OPERATIVES

Co-operatives are one of the oldest and most enduring forms of business, which can be traced back to at least 1498 with the formation of the Shore Porters' Society in Aberdeen, Scotland (10). Cooperatives play an important role in the economies of many industrialised nations. In 2018, the combined global turnover for the world's top 300 co-operatives was USD 2.1 trillion. Co-operatives generate partial or full-time employment for at least 280 million individuals worldwide, either in or within the scope of co-operatives, making up almost 10% of the entire employed population of the world (11). Globally, they supported the livelihoods of in the order of three billion people in 2018 (12), nearly 40% of the world's population in that year.

A Co-operative is an autonomous association of persons who unite voluntarily to meet common economic, social and cultural needs and aspirations through a jointly-owned and democratically-controlled enterprise, whose benefits go mainly to its members. Members are thus owner users. Co-operatives are based on the values of self-help, self-responsibility, democracy, equality, equity, and solidarity. In the tradition of their originators, co-operative members subscribe to the ideology (= core values) of honesty, openness, social responsibility, and caring for others (13).

A Co-operative is member-owned and organised with dual economic (= profit) AND social purposes (= an unfulfilled/poorly fulfilled societal need) in order to serve the interests of its members as customers to their benefit. It is set up with members' capital with the aim of satisfying a specific member need(s). Members: own the Co-operative; provide its capital; have one vote each; are typically the sole/primary customers of the organisation; may work in the organisation; and share in its profits on an equal basis. The major types of Co-operatives are consumer, producer/marketing, purchasing, employee/worker (14).

STOKVELS: SOUTH AFRICA'S PRIMARY EXAMPLE OF CO-OPERATIVES (15)

Stokvels in South Africa are invitation-only clubs of 12 or more people which serve as rotating credit unions or saving schemes, where members contribute fixed sums of money to a central fund on a weekly, fortnightly or monthly basis. Most of the money is paid out monthly to individuals, who spend it on consumables such as food and groceries.

The name "stokvel" originated from the term "stock fairs", as the rotating cattle auctions of English settlers in the Eastern Cape during the early 19th century were known.

Current estimates are that there are over 820,000 stokvels in SA, with a combined membership of 11.4 million people, about 20% of South Africa's population. About one in every two black adult South Africans is a member. In total stokvels handle over R44 billion per annum.

In summary: the Identity of the organisation forms the crucial starting point and foundation for the Strategic Design. In the above discussion, particular attention was given to the organisation's Purpose with its underlying Driver(s), which is framed by the organisation's chosen Core Values (see Figure 5.2). The organisation's Core Values therefore must also be architected into the organisation's design. This requirement is well illustrated in the case of Co-operatives, as described in the box. A fit-for-purpose

Organisational Design gives 'hands and feet' to the actualisation of the organisation's Purpose and Core Values as a concrete expression of its Identity.

Quality assurance questions for Stage A.0: Profile of Organisation – Nature of the organisation

QUALITY ASSURANCE QUESTIONS *Step A.0: Profile of Organisation – Nature of organisation*	DESIGN STEP	ADDRESSED: YES/ NO *(Yes: +; No: x)*
What design requirements do the organisation's **Purpose and Core Values** impose?	Step A.0.1	
By meeting these design requirements, will the delivery logic of the organisation enable the actualisation of the organisation's **Identity**?	Step A.0.1	

Step A.1: Foundation Construction

The objective of Step A.1: Foundation Construction is to establish the 'fundamentals' with respect to the organisation to be (re)designed. Metaphorically speaking, it is about bringing the necessary building materials for the design on site in order to prepare for the building that is to take place. These materials represent the essential inputs into the building of a robust fit-for-purpose design. The quality of the building materials will significantly affect the robustness of the final design, and determine whether it is fit-for-purpose (16).

From another perspective, the building materials are the contingency factors that determine when what design will be fit-for-purpose. The consideration of contingency factors debunks Myth 7: A chosen design can be the mere imitation of what others have done, that is applying their recipes uncritically. These factors result in inter-Organisational Design differences, as well as adaptations in the design of an organisation over time as fundamentals change.

The minimum necessary OD building materials to bring on site as sub-steps of Step A.1 of the design process are (see Figure 5.1):

- A.1.1: Profile Organisational Context
- A.1.2: Map Work Processes
- A.1.3: Determine Core Operating Technology with Enablers
- A.1.4: Identify Design Givens
- A.1.5: Formulate Design Criteria with Design Vision
- A.1.6: Diagnose Existing Design – Strengths and Weaknesses

Each step is discussed in turn.

Step A.1.1: Profile Organisational Context

The organisation has an external context – its Operating Arena, and internal context – for example, its Business/Value Model and Strategic Intent. A fit-for-purpose design requires an in-depth understanding of the key variables in the organisation's context that will affect its design requirements. The challenge is how to make the organisation contextually fit-for-purpose in terms of the requirements that the context imposes on the design *(17)*.

At a minimum the following key contextual variables have to be considered for design purposes:

- External context: (1) the Operating Arena of the organisation; (2) the contextual complexity of the organisation's Operating Arena; (3) Stakeholders; and (4) Critical Resources.

- Internal context: (5) Business/Value Model; (6) Strategic Intent; (7) Organisational Life Cycle; and (8) Organisational Rhythm.

Each is discussed in turn.

Contextual Variable 1: Operating Arena of the organisation

The following dimensions of the Operating Arena must be considered when architecting a fit-for-purpose design: (i) the substantive and qualitative characteristics of, and trends in the world at large affecting the organisation's Operating Arena; (ii) the specific, locational features of the Operating Arena; and (iii) the contextual complexity of the organisation's Operating Arena.

Dimension 1: Substantive and qualitative characteristics of, and trends in the world at large affecting the Operating Arena of the organisation

The substantive and qualitative characteristics of, and trends regarding the world at large affecting the Operating Arena of the organisation, and consequentially its delivery logic, must be identified and their design requirements must be thoroughly debated for the 'To-Be' design. Figure 2.2 provided a succinct orientation to the characteristics and trends of the emerging new order.

Substantively, by way of example, the deregulation of the cement industry in South Africa a number of years ago required branding and marketing – which was previously unnecessary – to become new, key work processes in these organisations. Similarly, the deregulation of the USA airline industry regarding fares, routes, and market entry during the late 1970s resulted in the need for different airline core organisational capabilities.

Qualitatively, and infusing the substantive trends, the emergence of the VICCAS world that is typified by increasing **V**ariety, **I**nterdependency, **C**omplexity, **C**hange, **A**mbiguity, and **S**eamlessness.

The emerging substantive and qualitative characteristics and trends of the emerging new order imply that overall design requirements must move from mechanistic to organic designs. A mechanistic design is well suited to a stable, predictable, simple context. This design is architected around hierarchy, formalisation, standardisation, specialisation (or differentiation), and top down, centralised decision-making. An organic design fits a rapidly changing, unpredictable, complex context better. This design is crafted around, for example, cross-functional integration, collaboration across organisational boundaries, flexibility, agility, responsiveness, and high autonomy at all organisational levels (18).

Dimension 2: Specific, locational features of the Operating Arena

The previous contextual dimension dealt with design requirements imposed by the world at large. This dimension addresses the specific, locational features of the organisation's Operating Arena, for example, developed vs. emerging economies. Emerging countries (ECs) will be used to illustrate how specific, locational features of the Operating Arena set design requirements.

Increasingly, emerging countries are becoming the chosen Operating Arena of many global (or globalising) organisations as they look into the future, given the predicted growing dominance and influence of ECs in the coming years in the globalising world. It is predicted that China and India will be respectively the first and second largest economies according to GDP by 2030, the USA being third.

Typically, ECs are countries in a state of rapid transition and fundamental transformation; are undergoing high economic growth; are experiencing a tighter integration of their localised, closed economies and societies into the global village; and are benefiting from the significant influx of high levels of foreign investment. The box depicts some of the more important unique features of ECs with their major consequences from an organisational and people perspective and some resultant, high level OD requirements (19).

EMERGING ECONOMY AS OPERATING ARENA		
UNIQUE FEATURES OF ECs	**MAJOR CONSEQUENCES**	**HIGH LEVEL OD REQUIREMENTS**
• A fundamental, normative *societal transformation* in terms of fundamental beliefs, values and norms resulting in divisive ideological tensions and conflicts. • The lead/lag development of *infrastructure*, with the commensurate incongruences and the absence of synergies across the country's infrastructure.	• The adoption as a non-negotiable vantage point of an *embeddedness* at all times into an organisation's mindset, thinking, decisions, and actions: 'We are part and parcel of the EC in which we are doing business, and not an intruder, gate crasher or exploiter.' • Given the fundamental, normative transformations EC societies are going through, with resultant normative ambiguities and ethics, having as an organisation a visible, clearly articulated and well communicated *values and beliefs stance*: 'This is who we are and what we stand for.' In other words, having an explicit, visible and robust *Organisational Identity*.	Architecting an organisation with a strong *relationship-centric delivery logic*, able to engage intensely – from an explicit, visible, and robust organisational Identity – with all of the organisation's stakeholders, both internally and externally (that is a geocentric attitude) on an ongoing basis.

UNIQUE FEATURES OF ECs	MAJOR CONSEQUENCES	HIGH LEVEL OD REQUIREMENTS
• Sophisticated *technology* pockets in a sea of poor/ outdated technology with newer technologies, for example, cell phones leapfrogging fixed telephone lines; the use of drones to overcome poor road infrastructure. • The dominant presence of *multi-national/global, capital-strong organisations* in ECs, threatening local, emerging industries. • A young, highly unemployed *population* with a severe brain drain of top talent to developed countries. • The wide, and in many cases widening, gap between the *'Haves' and the 'Have-nots'*.	• Crafting a proactive, well thought through *stakeholder engagement strategy*, because of the power struggles and ideological debates raging in these societies involving competing and diverse and multiple stakeholders, each seeking their fair and equitable share of the cake. Organisations within ECs have to significantly extend their view of their stakeholders. • Finding effective, pragmatic mechanisms to bring the *voices of different segments of the EC communities/societies into the organisations*, so that all parties can be fully heard. This necessitates opening up organisational boundaries so that stakeholders, internally and externally, can move effortlessly across these boundaries. • Visibly and concretely demonstrating good corporate citizenship through real, sustainable *social capacity building and upliftment interventions, addressing real societal needs and requirements* in EC communities. Local stakeholders need to be directly involved in real and meaningful ways of formally and informally engaging the 'Haves' and the 'Have-nots', employees and non-employees, communities, and non-government and private organisations. • *Assisting to smooth over and fill societal infrastructural underdevelopment/ mismatches and systemic imbalances,* enabling communities/societies and one's own organisation to function better, for example the upgrading of schools. • The adoption of a *geocentric attitude* by finding credible local partners with whom strong partnering relationships can be formed to jointly create wealth, globally. Also, giving local talent equal employment and career opportunities across all organisational levels/areas, both locally and globally.	Design must enable stakeholders to participate as *trusted partners* of the organisation who – jointly with the organisation – pursue mutual value unlocking and wealth creation, directed and guided by a co-generated, shared EC relevant, envisioned legacy. The relationship-centric transformation requires a radical shift in the organisational delivery logic from being a command-and-control, power-based organisation, to becoming a *distributed, network organisation* driven by joint value creation with trusted, local partners, both inside and outside of the organisation. In EC societies with collectivistic, national cultures, such *stakeholder engagement* becomes even more of a critical enabler to ensure legitimacy and credibility. In these societies, partnering is an innate societal expectation and norm. Given the (rapid) radical social transformation infusing ECs, an *agile, resilient, responsive design*, re-inventing itself on an ongoing basis in real time, is a necessity.

Contextual Variable 2: Contextual complexity of the organisation's Operating Arena (20)

Within its chosen/desired Operating Arena, an organisation – through its strategic choices – must deal with a certain degree of contextual complexity: the 'league' the organisation wants to play in. The degree of contextual complexity affects the nature and dynamics of the internal organisation context – the level at which the organisation wants to play the game within its selected league. The contextual complexity of an organisation's Operating Arena thus sets the requirements for the requisite complexity of the 'To-Be' design that must be given consideration.

The contextual complexity of an organisation is a function of five variables, namely: (i) its footprint, whether physical and/or virtual; (ii) the thinking time horizon within which the organisation has to/ wishes to operate; (iii) the scope of the organisation in terms of markets, customers and products/ services; (iv) the variety within the organisation with respect to aspects such as Strategic Intent, policies and standards, work processes and culture; and (v) the degree and rate of change the organisation is exposed to.

An organisation's contextual complexity grows exponentially as the chosen *footprint* of the organisation moves from a local to a global Operating Arena; the chosen *thinking time horizon* expands from short term (two to three years) to long term (more than ten years); the *scope* of the organisation extends from a single product/service, one type of customer/client and one market to multiple related (and even unrelated) products/services, customers/clients and markets; the *variety* within the organisation to lead and manage the organisation effectively increases from a single to multiple Strategic Intents, policies and standards, sets of work processes, functionalities and success metrics; and the *degree and rate of change* shift from incremental to revolutionary.

Table 5.2 highlights the respective complexity ranges of the five variables, enabling the reader to determine the contextual complexity they have to take into account when architecting the best contextual fit for a design.

Table 5.2: Degrees of Contextual Complexity

CONTEXTUAL COMPLEXITY VARIABLE	DEGREE OF CONTEXTUAL COMPLEXITY			
	1: Low	**2: Reasonable**	**3: High**	**4: Very High**
Footprint: Physical and/or Virtual	Local – Single location	National – Multiple locations, but one country	Multi-national – Locations in multiple countries with high local autonomy but little global integration	Global – Fully integrated global organisation

CONTEXTUAL COMPLEXITY VARIABLE	DEGREE OF CONTEXTUAL COMPLEXITY			
	1: Low	2: Reasonable	3: High	4: Very High
Thinking Time Horizon needed to look at world, industry and own organisation	2 to 3 years	3 to 5 years	5 to 10 years	10 years plus
Scope of the organisation in terms of Markets, Customers, Products/ Services	Single	Multiple but related	Multiple, related and unrelated	Multiple, unrelated
Variety within the organisation in terms of required Strategic Intent, policies and standards, work processes and practices, and outputs delivered	Uniform	Diverse but similar	Diverse but similar and dissimilar	Dissimilar
Degree and rate of change in context	Slow, incremental	Evolutionary – predictable trend shifts	Trend breaks	Revolutionary – re-creation and re-invention

The complexity variables form part of the Periodic Table of Basic Organisational Shapes to be discussed under Strategic Horizontal Design (see Figure 6.9). Generally speaking, the following complexity levels require the following Organisational Shapes (21):

- *Lower* contextual complexity: more of an Activity-based Shape – Functional or Process Shape.

- *Reasonable* contextual complexity: Multi-business (or Divisional) Shape.

- *High* contextual complexity: more of a Cluster (that is a Multi-organisational Unit or Portfolio) Shape.

Contextual Variable 3: Stakeholders

The types, stakes and interests of stakeholders, as well as the power (formal or informal) they have over the organisation, may set design requirements, such as the degree and intensity of interaction with stakeholders, as well the autonomy – perceived or actual – they award to an organisation. Or, put differently, the power through ownership or social media they have over the organisation (22). Social media has exponentially increased the power of stakeholders to exert pressure and influence, when and wherever, on organisations.

For example, a state-owned enterprise (where the state is the sole/major shareholder) typically demands the crafting of: (i) a CEO role to deal with the intense, time consuming interaction, lobbying, and reporting to parliament and politicians; and (2) a separate COO role to run the organisation on a daily basis. Or, for example, the involvement of a local community in (re)design at the organisation's operating sites, as part of an "Outside-In" design process, demonstrating social citizenship.

Contextual Variable 4: Critical Resources

Under consideration here is whether an organisation is critically dependent on a strategic resource supplier and/or alliance partner. For example, a stakeholder is the predominant or sole source of a key raw material or technology used by the organisation. This sets the design requirement of an assured, predictable supply or access. This can be achieved by architecting a Strategic Resourcing Unit/Role, a Client Executive Role, or a Strategic Technology Liaison Role into the design.

Contextual Variable 5: Business/Value Model

The Business/Value Model comprises how the organisation aims to make money and/or create value/ wealth as a key leadership task (see Figure 2.1) (23). Within the emerging new order, Business/Value Models are radically and fundamentally being re-invented (see Figure 2.3). Virtually no sector or industry remains untouched. This was Reason 5 offered in Chapter 2 for why OD has become a critical organisational discipline.

For example, Uber – the world's largest taxi company – owns no vehicles; Facebook – the world's most contemporary media owner – creates little, if any, content; Amazon – the most valuable global retailer – carries no inventory; the world's largest accommodation provider, Airbnb, owns no property; and the Khan Academy offers e-courses without any campuses, student residences, and class schedules.

The 'To-Be' Organisational Design must be aligned to the requirements of the organisation's Business/ Value Model, and must operationalise the Business/Value Model into a fit-for-purpose, delivery logic.

Contextual Variable 6: Strategic Intent

The Design must be aligned to, and be in support of, the requirements set by the organisation's Strategic Intent (24). The mantra of 'Structure follows Strategy' applies here. Organisations can pursue one of three Strategic Intents: product/service innovation, operational excellence or customer centricity (25) (26). Each Strategic Intent sets its own design requirements. Table 5.3 provides some of the OD requirements flowing from the three Strategic Intents respectively (27).

Table 5.3: The OD requirements of different Strategic Intents

STRATEGIC INTENT	ORGANISATIONAL DESIGN REQUIREMENTS
Product/service innovation *(28)*	• Create new/leading edge products/services faster than competitors • Build in-depth research and development expertise • Nurture an innovation-enabling organisational culture
Operational excellence	• A low cost producer • Continuous process efficiency improvement
Customer centricity	• Build long term, deep relationships with customers • Grow repeat business • Deliver high levels of customer satisfaction • Customise products/services upon request • Cross-sell and bundle products/services

Additionally, an organisation can decide strategically to grow organically and/or through mergers/acquisitions. Organic growth can be more of the same. For example, higher revenues from increased market share, and/or the addition of something new, for example, markets, clients and/or products/services. A merger implies the creation of a new organisation out of two standalone organisations, while an acquisition entails the total absorption of one organisation by another.

Whatever the growth strategy of the organisation, its crafted design must be 'growth friendly' such that it can accommodate the organisation's strategic growth aspirations. For example, the design must be merger/acquisition friendly by being able to incorporate new entities with ease.

Contextual Variable 7: Organisational Life Cycle (29)

At any point in time, every organisation is in a given life cycle stage. Two types of life cycle models exist: business and organisational models. Figure 5.3 gives an example of a composite life cycle stage model (that is a business and organisational model in combination) in the form of an S-curve, called an organisational life cycle model. Table 5.4 provides brief descriptions of the stages depicted in Figure 5.3. Each of the stages have stage specific OD requirements that have to be satisfied when crafting a design appropriate to the stage the organisation is in (30). It is thus critical for the organisation to correctly identify the stage it is at, and to also proactively foresee the next stage(s) the organisation is evolving to. A complicating factor is that different parts of the organisation may be in different stages of the Life Cycle. Under consideration here is the stage the *overall* organisation is in.

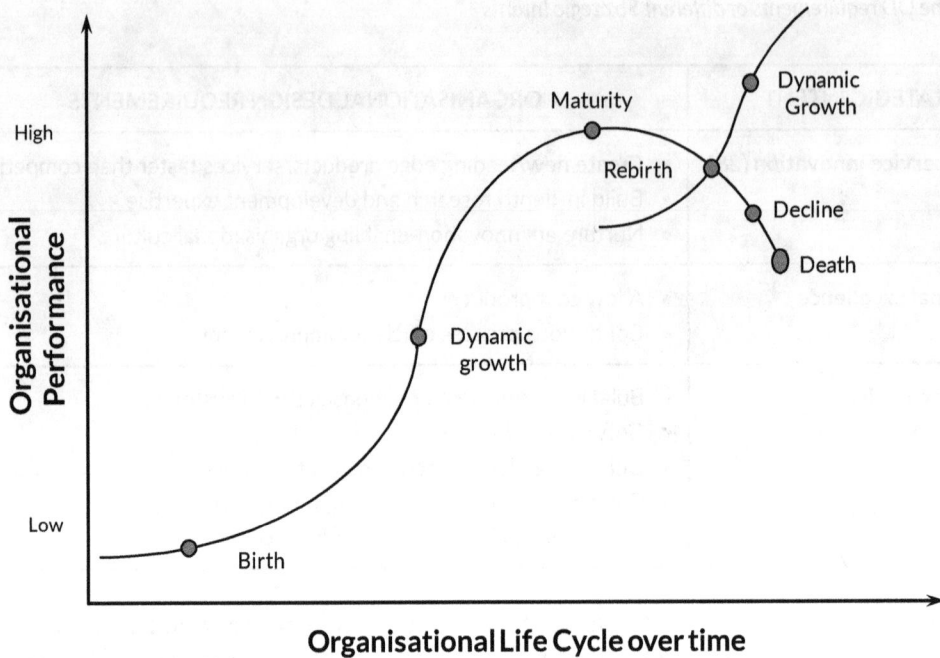

Figure 5.4: Organisational Life Cycle Stages

Table 5.4: Descriptions of Organisational Life Cycle stages

ORGANISATIONAL LIFE CYCLE STAGE	THEME(S)	DESCRIPTION	ORGANISATIONAL DESIGN REQUIREMENT BY STAGE
BIRTH	Entrepreneurial; Infancy; Adolescence	Variety of projects (or initiatives) with high financial risk. Broad, continuously changing product lines in new/changing markets/niches with low to weak competition. The pace is brisk. The emphasis is on innovation. Insufficient resources to satisfy all demands because of multiple priorities which have to be satisfied simultaneously. The focus is on the short term and establishing the organisation as a viable entity. Minimal policies, systems and procedures in place or being dismantled to encourage flexibility.	Requirement to formalise leadership: owners required to move from a hands–on, daily involvement in delivery to formalised leadership at requisite Levels of Work.

ORGANISATIONAL LIFE CYCLE STAGE	THEME(S)	DESCRIPTION	ORGANISATIONAL DESIGN REQUIREMENT BY STAGE
DYNAMIC GROWTH	Go-getter	Risk taking is more modest. Organisation is rapidly expanding within set parameters and guidelines. Product/service line(s) are changing and stable but around related lines. Growth mostly through market development in changing and predictable markets with varying degrees of competition. Constant dilemma exists between doing current work and engaging in future orientated projects. Policies, systems and procedures starting to be written or set up as there is a need for more control and structure for the ever expanding operation.	Requirement for autonomy: at all levels, organisational members want more freedom to act within well demarcated areas of accountability with clear hand-over points in order to make the organisation sufficiently responsive, flexible, and agile to meet client expectations and needs.
MATURITY	Stable; Creeping Bureaucracy	The focus is on maintaining existing profit levels. The organisation operates in predictable, clearly defined markets with stable, fierce competition. Growth is attained through market penetration and/or better operational efficiencies, resulting in cheaper products/services. Extensive policies, systems and procedures are in place. Structures and responsibilities are well defined. Modest cost-cutting efforts and employee terminations may be occurring.	Requirement for co-operation and collaboration: cross-functional/cross-unit integration in order to overcome silos, eliminate duplication and red tape, and create organisation-wide synergies.
DECLINE	Liquidation/ Divestiture	Assets are sold off, attempts are made to minimise losses, and there is a reduction in the staff complement. Little or no thought is given to trying to save organisation as declining profits are likely to continue because of disappearing/shifting markets and/ or obsolete product/service lines. All initiatives focus on the here-and-now.	Requirement for being lean and mean: simplified delivery logic in terms of Work Units, Roles, Levels of Work, work done.

ORGANISATIONAL LIFE CYCLE STAGE	THEME(S)	DESCRIPTION	ORGANISATIONAL DESIGN REQUIREMENT BY STAGE
RE-BIRTH	Turnaround; Transformation	The thrust is to save the organisation, which in principle is a viable entity. Although cost-cutting efforts and employee reductions are made, they are short term programmes aimed at long term survival. The organisation is repositioning and refocusing itself with respect to its product/services, markets, customers and competitors.	Requirement for radical innovation: a complete re-think and re-invention of the delivery logic to fit the reconceived organisation.
DEATH	In memoriam	Organisation has gone out of existence	None

The case study in the box is an example of an Organisational Life Cycle Design as applied by British Petroleum (31).

CASE STUDY: BUSINESS LIFE CYCLE DESIGN
Context
British Petroleum (BP), a global oil exploration, refining and oil-based manufacturing organisation.
OD Need
During the 1990s, BP was a politicised, top-heavy, bureaucratic organisation, with slow decision-making (financial proposals required 15 different approval signatures); high overheads (its head-office staff filled a 32 storey building in London); and massive time wastage (86 different committees absorbed virtually all the time of top executives). Business performance was declining and the company was heavily indebted. In 1992 the situation was so severe that the company almost went bankrupt.
OD Solution
For the purpose of this OD case study, the changes that were affected during this period within the upstream, exploration and production business, BP Exploration (BPX), are relevant. John Browne, who would later become CEO of BP, introduced a new Organisational Design called an 'Asset Federation'.
First, Browne refocused the *future, upstream strategy* on finding and exploiting large hydrocarbon deposits where the political and technical difficulties and attendant risks meant that BP's expertise and size gave it a relative advantage over smaller firms. This resulted in BPX's operations becoming increasingly dispersed around the globe in developing and transition economies.

The next move by Browne was to *redesign* BPX. The existing design was centred around a collection of geographically defined Regional Operating Companies (ROCs), with staffs of technical and business people overseeing the actual operations in the field. The heads of the ROCs and functions formed a Global Management Group, chaired by Browne. Performance data were aggregated to the level of ROCs. Managers of the actual fields had very limited discretion and little control over the resources in their units.

In terms of the new design, all the exploration and production operations were divided into some 40 separate Business Units, called assets, each of which consisted of a major oil or gas field or a group of co-located fields. Each was headed by an Asset Manager (later called a Business Unit Leader). The ROCs were eliminated, with senior management of the stream being paired down to Browne and two others. As the BPX Executive Committee (ExCo), they together directly oversaw the assets, with no intermediate layers of managers. The technical and functional staffs of ROCs were also largely dispersed to the assets.

Asset Managers were given charters that set bounds on their activities, for example, limiting their drilling to their own sites. They also signed explicit, individual performance contracts with the ExCo with regard to production volumes, costs and capital expenditure. Within their charter bounds – and the limits of general corporate policy – Asset Managers were empowered to decided out how to achieve their promised performance. For example, they could take action regarding where and how to drill, who to hire, and which suppliers to use.

Browne pushed performance discussions down to the level of the individual fields. The performance of individual assets was not aggregated below the level of the stream itself, but was fully transparent to Browne and the ExCo members who tracked performance closely, especially through rigorous quarterly performance reviews. In these meetings Browne coached Asset Managers, helping them develop their managerial skills and inculcating the values and norms he sought to spread through BPX. The performance contracts at the asset level became the basis for performance contracts for all the individuals within the asset. All employees' compensation was tied to their asset's performance and the overall performance of the stream. This significantly increased pay variability and the intensity of incentives.

Asset Managers found the new system highly empowering. However, the leanness at the top meant they could not rely on the Stream Headquarters to advise and support them when technical and/or business difficulties arose. To respond to this need, the assets were aligned into four peer groups that were defined on the basis of the life stage of assets: (i) actual exploration activities, including obtaining the rights to develop fields; (ii) assets being developed and brought into production; (iii) assets in full, plateau production; and (iv) assets approaching the end of their economic viability. The key point was that assets within a group – although geographically dispersed – were likely to face similar technical and commercial problems.

Asset Managers were encouraged to rely on their asset peer group colleagues for support. The peer groups were designed to facilitate mutual assistance among their member assets and to promote the sharing of best practices. A system of peer assists was established, under which an asset facing a problem could call on people from other assets to come and help solve the issue. Additionally, numerous other 'federal groups' came into being, linking people with common interests and challenges across the different assets.

Peer groups were also given another role early on, called a peer challenge. Under it, peer group members could challenge one another on the targets that they negotiated individually with the ExCo. This process allowed the Asset Managers' collective expert knowledge to be brought to bear in establishing targets. Later, peer groups each took a collective responsibility for meeting the performance targets of member assets and for allocating capital among them.

OD OUTCOMES

New fields were found and developed, many of which were previously thought to be technically too difficult to be economically feasible. The cost of developing fields was reduced substantially and kept being squeezed, also in partnership with outsourcing partners. The productive life of assets was therefore extended long beyond what had been believed possible.

The above changes eventually led to fundamental organisational cultural changes. People developed a deep, intrinsic dedication to deliver ever-improving performance. Strong norms emerged of mutual trust; of admitting early when one faced difficulties ('no surprises') and seeking assistance when needed; of responding positively to requests for help; and of keeping promises about performance. All of this generated a high degree of cooperation while still encouraging great self-initiative.

Contextual Variable 8: Organisational Rhythm

Each organisation has a rhythm of work during a given work year: the order and timing of when what has to be done. For example, the seasonal harvesting and non-harvesting periods in an agricultural organisation; the intense Christmas season in a retail organisation; the financial year end; or the sequence and timing of considering matters at a Board of Directors meeting. If necessary, therefore, the design requirements of the organisation's rhythm must be considered.

In summary: in order to architect a fit-for-purpose design, it is critical to identify the 20% key contextual requirements arising from the eight contextual variables discussed above, which make up 80% of the difference that have to be considered in architecting the design. Typically this includes around five, but mostly not more than ten, contextual design requirements.

Step A.1.2: Map Work Processes

The scope of the work to be done by an organisation to define, deliver and satisfy stakeholder needs is reflected in its work processes – core, enabling and support (32). Essential for a fit-for-purpose design is to have available a high level, work process map that provides an overview of all of the required organisational work. 'High level' in process mapping language pertains to the 'first level of deconstruction'. That is identifying a process at the organisational level, and showing the activities making up such a process. The shaded box gives an example of the mapped, high level core work process (= core value chain) of a Fund Management Organisation (33). The shaded blocks in the work process map show groupings of interdependent activities.

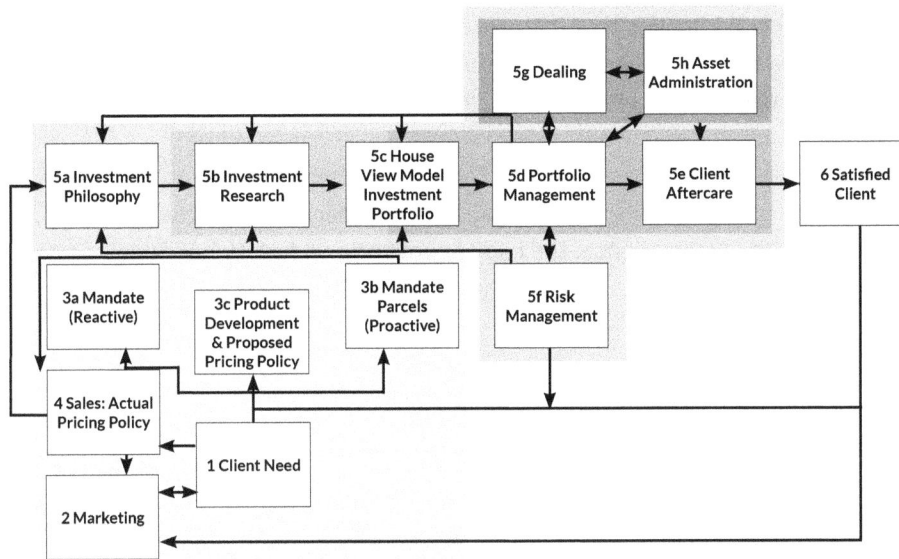

It is important to note regarding the high level mapping of the organisation's work process, of which the Fund Management Organisation is an example, that: (i) the process map must reflect *all* of its composite activities in terms of what should be done according to leading practices, and not only what is currently done in the organisation or is conventional in the sector/industry; (ii) the sequential order of executing the activities is correct; (iii) all of the interdependencies between activities are reflected; and (iv) for convenience sake, numbering the activities will help later on in the design process to check whether all activities are accommodated somewhere in a Room of the House (34). For example, regarding point (i), when I did my first major strategic design in the insurance industry 15 years ago, the conventional design was 'Inside-Out'. The organisation's actuaries decided what was good for customers. No fully fledged client needs determination process existed in the organisation: 'We know best what the client needs'.

The process map of the Fund Management Organisation (given above) only shows a high level core work process map. A complete organisational process map must include the core work, enabling *and* support processes – with their interdependencies – that the organisation requires in order to get all of its work done. Because the enabling/support processes are the focus of Stage B: Tactical Design, they need not be decomposed into their composite activities, but must merely be shown in the overall map as the necessary, enabling/support work processes.

Figure 5.4 depicts a generic portfolio of work processes – core, enabling and support – for the total organisation. Table 5.5 provides the purpose and expected outcome of each process depicted in Figure 5.4 *(35)*.

A sustainability vantage point is taken to the portfolio of work processes of the organisation. As already discussed in Chapter 2, sustainability entails four actions: the recovery, renewal, restoration and retention of existing value *whilst* delivering value going into the future. This vantage point has two implications for the work processes depicted in Figure 5.4: (i) sustainability infuses all work processes, hence its central placement in the figure; and (ii) the core value chain is seen as a circular, and not a linear process. Being circular implies that the process must produce zero waste. Produced waste must either be biodegradable or serve as an input to the same or another core value chain. In this way the organisation is seen as part of the overall ecological system of the earth (36).

Also important to note regarding Figure 5.4 and Table 5.5 is that the work process names must reflect the *task or work* the process actually entails, and to stay clear from functional names, for example, Marketing, Operations. In my experience, the use of conventional functional titles bias design solutions to take on a traditional form.

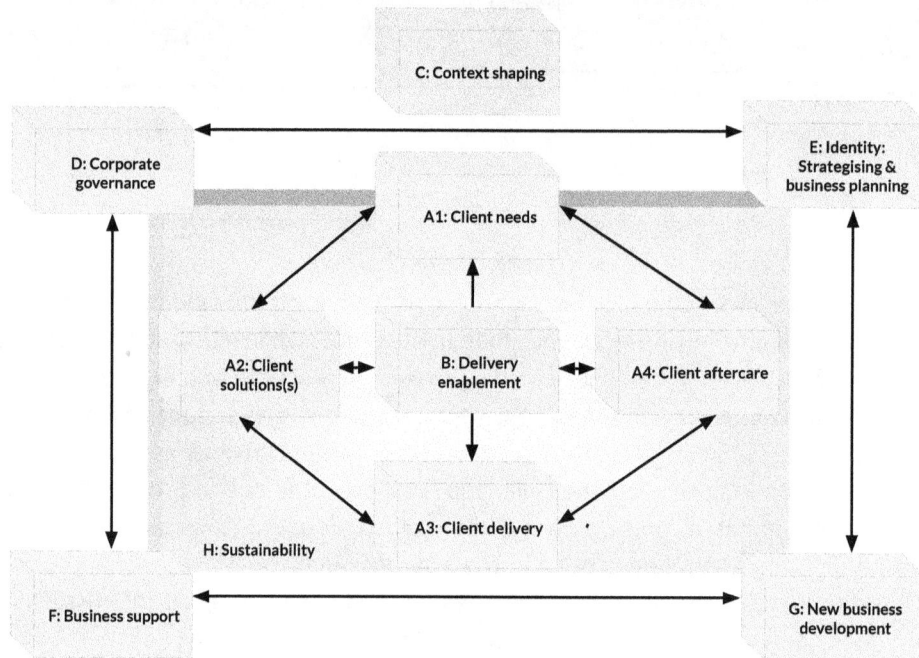

Figure 5.4: Portfolio of the generic work processes of the organisation

Table 5.5: Purpose and expected outcome of the organisation's generic work processes

PROCESS	PURPOSE	EXPECTED OUTCOME
A: Core value chain: A1: Client needs, A2: Client solution(s), A3: Client delivery, A4: Client aftercare	To identify, design and deliver the appropriate client solutions, and conduct client aftercare	Satisfied clients
B: Delivery Enablement	To acquire, deploy, maintain and enhance the resources required to ensure the delivery of client solutions, that is procurement, facilities, Core Operating Technology with Enablers	Affordable and available resources, appropriately deployed in support of the core value chain

PROCESS	PURPOSE	EXPECTED OUTCOME
C: Context shaping	To influence and participate in decisions affecting the form, shape and viability of the relevant industry (such as manufacturing), its direction, policies and standards	Conditions enabling an attractive and viable industry for the organisation concerned
D: Corporate governance	To act as custodians of the organisation's Identity, (that is its Purpose, Core Values, Vision Strategic Intent, Legacy), on behalf of stakeholders	A well governed organisation
E: Identity: Strategising and business planning	To craft, protect and enhance the organisation's Identity as a viable and profitable organisation within its Operating Arena	A viable and profitable organisation
F: Business Support	To satisfy specialist organisational needs regarding the continuity, assurance and protection of the entity as a going concern. For example, audit, public relations, corporate affairs, security, finance, people and corporate social investment	A well enabled organisation
G: New business development	To renew the organisation on an ongoing basis by identifying, assessing and taking up new organisational opportunities to sustain and enhance it	Successfully actualised organisational opportunities, extending its life span (37)
H: Sustainability	To ensure that all of the above work processes contribute towards sustainability through the recovery, renewal, restoration and retention of existing value *whilst* delivering value going into the future.	Consumed/Delivered Value < Replaced Value throughout all of the above work processes, but in particular the core value chain

The generic portfolio of work processes for the total organisation, as given in Figure 5.4 and Table 5.5, must be made organisation-specific during this design step by crafting an organisation-specific work process map that can be visually displayed as a complete work process model of the organisational work to be done. The shaded boxes respectively give examples of the complete work process map of: (i) an infrastructure construction and maintenance organisation (38); and (ii) a nickle mine/smelter (39). (See also the visual map of the Fund Management Organisation above.)

WORK PROCESSES: INFRASTRUCTURE AND CONSTRUCTION ORGANISATION

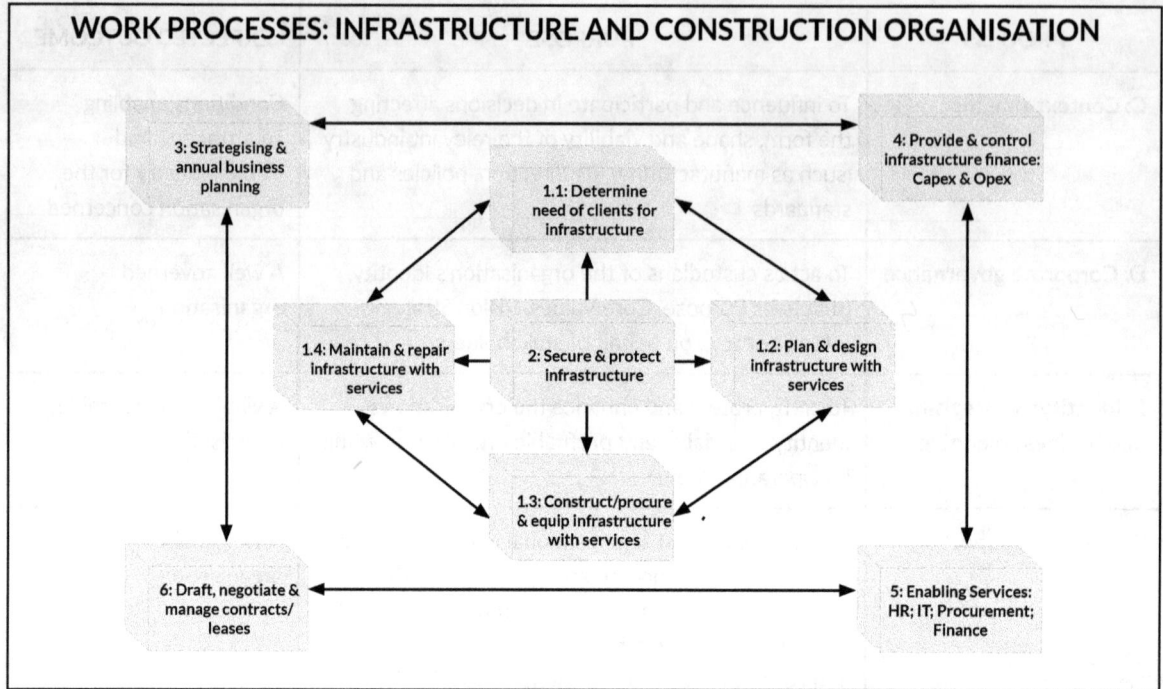

WORK PROCESSES: NICKLE MINE AND SMELTER

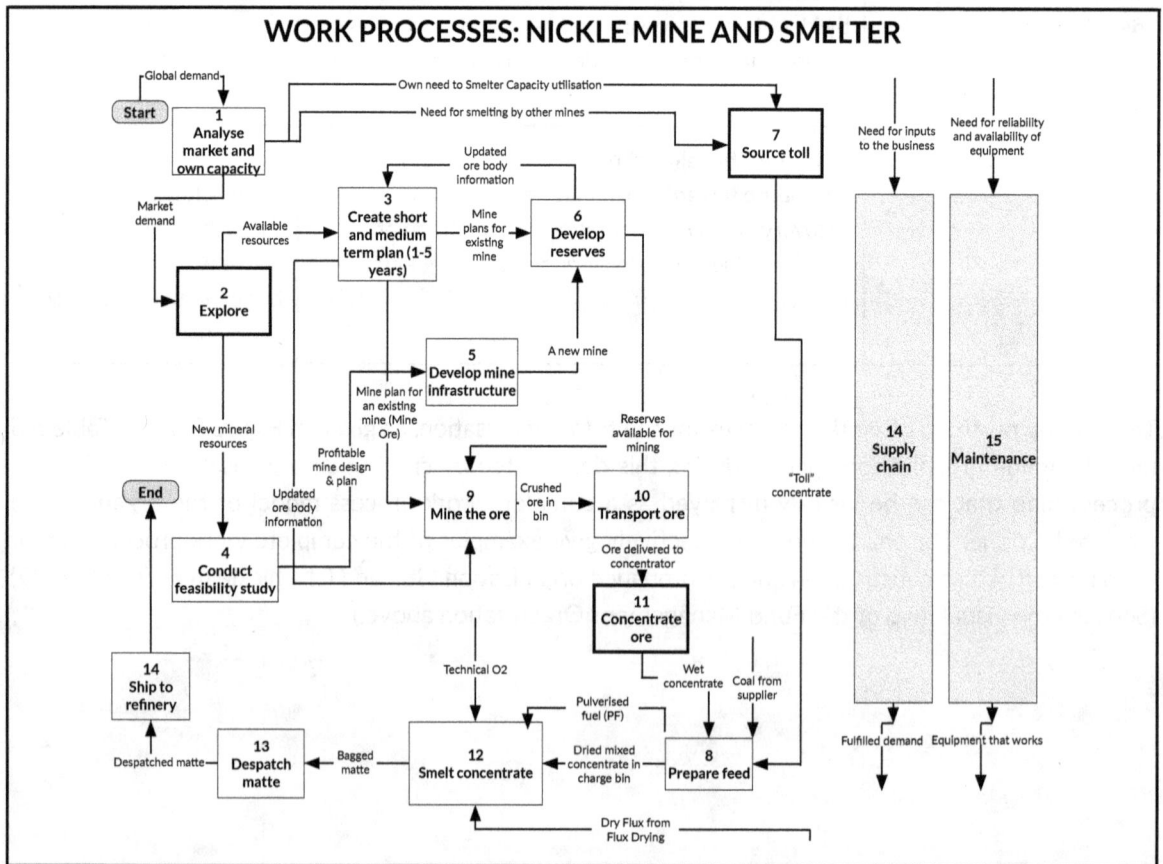

Reason 2 (see Chapter 2) for OD becoming a critical organisational discipline referred to the emerging 'compelling, memorable experience-based' economy. This economy is aimed at creating compelling, memorable customer and employee experiences by re-imaging how customers and employees can be delighted beyond their expectations. To graphically represent this shift, the portfolio of generic work processes for the organisation depicted in Figure 5.4 can be reconfigured in the form of concentric circles like the layers of an onion, with client experiences at the centre of the onion. Figure 5.5 gives this reconfiguration of the work processes. The strength of this configuration of the work processes is that it visually reinforces the point that all work processes must contribute to creating compelling, memorable customer (and employee) experiences. As already explicated in Figure 5.4, sustainability embraces all of the preceding work processes.

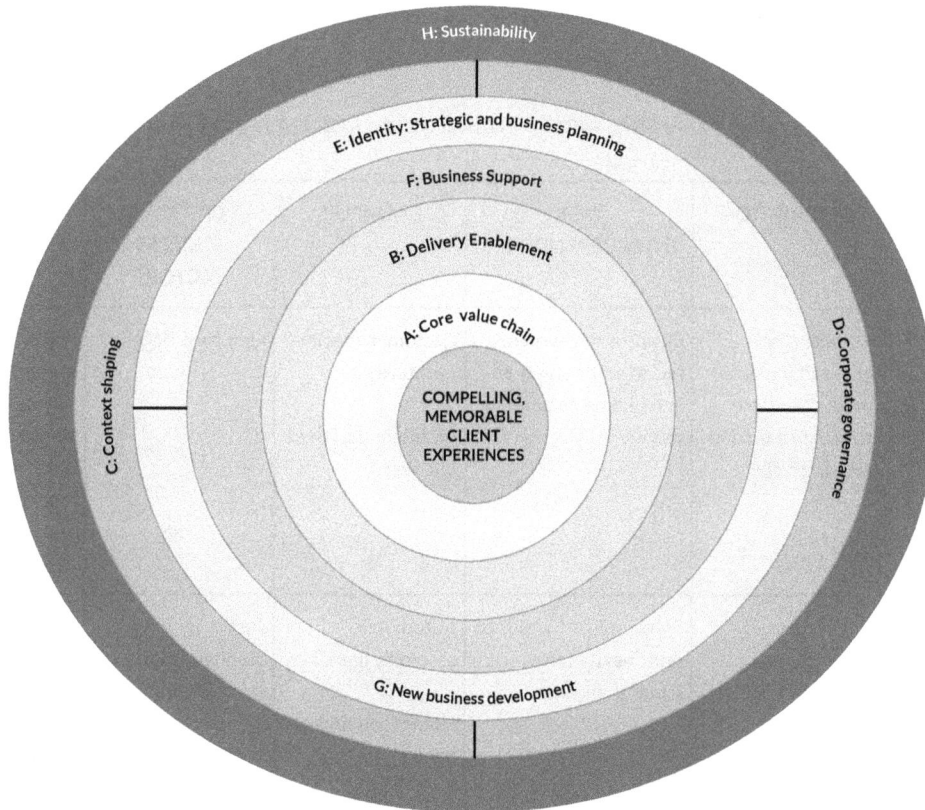

Figure 5.5: Reconfiguration of work processes around the delivery of compelling, memorable Client experiences

In conclusion, when designing a fit-for-purpose design, the importance of having a complete and comprehensive portfolio of the work processes – correctly configured – required by the organisation, as an expression of the work to be done, cannot be overemphasised.

Step A.1.3: Determine Core Operating Technology with Enablers

Core Operating Technology

The Core Operating Technology of an organisation forms the basis (or platform) of the delivery logic. It entails the means used to produce the organisation's products/services *(40) (41)*. The work processes discussed above are leveraged by a certain Core Operating Technology. The critical success factors of different types of Core Operating Technologies impose certain OD requirements, the so-called 'technological imperative' imposed by a Core Operating Technology on the intended design. This technological imperative has to be taken into account in architecting a fit-for-purpose design. Table 5.6 gives the critical success factors of different types of Core Operating Technologies with their resultant design requirements *(42)*.

Table 5.6: Types of Core Operating Technologies with their critical success factors and design requirements

TYPE OF CORE OPERATING TECHNOLOGY	DESCRIPTION	TASK INTERDEPENDENCE	EXAMPLES	CRITICAL SUCCESS FACTORS	DESIGN REQUIREMENTS
Batch	Producing a once-off, unique product/service to satisfy a unique customer/client	Reciprocal – everyone has to work together in real time to produce output	Customer specified furniture Architect designed building	First time right	Highly focused, in-depth, specialist self-designing, competency units, acting independently and with high autonomy
Assembly (or Relay)	The progressive assembly of a product/service through the sequential adding of components/ sub-assemblies	Sequential – Output of one linearly forms the input of another	Automobile assembly line Home loan unit of bank	Just in time Standardisation Specialisation	Well mapped, efficient process with clear hand-over points and specifications, being continuously improved
Continuous	Irreversible, sequential changes in substances to bring about something completely different to the input substances	Sequential – Output of one linearly forms the input of another	Chemical plant	Up time	Front line, real time diagnostic capabilities, enabling autonomous, rapid proactive/reactive responses – in line or from elsewhere – in case of down time

TYPE OF CORE OPERATING TECHNOLOGY	DESCRIPTION	TASK INTERDEPENDENCE	EXAMPLES	CRITICAL SUCCESS FACTORS	DESIGN REQUIREMENTS
Intensive, interdependent	A group of experts co-performing in real time a set of collective, co-ordinated actions to jointly produce an outcome	Reciprocal – everyone has to work together in real time to produce output	Medical operation Multi-disciplinary, multi-work stream, consulting assignment	Right expertise at the right time in the right place	Clearly specified client needs with well demarcated delivery roles and competencies necessary to satisfy client need effectively and efficiently
Independent contributing	A group of independent specialists/ contributors, producing an overall output	Pooled – each person contributes relatively interdependently to produce the overall output	Supermarket Retail banking	Complete range of Work Roles in right numbers, correctly matched to varying work demands	Clearly specified Work Roles in right numbers matched to work demand variability

Two significant intervening variables exist with respect to all of the Core Operating Technologies listed in Table 5.6. These variables infuse the Core Operating Technology with a certain level of 'manageability', in turn imposing certain design requirements (43):

- *Task Uncertainty (or Variability):* frequency of exceptions in the standard mode of use of the Core Operating Technology. The frequency can be innate to the Core Operating Technology or temporary because of a change in the technological means used to operate the technology.

- *Task Analysability:* the availability of known intervention methodologies and practices to deal with exceptions within the Core Operating Technology.

Combining these two intervening variables, each with a high/low status, results in four categories of Technology Manageability, given in Figure 5.6. The Core Operating Technology (COT) (see Table 5.5) typically associated with each category is given for each type. Design requirements are given within a cell in italics for each type of Technology Manageability.

		TASK UNCERTAINTY	
		Low Few exceptions	**High** Many exceptions
TASK ANALYSABILITY	**Low** Unknown methodologies and practices	**Craft Technology** Typical COT: Continuous *Design requirements:* Responsiveness, Agility, Flexibility, Specialisation	**Exclusive Technology** Typical COT: Batch *Design requirements:* Autonomous, Self-designing, Cross-functional, Cross-multi-disciplinary teams
	High Known methodologies and practices	**Routine Technology** Typical COT: Assembly; Independent contributing *Design requirements:* Standardisation, Formalisation, Specialisation, Centralisation	**Controllable Technology** Typical COT: Intensive, interdependent *Design requirements:* Autonomous, Responsive, Agile, Cross-functional teams

Figure 5.6: Types of Technology Manageability

To summarise: the organisation's Core Operating Technology with its associated type of Technology Manageability has to be determined. Once determined, its design requirements must be uncovered in terms of the Technology's critical success factors.

Technology Enablers

> *"Law of Robotics: A robot may not harm humanity. Or, by inaction, allow humanity to come to harm."*
>
> (Isaac Asimov)

The Core Operating Technology is given 'hands and feet' through the Technology Enablers, leveraging its execution. The organisation must debate and decide – thoroughly and upfront – which Enablers it wishes to apply to its Core Operating Technology and why. And then, consequently determine the design requirements arising out of their choices.

At present the emerging order world is in the throes of the Fourth Industrial Revolution (4IR), a term coined by Klaus Schwab – the Founder and Executive Chairman of the World Economic Forum. He uses the term to signify the current technological revolution that people live in, as well as to explore how the world is transforming that is inevitably affecting the way people see themselves live, interact and work (44). The First Industrial Revolution had steam as a power source; the Second, electricity; and the Third, information. The Fourth Industrial Revolution embraces the seamless, intelligent (or smart) integration of multiple disciplines (like biotechnology, or information technology) and sectors into a seamless whole in order to enhance, extend or change society's mode of existence, functioning and delivery in radically new and different ways (45). In designing a fit-for-purpose organisation, serious attention must be given to the implications of this revolution for possible Technology Enablers of the organisation's Core Operating Technology, and the resultant design requirements.

The Fourth Industrial Revolution can be characterised by the acronym DIVAS (46), which provides a handy way to depict the Technology Enablers that can be applied to the Core Operating Technology of the organisation:

- **Di**gitisation: making everything, anything and anywhere computer readable and processable.

- **I**nterconnectivity: everyone/everything talking to everyone/everything.

- **V**irtualisation: being present and delivering on an ongoing basis in cyberspace anything, anywhere, anytime, anyhow, for anyone.

- **A**utomation: performing a process or practice, and taking decisions and actions, through technological means with no/minimal human mediation.

- **S**mart: generating data from everything/anyone, affecting machine learning through feedback and/or turning data into intelligence through decision-making algorithms in order to take focused real time, in time, validated, predictive actions.

Table 5.7 provides an overview of some of the more important Organisational Design considerations arising out of the DIVAS Technology Enablers (47). The criticality of optimising the technology-people relationship and interaction through a fit-for-purpose design has become a real burning platform in architecting future-fit organisations. The challenge is to build a 'humane' organisation. Organisations have to become proactive, value-referenced masters of the Fourth Industrial Revolution (48). Hence the need to adopt a TSV delivery logic that infuses the Operating Model of the organisation.

Table 5.7: Possible Organisational Design considerations flowing from the emerging DIVAS technology enablers

TECHNOLOGY ENABLERS: DIVAS ("Fourth Industrial Revolution")		POSSIBLE ORGANISATIONAL DESIGN CONSIDERATIONS		
ENABLER	**SCOPE**	**HORIZONTAL DESIGN** (Work to be done)	**VERTICAL DESIGN** (Levels of Work) (LOW)	**LATERAL DESIGN** (Co-ordination; Integration; Governance)
DIGITISATION/ VIRTUALISATION (For example, smart phones, voice and facial recognition, augmented reality)	Migration of interactions, products/services and events from the physical to virtual reality (that is cyberspace) by making everything/ anything/anyone computer readable, manipulable, and processable	Real time, flexible product/service innovation and continuous improvement at ever accelerating speed Digitised virtualisation (= augmented reality) of end-to-end work processes with associated	Seamless space/time working together in real time, all the time More equalised, participative relationships across hierarchy Real time, agile, self-designing networking replacing hierarchy	Wide, boundaryless, cross-functional and multi-disciplinary collaboration in all directions, virtually enabled, working in real time together, unconstrained by space/ time boundaries (49)

TECHNOLOGY ENABLERS: DIVAS ("Fourth Industrial Revolution")		POSSIBLE ORGANISATIONAL DESIGN CONSIDERATIONS		
ENABLER	**SCOPE**	**HORIZONTAL DESIGN** (Work to be done)	**VERTICAL DESIGN** (Levels of Work) (LOW)	**LATERAL DESIGN** (Co-ordination; Integration; Governance)
DIGITISATION/ VIRTUALISATION (Continued)	'e' (that is 'online') prefix can be added to everything/ anything/any place/ anyone/anyhow Everything/ anything/ anyone talking to everything/ anything/anyone/ anywhere. Being present, communicating and delivering on an ongoing basis, anything, anywhere, anytime, anyhow, for anyone By heightening the density of connections in cyber-space/time in all directions, turning the world/ organisations into a single, dynamic, dense (or thick), organic, relationship network based on teaming and partnering	data/intelligence in real time, allowing real time doing, monitoring, tracking and intervention, being space/time free Wide, multi-disciplinary/ multi-functional collaboration, along and around core value chain Virtually enabled, working together, freed from space/time boundaries Teleworking 'Appli-fied,' self-help Space/time free, boundaryless expertise Provision of real time intelligence to clients in order to make them 'smarter' with respect to the product/service when using it	Fewer organisational levels – flatter organisation Wider spans of control Automation of work at least at LOWs 1, 2 and 3 Greater autonomy/ self-management to role incumbents and teams Higher level, soft skills become more important. For example, critical thinking; inquisitiveness; imagination; solving complex problems; interacting with others more collaboratively; teaming; empathy; thinking and acting innovatively; systemic/holistic thinking; learning how to question paradigms and mindsets; learning how to learn; resilience; agility; and inclusivity	'Appli-fied,' self-help Power shift from those with authority to those with expertise Boundaryless, real time, stakeholder involvement Biometric identification Rapid, real time communication, problem-solving, decision-making Seamless space/time working together in real time, all the time Crowdsourcing, of internally and externally of ideas, opportunities, product/ service enhancements, resources, funding Downside: over-connectivity Intelligently automate planning, co-ordination and interactions: who is to meet, when, where, and why

TECHNOLOGY ENABLERS: DIVAS ("Fourth Industrial Revolution")		POSSIBLE ORGANISATIONAL DESIGN CONSIDERATIONS		
ENABLER	**SCOPE**	**HORIZONTAL DESIGN** (Work to be done)	**VERTICAL DESIGN** (Levels of Work) (LOW)	**LATERAL DESIGN** (Co-ordination; Integration; Governance)
INTERCONNECTIVITY (For example, World Wide Web, social media, the Internet of Things, cloud computing, virtual collaboration platforms, like Skype, Zoom)	Production, delivery and maintenance of products/services with no/minimal human intervention in terms of human thinking, decisions and/or actions Algorithmic delivery/ management of work Generating data from each and every critical event/transaction/ outcome in order to: (i) improve machine learning through feedback and/or (ii) turn data into intelligence through fit-for-purpose decision-making algorithms. Intelligence is used to take focused, real time, in time, proactive/predictive action	Complementary humans and machines working together, supplementing each other with knowledge, expertise, and skills Division of work: humans defining the problems/desired outcomes; machines help find, but mainly produce, solutions; and humans verify acceptability of solutions in satisfying needs Seamless, space/ time, flexible working together in real time, all the time (= 'jazz band making music') Fluid, autonomous, self-organising as demanded by changing customer and work requirements Shortened innovation cycle: from conception to market introduction Downside: intensity of work increases because boundaries between work and private life disappear: 'Always on duty'	'Soft' abilities will grow in demand. 'Hard' abilities will be accepted as givens. Converting knowledge work done by professionals into decision-making algorithms, either automated or used by para-professionals Intelligence based, real time, in time validated, predictive, 'what if', proactive decision-making More intelligence-informed interactions Real time, digitised augmented transparency with regard to interactions, decisions, actions and outcomes Greater collaboration by broader group because of information rich work setting: wider. More participation	Appli-fy interactions Automated Integration Mechanisms, for example work scheduling Faster problem-solving and decision-making Downside: Machines and decision-making algorithms 'taking over'

TECHNOLOGY ENABLERS: DIVAS ("Fourth Industrial Revolution")		POSSIBLE ORGANISATIONAL DESIGN CONSIDERATIONS		
ENABLER	**SCOPE**	**HORIZONTAL DESIGN** (Work to be done)	**VERTICAL DESIGN** (Levels of Work) (LOW)	**LATERAL DESIGN** (Co-ordination; Integration; Governance)
AUTOMATION (For example, Robotics; 3D printing)		More reliably deliver, control, predict, monitor and track processes than humans, also removing need for governance as oversight process Algorithmicise (= automate) routine tasks – building 'routine smartness' in operations – enabling workers to focus on higher level, more meaningful tasks Downside: machine management with no human touch Downside: rigid automated, delivery, downplaying customer centricity, and compromising agility Real time, in time stakeholder intelligence, for example, clients, suppliers, regulators, communities	Potential to trigger real time, in time re-generation, innovation and entrepreneurialism Just-in-time, real time training and development as and when needed Downside: Intelligence overload and 'pollution'; choice fatigue Downside: Invasion of privacy Downside: misinformation, false truths, post-truths, cyber hacking, data security breaches	

TECHNOLOGY ENABLERS: DIVAS ("Fourth Industrial Revolution")		POSSIBLE ORGANISATIONAL DESIGN CONSIDERATIONS		
ENABLER	SCOPE	HORIZONTAL DESIGN (Work to be done)	VERTICAL DESIGN (Levels of Work) (LOW)	LATERAL DESIGN (Co-ordination; Integration; Governance)
SMART (For example, Artificial Intelligence (AI) *(50)*, Machine learning, Decision-making algorithms, Cloud)		Real time, in time intelligence rich work setting, enabling and empowering people to act in smarter manner Personalised, customisation, based on 360 degree customer insights in real time, all the time Downside: closer management/ supervision in real time, all the time through automated inspection – 'Big Brother is watching you' Downside: biases in data replicated and reinforced in decision-making algorithms		
EXPECTED OUTCOMES				
Faster; Better; Different; New; Cheaper; More predictability; Greater experiences; Less risk; Less errors; Greater access				

In practice, all of the work processes must be evaluated in terms of their potential DIVAS enablement: which work process, or part thereof, can be digitised, interconnected, virtualised, automated and made smart, and in what manner? To this end, work processes can be assessed on two continua, enabling the assessment of the degree of DIVAS enablement that can be considered (51):

- *Capabilities requirements*: Logical-cognitive and/or Compassionate-spiritual (that is purpose/ meaning giving).

- *Thinking/Doing requirements*: Repetitive/Predictable – Rule following and/or Innovative/Experimenting – Rule invention.

Using these two continua with their respective categories, Figure 5.7 depicts four possible Technological Enablement Models. A decision must be taken, given the Identity of the organisation, which Model(s) is/are relevant to which work process. For example, one model may be applicable to Client Needs and another to Client Delivery in the same organisation (refer to Figure 5.4 for the generic portfolio of work processes).

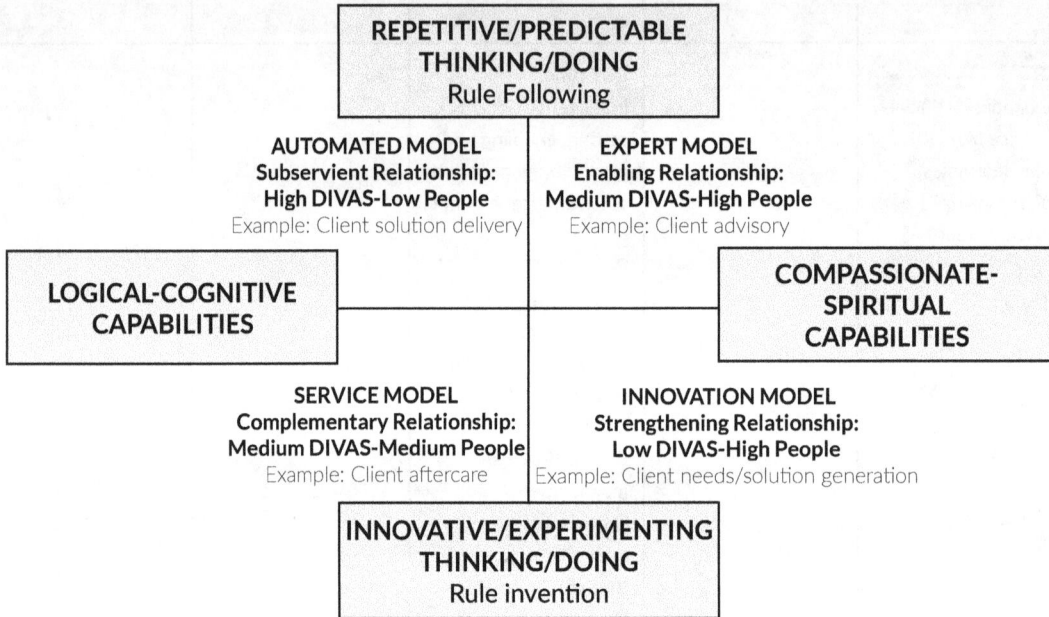

Figure 5.7: Possible Technological Enablement Models

A Technology Enablement Model by Work Process Matrix can be constructed to determine with respect to what Work Process, or portion thereof, which Technology Enablement Model will be applied. The Matrix provides high level design requirements for the applicable Technology Enablement. The set Design Criteria and Vision must be used as a reference point in deciding which model is applicable where. Table 5.8 gives an example of such a Matrix, assuming an Outside-In, client-centricity Design Criteria and Vision. An X indicates the primary Enablement Model for a Work Process.

Table 5.8: Technology Enablement Model by Work Process Matrix: An example

WORK PROCESSES (see Figure 5.4)	TECHNOLOGY ENABLEMENT MODEL (see Figure 5.7)			
	Automated Model	Service Model	Expert Model	Innovation Model
Client Needs				X
Client Solutions				X
Client Delivery	X: Manufacturing of Product/Service	X: Client facing		
Client Aftercare	X: Back office	X: Client facing		
Delivery Enablement: Engineering	X: Back office	X: Client facing	X: Centre of expertise	
Business Support: People	X: Back office	X: Client facing	X: Centre of expertise	

In a similar fashion, a Technology Enablement Model by Core Operating Technology Matrix can be constructed to determine which Technology Enablement Model will be applied to what Core Operating Technology. Again, the set Design Criteria and Vision must be used as a reference point in deciding which model is applicable where. Table 5.9 gives an example of such a Matrix. An X indicates the possible model for the type of Core Operating Technology concerned.

Table 5.9: An example of a Technology Enablement Model by Core Operating Technology

CORE OPERATING TECHNOLOGY (see Table 5.5)	TECHNOLOGY ENABLEMENT MODEL (see Figure 5.7)			
	Automated Model	Service Model	Expert Model	Innovation Model
Batch				X
Assembly (or Relay)	X			
Continuous	X			
Intensive, interdependent			X	
Independent contributing		X		

Step A.1.4: Identify Design Givens

Design Givens impose constraints on, and/or set parameters for, the organisation's design. For example, basic product/service/market/client groupings, geography, technology, regulatory requirements, organisational autonomy, or the contextual complexity faced by the organisation (see the above discussion). In the case of the Design Given of a geographically dispersed organisation, for example, a regionalised design will have to be considered. In another example, the regulatory requirement in the South African pharmaceutical manufacturing industry is that real time, quality assurance must occur after each step in the manufacturing value chain. This prescribed requirement thus has to be built into the delivery logic of such organisations.

The Design Givens hence are design requirements that are impossible or very difficult to change, and therefore *must* be incorporated into the design. Metaphorically, they are like the sun always coming up in the east – it is impossible to change. The above discussion on the Core Operating Technologies with their Technology Enablers, resulting in certain technological imperatives, is a clear case in point.

At a minimum, a Design Given must be accounted for in the design for the time period for which the crafted design will be in place, after which its relevance may be reconsidered. In the case of Strategic Design, this would mean at least five years. At a maximum, a Design Given must form part of a design for the period for which it is in force, for example a regulation.

Step A.1.5: Formulate Design Criteria with Design Vision

Choosing the Design Criteria is the penultimate critical step in bringing all of the necessary design building materials on site. Design Criteria are analogous to the specifications that a client would give an architect when instructing him/her to design a House for a client, for example, 'I would like to have a House of 200 square meters, north facing, open plan lounge/dining room/kitchen; three bedrooms'. Formally defined, a Design Criterion is the specification of a condition that the organisation's design must facilitate, enable, encourage and provide for (52).

Sound Design Criteria are comprehensive, specific, clear, aspirational/inspirational, actionable, positive, and future orientated (53). The requirement of 'comprehensive' needs to be further elucidated. 'Comprehensive' relates to the necessity that the Design Criteria must cover all three of the delivery modes as explicated in Chapter 2: Technical-Social-Virtuous. The sum total of Criteria cannot cover only one or two of the delivery modes.

The Design Criteria bring together and incorporate the design requirements arising out of the Context, Work Processes, Core Operating Technology with its Enablers, and Design Givens. From a certain perspective, Design Criteria represent the core organisational capabilities that the organisation wishes to build in order to give it a competitive edge through its delivery logic (54). Formulating the Design Criteria and Vision is the ultimate climax of Step A.1: Foundation Construction.

Ultimately, Design Criteria give the specifications of what a fit-for-purpose design for the organisation would look like. For example, the design must facilitate, enable, encourage and provide for the capacity to act; build focused competencies; enhance customer-centricity; promote teaming; minimise duplication; and offer a one-stop, client service. In the final instance, Criteria must bring about a high network/high engagement/high responsibility organisation. The shared box gives some of the key features of such an organisation (55).

FEATURES OF A HIGH NETWORK/HIGH ENGAGEMENT/HIGH RESPONSIBILITY ORGANISATION

- Feature 1: A distinct organisation Identity translated into a powerful, differentiating internal and external brand
- Feature 2: A boundary busting Business/Value Model
- Feature 3: Ongoing stretch, future leveraged strategising, translated into, rolled out to, and owned by all at all organisational levels
- Feature 4: Ethical, authentic, shared leadership
- Feature 5: A customer centric, team-based organisational architecture
- Feature 6: A clear, desired people profile, supported by a powerful employee brand and philosophy
- Feature 7: A strong but flexible organisational culture
- Feature 8: Continuous innovation and learning
- Feature 9: Real time, in time, multi-dimensional performance management
- Feature 10: Partnering with diverse, multiple stakeholders

Short descriptions (or definitions) need to be given of each Criterion to clarify exactly what is meant by them. This will ensure the uniform understanding of each Criteria, and make their use easier when debating the merits and demerits of different design options. For example, the Criterion of client-centricity means a one stop service will be provided to clients.

Usually not more than ten, preferably prioritised, Criteria are formulated. These Criteria can be grouped into: (i) non-negotiable; (ii) desirable; and (iii) nice-to-be. The shaded box gives a sample of possible Design Criteria (56). Criteria related to a particular delivery mode are indicated respectively by a T: Technical; S: Social; and V: Virtuous.

SAMPLE DESIGN CRITERIA
Our 'To-Be' Design must:

- create and reinforce compelling, memorable customer and employee experiences (S);
- build focused organisational competencies (T);
- have clear boundaries to ensure unambiguous roles, accountabilities and responsibilities (T);
- minimise duplication in order to ensure economies of scale (T);
- be effectively technologically enabled by optimising the people-technology integration in a humane way (T/V);

- nurture disruptive innovation and ongoing organisational learning (S);
- be cost effective and lean (T);
- be simple but of the requisite complexity (T);
- be agile and responsive (S);
- ensure effective and efficient organisational processes, for example, easy communication and information flows; quick decision-making; rapid problem-solving (T);
- be flat: not more than x organisational levels from top to bottom, compliant to the requisite Levels of Work (S);
- enable flexible people deployment though multi-skilling and multi-tasking (T);
- empower, enable, and engage organisational members at all levels (S);
- allow for teaming and teamwork (S);
- engender a high performance commitment with clear links to rewards (S);
- encourage cross-functional collaboration (S);
- nurture deep, collaborative stakeholder relationships, build social capital (S);
- engender an ethical organisational culture (V);
- be aligned to the core values of the organisation (V); and
- strengthen/enhance sustainability (the five Ps of sustainability, raised in Chapter 2), leveraged from true stewardship (V).

The box gives the Design Criteria McDonald's South Africa are using at present to direct and guide their organisational culture transformation, and by implication their delivery logic (57).

DESIGN CRITERIA TO DIRECT AND GUIDE THE ORGANISATIONAL CULTURE TRANSFORMATION OF McDONALD'S SOUTH AFRICA

From	To
Operational Excellence	Customer Excellence
Serving burgers	Creating delicious feel-good moments
Gut-feel decision-making	Sharper, insight-driven decision-making
Slow to market	Fast to market
Risk adverse	Bold, calculated risks
Relationship-led	Relationship- and results-led
Initiative overload	Disciplined prioritisation and execution
Operating in silos	Integrated
Bureaucratic, inefficient, overly-complex	Lean, efficient, simple
Passionate	Being passionate about the right things

The set of selected, prioritised Design Criteria serves as the ultimate reference point and court of appeal when debating and deciding during the design process which, among several different design options, is the best fit-for-purpose design. No other reference point or court of appeal may be applied – only the agreed upon Criteria may be used. This function of Criteria in the choice of the best design option ensures that the debate about options is more objective, impersonal, impartial and factual. Otherwise, destructive organisational politics such as power plays, turf wars, the pulling of rank, lobbying, personal agendas and interpersonal conflicts take over the choice process. No agreed-upon reference point exists to direct and guide the design process (58).

Although the Design Criteria specify the key features of the 'To-Be' design, its essential nature is still vague and abstract. The crafting of a Design Vision – a one pager, 'A day in the life of...' – can assist significantly in concretising the 'To-Be' design in the minds of everyone, and provide an even more tangible illustration of the new design in reality. The Design Vision describes in narrative form how the organisation will look and function in terms of its delivery logic when it operates in accordance with the set Design Criteria.

What can assist even more in concretising the Design Criteria is to choose a metaphor (or mental model) to visualise more tangibly the new mode of organisational working as reflective of its delivery logic. Metaphors are a handy tool to make reality real (59), especially if two metaphors are chosen to contrast the 'As-Is' against the 'To-Be' . Two examples: A *music* metaphor: 'As-Is' Design – A Symphony Orchestra: Outstanding specialists, jointly working to the same 'score sheet' under the baton of a single, overall leader vs. 'To-Be' – a Jazz Band: Specialists working together creatively around a shared intention and outcome, taking clues from one another as the work unfolds. Or, a *ship* metaphor: 'As-Is' Design – a massive oil tanker, under direct command from the captain on the bridge vs. 'To-Be' – a fleet of specialised, autonomous but complementary ships under the command of their own captains moving in the same direction towards a common, agreed upon destination.

The use of metaphors aims to trigger an ongoing, powerful narrative in the organisation around the 'To-Be', in contrast to the 'As-Is' organisation (60). A succinct tag line – a short, punchy description of the new design – can also be formulated to express the Design Vision. An example is the above BP case study, where the new design was entitled an 'Asset Federation'.

Visual ways can also be deployed to make the desired, future Organisational Design real, like industrial theatre, creating a simulated, virtual reality of the 'As-Is' and 'To-Be' designs, or using gamification to act out a day in the life of the 'To-Be' design.

Step A.1.6: Diagnose Existing Design – Strengths and Weaknesses

In the case of a brownfield design, that is a redesign, a sound diagnosis must be conducted of the major OD strengths and weaknesses of the existing design against the set Design Criteria and Vision. These strengths and weaknesses must be prioritised (*61*) and the OD 'mess' must be made systemically visible (*62*).

It is important to stress that the identified strengths and weaknesses must be design-related. For example, strengths: in-depth organisational capability, deep customer relationships; weaknesses: poor economies of scale, low agility. One must be careful not to include strengths and weaknesses unrelated to the existing design, for example, poor skills or the wrong products/services, although often these could be the symptoms of the underlying, *unfit*-for-purpose design.

The diagnosis is also placed as the last step in Step A.1: Foundation Construction. The diagnosis of the 'As-Is' design must be referenced against the 'To-Be' design as concretised in the Design Criteria and Vision in order to uncover *relevant* strengths and weaknesses with respect to the current vs. the desired.

A sound guideline is to identify the 20% strengths/weaknesses that are making 80% of the difference – usually about three to five of each. Frequently weaknesses trigger the OD need, hence the design intervention. The aim of the OD intervention is to build on the strengths and minimise/eliminate the weaknesses of the existing design.

This concludes Step A.1: Foundation Construction. The expected outcome of this step is to bring the necessary building material for the Strategic Design on site.

Quality assurance questions for Stage A.1: Foundation Construction

QUALITY ASSURANCE QUESTIONS *Step A.1: Foundation Construction – Building Materials of the House*	DESIGN STEP	ADDRESSED: YES/ NO *(Yes: +; No: x)*
Have the critical **contextual factors** (5 to 10) which impact on the design, with their implications for the design, been identified: Features/trends in the organisation's Operating Arena; the contextual complexity of the Operating Arena; Stakeholders; Contextual complexity; Stakeholders; Critical Resources; Business/Value Model; Strategic Intent; Organisational Life Cycle; Organisational Rhythm?	Step A.1.1	
Does a complete **work process map** exist, covering all of the core, enabling and support work processes required to define, deliver and satisfy client needs? Has an organisational **work process model** been constructed? Does the model incorporate the latest thinking about these work processes?	Step A.1.2	
Has the **Core Operating Technology** with its critical success factors been determined?	Step A.1.3	
Have clear choices been made regarding DIVAS **technology enablers** regarding the work processes? Which work process, or part thereof, must be in principle digitised, interconnected, virtualised, automated and made smart, and in what manner?	Step A.1.3	
Have all of the major **Design Givens,** which set constraints on the design with their implications for the design, been identified?	Step A.1.4	

QUALITY ASSURANCE QUESTIONS *Step A.1: Foundation Construction – Building Materials of the House*	DESIGN STEP	ADDRESSED: YES/ NO *(Yes: +; No: x)*
Are the **Design Criteria** (up to 10) appropriate to the conditions the design must facilitate, enable, encourage, and provide for? Are they clearly defined and prioritised (= non-negotiable, desirable, nice-to-be)?	Step A.1.5	
Does the **Design Vision** (= Day in the life of....) describe accurately what the organisation will look like when it operates in terms of the Design Criteria? Has a powerful **Metaphor** been selected to represent the Design Vision, and make it real?	Step A.1.5	
Have the major **strengths and weaknesses** of the existing design been identified, the 20% that makes 80% of the difference?	Step A.1.6	

Conclusion

This chapter dealt with Step A.0: Profile of Organisation – Nature of Organisation, and Step A.1: Foundation Construction – The Building Materials of the House, of the strategic design process. The objective of the *first step* is to demarcate the essential nature of the organisation under consideration as contained in its Identity. The objective of the *second step* is to establish the 'fundamentals' with respect to the organisation to be (re)designed, that is to bring the necessary building materials needed for the design on site in order to prepare for the building that is to take place. The building materials represent contingency design requirements which would result in inter-organisational design variations.

The critical building materials covered include: the key contextual features to be considered as design requirements (Step A.1.1); the Work Process Map (Step A.1.2); the Core Operating Technology with Enablers (Step A.1.3); the Design Givens (Step A.1.4); the Design Criteria with the Design Vision and Design Metaphor (Step A.1.5); and the Existing Design with its Strengths and Weaknesses (Step A.1.6). The importance of bringing good quality building materials on site cannot be overemphasised.

The next chapter addresses the next step in the Strategic Design Process: Strategic Horizontal Design.

Endnotes

(1) In general, this chapter draws on the author's experience, supplemented and enriched by Anand & Daft (2007); Bellerby (2017); Burton & Obel (2018); Burton, Obel & Håkonsson (2015); Galbraith (1997); (2006); (2008); (2014); Galbraith, Downey & Kates (2005); Kesler & Kates (2011); MacKenzie (1986); Mintzberg (1993); (1997); Nadler & Tushman (1997); Roberts, (2004); Stanford (2007) and Veldsman (2002).

(2) Chandler (1962).

(3) For example, Galbraith (1997); (2006); (2008); (2014); Galbraith, Downey & Kates (2005); Goold & Andrew (2002a); (2002b) Nadler & Tushman (1997); Stanford (2007).

(4) For example, Jacques (2006); Shephard, Gray, Hunt & McArthur (2007).

(5) Burton, Obel & Håkonsson (2015); Hanna (1988); Smith & Lankosi (2018); Yeoman & O'Hara (2017).

(6) Santos, Pache & Birkholz (2015); Saporito (2015); Smith & Lankosi (2018); Veldsman (2015a).

(7) Lankoski & Smith (2017); Smith & Lankosi (2018).

(8) Sourced from Smith & Lankosi (2018).

(9) Veldsman (2015a).

(10) Mazzarol, Limnios & Reboud, (2011).

(11) International Co-operative Alliance (accessed on 5 June 2018).

(12) Mazzarol, Limnios & Reboud (2011).

(13) Birchall (2011); ICA (1995) as quoted in Skurnik (1999).

(14) Bateman & Novkovic (2015); Birchall (2011); Davis (2001); Dubb (2016); Mazzarol, Limnios & Reboud (2011); Normark (1996); Novkovic (2008); Puusa, Mönkkönen & Varis (2013); Skurnik (1999); Spear (2000).

(15) Mulaudzi (2019); Stokvels (2019).

(16) Mintzberg (1993); (1997) sees environment (= context) as a contingency factor in Organisational Design.

(17) The law of requisite variety (Ashby, 1956) states that the variety of the internal organisational context must match the variety of the external organisational context, its Operating Arena, and vice versa (quoted by Fjeldstad, Snow, Miles & Lettl, 2012).

(18) First propagated by T. Burns and G.M. Stalker as quoted in Burton, Obel & Håkonsson (2015); Luhman & Cunlife (2013); Mintzberg (1993); (1997).

(19) Geldenhuys & Veldsman (2010); Veldsman (2013).

(20) This discussion draws heavily on Veldsman (2016). See also Bellerby (2017); Burton, Obel & Håkonsson (2015) and Pasmore (1988).

(21) Cf. Bellerby (2017). He interprets an increase in the complexity of an organisation very much as a growth in the size of the organisation. Mintzberg (1993); (1997) sees organisational size as a contingency factor in organisational design.

(22) Mintzberg (1993); (1997) sees power (including ownership) as a contingency factor in Organisational Design.

(23) Bussin (2017a); (2017c); Stanford (2015).

(24) Cf. Burton, Obel & Håkonsson (2015); Bussin (2017b); (2017d); Galbraith (1997); (2006); (2008); (2014) .

(25) Galbraith, Downey & Kates (2005).

(26) R.E. Miles and C.C. Snow offer another well-known and accepted strategy typology consisting of four Strategic Intents, namely: *Reactor*: adjust to context; *Defender*: maintain status quo; *Prospector*: discover/create new opportunities/being market leaders; and *Analyser* with (combination of Defender and Prospector) or without innovation (imitates what others are doing successfully by doing more efficiently/quick second mover) (quoted in Burton, Obel & Håkonsson, 2015).

(27) Adapted from Galbraith, Downey & Kates (2005); Kates & Galbraith (2007).

(28) An ambidextrous Organisational Design is one that concurrently accommodates and enables, along an innovation spectrum, sustaining *and* breakthrough with respect to product/service development as reflected in the table below (Kates & Galbraith, 2007)

Sustaining			Breakthrough		
Product improvement	Line extension	Next generation	New product	New technology	New business model
Close					**Far**
Distance from core business					

(29) Bellerby (2017); Burton, Obel & Håkonsson (2015); Bussin, M. (2017c); Stanford (2015)

(30) The figure and table was constructed by the author, based on Adizes (1988); Bellerby (2017); Burton, Obel & Håkonsson (2015); Bussin (2017b); Greiner (quoted in Luhman & Cunliffe, 2013); Mintzberg (1993); (1997); Stanford (2015)

(31) Roberts (2004)

(32) Bellerby (2017); Boynton & Victor (1991); Denison, quoted by Fenton & Pettigrew (2000); Christensen & Overdorf (2000); Cross (1990); De Guerre, Se Guin, Pace & Burkeida (2013); Galbraith (2014); Hanna (1988); Harbou & Schmidt (2018); ICI Chemical & Polymers Ltd. (1989); Kates & Galbraith (2007); MacKenzie (1986); Pasmore (1988); Porter (1985); Ramos (2012)

(33) Source: Author

(34) For example, MacKenzie (1986)

(35) ICI Chemical & Polymers Ltd. (1989) classifies work processes for design purposes into basic transformations, supplementary transformations, ancillary operations, transportation, and storage. This classification will be used in latter chapters to group work processes into Work Units and Teams

(36) Hawken (2010), but also Brown (2019)

(37) Refer to Contextual Variable 7: Organisational Life Cycle

(38) Source: Author

(39) Kindly supplied by a colleague, Andre Parker

(40) J. Woodward was the pioneer in first investigating the relationship between the Core Operating Technology of an organisation and its required design, linking technological complexity to design requirements (quoted in Luhman & Cunliffe, 2013; Mintzberg, 1993; 1997)

(41) Mintzberg (1993; 1997) sees technology as a contingency factor in the design of the organisation

(42) Based primarily on Thompson's (1967) and Woodward's typologies of technology, as quoted in Goodman & Associates (1986) and Luhman & Cunliffe (2013). See also Huber (2011) and Mintzberg (1993); (1997)

(43) Adapted from C. Perrow (quoted in Luhman & Cunliffe (2013). See also Donaldson & Joffe (2015)

(44) Hawryszkiewycz (2017); Okechukwu (2016)

(45) Distilled from the references given under Note (46)

(46) Conceived by the author

(47) Anderson & Van der Heyden (2017); Agarwal, Bersin, Lahiri, Schwartz & Volini (2018); Autor (2015); Bartleby (2018); Bhalla, Dyrchs & Strack (2017); Christos (2017); Christos & Bussin (2017); Covin (2015); Davenport (2017); Evans-Greenwood, Lewis & Guszcza (2017); Friedman (2016); Galbraith (2014); Garud, Kumaraswamy & Sambamurthy (2006); Hawryszkiewycz (2017); Hirschi (2018); Kiron (2017); Ludik (2019); Mariani, Sniderman & Harr (2017); McAfee & Brynjolfsson (2017); Okechukwu (2016); Reddy, (2019); Reddy (2019); Schwarzmüller, Brosi, Duman & Welpe (2018); The Economist (2016); (2018a); (2018b); Schildt (2017); Zammuto, Griffith, Majchrzak, Dougherty & Faraj (2007)

(48) Schwab (2016)

(49)   Based on a global survey of more than 3,500 managers and executives, MIT Sloan Management Review and Deloitte's third annual report on digital business found that the most digitally advanced organisations — those successfully deploying digital technologies and capabilities to improve work processes, engage talent across the organisation, and drive new value-generating business models — are far more likely to engage in cross-functional collaboration. More than 70% of these organisations use cross-functional teams to organise work and charge them with implementing digital, organisational priorities (Quoted by Kiron, 2017)

(50)   A survey by Sloan Management Review and Boston Consulting showed that 85% of companies think AI will offer a competitive advantage, but only one in 20 is extensively employing AI today (The Economist, 2018)

(51)   Based on insights gained and extended from Ludik (2019)

(52)   Bellerby (2017); Cross (1990); Kates & Galbraith (2007); Kesler & Kates (2011); Nadler & Tushman (1988); Veldsman (2002); (2015a)

(53)   Kates & Galbraith (2007); Kesler & Kates (2011); Miles, Snow, Fjeldstad, Miles & Lettl (2010)

(54)   Kates & Galbraith (2007)

(55)   Veldsman (2013)

(56)   Da Gama (2019)

(57)   Builds on the author's client assignments, enriched by, for example, Bellerby (2017); Kesler & Kates (2011); Lawler & Worley (2012); Mutuality Yeoman & O'Hara (2017); Petković, Mirić & Čudanov (2014)

(58)   Goold & Campbell (2002)

(59)   Ramos (2012)

(60)   Gruber, De Leon, George & Thompson (2015)

(61)   MacKenzie (1986) and Mosley & Meaney (2017) all emphasise the importance of a thorough diagnosis and assessment of the 'As-Is' design

(62)   Gharajedaghi (2011)

6

STRATEGIC ORGANISATIONAL DESIGN

Architecting the overall Organisational Shape: Strategic Horizontal Design

---

"Simplicity is the ultimate sophistication."

(Leonardo da Vinci)

"Make everything as simple as possible, but not simpler."

(Albert Einstein)

"It is vain to do with more, what can be done with less."

(William of Occam)

The purpose of Step A.1: Foundation Construction of the Strategic Design process was to bring the necessary, good quality building materials onto the site where the design has to be built, as referenced against the demarcated Purpose of the organisation (Step A.0.1). Now the design process can commence formally.

The purpose of this chapter is to deal with the first formal stage in the strategic design process – Step A.2: Strategic Horizontal Design (1). Figure 6.1 depicts by arrow the relative location of this step in the overall Strategic Design Route Map.

Step A.0: Profile of Organisation – Nature of organisation

A.0.1: Demarcate Organisation

Step A.1: Foundation Construction – Building materials of House

A.1.1: Profile Organisational Context
A.1.2: Map Work Processes
A.1.3: Determine Core Operating Technology with Enablers
A.1.4: Identify Design Givens
A.1.5: Formulate Design Criteria with Design Vision
A.1.6: Diagnose Existing Design – Strengths & Weaknesses

Step A.2: Strategic Horizontal Design – Rooms making up the House

A.2.1: Group Work Processes into Work Units
A.2.2: Configure Work Units into an Organisational Shape
A.2.3: Allocate Crown Jewels
A.2.4: Identify Partnering opportunities

Step A.3: Strategic Vertical Design – Type of ownership and owners of Rooms

A.3.1: Decide on requisite Level of Work of organisation overall
A.3.2: Architect House Ownership Model
A.3.3: Allocate requisite Levels of Work to Work Units
A.3.4: Identify mission critical Work Roles at Work Unit Leadership Level & generate high level Role Profiles

Step A.4: Strategic Lateral Design – Living together in the House

A.4.1: Construct an Interdependency Matrix
A.4.2: Decide on Integration Mechanisms
A.4.3: Set up Governance Model

Step A.5: Integrated Strategic Design and Charter – Overall House Plan

A.5.1: Compile Organisational Map
A.5.2: Draw high level Organogram
A.5.3: Draft Organisational Charter

Step A.6: Strategic Organisational Alignment – Fitting House into Town House Complex

A.6.1: Leadership Alignment
A.6.2: Cultural Alignment
A.6.3: People Alignment
A.6.4: Resources Alignment
A.6.5: Performance Alignment
A.6.6: Work Place Alignment

Step A.7: Strategic Design Impact Assessment – Existing vs. New Houses

A.7.1: Conduct Gap & Risk Analysis

Step A.8: Strategic Design Implementation Road Map – Planning how to build the House

A.8.1: Craft Design Roll Out Strategy & Plan
A.8.2: Craft Organisational Change Navigation Strategy & Plan

Step A.9: Strategic Design Solution Report

Step A.10: Strategic Design Implementation – Building the House

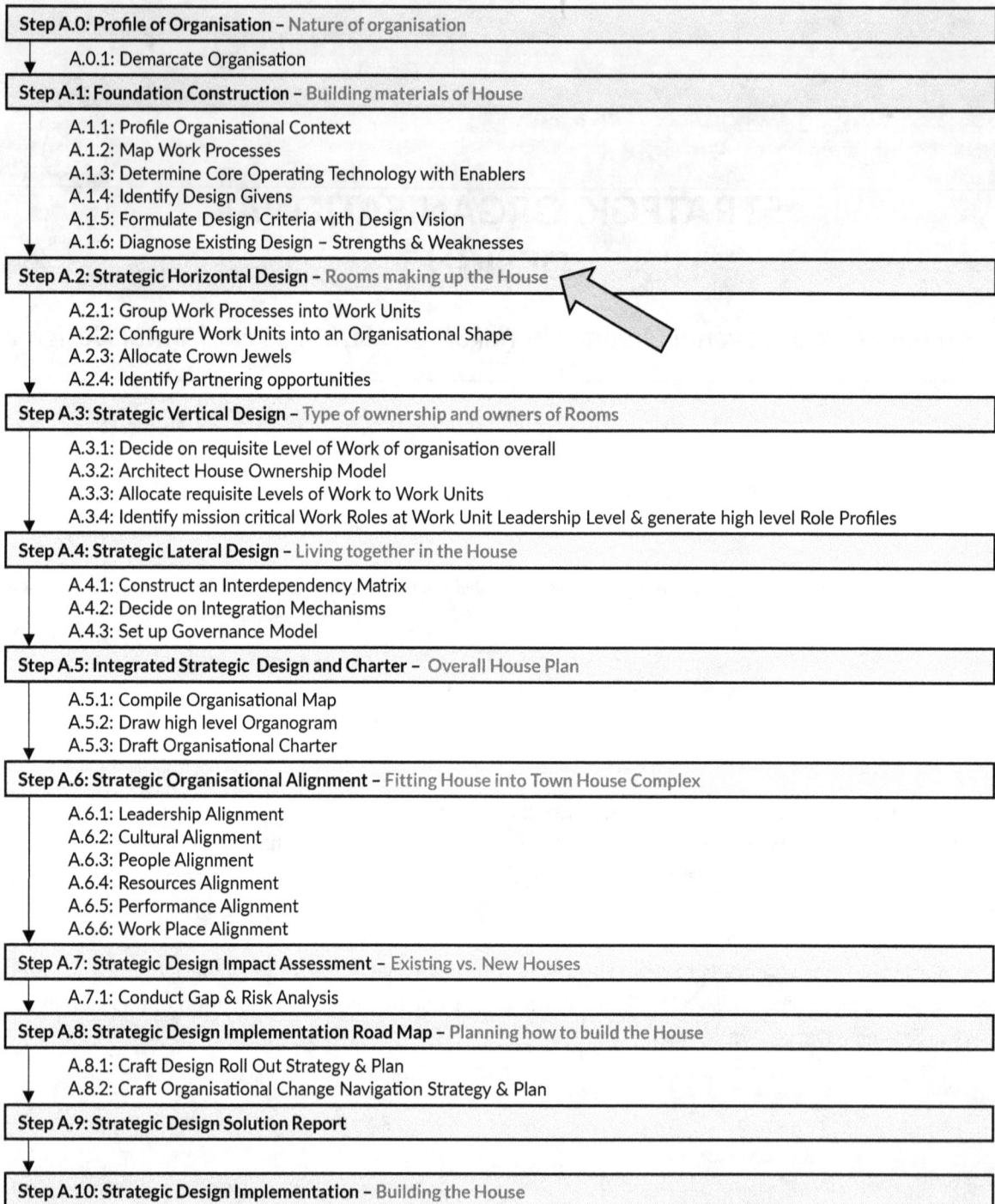

Figure 6.1: Strategic OD route map
Note: Part of Phase 3: Step 3.2 of the OD life cycle (see Chapter 4)

Step A.2: Strategic Horizontal Design – Rooms making up the House

The objective of Step A.2 is to determine the Work Units making up the organisation, and configure them into a fit-for-purpose Organisational Shape. Metaphorically speaking: identify and demarcate *all* of the Rooms making up the House and architect the House Plan – how do all of the Rooms fit together relative to each other? The key issue is: What Organisational Shape must be chosen in terms of a fit-for-purpose organisational delivery logic?

According to Figure 6.1, this step is made up of four sub-steps:

- A.2.1: Group work processes into Work Units.

- A.2.2: Configure Work Units into an Organisational Shape, for example: Functional, Strategic Business Units or Front-Back.

- A.2.3: Allocate crown jewels. That is, ensure that single accountabilities exist for the organisation's crown jewels.

- A.2.4: Identify partnering opportunities, that is our organisation best at doing a piece of work or will another party outside of the organisation be able to do it better?

Similar to the previous chapter, the step numbering in Figure 6.1 is used as a chapter numbering system.

Step A.2.1: Group Work Processes into Work Units

The first step in the Horizontal Design process is to group *all* of the work processes contained in the Work Process Map (see Figure 5.4, Step A.1.2, Chapter 5) into distinct Work Units (= Rooms in the House), applying throughout as reference the Design Criteria and Vision as decision-making guidelines (Step A.1.5). A Work Unit represents a distinct area of accountability around a focused, organisational capability. A Work Unit Purpose (or mandate) must be crafted for each identified Work Unit as a core statement of the work to be performed by the Unit. The Work Unit Purposes are a good aid in allocating work processes to Work Units.

At least five types of Work Units can be distinguished *(2):*

- *Board:* the unit that plays an *independent, oversight governance role over the organisation and its leadership.*
- *Corporate Centre (in conventional language, the Head Office):* the unit that *provides direction, guidance and governance to the total organisation.*
- *Operating Unit(s):* a unit containing the total core work process, the *client delivery process,* or a portion thereof.
- *Enabling Unit(s):* a unit containing the support processes that *enable delivery by the Operating Entity/ Entities.* For example, in the case of a manufacturing organisation, the maintenance of production equipment.

- *Support Units:* units containing the processes that *enable the organisation to function as an organisation*, for example, Finance, People, IT.

Figure 6.2 depicts these Work Units graphically.

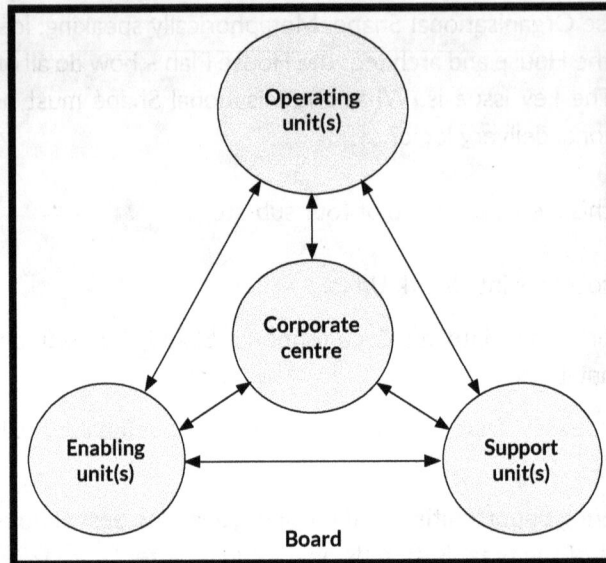

Figure 6.2: Types of Work Units

The shaded box provides guidelines for the creation of distinct, powerful Work Units (3).

GUIDELINES FOR THE CREATION OF DISTINCT, POWERFUL WORK UNITS
A Work Unit must:

- have a distinct *Core Purpose* that is clearly defined;

- represent a *whole piece of work* for clearly defined customer(s), internally and/or externally;

- contain at least one *Core Transformation*: an activity that adds value and creates wealth for the organisation, and/or at least one *Core Organisational Competency*;

- have clear *boundaries* at natural break points and handover points (for example, storage), allowing for clear ownership and accountability. Boundaries must be drawn in terms of the principle of control of variance at source: all of the activities that have a direct influence on the performance of a Work Unit, or are highly interdependent in their execution, must be under the Work Unit's immediate control. Otherwise the Work Unit cannot be held accountable for its performance;

- have identifiable, measurable *outputs*;

- *size-wise* not be bigger than an estimated 100 employees, with teams of about 8-10 persons each (= Operational Design). These sizes allow employees to better identify and relate to their Work Unit, co-employees, and the customers they are serving;

- have a *name* that is a true reflection of the work done by the Work Unit.

At the end of this step, each work process in the organisation's portfolio of Work Processes – in its totality or portions thereof – will have been allocated to a Work Unit as per type of Work Unit depicted in Figure 6.2.

Step A.2.2: Configure Work Units into an Organisational Shape

The Work Units (the Rooms in the House) have been created by allocating all of the work processes, according to the Work Unit Purposes. Next, the Work Units have to be configured into a Basic Organisational Shape (a House Plan) that is reflective of the desired delivery logic for the organisation. The chosen Organisational Shape represents the Strategic Horizontal Design. The final Organisational Shape is the outcome of having considered a set of different possible Organisational Design delivery logics as referenced against the set of chosen Design Criteria and the Design Vision, expressing the organisation's 'To-Be' design.

Figure 6.3 gives a graphic overview of the different categories of Organisational Shapes – reflective of different design delivery logics – that have to be considered:

- The general trend in Organisational Shapes.

- The context in which the organisation has to function, specifically sector-/industry-related Organisational Shapes.

- Organisational Shapes aligned to different Strategic Intents.

- Basic delivery logic axes on which to profile the desired 'To-Be' Organisational Shape.

- Having considered all of the above categories, the choice of a specific 'To-Be' Organisational Shape.

The movement through the five categories of Organisational Shapes – with their respective design delivery logics – is from the macro/general to the micro/specific in order to arrive at a specific, fit-for-purpose Organisational Shape for one's organisation. The shaded box provide some guidelines for choosing a fit-for-purpose Organisational Shape. In making choices along the way, the use of the set of selected Design Criteria and Vision with the Design Metaphor to provide decision-making guidelines stand central as a reference point and final arbiter, and again cannot be overstressed.

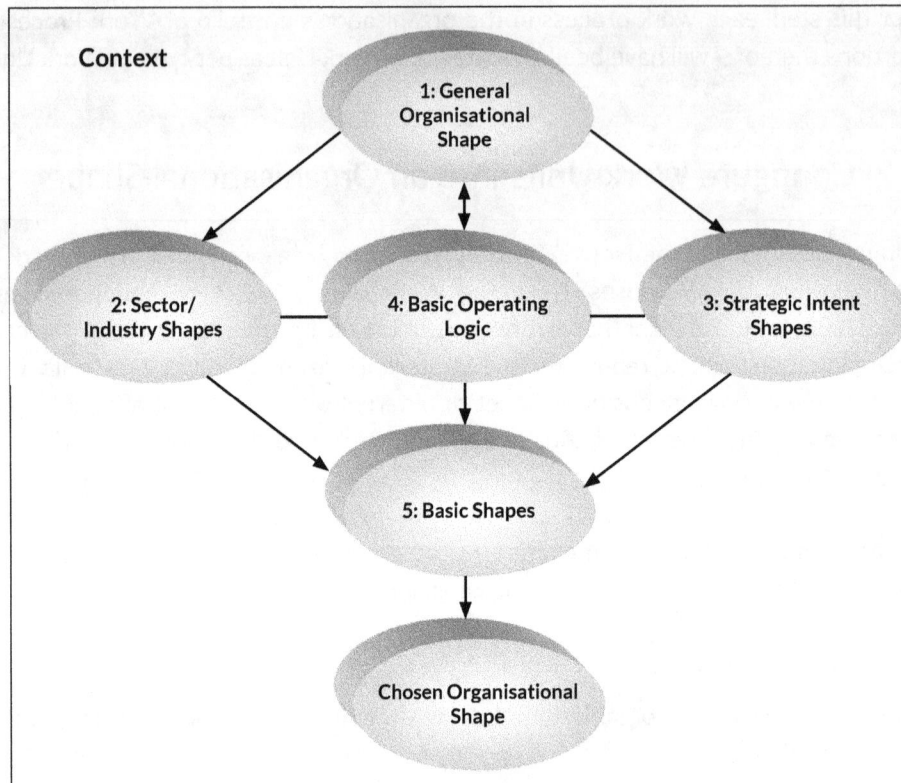

Figure 6.3: Different categories of Organisational Shapes to be considered in configuring Work Units into a final 'To-Be' Organisational Shape

---

GUIDELINES FOR CHOOSING A FIT-FOR-PURPOSE, ORGANISATIONAL SHAPE

- Choose the Organisational Shape that best meets the set Design Criteria and Vision, regardless of the current Organisational Shape and possible implementation barriers, like regulations, uncovered during Step A.1.

- When the gap between the 'As-Is' and 'To-Be' designs has been determined in Step A.7 and is vast, one may decide to architect interim designs to put in place for defined periods of time to take one to the final design.

Step A.2.2.1: Gain a general understanding of the broad mind shifts in Organisational Shapes

Because of the characteristics of the emerging new order as depicted in Figure 2.2., Chapter 2, the broad trend currently in design delivery logics is a mindset shift in the thinking about the critical ingredients of future-fit organisations, in contrast to those making up traditional organisations. This mindset shift debunks OD Myth 2, Chapter 2, which states that Organisational Designs befitting the future can be merely more of the same. Figure 6.4 depicts this mindset shift about organisations in general, going into the future (4).

TRADITIONAL ORGANISATION		EMERGING ORGANISATION
Objectives, plans, standards	→	Identity (= Purpose, Dream, Strategic Intent, Core Values, Legacy)
Tangible assets/Capital intensive	→	Intangible assets/people intensive
Static, self-sufficient	→	Self-designing, distributed value web
Local, physical	→	Global, virtual
Standardised, formalised	→	Flexible, unit-specific
Jobs, functions, individual	→	Roles, Work Domains, Teams
Procedures	→	Culture
Positional power	→	Relationship/Expert power
Top down decisions/relationships	→	Multi-directional decisions/relationships
Management: Efficiency	→	Leadership: Effectiveness
Over-inspection	→	Self management/governance
Information-scarce	→	Information-rich
Activities	→	Outcomes
Products/Service	→	Customer experience
Permanent employment	→	Temporary/Assignment employment
Compliant loyalty	→	Negotiated contributions
Engaging only Body and Head	→	Engaging total person, including Heart and Spirit
Self interest	→	Social citizen

Figure 6.4: General trend in mindsets about organisations: an OD perspective

In terms of Figure 6.4, the traditional organisation depicted on the left in the figure represents the traditional Command-and-Control Organisational Shape as graphically illustrated in Figure 6.5 (5).

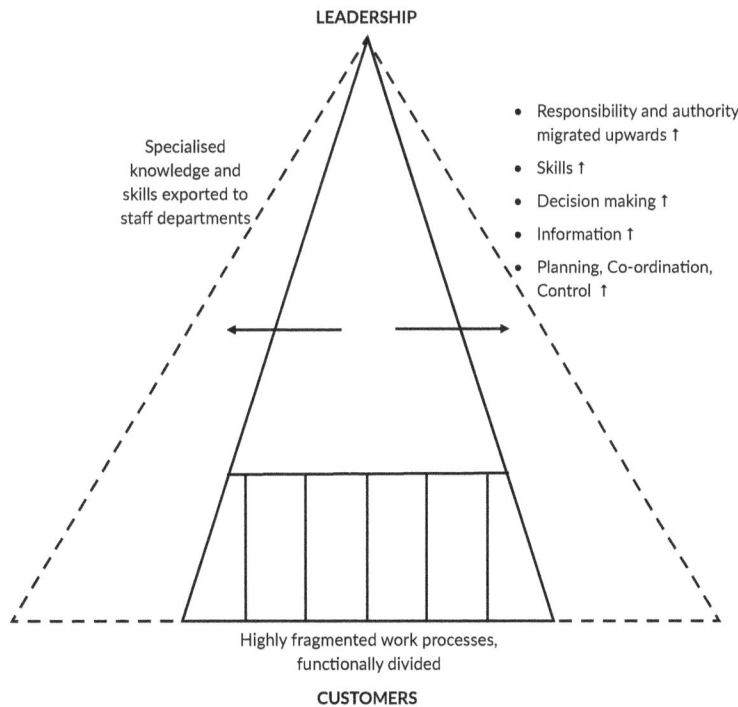

Figure 6.5: 'Pyramid' as a metaphor for the vision of the Traditional Organisational Shape: Command-and-Control delivery logic

According to Figure 6.5, the delivery logic of the Command-and-Control Organisational Shape entails: One person to one prescribed task (= job) with few skills; little decision-making power; little information; controlled by rules, procedures and rank; linked to others through the hierarchy; focusing on efficiency and quantity.

An adaptation of the Traditional Organisational Shape is the 'Inverted Pyramid' (or 'Individualised Corporation'), shown in Figure 6.6: the organisational hierarchy is turned upside down with higher organisational levels supporting the front line, who are in direct contact with the customer. Individuals at the front line is empowered by high levels of responsibility and authority; skills; decision-making; information; planning; co-ordination; and control to serve customers as best they can and need to (6).

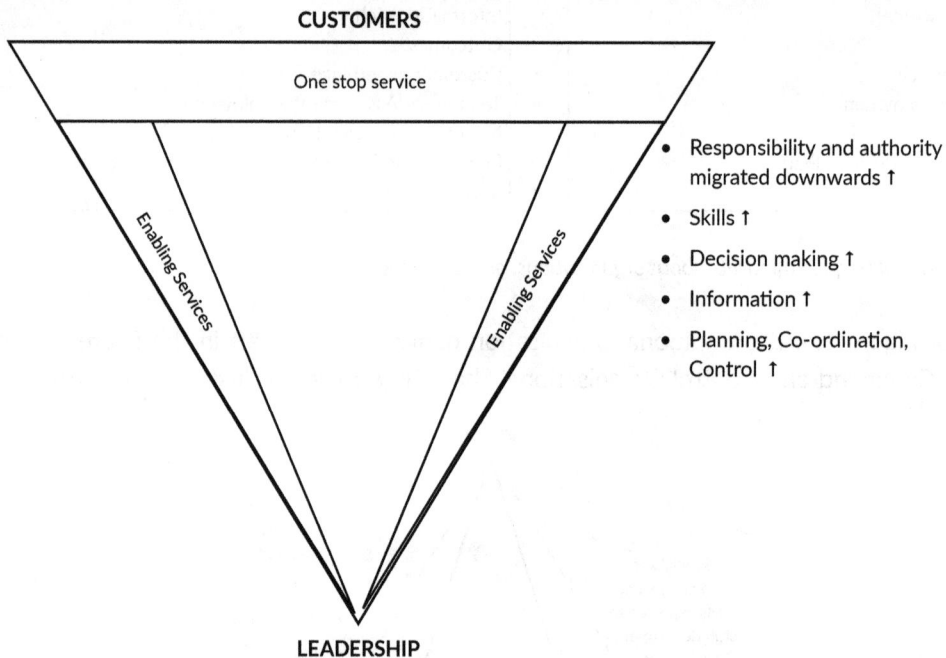

CUSTOMERS

One stop service

Enabling Services

Enabling Services

- Responsibility and authority migrated downwards ↑
- Skills ↑
- Decision making ↑
- Information ↑
- Planning, Co-ordination, Control ↑

LEADERSHIP

Figure 6.6: 'Inverted Pyramid' as a metaphor for the vision of the adapted Traditional Organisational Shape: Organisational hierarchy supporting the client-serving, front line delivery logic

The emerging organisation on the right side of Figure 6.4 represents the High Network/High Engagement/High Responsible Organisational Shape as illustrated in Figure 6.7 (7). The dotted circles depict the work to be done by each organisational entity or level.

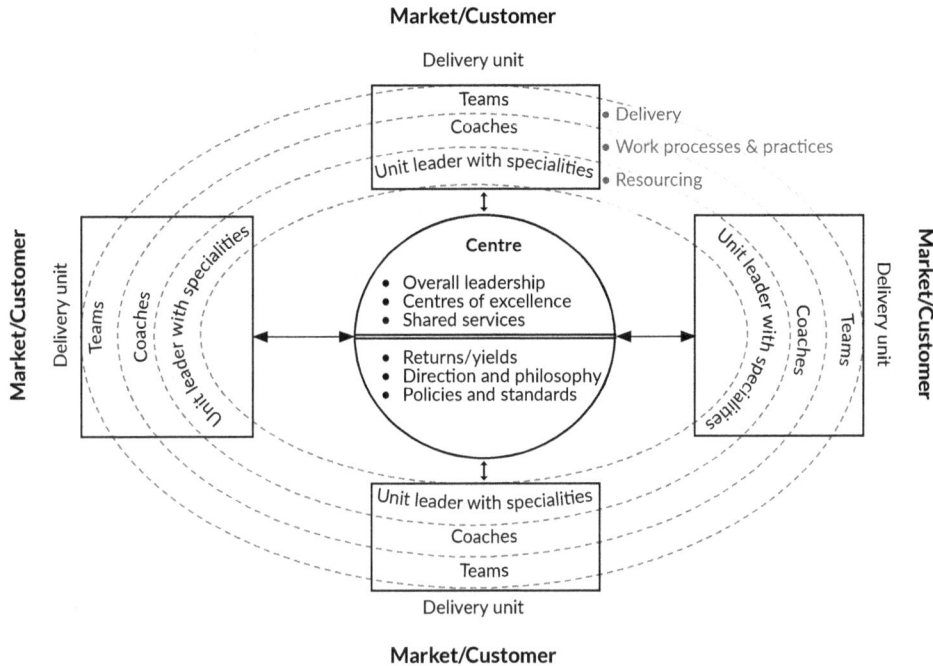

Figure 6.7: 'Spider Web' (or 'Distributed Network') as a metaphor for the vision of the emerging Organisational Shape: High Network/High Engagement/High Responsible delivery logic

According to Figure 6.7, the delivery logic of the High Network/High Engagement/High Responsible Organisational Shape entails: highly autonomous, multi-disciplinary/multi-skilled/mini-Business Units/ Teams performing broad chunks of the organisation's overall core work processes (or the total core work process for a product/service/client/market) with a high degree of decision-making power, self-generated information, driven by and linked to others by an internalised Organisational Identity, focusing on customers and quality, whilst acting as a true, genuine citizen.

The organisational shape given in Figure 6.7 is a manifestation of the Modularity Design Criterion: the organisation is disaggregated into Organisational Units, that is autonomous mini-Business Units/Teams, which are loosely coupled. That is, they have a high degree of independence and hence can easily be recombined into new configurations, possibly with newly introduced components, with little loss of functionality (8).

The Modular Design Criterion is also a key consideration for the Networking Organisational Shape (see Step A.2.2.5 (vi)) and for pursuing possible partnering opportunities (including outsourcing) (see Step A.2.4) (9). The Modularity Design Criterion allows for organisational agility, a critical organisational capability in a hyper-turbulent and hyper-fluid Operating Arena. It also enables the organisation to stick to its 'knitting' by readily outsourcing non-core activities.

The box gives a case study of Semco, a Brazilian company, which thanks to the inspiration of Ricardo Semler was a pioneer in embarking on an Organisational Shape strongly indicative of a High Network/ High Engagement/High Responsible Design (10).

CASE STUDY: SEMCO – AN EARLY EXAMPLE OF A HIGH NETWORK/HIGH ENGAGEMENT/HIGH RESPONSIBLE ORGANISATIONAL SHAPE

CONTEXT

When still in his teens, Ricardo Semler went to work for his father's company in São Paulo, Brazil, originally called Semler & Company, then a mixer and agitator supplier. He clashed with his father, Antonio Semler, a staunch supporter of the traditional autocratic style of management, because he favoured a decentralised, participatory style. He also aspired to diversify away from the struggling shipbuilding industry, which his father opposed.

Ricardo threatened to leave the company after heated clashes with his father. Rather than see this happen, Antonio Semler resigned as CEO and vested majority ownership in his son in 1980 when Ricardo was only 21 years old. On his first day as CEO, Ricardo fired 60% of all top managers in one afternoon. He began to work intensively on a diversification programme to rescue the company. He experienced serious health issues at the age of 25. After seeing a doctor, he was diagnosed with an advanced case of stress. This inspired him to want a greater work-life balance for his employees and himself.

DESIGN

Ricardo decided to embark on a radical redesign of industrial democracy. The essence of the new design was: *Power to the people; give people the freedom to do what they want, and over the long haul their successes will far outnumber their failures.*

Five *Principles*, each with associated *Pillars*, informed the new design, as outlined in the table below. Examples are given of practices illustrative of the Principles and Pillars concerned.

PRINCIPLES	PILLARS	PRACTICES: SOME EXAMPLES
TRUST	Treat people as responsible adults	People own their own attitudes; are expected to use their common sense and good judgement, and control their own work that they must do in the best way they see fit; no corporate value statement; no time clocks; no security checks; no travel expense approval
	Unfiltered transparency to promote openness and fairness	All information belongs to everyone; open reporting – receive financial information on own unit every month; simple reports
	Reduce power distance gap in all directions	No silos; flat hierarchy: three management levels – counsellors; partners; and team leaders (management levels) with associates; open meetings which anyone can join; floating offices; no differentiating privileges; live Board meetings; employees have seats on Board

PRINCIPLES	PILLARS	PRACTICES: SOME EXAMPLES
ALTERNATIVE CONTROL	Autonomy	No headquarters; teams of 10 with Work Units not being larger than 150 persons; all round participation; shared decision-making; employees decide themselves how to do their work; set own working hours with team; quality of life takes priority
	Shared control	All employees vote on important company decisions, like acquisitions; prospective leaders are interviewed and approved by the persons they will lead; rotating CEO, voted on by employees
	Busting bureaucracy	No policies or manuals, only a Survival Manual, explaining in comic form the 'Semco Way of Doing Things'; keep rules to a bare minimum so that employees can focus on the tasks that really matter; no organograms; no dress code; roll-over, flexible budgeting every six months
SELF-MANAGEMENT	Culture of commitment	No five year plans; employees and teams set their own goals; skills-based pay commensurate with employee's expertise and contribution; employees set their own salaries, linked to what he/she wants to contribute, approved by peers; profit-sharing with everyone bi-annually deciding how to distribute; salary cuts over job cuts
	Peer power	Team members hold each other accountable for results, achievement and behaviour, with clarity on what everybody's role and contribution is; teams recruit own members; bottom-up leadership assessment; peer assessment
	Talent development	Everyone is talent; multi-skilling; job rotation every 3-5 years; career self-navigation; ongoing training and development; entry level management trainees have no job descriptions but float for one year during which they have to try at least 12 organisational areas/units before they decide where they want to settle
EXTREME STAKEHOLDER ALIGNMENT	Outside-in perspective	Know clients and other external stakeholders, inside out; involve them as much as possible, for example, in product development; open books to external stakeholders; unions are stakeholders
	Finding common ground	Find shared interests and common ground, in shared dreams/objectives with stakeholders; show appreciation
	Assured consistency	Fully transparent, interdepartmental and team sharing; walking and talking must be the same; co-defined roles and responsibilities
CREATIVE INNOVATION	Continuous experimentation	Continuous improvement; asking 'why?'; rewarding good ideas
	Creative space	Innovation Forums to provoke dynamic equilibrium; make your space your own; make time to celebrate at work
	Entrepreneurship	All-round networking and partnering that thrive on blended and hybrid working practices

OUTCOMES
As at 2003, Semco had an annual revenue of $212 million, up from $4 million in 1982, with an annual growth rate of over 40% percent a year. In contrast to 90 employees in 1982, it employed 3,000 workers in 2003. Average turnover amongst employees was 2%.

Step A.2.2.2: Consider relevant Sector/Industry Organisational Shape

These Organisational Shapes relate to a particular sector/industry, which may have specific preferred delivery logics. As an illustration of these types of Shapes, the manufacturing sector with its two contrasting delivery logics of Fordism vs. Lean/Flexible manufacturing will be used. Table 6.1 gives a comparison of these two manufacturing delivery logics (11).

Table 6.1: Fordism vs. Lean/Flexible manufacturing delivery logics

Mass Production Logic: Assembly line, interchangeable parts, and economies of scale	Flexible, Lean Production Logic: Flexibility, speed, economies of scope, and core competencies
Specialised machinery	Flexible machines, low set-up costs
Long production runs	Short production runs
Infrequent product changes	Frequent product improvements
Narrow product lines	Broad product lines
Mass marketing	Targeted markets
Low working skill requirements	Highly skilled, cross-trained workers
Specialised skill jobs	Multi-skilled, multi-tasked jobs
Central expertise and coordination	Workers initiative
Hierarchic planning and control	Local information and self-regulation
Vertical internal communication	Horizontal communication
Sequential product development	Cross-functional development teams
Static optimisation	Continuous improvement
Accent on volume	Accent on cost and quality
High inventories	Low inventories (= Just-in-Time delivery)
Supply management	Demand management
Make to stock, limited communication with customers	Make to order, extensive communications with customers
Market dealings with employees and suppliers	Long-team, trust-based personal relationships
Vertical integration	Horizontal integration: Reliance on outside suppliers

Step A.2.2.3: Consider Organisational Shape for chosen Strategic Intents

As already discussed, the Organisational Design must in support of, and aligned to, the organisation's Strategic Intent *(12) (13)*. The respective delivery logics, and hence Organisational Shapes, associated with different Strategic Intents of Product/Service Innovation, Client Centricity and Operational Excellence are given in Table 6.2.

Table 6.2: Product/Service Innovation-centric vs. Customer-centric vs. Cost-centric Strategic-based Organisational Shapes

ORGANISATIONAL INGREDIENTS		ORGANISATIONAL SHAPES		
		Product/Service-centric Strategic Intent	Customer-Centric Strategic Intent	Cost-Centric Strategic Intent
STRATEGIC INTENT	**Goal**	Best product/service for customer	Best solution for customer	Lowest total cost
	Main offering	New products	Personalised packages of product, service, support, education, training, consulting	An acceptable product at the lowest price
	Value creation route	Cutting-edge products, useful features, new applications	Customising for the total solution	No-frills offering for the middle of the market
	Most important customer	Most advanced customer	Most profitable, loyal customer	Value shopper
	Priority setting basis	Portfolio of products – product profitability	Portfolio of customers – customer profitability	Find the most efficient way to do everything – product/market share
	Pricing	Price to market	Price for value, risk	Guaranteed lowest price or everyday low price
DESIGN	**Organisational concept**	Product profit centres, product reviews, product teams	Customer segments, customer teams, customer profit and loss	Strong centralised functions to standardise, economise, and achieve scale
	Most important process	New product development	Customer relationship management and solution development	Order-to-cash All transaction processes are efficiently re-engineered

Step A.2.2.4: Decide on the organisation's basic delivery logic in terms of which Work Units must be configured

At this point, an understanding has been gained into the mindset shift with regard to thinking about organisations in general. Additionally, sector/industry and Strategic Intent-specific Organisational Shapes have been considered. Against this background, the 'To-Be' basic delivery logic of the organisation concerned must now be considered. What is required at this point in the design process is to plot the organisation's position on the basic delivery logic axes, as per Figure 6.8 (14).

This plot establishes the basic delivery logic in terms of which the organisation wishes to operate. The choice of a fit-for-purpose logic finds its justification in the organisation's Purpose, Strategic Intent, Design Criteria and Vision.

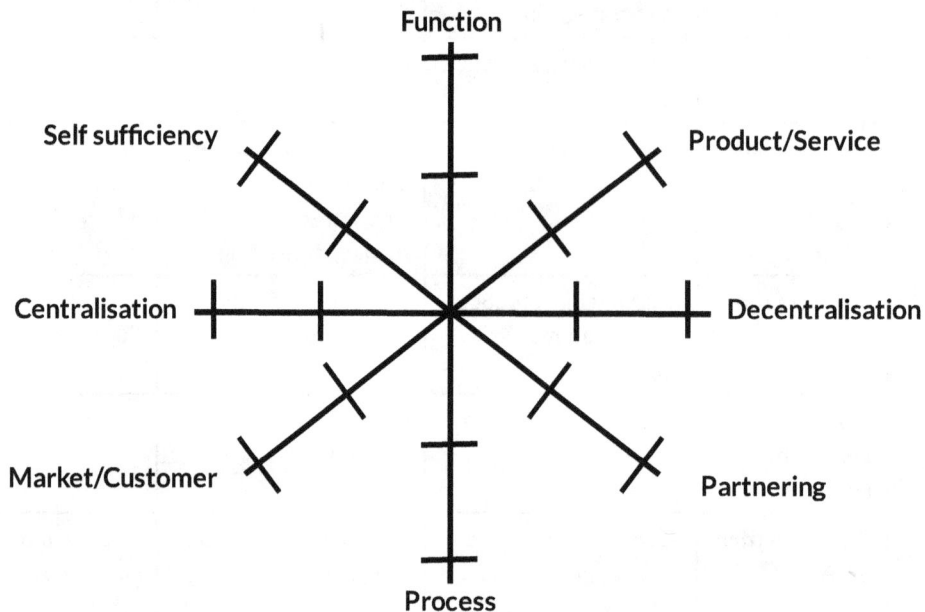

Figure 6.8: Basic delivery logic axes

Table 6.3 provides the prime strengths and weaknesses of each of the extreme positions on the axes given in Figure 6.8 (15).

Table 6.3: Prime strengths and weaknesses of the extreme positions on the Basic Delivery Axes

POSITION ON AXIS	STRENGTHS	WEAKNESSES
Function	Deep expertise Specialisation	Fragmented, specialist silos Fierce functional loyalty
Process	Direct line of sight of customer End-to-end accountability	Dominance of core work process to detriment of support processes, that is, process silos
Product/Service	In-depth product/service expertise	Product/service loyalty supersedes client and organisational needs
Market/Customer	Strong customer relationships	Client customisation may detract from product/service standardisation, undermining economies of scale
Self Sufficiency	Lower 'cost' of co-ordination and high speed of execution because everything is in house	Cannot be an expert in everything High investment cost to keep at forefront
Outsourcing/ Partnering	Complementary in-depth expertise Agility to renew/supplement expertise rapidly	Higher time investment in relationship building and maintenance Risks of misunderstood needs and under-delivery
Centralisation	Economies of scale Standardisation Quick decision-making Common culture	Uniformity to detriment of localisation Removed from customers/markets
Decentralisation	Local responsiveness enhancing speed, creativity, innovation	Duplication Variation in standards Difficulty of migrating innovation across organisation Fragmented approach to cross-national clients

The emerging new order is forcing organisations to move away from 'Either-Or' choices, for example, a Product/Service *or* Market/Customer basic delivery logic. Instead, they have to consider 'And' delivery logic choices which nowadays are essential for fitness-for-purpose, for example, a Product/Service *and* Market/Customer delivery logic (see Figure 6.8).

What is most helpful in using the simple but powerful graphic of plotting the basic delivery logic axes, given in Figure 6.8, is to specify what is meant by a particular choice on an axis, for example, a Functional/ Process choice can be specified such as: 'Functionalised specialised, enabling support services with Market/Customer, whole process delivery'. Alternatively: 'The centralisation of the functionalised specialised, enabling support services and decentralised Market/Customer delivery'. Of course, a given is that choices must be made in accordance with the set Design Criteria and Vision.

The basic delivery logic plot becomes the critical, guiding compass in choosing an eventual fit-for-purpose, To-Be Organisational Shape, which is covered in the next step.

Step A.2.2.5: Choose an Organisational Shape in accordance with the selected basic delivery logic

One is now in a sound position to choose an Organisational Shape, for example, Activity-based (for example, Functional or Process), Strategic Business Units/Divisional, Front-Back, Matrix, or Cluster. Figure 6.9 provides a 'Periodic Table' of generic Organisational Shapes with the conditions under they can be considered (16). The Integration requirements and Governance Models commensurate with each Shape are also reflected in the figure. The value of the Periodic Table lies in guiding one to make the appropriate choice with regard to a fit-for-purpose Organisational Shape to be used in configuring Work Units.

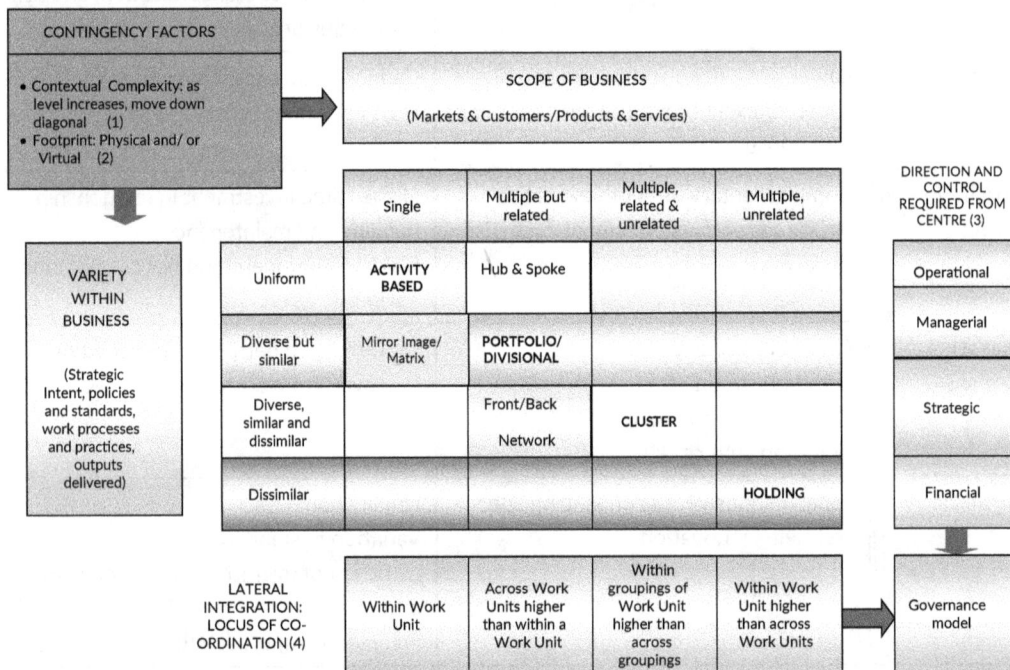

Figure 6.9: Periodic Table of Generic Organisational Shapes (17)

Notes: (1) See discussion Step A.1.1: Organisational Context – Contextual complexity, Chapter 5; (2) To be discussed in this chapter, at the end of this Step; (3) To be discussed under Step A.3: Strategic Vertical Design, Chapter 7; (4) To be discussed under Step A.4: Strategic Lateral Design, Chapter 7

In Figure 6.9, simple to complex Organisational Shapes are given by moving along the diagonal from top left to bottom right, and vice versa. The choice of an Organisational Shape in moving from simple to complex – from an Activity-based to a Holding Organisational Shape – is a function of:

- in general an increase in *contextual complexity* in terms of footprint and time boundaries, the scope of and variety in the organisation, and the degree and rate of change the organisation is exposed to (discussed under Step A.1.1: Organisational Context – Contextual Complexity). Essentially, this movement is about de-aggregating the organisation into smaller, agile, autonomous organisational entities, in contrast to a single, monolithic organisational entity;

- an extension in the *scope of the organisation*: from a single uniform Market/Customer or Product/ Service to diverse, unrelated Markets/Customers or Products/Services;

- an extension in the *variety within the organisation* as manifested in Strategic Intent, policies and standards, work processes and practices, and outputs delivered, from a single, uniform to a diverse, unrelated set.

As one moves along the diagonal from top left to bottom right in Figure 6.9 when selecting an appropriate Basic Organisational Shape, two other design logic variables shift in tandem, i.e.:

- the *direction and control from the Corporate Centre* from Operational to Financial (to be discussed later under Strategic Vertical Design, Chapter 7); and

- *lateral integration – the locus of co-ordination*: the locus varies depending on the extent to which Work Units (or groupings thereof) have to act in concert or not (also to be discussed later under Strategic Lateral Design, Chapter 7).

Moving along the diagonal from top left to bottom right in Figure 6.9, each of the Basic Organisational Shapes given in the above Periodic Table are next discussed in terms of the following:

- A *description* of the Shape.

- A graphic illustration of the Shape in the form of an *Organisational Map*, architected from the portfolio of generic work processes for the organisation (see Figure 5.4 and Table 5.5). The Map must contain all of the work processes of the organisation. An Organisational Map graphically depicts the configuration of Work Units, illustrating the overall 'House Plan' pictorially.

  The use of Organisational Maps to depict Organisational Shapes is contrary to the convention in the OD literature to present Organisational Shapes in the form of organograms. This practice only reinforces OD Myth 4 that OD equates to the redrawing of boxes and changing reporting lines on an organogram. It is contended that an Organisational Map gives a truer picture of the way the organisation is set up to deliver than an organogram, which essentially only gives reporting lines.

  Important to note in an Organisational Map are the relative locations of Rooms (= Work Processes) to each other: next to; in front of; and to the back of, with the overlaps between Rooms. All of these depict critical interdependencies have to be considered in Step A.4: Strategic Lateral Design.

- The *applicability of the Shape*, that is the choice of a fit-for-purpose Shape in terms of applicability has to be referenced against the chosen Design Criteria and Vision (Step A.1.5), as well as the selected basic design logic (the predominant basic design logic is indicated in each case for a Shape) (Step A.2.2.4).

- The *strengths and weaknesses* of the Shape. One has to build on the strengths of a Shape and proactively decide how to overcome its weaknesses.

In working through the nine Organisational Shapes, you as the reader can follow one of two approaches: (i) peruse each, one after the other; or (ii) pick the one(s) of interest and only peruse it/them. In terms of the latter, the box gives a table of the discussed Organisational Shapes, with their associated types if relevant, and the section in which each Shape is covered.

LOCATION IN PERIODIC TABLE (see Figure 6.9)	ORGANISATIONAL SHAPE	TYPES	SECTION
Single Organisational Scope with Uniform Organisational Variety	Activity-based	• Common activities: Functional Shape • End-to-end work flow(s): Process Shape • Projects: Projects Shape • Membership: Co-operative Shape	(i)
Single Organisational Scope with Diverse, Similar Organisational Variety	Mirror Image/ Matrix	-	(ii)
Multiple, Related Organisational Scope with Uniform Organisational Variety	Hub and Spoke	-	(iii)
Multiple, Related Organisational Scope with Diverse, Similar Organisational Variety	Portfolio/Divisional	• Groupings by *related products/ services*, each with its own set of activities that can be either be organised functionally or by process; or • groupings by *related clients/markets*, each with its own set of activities, that again can be organised either functionally or by process	(iv)
Multiple, Related Organisational Scope with Diverse, Similar and Dissimilar Organisational Variety	Front-Back	-	(v)
Multiple, Related and Unrelated Organisational Scope with Diverse, Similar and Dissimilar Organisational Variety	Network	• Tightly coupled/Negotiated movement: contracted ecosystems, for example, Outsourcing and Joint Venture • Loosely coupled/Negotiated movement: synergistic ecosystems, for example, Strategic Alliance • Tightly coupled/Free movement: managed ecosystems, for example, Linux, Wikipedia	(vi)

LOCATION IN PERIODIC TABLE (see Figure 6.9)	ORGANISATIONAL SHAPE	TYPES	SECTION
		• Loosely coupled/Free movement: instantaneous ecosystems, for example, Crowdsourcing, Social Movement Campaigns, Leaderless Revolutions	
Multiple, Related and Unrelated Organisational Scope with Diverse, Similar and Dissimilar Organisational Variety	Cluster		(vii)
Multiple, Unrelated Organisational Scope with Dissimilar Organisational Variety	Holding		(viii)
Any combination of the above Organisational Shapes	Hybrid		(ix)

(i)   Single Organisational Scope with Uniform Organisational Variety: Activity-based Organisational Shape

The Activity-based Organisational Shape – see the Periodic Table of Generic Organisational Shapes above – revolves around the work (= activities) that has to be done. Four types of Activity-based Organisational Shapes can be distinguished according to groupings of activities in terms of:

- common activities: Functional Shape *(18)*;

- end-to-end work flow(s): Process Shape *(19)*;

- projects: Projects Shape *(20)*; or

- membership: Co-operative Shape.

Each is discussed in turn.

(i.a)   Groupings around common activities: Functional Shape

Figure 6.10 illustrates the Functional Organisational Map.

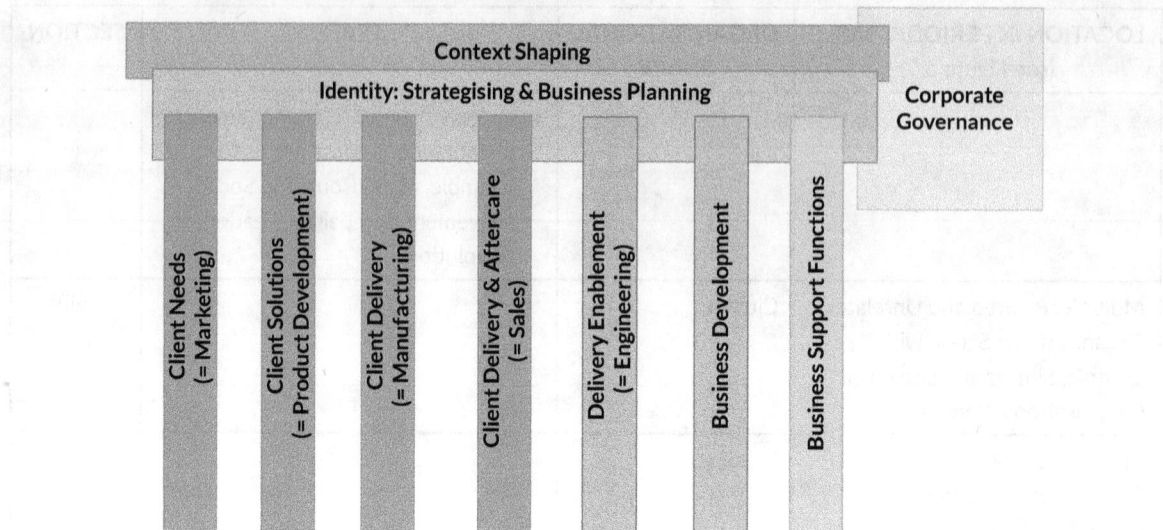

Figures 6.10: Groupings around common activities – Functional Organisational Map

As can be seen from Figure 6.10, each Work Unit represents a grouping of common activities set up to create and build in-depth organisational capabilities. The functional units only come together at the top of the organisation in the overarching Strategising and Business Planning Functional Unit, which typically equates to the office of the CEO (or MD).

Table 6.4 gives the applicability, strengths and weaknesses of the Activity-based Organisational Shape: Functional.

Table 6.4: Activity-based Organisational Shape – Functional: applicability, strengths and weaknesses

ORGANISATIONAL SHAPE	APPLICABILITY	STRENGTHS	WEAKNESSES
Groupings around common activities: Functional *Predominant Basic Design Logic:* Function; Products/Services; Centralised; Self-sufficient and/or Partnering (U-form)	• Undifferentiated products/services, clients and/or markets • In-depth competence and specialisation required • Long product/service life cycles • Common standards • Stable organisational context	• Economies of scale • Standardisation of operations and procedures • Specialisation • In-depth capabilities • Predictability	• Functional silos detract from rapid communication, decision-making and information sharing, also laterally • Hard to determine accountability and performance in the 'white spaces' between functions

ORGANISATIONAL SHAPE	APPLICABILITY	STRENGTHS	WEAKNESSES
			• Fierce functional loyalty over organisational loyalty • Cross-functional processes cause turf wars • Slow response to external changes • Hierarchical information and decision-making overload • Restricted view of whole

(i.b)   Groupings around end-to-end work flow(s): Process Shape

Figure 6.11 depicts the Process Organisational Map.

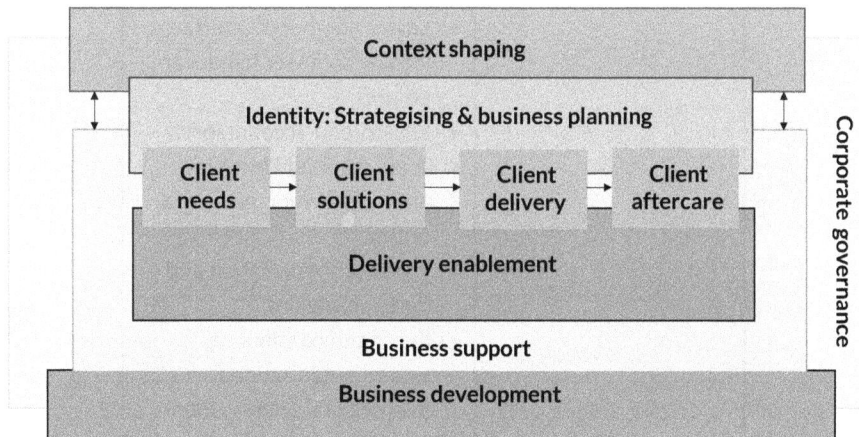

Figures 6.11: Groupings around common activities – Process Organisational Map

According to Figure 6.11, in the Process Organisational Shape the organisation is configured around the client delivery process, that is the core work process of the organisation that can be made up of more than one Process Work Unit. Each of the other Work Units are also configured in terms of their respective work processes.

In the originally proposed Process Organisational Shape, these process-based Work Units function relatively independently and in parallel to each other, creating process silos. The Organisational Map given in Figure 6.11 presumes interdependencies between all of the Work Units, hence the overlap between Work Units.

Table 6.5 provides the applicability, strengths and weaknesses of the Activity-based Organisational Shape: Process (21).

Table 6.5: Activity-based Organisational Shape – Process: Applicability, strengths and weaknesses

ORGANISATIONAL SHAPE	APPLICABILITY	STRENGTHS	WEAKNESSES
Groupings around end-to-end work flow(s): Process Shape *Predominant Basic Design Logic:* Process; Markets/Customers; Centralised; Self-sufficient; and/or Partnering	• High internal co-ordination to tailor responses to fit customer needs in flexible and rapid manner • Ongoing supplier-client interface critical • Ongoing reduced process cycle times	• High customer responsiveness: direct line of sight to customers • Higher product quality aligned with customer requirements, leading to higher customer satisfaction • Elimination of non-value adding activities, resulting in greater process efficiencies and cost reduction • Reductions in throughput time • Better delivery reliability • Lower number of interfaces, leading to fewer handover points • End-to-end accountability • Team work and learning around common goals and output • Rapid communication and decision-making • Enhanced continuous, shared organisational learning and improvement • Broader organisational overview and perspective • Flexible deployment of roles, people and resources • More opportunities for multi-skilling and multi-tasking • More potential to enable and empower people	• Dominance of core work process to detriment of support processes • Interface between core and support processes can become problematic: 'Process silos'

(i.c) Groupings around projects: Projects Shape (22)

The emerging new world order is becoming increasingly 'projectified'. It is estimated that at present around 40% of the global economy is project-based, using project management as the core work process for producing products/services (23). This Organisational Shape is called, amongst others, project-based, project-orientated, project-led or multiple-project. Figure 6.12 depicts the Projects Organisational Map.

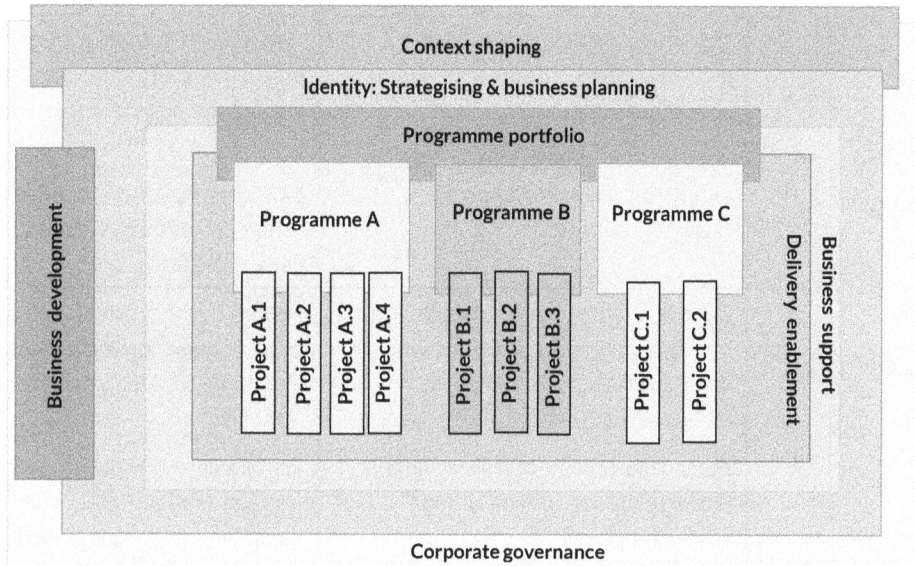

Figures 6.12: Groupings around common activities – Projects Organisational Map

According to Figure 6.12, in the Projects Organisational Shape the organisation is shaped predominantly around distinct, autonomous, self-designing, multi-disciplinary projects aimed at developing and rolling out innovative products/services within fixed time periods for defined customers. Related projects are grouped into programmes aimed at achieving set strategic objectives that cannot be fulfilled by a single project. Delivery Enablement processes are to a greater or lesser extent incorporated into projects and programmes.

Projects and programmes represent the *temporary* organisation. Collectively programmes are managed by the organisation as a portfolio of programmes which represents the *permanent* organisation, aligned to and in support of the organisation's Strategic Intent. Project, programme and portfolio management thus form the core work processes of the organisation. At the end of a project/programme, people, resources and tasks are reassigned to new projects/programmes, with reporting relationships and roles changing accordingly.

In terms of permanency, a Projects Organisation may have a permanent, legal status, like a consulting engineering firm. Or, be set up as a temporary, legal entity for a defined period of time to deliver a specific programme/project, like a infrastructure project. Once completed, the organisation is disbanded. Against this backdrop, different types of Projects Organisations can be distinguished, as per Table 6.6 (24).

Table 6.6: Types of Projects Organisations (POs)

		SINGULARITY OF GOALS AND OUTPUTS The extent to which the organisation focuses on developing unusual, sometimes once-off, products and services for varied, and often uncertain, markets	
		Low	**High**
SEPARATION AND STABILITY OF WORK ROLES The extent to which the organising of expertise, tasks and roles is predictable and stable over projects	**Low**	*Organisational* POs that produce multiple, varied outputs with different, changeable skills and roles For example, strategic consultancies, enterprise software, innovative business services	*Precarious* POs that produce risky, unusual outputs with varied, changeable skills and roles For example, some dedicated biotechnology firms, internet software firms such as many Silicon Valley companies
	High	*Craft* POs that produce multiple, incrementally related outputs with distinct, stable roles and skills For example, some business and professional services including advertising firms, IT consulting organisations, furniture and machinery firms	*Hollow* POs that produce single outputs and coordinate tasks through standardised, separate and stable roles and skills For example, complex construction projects or many feature film companies in the UK and USA

Table 6.7 depicts the applicability, strengths and weaknesses of the Activity-based Organisational Shape: Projects (25).

Table 6.7: Activity-based Organisational Shape – Projects: Applicability, strengths and weaknesses

ORGANISATIONAL SHAPE	APPLICABILITY	STRENGTHS	WEAKNESSES
Groupings around Projects: Project Shape (P-form) *Predominant Basic Design Logic:* Process; Markets/ Customers; Decentralised; Self-sufficient; and/or Partnering	Organisations using projects, programmes and portfolios as the primary means of delivering new products and services.	• High flexibility to respond rapidly to changing customer demands, expectations and needs • High integration of diverse bodies of knowledge, skills and expertise • Undertaking of complex, unpredictable, non-routine tasks • High innovation potential • Learning/teaching organisation	• Risk of misunderstood deliverables, disagreement whether output specifications have been met, and overruns in terms of timelines and costs, especially on complex, unpredictable projects/ programmes • Unclear career paths because of the continuous reconfiguration of projects/programmes and reallocation • Employment insecurity because of uncertainty about future projects

(i.d) Grouping around Membership: Co-operative Shape

Figure 6.13 illustrates the Co-operative (that is Membership) Organisational Map (26). The left-hand shape given in Figure 6.13 depicts the conventional (or classic) Co-operative Shape, which is made up of members as capital providers and clients simultaneously. The right-hand shape in the same figure shows a hybrid shape, which is a mix between the conventional Co-operative and (Pty) Ltd company.

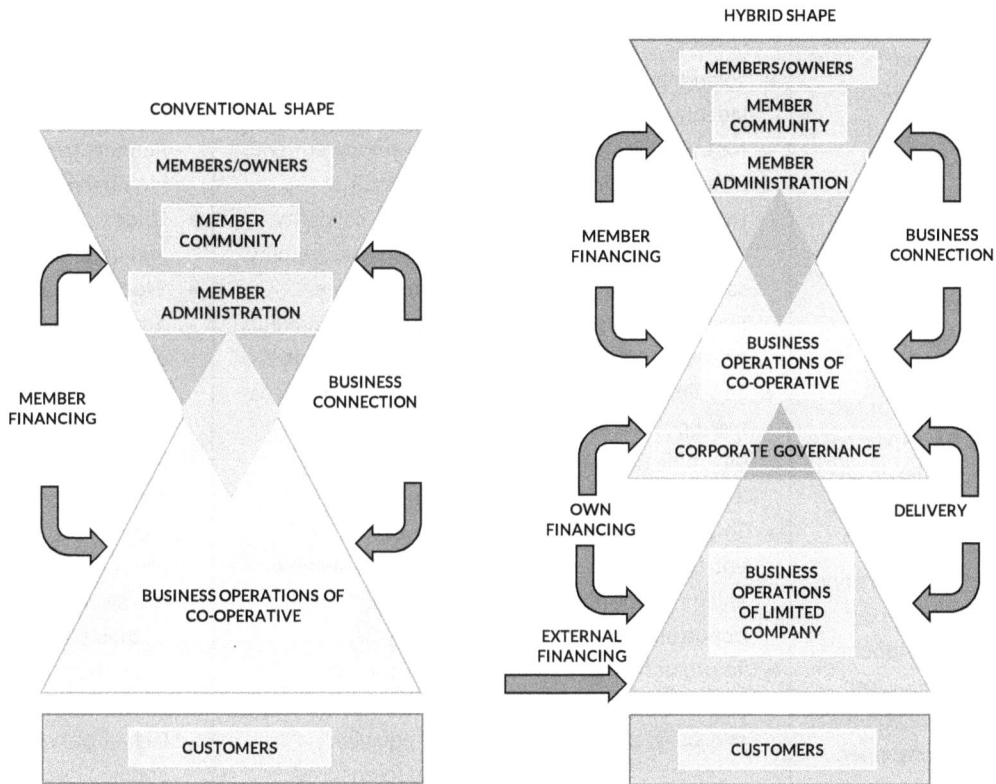

Figures 6.13: Grouping around common activities – Co-operative Organisational Map

Given the democratic, participative nature of co-operatives, they usually have a very flat structure led by an elected Exco or Management Committee. Work processes (termed 'business operations' in Figure 6.13) are voluntarily taken up by members to be performed for longer or shorter time periods (especially in the case of the Conventional Shape). In the case of the Hybrid Shape of a Pty Ltd company, members would be legally required to be appointed to specified positions.

Table 6.8 lists the applicability, strengths and weaknesses of the Co-operative Organisational Shape (27).

Table 6.8: Activity-based Organisational Shape – Co-operative: Applicability, strengths and weaknesses

ORGANISATIONAL SHAPE	APPLICABILITY	STRENGTHS	WEAKNESSES
Organised according to at least the following principles: • *Autonomy and Independence:* Co-operatives are autonomous, self-help organisations controlled by their members. If they enter into agreements with other organisations, including governments, or raise capital from external sources, they do so on terms that ensure democratic control by their members and maintain their co-operative autonomy. • *Voluntary and Open Membership:* Voluntary organisations, open to all persons able to use their services and willing to accept the responsibilities of membership. • *Democratic Member Control:* Controlled by members, who actively participate in setting their policies and making decisions. Elected member representatives are accountable to the membership. One vote per member.	• Any economic activity, from primary through secondary to tertiary sectors. • To address need(s) not (adequately) provided for by the state and/or business. Or, not trusted to address a need to the complete satisfaction of customers, in general or specifically. • To gain power in monopolistic and oligopolistic markets: 'Freedom from'. • To pursue social entrepreneurship and innovation opportunities. • To promote and pursue both economic and social goals.	• People need-centred as opposed to capital/profit-centred organisation. • Value-based/driven organisation: self-help, empowerment, democracy, equality, solidarity, openness, autonomy, independence, mutuality, community. • Embed democratic principles in the local community. • Promote local economic development to secure sustainable and decent local employment opportunities, common prosperity and equality. • Help to ensure a sustainable and more equitable future for communities as a whole by empowering (weaker) members of communities and societies to affect and control their own destinies. • Strong vehicle to build trusted networks and social capital in society. • Make cost of economic ownership affordable.	• 'Free riding', in which some members engage more passively than others who are more active, but still gain similar benefits from their membership. • Under-capitalisation and underinvestment. • 'Horizon problem': a member's residual claims over the assets of the co-operative are shorter than the life of the asset. This reduces members' incentive to invest in them as they cannot realise the full value of their share capital upon departure. • Portfolio problem: a lack of transferability and liquidity of member equity, which is tied to the patronage decision. Members are therefore unable to adjust their holding to their personal level of risk.

ORGANISATIONAL SHAPE	APPLICABILITY	STRENGTHS	WEAKNESSES
• *Member Economic Participation:* Members contribute equitably to, and democratically control, the capital of the co-operative. At least part of that capital is usually the common property of the co-operative. Members usually receive limited compensation, if any, on the capital subscribed as a condition of membership. • *Concern for Community:* Co-operatives work for the sustainable development of their communities through policies approved by their members. *Predominant Basic Design Logic:* Process; Markets/Customers; Decentralised; Self-sufficient		• Stronger, tighter interests and relationships between owners and customers of organisation, because both are the same. • Breeding ground for social entrepreneurship and innovation.	• Control problem: arises from a divergence of interests between members and the co-operative's management. This is due to the need to simultaneously maintain the co-operative's dual functions of delivering benefits to members while running a sustainable and profitable business. • Influence cost problem: the co-operative's strategic focus becomes fuzzy as it seeks to balance returns to the enterprise and to members.

(ii) Single Organisational Scope with Diverse, Similar Organisational Variety: Mirror Image/Matrix Organisational Shape

The Mirror Image/Matrix Organisational Shape – see the Periodic Table of Generic Organisational Shapes above – consists of simultaneously vertically and horizontally overlaid groupings. The one grouping (whether horizontal or vertical) represents the core work process activity domains. The other grouping represents a product/service (or a client). Figure 6.14 gives the Mirror Image/Matrix Organisational Map.

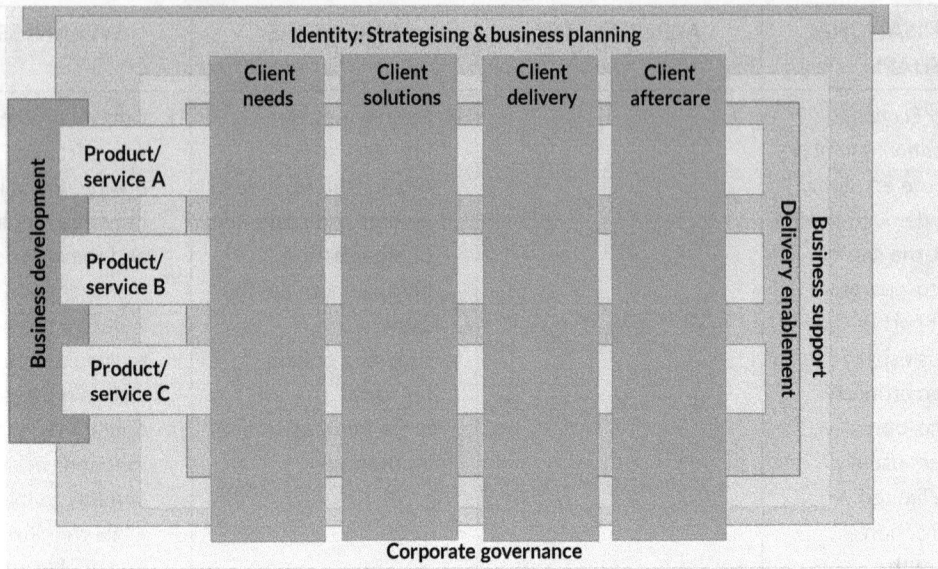

Figure 6.14: Mirror Image/Matrix Organisational Map
Note: For simplicity sake only Products/Services are shown horizontally. A similar Organisational Map can be drawn where Products/Services are replaced by Clients.

According to Figure 6.14, each core work process activity is performed 'vertically', for example, Client Needs, with respect to each Product/Service Work Unit that runs in parallel horizontally.

Table 6.9 highlights the applicability, strengths and weaknesses of the Mirror Image/Matrix Organisational Shape.

Table 6.9: Mirror Image/Matrix Organisational Shape: Applicability, strengths and weaknesses

ORGANISATIONAL SHAPE	APPLICABILITY	STRENGTHS	WEAKNESSES (28)
Simultaneously vertically and horizontally overlaid groupings. One grouping represents the activity domains of the core work process, such as technical expertise. The other grouping represents product/service expertise (or clients)	• Co-ordination in terms of dual demands by activity domains of core value process and products/services (or clients) required simultaneously	• Flexible sharing of resources • Standardisation of processes, procedures and standards by activity, clients and products/services concurrently	• Decision-making may be slowed down or derailed because of dual hierarchy • Two superiors simultaneously which can be frustrating, stressful and confusing to subordinates

ORGANISATIONAL SHAPE	APPLICABILITY	STRENGTHS	WEAKNESSES (28)
Predominant Basic Design Logic: Function; Markets/ Customers and Products/ Services; Decentralised; Self-sufficient; and/or Partnering	• Complex, multi-dimensional co-ordination, planning, decision-making and control of activities in a frequently changing organisational setting	• Cross-functional integration • Organisation wide learning • Development of functional, product/ service and/or client knowledge concurrently	• Time-consuming because frequent co-ordination and conflict resolution sessions are required. High transaction costs • Continuous input in real time to maintain power balance • Constant trade-off of priorities

(iii) Multiple, Related Organisational Scope with Uniform Organisational Variety: Hub and Spoke Organisational Shape

The Hub and Spoke Organisational Shape – see the Periodic Table of Generic Organisational Shapes above – is essentially an enhanced regionally based design. In this design, Regions are set up as independent businesses, containing the total business within that Region. Siloed regional 'empires' are hence created with, *inter alia*, resultant duplication; little interregional co-ordination and sharing; divergent policies and standards; and poor economies of scale. The Hub and Spoke Organisational Shape is an attempt to counter these weaknesses of the traditional regional design.

Two Organisational Maps are provided for the Hub and Spoke Organisational Shape, as per Figures 6.15 and 6.16 respectively. Figure 6.15 depicts a Regional Hub and Spoke Organisational Map, strengthened by global, lateral functions.

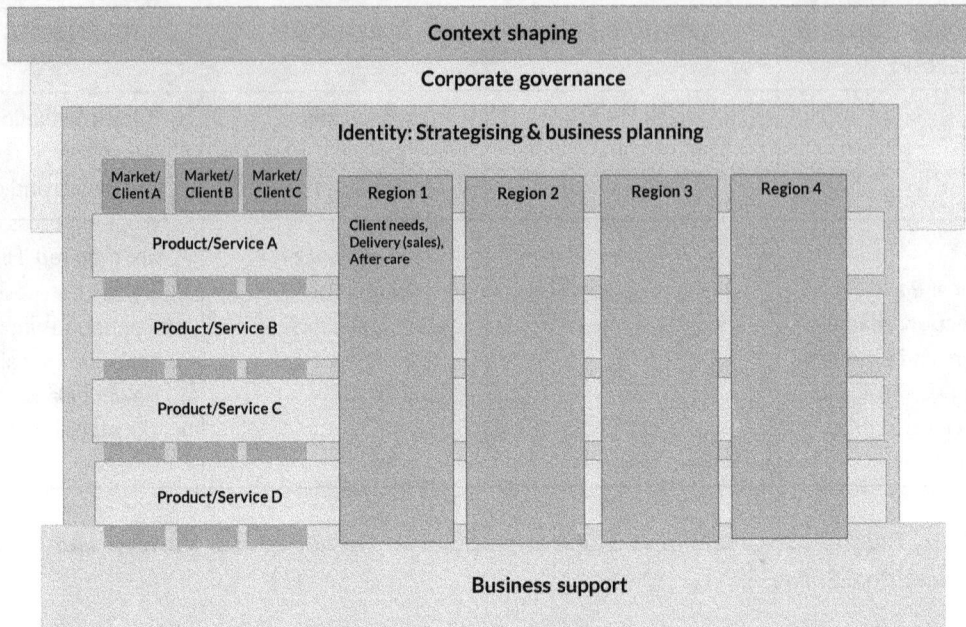

Figures 6.15: Regional Hub and Spoke Organisational Map, strengthened by globalised, lateral functions

According to Figure 6.15, in this Shape the traditional Regional Design is strengthened by globalised, lateral functions (given on the left of the figure) to provide across-regional direction, policies, standards, tools for a product/service area, and markets. Manufacturing also happens outside the Regions, globally. In the case of global clients (= markets), Global Account Executives can also be appointed.

Figure 6.16 gives a full Hub and Spoke Organisational Shape. In this case, Regional Hubs exist with the mandate to localise in a Region, *inter alia*, the organisational strategic direction, policies and standards for the Region concerned. They also centralise specialised and administrative services at the regional level, which are provided to the Operating Units making up the Region in order to attain economies of scale. From the Regional Hub, resources can also be flexed between the regional Operating Units as and where needs arise.

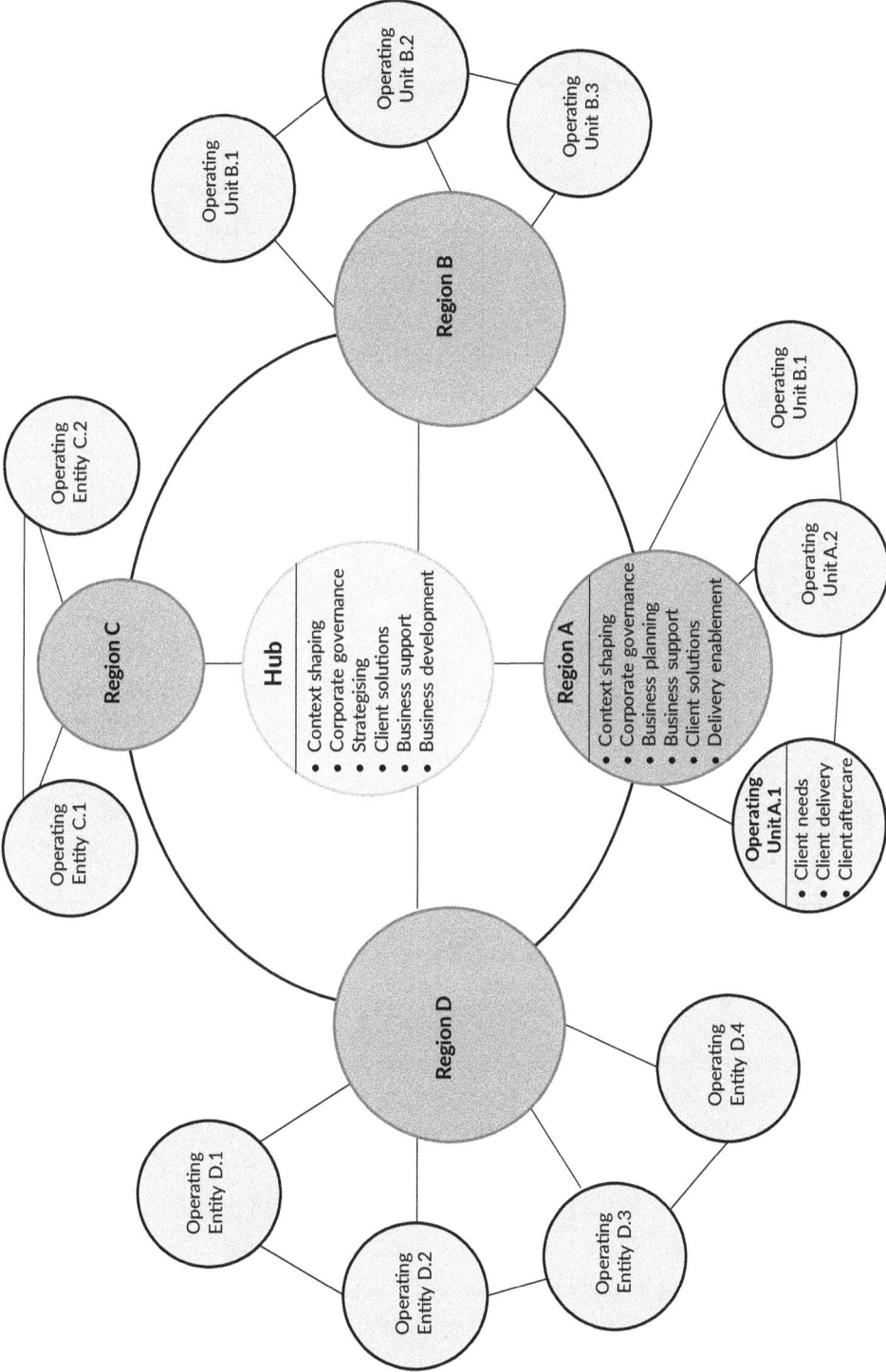

Figure 6.16: Full Hub and Spoke Organisational Map

Table 6.10 gives the applicability, strengths and weaknesses of the Hub and Spoke Organisational Shape.

Table 6.10: Hub and Spoke Organisational Shape: Applicability, strengths and weaknesses

ORGANISATIONAL SHAPE	APPLICABILITY	STRENGTHS	WEAKNESSES
Groupings of activities by geographical regions into Hubs (= Regions) *Predominant Basic Design Logic:* Function and Process; Markets/Customers; Decentralised; Self-sufficient; and/or Partnering	• Organisation with a national or global reach in terms of clients, markets and/or products/services • Significant differences between regions in terms of clients, markets and/or products/services	• Localised service delivery on site • Closeness to clients and markets • Gives organisation a local flavour • Economies of scale if specialised and administrative services are centralised at regional level, from where they then support the operating units making up a Region • Low value-to-transport cost ratio	• Geographical silos prevent rapid organisation-wide communication and decision-making, except if cross-regional lateral functions are set up • Real risk of differing processes, procedures and standards across regions • Duplication of activities and re-invention of the "wheel" across regions • Monopolising of resources by regions – difficult to mobilise and share resources across regions • Poor organisation-wide learning, except if cross-regional lateral functions are set up

(iv) Multiple, Related Organisational Scope with Diverse, Similar Organisational Variety: Portfolio/Divisional based Organisational Shape (29)

The Portfolio/Divisional based Organisational Shape – see the Periodic Table of Generic Organisational Shapes above – is formed around portfolios of activities related to products/services or clients/markets. Two types of Portfolio (or Divisional/Business Unit) based Organisational Shapes can be distinguished:

• Groupings by *related products/services*, each with its own set of activities that can be either be functional or process organised.

• Groupings by *related clients/markets*, each with its own set of activities that can again be either functional or process organised.

Figure 6.17 shows the Products/Services Portfolio Organisational Map.

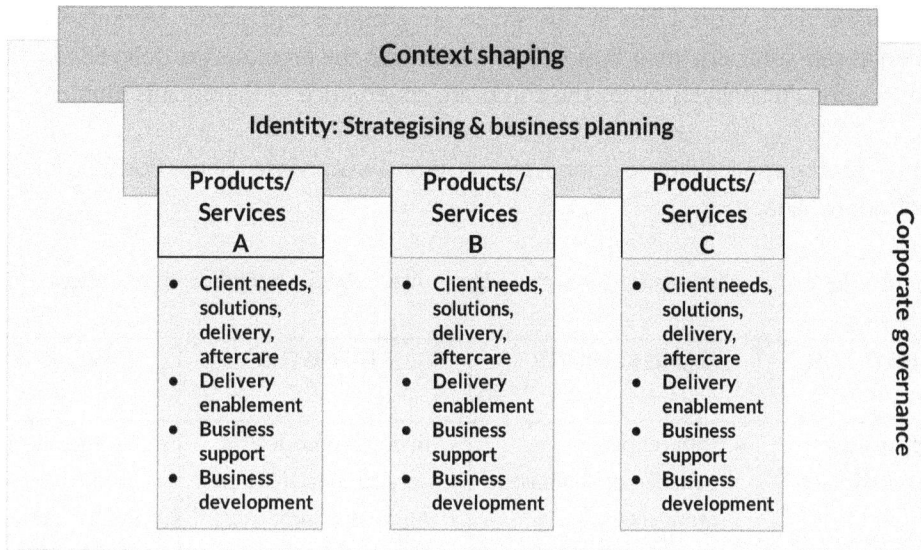

Figure 6.17: Groupings by related products/services, each with its own set of activities that can either be functional or process organised

According to Figure 6.17, in this Shape, Work Units are grouped into similar Products/Services Groups, which function as self-sufficient 'mini-businesses'. Their degree of autonomy is set by the prescribed corporate governance (read, the Corporate Centre) of the organisation: from little (= Groups are told what to do) to high (= Groups are highly autonomous).

Figure 6.18 gives the Markets/Clients Portfolio Organisational Map.

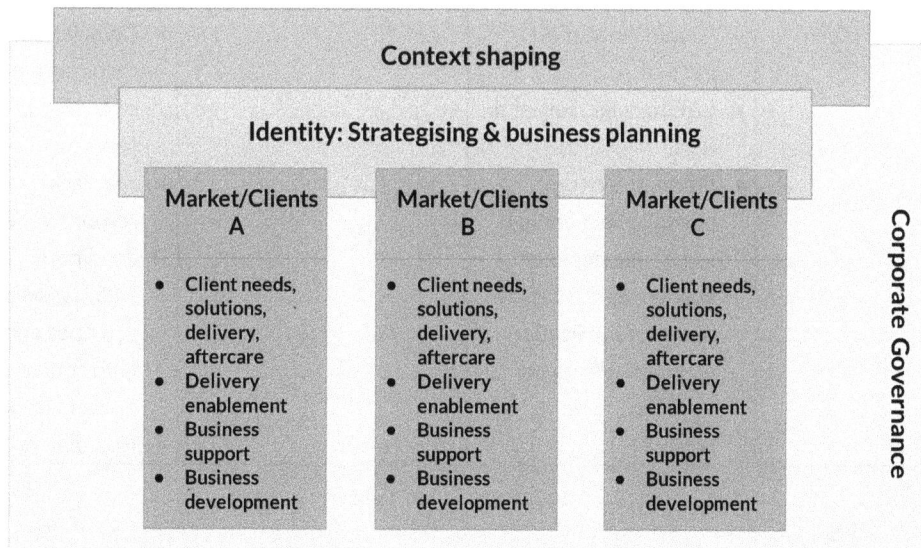

Figures 6.18: Groupings by related clients/markets, each with their own sets of activities that can be either functionally or process organised

According to Figure 6.18, Work Units in this Shape are grouped into similar Markets/Clients Groups, which function as self-sufficient 'mini-businesses'. Similarly to the previous Portfolio Shape, their degree of autonomy (= self-sufficiency) is set by the corporate governance of the organisation.

Table 6.11 provides the applicability specified, strengths and weaknesses of the Portfolio (or Divisionally) based Organisational Shape.

Table 6.11: Portfolio (or Divisionally) based Organisational Shape: Applicability, strengths and weaknesses

ORGANISATIONAL SHAPE	APPLICABILITY	STRENGTHS	WEAKNESSES
Groupings by related products/services, each with its own set of activities (functional or process groupings)	• Differentiated portfolio of standalone products/services for different clients with product/service specialisation • Product/services requiring different underlying business models • Strong product/service branding/brands • Shortened product/service life cycles – rapid innovation needed • Cutting edge, focused R& D • Product/services portfolios big enough to provide minimum economies of scale in order for duplication of enabling/support functions to not be too costly	• In depth product/service specialisation • Aggressive product/service branding • Encourages more entrepreneurial attitude	• Divergence amongst product/service lines in focus, process and standards • Fierce loyalty to product/service brands to detriment of broader organisational loyalty and needed product/service change/termination • Product/service takes dominance over client needs • Complex client needs requiring a portfolio of diverse products/services • May lack responsiveness to local conditions • Duplication of activities and resources with concurrent loss of economies of scale • Hoarding of resources

OR			
Groupings by related clients/markets. Each with its own set of activities (functional or process groupings) (M-form) *Predominant Basic Design Logic:* Function; .Markets/ Customers; Decentralised; Self-sufficient	• Differentiated portfolio of clients/ markets requiring in-depth client/market knowledge • Complex, diverse client needs demanding a portfolio of diverse products/services • In-depth client/market knowledge • Strong client/market identification • Buyer strength • Rapid client service • Ongoing, rapidly changing client needs/ expectations • Market/Client portfolios big enough to provide minimum economies of scale in order for duplication of enabling/support functions to not be too costly	• Quick pick-up of shifts in client needs/ expectations • Strong client relationships • Powerful clients • High client customisation • Rapid adjustment to fast change in an unstable setting • One stop client interface • Decentralised decision-making, problem solving and troubleshooting to where "moments of truth" with clients are created • Encourages more entrepreneurial attitude	• Divergence amongst clients in focus, processes and standards • Fierce loyalty to clients to detriment of broader organisational loyalty and client termination • Duplication of activities and resources with concurrent loss of economies of scale • Client customisation may detract from common product/ service standards • Duplication of product/ service knowledge • Hoarding of resources

(v) Multiple, Related Organisational Scope with Diverse, Similar and Dissimilar Organisational Variety: Front-Back Organisational Shape

The Front-Back Organisational Shape – see the Periodic Table of Generic Organisational Shapes – consists on the client facing side of organisation (the 'Front' of the organisation) of groupings in terms of distinct segments of client and/or markets, typically spread over a number of countries. The 'Back' of the organisation is made up of groupings in terms of different products/services, made up of one or more manufacturing entities. Figure 6.19 gives the Front-Back Organisational Map.

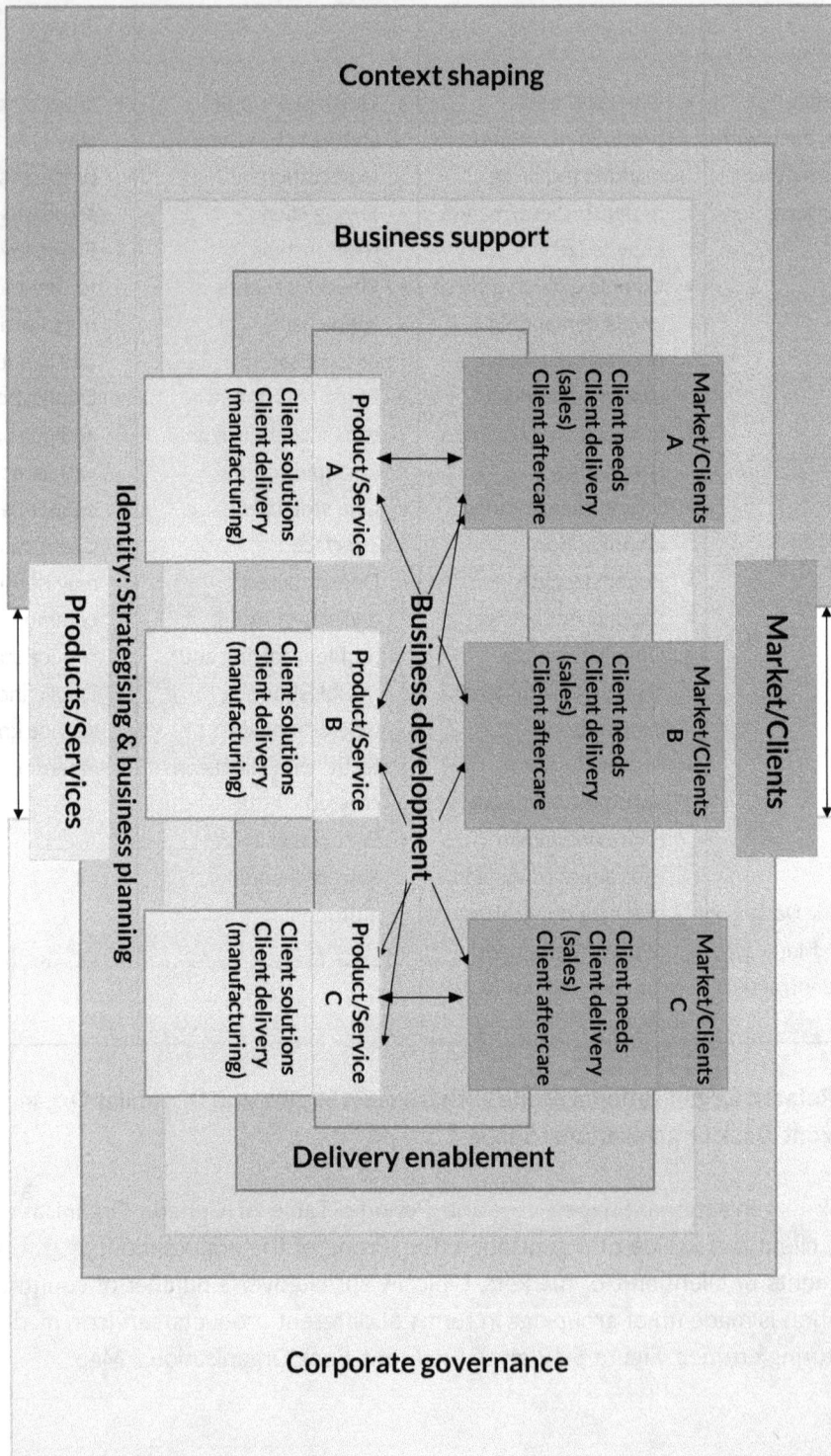

Figure 6.19: Front-Back Organisational Map

According to Figure 6.19, client/market groupings (or segments) (the 'Front' of the organisation) decide which portfolio of products/services are appropriate for that segment. They source those products/services from the products/services groupings concerned (the 'Back' of the organisation) (represented by arrows in the figure) which either deliver the products/services themselves or insource them from external providers.

Table 6.12 gives the applicability, strengths and weaknesses of the Front-Back Organisational Shape.

Table 6.12: Front-Back Organisational Shape: Applicability, strengths and weaknesses

ORGANISATIONAL SHAPE	APPLICABILITY	STRENGTHS	WEAKNESSES
On client facing side of organisation, groupings in terms of client and/or markets (Front of organisation). On product/service side of organisation, groupings in terms of products/services (Back of organisation) *Predominant Basic Design Logic:* Function; Markets/Customers and Products/Services; Decentralised; Self-sufficient; and Partnering	• Simultaneous matching of a portfolio of diverse clients/markets with diverse portfolio of products/services	• Focused attention to multiple objectives • Satisfaction of rapidly changing and diverse, localised client needs • Constantly redefined and enhanced client value proposition through the cross selling of products/services • Addition of value-added services/systems to clients when products have become commodities • Simultaneous client *and* product/service focus • Use of variety of distribution channels	• Dynamic tension between what takes priority: Front or Back • Disagreements over prices and customer needs • High co-ordination between support activities split between Front and Back • Conflicting/competing metrics • Information sharing and accounting complexity

(vi) Multiple, Related and Unrelated Organisational Scope with Diverse, Similar and Dissimilar Organisational Variety: Network Organisational Shape (30)

The Network Organisational Shape – see the Periodic Table of Generic Organisational Shapes above – centres around partnering: a set of independent organisations, teams and/or individuals who form relationships in a common space in order to jointly unlock value and create wealth for synergistic, mutual benefit, whether organisationally or publicly. The reasons for partnering could be to enable an organisation to do only what it is good at (that is 'Stick to its knitting'); to reduce risks; to co-create a public good; and/or to pursue a common, superordinate goal(s).

The demands of the VUCCAS world, with its imperative of disruptive innovation, are forcing organisations to form relationships beyond their boundaries in the inter-organisational space in order to: gain access to opportunities, knowledge, skills, expertise and resources with partners in order to at least learn jointly at the pace of change; retain their competitive edge; and/or add value for more demanding stakeholders with shifting expectations and needs on a continual basis (31). It has been found that successful organisations are more relationship driven. Organisations that focus on 'relationship centric' activities, whilst emphasising growth opportunities and adapting to a changing marketplace, are more likely to be better performers than organisations that focus only on decreasing working capital, improving supply chain efficiency, and spinning off non-core businesses (32).

The Network Organisational Shape is also called the "meta-organisation" (33), "multi-firm network" (34) or "multi-team system" (35). Meta-organisations are like a biological superorganism: a multitude of individual organisms that coexist, collaborate, and co-evolve by means of a complex set of symbiotic and reciprocal relationships, forming together a larger organism (36). Following this analogy, the Network Organisational Shape will be referred to as an ecosystem in the below discussion.

Design decisions regarding whether to partner or not will be considered formally, OD process-wise, in detail in Step A.2.4. However, the Network Organisational Shape – relating to partnering – is discussed here for completeness sake, given its criticality in the emerging new order.

The Network Organisational Shape varies on two design dimensions (37):

- *Closeness of the relationship:* tightly vs. loosely coupled.
- *Permeability of the boundaries regarding membership*: negotiated vs. free movement.

Based on the two dimensions, four types of Network Organisations – in the form of ecosystems – can be distinguished, as shown in Table 6.13.

Table 6.13: Types of Network Organisations

		CLOSENESS OF RELATIONSHIP	
		Tightly coupled	**Loosely coupled**
PERMEABILITY OF BOUNDARY REGARDING MEMBERSHIP	**Negotiated movement**	*Contracted Ecosystems*: Formalised, permanent relationships with a fixed set of members, contractually bound to each other for agreed upon, fixed periods of time Examples: Outsourcing, Joint Venture, Franchising Network, Multi-team System	*Synergistic Ecosystems*: Informal, temporary relationship with a fixed set of members, bound to each other through a verbal/written agreement for mutually, agreed-upon times Example: Strategic Alliance
	Free movement	*Managed Ecosystems*: Formalised, self-organising relationships within a varying, set of members for mutually agreed-upon, but varying periods of time Examples: Linux – an open-source software community; Wikipedia – the free, online encyclopaedia; g-economy; on demand economy	*Instantaneous Ecosystems*: Informal, temporary relationships within a set of varying members who join and leave of their own volition at any time it suits them Examples: Leaderless Ecosystems such as Leaderless Revolutions, Social Movements, Crowdsourcing, Crowdfunding

Each type of Network Organisational Shapes, as given in Table 6.13, is further explicated below.

(vi.a) Tightly coupled/Negotiated Movement: Contracted Ecosystems

This type of Network Shape – also called the modular organisation (38) – is shaped around formalised relationships, which are contractually and legally set-out, within a set of defined partners for a fixed period of time, in order to pursue an inter-organisational good. Design elements such as roles, contributions, authorities and responsibilities, standards, protocols, deliverables, fees and penalties, governance, and the period in force are all contractually and legally codified and enforceable.

Two examples of these Network Shapes will be briefly touched on: Outsourcing and Joint Ventures.

Outsourcing

Outsourcing relates to formally contracting out to partners portions of, or a complete, work process. Its purpose is for the organisation to stick to what it is good at – its strategic, core capabilities – and contract with other parties to do on its behalf what it is poor at, but they are good at. In the case of the Client Core Value Chain, for example, a subassembly of a product. In the case of Delivery Enablement, it could be outsourcing Maintenance or Supply Chain/Logistics activities. Or, in the case of Business Support, outsourcing IT or HR activities. This is why outsourcing is also referred to as the 'hollowed out' or 'modular' organisation, because portions of the organisation's work are farmed out to others in the form of 'parcels' of work.

Partnering through the Outsourcing Shape is illustrated through two Organisational Maps, given respectively in Figures 6.20 and 6.21. Figure 6.20 depicts the Outsourcing Map for the Delivery Enabling and Business Support processes, while Figure 6.21 gives the Outsourcing Map for the Client Core Value Chain. By way of illustration, the Partner Blocks given in the two figures represent a piece of work outsourced to a partner.

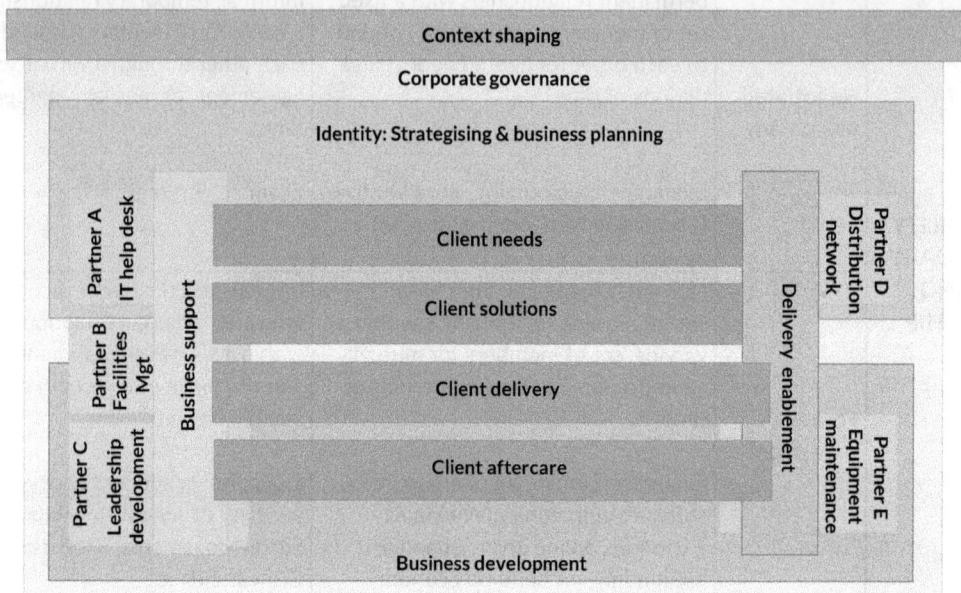

Figure 6.20: Network Organisational Shape: Outsourcing of Delivery Enabling and Business Support processes

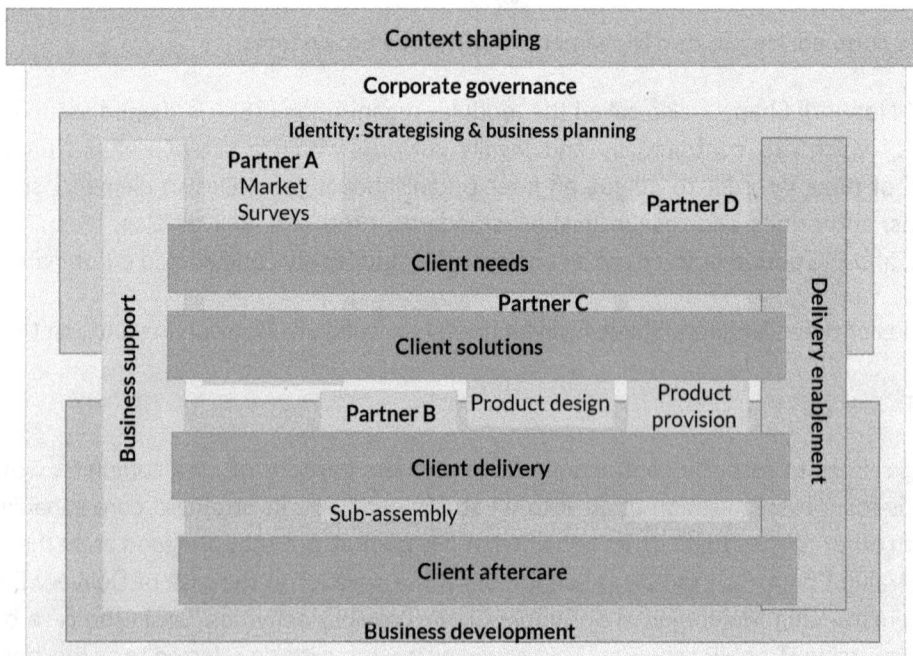

Figure 6.21: Network Organisational Shape: Outsourcing portions of the Client Core Value Chain

Table 6.14 shows the applicability, strengths and weaknesses of the Network Organisational Shape: Outsourcing as Contracted Ecosystem.

Table 6.14: Network Organisational Shape: Outsourcing as Contracted Ecosystem – Applicability, strengths and weaknesses

ORGANISATIONAL SHAPE	APPLICABILITY	STRENGTHS	WEAKNESSES
Work is outsourced to subcontractors with respect to business support and delivery enablement processes – 'Make/Do or Buy'	• High demand to focus on core capabilities only • Fierce price competition and consequently pressure to cut costs • More cost-effective to have non-core activities performed by external specialists	• Significant cost savings in the external provision of non-core activities: 'stick to knitting' • Access to best specialists and technology in non-core activities who are investing in product/service innovation • Vendor competition, resulting in constant and significant innovation in non-core processes • Enhanced organisational product/service/resource flexibility: switching between vendors as competitive circumstances change	• Loss of in-house LOW4 specialist skills to render judgment with regard to quality of services rendered and appropriateness to Strategic Intent • Higher transaction costs, for example, planning and co-ordination costs • Over-dependency on a single vendor where there is a lack of vendor competition
Work is outsourced to subcontractors with respect to the products/services activities of the core value chain *Predominant Basic Design Logic:* Function and Process; Markets/Customers and Products/Services; Decentralised; Self-sufficient and Partnering	• Rapidly changing market and/or client expectations requiring constant product/service innovation • Complex products/services • Possible to break up products/services into self-constrained modules (or chunks)	• Cost savings • Speed of responsiveness • Mobilisation of competence beyond own organisation • Low innovation-to-investment ratio • Joint product/service experimentation and innovation	• Higher planning and co-ordination costs • Loss of in-house LOW4 specialist skills • Competitive threat to outsourcing organisation of being supplanted by suppliers if outsourcing organisation only becomes 'assembler' of final product • Laggards can hold up delivery across total value chain, and/or undermine innovation • Disasters disrupting the supply chain, for example, a natural disaster

Joint Venture

A Joint Venture is an independent, legal entity with its own leadership and resources, with Board representation in the form of independent partners as co-owners who share in the returns and risks. Joint Ventures are set up, for example, to access critical skills or technology; to open up market opportunities; to achieve economies of scale; or to share major risks, like an investment. Figure 6.22 depicts the Organisational Map for a Joint Venture.

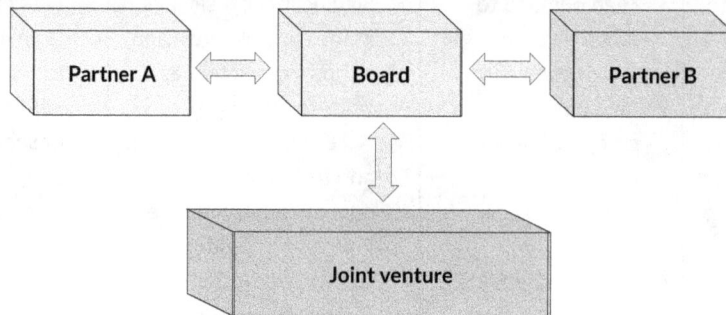

Figure 6.22: Network Organisational Shape: Joint Venture as Contracted Ecosystem

Table 6.15 gives the applicability, strengths and weaknesses of the Network Organisational Shape: Joint Venture.

Table 6.15: Network Organisational Shape: Joint Venture as Contracted Ecosystem – Applicability, strengths and weaknesses

ORGANISATIONAL SHAPE	APPLICABILITY	STRENGTHS	WEAKNESSES
Work is co-managed by two or more organisations through an intermediary, legally set-up, organisation *Predominant Basic Design Logic:* Function; Markets/ Customers and Products/Services; Decentralised; Self-sufficient	• Rapidly changing market and/ or client expectations requiring constant product/service innovation • High risk and/or high investment which is shared in order to make an opportunity viable	• Manageable risks • Cost savings • Economies of scale • Speed of responsiveness • Mobilisation of competence beyond own organisation • Low innovation-to-investment ratio • Joint product/service experimentation • Ability to move speedily to respond to market opportunities • A dedicated organisation focused on an opportunity, which can be disbanded once opportunity has been realised	• Loss of in-house specialist skills if transferred to Joint Venture • Difficult to build strong organisational Identity because of divided organisational loyalties or partisanship between home organisation and Joint Venture • High people/time investment in building trust and shared culture

(vi.b) Loosely coupled/Negotiated movement: Synergistic Ecosystems

This type of Network Shape centres around informal, temporary relationships within a fixed set of members, bound to one another through verbal agreement for mutually agreed-upon times to pursue an interorganisational good, for example, a Strategic Alliance. In the case of a Strategic Alliance, an agreement – somewhat contracted or a gentlemen's agreement – is reached between two or more independent partners to jointly pursue shared goals for mutual benefit. For example, by co-deploying assets and/or expertise; sharing technology and/or intellectual capital; and joint access to markets/clients, synergistically where one has something the other needs and vice versa, in order to enhance each other's independent businesses.

Being a closely coupled partnership, the purpose of the Strategic Alliance, its expected value-add and duration are usually clearly defined as applied to the fixed members belonging to the Alliance. However, roles with their associated authorities and responsibilities, standards and protocols evolve over time in a dynamic manner.

Figure 6.23 provides the Organisational Map for a Strategic Alliance.

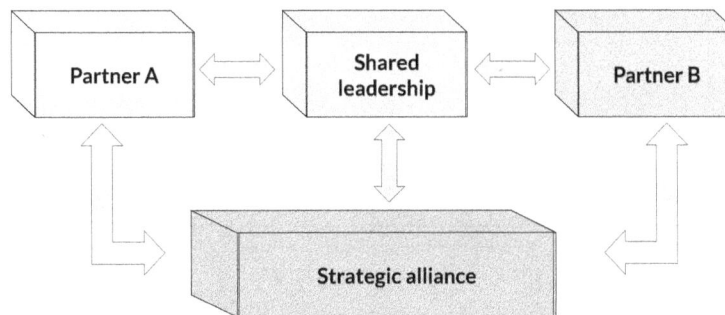

Figure 6.23: Network Organisational Shape: Strategic Alliance Synergistic Ecosystem

Table 6.16 gives the applicability, strengths and weaknesses of the Network Organisational Shape: Strategic Alliance as Synergistic Ecosystem.

Table 6.16: Network Organisational Shape: Strategic Alliance as Contracted Ecosystem – Applicability, strengths and weaknesses

ORGANISATIONAL SHAPE	APPLICABILITY	STRENGTHS	WEAKNESSES
Work is co-managed by two or more organisations through a contractual or verbal agreement, in force for a certain period of time	• Rapidly changing market and/or client expectations requiring constant product/service innovation	• Ability to respond better with an enhanced value proposition to market opportunities and client needs	• Higher planning and co-ordination costs • Difficult to build strong organisational Identity because of divided organisational loyalties or partisanship

ORGANISATIONAL SHAPE	APPLICABILITY	STRENGTHS	WEAKNESSES
Predominant Basic Design Logic: Process; Products/ Services and/or Markets/Customers; Decentralised; Self-sufficient	• High interorganisational synergy opportunities in terms of products/ services and resources: win-win opportunities • High organisational cultural compatibility	• Co-mobilisation of competence beyond own organisation • Enhanced leveraging of (specialist) resources across organisations • Low innovation-to-investment ratio • Joint product/ service experimentation • Cost savings • Economies of scale • Alliance focused on an opportunity, which can be terminated once opportunity has been realised • Risk mitigation	• Clashes between interorganisational priorities and goals, and time allocation • High people/time investment in building trust and shared culture • Transitory nature of agreement makes all of the above even tougher • An exploitative relationship: one partner(s) only takes out of the relationship and does not invest in the relationship • Misleading partners: withholding and/or distorting information • Partner(s) shirking responsibilities/not meeting expectations • Redundant/unnecessary relationships/partners • The value gained from the relationship is less than the costs of investing in the relationship

(vi.c) Tightly coupled/Free movement: Managed Ecosystems

This type of Network Shape – also called a Public Good, Community of Practice (39) – entails formalised, self-organising relationships within a varying set of members for mutually agreed-upon, varying periods of time in pursuit of a public good. The purpose of the self-organising partnering, its expected value-add, membership requirements, tasks, roles with associated authorities and responsibilities, standards and protocols are relatively clearly defined, providing order and discipline to interactions. However, partners can move in and out of the network as they see fit at any time that suits them. No hierarchical based authority and/or employment contract exists in the partnering common space. However, a lead partner(s) may direct and guide the network, as well as ensure that minimum partnering requirements are met.

Two examples of the Network Shape are open-source software (OSS) communities such as Linux and Wikipedia, the free online encyclopaedia. The shaded box provides descriptions of both these partnering communities (40).

LINUX: OPEN SOURCE SOFTWARE COMMUNITY

Linux is a global open source software community which aims to develop a free computer operating system by leveraging the capabilities of anyone who wants to contribute. Contributors, by personal choice, participate in creating software versions that are adapted to particular needs. All such adaptations are available to the entire community.

Protocols and norms exist for activities, such as access, use, submission, and commitment of code, as well as strong norms of good community citizenship, enabling the orderly development of code. Processes exist for integrating the source code from those separate versions into the common operating system.

Anyone can join the community and use its outputs. However, the vast majority of members are individuals. They voluntarily contribute to the provision of a public good, namely freely shared source code. In doing so they gain personal benefits in the form of intrinsic rewards such as the enjoyment of intellectual challenge, and/or non-monetary extrinsic rewards such as peer recognition; a sense of belonging; learning from feedback; and the signalling of technical excellence to peers and software firms.

In many cities and regions local associations exist, known as Linux User Groups (LUGs), as well as Internet communities and online support, which seek to promote the distribution and use of Linux. The LUGs hold meetings and provide free demonstrations and training, technical support, and operating system installations for new users.

WIKIPEDIA: ONLINE, OPEN SOURCE ENCYCLOPAEDIA

Wikipedia is the 5th most popular site on earth, having attracted 465 million unique visitors in April 2018. With 18 billion page views and nearly 500 million unique visitors a month, Wikipedia trails just behind Yahoo, Facebook, Microsoft, and Google, the largest with 1.2 billion unique visitors. It has over 5.6 million articles in English (41).

Wikipedia was initially constructed as a Loosely Coupled/Open Boundary Network Shape; a Synergistic Ecosystem. Much of the encyclopaedia was written, edited, formatted, and organised by volunteer members of the community at any time, all the time. Anarchy ruled.

Over time, however, Wikipedia has differentiated roles and editing rights in the community, moving toward a Managed Ecosystem: a Tightly Coupled/Open Boundary Network. The larger majority of members contribute to Wikipedia's input in the form of 'draft' articles — the open boundary, whilst a smaller group of editors is responsible for most of the pruning, quality assurance, and policing of the submitted drafts — the tightly coupled mode of working in terms of selection and retention processes laid down and used regarding submissions. For example, one quality standard is "Notability": does a concept merit an article in Wikipedia?

Consensus decision-making is the norm for establishing agreement, while straw polls and other conversation tools advance the discussion. An article is not considered to be owned by its creator or any other editor, and is not vetted by any recognised authority. Wikipedia's own hierarchy of formal roles is named and ordered as: steward, check-user, oversighter, bureaucrat, administrator, rollbacker, registered user, newly registered user, unregistered user, blocked user.

Wikipedia had about 40,000 featured articles and good articles as of March 2017, covering various vital topics. In 2005, *Nature Magazine* published a peer review comparing 42 science articles from Encyclopaedia Britannica and Wikipedia, and found that Wikipedia's level of accuracy approached that of Encyclopaedia Britannica. *Time* magazine stated that the open-door policy of allowing anyone to edit had made Wikipedia the biggest and possibly the best encyclopaedia in the world, which is a testament to the vision of Jimmy Wales, its founder.

The English Wikipedia passed the mark of two million articles on September 9, 2007, making it the largest encyclopaedia ever assembled, surpassing even the 1408 Yongle Encyclopaedia, which had held the record for almost 600 years.

Table 6.17 gives the applicability, strengths and weaknesses of the Network Organisational Shape: Managed Ecosystem.

Table 6.17: Network Organisational Shape: Managed Ecosystem – Applicability, strengths and weaknesses

ORGANISATIONAL SHAPE	APPLICABILITY	STRENGTHS	WEAKNESSES
Work is done through a public community of practice, centring around a free public good *Predominant Basic Design Logic:* Process; Products/Services; Decentralised; Self-sufficient	• Rapid participative/ democratic response, in real time, to an emerging need for a specific public good, either not addressed or commercially monopolised by profit seeking organisations • Dynamic mobilisation of specialist, focused knowledge, skills and expertise with the aim of creating and maintaining a free-of-charge, public good for the common good	• Real time, dynamic self re-organising in response to changing requirements and circumstances with respect to a public good need: agility • Constant re-innovation of public offering • Top knowledge, skills and expertise, voluntarily applied, at no cost	• Implosion of the offering if its evolving, increasing comprehensiveness and complexity are not matched by the requisite complexity levels of shared leadership, Work Roles, protocols and processes, as well as their formalisation and codification • Inversely, the over-formalisation and -codification of the above-mentioned may turn them into ends-in-themselves, instead of means, in this way suffocating the agile, creativity within the community • The 'tyranny of virtual democracy' in which the majority rules may constrain/ sabotage the full innovative deployment of knowledge, skills and expertise available within the community of practice

(vi.d) Loosely coupled/Free movement: Instantaneous Ecosystems

This type of Network Shape encompasses informal, temporary relationships within a set of varying members, mobilised around an issue, problem or challenge arising in the public domain in pursuit of an economic or social good. Members join and leave the instantaneously mobilised network of their own volition at any time it suits them. The Internet and social media provide critical enabling platforms for the triggering and sustaining of the temporary, Instantaneous Ecosystem.

Instantaneous Ecosystems can be differentiated on a continuum of the relative weight given to an Organisational or Social Good, as shown in Figure 6.24 *(42) (43)*.

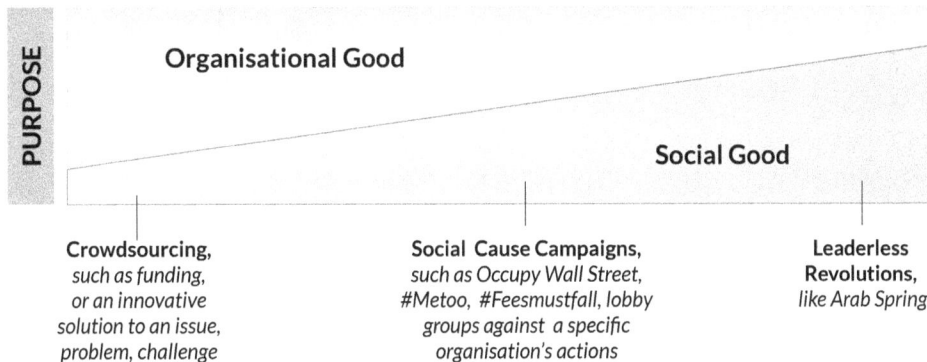

Figure 6.24: Types of Instantaneous Ecosystems as a function of the relative weight given to an Organisational or Social Good

The increasing frequency of the mobilisation of Instantaneous Ecosystems makes it imperative that organisations understand this Network Shape in order to know how to use it to their benefit and/or how to engage with it if it targets the organisation.

Table 6.18 gives the applicability, strengths and weaknesses of the Network Organisational Shape: Instantaneous Ecosystems.

Table 6.18: Network Organisational Shape: Instantaneous Ecosystem – Applicability, strengths and weaknesses

ORGANISATIONAL SHAPE	APPLICABILITY	STRENGTHS	WEAKNESSES
Work is done within the public domain by a voluntary, socially mobilised group of individuals centring around a public need, cause, or issue – either organisationally or socially located – giving the ecosystem a temporary collective identity	• Rapid democratic mobilisation to a real time, emerging need/cause/issue in order to bring about a specific, perceived public good	• Real time, agile and self re-organising in response to changing requirements and circumstances	• Absence of formalised, publicly recognised/ endorsed leadership makes as mobilised network unpredictable in terms of its actions and direction, and nearly impossible to engage with constructively as a formally led collective

ORGANISATIONAL SHAPE	APPLICABILITY	STRENGTHS	WEAKNESSES
Predominant Basic Design Logic: Process; Public good; Decentralised; Self-sufficient	• Unbounded, dynamic mobilisation of knowledge, skills and expertise, fuelled by inexhaustible pools of passion and dedication, even fanaticism	• Ongoing re-invention, in real time, of means and ends to achieve real time, instantaneously expected results • Unbounded mobilisation of knowledge, skills and expertise, and resources, voluntarily applied at no cost at anytime and anywhere	• Poor sustainability: Runs out of energy over time as passion and dedication run down and the need/issue/cause loses its public appeal

(vii) Multiple, Related and Unrelated Organisational Scope with Diverse, Similar and Dissimilar Organisational Variety: Cluster Organisational Shape

The Cluster Organisational Shape – see the Periodic Table of Generic Organisational Shapes above – consists of groupings of the same types of business/organisational units into clusters, typically sector-/industry-based. This shape is also called the 'Diversified Corporation'. Clusters differ in the nature of the businesses they represent, and can be designed in terms of any of the preceding Organisational Shapes. Figure 6.25 provides a Cluster Organisational Map.

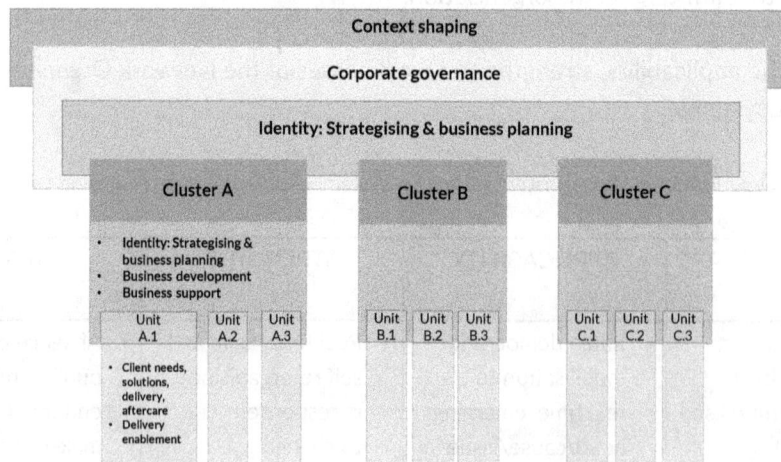

Figure 6.25: Cluster Organisational Map

Figure 6.25 shows different clusters made up of various operating units. For example, the clusters can represent different mining sectors: iron, coal, platinum, gold. Or, it can represent, in the case of the true conglomerate, different sectors altogether: Finance, ITC, Manufacturing.

Table 6.19 gives the applicability, strengths and weaknesses of the Cluster Organisational Shape.

Table 6.19: Cluster Organisational Shape: Applicability, strengths and weaknesses

ORGANISATIONAL SHAPE	APPLICABILITY	STRENGTHS	WEAKNESSES
Grouping of the same business/organisational units into clusters, typically based on sector/industry *Predominant Basic Design Logic:* Function; Products/Services and Markets/Customers; Decentralised; Self-sufficient	• Wide range of similar/dissimilar Business Units • Desire to enhance synergy amongst similar businesses in the form of groupings	• Sharing of resources and infrastructure, enhancing cost-effectiveness • Building of in-depth sector/industry expertise which can be shared • Greater critical mass in sector/industry, which allows for greater negotiation power • Reduction in span of control at organisation-wide level • Standardisation of operating processes and procedures within Cluster	• Internal parochial sector/industry perspective • Cluster loyalty takes precedence over organisation identification • Hogging of resources by a Cluster

(viii) Multiple, Unrelated Organisational Scope with Dissimilar Organisational Variety: Holding Organisational Shape

The Holding Organisational Shape – see the Periodic Table of Generic Organisational Shapes above – consists of the grouping of similar businesses/companies according to investment portfolio principles. Figure 6.26 gives the Holding Organisational Map.

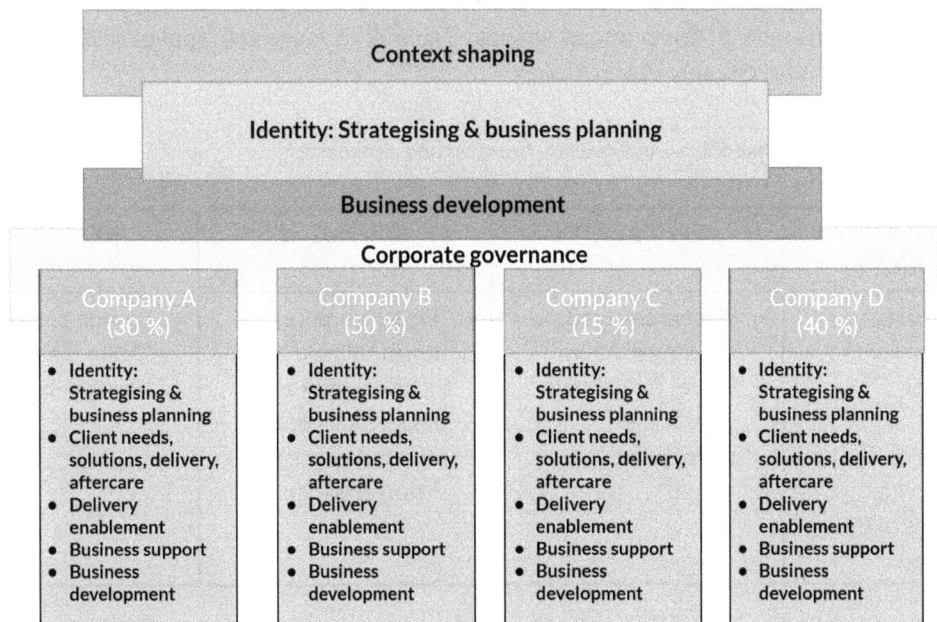

Figure 6.26: Holding Organisational Map

Figure 6.26 shows different companies in which a certain percentage of investments are held. Often the investments are chosen to provide collectively the best returns across economic/seasonal cycles.

Table 6.20 gives the applicability, strengths and weaknesses of the Holding Organisational Shape.

Table 6.20: Holding Organisational Shape: Applicability, strengths and weaknesses

ORGANISATIONAL SHAPE	APPLICABILITY	STRENGTHS	WEAKNESSES
Grouping of similar businesses/companies according to investment portfolio principles *Predominant Basic Design Logic:* Function; Products/Services and Markets/Customers; Decentralised; Self-sufficient	• Pure investment portfolio financial return interest	• Allows leadership of companies to take full responsibility and accountability to run their companies autonomously as they see fit • Flexibility to maximise investment portfolio financial returns by buying and selling stakes in companies	• 'Arms-length' financial returns and interest in companies invested in • Non-realisation of opportunities and synergies across organisations

(ix) Hybrid Organisational Shape

This is the Organisational Shape where groupings of activities are based on a mixture of any of the Shapes discussed above. Sometimes this Shape is called the 'ambidextrous' organisation, given that it is composed of different, fit-for-purpose shapes. Table 6.21 gives the applicability, strengths and weaknesses of the Hybrid Organisational Shape.

Table 6.21: Hybrid Organisational Shape: Applicability, strengths and weaknesses

ORGANISATIONAL SHAPE	APPLICABILITY	STRENGTHS	WEAKNESSES
Groupings based on a mixture of any of the above shapes *Predominant Basic Design Logic:* Any permutations of Design Axes options	• Diverse organisation requiring different Shapes for different parts of the organisation	• "Fit-for-purpose" design suitable to niche, Identity and design requirements for different parts of the organisation	• Tension between "Being the same" and "Being different"

This concludes the overview of Organisational Shapes. At the end of this design step, a specific Shape must have been chosen that fits the Design Criteria, Design Vision and basic delivery logic. Mediating factors with respect to the chosen Shape are the footprint the organisation aspires to have globally; what delivery mode will enable the desired footprint; and its sustainability footprint.

Step A.2.2.6: Decide on the appropriate delivery mode with its commensurate design to attain a global presence and reach

The world is increasingly becoming – and will be even more so in future – a global village. Many, if not most, boundaries restricting the movement of information, knowledge, people, stakeholders, products/services and resources (for example, raw materials, finance, technology) across the world are disappearing/will disappear – or at least are becoming more permeable – at varying speeds across the world.

It can be predicted that this trend will continue unabated, even though there is at present a worldwide counter-trend to globalisation. Currently there is a rise across the world in nationalism and populism: a growing internal focus of 'Put the interests of our country first'; inter-nation tensions; and global security fears/threats. These trends may slow down boundarylessness, and in some cases even counter globalisation. However, current and future organisations still will, or will want to, operate globally through a physical and/or virtual presence and reach. Burning platforms such as global warming; the depletion of scarce natural resources; threats to global security; and access to technology will force states and organisations into a global mindset and actions again, even if it is for the mere sake of survival.

Being a global organisation, or having the intent to become a global player, will become increasingly common in the emerging world order of a progressively interconnected world (44). Being a global/globalising organisation imposes its own design challenges, such as the location of accountabilities across countries; creating and managing global, seamless talent pools; bridging operationally different time and physical zones; migrating innovations globally across an organisation; ensuring inclusivity across different national cultures; and attaining high performance in culturally diverse teams.

Given the need for organisations to attain a global presence and reach, three delivery modes can be distinguished, each with its own delivery logic requirements:

- Having a *physical footprint* in the countries in which the organisation operates/wishes to operate.

- Having a *virtual footprint* on an ongoing basis, anywhere, anytime, anyhow, anything, for anyone as an organisation.

- Having a *sustainability* footprint to leave the world a better a place for current and upcoming generations.

The first two modes are not stand-alone (Either/Or), but can be used in a complementary fashion – And/Both. However, organisations have emerged that have a largely virtual footprint globally, having a minimum physical footprint or nothing at all in all of the countries in which they operate, such as Airbnb, Amazon, Uber, Facebook, Google and Shopify.

Physical footprint to attain a global presence and reach

The typical physical evolution path of globalising organisations is made up of four stages, as per Figure 6.27. Different Organisational Designs are associated with each of the four evolutionary stages set out in the figure.

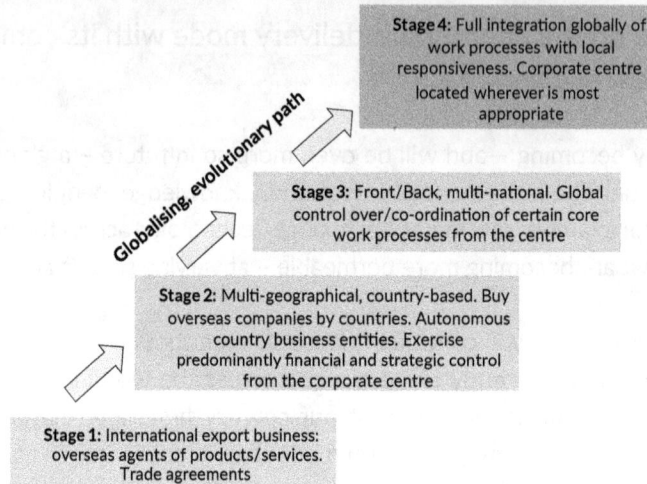

Stage 4: Full integration globally of work processes with local responsiveness. Corporate centre located wherever is most appropriate

Stage 3: Front/Back, multi-national. Global control over/co-ordination of certain core work processes from the centre

Stage 2: Multi-geographical, country-based. Buy overseas companies by countries. Autonomous country business entities. Exercise predominantly financial and strategic control from the corporate centre

Stage 1: International export business: overseas agents of products/services. Trade agreements

Globalising, evolutionary path

Figure 6.27: Typical evolution of a physically globalising organisation

At each evolutionary stage reflected in Figure 6.27, the major challenge to globalising organisations is to find the right balance between a *Reach Need* (the local and/or global integration of work) and an *Acting Need* (the local and/or global responsiveness on the ground in the locations where the organisation has an operational presence) (45). Figure 6.28 presents the different permutations of these two needs (46).

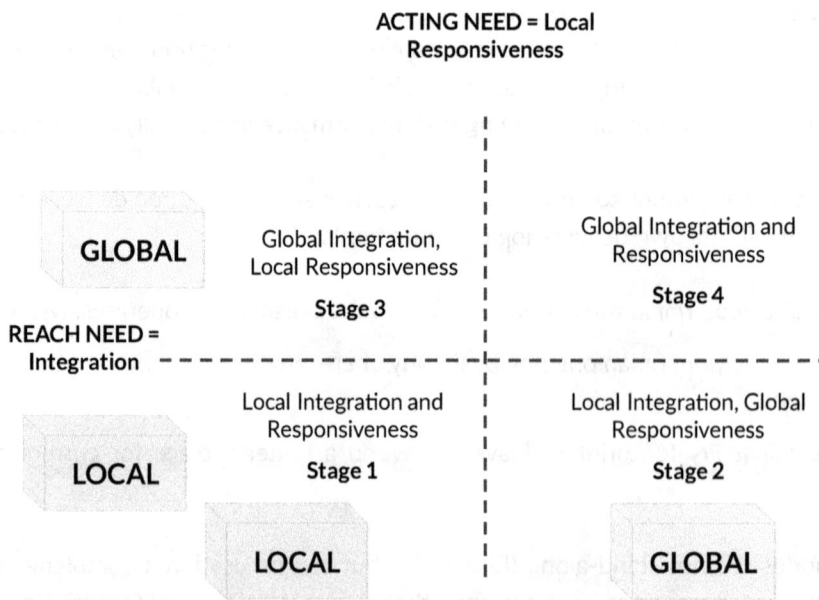

ACTING NEED = Local Responsiveness

REACH NEED = Integration

GLOBAL	Global Integration, Local Responsiveness **Stage 3**	Global Integration and Responsiveness **Stage 4**
LOCAL	Local Integration and Responsiveness **Stage 1**	Local Integration, Global Responsiveness **Stage 2**
	LOCAL	GLOBAL

Figure 6.28: Finding the right balance between Reach and Acting Needs relative to the stages of the globalising, evolutionary path, leveraged from the appropriate mix of a Local and/or Global Presence

In terms of balancing Reach and Acting Needs, Figure 6.29 depicts the typical way in which Work Processes (see Figure 5.4) can be distributed.

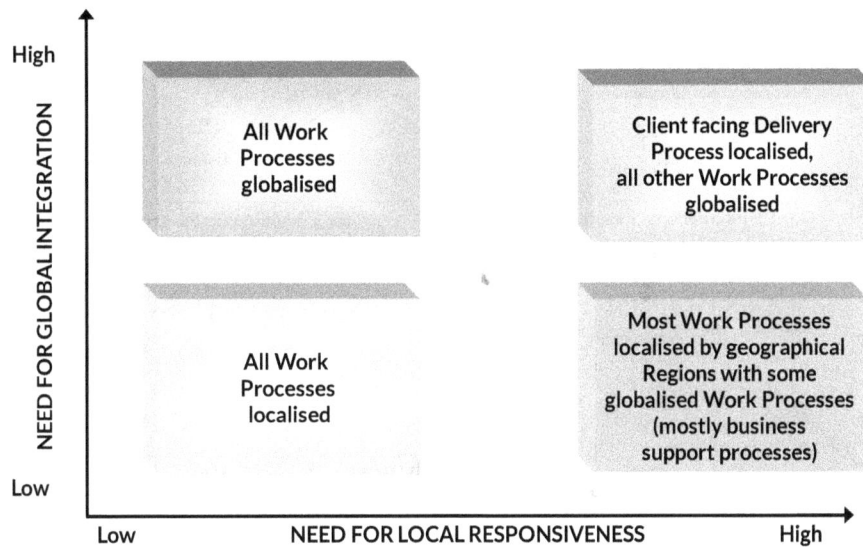

Figure 6.29: Typical distribution of Work Processes in terms of the different mixes of Reach and Acting Needs relative to the stages of the globalising, evolutionary path

Figure 6.30 highlights the various Organisational Shapes associated with the different mixes of Reach and Acting Needs in terms of the generic Work Processes, relative to the organisation's place on the globalising, evolutionary path. A critical success factor for a global/globalising organisation and its design to be effective is a global mindset: seeing, thinking, and acting seamlessly across the total global Operating Arena of the organisation with reference to its physical locations within its Operating Arena.

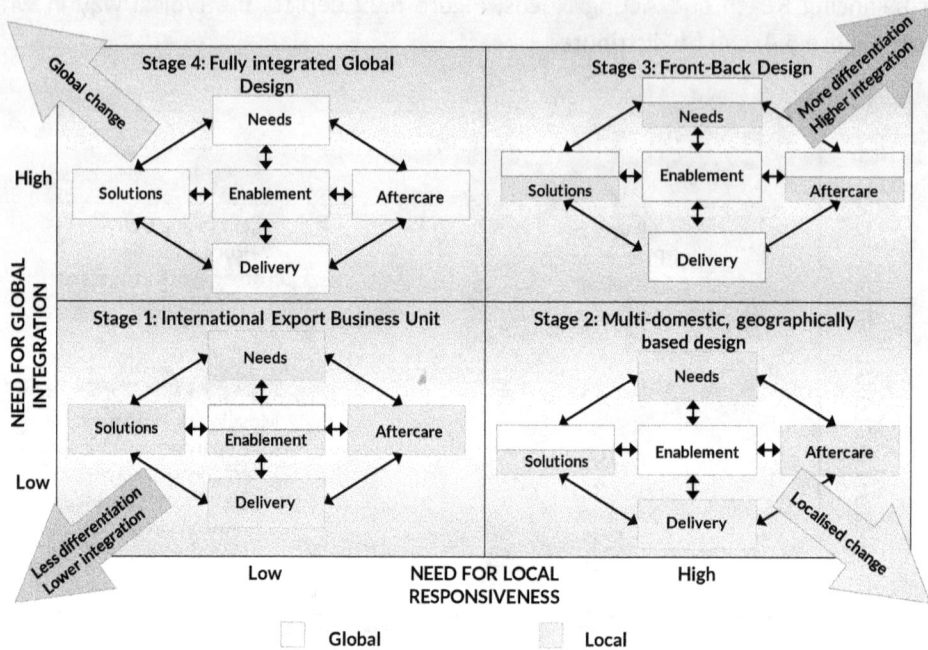

Figure 6.30: Different Organisational Shapes for the different needs of Global Integration and Local Responsiveness relative to the organisation's stage on the globalising, evolutionary path

Virtual footprint to attain a global presence and reach

The maths of the emerging new order – highlighted in Figure 2.2, Chapter 2 – demands delivery by organisations on an ongoing basis, anywhere, anytime, anyhow, anything for anyone. In other words, there is a global need for organisations with virtual footprints and reach. Figure 6.31 provides a number of basic delivery continua according to which the organisation can be mapped. Using these continua, the delivery logic of the virtual organisation can be profiled as indicated by the stars in the figure (47). Mostly frequently, virtual teams form the key building blocks of virtual organisations.

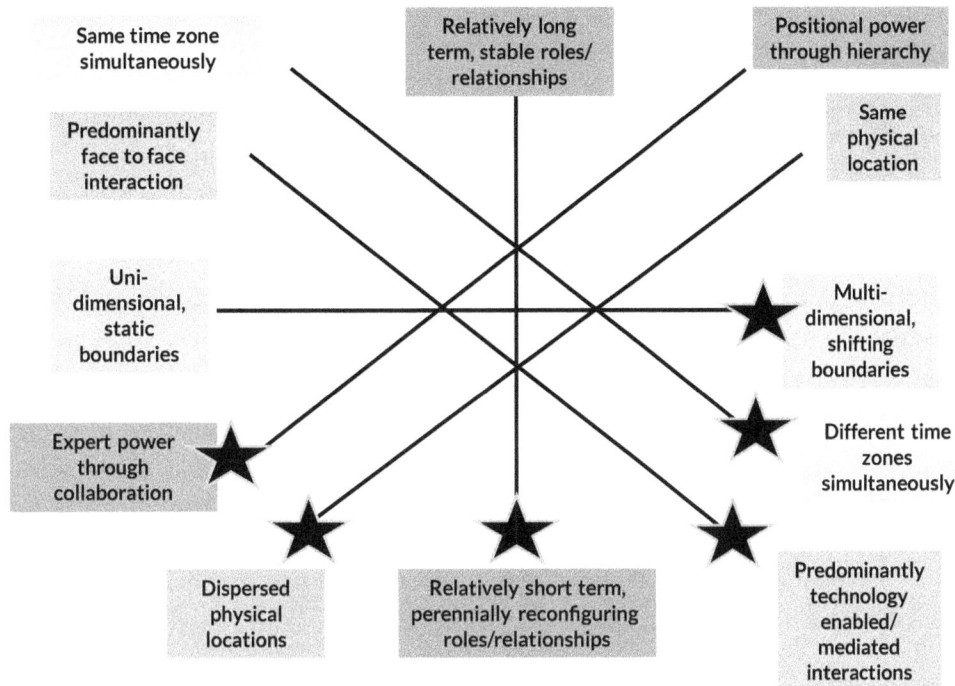

Figure 6.31: Profile of the virtual organisation

Using Figure 6.31 as a basis, a virtually connected organisation can be described as an organisation (48):

- in which 50% plus of organisational members of the total organisation/organisational unit work more than 75% of the time in different time zones, concurrently;

- that is located in dispersed physical locations across multi-dimensional, shifting boundaries. For example, different organisational functions/levels/regions and/or national cultures/countries;

- that has relatively short term, perennially reconfiguring, roles/relationships;

- that has predominantly technology enabled/mediated interactions in order get the work done. Also called remote, digital, distributed, or mobile work (49); and

- that applies their expert power in a collaborative mode.

Degrees of virtuality can also be distinguished: from the formal organisation that increasingly becomes virtually connected in doing its work, to 'organisations' designed around a technological, network-based application. These are organisations that are completely virtual from inception, like Uber, Lyft, Washio, Handy, Amazon's Mechanical Turk, and Airbnb. These completely (globalised) virtual organisations are manifestations of the snowballing rise of the new on-demand or shared economy.

Figure 6.32 provides an overview of the typical core values, critical success factors, and infrastructures required by the delivery logic of a globally virtual organisation (50):

- The *core values* are given in the inner, shaded portion of the star, for example, trust, identity, growth, and so forth.

- The *critical success factors* are in the points of the star, for example framing, sharing, value-add.

- The *types of infrastructure* required to enable delivery are in the rectangular blocks.

- A *critical success factor* adjacent to an *infrastructure block* informs that particular infrastructure, for example, framing (= the critical success factor) informing business infrastructure.

- Contained in each infrastructure block are the *typical design elements* making up that infrastructure. For example, the Communication Infrastructure has an Internal Network Website as a design element.

- All of the above are embedded in and framed by a *Virtual Mindset and Intelligence*, the overarching critical success factor of the virtual organisation. A Virtual Mindset entails the capability to see, think and act on an ongoing basis in terms of anywhere, anytime, anyhow, anything for anyone, as enabled and leveraged by technology (51). Virtual Intelligence relates to the capacity of the individuals and teams in the virtual organisation to successfully operate and perform in cyberspace unbounded by space or time (52).

Sustainability footprint of leaving the world a better a place for current and upcoming generations

As elucidated under Reason 2, Chapter 2 for OD becoming a mission-critical organisational discipline, the trend is towards the Operating Models of organisations being reflective and in support of true, genuine citizenship within communities and society. Organisations have to transform themselves into social enterprises, driven by the core value orientation of sustainability through stewardship *(53)*. Going into the future, as discussed in Chapter 2, it will be imperative to position the delivery logic of the organisation within a TSV design logic, where 'Virtuous' refers, *inter alia*, to doing the right things right in terms of a sustainability perspective: recover, renew, restore and retain existing value *whilst* delivering value going into the future, with respect to the five Ps of Productivity, Prosperity, People, Peace and Planet.

From a design perspective, the above implies at least the following: (i) sustainability must become part of the very DNA of the organisation, (ii) a Sustainability Work Process must be included in the organisation's portfolio of Work Processes (see Figure 5.4 and Table 5.5, Chapter 5), headed up by a Executive Work Role, which could be entitled something like 'Chief Sustainability Officer'; (iii) with a mandate of scrutinising each and every work process and all decisions and actions taken by the organisation for its impact on sustainability (similar to Internal Audit); and (iv) reporting directly into the organisation's Board of Directors. Only in this way will the sustainability footprint of an organisation really be promoted and enhanced. In the end, this Executive must ensure that Consumed/Delivered Value – Replaced Value for all of the organisation's work processes.

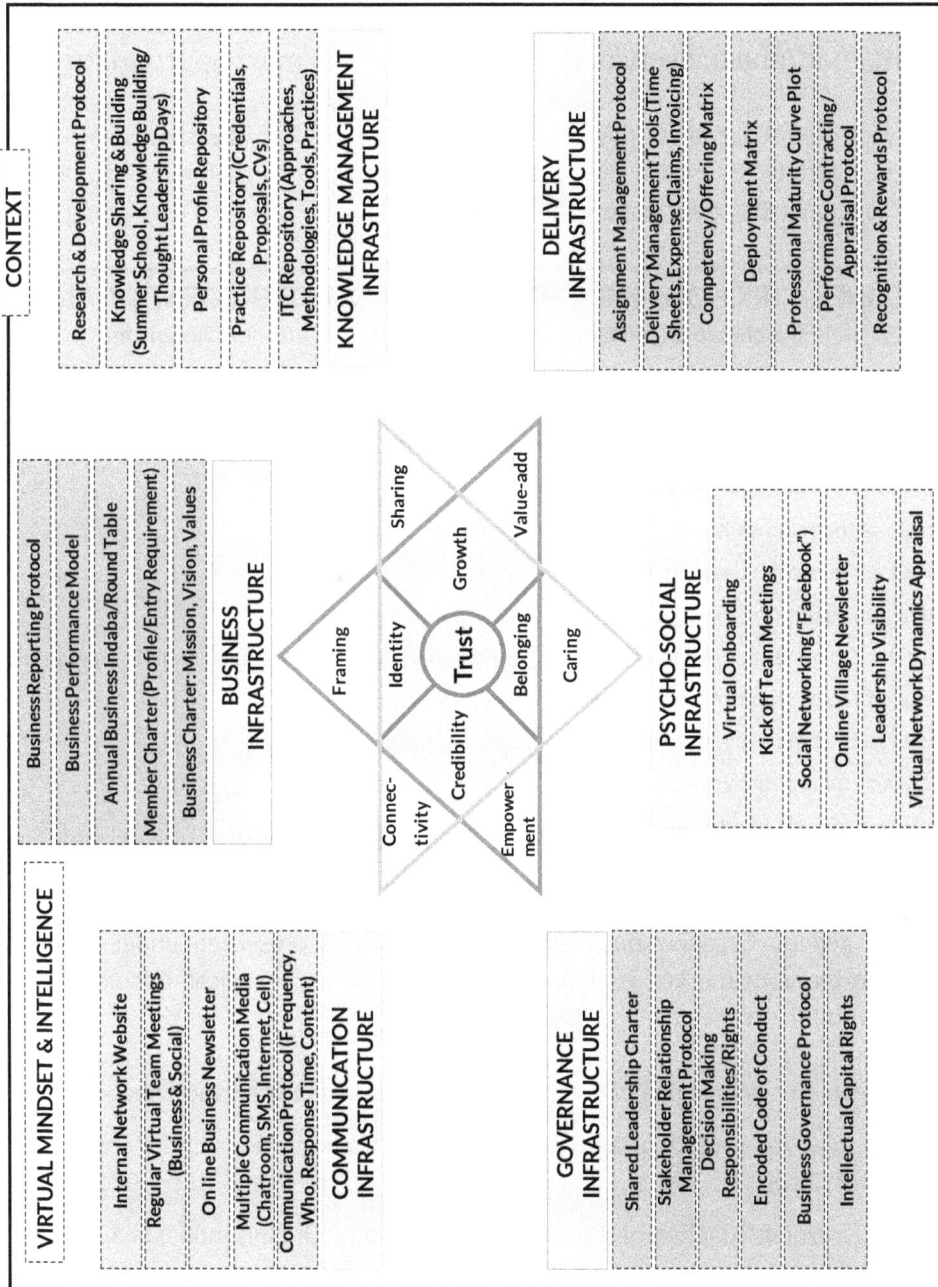

Figure 6.32: Typical core values, critical success factors, and infrastructure required by the delivery logic of a virtual organisation, embedded in and framed by a Virtual Mindset and Virtual Intelligence

Step A.2.2.7: Generate at least three possible Organisational Shapes – radical, middle of the road, and conservative – and choose the most appropriate

As a summary of Step A.2.2 up to this point of the design process, the shaded box gives a set of distilled key guidelines to ensure the choice of a fit-for-purpose Organisational Shape that equates to the Strategic Horizontal Design of the organisation.

GUIDELINES FOR CHOOSING A FIT-FOR-PURPOSE ORGANISATIONAL SHAPE
The chosen Organisational Shape, its Strategic Horizontal Design, must:

- meet the Design Criteria and Vision as expressed in the Design Metaphor;
- fit the specific sector/industry in which the organisation is operating/will operate;
- be aligned to the organisation's Strategic Intent, and broader, its Purpose;
- take note of the mind shift in thinking about organisations in general;
- be based on its chosen basic delivery logic;
- give due consideration to the Shape's, strengths and weaknesses;
- include the design requirements of its physical and/or virtual, as well as sustainability, footprints;
- house all of the work processes somewhere in a Work Unit;
- be of requisite complexity: not too simple nor too complex;
- be cost- and time-effective; and
- be easy to lead and operate.

To encourage out-of-the-box, zero base, no holy cows design thinking, at least three possible options for the chosen, generic Organisational Shape (the Shapes as presented under Step A.2.2.5) can be architected in terms of the key guidelines in the shaded box – radical, middle of the road, and conservative – with their respective pros and cons (54):

- *Radical:* a completely re-imaging of the chosen, conventional Organisation Shape.
- *Middle of the road:* an adaptation/recreation of the significant portions of the chosen, conventional Organisational Shape.
- *Conservative:* a tuning/adaption of the chosen, conventional Organisational Shape.

The box gives two examples of options regarding chosen generic Organisational Shapes, with their pros and cons.

CHOSEN GENERIC SHAPE	OPTIONS	SOLUTIONS	PROS	CONS
Functional (see (i) under Generic Organisational Shapes)	Radical	Populating design with cross-functional project teams, doing the organisational work	Integrated business solutions	Possible loss in in-depth, functional expertise
	Middle of the road	Switching to a Process Design within Functions	End-to-end flow of work	Process silos
	Conservative	Minimising the functional silos by lateral, co-ordinating roles	Maintain in-depth functional expertise, alongside cross-functional co-ordination	Power games/struggles between functions and liaison roles: who is calling the shots
Front-Back (see (v) under Generic Organisational Shapes)	Radical	A completely outsourced, virtual design, only retaining the executive level	High flexibility and agility in terms of innovating the client offering	At mercy of vendors who have relationships with customers and suppliers
	Middle of the road	Converting the Business Support and Delivery Enablement Processes into Global Shared Services	Economies of scale; in-depth, centralised competencies; partnering opportunities	Far removed from clients; unclear accountability/ responsibility handover points
	Conservative	Redrawing the boundaries of the market/client facing units (= Front); giving them greater autonomy to make local decisions; and placing all the back manufacturing units under one global executive	Front: Faster decision-making; localisation Back: Economies of scale; standardisation	Front: Differing customer treatments and standards across regions; duplication of activities Back: Slow rate of innovation because not in direct contact with customers and markets

Having considered different optional Organisational Shapes, the best fit-for-purpose Organisational Shape option – the Strategic Horizontal Design – must be chosen.

Step A.2.2.8: Construct an Organisational Map depicting the chosen Strategic Horizontal Design

This Design Step is concluded by drawing an Organisational Map, which visually depicts the chosen Strategic Horizontal Design. The Organisational Map represents the overall 'House Plan' of the organisation, reflecting the different Rooms and their relative placement to each other. This is the climax of the Strategic Horizontal Design process: the House Plan has come together.

The map must provide a true representation of the chosen Strategic Horizontal Design, similar to a House Plan, depicting the correct locations of Rooms relative to each other, showing interdependencies though overlaps between Rooms, or front-back relationships, that is where one Room is supported by another Room. The shaded box gives guidelines for a powerful Organisational Map of the chosen Strategic Horizontal Map. The further shaded boxes give three examples of such maps for: (i) a Banking/Financial Services Organisation (55); (ii) an IT Outsourcing Organisation (56); and (iii) a Refinery Organisation (57) *(58)*.

GUIDELINES FOR A POWERFUL ORGANISATIONAL MAP OF THE CHOSEN STRATEGIC HORIZONTAL MAP

- Simple but complete, reflecting the correct locations of Work Units relative to each other – top of, alongside, to the bottom of – with overlaps showing interdependencies
- Visual
- The different Rooms can also be colour coded in terms of their nature: Operating, Enabling, Supporting, Corporate Centre, Board (59)
- Fit a single page

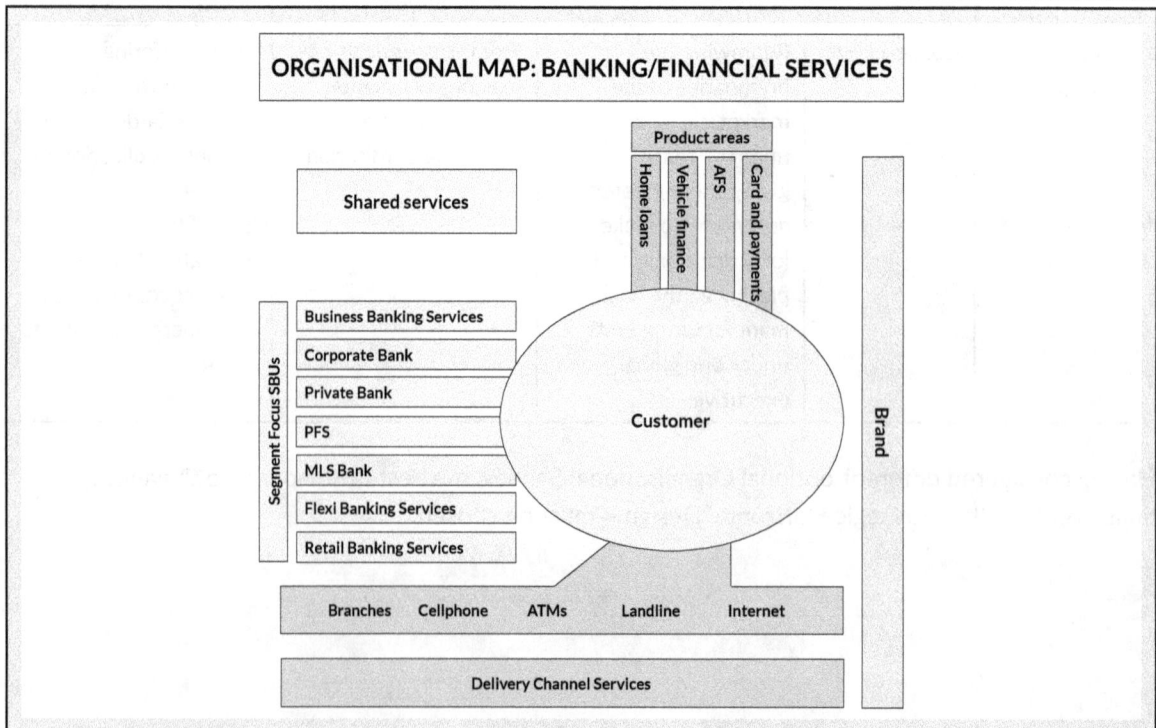

ORGANISATIONAL MAP: BANKING/FINANCIAL SERVICES

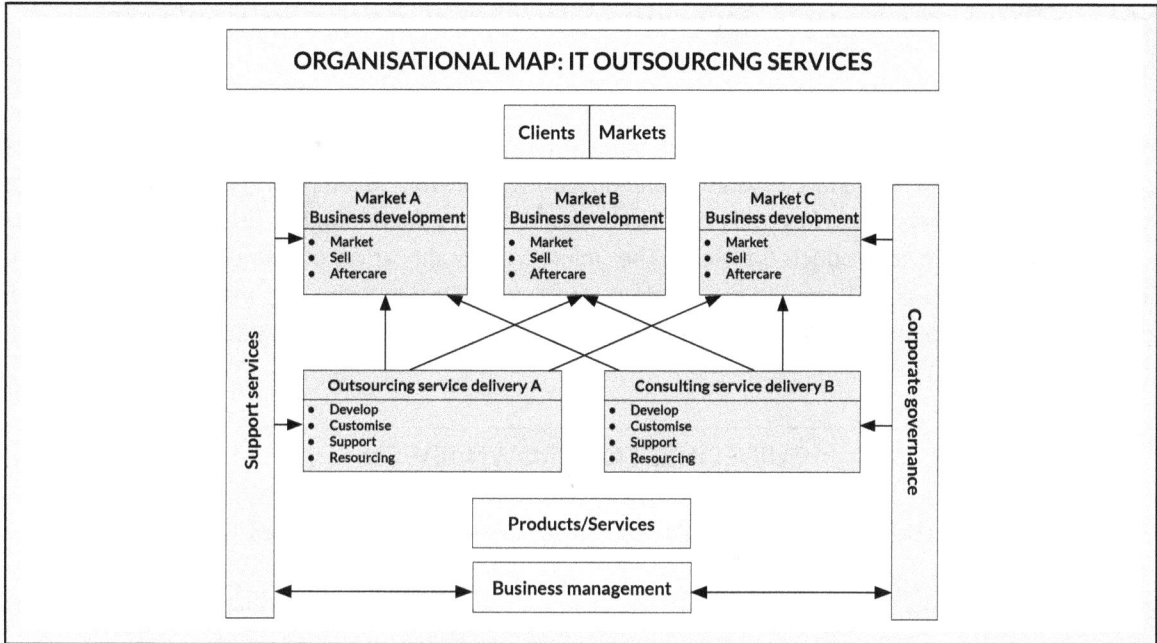

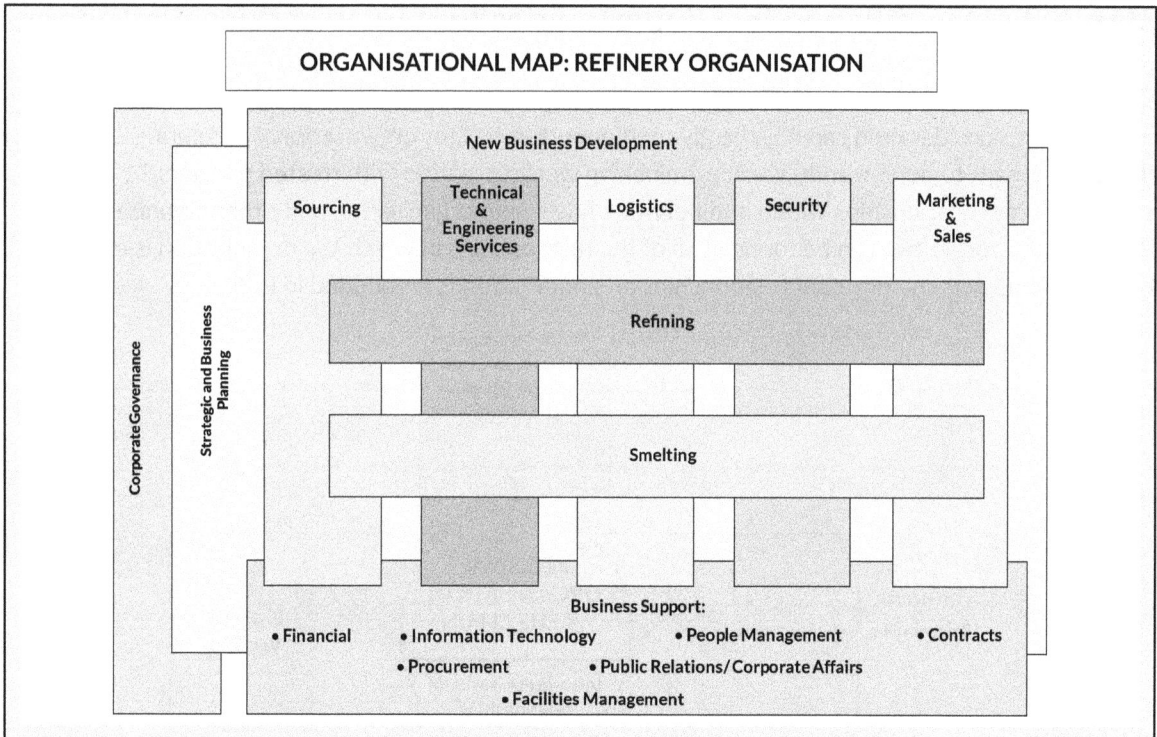

Step A.2.3: Ensure single accountabilities for the organisation's crown jewels

A crown jewel is a strategic organisational capability of the organisation, giving the organisation a competitive edge or a head start in creating and delivering value (60). Examples of such jewels are: core organisational competencies, key talent, critical resources, key technologies, brand(s), key markets/clients, and/or strategic products/services. The unambiguous allocation of ownership must be given to a specific Work Unit (= Room) in the Strategic Horizontal Design, using the mandate of Units as a guiding principle to make the allocation. Guidelines for dealing with the organisation's crown jewels are given in the shaded box.

GUIDELINES FOR CROWN JEWELS

- Certainty must exist that all of the organisation's crown jewels have been identified.

- A single 'owner' must exist for a specific crown jewel of the organisation.

Step A.2.4: Identify possible opportunities for Organisational Partnering

Given the Strategic Horizontal Design, representing the sum total of work to be done by the organisation, consideration can now be given to opportunities for organisational partnering. The aim of this partnering is to pursue mutual value, unlocking wealth creation with trusted partners, by setting up value exchange relationships within and between one's own organisation and other organisations (61). Partnering opportunities can be found in all of the relationships in which the organisation is embedded. Figure 6.33 depicts the different relationships an organisation is embedded in (62).

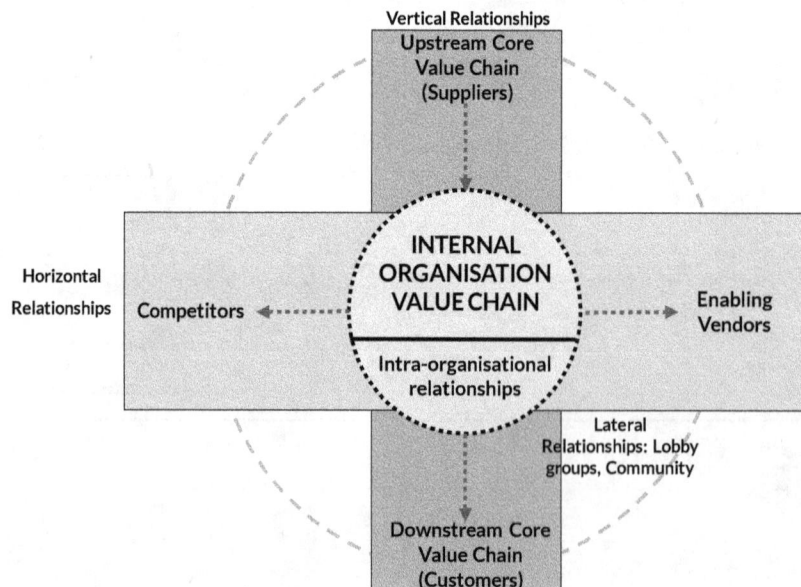

Figure 6.33: Different relationships the organisation is embedded in

From Figure 6.33 it should be clear that the organisation is made up in its very essence by relationships. As was reported in the discussion of the Network Organisational Shape, it has been found that successful organisations are more relationship driven. Partnering – as the concrete manifestation of a relationship-centric organisation – pertains to two or more individuals, groups or organisations that are able and willing to engage in mutually beneficial, two-way, value-exchange, cross-boundary relationships based on trust.

Five strategic reasons for partnering can be distinguished: (i) Capitalising on opportunities; (ii) Extending/enhancing capabilities; (iii) Accessing expertise and know-how; (iv) Mitigating risks; and/or (v) Focusing on core business (including outsourcing). Figure 6.34 depicts prime examples for each type of partnering with their associated Value Focus and Value Outcome (63).

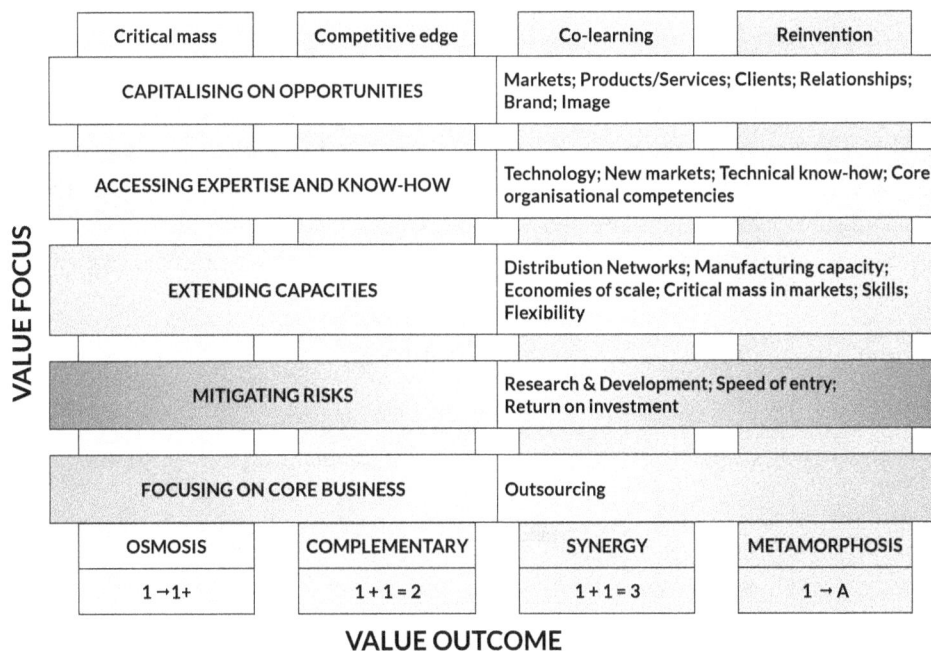

Critical mass	Competitive edge	Co-learning	Reinvention
CAPITALISING ON OPPORTUNITIES		Markets; Products/Services; Clients; Relationships; Brand; Image	
ACCESSING EXPERTISE AND KNOW-HOW		Technology; New markets; Technical know-how; Core organisational competencies	
EXTENDING CAPACITIES		Distribution Networks; Manufacturing capacity; Economies of scale; Critical mass in markets; Skills; Flexibility	
MITIGATING RISKS		Research & Development; Speed of entry; Return on investment	
FOCUSING ON CORE BUSINESS		Outsourcing	
OSMOSIS	COMPLEMENTARY	SYNERGY	METAMORPHOSIS
$1 \rightarrow 1+$	$1 + 1 = 2$	$1 + 1 = 3$	$1 \rightarrow A$

VALUE FOCUS (vertical axis label) — *VALUE OUTCOME* (horizontal axis label)

Figure 6.34: Prime examples of different types of partnering

Being a relationship-centric organisation requires a radical shift in the Organisational Design logic: from being a command-and-control, power-based organisation, to becoming a distributed, network organisation driven by joint value creation with trusted partners, both inside and outside the organisation. Figure 6.35 shows the contrast between the design delivery logic of the traditional command-and-control Organisational Design (see Figure 6.5) and a partnering design, based on a distributed, network organisation (see Figure 6.7) (64).

COMMAND-AND-CONTROL
Hierarchy and Authority
Policies and Standards
Rules and Procedures
Legal Contract and Recourse
Standardisation and Formalisation
Control and Dependency
Competition

PARTNERING
Reputation
Access Restriction
Collective Sanctions
Socialisation
Vision and Core Values driven
Autonomy and Interdependency
Collaboration/Co-opetition

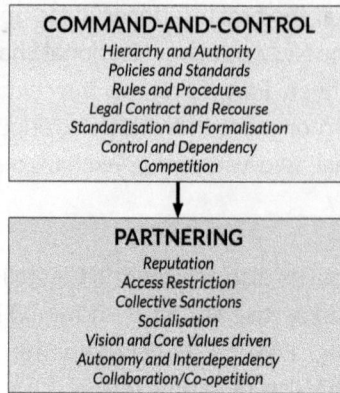

Figure 6.35: Contrast between the design delivery logic of the traditional Command-and-Control Organisational Design and Partnering Organisational Design reflective of a Distributed Network Organisation Design

Typical Partnering Organisational Shapes, as a function of the value to be created, are given in Figure 6.36 (65). At the bottom of the figure, continua of Design Criteria are given that specify the 'location' for a specific Shape, for example Formal to Informal; Dependence to Interdependence. Two differentiating axes, for example, Known, Present Defined Value vs. Unknown, Evolving Future Defined Value, define the parameters of four partnering locations, each with their associated possible Organisational Shapes.

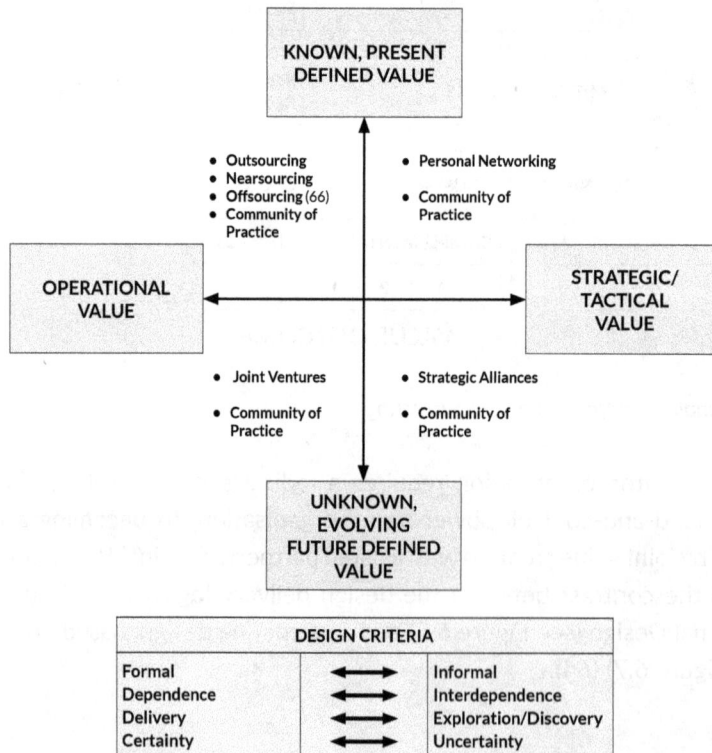

KNOWN, PRESENT DEFINED VALUE

- Outsourcing
- Nearsourcing
- Offsourcing (66)
- Community of Practice

- Personal Networking
- Community of Practice

OPERATIONAL VALUE

STRATEGIC/ TACTICAL VALUE

- Joint Ventures
- Community of Practice

- Strategic Alliances
- Community of Practice

UNKNOWN, EVOLVING FUTURE DEFINED VALUE

DESIGN CRITERIA		
Formal	⟷	Informal
Dependence	⟷	Interdependence
Delivery	⟷	Exploration/Discovery
Certainty	⟷	Uncertainty

Figure 6.36: Typical Partnering Organisational Shapes as a function of the value to be created

In identifying partnering opportunities with respect to the Strategic Horizontal Design, the necessary steps are as follows: (i) identify the strategic rationale for partnering relative to relationship(s) and value (see Figures 6.33 and 6.34); (ii) set up a basic partnering design delivery logic, based on a distributed, network organisation design (see Figure 6.35); and (iii) choose a fit-for-purpose Organisational Shape(s) as a function of the value to be created (see Figure 6.36).

The sole aim of Step A.2.4 is to identify partnering opportunities. In the Tactical Design, partnering designs will be architected for the opportunities selected. A detailed, outsourcing case study of Purchasing and Supply Management will be explicated in Chapter 9: Tactical Design.

The box gives an example of a total core value chain outsourcing by Benetton (67).

CASE STUDY: COMPLETE, TOTAL CORE VALUE CHAIN OUTSOURCING
Context
Benetton, the global fashion organisation
Organisational Design
Benetton has adopted the strategic role of 'Core value chain organiser'. This role involves the lead firm's organisation and management of its value chain in fashion wear, while actually owning few of the assets involved, and carrying out a limited set of strategic activities needed to create value. Prior to each fashion season, based on self-generated fashion intelligence, Benetton reconfigures its core fashion value chain given the predicted fashion needs of the upcoming season. Fashion Intelligence is its strategic, core organisational capability. It takes care of creating the patterns from the designers' drawings, dyes, the clothing, handles the logistics of distribution, and runs the advertising and marketing for the brand. It outsources the basic design work and most of the manufacturing for its products. It relies on retail outlets that are independently owned, although selling only Benetton products. It deals with these retailers through agents who are not Benetton employees. However, the outlets are linked to Benetton's information systems to track sales.

Design guidelines for partnering are given in the shaded box.

DESIGN GUIDELINES FOR PARTNERING

- A clear strategic rationale must exist for partnering.

- Choose a fit-for-purpose, patterning Organisational Shape(s) as a function of the value to be created.

- Never let go in a partnering relationship – that is, never 'outsource' – the Levels of Work: Strategic Intent and Strategic Translation (to be discussed under Strategic Vertical Design, Chapter 7) to an external partner(s). These Levels of Work are to remain at all times in the organisation. If the organisation does outsource them, it loses the strategic capability to render a proper judgement about the value delivered by the partnership relative to the organisational need to be satisfied by partnering.

- The 'outsourcing' organisation still remains ultimately *accountable* for the 'outsourced' work, although a partner is responsible for its delivery.

Quality assurance: Stage A.2: Strategic Horizontal Design

QUALITY ASSURANCE QUESTIONS *Step A.2: Strategic Horizontal Design – The Rooms making up the House*	DESIGN STEP	ADDRESSED: YES/NO *(Yes: +; No: x)*
Have **distinct Work Units with clear mandates and boundaries** been constructed – Operating, Enabling and Support Entities, a Corporate Centre and Board (if applicable)?	Step A.2.1	
Do the Work Units in total include all of the **work processes** required by the organisation to define, deliver and satisfy client needs?	Step A.2.1	
Has the **basic delivery logic** been clearly defined for the 'To-Be' design?	Step A.2.2.4	
Has the best **fit-for-purpose Organisational Shape** in light of the chosen basic delivery logic been chosen to configure the Work Units, (i) aligned to the organisation's Strategic Intent, meeting any (ii) sector/industry requirements, and (iii) fulfilling the Design Criteria and Design Vision with the Design Metaphor?	Step A.2.2.5	
Are the **strengths of the chosen Organisational Design** truly capitalised on?	Step A.2.2.5	
Have any possible **weaknesses of the chosen Organisational Shape** been countered?	Step A.2.2.5	
Has a comprehensive but simple **Organisational Map** been drawn that visually represents the Strategic Horizontal Design faithfully?	Step A.2.2.8	
Has clear custodianship been established for the **crown jewels** of the organisation?	Step A.2.3	
Have possible **partnering opportunities** been identified for value-adding partnering?	Step A.2.4	

Conclusion

This chapter dealt with Step A.2: Strategic Horizontal Design – The Rooms making up the House. The objective of Step A.2 was to determine the Work Units making up the organisation and configure them into a fit-for-purpose Organisational Shape, resulting in the Strategic Horizontal Design. Metaphorically speaking, the aim is to identify and demarcate *all* of the Rooms making up the House, and architect the House Plan: how do all of the Rooms fit together relative to each other?

More specifically, the outcomes of Step A.2.1 would be: (i) clearly mandated and demarcated Work Units, containing all of the work processes of the organisation; (ii) a clear basic delivery logic for the organisation; (iii) an overall Organisational Shape; (iii) single accountabilities for the organisation's crown jewels; and (iv) organisational partnering possibilities.

The next chapter addresses the Strategic Vertical and Lateral Designs as the next steps in the Strategic Design process.

Endnotes

(1) Overall references for this chapter are as per (1) in the previous chapter, with additionally Goold & Campbell (2002b).

(2) Three other typologies of organisational units are given below. It is interesting to note that none of them include the Board as a Work Unit.

(i) Mintzberg (see Mintzberg, 1993; 1997; Matheson, 2009).

For Mintzberg, the organisation is the sum total of the ways in which it divides its work into distinct tasks and then sets up coordination among them. Six *coordinating mechanisms* are distinguished: (1) mutual adjustment; (2) direct supervision; (3) standardisation of work processes; (4) standardisation of work outputs; (5) standardisation of skills; and (6) standardisation of norms.

The different coordinating mechanisms result in different organisational structures, which comprise nine design parameters and six basic organisational parts. The nine *design parameters* are: job specialisation; formalisation; training and indoctrination; unit grouping; unit size; planning and control systems; and liaison devices.

The six *organisational parts* – directly relevant here – are: (1) the *operating core* that does the basic work of the organisation; (2) the strategic apex: managers who are located at the top of the organisation; (3) the middle line that links the strategic apex to the operating core; (4) the technostructure: analysts who standardise others' work; (5) the support staff who enable the functioning of the operating core indirectly, such Finance, R&D, HR, Legal; and (6) the organisation's "ideology", which is a force rather than a part because it is all-pervasive within the organisation.

(ii) Goold & Campbell (2002b).

Type of Unit*	Description	Examples
Parent	Upper unit levels that carry out obligatory corporate tasks and influence and add value to other units	Corporate/Divisional HQs
Business Units	Market-focused, profit-responsible units	Business Divisions
Business Functions	Operating functions	Manufacturing, Sales
Overlay Units	Market-focused units, serving segments defined along dimensions that cut across Business Units	Country Unit
Sub-businesses	Market-focused units, serving segments defined at a more disaggregated level than Business Units	Regional Unit
Core Resource Units	Units that develop and nurture scarce resources that are key to the competitive advantage of Business Units	R&D

| Shared Service Units | Units that provide services needed by other units | Finance, HRM, IT |
| Project Units | Units which carry out tasks/projects that cut across other units, normally for a finite period of time | Enterprise Resource Planning (ERP) system for organisation |

*A decision has to be taken whether a unit will be a cost, revenue, or profit centre.

    (iii)   Bellerby (2017): Business Units, Service Units, Project Units, Corporate Centre, Integrating Units, Strategic Units, Global Strategic Centre.

   (3)   Based on the author's experience, drawn on and enriched by socio-technical systems design principles (cf. Pasmore, 1988; Daniels, Le Blanc & Davis, 2014; Parker, Morgeson & Johns, 2017), as well as Mintzberg (1993); (1997); ICI Chemical & Polymers Ltd. (1989) and Nadler & Tushman (1988).

   (4)   Updated and expanded from Veldsman (2015a).

   (5)   Author constructed. See also Silva & Guerrini (2018).

   (6)   Ghosal & Bartlett (1998).

   (7)   Cf. Bersin, O'Reilly, Magoulas & Loukides (2019); Burton, Obel & Håkonsson (2015); Fjeldstad, Snow, Miles & Lettl (2012); Goold & Campbell (2002b); Goold & Campbell (2003); Gulati, Puranam & Tushman (2012).

   (8)   Bals (2017); Lee & Edmondson (2018); Loñar (2005); McDowell, Agarwal, Miller, Okamoto & Page (2016); Schilling & Steensma (2000).

   (9)   Bals (2017).

  (10) Fisher (2005); Semco (2019); Semler (1989); (1994); Van Eeden (2019).

  (11) Adapted from Roberts (2004) and supplemented with Inamizu, Fukuzawa, Fujimoto, Shintaku & Suzuki (2014).

  (12) Galbraith (2008); (2014); Kates & Galbraith (2007); Kessler & Kates (2010). This Strategic Intent typology resembles losely Porter's (1980) well known strategy typology of cost leadership, product differentiation, market focus.

  (13) R.E. Miles and C.C. Snow match the following Organisational Shapes to their four Strategic Intents as per the table below (Burton, Obel & Håkonsson, 2015). The Shapes mentioned in the table will be discussed in detail under Step A.2.2.5.

STRATEGIC INTENT	ORGANISATIONAL SHAPE
Reactor: adjust to context	Simple – low on functional and customer/product/ service differentiation. Typical start-up, entrepreneurial organisation, led by a single leader
Defender: maintain status quo	Functional
Prospector: discover/create new opportunities – a market leader	Divisional
Analyser: with (combination of Defender and Prospector) or without innovation (imitates what others are doing successfully by doing more efficiently, quick second mover)	Matrix

  (14) For example, Bellerby (2017); Brickley, Smith & Zimmerman (2003); Capelle (2017); Burton, Obel & Håkonsson (2015); Kates & Galbraith (2007); Nadler & Tushman (1988).

  (15) Same references as per (13).

  (16) Constructed by the author, based on Goold & Campbell (2002b); Stanford (2015); Brickley, Smith & Zimmerman (2003); Bellerby (2017); Galbraith (2014); Huber (2011); Kesler & Kates (2011); Galbraith, Lawler & Associates (1993); Burton, Obel & Håkonsson (2015); Kates, A. & Galbraith, J.R. (2007); Miles, Snow, Fjeldstad, Miles & Lettl (2010); Nadler & Tushman (1988). The subsequent discussion of the respective organisational shapes are also based on these references. For some Organisational Shapes, additional references were used and are listed.

  (17) Instead of the conventional Shapes given in Figure 6.9, Mintzberg (1981); (1993); (1997) proposes five Organisational Configurations (= Shapes): (i) Simple Structure – autocratic or charismatic (direct supervision, strategic apex); (ii) Machine Bureaucracy (standardisation of work processes, technostructure); (iii) Professional Bureaucracy (standardisation of skills, operating core); (iv) Divisional Form (standardisation of work outputs, middle line); and (v) Adhocracy (mutual adjustment, support staff). See above Note (2) for an explanation of the terms in brackets that indicate the core element(s) of a configuration.

  (18) Also called the Unitary-form, U-form (Miles, Snow, Fjeldstad, Miles & Lettl, 2010).

(19) Also called the horizontal organisation (Ostroff, 1999), process-centred organisation (Hammer, 1996), enterprise organisation (Hammer & Stanton, 1999), process-focused organisation (Gardner, 2004), or simply the process organisation (quoted in Kohlbacher & Reijers, 2013).

(20) There are various names in the literature for this organisational shape, like project-based organisation (Hobday, 2000; Turner & Keegan, 2001, Sydow et al., 2004), firm (Lindkvist, 2004; Prencipe & Tell, 2001; Whitley, 2006) or company (Jerbrant, 2013; Lundin et al., 2015), multi-project firm (Geraldi, 2008; 2009), multi-project organisation/firm (Canonico & Söderlund, 2010), project-intensive firm (Söderlund & Bredin 2006), projectified matrix organisation (Arvidsson, 2009), project-oriented organisation (Huemann, 2014; 2015) or company (Gareis, 1990, 2005; Gareis & Huemann, 2007; Huemann et al., 2007) (quoted by Miterev, Turner & Mancini, 2017a; 2017b).

(21) See additionally Kohlbacher & Reijers (2013) and Leyer, Stumpf-Wollersheim & Pisani (2017).

(22) Draws on Aubry & Lavoie-Tremblay (2018); Miterev, Mancini & Turner (2017a); (2017b) and Whitley (2006).

(23) Turner et al. (2010) (Quoted by Miterev, Turner & Mancini, 2017a).

(24) Sourced from Whitley (2006).

(25) Draws on the references listed under (22).

(26) A description of co-operatives was given under Step A.0: Profile of Organisation – Nature of organisation, Chapter 5. The map was sourced from Skurnik (1999), obtained from www.pellervo.fi.

(27) Bateman & Novkovic (2015); Birchall (2011); Davis (2001); Dubb (2016); Mazzarol, Limnios & Reboud (2011); Normark (1996); Novkovic (2008); Puusa, Mönkkönen & Varis (2013); Skurnik (1999); Spear (2000); Zamagni & Zamagani (2010).

(28) Given this significant weakness of the Mirror Image/Matrix Shape, Goold & Campbell (2003) suggest the Structured Network shape as a modified, matrix shape. In structured networks, the self-managing organisational units retain considerable autonomy as in a matrix, but are supplemented by extensive, formalised collaboration though voluntary networking between units. The aim is to reap the benefits of interdependence of a typical matrix, but without sacrificing clear responsibilities, managerial initiative and accountability, speed of decision-making, and a lean hierarchy between units. Structured networks avoid the problems of matrices by keeping the amount of structure, process and central influence to a minimum, but simultaneously complement their autonomy with enough shared structure and process to enable structured collaboration.

(29) Also called multi-divisional shape, the M-form (Miles, Snow, Fjeldstad, Miles & Lettl, 2010).

(30) Discussion draws on Burton, Obel & Håkonsson (2015); Fjeldstad, Snow, Miles & Lettl (2012); Gulati, Puranam & Tushman (2012); Mathieu (2012); Miles & Snow (1995); Miles, Snow, Fjeldstad, Miles & Lettl (2010); Poole & Contractor (2012); Schilling & Steensma (2001); Silva & Guerrini (2018); Thorelli (1986); Zaccaro, Marks & DeChurch (2012).

(31) See references given under (29).

(32) Booz Allen Hamilton & Kellogg School of Management, Northwestern University (Unfortunately the specific reference could not be tracked down).

(33) Gulati, Puranam & Tushman (2012).

(34) Miles, Snow, Fjeldstad, Miles & Lettl (2010).

(35) Mathieu (2012); Poole & Contractor (2012); Zaccaro, Marks & DeChurch (2012).

(36) Gulati, Puranam & Tushman (2012), but also Burton, Obel & Håkonsson (2015).

(37) Adapted and expanded from Gulati, Puranam & Tushman (2012).

(38) Bals (2017); Lee & Edmondson (2018); Loñar (2005); McDowell, Agarwal, Miller, Okamoto & Page (2016); Schilling & Steensma (2000).

(39) Gulati, Puranam & Tushman (2012).

(40) Fjeldstad, Snow, Miles & Lettl (2012); Gulati, Puranam & Tushman (2012); Jemielniak (2014).

(41) Cf. Jemielniak, 2014.

(42) See Nielsen (2018) for an insightful discussion of crowdfunding, which he calls in design language, a "partial organisation".

(43) Crowdsourcing is but one example of the sharing economy, according to Sundararajan (2016) (see MacDonald's (2018) book review). It is represented by organisations such as Uber, Airbnb, Lyft, Etsy, TaskRabbit, BlaBlaCar, EatWith, and Thumbtack, to name but a few. According to MacDonald, Sundararajan argues that the sharing economy has these five characteristics, two of which are relevant here for the purpose of my book: (i) crowd-based 'networks' rather than centralised institutions

or 'hierarchies': the supply of capital and labour comes from decentralised crowds of individuals rather than corporate or state aggregates. Future exchange may be mediated by distributed crowd-based marketplaces rather than by centralised third parties; and (ii) the blurring of lines between fully employed and casual labour, between independent and dependent employment, and between work and leisure. Many traditionally full-time jobs are being supplanted by contract work that features a continuum of levels of time commitment, granularity, economic dependence, and entrepreneurship.

According to MacDonald, Sundararajan further contends that efficiency has a morally significant value: firms and services within the sharing economy have found innovative ways to free up underutilised capital and labour by leveraging digital technology to connect under-served consumers with under-utilised goods and labour. According to Sundararajan, our society is characterised by massive, pervasive waste in the form of excess, unused capacity. Using that capacity in order to improve lives would be good. The value-add of the shared economy efficiency-wise is potentially enormous and morally important. This contention of Sundararajan is an excellent example of the virtuous delivery logic mode (see Chapter 2 regarding the TSV delivery logic incorporated in the Operating Model of the organisation).

(44) Burton, Obel & Håkonsson (2015); Collis, Young & Goold (2012); Galbraith (2000); Kates & Galbraith (2007).

(45) Collis, Young & Goold (2012); Donaldson & Joffe (2015); Galbraith (2000); Liao (2017); Owen (2017); Perlmutter (1969).

(46) This figure, and the subsequent Figures 6.28 and 6.29, were constructed by the author.

(47) Author's own consulting work on virtual organisations, sourced from and complemented by Curseu (2006); Ferazzi (2014); Gilson, Maynard, Jones Young, Vartiainen & Hakonen (2015); Kelliher & Richardson (2012); Lee et al. (2007); Liao (2017); Lu et al. (2006); Makarius & Larson (2017); Orhan (2014); Rosen (2009); Schmidtke & Cummings (2017); Skekhar (2006); Walters (2005); Webster & Wong (2008); Zaccaro, Marks & DeChurch (2012); Zhang & Fjermestad (2006).

(48) Murray (2015); Stein (2015); The Economist (2015).

(49) Makarius & Larson (2017).

(50) References the same as for (11).

(51) Schmidtke & Cummings (2017).

(52) Makarius & Larson (2017).

(53) See Hawken (2010); Lawler & Worley (2012) and Lawler & Conger (2015), who clearly elucidate how sustainability must infuse the organisation into its very being. Cf. also Veldsman (2015b).

(54) Stanford (2015) also suggests developing options before deciding on a final design.

(55) Source: Author.

(56) Source: Author.

(57) Source: Author.

(58) De Guerre, Se Guin, Pace & Burkeida (2013) in their discussion of their redesign journey of the School of Extended Learning at Concordia University, Montreal, give a good example of the use of an Organisational Map to graphically depict their design solution, called Institutional Goals.

(59) Goold & Campbell (2000b).

(60) For example, Eisenhardt & Martin (2000); Gottschalk (2014) and Prahalad & Hamel (1990).

(61) This section draws heavily on ASHE Higher Education Report (2010); Bugnar, Mester & Petrica Dana (2009); Doz & Hamel (1998); Eckel & Hartley (2009); Elmuti, Abebe & Nicolosi (2005); Gadman & Cooper (2005); Jarillo (1993); Kale & Singh (2009); Nohri & Eccles (1992); Stein (2015); The Economist (2010); Veldsman (2011); (2015a);.

(62) Constructed by the author.

(63) Constructed by the author.

(64) Constructed by the author.

(65) Constructed by the author. Cf. also Liu, Sarala, Xing & Cooper (2017).

(66) Offshoring refers to the relocation of organisational tasks and services to foreign locations. The rationale for offshoring is lower manufacturing wages, lower delivery costs of work processes and high level talent shortages. The challenge for the offshoring organisation is how to coordinate and integrate geographically dispersed activities across far distances (Ørberg Jensen, Larsen & Pedersen, 2013). Nearshoring is within-country outsourcing.

(67) Roberts (2004).

7

STRATEGIC ORGANISATIONAL DESIGN

Architecting the overall Organisational Shape: Strategic Vertical and Lateral Designs

---

"Leaders are not responsible for success. Leaders are responsible for the people who are responsible for the results."

(Simon Sinek)

"Coming together is a beginning;
Keeping together is progress;
Working together is success"

(Henry Ford)

The purpose of Step A.2: Strategic Horizontal Design was to architect a House Plan for the organisation, in this way arriving at the organisation's overall Organisational Shape. The crafting of the Strategic Vertical and Lateral Designs come next respectively in the Strategic Design process. The purpose of this chapter is to elucidate these two designs (1).

Strategic Vertical Design encompasses architecting the requisite Levels of Work to be performed by the organisational overall, as well as each of its Work Units. The Strategic Horizontal and Vertical Designs demarcate the work of the organisation into Work Units and Levels of Work with the commensurate governance model, respectively, the differentiating dimension (or division of labour) of the design process. Strategic Lateral Design pertains to architecting the Integration Mechanisms for the interdependencies across Work Units and crafting the organisation's Governance Model: how we must live together in the House. Strategic Lateral Design integrates the differentiated parts of the organisation resulting from the Strategic Horizontal and Vertical Design into a systemic whole.

Figure 7.1 depicts the relative location by arrows of the steps making up the Strategic Vertical and Lateral Designs in the Strategic Design Route Map.

Step A.0: Profile of Organisation – Nature of organisation

A.0.1: Demarcate Organisation

Step A.1: Foundation Construction – Building materials of House

A.1.1: Profile Organisational Context
A.1.2: Map Work Processes
A.1.3: Determine Core Operating Technology with Enablers
A.1.4: Identify Design Givens
A.1.5: Formulate Design Criteria with Design Vision
A.1.6: Diagnose Existing Design – Strengths & Weaknesses

Step A.2: Strategic Horizontal Design – Rooms making up the House

A.2.1: Group Work Processes into Work Units
A.2.2: Configure Work Units into an Organisational Shape
A.2.3: Allocate Crown Jewels
A.2.4: Identify Partnering opportunities

Step A.3: Strategic Vertical Design – Type of ownership and owners of Rooms

A.3.1: Decide on requisite Level of Work of organisation overall
A.3.2: Architect House Ownership Model
A.3.3: Allocate requisite Levels of Work to Work Units
A.3.4: Identify mission critical Work Roles at Work Unit Leadership Level & generate high level Role Profiles

Step A.4: Strategic Lateral Design – Living together in the House

A.4.1: Construct an Interdependency Matrix
A.4.2: Decide on Integration Mechanisms
A.4.3: Set up Governance Model

Step A.5: Integrated Strategic Design and Charter – Overall House Plan

A.5.1: Compile Organisational Map
A.5.2: Draw high level Organogram
A.5.3: Draft Organisational Charter

Step A.6: Strategic Organisational Alignment – Fitting House into Town House Complex

A.6.1: Leadership Alignment
A.6.2: Cultural Alignment
A.6.3: People Alignment
A.6.4: Resources Alignment
A.6.5: Performance Alignment
A.6.6: Work Place Alignment

Step A.7: Strategic Design Impact Assessment – Existing vs. New Houses

A.7.1: Conduct Gap & Risk Analysis

Step A.8: Strategic Design Implementation Road Map – Planning how to build the House

A.8.1: Craft Design Roll Out Strategy & Plan
A.8.2: Craft Organisational Change Navigation Strategy & Plan

Step A.9: Strategic Design Solution Report

Step A.10: Strategic Design Implementation – Building the House

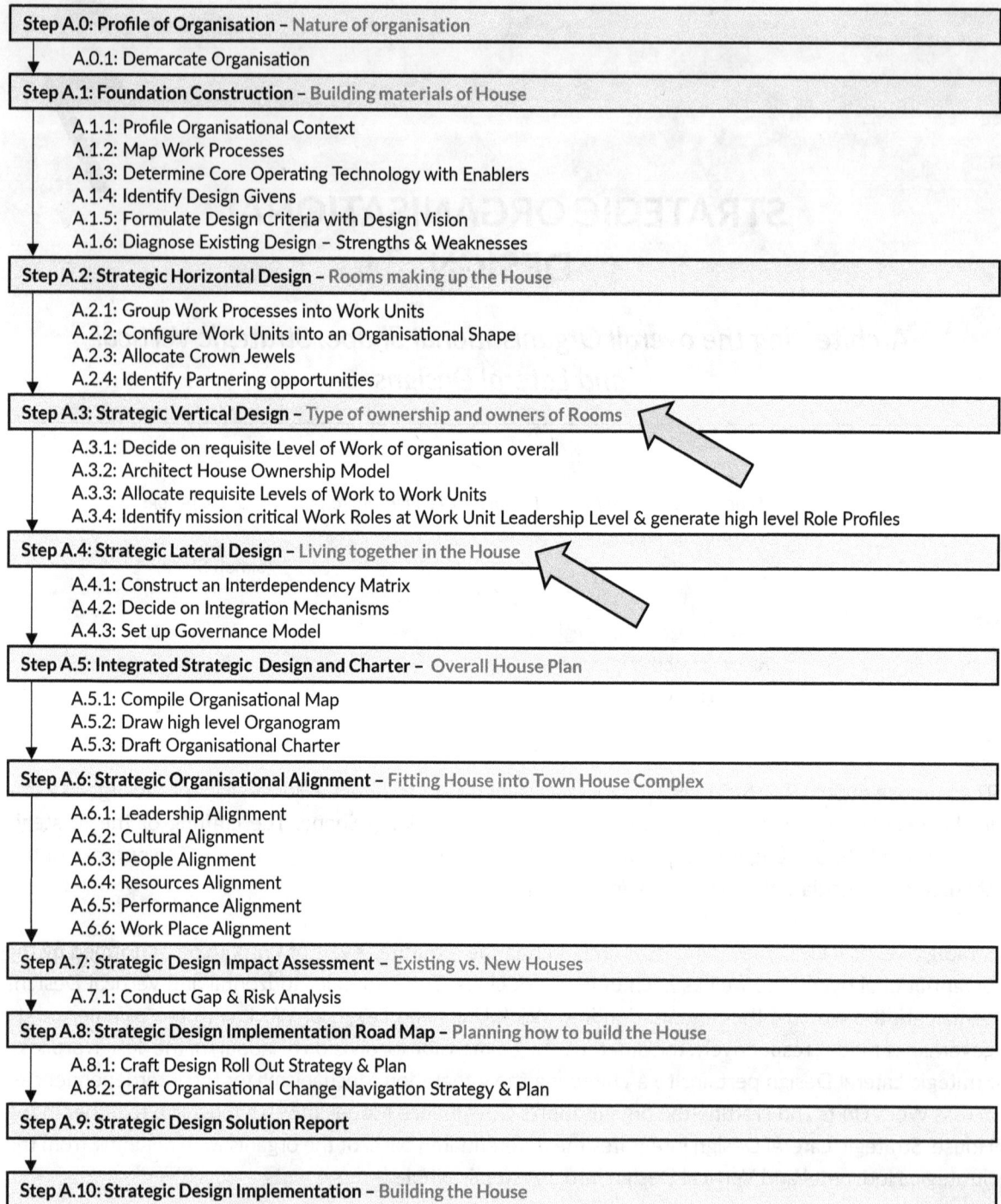

Figure 7.1: Strategic OD route map
Note: Part of Phase 3: Step 3.2 of the OD life cycle (see Chapter 4)

Strategic Vertical Design will first be discussed, followed by Strategic Lateral Design.

Step A.3: Strategic Vertical Design (2)

The objective of Step A.3: Strategic Vertical Design is to define the requisite Levels of Work for the organisation overall, as well as the respective Work Units, with their commensurate Work Roles as contained in Strategic Horizontal Design. The key issue is: what requisite Levels of Work are required for the organisation overall and each Room in the House and their associated Work Roles?

The crux of Strategic Vertical Design revolves around deciding on the requisite Levels of Work (LOW) to be performed:

- *First*, the LOW of the organisation overall.

- *Second*, the distribution of LOWs between the Board of Directors (hereafter called 'Board') relative to the organisation, as well as the Corporate Centre (traditionally called the 'Head Office') and its Work Units: the House Ownership Model of the organisation.

- *Third*, the allocation of the requisite LOWs to Work Units.

- *Fourth*, the identification and profiling of the mission-critical Work Roles with their commensurate LOWs in order to 'anchor' the design at a Strategic level.

This action is made up of four sub-steps (see Figure 7.1 above):

- A.3.1: Decide on the requisite LOW for the organisation overall.

- A.3.2: Architect the House Ownership Model.

- A.3.3: Allocate the requisite LOWs to Work Units.

- A.3.4: Identify the mission-critical Work Roles with their LOWs at Work Unit Leadership Level, and generate high level Role Profiles.

As a conceptual framework for Strategic Vertical Design, Stratified Systems Theory provides an insightful, handy way of conceptualising LOWs with their respective requisite complexities (3). Seven LOWs can be distinguished, from the highest LOW7: Corporate prescience (that is leading a global system) through to the lowest LOW1: Quality (that is daily operational delivery). Table 7.1 provides an overview of the seven LOWs (4).

Important to note with respect to Table 7.1 is the addition of *contextual complexity* (see Table 5.2) to the 'classic' LOWs as an essential, additional source of complexity. I would like to contend that the requisite complexity of the respective LOWs – which focuses on organisational Work Roles only – is mediated by the organisation's Operating Arena with its commensurate contextual complexity, in which the Work Roles with their LOWs are embedded and have to be performed. For example, LOW5: Strategic Intent will look qualitatively and significantly different complexity-wise than a high Contextual Complexity context, although it still remains strategic work at LOW5. Strategic Intent work at LOW5 is different for the solely owned supermarket in a suburb to that a national retailer, which in turn looks different for a global retailer operating over multiple countries. Yet it still remains LOW5 work despite the differences in contextual complexity across the three Operating Arenas.

Thus:

Total Work Requisite Complexity = Requisite LOW of Work Roles x Requisite Contextual Complexity of organisation's Operating Arena

Table 7.1: Overview of the respective Levels of Work

SHIFTS IN TYPICAL WORK CONTEXT CHARACTERISTICS	LEVEL OF WORK	THEME OF WORK	WORK SETTING	WORK ELEMENTS	TYPICAL DECISION TIME HORIZON	TYPICAL WORK ROLES
From LOW1 to LOW7 • Predictable, certain to unpredictable, ambiguous • Tangible, visible variables to intangible, invisible variables • Facts to fuzzy probabilities • Simple, ordered to complex, chaotic • Linear causality to systemic patterns • Single to multiple variables/dimensions • Past/present-into-future to future-into-present	7: Corporate Presence	Global influence and presence	World at large	• World/global mindsets, philosophies, policies, and systems	20 years plus	Global System Leader
	6: Corporate Citizenship	Industry protection and enhancement Business oversight/ longevity	Industry, locally and internationally Board	• Context shaping • Corporate Governance	10-20 years	Industry leader Board Director
	5: Strategic Intent	Strategy crafting	Organisation	• Returns/yields • Direction, objectives, philosophy	5 to 10 years	CEO/MD
	4: Strategic Translation/ Implementation	Strategy Realisation	Organisational Function	• Organisational policies and standards • Organisational systems • Organisation Functional direction, objectives, philosophy, return/yields	3-5 years	Enterprise/ Work Unit Executive Functional Executives
	3: Operational Execution	Practice	End-to-end Work (Unit) process	• Resourcing • Work delivery processes	2 to 3 years	Process Leader

SHIFTS IN TYPICAL WORK CONTEXT CHARACTERISTICS	LEVEL OF WORK	THEME OF WORK	WORK SETTING	WORK ELEMENTS	TYPICAL DECISION TIME HORIZON	TYPICAL WORK ROLES
	2: Operational Practices	Service	Work Sub-Unit	• Delivery standards	1 year	Front Line Leader (= Supervisor)
	1: Operational Delivery	Quality	Work station	• Daily delivery	Up to 3 months	Operator/ Practitioner
CONTEXTUAL COMPLEXITY **Low to High:** • Footprint: Physical and/or virtual • Thinking time horizon • Scope of, and variety within organisation • Degree and rate of change						

* Note: These are typical time horizons. It could be argued that the higher the contextual complexity, the longer the time horizon must be. Inversely, the more revolutionary the change, the shorter the horizon

In what follows, the LOWs depicted in Table 7.1 are used to architect the Vertical Design of the organisation. It is also an ideal way in which to broadband the organisation in terms of the appropriate number of organisational levels (5). The box gives a case study of such a broadbanding application in the Strategic Vertical Redesign of a niche bank (6).

CASE STUDY: BROADBANDING OF A NICHE BANK

Context: The niche bank had at least 8-10 organisational levels with close on 100 job descriptions, of which probably only 15% to 20% were up-to-date at any given point in time.

Need: To broadband the design and reduce the need for so many job descriptions.

Solution: The requisite LOW of the organisation was LOW5. Six LOW bands – in contrast to the existing 8-10 organisational levels – were designed, the out-of-the-ordinary exception being an Administrative LOW, for example, messengers, filers, tea makers, below the conventional LOW1. Five Competency Domains were defined, sitting vertically across the six LOWs: Business Mastery; Technical/Professional Competence; Leadership/ Managerial Competence; Personal, Interpersonal and Organisational Competencies; and Capacity to Learn and Apply Learning.

Behaviourally based competency outputs were written in the form of statements for each Competency Domain at the LOW concerned. A Work Profile was crafted for each LOW. Thus only six Profiles were created for the total organisation, in contrast to nearly 100 job descriptions. The additional advantage of the competency outputs was that they could be used for performance contracting and appraisal.

Altogether, the organisation was profiled on six pages in terms of a Matrix of LOWs by Competencies. An extract of the Matrix is given below as an example.

LEVEL OF WORK	BUSINESS MASTERY *Understanding of how business operates; what the key business issues are; and how they impact on the success of the business*	TECHNICAL/ PROFESSIONAL COMPETENCE *Ability to apply knowledge, skills and expertise appropriately to the complexity of the setting*	LEADERSHIP/MANAGERIAL COMPETENCE *Ability to develop and mobilise people around a shared vision and values, and lead people towards actualising the vision and living the values*
5: Strategic Formulation (SF) *Establish Strategic Intent for business; able to sustain the business within 3 to 5 year time horizon as a viable, profitable entity.*	• Understand the business of the business in an integrated manner, now and in the future, and its critical success factors. • Able to determine, attract and deploy business level resources effectively relative to business needs in the present and future.	• Able to understand, deal with, and influence general business and industry specific trends over longer term. • Able to expand and/or redefine existing mental models, business rules and systems in order to enhance/sustain the future viability of the business.	• Develop vision, mission and values for total business. • Mobilise the total organisation around the vision, mission and values. • Identify necessary Strategic Initiatives to actualise vision and mission and obtain organisation-wide-buy-in for these initiatives.

LEVEL OF WORK	BUSINESS MASTERY *Understanding of how business operates; what the key business issues are; and how they impact on the success of the business*	TECHNICAL/ PROFESSIONAL COMPETENCE *Ability to apply knowledge, skills and expertise appropriately to the complexity of the setting*	LEADERSHIP/MANAGERIAL COMPETENCE *Ability to develop and mobilise people around a shared vision and values, and lead people towards actualising the vision and living the values*
4: Strategic Execution (SE) *Translate Strategic Intent into necessary business requirements by aligning business functionalities to strategic intent within 2 to 3 year time horizon.*	• Understand Division/Discipline in an integrated manner, as well as its link to the business and the continued success of the business. • Able to determine, attract, deploy and grow Divisional/Disciplinary resources effectively in order to meet Divisional/Disciplinary needs.	• Able to understand and act upon industry and functional/discipline trends over the medium term. • Able to expand and/or redefine Divisional/Discipline operating models and rules in order to enhance/sustain the future contribution of Division/Discipline to the ongoing success of the business.	• Formulate and implement Divisional/Disciplinary goals and plans aligned to the business Strategic Intent and bought into by Divisional/Disciplinary members. • Appropriately allocate responsibility, authority and accountability within Division/Discipline to enable the Division/Discipline to achieve its set outcomes.

188

LEVEL OF WORK	PERSONAL, INTERPERSONAL, AND ORGANISATIONAL COMPETENCIES *Ability to manage oneself and one's interpersonal relationships successfully, and function effectively in an organisational setting*	CAPACITY TO LEARN AND APPLY LEARNING *Ability to learn new things and use learning effectively by changing oneself and the setting in which one operates*
5: Strategy Formulation (SF) *Establish Strategic Intent for business; able to sustain business within 3 to 5 year time horizon as a viable, profitable entity.*	• Ability to assess and handle multiple demands and shifting priorities in an ever changing environment, and adjust personal behaviour accordingly. • Ability to understand and accommodate other persons' concerns, values, needs and attitudes relative to the business direction, challenges and priorities.	• Ability to see/create new business opportunities and translate them into new business ventures. • Assess diverse information from multiple sources, identify patterns and connections, and arrive at integrated, future directed conclusions.
4: Strategic Execution (SE) *Translate Strategic Intent into necessary business requirements by aligning business functionalities to strategic intent within 2 to 3 year time horizon.*	• Able to accept change and adopt one's approach and style across situations, individuals and groups. • Able to establish and maintain internal and external interpersonal relationships based on trust and openness.	• Keep abreast with latest developments and thinking in Division/Discipline through reading, networking, and skills enhancement events. • Seek out/gather all relevant information required for problem solving and decision-making with respect to business requirements as they relate to the Strategic Intent of the business.

However, even if the appropriate, requisite LOWs are awarded, Work Role incumbents can 'undermine', 'sabotage' and/or 'corrupt' the requisite LOWs, often unbeknown to themselves. The box shows how the Requisite LOW and/or Requisite Contextual Complexity can go wrong in terms of people taking up their Work Roles in their organisation within its Operating Arena (7).

UNDERMINING, SABOTAGE AND CORRUPTION OF LOWs BY WORK ROLE INCUMBENTS		
TRAP	**DESCRIPTION**	**SYMPTOMS**
Compression	When a Work Role incumbent at a particular LOW does his/her work at a lower LOW	• Role incumbents at a LOW feel overworked and incapable of meeting work demands because their peers at the same LOW are operating at lower LOWs • Slow/wrong thinking and decisions • Continuous crisis management and fire-fighting because the LOW is not performed at the requisite level • Micro-management: a lack of trust and a fear culture because of the encroachment of higher LOW leadership into lower LOW leadership's areas of accountability/responsibility
Vacuum	A direct consequence of Compression. Requisite work missing because of compressed LOW(s). No adequate work investment at right LOWs	• No time invested in exploring the strategic challenges faced by the organisation • Perceived lack of strategic direction and/or translation/implementation by leadership at lower LOWs • Newly developing contextual/competitive challenges catch organisation unprepared • Frenetic work activity at the missing LOWs because leaders are exceptionally busy but with the wrong work
Depression	A combination of Compression and Vacuum: run-down energy levels in organisation because space for autonomy at lower LOWs have become hemmed-in	• Loss of faith in the strategic direction of the organisation and its success, because the strategic work is not being done • Feelings of disempowerment and disablement at lower LOWs because of encroachment by higher leadership into lower LOWs • Leaders at strategic levels – LOW5 and LOW4 – believe leaders at lower LOWs shirk responsibility, lack initiative, and fear innovation. However, the lower LOWs have been granted little freedom to act • Leaders at lower LOWs delegate their responsibilities upward through abdication and become passive ("waiting for instructions") because they do not have the necessary autonomy to act

UNDERMINING, SABOTAGE AND CORRUPTION OF LOWs BY WORK ROLE INCUMBENTS		
TRAP	**DESCRIPTION**	**SYMPTOMS**
Pull-down	Leaders at higher LOWs are pulled down by the inexperience or incompetence of leaders at lower LOWs – whose work they have to do and/or supervise them operationally more closely	• Leaders at higher LOWs are continuously involved doing the work that is supposed to be done by lower LOWS, and/or in dealing with crises at lower LOWs
Inflation	A push by role incumbents at lower LOWs to be involved in a hands-on way at a higher LOW(s), as if they are accountable for work at the higher Level(s). It could lead to an abdication of work at their LOW because they claim falsely that they cannot be held accountable for outputs at their LOW, because they are not adequately involved at the higher (strategic) LOW	• Never-ending upward consultation and relentless demands for the setting up of numerous, superfluous working groups/committees • Lack of strategic work getting done because of excessive demands to be consulted and overbearing interference by lower LOW leadership • Neglect of own LOW because of superfluous, over-extended involvement at higher LOWs
Showmanship	Role incumbent functions at their requisite LOW but overemphasises the short term, 'glamorous' work of their LOW that will earn them high public credit in the right places at the right time in order to promote their career ambitions	• Perennial grand standing and seeking of ongoing public recognition • Pursuit of predominantly short term gains, visible in the right places, to the detriment of invisible, longer term work investments and pay-back times • Always seeking an unnecessary presence with the 'right' people who will be able to open doors for them • Rationalisation of, and defensiveness to, failures and oversights because of not doing a full set of work at their LOW
Misfit	Inability to attain a good fit between LOW and the context with its commensurate contextual complexity, setting the requirements for the work that has to be delivered	• Narrowing down of the size of the LOW's contextual radar screen in order to make overwhelming contextual signals manageable for Work Role incumbent • Inability by Work Role incumbent to build a complete, 'big' picture that covers the full context at their requisite LOW • Overemphasis by Work Role incumbent of only certain contextual dimensions and trends – the easy to handle parts, at the cost of neglecting other significant dimensions and trends – the tough parts too difficult to handle

Step A.3.1: Decide on the requisite Level of Work for the organisation overall

The first step in Strategic Vertical Design is to identify the requisite LOW (that is the highest LOW) to be performed by the organisation overall, typically lodged in the Work Role of the top organisational leader, for example, the CEO/MD. Highly autonomous, independent organisations are at least LOW5 organisations. That is, they have to do the strategic work required by LOW5 independently. Organisations that dominate their sectors/industries, especially globally, are at least LOW6 or even LOW7 organisations when they are the unquestionable leaders in (re)inventing sectors/industries. Subsequently, the cascading, lower LOWs in the organisation are pegged against the highest requisite LOW awarded to the organisation overall.

The criticality of awarding the right requisite LOWs to an organisation, its Work Units, and Work Roles cannot be overemphasised. The severe implications of awarding LOWs incorrectly is illustrated in the box by a case study of an organisation – the Red Cross – having too low a LOW (8).

REDESIGNING A GLOBAL, COMMUNITY ORGANISATION TO DEAL WITH INCREASING COMPLEXITY
CONTEXT
The International Federation of Red Cross and Red Crescent Societies, simply known as the Red Cross, is the largest international humanitarian organisation in the world. Its purpose is to improve the situation of the most vulnerable people in the world through the coordination of disaster relief, and providing them with the capacity to cope. It delivers in some of the toughest conditions around the world.

The Red Cross operates directly and indirectly in nearly every country of the world through 16 regional offices and 185 national societies. The organisation has four official languages. At the time of the case study it comprised a total of 97 million members and volunteers and 298,000 paid staff members, who in turn provided service to 233 million people on an annual basis. It had some $24 billion (CND) in annual expenditures. The critical demand on the Red Cross is on how to effectively and efficiently use donor or taxpayer dollars in pursuing its purpose.

Beyond the need to have an organisation that can move swiftly in its relief operations, the International Federation also has the responsibility for the development of National Red Cross and Red Crescent Societies, with the intention of making them self-sufficient in terms of domestic programmes; enabling them to deal with disasters of a local nature; and having the capacity to be the first wave of response to cataclysmic disasters requiring international assistance.

The International Federation acts as a permanent body liaison amongst the National Societies. It also represents the collective interests of its member national societies in their dealings with other inter-governmental bodies and international organisations, such as the United Nations (UN). The International Federation is governed by a General Assembly that meets every two years. It is made up of the entire membership of national societies and observers (UN and other international organisations), with some 800 people in the body. The Secretary General is held to account to this body for the activities and operations of the International Federation.

OD NEED

When George Weber took over as Secretary General in 1992, the Red Cross was operating as a requisite LOW5 organisation. He inherited a Secretariat Headquarters in Geneva, Switzerland, with 12 regional offices. At that time the International Federation was assisting about 15 million people globally through its relief operations. It had 149 member national societies around the world.

During his mandate – from 1993 to 2000 – the regional offices grew by about 30 percent. In addition, there were 50+ country offices around the world, a number that rose or fell on almost a monthly basis, dependent upon various major relief operations in any country around the world. He had some 5,000+ Secretariat employees of 92 different nationalities working worldwide.

The organisation was faced with increasing demands. First, the sheer number of people who had been displaced by natural calamities and political upheavals was escalating. Second, the complexities were rising in dealing with different types and increasing numbers of security issues internationally. Third, as national societies were created and developed new capacities, they wanted different types of assistance to further evolve their capacity by having local people trained instead of bringing in foreigners to do the work. While this increased overall capability, it also increased the complexity of disaster operations, being now a combination of locals and foreigners. Fourth, there were also requests for the International Federation to provide more timely services and different types of services to the National Societies as they increased in strength.

Fifth, there were increasingly insistent calls from donors for more accountability and transparency by the Red Cross. As most of the funding was raised from governments, the Secretariat had to be accountable for reporting in their diverse formats and meeting their different standards. Having dealings with 30 different governments, each with its own systems, meant that the International Federation had to do intense, customised reporting.

Sixth, the Secretariat had greater volumes of information requiring specialised, customised diagnoses. Seventh, the context was increasingly competitive because more humanitarian organisations were developing international programming. Eighth, there was a desire to maximise effectiveness with available resources. There was money for direct assistance and operations, but not a lot more money to deal with the core infrastructure. There was a need to expand services, enhance competencies, and handle a larger and more difficult workload, but with very similar resources.

Despite these new, pressing needs, staffing at the Geneva Headquarters was not keeping pace. The Geneva staff complement remained relatively constant during Weber's term of office, while the delegated and locally hired staff fluctuated depending on the number and size of the disaster relief operations under way.

The Secretary General had 16 direct reports at different levels. Thus functional alignment was not ideal. As the new CEO, Weber needed to travel six to seven months a year in order to energise the organisation to realise its potential, to get the national societies and donors to cooperate with the Secretariat, and to deal with governments.

In summary, this period during Weber's tenure was marked by increasing complexities, increasing demand, higher standards of accountability, the restricting budgetary requirement to meet these needs with the same or only slightly more resources, and increasing specialist information needs.

OD SOLUTION
The Design Vision was to enhance the organisation's quick response capability in disaster situations; address the increasing complexity of its international operations; and build the leadership capability of local areas. Fundamental to the Vision was a desire to do less with internal Secretariat resources. Also to engage, borrow, and use more National Society capacity to do some of the work, so that the Secretariat could better cope with its mandate. This led to a new Organisational Design, embraced in the concept of "Working as a Federation". Apart from other supporting organisational change recommendations, design-wise the key recommendation was that the Secretariat – and by implication the Secretary General Role – had to be positioned at a LOW6 to match the requisite complexities faced by the organisation. At LOW5, four new Under Secretary General roles were created: two Under Secretary General roles to head up respectively two core operating units, namely Disaster Response and Operating Coordination (DROC), which was accountable for both disaster response and operations coordination, and National Society Cooperation and Development (NSCD), which was accountable for relations with national societies and for spearheading the concept of "Working as a Federation". Additionally, two support Under Secretary roles were created for Finance and Administration and Communication and Policy Coordination. In this way the Secretary General's span of control was reduced from 16 to 9 direct reports. The organisation was further strengthened by the creation of five LOW3 regional departments, with Regional Directors and some desk officers similar to the situation in a foreign ministry. They were accountable for the delegations and the National Societies in their region. The three roles of Deputy Director, Head of Country Delegation, and Head of Regional Delegation were direct reports into the LOW5 Regional Director role.
BENEFITS
Overall the change process was a great success. In 1992 the International Federation had been handling some $410 million (CND) annually in appeals. For example, to assist a country's population to cope after a natural disaster or to help a country reinforce its infrastructure to deal with the effects of an armed conflict situation, such as refugee movement or internally displaced persons. By early 2000, appeals had grown by 54% to $631 million (CND) in relief operations, but the number of beneficiaries assisted had doubled. There were also an additional 27 National Red Cross/Red Crescent Societies, about an 18% increase. The International Federation was thus able to help more people. The number of beneficiaries doubled while the quality of service also improved. The donors supporting the International Federation increased their financial donations and provided more people and materials to achieve the International Federation's objectives. National Societies were therefore able to do more work. This was critical because it is the local people, at the community level, who respond in the first hours of a disaster who make the biggest difference. The capacity of the national societies to handle a threshold of numbers of people affected by various situations increased by at least 50%. Because of this increased sustainability, the International Federation was able to increase the overall range and scope of its activities. There was also greater, all round staff satisfaction.

Step A.3.2: Architect the House Ownership Model

Having decided on the requisite LOW for the organisation overall, the LOW ownership model for the organisation must be architected. Essentially this model pertains to two vertical relationships:

- *The relationship between the Board of Directors and the organisation*, specifically with its CEO/MD. The foundation of this relationship is to be based on how the Board defines its role relative to the CEO/MD of the organisation it oversees. In turn, its adopted role specifies the specific design of the Board, the details of which will be addressed during the Tactical Design (see Chapter 9).

- *The relationship between the Corporate Centre – essentially the 'office of the CEO/MD' – and the organisation's Work Units*, whether Operating, Enabling or Support (see Figure 6.2). In traditional language, this covers the relationship between the Head Office and the Work Units of the organisation. This relationship is all about the direction and control that will be exercised by the Corporate Centre over Work Units. The decision on the direction and control exercised by Centre defines the expected role of the Centre, the details of which will be discussed under Tactical Design (see Chapter 9).

Each relationship is discussed below with respect to the design of the House Ownership Model of the organisation.

The Board – CEO/MD House Ownership Model (9)

As a collective body, the Board of Directors of an organisation carries the highest and ultimate authority and accountability for protecting the interests of the organisation's stakeholders regarding the actions – actual and intended, present and future – taken by an organisation and its leadership relative to the Identity of the organisation. The Board is ultimately accountable to stakeholders for the soundness of the organisation's corporate governance.

Corporate governance (from the Latin "to steer, direct") has been described as the biggest issue facing business in the 21st century, especially in light of a number of significant corporate failures attributed directly, in many instances, to breakdowns in governance (10). This in spite of an abundance of corporate governance codes. For example, the UK's Cadbury Code and Combined Code, South Africa's King Code, Germany's Cromme, and Holland's Tabaksblat, as well as legislation to ensure compliance like America's Sarbanes-Oxley, and stock exchange reporting requirements.

The challenge to following a deliberate, explicit design process for Boards of Directors is that Board design receives virtually no, if any, attention in the design literature itself. Design pieces are considered but not shaped into a deliberate, comprehensive and integrated design process. It is readily assumed that given prescriptions – mostly regulatory, legislative and governance codes – are suffice design-wise to set up an effective and efficient Board. Such as, that design will happen automatically by mere compliance. I would like to strongly contend that this view is hugely detrimental to the likelihood of effective and efficient Boards. To have a truly fit-for-purpose Board, a deliberate, explicit design process is more than necessary – it is essential. This is the reason for the endeavour to map such a design process, as per the discussion below.

From a Strategic Vertical Design perspective, the Board – CEO/MD House Ownership Model is to be found in how the Board positions itself: what will its Operating Framework be? This framework is constituted by six interdependent questions to be answered through explicit, intense Board deliberations, in order to arrive at a coherent framework:

- *Its purpose:* why does the Board exist? The answer to this question provides the *raison d'être* for the Board – how does the Board see its corporate governance role with respect to the organisation it has to exercise oversight over? Essentially the purpose of the Board is to direct and guide the affairs of the organisation by meeting the legitimate interests/needs of its stakeholders in a fair and balanced fashion, such that the business is/remains prosperous and sustainable in the long term relative to its Identity. In terms of a Virtuous delivery logic mode (see the definition of OD, Chapter 2), Boards must be (re)purposed from a multi-stakeholder, sustainability effectiveness vantage point, necessitating that all of the organisation's most important stakeholders are represented on it (11). This is also the recommended route for organisations operating in emerging economies (see Contextual Variable 1, Chapter 5 regarding the organisation's Operating Arena).

- *Its vision:* what 'dream' does the Board have for the organisation for which it is performing this oversight role? What is the desired end state the Board wants to bring about through its value-adding contribution?

- *Its mandate:* who can act with what degree of autonomy? The answer to this question defines what type of Board it wishes to be in terms of its sphere of influence, relative to that of the CEO/MD and the organisation's executive team. Figure 7.2 depicts who the players are in the Board space, implicated by the mandate answer.

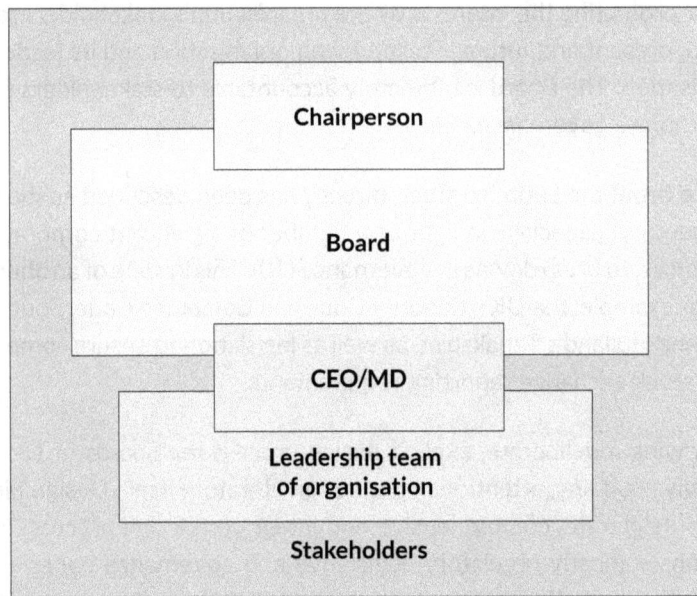

Figure 7.2: Players in the Board space

It is important to note with respect to the relative relationship between the different players that the Board's sole official connection with the organisation is through its CEO/MD. He/she is the only employee of the Board who is accountable for his/her appointment, orientation, development, performance and rewards. Only Board-passed motions are binding on the CEO/MD. From the Board's perspective, all authority, responsibility, accountability, and performance of the organisation's leadership equates to all the authority, accountability and performance of the CEO/MD. Thus the answer given to the mandate question by the Board impacts solely on the Board –

CEO/MD relationship. Of course, by implication upon the CEO/MD shoulders rests the quality of the organisation's relationship with the Board.

Figure 7.3 depicts three types of Boards in terms of their mandates, forming the basis of the Board – CEO/MD House Ownership Model.

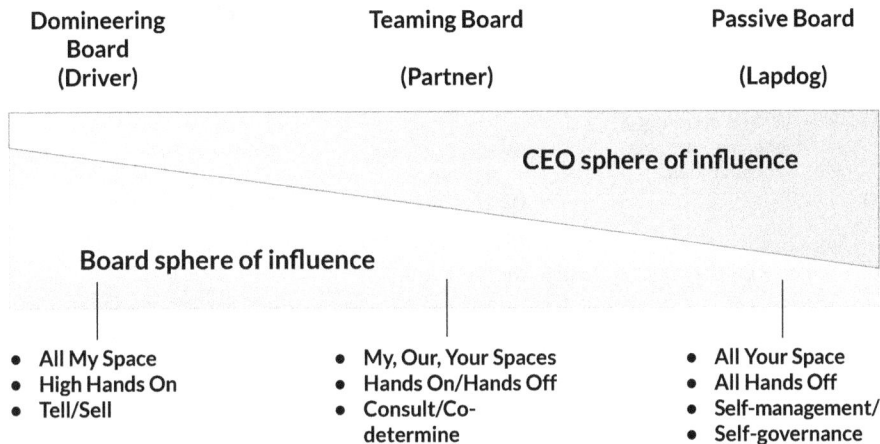

Domineering Board (Driver)	Teaming Board (Partner)	Passive Board (Lapdog)

CEO sphere of influence

Board sphere of influence

- All My Space
- High Hands On
- Tell/Sell

- My, Our, Your Spaces
- Hands On/Hands Off
- Consult/Co-determine

- All Your Space
- All Hands Off
- Self-management/ Self-governance

Figure 7.3: Three types of Boards

The mandate adopted by the Board will determine the decision rights and styles at the Board/CEO interface – who plays where and how? This design aspect will be covered below under the Strategic Lateral Design: Governance Model in this chapter.

- *Vantage point:* from what perspective will the Board view the world, and the way the world works? To be debated here by the Board, is at least two views regarding the world. Firstly, what is the right set of lenses to use when looking at the world in which the Board has to lead? Secondly, in terms of what dimensions does a Board wish to chart the world? The second question is relevant here because it gives the basic demarcation of the Board's intended work, to be further discussed under the Tactical Design of the Board (see Chapter 9).

Figure 7.4 graphically depicts the possible dimensions a Board can use to chart the world. The selected dimensions determine what shape the Board's radar screen will take, allowing certain matters to be observed and debated, or not. At issue here is what matters Board members will regard as relevant or not, depending on the dimensions Board members award to the world.

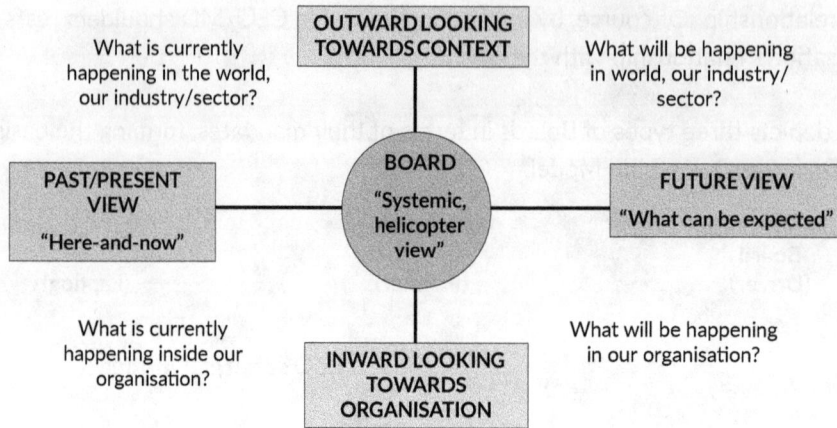

Figure 7.4: Possible dimensions the Board can use to chart the world

- *Identity:* who and what are we as a Board? What is our 'brand' as a Board? One way of profiling a Board's Identity – who and what a Board is/wishes to be – is by plotting its Identity in terms of a two-dimensional focus a Board may adopt: Performance vs. Relationship *and* Compliance vs. Commitment. Four 'pure', predominantly constructive, Identities flow from the combination of these two foci: a Role-, Achievement-, Power-, or Support-based Identity (12). The corresponding negative Identities are: Conformist (counter to Role), Run Away Train (counter to Achievement), Feudal Lord (counter to Power), and Old Boys Club/Group Think (counter to Support) based Identities. Typically, a Board's Identity is a mixture of all four Identities, although one Identity is usually dominant. Figure 7.5 illustrates the above discussion with examples of the constructive Identities.

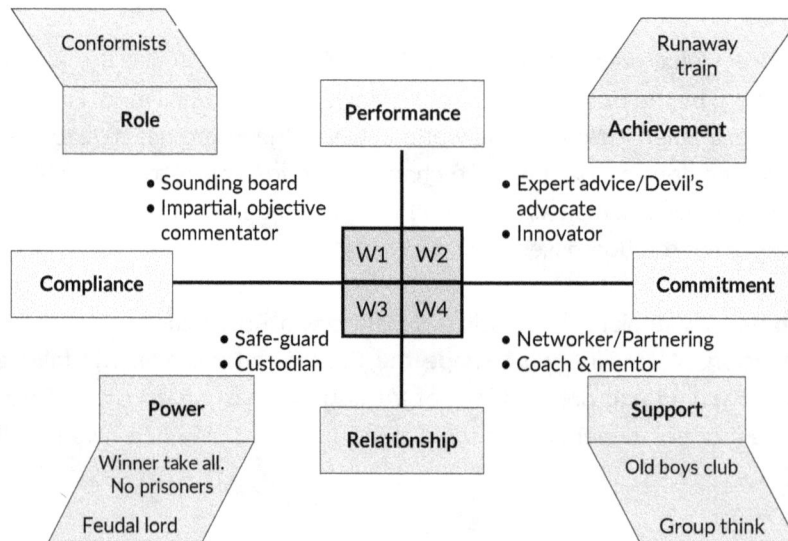

Figure 7.5: Possible Board Identities

Note: W1 to W4 refers to the weights given by the Board to an Identity. The weights must sum to 100 across the four quadrants

- *Core values*: How should we conduct ourselves as a Board? What is right/wrong; important/ unimportant; good/bad? Typical Board values are: *Stewardship:* Looking after stakeholders' interests as if they are our own; *Sustainability:* Leaving the world a better place for current/upcoming generations; *Integrity:* Acting in an honest, consistent and trustworthy manner; *Fairness:* Being just and equitable in our dealings; *Accountability:* Taking full responsibility for our actions; and *Transparency:* Being open and accessible about the why, what and how of our actions.

In summary: from a Strategic Vertical Design perspective, the Board – CEO/MD House Ownership Model is to be found in the Board's Operating Framework, constituted by six interdependent design elements: Purpose, Vision, Mandate, Vantage Point, Identity, and Core Values. A sound Vertical Design for the Board requires an explicit, well-formulated, well-communicated, fit-for-purpose Operating Framework, meeting the set Strategic Design Criteria and Vision with its Design Metaphor.

The Corporate Centre – Work Unit Ownership Model

With respect to the Corporate Centre-Work Units relationship, five basic types of House Ownership exist as design options. These options are given in Table 7.2 (13). A tick (✓) indicates the Centre taking accountability for a given LOW work element, although a Work Unit may be responsible for its execution. A dash (-) indicates a Work Unit being accountable for that work element. The typical – but not necessarily so – Organisational Shapes associated with a certain type of House Ownership are indicated in the last column (also refer back to Figure 6.9: Periodic Table of Generic Organisational Shapes).

Table 7.2: Basic types of House Ownership based on the direction and control exercised by the Centre over the organisation's Work Units

LEVEL OF WORK: ACCOUNTABILITY / DIRECTION AND CONTROL FROM CENTRE	LOW5: Returns/Yields	LOW5: Organisational Strategic Intent	LOW4: Work Unit Strategic Translation/Implementation	LOW4: Policies and Standards	LOW4: Resourcing	LOW4: Systems and methodologies	LOWs3 & 2: Work processes and practices	LOW1: Delivery	TYPICAL ORGANISATIONAL SHAPES ASSOCIATED WITH TYPE OF DIRECTION AND CONTROL
Financial	✓	-	-	-	-	-	-	-	Holding
Strategic: Loose	✓	✓	-	-	-	-	-	-	Cluster; Front-Back; Network; Portfolio/Divisional
Strategic: Tight	✓	✓	✓	✓	✓	✓	-	-	Portfolio/Divisional
Managerial	✓	✓	✓	✓	✓	✓	✓	-	Hub & Spoke; Mirror Image; Activity: Process/Project
Operational	✓	✓	✓	✓	✓	✓	✓	✓	Activity: Functional; Process; Project

The movement in Table 7.2 is from a 'hands-off owner' – Financial Direction and Control – to an 'Hands-on manager' of Work Units – Operational Direction and Control (14).

Figure 7.6 shows the factors that could influence the required degree of direction and control to be exercised by the Centre over its Work Units. The personality, leadership philosophy and style of the CEO/MD could mediate the actual degree of direction and control exercised by the Centre, regardless of the chosen design. The more democratic the leader, the less the control. The more autocratic the leader, the more the direction and control from the top (15). A complete Vertical Design requires deciding which Corporate Centre – Work Unit Ownership Model is fit-for-purpose, given the set Strategic Design Criteria and Vision with its Design Metaphor.

PERSONALITY, LEADERSHIP PHILOSOPHY AND STYLE OF CEO/MD (Mediating variable)		DEGREE OF DIRECTION FROM CENTRE	
		Less Strategic Direction	More Strategic Direction
DEGREE OF CONTROL FROM CENTRE	Less Operational Control	• Open, unpredictable, fluid competition • Higher diversity of Work Units, each with a unique niche	• More dense linkages between Work Units, driven by the desire for higher inter-unit synergies • Greater investments over a longer payback period in a Work Unit(s) • Fierce competition responded to by an organisational 'Win' Strategic Intent
	More Operational Control	• Fierce competition responded to by an organisational 'Withdrawal' or 'Stable' Strategic Intent • Work Unit is the custodian of a mission-critical, organisational crown jewel	• Greater investments over a shorter payback period in a Work Unit(s) • Less diverse Work Units, triggering the need to keep Work Units within their designated Operating Arenas and circumvent 'border wars' • Less capable, less experienced Work Unit leadership • High financial/resources stress in organisation • Fierce competition responded to by an organisational 'Hold' Strategic Intent

Figure 7.6: Factors influencing the degree of direction and control exercised by the Centre over its Work Units

Step A.3.3: Allocate the requisite Level of Work to each Work Unit

Based on the requisite LOW of the organisation and its chosen House Ownership Model, the requisite LOW must be allocated to each Work Unit contained in the House Plan in terms of its expected contribution. For example, must the IT Work Unit of the organisation make a LOW3 contribution, being 'merely' an IT Data Processing Unit? Or, must it make a LOW4 contribution, being a Business Intelligence Unit? Is the People Function merely a transactional function or a strategic partner?

The shaded box depicts the House Plan of a LOW4 IT Work Unit, using a Front/Back Organisational Shape. The Front is represented by the IT Needs and Solutions Work Unit, and the Back by the IT Operations Work Unit. As can be seen, the LOWs of the Business Partners (= Enabling/Support Work Units) that provide a service to the IT Work Units concerned also need to be specified (16).

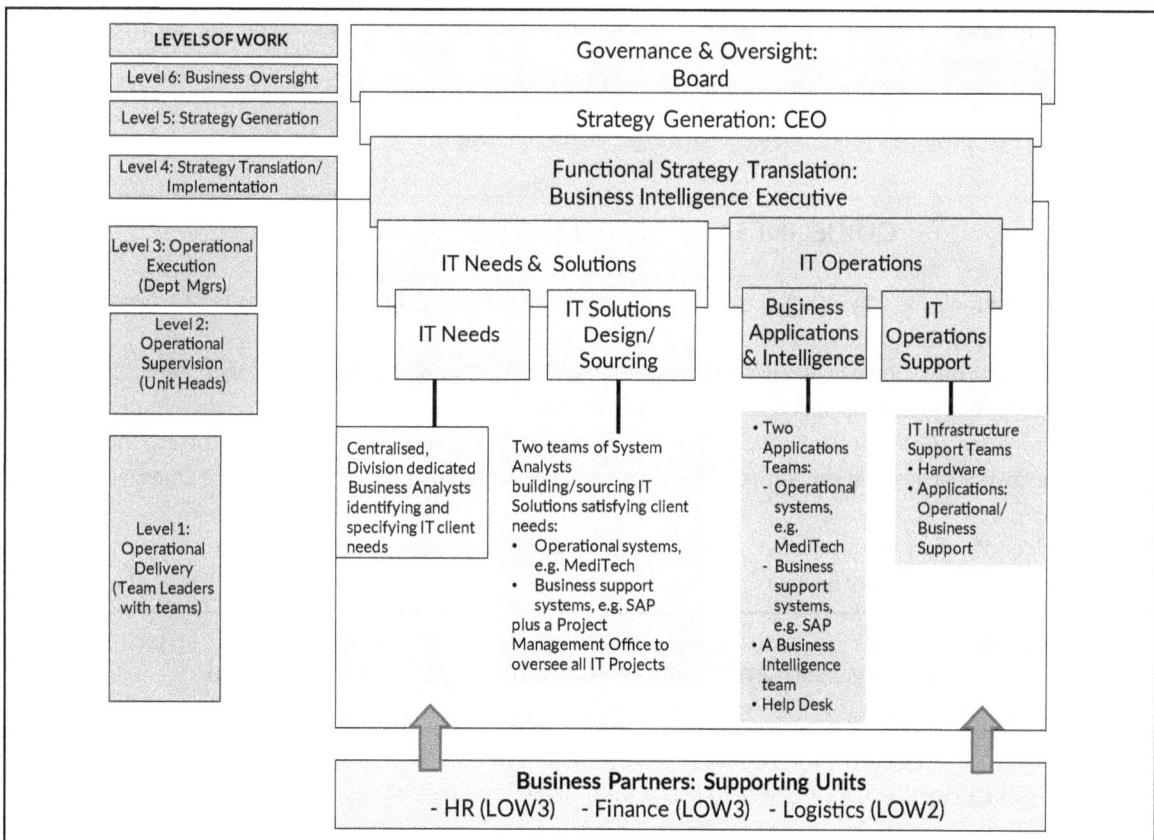

LEVELS OF WORK	Governance & Oversight: Board		
Level 6: Business Oversight			
Level 5: Strategy Generation	Strategy Generation: CEO		
Level 4: Strategy Translation/ Implementation	Functional Strategy Translation: Business Intelligence Executive		
Level 3: Operational Execution (Dept Mgrs)	IT Needs & Solutions		IT Operations
Level 2: Operational Supervision (Unit Heads)	IT Needs	IT Solutions Design/ Sourcing	Business Applications & Intelligence — IT Operations Support
Level 1: Operational Delivery (Team Leaders with teams)	Centralised, Division dedicated Business Analysts identifying and specifying IT client needs	Two teams of System Analysts building/sourcing IT Solutions satisfying client needs: • Operational systems, e.g. MediTech • Business support systems, e.g. SAP plus a Project Management Office to oversee all IT Projects	• Two Applications Teams: - Operational systems, e.g. MediTech - Business support systems, e.g. SAP • A Business Intelligence team • Help Desk	IT Infrastructure Support Teams • Hardware • Applications: Operational/ Business Support

Business Partners: Supporting Units
- HR (LOW3)   - Finance (LOW3) - Logistics (LOW2)

Step A.3.4: Identify the mission-critical Work Roles at the Work Unit Leadership Level and generate high level Role Profiles

A Work Role refers to what needs to be done and delivered by its incumbent. In order to 'anchor' the Strategic Design, mission-critical Work Roles with their requisite LOWs have to be identified and profiled at a high level, usually a one-pager. (The detailed design of Work Roles will be discussed under Operational Design, Chapter 10.)

These roles include the CEO/MD of the organisation and the Heads of the respective Work Units (= Rooms) as contained in the Organisational Map (= House Plan), usually LOW5, 4 and 3 Work Roles (if LOW3 Work Units exist). Typically a high level Work Role Profile covers three sections, namely:

- Core Purpose;
- Critical Tasks (= Key Performance Areas); and
- Key Outputs.

A Work Role Profile template is given in Appendix B: Design Template 3.

Comparing the Core Purposes of all of the Work Roles is a handy way to confirm and verify that: (i) the mandates of the Work Units are aligned and do not overlap; and (ii) all of the work of the organisation is covered because the Work Unit Leader Work Role represents, at a high level, the sum total of the organisation's work.

The shaded box provides guidelines for Strategic Vertical Design.

GUIDELINES FOR STRATEGIC VERTICAL DESIGN

- Given the requisite LOW of the organisation overall, ensure that all of the lower, requisite LOWs are in place. A LOW cannot be skipped.
- Ensure that the Home Ownership Models of the Board and Corporate Centre are congruent with the set Strategic Design Criteria and Vision with its Design Metaphor.
- The requisite LOWs for the Delivery Enabling and Business Support Work Units must correspond to the respective enabling and support roles they have to play in the organisation regarding its Operating Work Units.
- The identification and profiling of unambiguous, value-adding, mission-critical Work Roles with clear boundaries and accountabilities.

Quality assurance: Stage A.3: Strategic Vertical Design

QUALITY ASSURANCE QUESTIONS *Step A.3: Strategic Vertical Design – The type of ownership and owners of the House Plan and its Rooms*	DESIGN STEP	ADDRESSED: YES/NO *(Yes: +; No: x)*
Have the requisite Levels of Work been identified for the **organisation overall?**	Step A.3.1	
Has a clear **LOW Home Ownership Model** been architected for the organisation?	Step A.3.2	
Have the requisite Levels of Work been allocated to **Work Units** in accordance with this Ownership model?	Step A.3.2	

QUALITY ASSURANCE QUESTIONS *Step A.3: Strategic Vertical Design – The type of ownership and owners of the House Plan and its Rooms*	DESIGN STEP	ADDRESSED: YES/NO *(Yes: +; No: x)*
Have the minimum **mission-critical Work Roles** with their requisite Levels of Work with respect to all of the Work Units and the organisation been identified?	Step A.3.3	
Have **high level Role Profiles** been generated for these mission-critical Work Roles?	Step A.3.4	
Are these Work Roles across Work Units and within the Levels of Work **aligned and congruent** in terms of their Core Purposes?	Step A.3.4	
Does the Strategic Vertical Design meet the set **Strategic Design Criteria**, reflect the **Design Vision**, and resonate with the **Metaphor** representing the Design Vision?	Stage A.3 in total	

Step A.4: Strategic Lateral Design (17)

The objective of Step A.4: Strategic Lateral Design is to create a strategically integrated overall thrust and synergy across the Work Units, Levels of Work, and Work Roles. The key issues are twofold: What is the necessary integration between Work Units, as well as and the overall Governance Model of the organisation?

This step entails: firstly, mapping the interdependencies between Work Units (or their proxies, namely Work Roles); secondly, crafting Integration Mechanisms for the identified interdependencies; and thirdly, deciding on the appropriate overall Governance Model of the organisation. This step is thus made up of three sub-steps (see Figure 7.1 above):

- A.4.1: Construct an Interdependency Matrix;
- A.4.2: Decide on Integration Mechanisms; and
- A.4.3: Set up the Governance Model of the organisation.

Step A.4.1: Construct an Interdependency Matrix for the respective Work Units/Roles in order to determine their interdependencies

The lateral integration relative to the different Organisational Shapes was included in the Periodic Table of Generic Organisational Shapes (see Figure 6.9). For ease of reference, it is repeated here again in Table 7.3.

Table 7.3: Required lateral integration relative to different Organisational Shapes

GENERIC ORGANISATIONAL SHAPE	Activity based (Functional, Process, Project, Membership) Mirror Image/ Matrix	Portfolio/ Divisional, Hub and Spoke, Front/Back, Network	Cluster	Holding
LATERAL INTEGRATION Locus of Organisational Co-ordination	Within Work Unit (Activity based: Functional, Process, Project, Membership) Within Work Unit AND across Work Units (Mirror Image/Matrix)	Across Work Units higher than within Work Units	Within groupings of Work Units (= Clusters), higher than across groupings	Within Work Unit (= organisation) higher than across Work Units (= organisation)

Five basic types of interdependencies can be distinguished between Work Units/Roles (18):

- *Pooled:* A Work Unit/Role functions highly independently; its performance output does not affect another Work Unit/Role and is added to the overall output.

- *Sequential:* The performance output of a Work Unit/Role is the input to another Unit/Role; the one Unit delivers work to another.

- *Reciprocal:* The performance output of one Unit/Role becomes the input of another Unit/Role, whose performance output in turn becomes the input to the first Unit/Role. Mutual interdependency exists between parties to get the work done.

- *Enabling:* One Work Unit/Role provides and maintains the direct means required by another Work Unit/Role to get the work done.

- *Supporting:* One Work Unit/Role provides specialist advice, counselling, knowledge and/or expertise to another Work Unit/Role, enabling it to make the right decisions and take the right actions.

A handy way of mapping the interdependencies between Work Units and Roles – making up the Strategic Horizontal and Vertical Designs – is to generate an Interdependency Matrix that reflects the nature of those interdependencies. Table 7.4 gives the format of such a matrix. The types of interdependencies between a pair of Work Units have to be described in each cell of the matrix – pooled, sequential, reciprocal, enabling or supportive – in concrete terms. For example: 'Unit 1 provides this product of this quality and quantity to Work Unit 3 at a specific monthly date'. The box provides guidelines for the generation of an Interdependency Matrix.

Table 7.4: Interdependency Matrix

	UNIT 1*	UNIT 2	UNIT 3	UNIT 4	UNIT 5	Etc.
UNIT 1	---					
UNIT 2		---				
UNIT 3			---			
UNIT 4				---		
UNIT 5					---	
Etc.						---

* Note: Work Units act as proxies for the associated Work Roles that head up Units. If required, a Work Role Interdependency Matrix can also be generated.

GUIDELINES FOR THE GENERATION OF AN INTERDEPENDENCY MATRIX

- All Work Units (or Work Roles as their proxy) – as contained in the Strategic Horizontal Design – must be included in the Matrix.

- Interdependencies for pairs of Work Units must be considered in both directions: from one Work Unit to another, and vice versa because the interdependencies may differ in the two directions.

- Organisation-wide Integration Mechanisms, taking account of the nature of the chosen Organisational Shape (see Table 7.3), must also be architected. For example, the Investment Committee of a Holding organisation.

Step A.4.2: Decide on the most appropriate Integration Mechanisms to link Work Units, individually and as a whole, in order to create a strategically integrated thrust and synergy for the organisation

Using the Interdependency Matrix – given the inter-Work Unit interdependencies as well as organisation-wide interdependencies – Integration Mechanisms must be architected in order to create an overall, integrated strategic thrust and synergy for the total organisation. Figure 7.7 provides a two-dimensional typology of possible Integration Mechanisms (19), Table 7.5 lists the strengths and weaknesses of the respective Mechanisms (20).

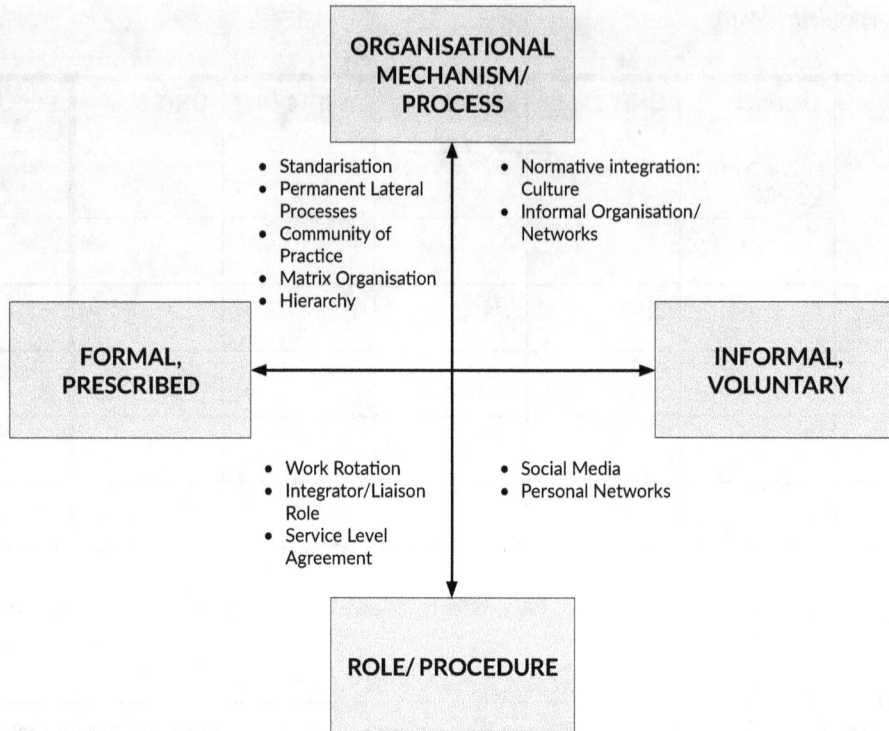

Figure 7.7: Typology of possible Integration Mechanisms

Table 7.5: Strengths and weaknesses of Integration Mechanisms

TYPE	STRENGTHS	WEAKNESSES
INFORMAL VOLUNTARY ROLE/PROCEDURE		
Social media	• Real time, immediate, anyone, anywhere, anytime • Cost-effective	• Hijacked for personal use (= abuse) • Information overload • Spread of untruths, misinformation and lies that cannot be prevented • Lacks face-to-face, interpersonal interaction • Difficult to build trust
Personal networks	• Face-to-face interpersonal interaction • Good at building trust • Innovation and continuous improvement	• Time consuming • High investment to set up and maintain
INFORMAL VOLUNTARY ORGANISATIONAL MECHANISM/PROCESS		
Normative integration: Culture	• Empowering • Organisation-wide • Internalisation of values, norms and beliefs	• Challenge to embed and difficult to change • Presence of subcultures may undermine integration

TYPE	STRENGTHS	WEAKNESSES
Informal Organisation/ Networks	• Tend to occur naturally • People are eager to form them, since they provide personal and organisational benefits • Relatively inexpensive to foster • Rely on simple communication • Do not add formal levels or meetings	• Dependent on eagerness to spontaneously interact • Too risky to rely on for critical processes • No formalised, agreed upon processes • Too informal to capture learning across the organisation
FORMAL PRESCRIBED ROLE/PROCEDURE		
Work rotation	• Developing a cross-functional and cross-disciplinary perspective: big picture formation • Basis of multi-skilling and multi-tasking	• Erosion of specialist focus and depth • If not specified as a requirement for career advancement, may be seen as an unnecessary nuisance
Integrator/Liaison Role	• Single point of integration at cross-over of boundaries • Create formal responsibility for the integration of multiple inputs and perspectives	• Availability of persons able to work effectively in boundary spanning roles
Service Level Agreements	• Formalised roles, responsibilities, accountabilities and expectations • Provide metrics to measure delivery and deliverables • Clarifies competencies, expertise and resources needed to satisfy client demands	• Tendency to act in terms of letter but not spirit of the agreement • Emphasis on agreement and measurables, and not client relationship and non-measurables • Not highly responsive to changing circumstances and shifting client needs/ expectations
FORMAL PRESCRIBED ORGANISATIONAL MECHANISM/PROCESS		
Standardisation: for example of work processes, outputs, skills	• Clear standards, giving predictability	• Loss of flexibility and responsiveness to deal with unique and/or changing situations • Standardisation becomes the end and not the means, that is means-ends reversal
Temporary Lateral Processes: for example, Cross-functional Teams/ Task forces/Work Groups	• In time, problem solving utilising multiple organisational perspectives and resources • Push decision-making downward • Create common goals and mental models • Utilise existing staff, thus do not increase staff complement	• May bring hidden/suppressed conflicts in the organisation into the open • Requires a team and teaming culture • May waste resources if there is no clear leadership, mandate and/or mode of working • Dependent on healthy, informal networks

TYPE	STRENGTHS	WEAKNESSES
Permanent Lateral Processes, for example Forums, Joint Planning Centres, Standing Committees	• Formalise interactions across organisational boundaries • Create focus on the critical issues within the organisation • Reduce reliance on individual managers to ensure organisation-wide integration	• Takes dedicated resources to make it work • Cross-functional processes may not have a clear owner • May bureaucratise what should be happening spontaneously in any event • May be seen as a necessary nuisance because it sits outside formal hierarchy
Community of Practice	• Formalised interaction • Sharing of best practices • Standardisation of processes and procedures • More effective allocation and deployment of resources • Encourage organisation-wide learning	• Takes dedication to maintain and sustain because it sits outside of formal hierarchy
Matrix Organisation	• Mirror the multi-dimensionality of the organisational reality • Enable more flexible utilisation of technical expertise • Enable/enforce a multi-functional perspective • Enhance organisational learning through multiple channels	• Enhanced chances of conflict because of dual reporting relationships • "Them-Us" dynamics may be heightened • Lack ability to handle more complex information sharing, decision-making, problem solving and conflict resolution • Employees may feel lost without a permanent 'home'
Hierarchy	• Formally allocated authority, responsibility and accountability allocated to formal positions, using the optimal span of control (see the shaded box for guidelines on spans of control)	• Hierarchical information and decision-making overload, as well as slowing down communication, decision-making, and conflict resolution • Functional silos resulting in fragmented approaches to organisation wide challenges, issues and problems • Does not formally acknowledge the growing importance of lateral interactions to get things done in the organisation • Disregards/downplays insights, knowledge, expertise and experience at lower levels in the organisation

According to Figure 7.7 and Table 7.5, a wide range of Integration Mechanisms are available. What should be clear from this figure and table is that the hierarchy is not, and should not be, the only Integration Mechanism. The movement from the Command-and-Control (= Pyramid) Organisational Shape (see Figure 6.5) to the High Network/High Engagement/High Responsible (= Distributed

Network) Organisational Shape (see Figure 6.7), because of the VICCAS world, is also a movement towards the use of multiple/different Integration Mechanisms. Hierarchy is no longer, and perhaps was never, good enough on its own to integrate the organisation. The set Strategic Design Criteria and Vision with its commensurate Design Metaphor must also be applied in choosing fit-for-purpose Integration Mechanisms. Teaming and teamwork as a Criterion demands more person-centric, face-to-face Mechanisms.

A template to assist in designing the Integration Mechanisms is given in Appendix B: Design Template 4.

GUIDELINES FOR AN OPTIMAL SPAN OF CONTROL (21)

Narrow (less people can be led) (4-6 reportees)

- Complex work with high variety
- High interdependence between Work Roles
- Unpredictable work processes
- Work requires close, personal co-ordination
- Work output difficult to measure and assess, usually more intangible
- Highly turbulent and fluid work setting, requiring rapid responses

Wide (more people can be led) (6-12 reportees)

- Simple, similar work with low variability
- Low interdependence between Work Roles
- Routine work processes
- Work can be managed by rules and standard operating procedures
- Work output easy to measure and assess, usually more tangible
- Incrementally and/or predictably changing work setting

An example of a crafted Integration Mechanism for a Hub and Spoke Organisational Shape (see Step A.2.2.5 (iii) and Figure 6.16) for a global gold mining company is given in the shaded box (22).

Design guidelines for Integration Mechanisms are given in the shaded box.

GUIDELINES FOR INTEGRATION MECHANISMS

- For each identified interdependency between Work Units, an Integration Mechanism must be architected in order to ensure an integrated strategic thrust and synergy at the Work Unit level.

- Overall Organisational Integration Mechanisms must also be designed in order to create an overall integrated strategic thrust and synergy for the total organisation.

- Keep Integration Mechanisms as few and simple as possible, but not more simple or more complex than required.

- The chosen Integration Mechanisms must be compliant to the set Strategic Design Criteria and Vision with its commensurate Design Metaphor.

EXAMPLE: CRAFTED, INTEGRATION MECHANISMS FOR A GLOBAL HUB AND SPOKE SHAPE					
Integrating Mechanism: Hierarchy	**Purpose/ Mandate**	**Work Domain/ Agenda covered**	**Owner**	**Attendees**	**Frequency**
Executive Team	Overall strategic direction	• Strategy Intent/ initiative • Overall business performance • Business synergy	CEO	• CEO • Business Support Services • Business Development • Regional Heads	Quarterly
Operational Leadership Team	Overall strategic implementation	• Strategy execution/fine tuning • Overall business performance	CEO	• CEO • Business Support Services • Business Development	Monthly
Regional Leadership Team	Regional Resource Deployment	• Regional Resource Synergies	Regional Heads	• Regional Heads	Quarterly
Management Team (by Region)	Operational Execution	• Strategy implementation • Regional performance • Regional synergy	Regional Director	• Regional Heads • Regional Operational Support Services • Managers, Operating Business Entities	Monthly
Leadership Forum (meeting back to back with Executive Leadership)	Informed leadership community	• Business overview/review	CEO	All of the above except the Managers of the Operating Business Entities	Quarterly

Step A.4.3: Set up the Governance Model for the design

This step addresses: (i) the allocation of decision-making rights to Work Units – and by implication their lead Work Role with its requisite LOW (see Table 7.1) – with respect to a work process or element thereof; and (ii) deciding on the decision-making style by which these rights have to be exercised. Together decision-making rights and style form the Governance Model of the design.

The purpose of the organisation's Governance Model is to ensure that the right Units/Roles do the right things, for the right reasons, in the right ways, at the right times, with the right autonomy. 'Right' has to be referenced against the set Strategic Design Criteria and Vision.

Decision-making Rights

The Decision-making Rights can be defined in terms of **VARII** (23):

- **V**eto (or Ratify): Go/No Go – approval of, or compliance to, a policy, standard or practice.

- **A**ccountability: Final decision maker regarding the work process or element thereof who is accountable for the decision/action (only one Work Unit/Role).

- **R**esponsible: Who does the work regarding the work process or element thereof, for example, Policies and Standards (can be more than one Work Unit/Role)?

- **I**nput (or Consult): Who must be provided input to the decision/action, before and whilst the work is being done, regarding the work process or element thereof?

- **I**nformed: Who must be informed once the decision has been taken regarding a work process or element thereof, and during its implementation?

Decision-making Styles

The decision-making styles with which the accountable party has to exercise its decision-making rights have to be specified. Five styles are possible (24):

- *Tell:* The accountable party makes the decision and instructs those responsible to do the work.

- *Consult:* The accountable party asks for input from the responsible parties, considers their input, makes the decision, and instructs them.

- *Co-determine:* The accountable and responsible parties jointly debate the intended action and make the decision together.

- *Self-manage* (that is Upward Consultation): The responsible party (or parties) consults upwards with the accountable party, makes the decision and informs the accountable party accordingly.

- *Self-govern* (that is Upward Telling/Selling): The responsible party (or parties) takes the decision and informs the accountable party upwards.

Figure 7.8 graphically depicts the above discussion regarding decision-making style.

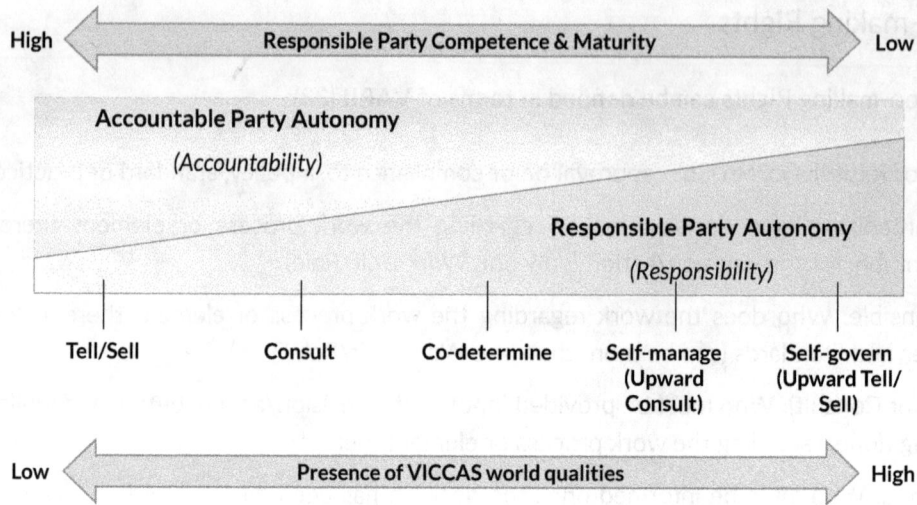

Figure 7.8: Decision-making Styles

Generally speaking, the trend in the emerging new order – given the demand for responsiveness and agility – is towards at least Consult, but more strongly towards Co-determine, Self-manage and Self-govern. Figure 7.9 graphically illustrates this trend, using 'Myself' as a reference point outwards from a given leader in a Work Role (25).

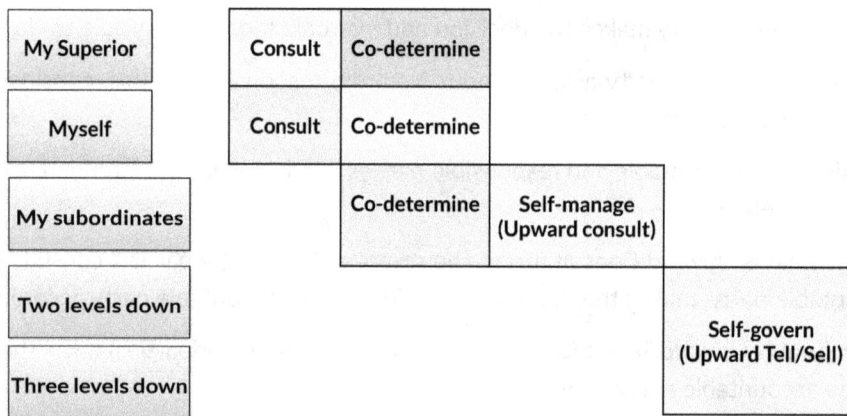

Figure 7.9: Emerging pattern regarding Decision-making Styles

Decision-making Rights by Decision Styles: Governance Model of organisation

Putting the Decision-making Rights and Styles together gives one a Decision-making Rights X Styles Matrix. This Matrix has to be (i) populated with the relevant Work Units/Work Roles and Integration Mechanisms; and (ii) Decision-making Rights and Styles have to be awarded to them using the set Strategic Design Criteria and Vision as reference. The completed Matrix represents the Organisational Governance Model. Table 7.6 gives an example of what such a hypothetical Organisation Governance

Model could look like. A template for architecting the organisation's Governance Model is given in Appendix B: Design Template 5.

Table 7.6: Organisation Governance Model: Extract based on a hypothetical example

LEVEL OF WORK/ WORK PROCESS (OR ELEMENT THEREOF)	DECISION-MAKING RIGHTS *Relevant Work Unit/Work Role*					
	Veto/Ratify	**Accountable**	**Responsible**	**Input**	**Informed**	
6 **Context shaping**	Stake-holders (at AGM)	Board	Board sub-committees	Stakeholders CEO/MD with team	Stakeholders CEO/MD with team	**DECISION-MAKING RIGHTS**
	Consult	Consult	Consult	Consult	Consult	**DECISION-MAKING STYLE**
5 **Direction, Objectives, Philosophy**	Board	CEO/MD with team	All Work Units' Heads	All Work Units' Heads	Total Organisation	**DECISION-MAKING RIGHTS**
	Consult	Co-determine	Co-determine	Co-determine	Consult	**DECISION-MAKING STYLE**
4 **Organisational Policies & Standards** *(specify which)*	CEO/MD with team	All Work Units' Heads	Reportees into Work Unit Heads	Reportees into Work Unit Heads	Total Organisation	**DECISION-MAKING RIGHTS**
	Consult	Co-determine	Co-determine	Consult	Tell	**DECISION-MAKING STYLE**

The shaded box gives the Design Guidelines for a Governance Model.

An example of typical Decision-making Rights and Styles at the Board/CEO interface – who plays where and how – for a Teaming (or Partnering) Board (see Figure 7.3) is given in the shaded box (26).

GUIDELINES FOR A GOVERNANCE MODEL

- Clear Decision-making Rights and Style Matrix
- Minimum critical specification: not making decisions for another Work Unit/Work Role which ought to make them for themselves.
- Clear hand-over points: the when, what and how with clear quality requirements.

EXAMPLE: BOARD – CEO/MD GOVERNANCE MODEL

Decision making rights

Hands on	Accountable/ Responsible	Where does business need to go/is going?
	Approve/ Ratify	**Board to CEO perspective** Prescriptive, affirmative "Thou shalt"
Hands off	Understand/ Insight	**Board to CEO perspective** Prohibitive, constraining "Thou shalt not"
	Aware of/ Unsighted	What does business do to get there?

1: Business protection, enhancement & sustainability — **Board's space ("Mine")**

2: Business identity, positioning, direction, yield
3: Business policies & standards — **Common space ('Ours")**

4: Business requirements/ resourcing
5: Work processes
6: Operational practices
7: Operational delivery — **CEO's space ("Yours")**

Decision making styles

- Tell
- Sell
- Consult
- Co-determine
- Self management
- Self government

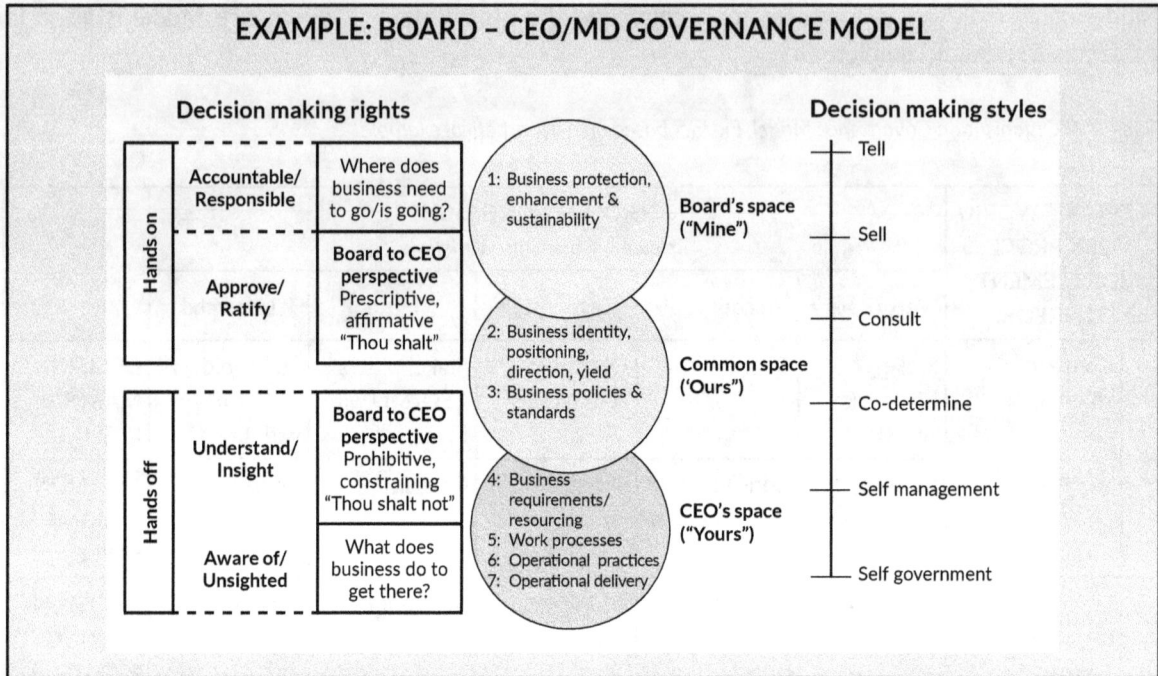

Quality assurance: Stage A.4: Strategic Lateral Design

QUALITY ASSURANCE QUESTIONS Step A.4: Strategic Lateral Design – Living together in the House	DESIGN STEP	ADDRESSED: YES/NO (Yes: +; No: x)
Have the **interdependencies** between all Work Units/Roles and the organisation as a whole been identified?	Step A.4.1	
Have the most appropriate **Integration Mechanisms** relative to these interdependencies been chosen to link Work Units/Roles and the organisation as a whole, in order to create an overall strategically integrated thrust and synergy for the organisation?	Step A.4.2	
Is the allocation of **Decision-making Rights and Styles** unambiguous, that is the **Governance Model** for the design clear? Have the necessary checks and balances been built into the Governance Model?	Step A.4.3	
Are **Decision-making Rights** well distributed across the organisation, that is will decisions be taken in the right place by the right person at the right time?	Step A.4.3	
Does the Strategic Vertical Design meet the set **Strategic Design Criteria**, reflect the **Strategic Design Vision**, and resonate with the **Design Metaphor** representing the Design Vision?	Stage A.4 overall	

Conclusion

This chapter dealt with Step A.3: Strategic Vertical Design and Step A.4: Strategic Lateral Design. The objective of Step A.3: Strategic Vertical Design is to define the requisite Levels of Work of the organisation overall and its Work Units, with the commensurate mission-critical Work Roles regarding each Work Unit as contained in Strategic Horizontal Design. Step A.4: Lateral Design's objective is to create overall strategically integrated thrust and synergy for the organisation across Work Units/Work Roles.

The outcomes of Step A.3 outcomes are: (i) requisite LOWs for the organisation overall requisite; (ii) a House Ownership Model: the strategic positioning of the Board and Corporate Centre; (iii) the requisite LOWs for Work Units; and (iv) profiles of mission-critical Work Roles. The Step A.4 outcomes are: (i) Organisational and inter-Work Unit Integration Mechanisms; and (ii) the Governance Model of the organisation.

From the perspective of the overall Integrated Strategic Design, the next chapter addresses the final steps in the Strategic Design: an Integrated Strategic Design and Charter; Strategic Organisational Alignment; Strategic Design Impact Assessment; as well as the Strategic Design Implementation Road Map, and its implementation.

Endnotes

(1) In general, this chapter draws on the author's experience, supplemented and enriched by Anand & Daft (2007); Burton & Obel (2018); Burton, Obel & Håkonsson (2015); Galbraith (1997); (2006); (2008); (2014); Galbraith, Downey & Kates (2005); Jaques (2006); Jaques & Clement (1994); Kesler & Kates (2011); MacKenzie (1986); Nadler & Tushman (1997); Roberts, (2004); Rowbottom & Billis (1987); Stanford (2007); Shephard, Gray, Hunt & McArthur (2007); Veldsman (2002).

(2) Specific discussions on Vertical Design (= Levels of Work) can be found primarily in Jaques (2006); Jaques & Clement (1994); Rowbottom & Billis (1987) and Shephard, Gray, Hunt & McArthur (2007), but also in Capelle (2014); Goold & Campbell (2002b) and Kesler & Kates (2011), although much more superficially.

(3) Jaques (2006); Jaques & Clement (1994); Shephard, Gray, Hunt & McArthur (2007).

(4) Based on the same references as (3), as well as Bussin (2017d) and Capelle (2017).

(5) Bussin (2017d).

(6) Based on a consulting assignment by the author.

(7) The original source of the table given in the shaded box is unknown. Adapted and expanded from the original, and enriched by Price (2013).

(8) Weber & Mihalicz (2007).

(9) This discussion draws heavily on Veldsman (2012b); (2012c).

(10) King (2002); Rezaee (2009).

(11) Bersin, O'Reilly, Magoulas & Loukides (2019); Lawler & Worley (2012).

(12) Based on Harrison (1972).

(13) Based on Bellerby (2017); Collis, Young & Goold (2012); Goold & Campbell (1987); Goold & Campbell (2002b); (2002c) and Goold, Pettifer & Young (2001). Goold and Campbell were the pioneers in researching the design of Corporate Centres, systematically and in-depth.

(14) Roghé, Pidun, Stange & Krühler (2013). In-between the two extremes, the authors distinguish financial sponsors, family builders, strategic guides and functional leaders to typify the direction and control from the Corporate Centre over the Work Units.

(15) Based on Goold & Campbell (1987).

(16) Source: Author.

(17) Specific discussions on Lateral Design, and co-ordinating mechanisms as a synonymous term for Lateral Design, can be found in Brophy (2017); Galbraith (1994); Goold & Campbell (2002b); Kesler & Kates (2011) and Mintzberg (1993); (1997). For Mintzberg, co-ordinating mechanisms are the centrepieces holding the organisation together and enabling it to get its work done.

(18) The first three interdependencies were originally proposed by Thompson (1967) (Quoted by Mintzberg, 1993; 1997; Nadler & Tushman, 1988). The fourth and fifth were added by myself, based on Kates & Galbraith's (2007) suggested relationship map.

(19) Constructed by the author.

(20) Based on Burton, Obel & Håkonsson (2015); Galbraith (2014); Nadler & Tushman (1988); Kates & Galbraith (2007); Kesler & Kates (2011); Mintzberg (1993); (1997); Szilagyi & Wallace (1983).

(21) See, for example, ICI Chemical & Polymers Ltd. (1989).

(22) Source: Author.

(23) Author constructed, also drawing on Kates & Galbraith (2007).

(24) Adapted and expanded from Tannenbaum & Schmidt (1958), with elements of the situational leadership theory of Hersey and Blanchard (1982) incorporated.

(25) Author constructed.

(26) Author constructed.

STRATEGIC ORGANISATIONAL DESIGN

8

Architecting the overall Organisational Shape: Integration, Alignment, Impact and Implementation

---

"To accomplish great things,
We must not only act but dream,
Not only plan but also believe."

(Anatole France)

"If you want to truly understand something, try to change it."

(Kurt Lewin)

Strategic Design aims to architect the design of the organisation as a total operating entity – the complete House Plan of the organisation – resulting in a total Organisational Design. The ultimate outcome of this processes, specifically:

- the *Work Units* making up the organisation, and their configuration into an *Organisational Shape*: its Strategic Horizontal Design;

- the requisite *Levels of Work* and the *Home Owner Model* of the organisation: its Strategic Vertical Design; and

- the organisation's Integration *Mechanisms and Governance Model*: its Strategic Lateral Design.

At this point in the Strategic Design Process, the Strategic Design is complete, having covered the Identity of the organisation and Foundation of the Design (Chapter 5); the Strategic Horizontal Design (Chapter 6); and the Strategic Vertical and Lateral Designs (Chapter 7). What remains now in the Strategic Design Process can be summarised in four words: Integration, Alignment, Impact and Implementation. The purpose of this chapter is to address these final steps in the process (1).

The arrows in Figure 8.1 depict the outstanding six sub-steps in the Strategic Design Route Map. This chapter will cover these steps, that is Step A.5: Integrated Strategic Design and Organisational Charter to Step A.10: Strategic Design Implementation.

Step A.0: Profile of Organisation – Nature of organisation

A.0.1: Demarcate Organisation

Step A.1: Foundation Construction – Building materials of House

A.1.1: Profile Organisational Context
A.1.2: Map Work Processes
A.1.3: Determine Core Operating Technology with Enablers
A.1.4: Identify Design Givens
A.1.5: Formulate Design Criteria with Design Vision
A.1.6: Diagnose Existing Design – Strengths & Weaknesses

Step A.2: Strategic Horizontal Design – Rooms making up the House

A.2.1: Group Work Processes into Work Units
A.2.2: Configure Work Units into an Organisational Shape
A.2.3: Allocate Crown Jewels
A.2.4: Identify Partnering opportunities

Step A.3: Strategic Vertical Design – Type of ownership and owners of Rooms

A.3.1: Decide on requisite Level of Work of organisation overall
A.3.2: Architect House Ownership Model
A.3.3: Allocate requisite Levels of Work to Work Units
A.3.4: Identify mission critical Work Roles at Work Unit Leadership Level & generate high level Role Profiles

Step A.4: Strategic Lateral Design – Living together in the House

A.4.1: Construct an Interdependency Matrix
A.4.2: Decide on Integration Mechanisms
A.4.3: Set up Governance Model

Step A.5: Integrated Strategic Design and Charter – Overall House Plan

A.5.1: Compile Organisational Map
A.5.2: Draw high level Organogram
A.5.3: Draft Organisational Charter

Step A.6: Strategic Organisational Alignment – Fitting House into Town House Complex

A.6.1: Leadership Alignment
A.6.2: Cultural Alignment
A.6.3: People Alignment
A.6.4: Resources Alignment
A.6.5: Performance Alignment
A.6.6: Work Place Alignment

Step A.7: Strategic Design Impact Assessment – Existing vs. New Houses

A.7.1: Conduct Gap & Risk Analysis

Step A.8: Strategic Design Implementation Road Map – Planning how to build the House

A.8.1: Craft Design Roll Out Strategy & Plan
A.8.2: Craft Organisational Change Navigation Strategy & Plan

Step A.9: Strategic Design Solution Report

Step A.10: Strategic Design Implementation – Building the House

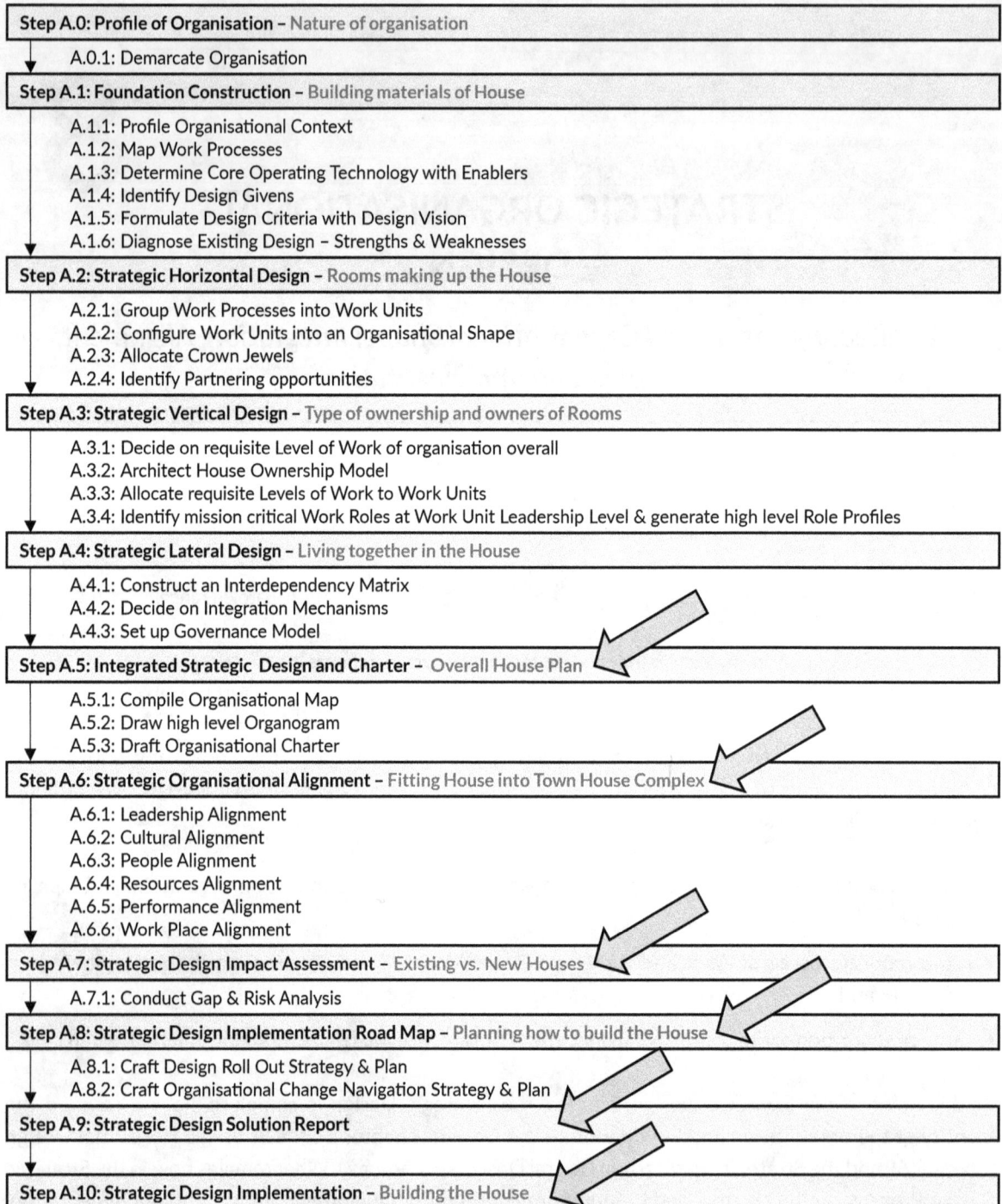

Figure 8.1: Strategic OD route map
Note: Part of Phase 3: Step 3.2 of the OD life cycle (see Chapter 4)

Step A.5: Generate the Integrated Strategic Design and Charter

This step consists of three sub-steps:

- Step A.5.1: Compile Organisational Map of the Integrated Strategic Design

- Step A.5.2 Draw a high level Organogram

- Step A.5.3: Draft an Organisational Charter

Step A.5.1: Compile an Organisational Map of the Integrated Strategic Design

Upon completion of Step A.2: Strategic Horizontal Design, an Organisational Map was drawn to visually represent the design, that is the House Plan (see Step A.2.2.8). This graphic representation of the Organisational Design now has to be extended with the outcomes of Step A.3: Vertical and Step A.4: Lateral Designs. That is including the requisite LOWs by Work Units with the mission-critical Work Roles into the Map (2). The Work Roles (see Design Template 3, Appendix B); Integration Mechanisms (see Design Template 4, Appendix B) and Governance Model (Design Template 5, Appendix B) can be attached to the Organisational Map as critical supporting documents.

In this way, a visual picture and record of the Integrated Strategic Design as a handy reference exists in a single place. This is analogous to having a comprehensive House Plan of the House one wishes to build. The shaded box provides an example of such an Organisational Map for the National Housing Corporation of a national government in Southern Africa. The Integration Mechanisms and Governance Model – Lateral Design – are not shown.

The shaded box provides Guidelines for the Integrated Strategic Organisational Design.

GUIDELINES FOR THE INTEGRATED STRATEGIC ORGANISATIONAL DESIGN

- The Integrated Strategic Organisational Map must be complete, including the Strategic Horizontal and Vertical Designs with the Lateral Design (the Integration Mechanisms and Governance Model), to depict the desired end state of the 'To-Be' Organisation.

- The Map must fit on one page.

- Depict the Map in a visual format to give it greater impact.

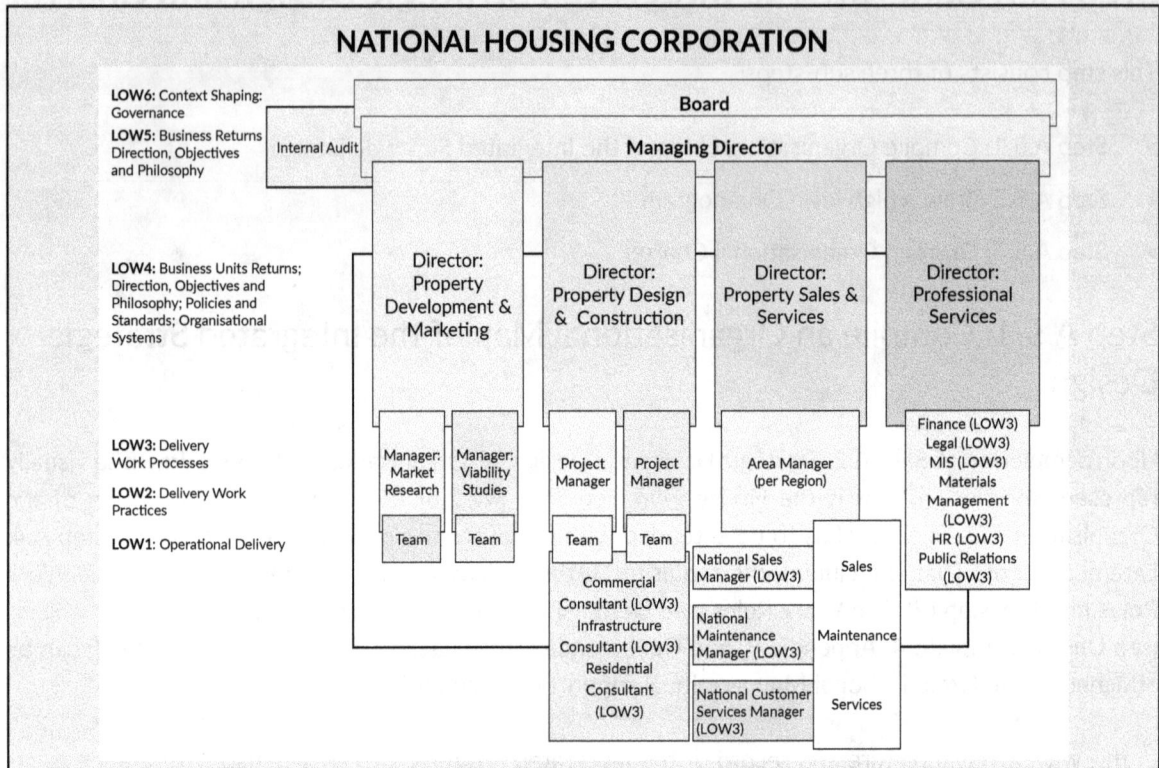

Step A.5.2: Draw a high level Organogram

Only at this point in the Strategic Design Process can and does one draw a high level organogram (or organisational chart) of the top two to three organisational levels, showing the reporting relationships with respect to the mission critical Work Roles. Why only now? Because only at this point in the design process, after five major design steps with 20 sub-steps (see Figure 8.1), has the delivery logic of the organisation been finalised. The organogram has to be based on, and be directly reflective of, this logic.

If it is done any time earlier, the organogram will be based on half-baked insights, political horse trading and personal preferences and wishes, because the rigour and discipline of the Strategic Design Process has not been followed. Therefore, it must be readily apparent that OD cannot be equated to merely drawing an organogram on the back of serviettes or cigarette boxes, as per Myths 3 and 4, debunked in Chapter 2.

The shaded box gives the organogram for the Organisational Map of the National Housing Corporation, whose Strategic Organisational Map was given above.

NATIONAL HOUSING CORPORATION

NATIONAL HOUSING CORPORATION

LOW6: Context Shaping: Governance

LOW5: Business Returns Direction, Objectives and Philosophy

LOW4: Business Units Returns; Direction, Objectives and Philosophy; Policies and Standards; Organisational Systems

LOW3: Delivery Work Processes

LOW2: Delivery Work Practices

Board

Internal Audit — Managing Director

Director: Property Development & Marketing | Director: Property Design & Construction | Director: Property Sales & Services | Director: Professional Services

Manager: Market Research | Manager: Viability Studies | Project Manager | Project Manager | Commercial Consultant | Infrastructure Consultant | Residential Consultant | Finance (LOW3)

Team | Project Team(s) | Legal (LOW3)

MIS (LOW3)

LOW3: Delivery Work Processes

AM* | AM | AM | AM | Materials Management (LOW3)

LOW2: Delivery Work Practices

National Sales Manager (LOW3) | Sales | Sales | Sales | Sales | HR (LOW3)

LOW1: Operational Delivery

National Maintenance Manager (LOW3) | Mainte-nance | Mainte-nance | Mainte-nance | Mainte-nance | Public Relations (LOW3)

National Customer Services Manager (LOW3) | Services | Services | Services | Services

* Area Manager

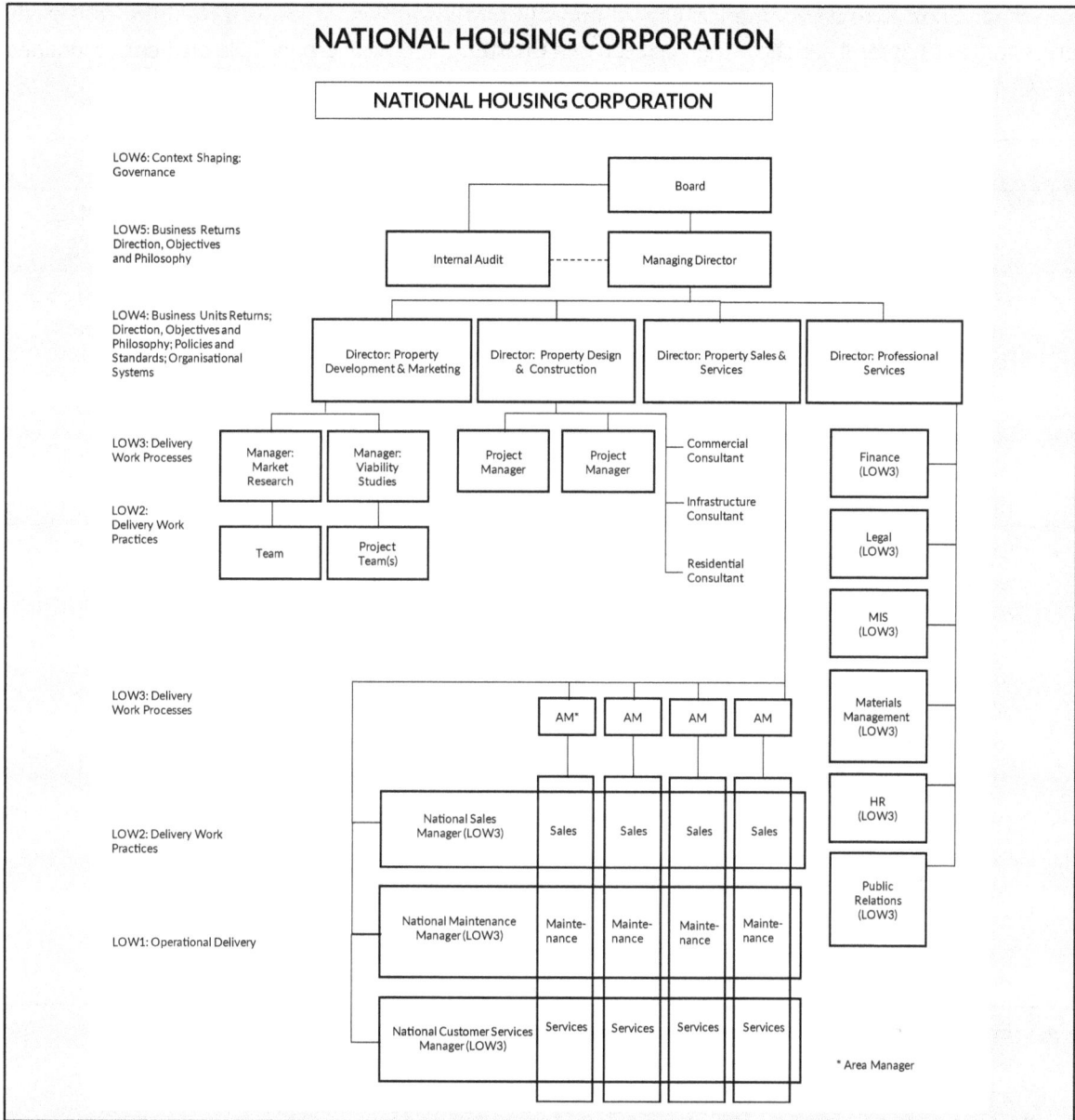

Step A.5.3: Draft an Organisational Charter

A concrete expression of the ground rules of the Operating Model of the 'To-Be' Organisation – its delivery logic – can be given in the form of an Organisational Charter. A Charter forms the 'constitution' of how the organisation will operate. It aims to direct, guide and monitor the stakeholders' thinking, deciding, and doing regarding the organisation's delivery. It can also be called the 'Operating and Philosophy' of the organisation (3). An Organisational Charter must be simple, clear, and inspiring, preferably not contain more than ten statements, that is 'Less is more'.

The shaded box gives a hypothetical Organisational Charter for Swatch, derived from the case study presented in Chapter 4. To show the make-up of a Charter, the typical ground rule elements contained in a Charter are indicated in the right hand column. This column will not be shown in a Charter.

HYPOTHETICAL ORGANISATIONAL CHARTER OF SWATCH	
ORGANISATIONAL CHARTER	**GROUND RULE ELEMENTS**
• Why do we exist and for whose benefit? The Purpose of our organisation is our secure anchor and fixed reference point against which we judge all of our thinking, decisions and actions. *Our Purpose is to make our innovative, inexpensively priced watch – the Swatch – the most popular watch brand in the world.*	*Purpose of Organisation as part of its Identity*
• In pursuit of our Purpose we will operate like an armada of unique, autonomous ships in mutual support of each other in real time, directed and guided by our shared, overarching Purpose, destination and core values.	*Design Vision and Metaphor*
• On the customer-facing side of our business, we are highly decentralised, organised along clearly differentiated product lines with distinct brands, and headed up by highly autonomous Global Product Managers, each being accountable for a specific product line. Where feasible, autonomous Country Managers are in place to give us strong, localised customer connectivity and feedback. They have a deep understanding of customer needs, expectations and satisfaction in order to decide independently what product, for which customer, at what time, and at what price, will delight them in their countries.	*Mode of Working: Horizontally*
• On the R&D and Manufacturing sides of our business – designing and producing our products – we are highly centralised into single, autonomous operating entities – headed up by single, global leaders – to give us respectively innovation depth and economies of scale. These entities supply to our market-facing roles and units, providing the right product for the right customers, at the right time, in the right place, at the right price, at the right quality.	
• Everyone at all levels everywhere collaborate seamlessly with whoever, whenever, and in whatever form – across the boundaries of function, product, and geography – in delighting our customers, both internal and external, and exceeding their expectations.	*Mode of Working: Laterally*
• Everyone at any level has the authority and autonomy to do whatever it takes to delight our customers and keep our promises to them by challenging, changing, and transforming – without any fear – the existing into the better, even if it is different.	*Governance Model: Decision-making Rights and Style*
• We see our people as responsible, self-motivated, trustworthy adults who are the only true value unlockers and wealth creators in our organisation, inspiring and driving our relentless innovation and customer delight, in this way making our Purpose an everyday reality for all of our stakeholders.	*View of People*

Quality assurance: Stage A.5: Integrated Strategic Design

QUALITY ASSURANCE QUESTIONS *Step A.5: Integrated Strategic Design – Complete House Plan*	DESIGN STEP	ADDRESSED: YES/NO *(Yes: +; No: x)*
Is the **Organisational Map** of the **Integrated Strategic Design** a correct, visual representation of the desired overall delivery logic of the organisation?	Step A.5.1	
Is the **organogram** a true reflection of the Integrated Strategic Design, that is the delivery logic of the organisation? Does the **organogram** contain all of the **mission critical Work Roles?**	Step A.5.2	
Is the **Organisational Charter** a true and complete reflection and philosophy of the organisation's 'To-Be' Design, its Operating Model?	Step A.5.3	
Does the Integrated Strategic Design meet the set **Strategic Design Criteria**, reflect the **Strategic Design Vision**, and resonate with the **Design Metaphor** representing the Design Vision?	Stage A.5 overall	

Step A.6: Ensure Strategic Organisational Alignment

The Design of the organisation is one of the building blocks of the Organisational Landscape, as depicted in Figure 8.2. This figure was also given in Chapter 3 (Figure 3.2) where the positioning of Design in the Landscape was discussed.

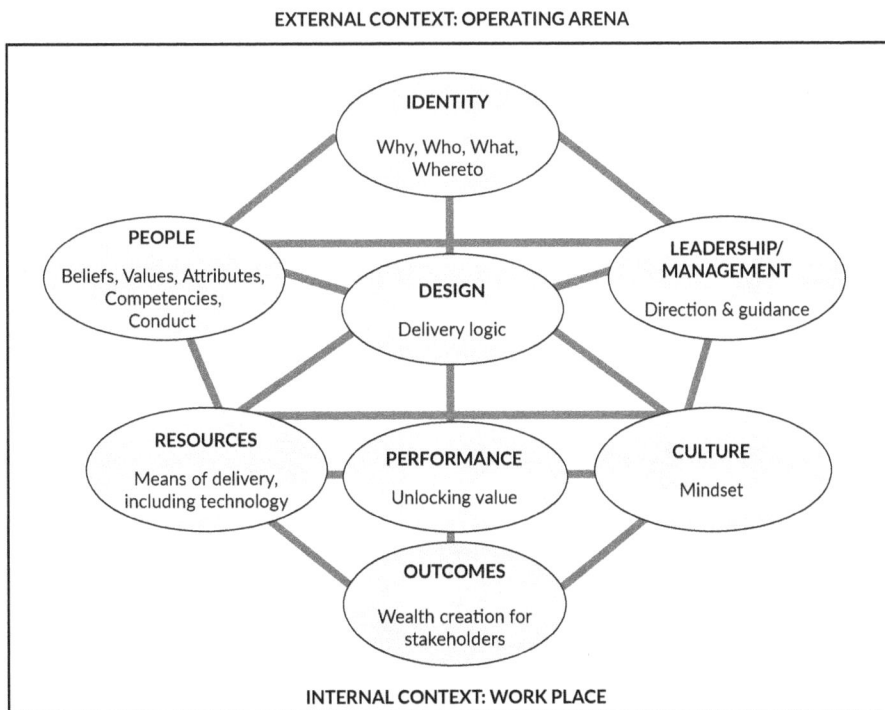

Figure 8.2: Design as part of the Organisational Landscape

According to the discussion in Chapter 3, and as can be seen from Figure 8.2, the Organisational Landscape forms a dynamic, systemic interconnected whole of reciprocally influencing, interacting building blocks. Given the nature of the Organisational Landscape, the objective of this design step is to ensure that Organisational Landscape building blocks support/reinforce the proposed Design. Metaphorically, it is about fitting the House (= Design) into the Town House Complex (= Organisational Landscape). The key issue is: *In terms of the Organisational Landscape in which the 'To-Be' Design is embedded, what alignments (or fit) are required in the other organisational components making up the Organisational Landscape?*

The alignment of the 'To-Be' Organisational Design to the respective building blocks of the Organisational Landscape to ensure a congruent Organisational Landscape – supporting and reinforcing the Design – is critical if the fit-for-purpose design is to be effective and efficient (4) (5). In a sense, a fit-for-purpose design is only fit in the final instance if the Organisational Landscape is aligned to the Design. The alignment of the building blocks of the Organisational Landscape – particularly, the fit-for-purpose Design and the other building blocks – correlates with significantly higher organisational performance and success (6).

Table 8.1 gives examples of the Organisational Landscape alignments required for different Strategic Intent Organisational Designs, namely Product/Service Innovation-centric, Customer-centric or Cost-centric. This table is a further extension of Table 6.2, which only dealt with the Strategic Intent – Design alignment. Table 8.1 covers the complete alignment across the total Organisational Landscape (7).

Table 8.1: Organisational Landscape Alignment for different Strategic Intent-Organisational Designs: Product/Service Innovation-centric, Customer-centric or Cost-centric

ORGANISATIONAL INGREDIENTS		ORGANISATIONAL SHAPES		
		Product/Service Innovation-Centric	**Customer-Centric**	**Cost-Centric**
STRATEGIC INTENT	**Goal**	Best product/service for customer	Best solution for customer	Lowest total cost
	Main offering	New products/service	Personalised packages of product, service, support, education, training, consulting	An acceptable product at the lowest price
	Value creation route	Cutting-edge products/ services, useful features, new applications	Customising for the total solution	No-frills offering for the middle of the market
	Most important customer	Most advanced customer	Most profitable, loyal customer	The value shopper
	Priority setting basis	Portfolio of products/ services – product/service profitability	Portfolio of customers – customer profitability	Find the most efficient way to do everything – product/market share

ORGANISATIONAL INGREDIENTS		ORGANISATIONAL SHAPES		
		Product/Service Innovation-Centric	Customer-Centric	Cost-Centric
	Pricing	Price to market	Price for value, risk	Guaranteed lowest price or everyday low price
DESIGN	Organisational concept	Product/Service profit centres, product reviews, product teams	Customer segments, customer teams, customer profit and loss	Strong centralised functions to standardise, economise, and achieve scale
	Most important process	New product/service development	Customer relationship management and solution development	Order-to-cash All transactions processes are efficiently re-engineered
LEADERSHIP	Leadership stance	Transcendental: meaning, purpose, beliefs	Transformational: vision, philosophy, values	Transactional: goals, plans, standards
CULTURE	Mind set	Innovative-entrepreneurial: new product/service culture – open to new ideas, experimentation	Relationship management: searching for more customer needs to satisfy	Achievement-efficiency-continuous improvement: constant search for improvement of costs through eliminating waste and variety and implementing repeatable processes
RESOURCES	Core organisational capabilities	• New product/service development • Market research • R & D Pipeline	• Key customer relationship management • Customisation • Client knowledge management	• Supply chain: inward and outward bound logistics • Management/cost accounting • Core technology enablement/automation
	Technology Enablement Model	• Innovation Model	• Service Model	• Automation Model
PERFORMANCE	Measures	• Number of new products/services • Percent of revenue from products/services less than two years old • Market share	• Profit per customer • Customer share of most valuable customers • Customer satisfaction • Lifetime value of a customer • Customer retention	• Productivity per core process • Detailed costs per core process/transaction • Total delivered cost • Constant improvement and cost reduction • Quality/wastage • Up time and utilisation of equipment

ORGANISATIONAL INGREDIENTS		ORGANISATIONAL SHAPES		
		Product/Service Innovation-Centric	Customer-Centric	Cost-Centric
PEOPLE	Approach to people	People Profile: • R & D specialists • Creative and innovative • Self-driven with internal locus of control	People Profile: • Customer specialists • Relationship driven • Service orientation • Empathy	People Profile: • Operations management • Cost effectiveness/ Efficiency orientation • Planning, co-ordination and control
		Power to people who conceive and develop products/services: highest reward is working on next, most challenging product	Power to people with in-depth knowledge of customer's business: highest rewards to relationship managers who save the customer's business	Power to discoverers of how to use scale and leverage: highest rewards to the proposers of cost-reduction ideas
		Manage creative people through challenges with a stretch deadline	Enable and empower people to delight customers	Best if it is the frugal person who prefers to work for the organisation
	Mental process	Divergent thinking: *How many possible uses of this product/service?*	Convergent thinking: *What combination of products/services is best for this customer?*	Lean thinking: *How to eliminate time, waste, cost?*
	Sales bias	On the side of the seller in a transaction	On the side of the buyer in a transaction	Anything that increases constant, level volume

Excluded from Table 8.1, but a key building block of the Organisational Landscape, is the Internal Context: Workplace (see Figure 8.2). The Workplace – in particular, the Physical Workplace – must also be aligned to the 'To-Be' design in its appearance and lay-out. This implies working with the likes of architects to redesign the workplace to fit the design. For example, a team-based design demands team-based working spaces, while a process flow design must allow organisational members to work in a process flow way.

The shaded box provides guidelines for Strategic Organisational Alignment. A template to assist in the consideration of the various Organisational Alignments across the Organisational Landscape is given in Appendix B: Design Template 6.

GUIDELINES FOR STRATEGIC ORGANISATIONAL ALIGNMENT

- Ensure that all building blocks of the whole Organisational Landscape are covered.
- Organisational Alignments must fit the set Strategic Design Criteria and Vision with its accompanying Design Metaphor.

Quality assurance: Stage A.6: Strategic Organisational Alignment

QUALITY ASSURANCE QUESTIONS *Step A.6: Organisational Alignment – Fitting the House into the Town House Complex*	DESIGN STEP	ADDRESSED: YES/NO *(Yes: +; No: x)*
Has the **Strategic Intent-Organisational Design Alignment** been re-validated?	Stage A.5	
Have the necessary **Organisational Alignments** across the Organisational Landscape – that are required to support/reinforce the proposed Design – been identified and crafted? • Leadership Alignment • Culture Alignment • People Alignment • Resources (including Systems, Core Operating Technology) Alignment • Performance Alignment • Work Place Alignment	Stage A.5	
Does the crafted organisational alignment meet the set **Design Criteria**, reflect the **Design Vision**, and resonate with the **Design Metaphor** representing the Design Vision?	Stage A.5 overall	

Step A.7: Conduct a Strategic Design Impact Assessment: 'As-Is' vs. 'To-Be' Designs

In the previous step, the required Strategic Organisational Alignment was established across the Organisational Landscape to support and reinforce the new design. The aim of this step is to determine the difference between the Existing and the Future Desired Designs: the current House ('As-Is') vs. the new House ('To-Be'). The key issue is: where are the gaps with their associated risks between the two designs, and what actions must be taken to close them?

The gap assessment of the Current vs. Future Desired Designs must cover, at a minimum, the following: the Mental Model required by the design; the Design Criteria; the Design Vision with its commensurate Design Metaphor; the Horizontal, Vertical and Lateral Designs; the required Organisational Alignments (which only applies to the new design); and finally, the Costing of the two Designs. The major risks associated with the gaps must also assessed and the actions must be decided upon to close the gaps and minimise/eliminate the commensurate risks.

Table 8.2 gives an example of an extract of what such a Strategic Design Impact Assessment could look like. A template to assist in the Impact Assessment is given in Appendix B: Design Template 7.

Table 8.2: Example of an extract of a Strategic Design Impact Assessment

CRITICAL DESIGN VARIABLE	CURRENT DESIGN	FUTURE, DESIRED DESIGN	ASSESSED GAP TRANSLATED INTO CHANGE NEED	RISK ASSESSMENT 1=High; 2=Medium; 3=Low	IMPLEMEN-TATION PRIORITY 1=High; 2=Medium; 3=Low	REQUIRED ACTIONS TO CLOSE CRITICAL GAPS
Mental Model required by Design Beliefs, Assumptions, Values, Norms, Attitudes						
Design Criteria						
Design Vision with Metaphor						
Horizontal Design						

The Assessed Gap given in Table 8.2 has to be translated into an overall organisational change need to be addressed through a change navigation strategy and plan (see Step A.8.2 below). Four types of needs can be distinguished as given in Figure 8.3 (8):

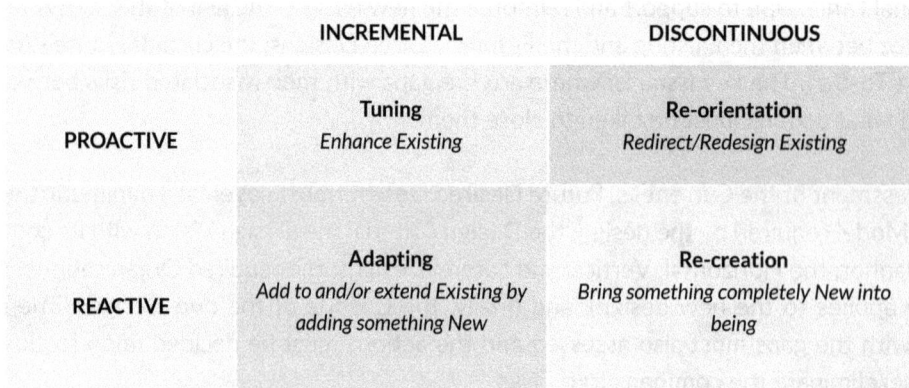

	INCREMENTAL	DISCONTINUOUS
PROACTIVE	**Tuning** *Enhance Existing*	**Re-orientation** *Redirect/Redesign Existing*
REACTIVE	**Adapting** *Add to and/or extend Existing by adding something New*	**Re-creation** *Bring something completely New into being*

Figure 8.3: Typology of Change Needs

Guidelines for the Strategic Design Impact Assessment are given in the shaded box.

GUIDELINES FOR THE STRATEGIC DESIGN IMPACT ASSESSMENT

- Be brutally honest in terms of the assessment: face the true reality. Not the 'nice to be' or a make-believe reality.

- Focus on the make-or-break gaps with high risks which must form the basis of the priorities.

- Do not underestimate the required actions to close the gaps, especially resource-wise. Rather be conservative and err on the generous side, resource-wise.

- If the gap between the current and future desired designs is too big and overwhelming, DO NOT change the future desired design. This is the design that a robust, thorough design process has shown to be fit-for-purpose. Rather architect interim designs that will take the organisation progressively to the future desired design.

Quality assurance: Stage A.7: Strategic Design Impact Assessment

QUALITY ASSURANCE QUESTIONS *Step A.7: Strategic Design Impact Assessment – 'The existing vs. the new House'*	DESIGN STEP	ADDRESSED: YES/NO *(Yes: +; No: x)*
Have the **make-or-break gaps with high risks and the actions** *necessary* to close the gap between the current and future desired designs been identified and prioritised?	Stage A.7	
Does the Impact Assessment address the **true reality**? Is it brutally honest?	Stage A.7	

Step A.8: Craft a Strategic Design Implementation Road Map

The Design Implementation Road Map consists of two components: (i) the roll out strategy and plan for the 'To-Be' Design; and (ii) a change navigation strategy and plan to increase the likelihood that all stakeholders will buy-in and take ownership of the new design Metaphorically put: 'Planning how to build the House with committed tenants'. The key issue is how to maximise the likelihood of a successful implementation of the new design within the strategic window of opportunity.

This step thus consists of two steps:

- Step A.8.1: Craft a Design Roll Out Strategy and Plan
- Step A.8.2: Craft a Change Navigation Strategy and Plan

Step A.8.1: Craft a Design Roll Out Strategy and Plan

The objective of this design step is to plan how to roll out the proposed design and build the measurement model necessary to track and monitor the implementation. The typical aspects of a sound Roll Out

Strategy and Plan have to be covered, i.e.: (i) an overall Roll Out Strategy (such as big bang vs. incremental); (ii) the Plan itself, consisting of the what, by when, how, who, and a handover log, based on the actions identified in the Impact Assessment; (iii) a Roll Out measurement model; and (iv) the Roll Out governance structure and process. A template for a Strategic Design Roll Out Strategy and Plan is given in Appendix B: Design Template 8.

The Roll Out measurement model requires some further elucidation. A comprehensive measurement model consists of three types of metrics:

- *Design roll out implementation metrics:* the usual project roll out metrics of time, achievements of deadlines/milestones, deliverables and budget.

- *People adoption metrics:* metrics derived from the new delivery logic, indicating whether people are working as per the new delivery logic.
- *Organisational performance metrics:* metrics indicating whether the new design is delivering the expected benefits and making the intended value-add, including sustainability metrics

The shaded box provides Guidelines for a Strategic Design Roll Out Plan.

GUIDELINES FOR A STRATEGIC DESIGN ROLL OUT PLAN (9)

Caveat: The bias of the author in the implementation guidelines given below is towards an incremental roll out of a brownfield redesign, and a big bang roll out in the case of a greenfield design, based on his observation over many years of:

- the chaos of the (unintended, positive and negative) consequences of implementation impatience;
- the under-assessment of the complexity of the new design, as well as the responses of organisations/ people in general to redesign. The typical roll out approach to the introduction of a new design in many organisations is: *'Friday we announce the new design (usually only a revised organogram is communicated) which in its totality will become effective coming Monday from 8h00 onwards. Thank you very much.'*; and
- the misjudgement of the actual resources required – time, money, people – to put the new Design in place.

Brownfield: Strategic Redesign

Incremental Roll Out Strategy and Plan by Organisational Level (not to be confused with LOWs) of the new design:

LAUNCH: First 30-90 days: Reshape organisation and activate natural Work Teams making up the Work Units

- **Action 1:** *Road show/workshop* with finalised revised OD. (It is assumed that everyone was kept informed/ consulted as the Horizontal, Vertical and Lateral Designs were being architected. There should not be any major surprises at this stage.)
- **Action 2:** Identify, assess and appoint *Work Role incumbents* to Design Levels 1 and 2, and possibly Level 3 Work Roles, for the mission-critical Work Roles for which Profiles were generated (see Step A.3.4).

- **Action 3:** Go live at Design Levels 1 and 2 with the new design by merely *regrouping existing Work Units* at Design Level 2 by changing reporting relationships in order to set up the organisation for the Tactical Design process of Work Units. Look for quick wins from the new design.
- **Action 4:** Conduct Team Building Sessions with each natural team at Design Levels 1 and 2, focusing on the hardware (that is the design with enabling organisational processes) and software (the change journey to date and how the team is going to work together as a team). (See the suggested two day programme in Appendix C: Programme Template 1: Teaming and Alignment Design Workshop Programme.)
- **Action 5:** Monitor and track implementation against Design Measurement Model, and take corrective action.

MOMENTUM: Months 4 to 6: Organisational Alignment

- **Action 6**: Do progressive Organisational Alignments, for example budgets, performance contracts and personal development plans, as directed by priorities from the Impact Assessment.
- **Action 7** (in parallel to Actions 2 to 5): Specify/define changing operating requirements, for example communication flows, information requirements and authorisation levels.
- **Action 8:** (in parallel to Actions 5 and 6): Once a Work Unit team has entered into the Performing Team Stage, initiate the Tactical and Operational Designs of the Work Unit in chronological sequence.

REFINE AND LEARN: Months 6 to 9 and beyond: Making Design work to its fullest potential

- **Action 9:** Roll out Tactical and Operational Designs sequentially in a similar fashion to Actions 1 to 4 of the Strategic Design roll out.
- **Action 10:** Fine tune design as operating bugs appear. Allow for localisation in specific organisational areas in order to meet unique circumstances.
- **Action 11:** Learn how to reap the full benefits of the new design.

Greenfield: First time ever Strategic Design

LAUNCH: First 60-90 days

- **Action 1:** Big bang, cascading from top level down in terms of staffing up the new design, across all Work Units simultaneously and in parallel, in the logical sequence of setting up Work Units: Strategic-Tactical-Operational Designs.
- **Action 2:** Conduct Team Building Sessions with each natural team at Levels 1 and 2, focusing on the hardware (that is the design with enabling organisational processes) and software (the change journey to date and how the team is going to work together as a team). (See the suggested two day programme in Appendix C: Programme Template 1: Teaming and Alignment Design Workshop Programme.)
- **Action 3:** Monitor and track implementation against Design Measurement Model, and take corrective action.

REFINE AND LEARN: Months 4 to 12 and beyond: Making Design work to its fullest potential

- **Action 4:** Fine tune design as operating bugs appear. Allow localisation in specific organisational areas in order to meet unique circumstances.
- **Action 5:** Learn how to reap the full benefits of the new design.

Step A.8.2: Craft a Change Navigation Strategy and Plan

Although only discussed now under this step, a change navigation strategy and plan must be in place to support and enable the total strategic design process throughout from the word 'Go'. That is, from the time the OD intervention is first communicated. (In this regard, refer back to Figure 3.6 which provides an overview of the generic overall OD process, and Chapter 4: Phase 2.8 of the OD process as an organisational intervention, which deals with the issuing of a communication brief informing all parties concerned regarding the pending OD intervention.)

The aim of the change navigation strategy and plan is:

- firstly, to build the needed *buy-in and commitment* amongst stakeholders to undertake the change journey;

- secondly, to enable the successful navigation of the three *change states* (see discussion below), such that the 'To-Be' state would become the 'As-Is' state; and

- thirdly, to ensure that the *parties* impacted by the change arrives transformed in the new 'As-Is' state able, willing and engaged to perform and contribute.

Because the focus of my book is on Organisational Design, *not* change navigation, a full blown discussion of change navigation will not be undertaken here. However, a number of pertinent points will be highlighted.

Change navigation as organisational journey encompasses the 'As-Is', 'To-Be', and 'In-Between' States

The journey towards a desired future change – in this case a new Organisational Design – pertains to the conversion of the *'As-Is'* state – the existing design, into the *'To-Be'* state – the future, desired design. Between the 'As-Is' and 'To-Be' states another state exists, namely the *'In-Between'* state – the state of transition: the time/space during which and where the change journey occurs and unfolds as the new design is being rolled out.

Within the 'In-Between' state, the 'As-Is' state – the existing design – is increasingly becoming 'unreal', while in tandem the 'To-Be' state (or derivatives and/or corruptions of this state) – the future desired design – is becoming 'real'. Subsequent to the conversion of the 'As-Is' state into the 'To-Be' state, having passed through the 'In-Between' state, the organisation will be different to a greater or lesser degree in terms of its character, dynamics, functioning, performance and/or trajectory as a function of the new design.

Figure 8.4 graphically illustrates the above discussion (10). W1 to W4 will be explicated in the next section.

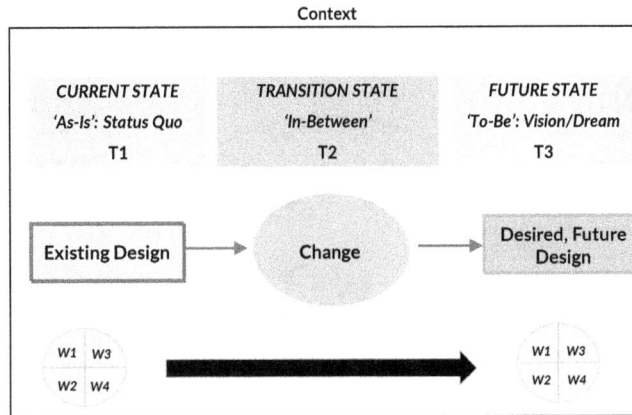

Figure 8.4: Change navigation as an organisational journey encompassing the 'As-Is', 'To-Be', and 'In-Between' States

Change navigation as a journey affecting the four Worlds populated by the organisation's Action Community

The Organisational Landscape – as a dynamic, systemic network – is conceived, constituted, moulded together, sustained, and frequently destroyed by the psycho-social dynamics infusing the set of interacting stakeholders of the organisation – its action community – populating the Organisational Landscape. Individually and severally, stakeholders create and sustain, but also can destroy, the organisation. In turn, the organisation, once created, 'forces' stakeholders to relate and interact with each other in terms of established patterns – virtuous or vicious – within the Organisational Landscape.

As an action community, the stakeholders populate four reciprocally interdependent Worlds simultaneously – all affected to a greater or lesser extent by the context of the emerging new order (see Figure 2.2.) – and the corresponding change to be navigated. The four Worlds were included in Figure 8.4 in two circles as W1 to W4 at the bottom of the figure. Figure 8.5 depicts in detail the make-up of the four Worlds (11). In the figure the Context of World 3 refers to the organisation's Operating Arena, whilst the Context as outer border embracing all four Worlds refer to the world at large.

Context

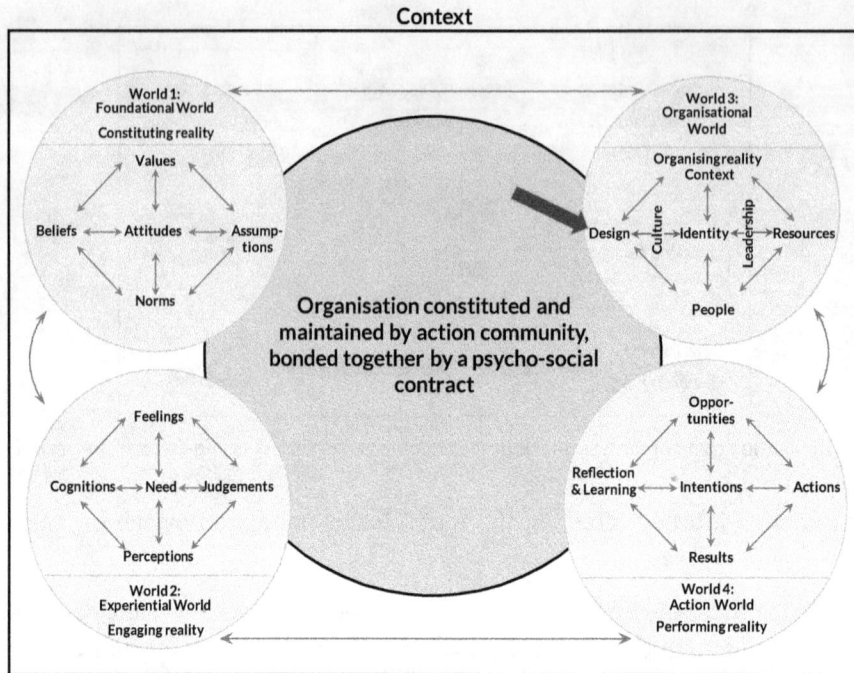

Figure 8.5: Four Worlds populated by stakeholders as the Action Community of the Organisation

According to Figure 8.5, the design (indicated by the arrow) of the organisation forms part of World 3: Organisational World. The more radical the change need – moving from Tuning to Recreation (see Figure 8.3 above) – the greater the degree of change required; not only in World 3, but also in Worlds 1: Foundational World and 2: Experiential World. The future desired design, being a totally different design to the existing one, will demand changes in some or all of the elements making up Worlds 1 and 2. This insight also debarks Myth 2 that OD does not require the shifting of mindsets, flames of reference and attitudes.

Change Navigation Value Chain

The change journey can be depicted in the form of a Change Value Chain. An example of such a Value Chain is depicted in Figure 8.6, premised on a Complexity/Chaos world view (12).

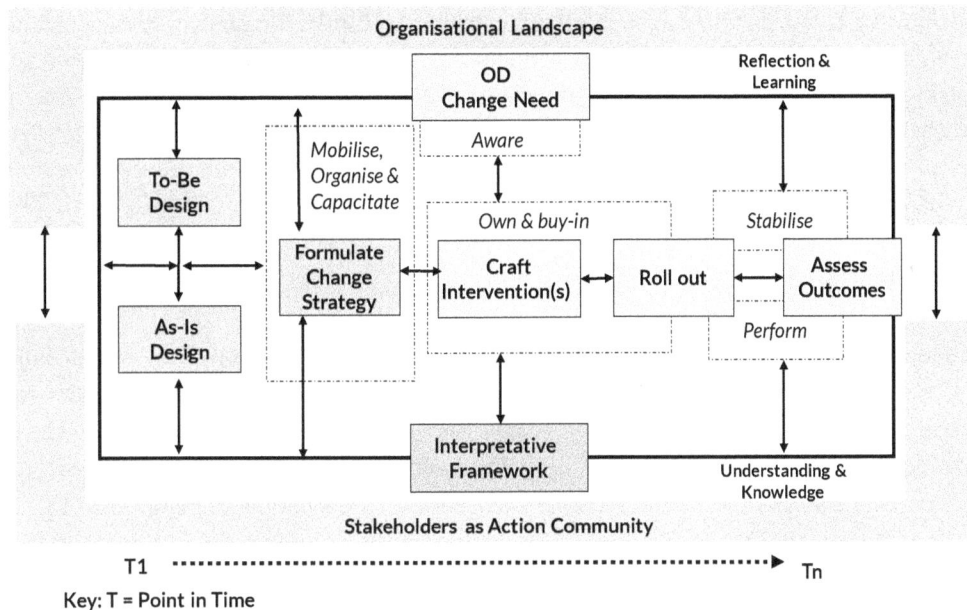

Figure 8.6: Typical Change Navigation Value Chain

According to Figure 8.6, the Change Navigation Value Chain consists of a set of interdependent, reciprocally influencing actions. This process – with its associated actions – forms an organic and dynamic whole. Although the process depicted in Figure 8.6 appears linear and sequential with feedback loops, giving the process an input-throughput-output-like (or systems or cybernetic) appearance, the process must be viewed from the perspective of a Complexity/Chaos world view. This systemic, interconnected patterned view of reality, as applied to the change navigation process, is represented in Figure 8.6 in the form of two way arrows.

The two way arrows in Figure 8.6 hence represent dynamic relationships that not only indicate 'approximate' sequencing, but also the (re)validation and (re)confirmation of what has gone before. This may imply a return to reconsider, reaffirm, and/or re-address an earlier action(s) in the change navigation process. For example, although the OD Change Need – and its scoping – sequentially triggers the change navigation process as shown in Figure 8.6, the subsequent stages revalidate and reconfirm in greater detail the validity of the initial understanding and scoping of the Change Need. It may need to be redefined reiteratively, given the insights gained through the unfolding of the subsequent change navigation stages.

Furthermore, the process illustrated in Figure 8.6 is based on an action research and learning approach to the change navigation process. This approach propagates that the change navigation process must be facilitated and enabled by deliberate, ongoing learning and reflection, as well as an internalised, deepening understanding and knowledge, as the change unfolds within the Organisational Landscape and its Action Community.

Metaphorically described, given a 'Chess' change navigation attitude, the game – the change navigation process – consists of a set of chess pieces: the actions making up the change navigation process as reflected in Figure 8.6. Any of the pieces can be played at any time. *Firstly*, according to certain rules, that is, change navigation and best practices. *Secondly*, accordingly to a bigger game plan that dynamically changes as the game unfolds. That is, as the organisation with its Action Community responding to the unfolding change.

Change Navigation Intelligence

Given an action research and learning approach to the change navigation process, real time change navigation intelligence must be generated during the change navigation journey in order to monitor and track the unfolding journey. In this way a progressively, deepening understanding of the unfolding journey can be built, and real time, in time, corrective action can be taken. Proper change navigation intelligence demands a balanced scorecard approach, such as the example in Figure 8.7 (13).

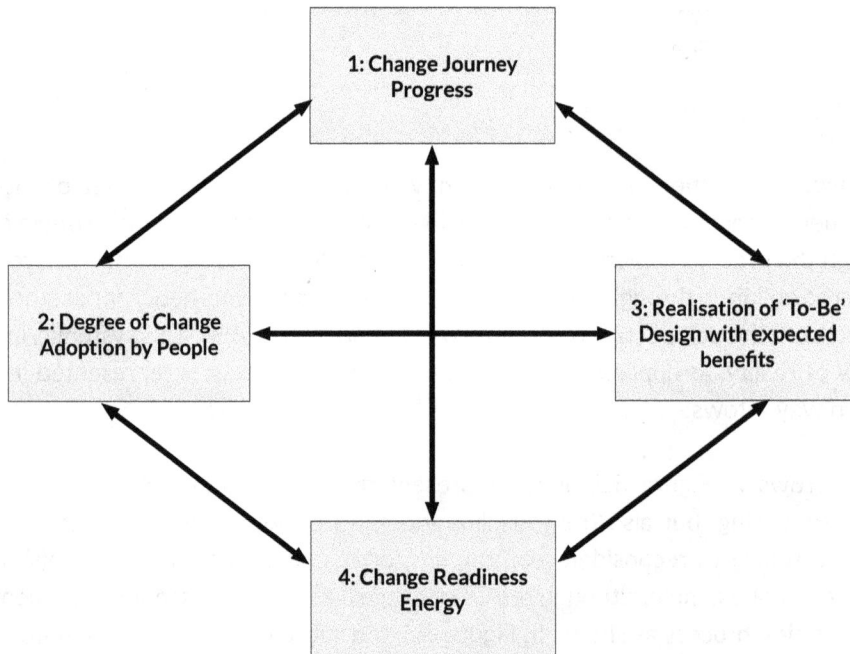

Figure 8.7: Change Navigation Intelligence: Balanced Scorecard Approach

In the discussion under Step A.8.1 of the implementation measurement model, Measurement Domains 1 to 3 in Figure 8.7 were explicated. In Figure 8.7 a fourth Measurement Domain is added: Change Readiness Energy. This dimension entails the energy present within the action community, individually and severally, during the unfolding change journey. This energy level has to be kept at the right level at all times if the likelihood of the successful conversion of the 'As-Is' state into the 'To-Be' state within the 'In-Between' state is to occur: no energy, no movement. The measures making up this dimension are given in Table 8.3. As the change journey unfolds, a real time picture must exist at all times of the energy level present within the action community of the organisation (14).

Table 8.3: Change Readiness Energy Dimension

Change Readiness Energy Measures
❑ Need for and desire to change
❑ Sponsorship and stakeholder commitment
❑ Leadership visibility
❑ Vision clarity
❑ Benefits of change relative to costs of change
❑ Resource availability (for example, time, people, money)
❑ Confidence in implementation capability
❑ Clear route map, roles and contributions
❑ Change adopter confidence and competence
❑ Recognition and celebration of successes

A real time, in time, revitalisation and alignment perspective of the Change Navigation Journey

Increasing the Change Navigation Value Chain (see Figure 8.6) is being approached from a revitalisation and alignment perspective. As the change is being navigated, affected stakeholders making up the action community are:

- assisted to *'Let go of the past, and embrace the future'* in order to eliminate/minimise the change baggage from the past and deal with 'unfinished business' resulting from past change, in order to prepare them to deal more ably with present/future change;

- enabled to understand where they are, individually and collectively, on the *change transitional cycle* in the 'In-Between' State, as well as what is needed to move along on the cycle. Figure 8.8 depicts such a cycle (15);

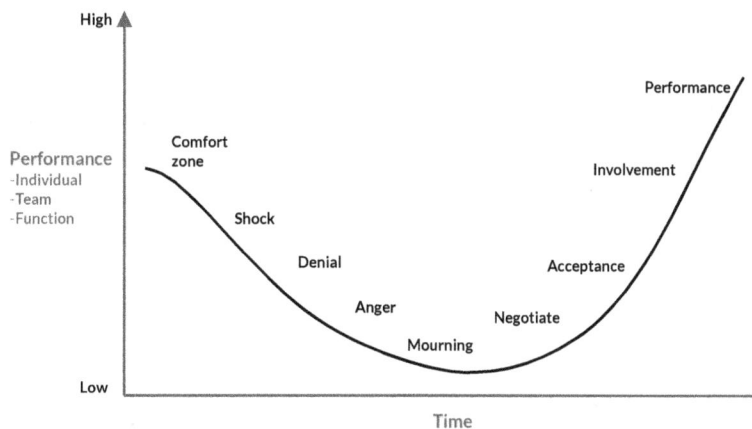

Figure 8.8: Change transitional cycle(s) in the 'In-Between' state

- *realigned as natural work teams* within the new design in terms of who they are as a team, how they want to work together, what their mutual expectations are, and the core values guiding their behaviour (the team 'software'). This is enabled through the restoration of the *organisational memory* within these teams regarding how to operate and do things in the organisation, which was 'destroyed' during the change (the team 'hardware') (see the suggested two day programme in Appendix C: Programme Template 1: Teaming and Alignment Design workshop programme); and

- re-energised though the organisation's *'Future Definition of Victory'*, which is customised by teams for themselves, with guidance on how to gain this victory within the transforming/transformed Organisational Landscape. The Future Definition of Victory equates in this instance to the realisation of the expected benefits of the new design.

A template for a Change Navigation Strategy and Plan is given in Appendix B: Design Template 9.

Quality assurance: Step A.8: Craft a Strategic Design Implementation Plan

QUALITY ASSURANCE QUESTIONS *Step A.8: Strategic Design Implementation Plan – 'Planning how to build the House with committed tenants'*	DESIGN STEPS	ADDRESSED: YES/NO *(Yes: +; No: x)*
Is the **Design Implementation Road Map – Roll Out and Change Navigation**, with its milestones, complete, clear and simple?	Stage 4.8 overall	
Is the **Roll Out/Change Intelligence Measurement Model** to track and monitor the implementation complete, covering all four measurement domains, but simple, focusing on the critical measures? Is the model being used in real time?	Step A.8.2 Figure 8.8	
Does the **Change Navigation Strategy and Plan** cover all of the key stakeholders?	Step A.8.2	
Is the **Change Navigation Strategy and Plan** powerful enough to obtain and sustain the necessary buy-in and continued commitment from all stakeholders in order to realise the 'To-Be' state?	Step A.8.2	

Step A.9: Compile a Strategic Design Solution Report

A detailed report on the Strategic Design Solution must be produced by the OD Expert, which will form the basis of implementation. Without proper documentation, the implementation has a high likelihood of derailment given the intensity of personal and organisational dynamics that OD invokes. The design process is completed with the delivery of the report. A typical Strategic Design Solution Report template is given in Appendix D: Report Template 1.

Step A.10: Implement Strategic Design

The aim of this step is to implement the Strategic Design Solution in accordance with the Implementation Road Map: Building the House with committed tenants. It is important to track the roll out and value-add of the new design at three, six and nine month intervals, fine tuning it where necessary. However, the re-architected design must be kept intact for at least five years because the new design, if done properly, should be aligned to the organisation's corresponding Identity.

Conclusion

This chapter covered the final steps of the strategic design process:

- Step A.5: Generate the Integrated Strategic Design and Organisational Charter
- Step A.6: Ensure Strategic Organisational Alignment
- Step A.7: Conduct Strategic Design Impact Assessment
- Step A.8: Craft Strategic Design Implementation Road Map
- Step A. 9: Compile Strategic Design Solution Report
- Step A.10: Implement Strategic Design

Typically the Strategic Design Process would have taken approximately three months up to the point of implementation.

The discussion of the strategic design process in Chapters 5 to 8 was based on Design Process Option 1: Expert generated (see Table 4.3). In this option the Client requires the OD Expert to craft a design and submit it to her/him for a decision.

With respect to the other three possible options, the Strategic Design Process would take on the following forms:

- *Option 1: Assurance:* The Client has already generated a desired design. The OD Expert merely has to quality assure the Client's proposed design, independently and in an impartial, objective manner, against leading OD practice. In this instance, the OD Expert can use the Quality Assurance Questions given at the end of each strategic design step to stress test the Client-proposed Strategic Design Solution. It is critically important in the case of this option that the OD Expert does not respond on the spot to the Client's proposed solution, but requests at least two full days to work through what is proposed at his/her leisure, and then have a work session with the Client to provide well-considered feedback.

- *Option 2: Straw Model:* The OD Expert crafts a 'straw model' design which is workshopped with the relevant key decision makers in the client system for a final decision, followed by a finalisation of the Strategic Design solution. Typically, this workshop – usually one to two day – would take place as an additional step after Step A.5: Integrated Strategic Organisational Design and Organisational Charter. After the workshop, the outstanding steps as outlined above (Steps A.6 to A.9) will be completed.

The personal experience of the author has shown that one needs to invite the top three levels of leaders of the organisation to participate. In LOW language – assuming a requisite LOW5 organisation – LOW5 to LOW3 to represent the Strategic Intent, Strategic Translation/Implementation, and Operational Execution. This will bring balanced, rich perspectives and expertise into the workshops.

A programme for Straw Model, Design Workshop is given in Appendix C: Programme Template 2.

- *Option 3: Co-design:* The OD Expert facilitates an OD co-design process with the relevant stakeholders in the client system, that is Steps A.1 to A.8 are executed through a series of workshops. Critically important in the selection is to consider bringing the organisation's high potential young leaders as observers into the workshop as a developmental exercise. After all, a number of them will in all probability lead the organisation in the future. A programme of the series of the strategic design workshops with their associated topics is given in Appendix C: Programme Template 3.

Based on a Strategic Design – the overall House Plan, the Tactical Design process – the Rooms making up the House, can now commence. This process will be elucidated in the next chapter.

Endnotes

(1)   This chapter draws heavily on the author's experience over many Strategic Design consulting assignments. Sources that supplement his experience will be referenced where relevant in what follows.

(2)   Ramos (2012) also stresses the value of an Organisational Map to make the design visually real in a simple fashion; a map tells a powerful story. Levin (2005) suggests organigraphs instead of organograms, following H. Mintzberg and I. van der Heyden quoted by the author.

(3)   Cross (1990); Kriek (2019); Laloux (2014); Thoren (2017). While the other authors refer to an Organisational Charter, Kriek refers to a Team Charter in his focus on Work Teams.

(4)   Adler & Hiromoto (2012); Ambroise, Prim-Allaz, Teyssier & Peillon (2018); Birken (2000); Burton & Obel (2018); Burton, Obel & Håkonsson (2015); Capelle (2014); Donaldson & Joffe (2015); Galbraith (2014); Hanna (1988); Jevtić, Jovanović & Krivokapić (2018); Kates & Galbraith (2007); Kesler & Kates (2011); Kohlbacher & Reijers (2013); Lawler & Conger (2015); Levin (2005); MacKenzie (1986); Mueller, Procter & Buchanan (2000); Nadler & Tushman (1988); (1997); Ramos (2012); Stanford (2015).

(5)   Miles & Snow (1978); (1984) (quoted by Fjeldstad, Snow, Miles & Lettl, 2012) distinguish between internal fit (alignment of Strategic Intent and Design), external fit (alignment of Strategic Intent and Context), and dynamic fit (maintenance and improvement of internal and external fit over time).

(6)   Donaldson & Joffe (2015); Jevtić, Jovanović & Krivokapić (2018); Lin (2014).

(7)   Expanded and adapted from Galbraith (2008); (2014); Kates & Galbraith (2007) and Kessler & Kates (2010).

(8)   Based on Nadler and Tushman's (1995) well known, change need typology. See also Boynton & Victor's (1991) discussion on evolutionary and revolutionary change.

(9)   See also a discussion on implementation phases by Kesler & Kates (2011) and on using natural Work Teams as the Unit of Implementation (Capelle, 2014).

(10)   Constructed by the author.

(11)   Veldsman (2002a).

(12)   Veldsman (2008c).

(13)   Constructed by the author.

(14)   Compiled by the author based on his experience.

(15)   Constructed by the author, drawing on Kübler-Ross and Gabarro; Fink, Beak & Taddeco as cited in Manderscheid & Ardichvili (2008); Nicholson (1990); Weiss (1990).

9

TACTICAL ORGANISATIONAL DESIGN

Architecting the Work Units of the Organisation

"And if a house is divided against itself, that house cannot stand."

(St Matthew, 3:25)

"For a man's house is his castle."

(Sir Edward Coke)

"A small body of determined spirits, fired by an unquenchable faith in their mission, can alter the course of history."

(Mahatma Gandhi)

The Strategic Design is in place. The House Plan – represented by the Integrated Strategic Design Map and Organisational Charter – has been architected, representing the culmination of the Strategic Design Process. The purpose of this chapter is to address the 'How' of Tactical Design, which is directed at the design of the different Work Units making up the Organisational Shape of the Strategic Design. Metaphorically, this involves architecting each of the Rooms making up the House Plan.

As Rooms, the Tactical Design represents the organisational functionalities of the organisation. Work Units are critical because they are accountable for the actualisation of the organisation's Identity through the strategic translation and implementation of the organisation's Strategic Intent. If these Units are not fit-for-purpose, or even worse are missing, the organisation's Strategic Intent, as part of its Identity, will have no 'hands and 'feet' in terms of strategic roll out. The vantage point of Tactical Design is standing 'inside a Room' in order to (re)design the Room that has been architected through the Strategic Design. If no explicit Integrated Strategic Design Map exists for the organisation to form the basis of the Tactical Design, a 'rough-and-ready' Integrated Strategic Design Map must be constructed.

In the mainstream design literature, Tactical Design receives little detailed attention. The dominant focus is on Strategic and Operational Design. In the Strategic Design literature, the discussion is intense and extensive about overall Organisational Shapes with their accompanying organisational entities, for example Functional, Divisional, Mirror Image/Matrix. However, most frequently, no 'drill down' detailed discussion is given regarding the design of the organisational entities making up the Strategic Design, that is the Tactical Design. From a practice perspective, this is ironic because Tactical Design – both in frequency and volume – is probably the most active, ongoing area of design in practice.

Typically, Tactical Design is rather dealt with separately within specialist/discipline-specific literatures addressing the make-up of a specific discipline. And, by consequence its place in the organisational setting as a Work Unit (= Function) representing that specialisation/discipline, for example, Board of Directors, Corporate Centre, People (or HRM), Information Technology, Supply Chain (or Logistics), or Finance. My intention with *Designing Fit-for-Purpose Organisations* in general, and this chapter specifically, is to show the necessary and essential link between Strategic Design and Tactical Design. I would like to contend that Tactical Design must be an inherent part of the mainstream design literature. How can the Room(s) of a House be architected separate from the House it forms part of?

As previously defined in Chapter 6, a Work Unit represents a distinct area of accountability around a focused, organisational competency. In that chapter at least five types of Work Units were distinguished (see Figure 6.2), which will all be addressed in this chapter:

- *Board of Directors* (abbreviated to 'Board' in what follows): the unit that plays an *independent, oversight governance role over the organisation and its leadership*.

- *Corporate Centre* (in the conventional language, the Head Office): the unit that *provides direction, guidance and governance to the total organisation*, led by the CEO/Managing Director.

- *Operating Unit(s):* the unit containing the total core work process, the *client delivery process*, or a portion thereof.

- *Enabling Unit(s):* the unit containing the support processes that *enable delivery by the Operating Entity/ Entities*. For example, in the case of a Manufacturing Organisation, the maintenance of production equipment.

- *Support Unit(s):* the unit containing the processes that *enable the organisation to function as an organisation*, for example, Finance, People and Information Technology.

In terms of requisite Level of Work (LOW), Work Units would typically vary between LOW6: Main Board or LOW5: Subsidiary Board; LOW5: Corporate Centre; and LOW4 to LOW3 for the Operating, Enabling and Support Units. While a Strategic Design needs to be in place for at least five years, corresponding to the strategic thinking horizon of the organisation, the shelf life of a Tactical Design must be for up to five years. It must remain in force at all times during the time the Strategic Design is in place.

The Tactical Design Process may be initiated in one of two situations:

- as the consequence of a Strategic (re)Design; or

- to architect a specific Work Unit because of a Work Unit-specific OD need. Such needs have been elucidated in Chapter 4 dealing with the OD life cycle (see Table 4.1). Examples are a change in Work Unit leadership; a revised Work Unit Strategic/Tactical Intent; or a major weakness in the existing Work Unit design, having a negative impact on its performance and success. As already alluded to above, for a fit-for-purpose Tactical Design to be architected and be able to make a value-adding contribution, a clear Strategic Design must be in place.

The critical assumption is that the Work Unit to-be-redesigned has been readied from an organisational change navigation perspective for the OD intervention. And to the extent that it is thought necessary, the rest of the organisation has been informed of the intention of the Work Unit to embark on a redesign intervention. Conditions are thus favourable for a successful OD intervention, or have been made favourable (see Phase 2.3, Chapter 4 of the design intervention life cycle).

This chapter uses the Tactical Design route map, introduced in Chapter 4 when addressing the OD life cycle, as its structure. For the sake of convenience, the map is reproduced here again as Figure 9.1. For the sake of easy reference and to avoid any confusion, the chapter numbering will follow the numbering system used for the design steps in Figure 9.1. May I remind the reader again, that in order to keep the Tactical Map given in Figure 9.1 simple, the Change Navigation and Project Management building blocks of the OD process have been left out (see Figure 3.6), but are essential, enabling elements in the Design route map.

The chapter structure is similar to that followed for the Strategic Design: each step in the route map, with any associated OD concepts, is defined; the action(s) with respect to the steps concerned are discussed; and guidelines to inform this step, based on OD thought leadership and leading practices, are provided to enhance the chances of a fit-for-purpose design solution. Quality assurance questions are given at the end of each major step in the Design route map in order to allow for the progressive stress testing of the robustness of the design as it is being architected. Again, where it can be helpful, templates are provided in Appendices B to D.

What should be immediately noticeable about the Tactical OD route map given in Figure 9.1 is that Steps B.1 to B.10 are exactly the same as Steps A.1 to A.10 of the Strategic Design. However, as applied within the context of Tactical Design. The Work Units of the organisation after all represent the organisational functionalities required by the organisation to deliver on its Identity, and thus Strategic Intent. The overall delivery logic of the organisation finds its concrete application in these Units. Hence in discussing the Tactical Design steps, only nuanced differences in comparison to the Strategic Design Process will be highlighted. The essence of these steps, however, remains essentially the same.

The first critical step in the Tactical Design Process – Step B.0 – is to establish the essential Purpose of the Work Unit concerned, that is its Identity: why does this Room exist? In addition, the aim is to determine the nature of the Room one is dealing with, that is Board, Corporate Centre, Operating, Enabling, or Support Work Unit. The Identity – expressed in its Purpose – of a Work Unit lies in the specifics of the actual Tactical Design route map to be followed. The generic Tactical Design route map, as given in Figure 9.1, therefore has to be adapted content-wise to suit the type of Work Unit under consideration. The essence of the map remains the same, however, although sub-steps may differ.

Step B.0: Profile of Work Unit – Nature of Room

    B.0.1: Demarcate Work Unit (WU)
    B.0.2: Align WUs

Step B.1: Foundation Construction – Building materials of Room

    B.1.1: Profile WU Context
    B.1.2: Map WU Processes
    B.1.3: Determine WU Core Operating Technology with enablers
    B.1.4: Identify WU Design Givens
    B.1.5: Formulate WU Design Criteria with Design Vision
    B.1.6: Diagnose Existing WU Design – Strengths & Weaknesses

Step B.2: Tactical Horizontal Design – Work Domains making up the Room

    B.2.1: Group WU Work Processes into Work Domains (WDs)
    B.2.2: Configure WDs into WU Shape
    B.2.3: Allocate WU Crown Jewels
    B.2.4: Construct Partnering Relationships

Step B.3: Tactical Vertical Design – Type of ownership & owners of Work Domains

    B.3.1: Decide on requisite Level of Work of Work Unit
    B.3.2: Architect WU House Ownership Model
    B.3.3: Allocate requisite Level of Work to Work Domains
    B.3.4: Identify mission-critical WU Work Roles & generate high level Role Profiles

Step B.4: Tactical Lateral Design – Living together in the Room

    B.4.1: Construct WU Interdependency Matrix
    B.4.2: Decide on WU Integration Mechanisms
    B.4.3: Set up WU Governance Model

Step B.5: Integrated Tactical Design and Charter – Overall Room Plan

    B.5.1: Compile Work Unit Map
    B.5.2: Draw Work Unit Organogram
    B.5.3: Draft Work Unit Charter

Step B.6: Tactical Organisational Alignment – Fitting Room into House Plan

    B.6.1: Leadership Alignment
    B.6.2: Cultural Alignment
    B.6.3: People Alignment
    B.6.4: Resources Alignment
    B.6.5: Performance Alignment
    B.6.6: Work Place Alignment

Step B.7: Tactical Design Impact Assessment – Existing vs. new Rooms

    B.7.1: Conduct Gap & Risks analysis

Step B.8: Tactical Design Implementation Road Map – Planning how to build Room

    B.8.1: Craft Design Roll Out Strategy & Plan
    B.8.2: Craft Organisational Change Navigation Strategy & Plan

Step B.9: Tactical Design Solution Report

Step B.10: Tactical Design Implementation – Building the Room

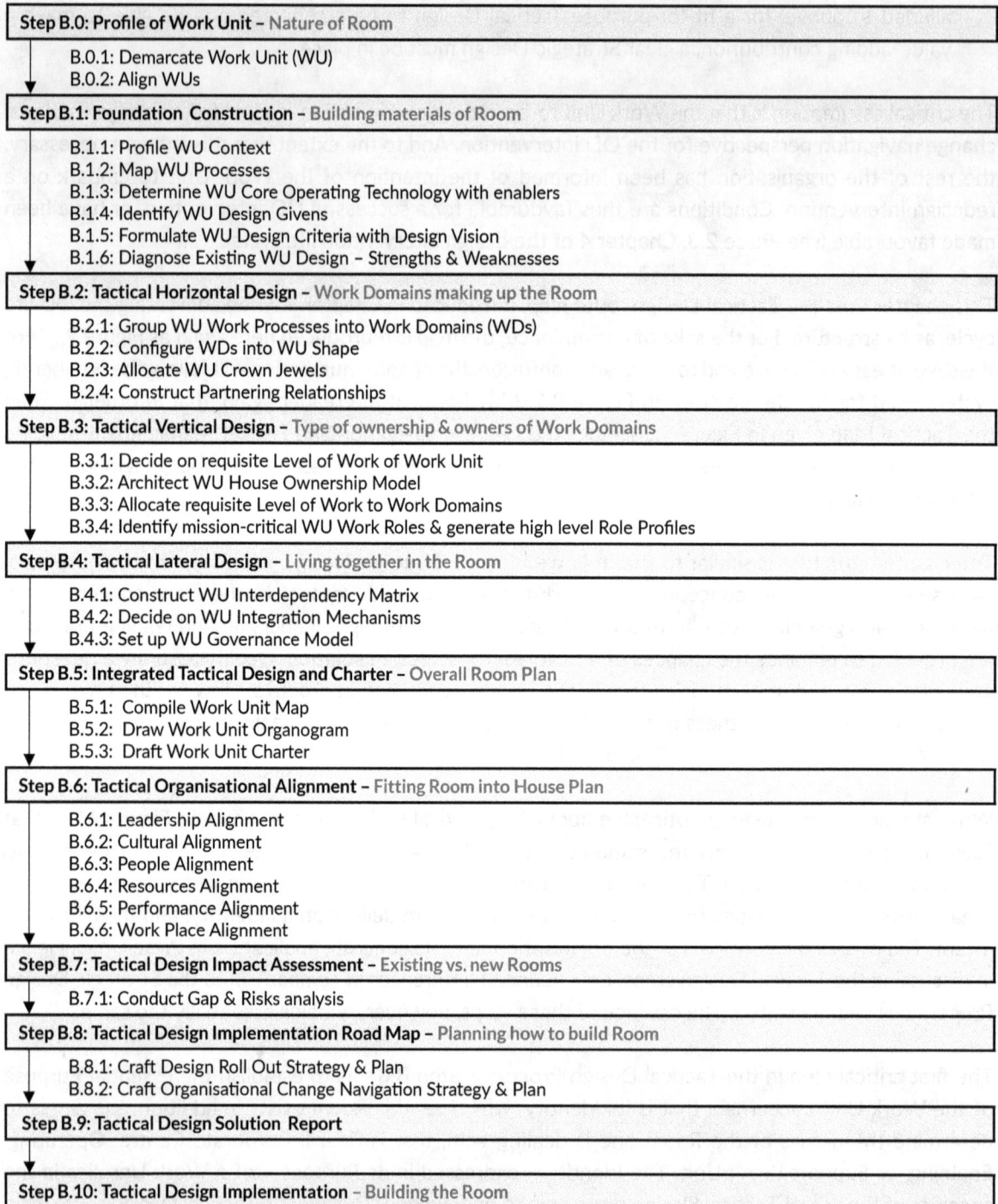

Figure 9.1: Overview of Tactical OD route map

Note: Part of Phase 3: Step 3.2 of the OD life cycle (see Chapter 4)

Given the differences in Purpose, a distinction is drawn in the ensuing discussion between five types of adapted Tactical Design route maps:

- Board
- Corporate Centre
- Operating Units
- Delivery Enabling Units
- Support Units *(1)*

Depending on your need as a reader, you may only want to look at the specific Work Unit requiring Tactical Design at present in your organisation. Or, look at the Work Unit that interests you, for example, the Corporate Centre. For this reason, you may not want to work in one go through all of the Tactical Designs covered in this chapter. Otherwise, work through the chapter end-to-end.

Tactical Design of the Board of Directors (2)

Step B.0: Profile Board as a Work Unit

The objective of this step is to determine the essential nature of the Work Unit under consideration – its Identity. In this case, the Board, and specifically the design elements making up the Tactical Design route map for the Board's design. In the introduction to this chapter, the Board was described as the Work Unit that plays an independent, oversight governance role over the organisation and its leadership.

The Board as a unique team

A Board of Directors exercises its authority as a group; it has to take shared, ultimate accountability and responsibility for the actions of the organisation, individually and severally, in the process 'owning' the organisation's overall governance. The objective of governance is to protect and enhance the Identity of the organisation on behalf of its stakeholders (3). The power of the Board lies in its collective wisdom, which is only released in a value-adding way when the Board functions as a collective body. That is when the Board speaks as one voice from many (4).

Being a collective body speaking with one voice implies that the Board as a group of individuals must transform itself into a proper (or true) team (5). A group refers to a mere collectivity of individuals. However, the Board, when acting as a genuine team, can be described as a limited number of persons who act in a mutually supportive and interdependent manner through the synergistic combination of individual competencies, expertise and experience. Through the different contributions of its respective members, the Board as a team strives to achieve shared intentions and goals within a certain context for which collective responsibility is taken. In the case of a Board the common, overarching goal is a well governed organisation which creates the intended value for stakeholders by overseeing the actualisation of its Identity (6).

The distinguishing character of the Board as a unique type of team is to be found in at least five dominant features. These features make it challenging for a Board to become a proper team, and not remain merely the sum total of a group of individuals:

- One becomes a Board member through a politically-based election (or, in some instances, a nomination process). Board members are expected, whether it is explicitly expressed or not, to represent and serve the parochial interests of the stakeholder(s) they represent (7).

- Board members have high personal profiles and strong personalities. They are often/have often been executive leaders in their own rights in other organisations. As members of the Board, they all are equal in standing, responsibility, and roles (8).

- Usually at least 50% of board members are not employed on a permanent basis by the organisations on whose board they serve as non-Executive Directors. Board members therefore do not have full time involvement in the organisation they oversee (9).

- A low number of regular face-to-face interactions amongst board members, perhaps twice a quarter for a few hours in Board and Board committee meetings, is common (10).

- The solving of complex challenges/issues under severe time constraints with imperfect information (11).

Design elements making up the Tactical Design of the Board

Under the Strategic Vertical Design (see Step A.3.2), the relationship between the Board of Directors and the organisation, specifically with its CEO/MD, was architected: how does the Board define its role relative to the CEO/MD of the organisation it oversees, the House Ownership Model (discussed in Chapter 7)? This Model is expressed in the Board's Positioning which is recapped below under 'Right Positioning'. With the 'Right Positioning', the Tactical Design of the Board can proceed.

A distinction can be drawn between the hardware and software of the Board. The hardware pertains to the formal aspects of the Board's functioning; it defines and frames the Board's scope, mode of working, and roles, while the software relates to the factors affecting the dynamics with the Board. The Board hardware sets the context (the playing field) for the Board's software: the players and game (12). This software has to support and reinforce the hardware.

Figure 9.2 depicts the Tactical Design elements making up the hard- and software of the Board. The hardware relates to the formal OD process elements (the numbers given in Figure 9.1 to the elements, for example B.2.1 and B.2.2, refer to the steps in the Tactical Design route map to which they belong) (13). The software relates to the OD alignment process elements (again, the numbers relate to the Tactical Design route map steps).

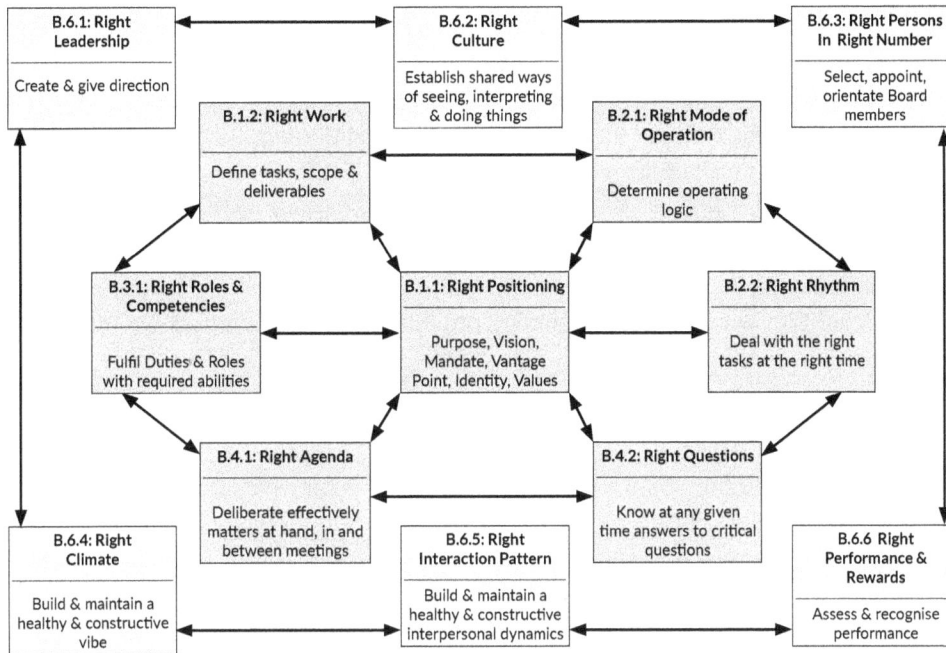

Figure 9.2: Hardware and software of the Board: Tactical Design elements

Note: Dark Grey Blocks = Hardware Elements; Light Grey Blocks = Software Elements

The design elements given in Figure 9.2 relate to the main design steps as follows:

- *Step B.1: Foundation construction* – Step B.1.1: Right Positioning; Step B.1.2: Right Work

- *Step B.2: Tactical Horizontal Design* – Step B.2.1: Right Mode of Operation; Step B.2.2: Right Rhythm

- *Step B.3: Tactical Vertical Design* – Step B.3.1: Right Roles and Competencies

- *Step B.4: Tactical Lateral Design* – Step B.4.1: Right Agenda; Step B.4.2: Right Questions

Each design element is discussed next relative to its location within the overall Tactical Design route map.

Step B.1: Foundation Construction – Building materials of the Board

The objective of this step is to bring the critical building materials onto site that will be used as the basis for the design process for the Board. In the case of a Board design, the Board's Positioning and Scope of Work. Two primary design steps make up this step: Steps B.1.1: Right Positioning and B.1.2: Right Work (see Figure 9.2), embedded in and followed by the further, necessary design steps of: Steps B.1.3: Determine Core Operating Technology and Enablers; B.1.4: Identify Design Givens; B.1.5: Formulate Design Criteria with Design Vision; and B.1.6: Diagnose Existing Design – Strengths and Weaknesses.

Step B.1.1: Right Positioning

The Right Positioning of the Board (see Figure 9.2) provides the frame of reference in accordance with which the Board's design must take place. The Right Positioning of the Board has already been discussed in Chapter 7: Vertical Design – Step A.3.2: Board – CEO/MD House Ownership Model. Since the Positioning of the Board is part of the Strategic Vertical Design of the organisation, its Tactical Design must of necessity be aligned to the former.

To briefly recap from Chapter 7, Right Positioning provides the Board with its Operating Framework. This encompasses:

- the Board's *Purpose*: why does the Board believe it exists?
- *vision*: what 'dream' does the Board have for the organisation for which it is performing this oversight role?
- *mandate:* who can act with what degree of autonomy?
- *vantage point:* from what perspective will the Board view the world and the way this world works?
- *identity:* who and what are we as a Board? What is our 'brand' as a Board? and
- *core values:* how should we conduct ourselves as Board?

Let us assume, for example, that a Board adopts the following Operating Framework: its *Purpose* is to serve all of the stakeholders of the organisation in a balanced, fair, and equitable manner; its *Dream* for the organisation is to be the leading innovator in its sector; its *Mandate* is to partner with the CEO; its *Vantage Point* is to be future-orientated/outward looking towards its context; its *Identity* is to be found in driving Achievement; and one of its Core Values is stewardship (see Chapter 7: Strategic Vertical Design: The Board – CEO/MD House Ownership Model for further optional considerations regarding the Board's Positioning as reflected in its Operating Framework).

Step B.1.2: Right Work

Right Work refers to the appropriate demarcation of the scope of work of the Board (see Figure 9.2); its Work Process Map. Put differently, what must be on the Board's agenda? What must it spend its time and energy on? The scope reflects the work to be done by the Board within its Operating Framework. In terms of this scope, the Board would set its agreed upon goals, agenda, and expected outcomes. The Right Work is directly affected by the set Design Criteria flowing from particularly the vantage point adopted by the Board. The vantage point refers to the possible dimensions of the world that it believes need to be taken into consideration: inward and outward looking; and past/present and future orientations (see Figure 7.4). Figure 9.3 depicts what would typically be seen as a comprehensive and complete scope of work for a Board (14).

Outward Looking

Task 1
Stakeholder Engagement &
Accountability

- Stakeholder Relationship
  Management & Goodwill
- Company Image/Reputation
- Networking & Brokering
- Fiduciary, Legal & Ethical
  Compliance/Obligations
- Sustainability

Task 2
Strategic Direction &
Philosophy

- Contextual Trends
- Opportunities & Threats
- Strategy Formulation & Execution
- Objectives, Plans, Milestones
- Values, Beliefs, Norms

Inward Looking

Task 4
Organisational & Management
Performance

- Resource Requirements, Procurement
  & Deployment
- Benchmarking
- Organisational & Management
  Performance Model & Metrics
- Policies & Standards
- Strengths & Weaknesses
- Organisational Enablers & Barriers

Task 3
Organisational & Leadership Continuity

- Business Risk Identification &
  Mitigation Management
- Key Talent Pool
- Compliance/Performance Checks &
  Balances
- Core Organisational Competencies/
  Capabilities
- Strategic Clients & Suppliers

Past/Present Orientation

Future Orientation

Figure 9.3: Comprehensive, complete scope of work for the Board

The requisite contextual complexity level to be adopted by the Board, from which the Board must consider its scope of work, must also be determined. Figure 9.4 depicts the axes in terms of which the requisite contextual complexity for a Board can be determined (15).

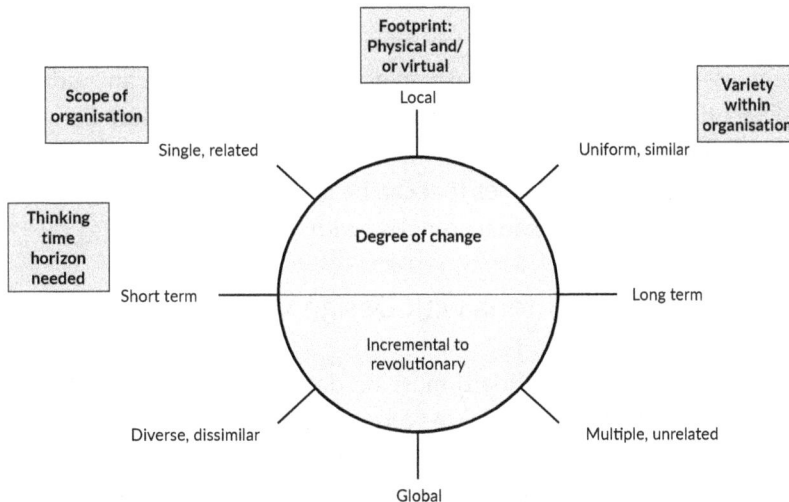

Footprint:
Physical and/
or virtual
Local

Scope of
organisation
Single, related

Variety
within
organisation
Uniform, similar

Thinking
time
horizon
needed
Short term

Degree of change

Long term

Incremental to
revolutionary

Diverse, dissimilar

Multiple, unrelated

Global

Figure 9.4: Complexity perspective axes to determine the requisite contextual complexity of the Board

In terms of Figure 9.4, the requisite contextual complexity of a Board's scope of work, both quantitatively and qualitatively, will increase significantly if its footprint shifts from a local to global context; its thinking time horizon moves from relatively short to long term; the scope of the organisation changes from a single/related set of products/services to multiple, unrelated sets of products/services; the variety within the organisation moves from uniform and similar to diverse and dissimilar; and the degree of change shifts from incremental to revolutionary.

The key point here is that the Board's scope of work – given in Figure 9.3 – must be viewed in terms of its requisite contextual complexity. The scope viewed at the requisite complexity will have a direct bearing on the profile of the desired Board members (refer to Step B.6.3: Right People in Right Numbers, Figure 9.2).

Step B.1.3: Determine Core Operating Technology and Enablers

The Core Operating Technology of a Board is typically *intensive and interdependent*. That is, a group of experts (= Directors) co-performing in real time a set of collective, co-ordinated actions to produce an outcome, jointly and reciprocally, with co-accountability. Its critical success factor is having the right expertise at the right time in the right place (see Table 5.6).

The Board's Core Operating Technology can be enabled by any of the DIVAS features of the Fourth Industrial Revolution explicated in Table 5.7: **D**igitisation, **I**nterconnectivity, **V**irtualisation, **A**utomation, and **S**mart. All of these Technology Enablers can be used to enhance the effectiveness and efficiency of the Board, given that Directors are not always physically together but still have full time accountability for the decisions and actions of the organisation they oversee. The appropriate Technology Enablement Model thus appears to be the Expert Model (see Figure 5.7).

Step B.1.4: Identify Design Givens

The Design Givens for the Board have to be identified. These are mostly found in the legislative and regulatory requirements set for Boards. For example, a Board must have an Audit Committee that is chaired by a non-Executive Director; at least two, preferably four, Board/Sub-Committee meetings per year; and preferably an independent Chairperson. Usually Corporate Governance Codes, although not enforceable, provide handy design guidelines that can be accepted as Design Givens that will stand the Board Reputation and Image in good stead if complied with.

Step B.1.5: Formulate Design Criteria with Design Vision

The Design Criteria and Vision for the Board must be derived from the Board's adopted Operating Framework (see Step B.1.1: Right Positioning). As a reminder: a Design Criterion is a specification of a delivery logic condition that the design must facilitate, enable, encourage and provide for. Usually not more than ten Criteria, preferably prioritised, are to be selected. In the case of the above described Operating Framework of a Board, examples of such Design Criteria could be: a Board Design that facilitates/enables/encourages/provides for the ongoing, intense involvement by diverse stakeholders (also propagated under the Strategic Vertical Design: Home Ownership Model of the Board – see Chapter 7); a high performance commitment with clear links to rewards; and high agility/responsiveness.

Again, the crafting of a Design Vision – a one page 'Day in the life of… ' – can assist significantly in concretising the 'To-Be' design of the Board in the minds of everyone, and provide a more tangible illustration of the new Board Design in reality. A Design Metaphor – to visualise more concretely the way in which the Board desires to operate – can be selected, for example, 'Trusted Stewards'.

All of the to-be-discussed, subsequent hard- and software design elements of the Board (see Figure 9.2) need to be aligned to the Board's adopted Right Positioning, as translated and operationalised into the Board's set Design Criteria and Vision with a corresponding Design Metaphor.

Step B.1.6: Diagnose Existing Design – Strengths and Weaknesses

The strengths and weaknesses of the existing Board have to be determined against the set Design Criteria and Vision. The strengths have to be built on, and the weaknesses minimised or eliminated in the new design.

Step B.2: Architect Tactical Horizontal Design

The previous step provided the foundation to the Board Design that now can start in all seriousness. The objective of this step is to architect the Horizontal Design of the Board. This step is made of two sub-steps: Steps B.2.1: Right Mode of Operation; and B.2.2: Right Rhythm.

Step B.2.1: Right Mode of Operation

The Right Mode of Operation (see Figure 9.2) deals with how the Board's work must be structured for optimal functioning relative to its requisite contextual complexity (16). Typically, the Right Mode of Operation embraces aspects such as the following (17):

- The division of work in the Board by means of work portfolios to be allocated to Board members.

- The subcommittee structure and composition of the Board. These elements are frequently to a lesser or greater extent prescribed/covered by corporate governance codes.

- The structuring of the Board's agenda.

- The Board's work processes, procedures, and modes of working within and between meetings.

- Information flows.

- Decision-making rules, rights and styles.

- Stakeholder management and interaction.

Figure 9.5 depicts a visual Board Map of a possible Right Mode of Operation for the Board (18). The map indicates the different Rooms making up the Board; what tasks fall within the boundaries of each Room; the decision-making powers of each Room; the flows between Rooms; and the logical rhythm and frequency of addressing tasks.

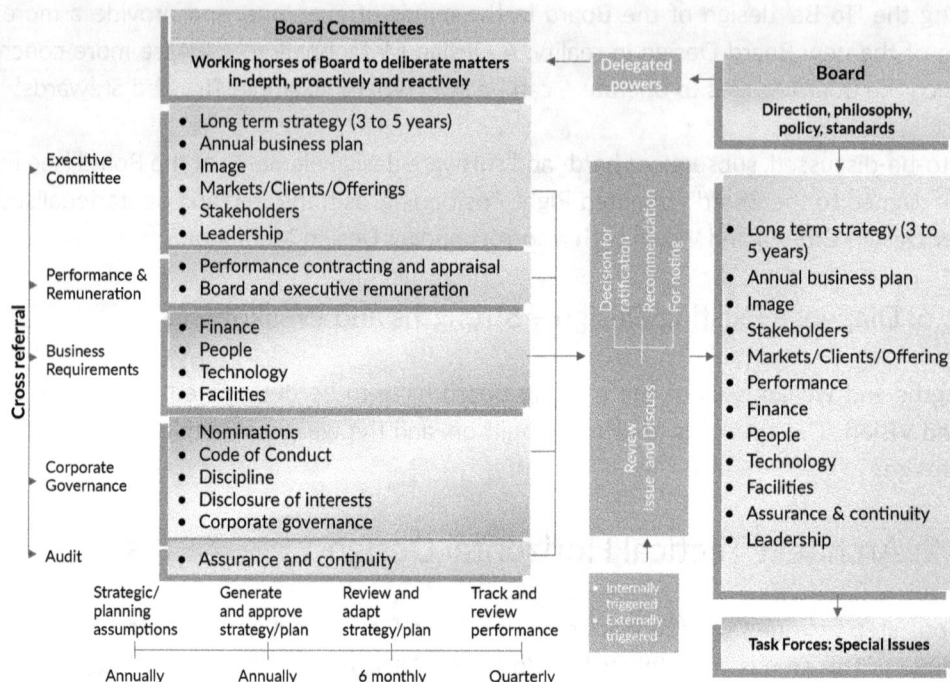

Figure 9.5: Right Mode of Operation: A visual Board Map

Step B.2.2: Right Rhythm

The sequence (see Figure 9.2) has to be architected in which the four task domains – with their related tasks that make up the scope of the Board's work (see Figure 9.3) – have to be addressed by the Board during its meetings over the course of a financial year. This sequence is critical in infusing the right rhythm into the Board's functioning. It would enable the Board in its meetings to deal with the right tasks at the right time in the right order.

For example, the right rhythm would include first considering the organisation's strategy, with the current year's business plan, *before* reviewing the budget in support of the strategy and business plan. Table 9.1 gives an example of what such a right rhythm could look like, assuming at least four Board meetings per year as required by good corporate governance (19). The shaded blocks in Table 9.1 indicate the point at which a specific task would be initiated in a financial year.

Table 9.1: Example: Board Right Rhythm – Right tasks at the right time in the right order

	1st Quarter of Financial year	2nd Quarter of Financial year	3rd Quarter of Financial year	4th Quarter of Financial year
Long term strategy	Progress review	Annual assessment ("State of the union") Planning assumptions signed-off	Plan approved/ adapted	-----
Annual business plan	Progress review	Progress review	Annual assessment Planning assumptions signed-off	Plan approved
Stakeholders	Progress review	-----	Annual assessment Stakeholder management plan approved	-----
CEO performance	Annual assessment	-----	Progress review	Contract set-up/ updated
Image	Plan approved	-----	Progress review	Annual assessment Planning assumptions signed-off
Markets, Clients, Products/ Services	-----	Progress review	Annual assessment Planning assumptions signed-off	Plan approved
Finance	Progress review	Progress review	Strategic budget approved/adapted Progress review Planning assumptions signed-off	Annual budget approved Annual assessment
People	Plan approved	-----	Progress review	Annual assessment Planning assumptions signed-off
Technology	Plan approved	-----	Progress review	Annual assessment Planning assumptions signed-off
Facilities	Plan approved	-----	Progress review	Annual assessment Planning assumptions signed-off
Company performance scoreboard	Achievement review	Achievement review	Achievement review	Annual performance review Performance indicators and goals signed-off
Board performance and remuneration/ Corporate governance	Annual performance assessment Remuneration approved	-----	-----	-----

	1st Quarter of Financial year	2nd Quarter of Financial year	3rd Quarter of Financial year	4th Quarter of Financial year
Assurance and continuity • **External audit**	-----	Annual financial statement Appointment of auditors	-----	Audit plan review
• **Internal audit**	Progress review	Annual assessment Planning assumptions signed-off	Plan approved	-----
• **Risks**	-----	Progress review	Annual assessment Planning assumptions signed-off	Plans approved/ adapted
Leadership Development	Annual assessment Plan	-----	Progress review	-----

Step B.3: Architect Tactical Vertical Design

This step addresses the Work Roles with their associated competencies that are necessary for the Board.

Step B.3.1: Right Roles and Competencies

This design step is about identifying and profiling the right roles for the Board with the associated competencies (see Figure 9.2). Firstly, the requisite LOW has to be re-validated as allocated to the Board. As explicated under the Strategic Vertical Design (Chapter 7), the requisite LOW for a Main and Subsidiary Board typically would be respectively LOW6 and LOW5, but they have to be re-validated during this step of the Board's Tactical Design.

The required duties and roles of a Board are generally laid down in common law, for example in legislation like the Companies Act, corporate governance codes, and the organisation's Memorandum and Articles of Association. Tables 9.2 and 9.3 provide overviews of the typical prescribed duties and roles with responsibilities of the Board and Directors (20).

Table 9.2: Typical prescribed duties of the Board

Prescribed Duties	**Common Law**	**Companies Act**	**Memorandum and Articles of Association**
Fiduciary duty	X		
Duty of care and skill	X		
Avoid conflict of interest	X		

Prescribed Duties	Common Law	Companies Act	Memorandum and Articles of Association
Maintain an unfettered discretion	X		
Administration of company's affairs		X	
Keeping of records and registers		X	
Share capital		X	
Preparation of financial statements		X	
Auditors		X	
AGM		X	X
Disclosure of interest		X	
Avoid insider trading		X	
Prohibition of loans to Directors		X	
Proper statutory specified accounting records			X
Annual financial statements			X

Table 9.3: Typical prescribed roles with responsibilities of the Board

Prescribed Role	Responsibilities
Chairperson	<ul><li>Maintain relations with company's stakeholders</li><li>Custodian of the organisation's Identity</li><li>Act as main informal link between Board, CEO and Senior Management</li><li>Establish an annual work plan for the Board against agreed objectives and conduct appraisals</li><li>Play lead role in setting agenda for Board meetings</li><li>Ensure all material facts are placed before the Board to enable Directors to reach informed decisions</li><li>Oversee succession plan for Board, CEO and Senior Management</li><li>Active participation in selection of Board Members</li><li>Ensure new Board members are inducted and orientated</li><li>Monitor and evaluate Board's and Directors' performance appraisals</li><li>Take a lead in removing under-performing or unsuitable Directors</li></ul>

Prescribed Role	Responsibilities
CEO	• Develop long term strategy and vision as part of the organisation's Identity • Develop an annual business plan and budgets in support of the long term strategy • Ensure the day-to-day affairs of the organisation are properly monitored and managed • Ensure continuous improvement in the quality and value of the organisation's products and services and maintenance of its competitive position • Ensure an effective leadership team • Formulate and oversee the implementation of major organisational policies • Act as chief spokesperson for the organisation • Foster an organisational culture which promotes ethical practices, individual integrity, and being a socially responsible citizen
Directors	• Devote ample time to organisation in order to diligently carry out responsibilities and duties • Exercise utmost good faith, honesty and integrity in all dealings • Exhibit highest degree of care and skill as may reasonably be expected • Act in the best interest of the organisation • Never permit a conflict of duties and interests; disclose potential conflicts of interest • Be informed about the financial, industrial and social milieu in which the organisation operates • Be able to make informed decisions • Treat confidential matters relating to the organisation with necessary circumspection • Must act with enterprise for and on behalf of the organisation, and always strive to increase shareholders' value and interests
Secretary	• Induct new and inexperienced Directors • Assist the Chairperson and CEO in determining the annual Board plan, meetings and agendas • Assist in other strategic issues of an administrative manner • Guide the Board and individual Directors in the proper discharge of their responsibilities • Act as a central source of guidance on matters of ethics, governance and codes of conduct for Boards • Run administrative affairs of Board efficiently
Co-opted non-voting members	• As contracted

The right work at the requisite LOW will form the basis of the profile of desired Board members, who are able to perform the laid-down duties (see Table 9.2) and fill their prescribed roles (see Table 9.3). Figure 9.6 gives a Director meta-competence model to be populated with specific competencies as deduced from the above Board design elements (21).

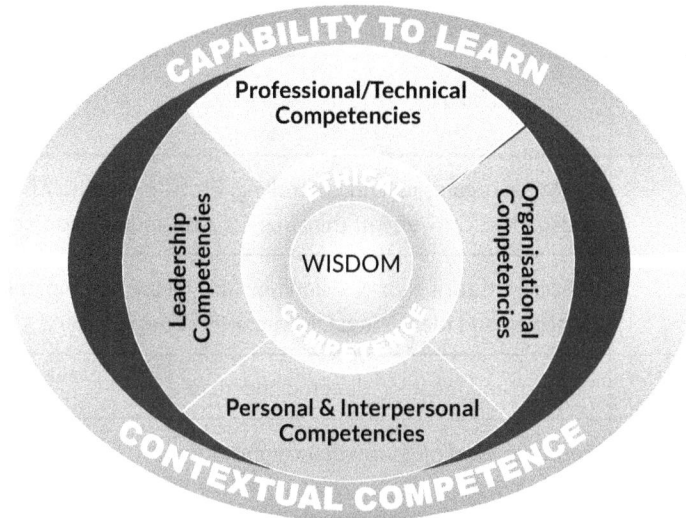

Figure 9.6: Meta-competence model for Directors

Given the respective competency domains of Directors as reflected in Figure 9.6, the box gives an overview of the typical competencies making up these domains (22).

COMPETENCY DOMAIN	COMPETENCIES
WISDOM	Contextual awareness; Stakeholder management; Helicopter view; Big picture thinking; Judgement
ETHICAL COMPETENCE	Stewardship; Integrity; Honesty; Consistency; Trustworthiness; Transparency; Sustainability
PERSONAL AND INTERPERSONAL COMPETENCIES	
• Personal	Critical faculty; Drive; Resilience; Flexibility; Decisiveness; Self-awareness
• Interpersonal	Persuasiveness; Empathy; Sociability; Communication; Active Listening
ORGANISATIONAL COMPETENCIES	Diversity sensitivity/Inclusivity; Teaming; Relationship building; Coalition formation; Networking
PROFESSIONAL/ TECHNICAL COMPETENCIES	Industry know-how; Business Acumen; Discipline-specific competencies; Role-specific competencies

COMPETENCY DOMAIN	COMPETENCIES
LEADERSHIP COMPETENCIES	
• Transactional	Planning, organising and controlling; Problem analysis/Trouble shooting; Delegation; Convergent thinking; Training and development
• Transformational	Proactive futuring (or envisioning); Risk taking; Championing and modelling; Coaching and mentoring; Divergent thinking; Advisory
• Transcendental	Purpose and meaning directed and guided
CONTEXTUAL COMPETENCE	Requisite level of contextual complexity
CAPABILITY TO LEARN	Learning attitude; Inquisitiveness/Curiosity; Learning how to learn

Step B.4: Architect Tactical Lateral Design

The objective of this step is to create an overall, strategically integrated thrust and synergy across the Horizontal and Vertical Designs of the Board as architected in the preceding steps, that is to build the Integration Mechanisms that will enable the Board to function as an integrated body, speaking as one voice from many.

Two critical Integration Mechanisms already been discussed:

- Step B.2.1: Right Mode of Operation – the flow of information and decisions through the Board (see Figure 9.5); and
- Step B.2.2: Right Rhythm – when does what gets discussed in the Board (see Table 9.1).

Two further Lateral Design steps are Steps B.4.1: Right Agenda and B.4.2: Right Questions.

Step B.4.1: Right Agenda

The Board discussions and interactions must be directed and guided by the Right Agendas (see Figure 9.2) based on the Right Rhythm (see Figure 9.2 and Step B.2.2). Meeting agendas in a sense become the concrete operationalisation of the Board rhythm, and hence need to form part of the Tactical Design process. They play a critical, enabling role in providing an overall, strategically integrated thrust and synergy to the Board. Figure 9.7 gives a typical agenda structure as reflective of the right agenda (23).

❶ Board Business Update	• Contextual/Sector trends • Opportunities/Threats • Organisational Update
❷ Matters arising	
❸ Current Business	• Executive overview with supporting documentation containing details: – For noting – For Ratification – For Decision
❹ Review of pending matters	• Work in progress • Matters still under consideration
❺ Look ahead to next meeting	• Standard agenda items as per Board annual rhythm • Invitation to submit agenda points
❻ Short review of effectiveness of Board meeting	• What worked/did not work

Figure 9.7: Typical Board Agenda Structure

Given that non-Executive Directors are not involved on a full time basis in the organisation, it is mission-critical that they are to be kept up-to-date between Board meetings on the significant events, decisions and actions affecting the organisation.

Ways and means therefore have to be formally architected to ensure that Board members are kept informed at all times, for example through a regular CEO Update Brief, virtually or via a written brief. The in-between meetings briefing also has to become part of the Right Agenda. The best, safest way to ensure that the briefings do happen is to schedule them into the Board rhythm at appropriate time slots.

Step B.4.2: Right Questions

To fulfill their oversight role properly and effectively, Board members need to have answers to a number of crucial 'right questions' at any given time (see Figure 9.2). The shaded box provides a suggested list of such questions. In this step of the Lateral Design, ways and means have to be architected to ensure this state of affairs (24).

RIGHT QUESTIONS

1. Do we understand and support where the organisation is going and how it is going to get there in meeting its identity?
2. How does/will the organisation make money/create value now and in the future?
3. Are our customers paying up?
4. How are we doing relative to our competitors? What level of customer satisfaction exists?
5. Are we living within our means, now and in the future?
6. What could really hurt or kill the organisation, now and over the next few years?

---

7. If the CEO is hit by a bus, who would run the organisation?

8. For what, and in what form, is the CEO rewarded, and how does it affect his/her decisions/conduct/performance?

9. What is the quality of the organisation's relations with its stakeholders? Are there any risks in these relationships?

10. How does bad news get to the top, if it all?

Step B.5: Map Integrated Tactical Board Design and Charter

At this point, all of the hardware design elements of the Board Tactical Design have been addressed. An integrated Board Tactical Design Map can now be drawn, visually displaying all the above, which provides the Room Plan of the Board. The picture drawn that reflects the Right Mode of Operation (see Figure 9.5) provides already a good basis for such a Design Map. A Board Charter must also be drafted containing the ground rules according to which the Board wants to operate design-wise. The Operating Framework of the Board (see Step B.1.1) provides a good starting point for such a Charter.

Step B.6: Ensure Tactical Board Alignment

This step of the Board Tactical Design addresses the software design elements of the Board that need to be in support of, and reinforce, the Integrated Tactical Board Design. In Figure 9.2 these software elements were given in Steps B.6.1 to B.6.6: Right Leadership, Right Culture, Right Persons in Right Number, Right Climate, Right Interaction Pattern, and Right Performance and Rewards. Jointly, the software design elements, in their reciprocal interdependency, affect the likelihood that the hardware of the Board Design will be effective and efficient.

Five examples are discussed to illustrate the flavour of this design step, namely the software elements of Right Leadership, Right Culture, Right Persons in Right Number, Right Climate, and Right Interaction Pattern. In each case, the right options have to be chosen to ensure alignment with the hardware of the Board's Design.

Step B.6.1: Right Leadership

At least one of four leadership modes can be adopted and institutionalised as dominant in the Board by the Chairperson (25):

- *Caretaking* Mode: influencing board members to believe that the "good old days" are still the best and that things should be kept as they are.

- *Crisis/Paranoid* Mode: influencing members to perform by mobilising them to respond to ongoing crises, real and/or artificially created.

- *Instrumental* Mode: influencing members by establishing clear links between efforts, goals, outcomes, and rewards/recognition.

- *Visionary/Purpose driven* Mode: influencing members' actions through the building and actualisation of a shared inspiring vision/cause that will contribute to leaving a lasting legacy through actualising the organisation's Identity.

Step B.6.2: Right Culture

The Culture – the shared ways of seeing, interpreting and doing things within the Board – must be aligned to, and be a reflection of, its chosen Identity: Role/Conformist; Achievement/Runaway; Power/Winner takes all; or Supporting/Old Boys Club (see Figure 7.5 that depicts possible Board Identities – a positive Identity with its negative counterpart).

Step B.6.3: Right Persons in Right Numbers

As was stated above, one of the unique features of a Board is that it is typically made up of members with many years of experience who have high personal profiles and strong personalities, who are often/have often been executive leaders in their own right in other organisations. It is thus critical that the 'Right Persons' are selected to serve on a Board if the Board is to be effective. In addition, the 'Right Number' of Directors is a perennially debated point in the literature.

The history of organisations imploding and failing because of unsuitable Directors, who are unable to effectively work together because of destructive Board politics, is rife. Additionally, the frequency of charismatic and/or toxic CEOs/MDs hijacking Boards for their own personal, self-serving interests and agendas. In this respect, a Director meta-competence model – as explicated above – plays a key role in selecting the Right Persons.

Step B.6.4: Right Climate

The climate in the Board deals with the prevailing mood (or vibe), which constantly permeates the Board's functioning and interactions. Figure 9.8 gives two contrasting prevailing moods that may infuse a Board (26).

The descriptors in light grey boxes indicate the mood that would be conducive to a teaming atmosphere amongst Board members, reflective of a psycho-social contract of partnering/identification amongst Board members (see Figure 7.3 on types of Boards), resulting in constructive and healthy Board dynamics. Descriptors in dark grey boxes indicate the opposite in terms of Board dynamics. These are more indicative of a coercive/instrumental psycho-social contract amongst Board members.

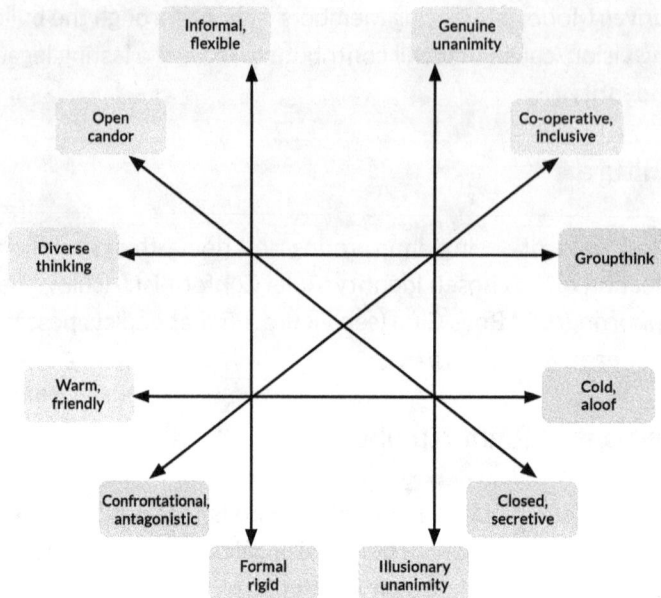

Figure 9.8: Possible, contrasting prevailing moods in a Board

Step B.6.5: Right Interaction Pattern

Board Interaction refers to the ways in which Board members work together in doing the Board's work: during and between Board meetings. Over time a certain interaction pattern becomes established and institutionalised in the Board, which is reflective of its culture. The interaction pattern manifests in the set ways in which the Board handles processes, such as information gathering/sharing, problem solving, decision-making, and conflict resolution.

Figure 9.9 depicts two contrasting interaction patterns – in light grey and dark grey boxes respectively – indicating more positive and more negative patterns. The former, by implication, is more conducive to constructive, healthy Board dynamics, reflective of a teaming Board (27).

• Shared Goods/Intentions/Frame of Reference	⟷	• Individual Goals/Intentions/Frame of Reference
• Facilitating Chairperson/CEO	⟷	• Forceful/imposing Chairperson/CEO
• Flexible, free flowing, organic mode of working ('Teaming')	⟷	• Rigid, predictable, linear mode of Working ('Meeting')
• Real business done inside the Board Room	⟷	• Real business done outside the Board Room
• Complementary, harmonious relationships/contributions ('Team players')	⟷	• Competitive, conflict ridden Relationships/contributions (Prima Donnas/Lone Rangers)
• Decisions based on sufficient consensus	⟷	• Decisions based on majority vote/ forceful personalities
• Ongoing action learning/teaching	⟷	• No/little action learning/teaching
• High/open information sharing	⟷	• Little/selective information sharing
• High collective commitment to decisions/actions and consequences thereof	⟷	• Low collective commitment to decisions/actions and consequences thereof

Figure 9.9: Contrasting Board Interaction Patterns

In summary, the Board software design elements – Steps B.6.1 to B.6.6 – must be set up to support and reinforce the Board hardware design elements; the outcomes of Steps B.1 to B.5. Without this alignment, the effectiveness of the hardware elements will be undermined and sabotaged.

Steps B.7: Conduct Tactical Design Impact Assessment to B.10: Tactical Design Implementation

The final steps in the Board Tactical Design process are:

- Step B.7: Conduct a *Tactical Design Impact Assessment*: (i) comparing the existing Board Design to the new Board Design to determine the gaps and risks; and (ii) deciding on the prioritised, required actions to close the gap.

- Step B.8: Generate a *Tactical Design Implementation Road Map* – planning how to build and roll out the new Board Design with the accountable and responsible parties, and creating a timetable and deadlines. The Roll out strategy and Plan must be enabled by a solid Charge Navigation Strategy and Plan.

- Step B.9: Draft a *Tactical Design Solution Report* – preparing a report on the proposed Board Design. A template for such a report is given in Appendix D: Report Template 2.

- Step B.10: Do the *Tactical Design Implementation* – implement the new design.

The approach and principles, as well as quality assurance questions, to these steps are highly similar to the equivalent steps in the Strategic Design process, as discussed in Chapter 8: Steps A.7 to A.9, thus they will not be discussed any further here. In most instances, one can merely replace the word 'Strategic Design' with the word 'Board Design' to make whatever is being considered applicable to the Board Design.

Quality assurance: Tactical Design – Board

QUALITY ASSURANCE QUESTIONS *Is the Tactical Design of the Board complete?*	DESIGN STEP	ADDRESSED: YES/NO *(Yes: +; No: x)*
Right Positioning: Does the Tactical Board Design meet the set **Design Criteria**, reflect the **Design Vision**, and resonate with the **Design Metaphor** representing the Design Vision, all as derived from the Board's Operating Framework?	Step B.1.1	
Right Work: Has a clear **scope of work** been demarcated for the Board?	Step B.1.2	
Right Mode of Operation: Are the following well demarcated: the different **Rooms making up the Board** (= decision-making and working bodies), as well as the tasks falling with the boundaries of each Room; the logical rhythm and frequency of addressing tasks; the decision-making rights of each Room; and flows between Rooms?	Step B.2.1	

QUALITY ASSURANCE QUESTIONS *Is the Tactical Design of the Board complete?*	DESIGN STEP	ADDRESSED: YES/ NO *(Yes: +; No: x)*
Right Rhythm: Has a **logical, annual sequence** been set up in which the Board will deal with the tasks contained in its scope of work?	Step B.2.2	
Right Roles and Competencies: Have clear (prescribed) **roles with their commensurate competencies** been crafted? Do these roles cover the **prescribed duties** of a Board?	Step B.3.1	
Right Agenda: Have a **Board and 'In between' Agendas** been constructed that are reflective of the laid down annual Board Rhythm?	Step B.4.1	
Right Questions: Will the Board get accurate and timeous **answers** to their critical questions by having the right information at any given time?	Step B.4.2	
Has an **Integrated Tactical Design** (including a visual **Tactical Board Design Map) and Charter** for the Board been generated, covering all of the above?	Step B.5	
Right Board Design Alignment: Is the **Integrated Tactical Board Design** – the **Board hardware** – aligned to the **Board software**: Right Leadership, Right Culture, Right Persons in Right Number, Right Climate, Right Interaction Pattern, Right Performance and Rewards?	Step B.6	
Has a **Tactical Design Impact Assessment** been done?	Step B.7	
Has a **Board Design Implementation Road Map** been generated?	Step B.8	
Has a **Board Design Solution Report** been drafted?	Step B.9	

Tactical Design of the Corporate Centre

The Corporate Centre provides governance, direction and guidance to the total organisation. In dealing with the Strategic Vertical Design: Corporate Centre – Work Units relationship, five types of House Ownership were distinguished: Financial through to Operational (see Table 7.2). These Ownership Models depict the different types of direction and control that the Corporate Centre can exercise over the organisation overall and its Work Units.

Based on the strategically chosen House Ownership Model for the Corporate Centre – contained in the Strategic Vertical Design – the Tactical Design of the Corporate Centre can now proceed. The Tactical Design of the Corporate Centre addresses the functional nature of the overall, direction, guidance and governance to be provided by the Centre. In turn this would affect, directly and indirectly, the demarcation and boundaries of the Corporate Centre in relation to the Work Units making up the organisation (28).

Step B.0: Profile Corporate Centre as Work Unit – Role and Mandate

The objective of this step is to determine the essential nature of the Corporate Centre as Work Unit, and specify the design elements making up the Tactical Design route map of its design. Against the backdrop of the Corporate Centre's chosen House Ownership Model – elucidated under Strategic Tactical Design in Chapter 7 – three design dimensions have to be considered in determining the role and mandate of a Corporate Centre:

- What *role* must the Corporate Centre fulfil?

- Who is the *client(s) of the Centre*: the CEO *and/or* the Work Units of the organisation?

- What is the *focus of the Centre*: Inward (= the internal organisation) *and/or* Outward (= the Operating Arena of the organisation)?

A Corporate Centre can fulfil at least the following roles (29):

- *Value and synergy creating* activities such as strategic oversight and guidance; access/allocation to valuable resources at the right time and in the right place; promoting inter-Work Unit synergies through the creation and sharing of core capabilities.

- *Capacity building* activities to install the required capacity in Operating Units to perform, for example, leadership, funding.

- *Obligatory/assurance/compliance* activities required of all Corporate Centres, for example, tax, treasury, financial reporting.

- *Shared services* to exploit scale economies; build specialised, focused core organisational capabilities.

- Promotion and protection of the *organisation's brand and reputation.*

Based on the above listed, two design dimensions – *client* and *focus* – each with two options, four possible positionings of the Corporate Centre can be distinguished relative to its role, as shown in Figure 9.10, each representing a Work Domain. A Corporate Centre can include one to all four of these positionings, defining its mandate. The typical functionalities that can be included in each quadrant are also given in the figure.

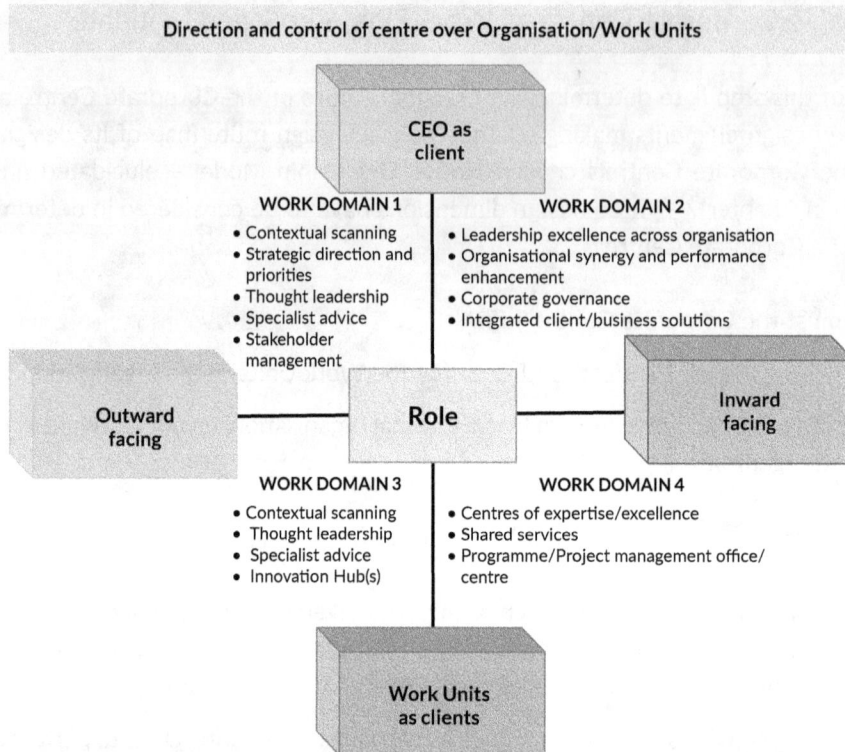

Direction and control of centre over Organisation/Work Units

CEO as client

WORK DOMAIN 1
- Contextual scanning
- Strategic direction and priorities
- Thought leadership
- Specialist advice
- Stakeholder management

WORK DOMAIN 2
- Leadership excellence across organisation
- Organisational synergy and performance enhancement
- Corporate governance
- Integrated client/business solutions

Outward facing

Role

Inward facing

WORK DOMAIN 3
- Contextual scanning
- Thought leadership
- Specialist advice
- Innovation Hub(s)

WORK DOMAIN 4
- Centres of expertise/excellence
- Shared services
- Programme/Project management office/ centre

Work Units as clients

Figure 9.10: Possible positionings of the Corporate Centre

Given its chosen Role – and within the framework of its chosen direction to, and control over, its Work Units – the Corporate Centre can have one or more of the positionings given in Figure 9.10. These positionings demarcate the Centre's mandate as a Work Unit in its own right *(30)*:

- Work Domain 1: Be outward facing, serving the CEO as its sole client.

- Work Domain 2: Be inward facing, but still with the CEO as its sole client.

- Work Domain 3: Be outward facing, with the other Work Units as its clients.

- Work Domain 4: Be inward facing, serving the other Work Units of the organisation as its clients.

Typically in practice, Work Domain 1 or Work Domains 1 and 2 jointly are called the 'Office of the CEO', with the CEO as its sole client. Given the chosen Corporate Centre mandate, the functionalities making up the Corporate Centre that have been allotted during Strategic Design (see Step A.3.2: Strategic Vertical Design) must be confirmed from a Tactical Design perspective, from 'inside the Room' so to speak. They form, individually and collectively, the focus of the Tactical Design of the Corporate Centre.

In general, the more the Corporate Centre exercises Financial or Strategic Direction and Control over Work Units, the more Work Domain 1 and/or Work Domain 2 of the Corporate Centre mandates will apply. The more Managerial and/or Operational Direction and Control is exercised by the Centre, the more all four Work Domains will have to be part of the Corporate Centre's mandate. The domains give the Corporate Centre the capacity with which to exercise its chosen direction and control, mandate and role.

Steps B.1: Construct Foundation to B.10: Do Tactical Design Implementation

Based on a chosen Corporate Centre role and mandate, as aligned to the chosen House Ownership Model for the Corporate Centre, the Tactical Design process now can proceed: Steps B.1 to B.10 (see Figure 9.1). Essentially, this process content-wise and quality assurance-wise takes on the same format as the Strategic Design Process – Steps A.1 to A.10 – discussed in Chapters 5 to 8, but now applied to the Corporate Centre.

There are, however, two important variations. Firstly, given the range of functionalities included in the Corporate Centre and the choice of Work Domains, one may have to first address the design of each Corporate Centre functionality individually and then look at the overall integrated Corporate Centre's Tactical Design, and vice versa. Secondly, when undertaking the Tactical Lateral Design, interdependencies and governances not only within the Corporate Centre must be considered, but also interdependencies and governances at the interfaces between the Centre and the Work Units of the organisation (Step B.5), although possibly already addressed at a high level during Strategic Design Step A.5: Integrated Strategic Design.

A template for a Tactical Design Solution Report on the Corporate Centre is given in Appendix D: Report Template 3.

Quality assurance: Tactical Design – Corporate Centre

QUALITY ASSURANCE QUESTIONS *Does the Tactical Design of the Corporate Centre meet the following requirements?*	DESIGN STEP	ADDRESSED: YES/ NO *(Yes: +; No: x)*
Has the **Role** of the Corporate Centre been clearly defined?	Step B.0	
Have the right **mix of Work Domains** been selected for the Corporate Centre relative to its Role, giving it its **Mandate**?	Step B.0	
Does the defined Role with the selected Work Domains, that is mandate, provide the **required capacity** to the Corporate Centre to exercise its chosen direction and control over Work Units?	Step B.0	
Have Design Steps B.1 to B.5 been completed for the design of the Corporate Centre – Tactical Horizontal, Vertical and Lateral Designs – in order to arrive at an **Integrated Tactical Design and Charter** for the Corporate Centre?	Steps B.1 to B.5	
Have Design Steps B.6 to B.9 been completed for the Corporate Centre: **Alignment; Impact assessment; Implementation roll out plan; and Report**?	Steps B.6 to B.9	

Tactical Design of Operating Units

As stated in the introduction of this chapter, an Operating Work Unit contains the total *core* work process – the client delivery process – or a portion thereof. That is, the factories of a manufacturing organisation or retail banking in a financial institution. An Operating Unit is the place where the value and wealth for the clients/customers of the organisation are created and delivered by the organisation. Put differently, these are the Units that 'own' the organisation's clients/customers because they serve them. The individual Operating Units are the outcome of the Strategic Design Step A.2: Horizontal Design.

The Tactical Design of Operating Units has to address each Unit from the 'inside-out' by standing inside the Room representing the Operating Unit, so to speak (31). As result of a comprehensive Strategic (re) Design, all of the Operating Units may have to be (re)designed, or the design need may be to architect the Tactical Design of a specific Operating Unit only.

Step B.0: Profile Operating Unit(s)

Step B.0.1 Demarcate Work Unit

The objective of this step is to determine the essential nature of an Operating Unit(s). Figure 9.11 gives a graphic lay-out of the design elements of an Operating Unit that can be used to profile the Unit (32). The Tactical Design Profile can be used to depict the essential design elements of an Operating Unit in a systemic, integrated manner. The numbering of the design elements indicates the order in which they must be addressed logically, given the reciprocal interdependency between the elements. The Operating Unit Profile provides the baseline information for the design of an Operating Unit.

The Operating Unit Profile has been included in Appendix B: Design Template 10.

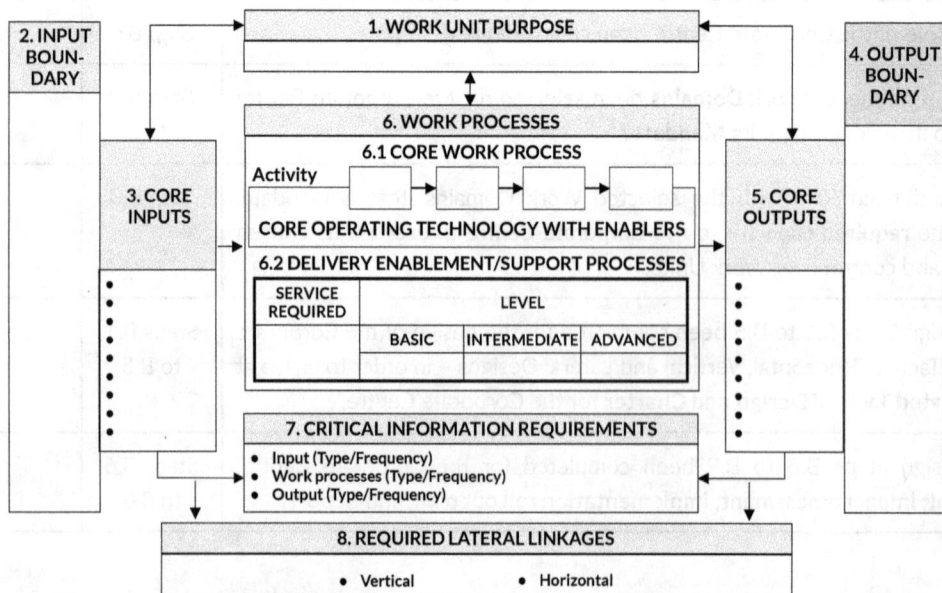

Figure 9.11: Profile of the Operating Unit

With reference to the Work Processes (Design Element 6 in Figure 9.11), a complete map must be generated, including Context Shaping, Corporate Governance, Identity: Strategic and Business Planning, and Sustainability (including policies and standards) (see Figure 5.4 and Table 5.5).

Table 9.4 provides descriptions of the design elements contained in the Operating Unit Profile, as given in Figure 9.11 (33).

Table 9.4: Descriptors of the Tactical Design elements of the Operating Unit

TACTICAL DESIGN ELEMENT	DESCRIPTION
1. Purpose of the Work Unit	Why does the Work Unit exist, i.e. what is the rationale for its existence?
2. Input Boundary	Where does the Unit's Area of Accountability start on the input side (the supplier side)?
3. Core Inputs	What inputs does the Work Unit receive from its Key Supplier(s) with their requirements to be acceptable, for example, timing, quantity, quality?
4. Output Boundary	Where does the Unit's Area of Accountability end on the output side (the customer side)?
5. Core Outputs	What outputs does this Work Unit supply to its key customer(s) with their requirements to be acceptable, for example, timing, quantity, quality?
6. Work Processes 6.1 Core Work Process, leveraged by Core Operating Technology and Enablers	The work to be done by the Operating Unit to define, deliver and satisfy customers' needs. A series of interdependent activities required to transform inputs into output(s), that is a product/service. A 'true' core process runs from a product-/service-related input to the export of the finished product and/or the delivery of a service. Classification of Core Work Process levels: • *Key transformations:* key points at which substantive changes take place in inputs. A key transformation represents the reason why Operating Work Unit activities take place: it embodies the essence of the core work process. It is the point in the core work process where the value-add is the greatest. A Work Unit is often named after the key transformation. • *Supplementary transformations:* significant but not essential changes to the composition of inputs. • *Ancillary operations:* peripheral or 'cosmetic' changes to the product/service in the process. • *Transportation:* geographical change only. • *Storage:* no change in the product/service.

TACTICAL DESIGN ELEMENT	DESCRIPTION

6.2 Delivery Enablement/ Support Work Processes	As one moves from Storage to Transformation, the degree of change and value-add to the inputs move from minimum to maximum. *Core Operating Technology and Enablers* through which the Core Work Process is delivered: the means used to produce the Work Unit's products/services. Series/sets of interdependent activities required to enable/support the execution of the core work process. Classification of the delivery levels of enablement/support processes:
	• *Basic:* Delivery of day-to-day, first line enablement/support activities (for example, ordering of consumables, performance appraisal, band aid repairs; data capturing; recruitment; training).
	• *Intermediate:*
	   o Delivery of focused enablement/support activity advice or expertise.
	   o Operation and maintenance of programmes, procedures, standards and/or courses associated with enablement/support process systems (for example, a specific Information Technology system, recruitment process).
	• *Advanced:*
	   o Delivery of enablement/support process systems level advice or advanced expertise with respect to enabling/support activities (for example, major maintenance, people assessment).
	   o Design, implementation and termination of overall enablement/ support process systems (for example, capital expansion, leadership development process).
	   o Generation of enablement/support process strategies, priorities and policies. As one moves from basic to advanced delivery enablement/support work processes, there is:
	   o a decrease in the frequency of the performance of the activities inside the Work Unit; and
	   o an increase in the degree of required, in-depth specialisation of the enablement/support activities that need to be performed. An important design consideration with respect to the delivery enablement/ support processes is at what delivery levels these processes must be available at all times within the Operating Unit – Basic, Intermediate, or Advanced – given also the requirements of the Operating Technology and Enablers used by the Unit.

7. Critical Information Requirements	What information does the Work Unit require to get the job done?
	   o Input information
	   o Work process information
	   o Output information

8. Required Lateral Linkages	What essential interfaces – horizontal and vertical – are needed by the Work Unit with the rest of the organisation in order to get its work done?

The first step in the Tactical Design of an Operating Unit is thus to complete the Operating Unit Profile as per Figure 9.11, using the descriptors of the design elements given in Table 9.4. At the end of this step, the Operating Unit has now been properly demarcated and mapped, and its profile has been generated.

Quality assurance: Operating Unit Profile

QUALITY ASSURANCE QUESTIONS	DESIGN ELEMENT (see Figure 9.11)	ADDRESSED: YES/NO (Yes: +; No: x)
PURPOSE OF WORK UNIT • Is the reason for existence defined to indicate a unique mandate (= scope of work)? • Does the Work Unit's mandate contribute to the organisation's Identity? • Is the scope of work meaningful and does it add value to the organisation? • Is the key transformation/value-adding process, owned by the Work Unit, clearly defined?	1	
INPUT AND OUTPUT BOUNDARIES OF WORK UNIT • Are the input and output boundaries well demarcated to ensure clear ownership? • Can control of variance at source be achieved within these boundaries? Control of variance refers to the principle that all of the activities that have a direct influence on the performance of a Work Unit must be under its control, otherwise it cannot be held accountable for its performance. • Do boundaries allow the domain to function as a self-contained entity within cost constraints?	2 & 4	
CORE INPUTS • Have the appropriate direct suppliers been defined? • Have the supplier input requirements been specified? • Have the supplier input requirements of the Work Unit been aligned with the customer output requirements of proceeding Work Unit(s)? • Are inputs identifiable and measurable?	3	

QUALITY ASSURANCE QUESTIONS	DESIGN ELEMENT (see Figure 9.11)	ADDRESSED: YES/NO (Yes: +; No: x)
CORE OUTPUTS • Have the appropriate direct customers been identified relative to the Work Unit's mandate? • Is the product/service to be delivered clearly defined? • Have the core outputs been specified in terms of quality, quantity, time and cost? • Have the customer output requirements of the Work Unit been aligned with the supplier requirements of the next Unit?	5	
WORK PROCESSES **Core Work Process** • Are the core work process activities fully listed and mapped? • Have the core work activities been properly classified: (transformation, transportation/ancillary/storage)? • Has the appropriate work process been described for achieving the desired outputs with the given inputs? **Core Operating Technology and Enablers** • Has the Core Operating Technology with its Enablers been correctly identified? • Have its critical success factors been listed? **Core Work Process Interfaces** • Are all operating interfaces with the Work Unit covered? • Are interface Integration Mechanisms fit for the purpose? • Do the integration benefits outweigh the costs thereof, its value-add? • Have only the relevant key stakeholders been included in the interface?	6.1	
WORK PROCESSES **Delivery Enablement/Support Processes** • Have the necessary delivery enablement processes been indicated? • Are the types of in-house enablement requirements with the corresponding level of enablement indicated? • Are the types of external enablement requirements indicated?	6.2	

QUALITY ASSURANCE QUESTIONS	DESIGN ELEMENT (see Figure 9.11)	ADDRESSED: YES/NO (Yes: +; No: x)
WORK PROCESSES (Cont.)		
Delivery Enablement/Support Process Interfaces • Are all the delivery enablement/support interfaces with the Work Unit covered? • Have only the relevant key stakeholders been included in the interface? • Do the interface Integration Mechanisms have a clear customer focus, and are they fit-for-purpose? • Do the integration benefits outweigh the costs thereof, its value-adding? • Are the interfaces pitched relative to the level and type of enabling delivery/support services required?	6.2	

CRITICAL INFORMATION REQUIREMENTS
 	
 • Have the critical information requirements with measures been identified for:
    o key inputs?
    o key outputs?
    o the core business processes?
 	
 • Are the measures chosen practical and relevant?
 • Does the intelligence provided by the above enable timeous, proactive action?
	7	

REQUIRED INTEGRATING MECHANISMS AND GOVERNANCE • Have the vertical linkages been identified and described, and the Integration Mechanisms specified? • Have the horizontal linkages been identified and described, and the Integration Mechanisms specified? • Is the Work Unit Governance Model clearly specified with a clear decision-making Style and Rights?	8	

Step B.0.2: Align Operating Work Unit to be (re)designed with other Work Units

All Operating Work Units must form a coherent whole along the core value chain. In particular: (i) the purposes and mandates of Operating Units must not overlap, that is they must be distinct; (ii) the Input and Output Boundaries relative to the Work Unit Purposes and Mandates must agree and be unambiguous in order to prevent 'turf wars'; and (iii) the supplier and customer handovers (what, when, to what specifications) must be clearly specified.

Steps B.1: Construct Foundation to B.10: Do Tactical Design Implementation

The purpose of Steps B.1 to B.10 is to architect and roll out the Tactical Operating Unit Design – the Room Plan of the Operating Unit. Essentially, this process content-wise and quality assurance-wise takes the same format as the Strategic Design Process already discussed in Chapters 5 to 8 – Steps A.1 to A.10 – but as applied to Operating Work Units. However, a number of step-specific comments with respect to the Tactical Design process (see Figure 9.1) regarding Operating Units should be highlighted. In the process, only *some* of the design steps will be lifted out.

Step B.1: Foundation Construction

Step B.1.1: Profile WU Context

The most important consideration to focus on in this step is the Strategic Design Criteria and Vision of the organisation which form the design frame of reference for the Operating Unit. The Operating Unit need not choose same Strategic Organisational Shape as the organisation, for example Functional or Front/Back. It must architect its own fit-for-purpose Tactical Horizontal Design. However, all of the other contextual factors listed under this Strategic Design step must be considered for their relevancy to the Operating Unit Design, as well as any other unique, Operating Unit-specific contextual factors.

Step B.1.2: Formulate Design Criteria with Design Vision

Based on the emergence of the High Network/High Engagement/High Responsible Organisational Shape (see Step A.2.2.1), the shaded box gives the emerging Tactical Design Delivery Logic of the Future Workplace. These features give strong clues to the Design Criteria and Design Vision of the Operating Unit with the commensurate Design Metaphor. Another source of Design Criteria can be Manufacturing Delivery Logics like Lean/Flexible Manufacturing (see Table 6.1).

EMERGING TACTICAL DESIGN DELIVERY LOGIC OF THE FUTURE WORKPLACE

- Purpose-driven
- Outside-In, client centric
- Broader skills repertoires and higher skills densities, that is multi-tasking/multi-skilling, flexibly applied
- Accessible, in time, real time, information ('Intelligence')
- High decision-making autonomy
- High interdependence through teaming
- Modularisation
- Increased involvement in wider organisational context
- Social responsibility
- Sustainability

Step B.2: Tactical Horizontal Design

B.2.1: Group WU Work Processes into Work Domains

As a departure point, it is important to note that the unit of design is the *Work Domain*: the Operating Unit's portfolio of work processes (see Figure 9.11) that must be grouped into *Work Domains*. A Work Domain equates to the Work Teams or Work Roles that will populate the Work Unit, to be architected in detail during the Operational Design (see Chapter 10). The shaded box contains guidelines for the creation of distinct, powerful Work Domains (34).

GUIDELINES FOR THE CREATION OF DISTINCT, POWERFUL WORK DOMAINS

A Work Domain of an Operating Unit must:

- represent a whole piece of work for clearly defined customer(s), internal and/or external to the Work Unit;
- contain at least one Core Transformation (an activity that adds value and creates wealth for the Operating Unit) and/or at least one Core Organisational Capacity;
- have a similar mode of working;
- have high mutual interdependencies between the work process activities, making up the Domain;
- have a high frequency of performance of the work process activities included in the Domain;
- be able to comply with technological imperatives imposed by the Core Operating Technology and its Enablers, used by the Operating Unit (see Table 5.6 and Figure 5.6):
  - task interdependence: pooled, sequential, reciprocal; and
  - technology manageability (= task uncertainty and task analysability).

  These technological imperatives particularly affect the level of the delivery by enabling and support processes needed on an immediate basis within the Domain – basic, intermediate or advanced. The lower the technology manageability, the higher the level of enabling delivery that must be immediately available within the Domain;
- have geographical proximity/ongoing and/or, virtual connectivity;
- have the potential for high levels of autonomy, that is decision-making freedom;
- have clear Domain boundaries at natural break and handover points (for example, storage), allowing for clear ownership and accountability. Boundaries must be drawn in terms of the principle of control of variance at source;
- have identifiable, measurable outputs;
- not be bigger than an estimated 100 employees, with teams of about 8-10 persons each. Such sizes allow employees to better identify and relate to their unit and co-employees;
- have a name that is a true reflection of the work done in the Domain; and
- leave scope for unique character. Do not fall into the trap of "One size fits all". Domains may differ because they face unique circumstances/challenges; have a unique niche; have different Tactical Intents; and are in different stages of the organisational life cycle.

In the case where a Work Domain is demarcated into more than one Work Team (the respective Work Teams represent 'Mini-Work Domains'), the guidelines given in the above shaded box are equally applicable.

Step B.2.2: Configure Work Domains into Work Unit Shape

The work processes of the Operating Unit have been grouped into Work Domains. Under this step, firstly, a decision must first be taken regarding the fit-for-purpose, basic delivery logic for the Work Unit by plotting the Operating Work Unit on the Basic Delivery Logic axes, as per Figure 9.12 (a recap of Figure 6.8). Repeating what was said above in another way: the Unit's chosen delivery logic may differ from that of the organisation overall.

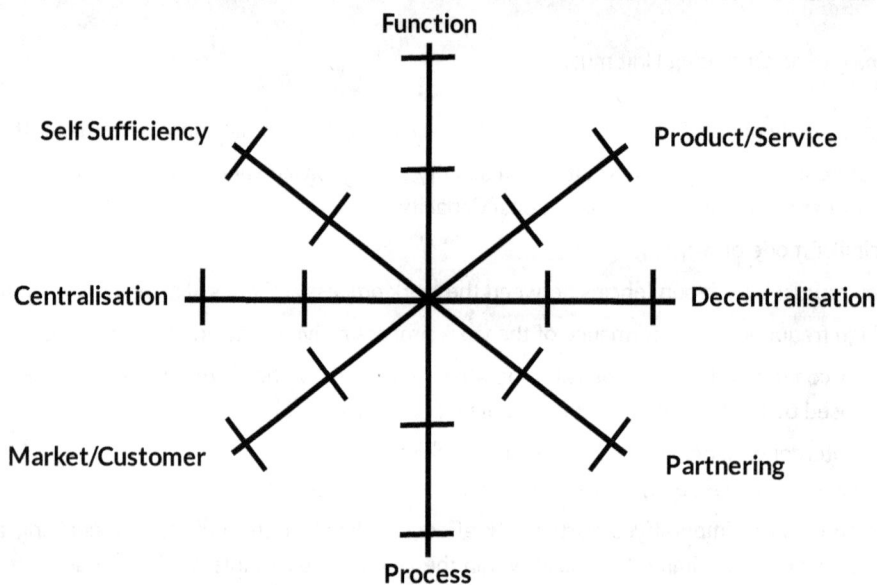

Figure 9.12: Basic Delivery Logic Axes

This plot establishes the Basic Delivery Logic in terms of which the Operating Unit desires to operate. The choice of a fit-for-purpose logic finds its justification in the Operating Unit's Tactical Intent. To remind the reader, Table 6.3 provides the prime strengths and weaknesses of each of the extreme positions on the axes given in Figure 9.12.

Secondly, as referenced against the chosen Unit's Basic Delivery Logic, an Operating Unit Shape must be architected in order to configure the Work Domains of the Unit into a fit-for-purpose Unit Shape. Useful clues regarding a Shape can be gained from the Organisational Shapes discussed under Step A.2.2.5. A Shape must be architected that befits the Unit Design Criteria and Vision, as well as its chosen Basic Delivery Logic.

The Shapes that can be considered for a Work Unit Shape are given in Table 9.5. In the table, a Work Domain in the Tactical Design can represent a Work Team(s) and/or Work Roles. In the Operational Design it will be decided whether a Work Domain equates to Work Team(s) or Work Role(s). The applicability, strengths and weaknesses of the Shapes listed in Table 9.5 can be found under Step A.2.2.5, Chapter 6, as applied to the context of the Tactical Operating Unit Design.

Table 9.5: Possible Operating Unit Shapes

PREDOMINANT BASIC DELIVERY LOGIC (based on Figure 9.12)	Function; Products/ Services; Centralised; Self-sufficient and/or Partnering	Process; Markets/ Customers; Centralised; Self-sufficient and/or Partnering	Process; Markets/ Customers; Decentralised; Self-sufficient and/or Partnering	Function and Process; Markets/ Customers; Decentralised; Self-sufficient and/or Partnering	Function; Markets/ Customers and Products/ Services; Decentralised; Self-sufficient and Partnering	Process; Markets/ Customers and Products/ Services; Decentralised; Self-sufficient
CORRESPONDING WORK UNIT SHAPE	**Functional**	**Process**	**Project/ Programme**	**Hub and Spoke**	**Front-Back**	**Network**
Description	Specialist Work Domains, each representing a single or set of related core competencies	Work Domains organised along the core work flow through the Operating Unit	All the of Work Domains are set up as projects and programmes	Decentralised regional Delivery Hubs with a centralised Hub with specialist support services	Customer serving Work Domains (= Front) with Solution Provision Work Domains (= Back)	Managed Ecosystem: Community of Practice

Step B.2.4: Construct Partnering Relationships

Whereas partnering possibilities would have been merely identified under Step A.2.4 in the Strategic Horizontal Design, in the Tactical Operating Unit Design these possibilities are converted into actual partnering relationships. A case study of outsourcing partnering with respect to Purchasing and Supply Management is discussed in the next section on the Tactical Design of Delivery Enabling Units.

Step B.5: Integrated Tactical Design and Charter

Step B.5.1: Compile Work Unit Map

Figure 9.11 can be used to construct a Tactical Work Unit Design Map with the following adaptations (see Appendix B: Design Template 11):

- *Design Element 6:* Replace the title 'Work Processes' with the title 'Horizontal and Vertical Designs'. In this box graphically depict the Horizontal Tactical Design: Configuration of Work Domains into an Operating Unit Shape, and the Vertical Tactical Design: Requisite Levels of Work.

- *Design Element 7:* Replace the title 'Critical Information Requirements' with the title 'Critical Unit Intelligence'. In this box list the critical intelligence the Operating Unit must have at its disposal at all times. A balanced scorecard can be used to depict this intelligence.
- *Design Element 8:* Replace the title 'Required Lateral Linkages' with the title 'Lateral Design'. In this box depict the lateral design, specifically the crafted Integration Mechanisms and Unit Governance Model.

A Work Unit Charter, outlining the ground rules according to which the Work Unit will operate, must be generated.

In summary: it cannot be overstressed that *all* of the Tactical Design steps, as reflected in Figure 9.1, *must* be followed regarding the architecting of the Operating Unit, using the Strategic Design Process steps discussed in Chapters 5 to 8 as a guide. Only Tactical Design steps that are different to the Strategic Design steps were explicated above.

Tactical Design of Delivery Enabling Units: Purchasing and Supply Management as Illustration

As stated in the introduction of this chapter, a Delivery Enabling Unit contains the support processes that enable delivery by the Operating Entity/Entities, such as equipment maintenance or supply chain/logistics. The Tactical Design for this type of Unit is illustrated through a case study regarding the outsourcing of Purchasing and Supply Management in a global chemical and pharmaceutical company (GCPC) (35). This Tactical Design Step is the next logical step of Strategic Step A.2.4: Identify possible opportunities for Organisational Partnering. In the case of Tactical Design, the equivalent step is Step B.2.4: Construct Partnering Relationships.

A caveat: although directly relevant to Tactical Design for a Delivery Enabling Unit, a limitation of the case study is that it discusses the design solution arrived at, and not the design process followed. However, what is particularly insightful regarding this case study is how the work (called 'activities' in the case study) of the Purchasing and Supply Organisations (PSO) was mapped and categorised in order to make informed outsourcing decisions.

Similar to the Tactical Designs discussed above, the Tactical Design Steps B.0 to B.10 (see Figure 9.1) must be followed, although they are not illustrated in this case study due to its exclusive focus on the design solution The following discussion of the Tactical Design of the People Function as an illustration of an Enabling Work Unit will again follow the Tactical Design route map.

Outsourcing Options for Purchasing and Supply Management

Outsourcing refers to the decision to move some of an organisation's internal activities and decision-making responsibilities to an external vendor: the choice of Make/Do or Buy. In this case, the PSO of GCPC. It is predicted that the outsourcing of Purchasing and Supply Management is expected to grow by 50% in the near future (36).

Four design options can be considered for PSOs: (i) by product/service/category; (ii) by business unit; (iii) by geography; and/or (iv) by activity. In the case of GCPC, the design option chosen for its PSO was an activity-based design, differentiating between:

- core: strategic sourcing activities;

- disposable, transactional activities: purchasing; and

- close-distinct: performance management activities.

The initial aim of the design intervention was to achieve process synergies, especially in transactional purchasing activities, in order to facilitate the shifting of internal resources into strategic sourcing activities.

Old vs. New Organisational Design

Figure 9.13 depicts the old and new design of the GCPC's PSO (37).

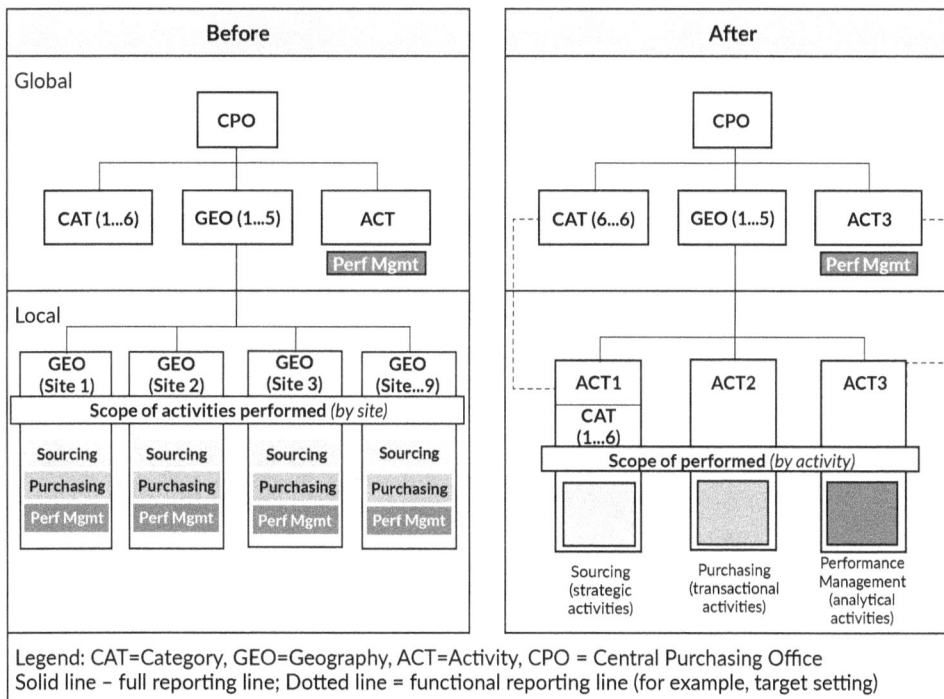

Figure 9.13: Old vs. New Organisational Design of GCPC's PSO
Note: Throughout the case study, the following colour coding applies to categorise activities in figures: light = sourcing – strategic; medium = purchasing – transactional; dark = performance management

Both before and after the redesign, GCPC's had at the global level a PSO with a small, centralised global procurement management team located at its headquarters. Its global level PSO was mainly structured according to categories (six major spend categories) and geographies (five major spend countries). The global category heads, the country heads, and the global performance management head formed part of the global management team of the PSO.

According to Figure 9.13, at the local level, three organisational activity clusters were established in the new PSO:

- 'Sourcing': strategic activities like provider selection and negotiations.
- 'Purchasing': operational activities such as purchase order processing.
- 'Performance management': analytical tasks, such as developing and checking on KPIs for the PSO, as well as spend analyses.

After its development in 2010, the new PSO design was implemented in most countries in 2011.

Clustering of activities in the new Organisational Design

Figure 9.14 shows the clustering of activities in the new Organisational Design (38).

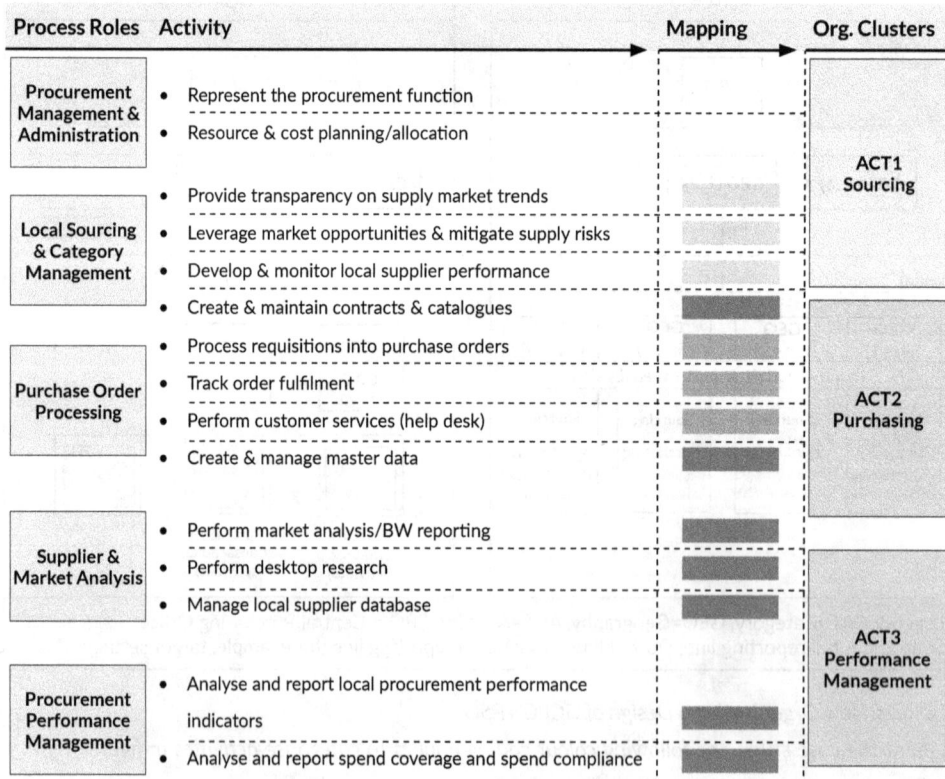

Figure 9.14: Clustering of activities in the new Organisational Design

In line with this, as well as the current distribution of capacities regarding activities in two of the major countries, GCPC developed and implemented a guideline of having personnel distribution as follows:

60% sourcing, 30% purchasing, and 10% performance management. The additional external provider capacity was intended to facilitate that change even further over time, so transactional and support activities could be even more outsourced to the external providers. Simultaneously, internal core employees could concentrate on PSO strategic tasks: sourcing and performance management.

New foci of activity clusters in new Organisational Design with realised benefits

The new activity-based PSO design provided increased effectiveness through transparency, and enhanced efficiency through the opportunity to increase standardisation and the harmonisation of PSO practices and processes on a global scale in GCPC. Figure 9.15 depicts the new foci of the activity clusters in the new design (39).

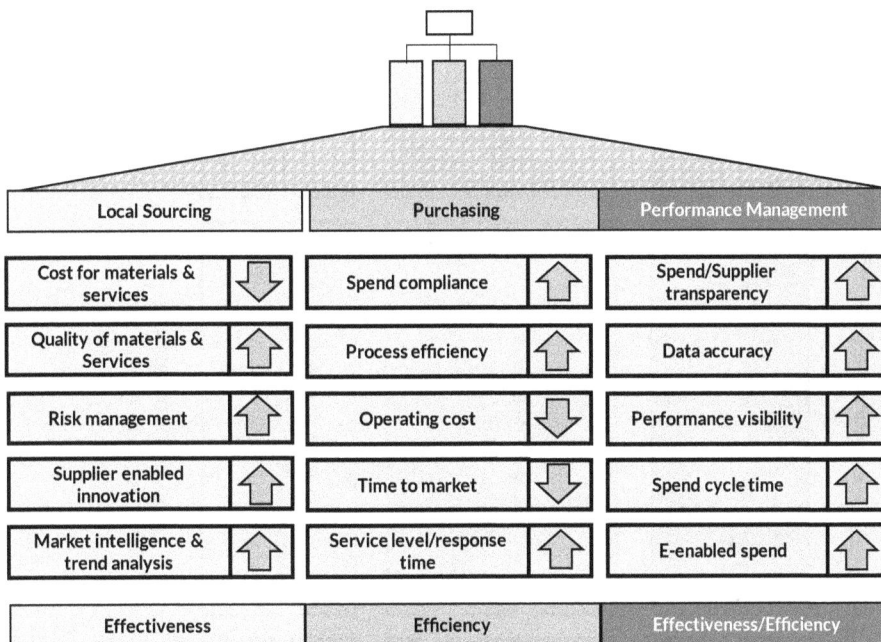

Local Sourcing	Purchasing	Performance Management
Cost for materials & services ⬇	Spend compliance ⬆	Spend/Supplier transparency ⬆
Quality of materials & Services ⬆	Process efficiency ⬆	Data accuracy ⬆
Risk management ⬆	Operating cost ⬇	Performance visibility ⬆
Supplier enabled innovation ⬆	Time to market ⬇	Spend cycle time ⬆
Market intelligence & trend analysis ⬆	Service level/response time ⬆	E-enabled spend ⬆
Effectiveness	Efficiency	Effectiveness/Efficiency

Figure 9.15: New foci of the Activity Clusters in the new PSO Design

Spectrum of Make or Buy decisions made by GCPC regarding its PSO

GCPC faced a significant growth scenario by 2012. The company needed PSO to better support its overall strategic targets, with sales challenged to provide enough supply to meet market demand. This implied, for example, that PSO would have to not only take a close look at all available options with existing suppliers to increase volumes, but also identify and quickly engage with new suppliers. In these efforts, an activity-based PSO design allowed it to outsource and engage external providers in parts of the PSO function.

The new modularised, activity-based Organisational Design thus enabled GCPC to consider the outsourcing of transactional PSO activities (see Figure 9.14). Figure 9.16 shows the spectrum of Make or Buy decisions that could be made by GCPC regarding its PSO (40).

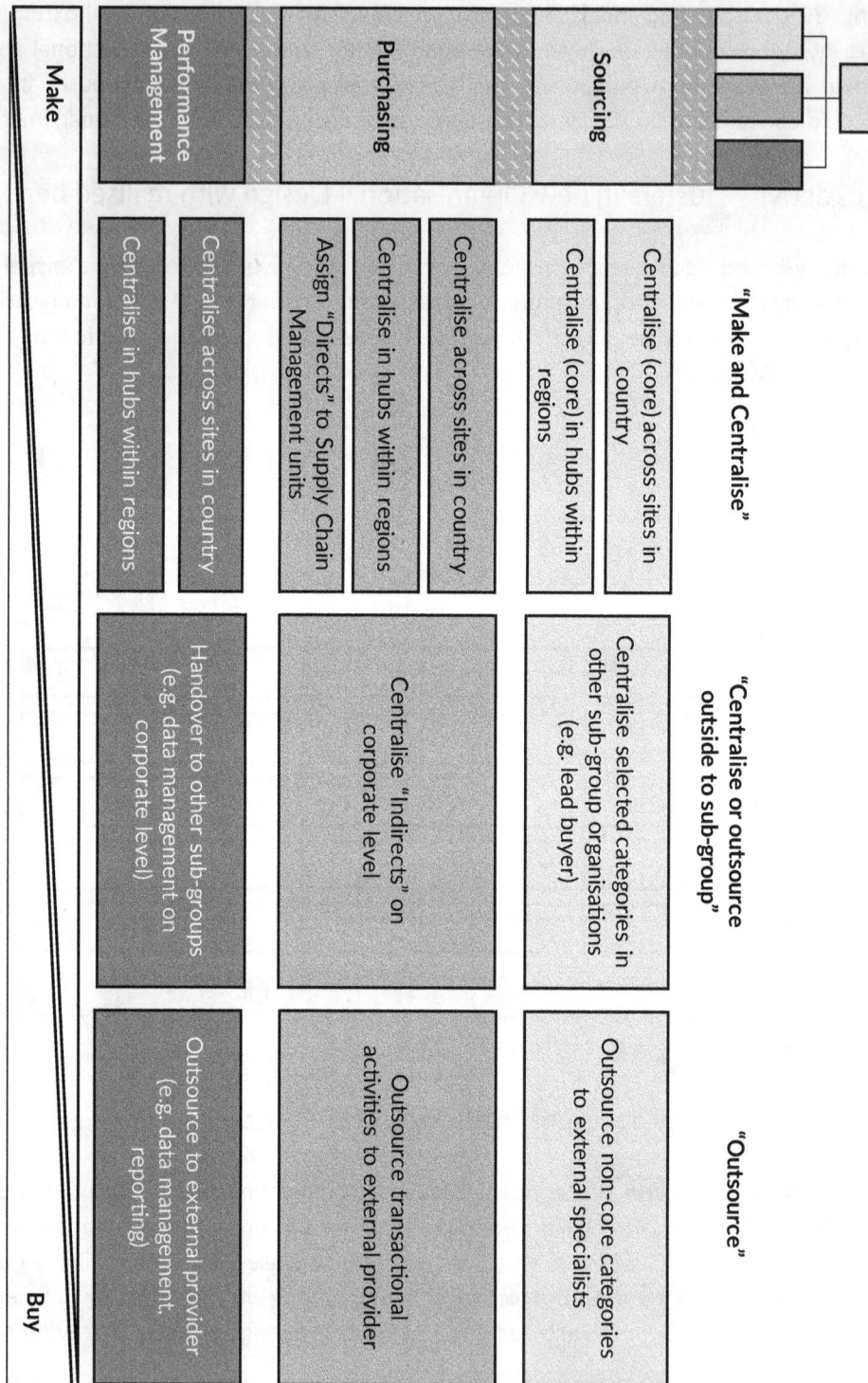

Figure 9.16: Spectrum of GCPC 'Make/Do' or 'Buy' GCPC decisions regarding its PSO

The scenario of the Make or Buy continuum for PSO activities – illustrated in Figure 9.16 – was created in 2010, but it was not until 2012 that parts of the PSO were outsourced and external providers were engaged. In 2012, GCPC decided to engage external support for parts of its activity cluster 'sourcing'. This focused especially on activities related to market intelligence and the preparation of RFPs and e-auctions. In addition, GCPC outsourced a part of the cluster 'performance management', particularly spend analysis and the provision of the KPI reporting tool via a web-based interface. These changes also involved changing the PSO. The new PSO was experienced in successfully outsourcing in the Purchasing and Supply Management context. It saw the engagement of external service providers as a cost effective means to address capacity challenges related to the growth scenario.

With these changes, GCPC expected to achieve the following capacity benefits regarding its PSO, which it later realised: first, improve process efficiency: external providers are experts at processing these activities in large volumes; second, leverage outsourcing to quickly scale up or scale down human resources capacities on the provider side as required. The external providers were considered to have better access to human resources for these activities, and contractually agreed to have a flexible organisation, that is to increase or decrease capable resources dedicated to GCPC's needs within a three month notice period. This facilitated both efficiency and effectiveness in GCPC operations.

Tactical Design of Support Work Units: The People Function as Illustration

As stated in the introduction of this chapter, a Support Unit contains the processes that enable the organisation to function as an organisation overall, for example, Finance, People, IT. To illustrate the balance of the design process for a Support Unit: Steps B.1 to B.10 as per Figure 9.1, the People Function will be used as an illustration (41) (42). Essentially, this design process – content-wise and quality assurance-wise – takes on the same format as the Strategic Design Process already discussed (Steps A.1 to A.10, Chapters 5 to 8), but as applied to the People Function as Support Work Unit.

Step B.0: Profile of Work Unit

The objective of this step is to determine the essential nature of the Work Unit under consideration – its Identity – as a Support Unit, in this case the People Function.

The purpose of the People Function is to bring about and maintain enabling and empowering conditions under which the organisation's people can contribute fully to its sustainable success by ensuring that the right people are in the right numbers at the right time in the right place, able, willing, wanting, and being allowed to perform with a sense of purpose, thereby giving the organisation a sustainable, competitive edge (or value-creation) in its chosen markets through its people.

In the discussion the People Tactical Design route map, the focus will be on lifting out specific design steps to provide insight into critical aspects regarding this Tactical Design. However, all of the steps with their associated sub-steps remain in force and have to be undertaken (that is Steps B.1 to B.10, Figure 9.1).

Step B.1: Foundation Construction

For the purposes of this discussion, only two sub-steps will be focused on in this step: Step B.1.2: Map Work Processes, and B.1.5: Formulate Design Criteria with Design Vision. All of the other steps have to be conducted as per the steps making up the Strategic Design: Steps A.1 to A.5, but will not be discussed here.

Step B.1.2: Map Work Processes

It is important in this step to construct a comprehensive and complete People Work Process. Figure 9.17 gives an example of such a high level Work Process Map for People Management, detailing its People Value Chain (43). The process map provides an overview of the work that needs to be done with regard to the people of the organisation. Critically important in arriving at a proper People Value Chain that is reflective of the latest thinking about People Management, is that it correctly maps the logical process flow of the work, and that it shows all of the interdependencies between process activities.

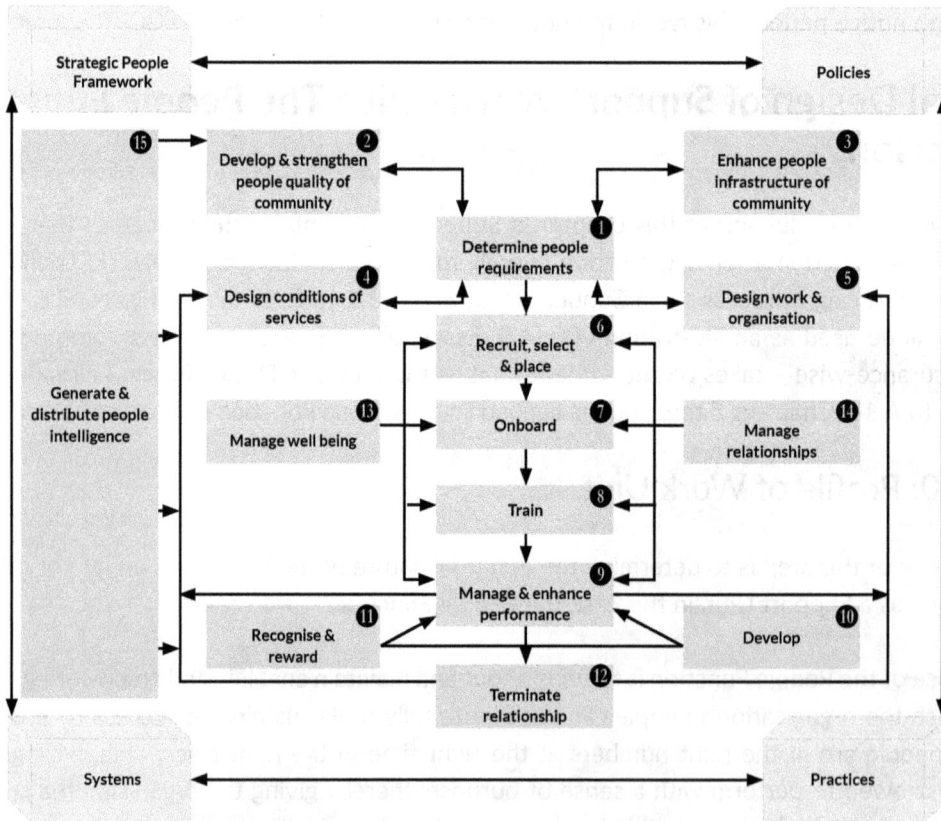

Figure 9.17: Work of the People Function – People Value Chain

Figure 9.18 gives an Employee Life Cycle Process of the work of the People Function, reflecting the emerging view of the idea that the People Function's mandate is all about creating and maintaining irresistible, memorable, end-to-end Employee Experiences (44) (45).

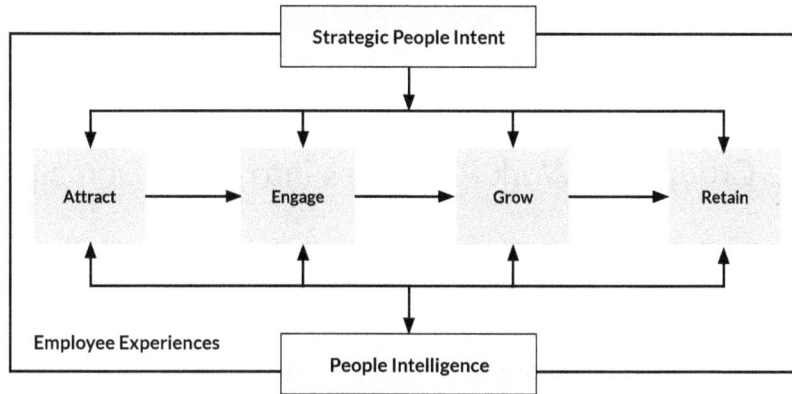

Figure 9.18: Work of the People Function – Employee Experiences relative to the Employee Life Cycle

B.1.5: Formulate Design Criteria with Design Vision

Currently the widely accepted departure point – the dominant Design Criterion – for the People Function and People Professionals is that of *(Strategic) Client-centric Partnering* (46). Partnering implies taking co-responsibility with clients to realise the People Function's Purpose as outlined above. Given Partnering as a Design Criterion, there has been a general mind shift in the *Overall Engagement Mode* that People Professionals must adopt when engaging with clients. The mind shift is from being a technical specialist in a support and service role, to being a genuine business partner. This mind shift is reflected in Table 9.6.

Table 9.6: Mind shift in the Overall Engagement Mode of future-fit People Professionals

From	To
• Product-centric	• Client-centric
• Technical solutions	• Business solutions
• Risk avoidance, reactive	• Risk-seeking, proactive
• Transactional contributions	• Transformational contributions
• Activity focus	• Output, value focus

Step B.2: Tactical Horizontal Design

The primary focus in the discussion will be on:

- Step B.2.1: Group WU Work Processes into Work Domains; and

- Step B.2.2: Configure Work Domains into Work Unit Shape with two relevant sub-steps, namely:

  o Step B.2.2.4: Decide on the Basic Delivery Logic of the WU in accordance with which its Work Domains must be configured into a WU Shape; and

  o Step B.2.2.5: Choose a Basic WU Shape that is congruent with the selected Basic Delivery Logic, including a possible global/globalising footprint.

To repeat, *all* of the steps of the Tactical Horizontal Design not discussed here as per Strategic Horizontal Design: Steps A.1 to A.5 also have to be conducted to arrive at a complete, fit-for-purpose Tactical People Function Design.

Step B.2.1: Group WU Work Processes into Work Domains

This step is about architecting the flow of the People Value Chain by creating areas of focused competencies and specialisation. That is, the Work Domains making up the People Function. The Work Domains must be demarcated in a such a way as to enable the organisation to make people its competitive edge. The Horizontal People Design in essence is about the best division of labour of the People Function's work.

The Work of the People Function – the People Value Chain (see Figure 9.17) or Employee Life Cycle (see Figure 9.18) – can be demarcated into four primary work domains, using the Design Criterion of Client-centric Partnering:

- *Domain 1:* People direction, philosophy and value add (or returns).
- *Domain 2:* People policies and standards.
- *Domain 3:* People work flow. The People Value Chain, depicted in Figure 9.15, subdivided into Need Satisfaction, Solutions and Enablers.
- *Domain 4:* People intelligence and reporting.

Domains 1 to 3 are the typical, conventional primary people work domains, and are readily apparent. Domain 4, however, perhaps requires further explication because it has been until recently somewhat out of the ordinary. If people are moving centre stage in securing the future sustainable success of organisations, then real-time people intelligence and reporting become mission-critical (for example, a people balanced scorecard or dashboard, and employee climate surveys). The analogy here is that of financial reporting, with its commensurate intelligence provided to make informed financial decisions at Executive and Board levels.

Step B.2.2: Configure Work Domains into Work Unit Shape

Step B.2.2.4: Decide on the Basic Delivery Logic of WU

A decision must be taken on the Basic Delivery Logic of the People Function in terms of which its Work Domains must be configured. As a memory jogger, Figure 9.19 (a replication of Figure 6.8) depicts the design axes in terms of which a Basic Logic Delivery can be plotted, in this case for the People Function. Table 6.3 provides the prime strengths and weaknesses of each of the extreme positions on the axes given in Figure 9.19.

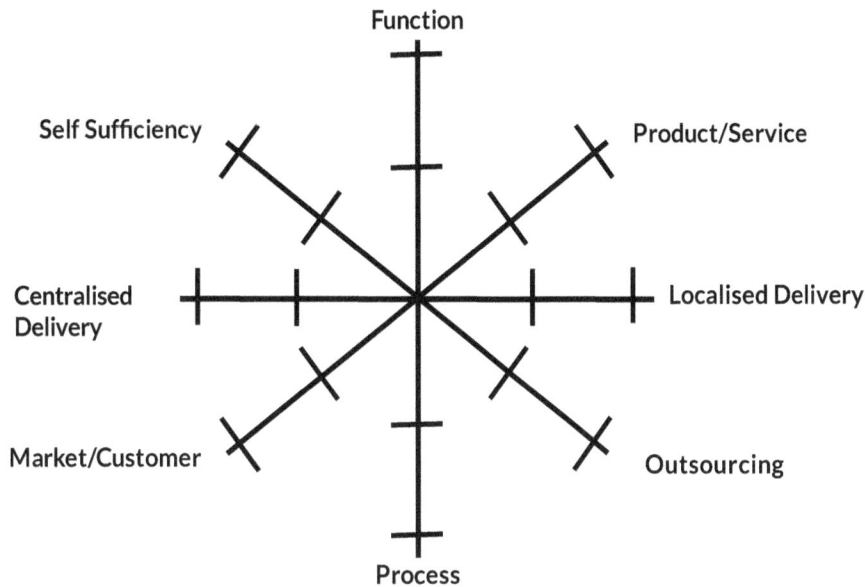

Figure 9.19: Design logic axes to decide on a Basic Design Delivery Logic for the Work Unit

In applying the design axes given in Figure 9.19 to the Basic Design Logic of the People Function, the following delivery logic choices are possible. The final choice must be referenced against the Design Criterion of Client-centric Partnering for the People Function, and any other Design Criteria decided on:

- *Function* (for example, the People Functional areas, such as talent sourcing, employment relations, rewards, training and development) and/or *Process* (for example, the People Client Delivery Process).

- *Market/Customer* (that is those Divisions/Work Units of the organisation to be serviced by the People Function) and/or the *Products/Services* delivered by the People Function (for example, reward packages, assessments, union collective agreements, leadership development programmes).

- *Centralised delivery* (that is a centralised People Function) and/or *Localised delivery* (that is a People Partner per Department/Divisions/Work Units of the organisation).

- *Self-sufficiency* (that is delivering all the people services from own, internal resources) and/or *Outsourcing* (that is, making use of external service providers).

Step B.2.2.5: Choose a WU Shape in accordance with the selected Basic Delivery Logic, including a possible global/globalising footprint

In the preceding steps of the Tactical Horizontal Design process, the Work Domains of People Management were demarcated and a Basic Delivery Logic decided on, as referenced against the set Design Criteria and Design Vision. Next, an Organisational Shape for the People Function – its Horizontal Design – must be configured using the basic Work Domains as input. Metaphorically, the Room (= Work Unit, that is the People Function) with its respective Work Domains (= Sub-Rooms) must configured.

Useful clues regarding a fit-for-purpose Shape can be gained from the Organisational Shapes discussed under Step A.2.2.5, Chapter 6. A Shape must be architected that befits the WU Design Criteria and Vision, as well as its chosen Basic Delivery Logic. The Shapes that can be considered as fit-for-purpose are given in Table 9.7. In the table, a Work Domain in the Tactical Design can represent a Work Team(s) and/or Work Role(s). In the Operational Design it will be decided whether a Work Domain equates to Work Team(s) or Work Role(s). (The applicability, strengths and weaknesses of the Shapes listed in Table 9.7 can be found under Step A.2.2.5, but applied to the context of the Tactical WU Design.)

Table 9.7: Possible Tactical WU Shapes

PREDOMINANT BASIC DELIVERY LOGIC (Based on Figure 9.19)	Function; Products/ Services; Centralised; Self-sufficient and/or Partnering	Process; Markets/ Customers; Centralised; Self-sufficient and/or Partnering	Process; Markets/ Customers; Decentralised; Self-sufficient and/or Partnering	Function and Process; Markets/ Customers; Decentralised; Self-sufficient and/or Partnering	Function; Markets/ Customers and Products/ Services; Decentralised; Self-sufficient and Partnering	Process; Markets/ Customers and Products/ Services; Decentralised; Self-sufficient
CORRESPONDING WORK UNIT SHAPE	**Functional**	**Process**	**Project/ Programme**	**Hub and Spoke**	**Front-Back**	**Network**
Description	Specialist Work Domains, each representing a single or set of related core competencies	Work Domains organised along the core work flow through the Support WUs	All the Work Domains are set up as projects and programmes	Decentralised regional Delivery Hubs with a centralised Hub with specialist support services	Customer serving, Work Domains (= Front) with Solution Provision Work Domains (= Back)	Managed Ecosystem: Community of Practice

In the light of the overall strategic Client-centric Partnering Criterion chosen above for the People Function, a leading practice Tactical Horizontal Design Shape for the People Function is given in Figure 9.20. This Shape represents a Front-Back Shape (see Table 9.7 above). The typical additional Design Criteria informing this Shape are shown in italics next to each of the Work Domains making up this Tactical Design Shape for the People Function (47).

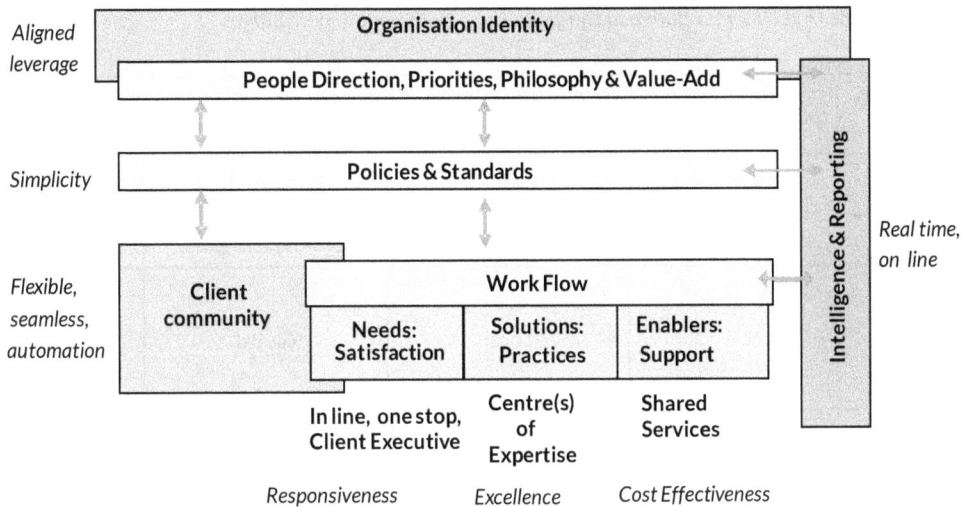

Figure 9.20: Tactical Horizontal Design for People Function

The Horizontal People Design given in Figure 9.20 can be called a *Client-centric, Expert-based, Organisational Enabling Design*. The essence of its delivery logic is to be found in a design centring around People Client Communities to be serviced in a 'one-stop' seamless manner by People Client Executives, endeavouring to optimally match the people needs of internal, organisational clients to people solutions provided by the People Function. The Design Metaphor that best informs this People Design is that of a soccer/rugby team, that is a group or specialists/generalists jointly working together to attain the overarching goal of organisational success to the benefit of their stakeholders.

Physical Footprint: Global/Globalising

If one's organisation operates globally, or intends becoming a global player, the design of the People Function must fit the global footprint of the organisation of which it forms part. It is important for the Function to be aligned to the stage of the evolutionary, globalising path of the organisation (see Figure 6.27) because different Organisational Designs are associated with each of the four stages (see Figure 6.30). Thus the Tactical Horizontal Design of the People Function will be different for each globalising, evolutionary stage (48).

To remind the reader: the major challenge to a globalising organisation (and by implication its People Function) at each evolutionary stage is to find the right balance between a *reach need*, that is the local and/or global integration of work, and an *acting need*, that is the local and/or global responsiveness on the ground at those locations where the organisation has an operational presence.

Table 9.8 depicts different typical Tactical Shapes for the People Function Unit Designs for the various permutations of reach and acting needs, relative to the stages of the globalising, evolutionary path.

Table 9.8: Typical People Unit Designs relative to the globalising, evolutionary path stages

PEOPLE WORK DOMAINS	BALANCING RESEARCH AND ACTING NEEDS RELATIVE TO THE GLOBALISING, EVOLUTIONARY PATH STAGES			
	Stage 1 Local integration and responsiveness	*Stage 2* Local integration, Global responsiveness	*Stage 3* Global integration, Local responsiveness	*Stage 4* Global integration and responsiveness
1: People direction, philosophy and value add/returns	Local	Local	Global	Global
2: People policies and standards	Local	Local	Global	Global
3A: People work flow: Need satisfaction	Local	Local	Local	Local
3B: People work flow: Solutions	Local	Regional	Regional	Global
3C: People work flow: Enablers	Local	Regional	Regional	Global
4: People intelligence and reporting	Local	Global	Global	Global
TACTICAL PEOPLE DESIGNS	Completely separate autonomous People Functions by country. All Work Domains (1 to 4) are country-based.	Local People Units handle Work Domains 1, 2 and 3A. Work Domains 3B and 3C are regionalised to cater for regional differences, for example, different tax regimes for the payroll. Work Domain 4 is globalised.	Work Domains 1, 2, 3B and 4 are globally integrated. Work Domain 3A is localised for in-country responsiveness. Some of Work Domains 3B and 3C may be regionalised to cater for regional differences, but also to achieve regional economies of scale.	Client-facing Work Domain 3A is localised. All other Work Domains are globally integrated (1, 2, 3B, 3C and 4), although some in-country autonomy may be given to localise Work Domains 2 and 3B to attain a better in-country fit.

Local	Regional	Global

Step B.3: Architect Tactical Vertical Design

The Tactical Vertical Design of the People Function aims to establish the requisite ownership of each of the Work Domains demarcated during the Tactical Horizontal Design in terms of the requisite Level of Work (LOW) and profiling mission-critical Work Roles. This means considering the Vertical Dimension of the People Function, that is organisational levels.

Four steps will be considered here:

- B.3.1 Decide on the requisite LOW for the WU overall.
- B.3.2 Architect the WU's House Ownership Model.
- B.3.3 Allocate the requisite LOWs to each Work Domain.
- B.3.4 Identify the mission-critical Work Roles and generate high level Role Profiles.

Step B.3.1: Decide on the requisite LOW for the WU overall

If the People Function is the outcome of a Strategic Design intervention, its requisite LOW would have been decided already. If the People Function is being designed as a stand-alone Tactical Design exercise, its requisite LOW has to be debated and decided on, aligned to the organisations' overall requisite LOW.

In the People Partnering model, the requisite LOW is typically LOW4. This implies a Strategic Translation/ Implementation contribution by the People Function. However, the People Function may only be expected to make a LOW3: Operational Execution contribution, that is transaction-administrative, which is contrary to the Design Criterion of Strategic Partnering (see Table 7.1).

Step B.3.2: Architect the WU's House Ownership Model

The People Domain 1: People direction, philosophy and value-add; and Domain 2: People policies and standards can be regarded as the Corporate Centre analogy for the People Function with respect to the other People Domains (see Figure 9.20). With this view as a departure point, the People Function's Ownership Model has to be crafted. Similar to the types of House Ownership delineated in Table 7.2 for a Corporate Centre over its Work Units, the House Ownership within the People Function can vary from Financial to Operational in terms of the direction and control exercised by the 'People Centre' (= Domains 1 and 2) over the balance of the People Work Domains.

Step B.3.3: Allocate requisite LOWs to Work Domains

The next critical design decision with respect to the Tactical Vertical Design of the People Function is the identification of the highest requisite LOW required by the respective People Work Domains, with their associated Work Roles. Figure 9.21 graphically depicts the above demarcated Work Domains with their suggested respective LOWs.

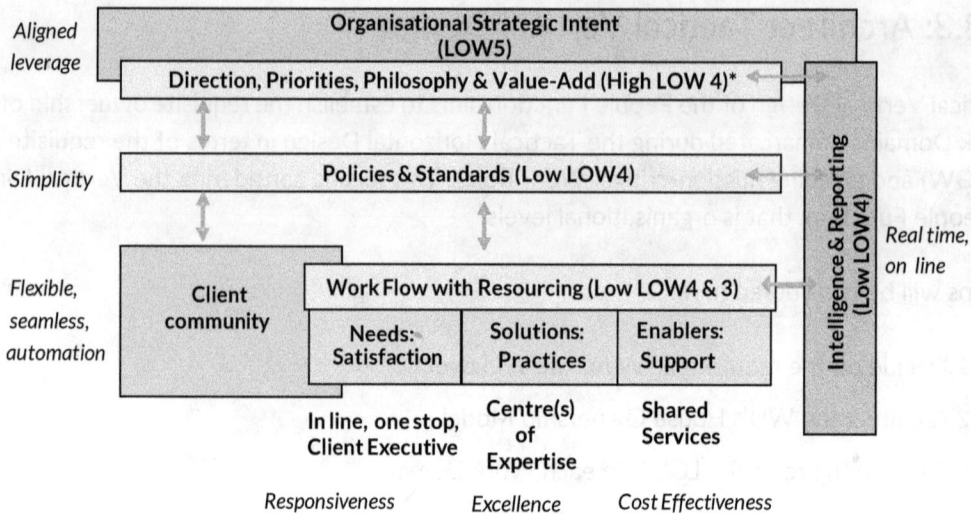

Figure 9.21: Vertical Tactical Design for People Function: House Ownership Model

Step B.3.4: Identify the mission-critical Work Roles and generate high level Role Profiles

An excellent way to anchor the Tactical Horizontal and Vertical Designs of the People Function, as well as to ensure the total coverage and alignment of the work that has to be done, is to generate a portfolio of Work Role Profiles for the respective generic Work Roles identified in the Tactical Horizontal Design. That is, profiling the owners of the respective Work Domains at their requisite LOWs, for example People Leadership or People Generalists. As discussed before, a Work Role refers to what needs to be done and delivered by a person fulfilling the role.

The Role Profile is a concise page to one-and-a-half page document, structured in terms of: (i) the core purpose of the Role (three to four lines); (ii) major task/key performance areas (no more than five task areas); and (iii) critical outcomes (no more than five outcomes). (See Appendix B: Design Template 3.) The next logical step, but part of the Operational and not Tactical Design, is to translate the Role Profiles into the required competencies needed by role incumbents.

The following design topics are addressed with regard to the People Professional Roles: Core Work Roles; Generic Work Roles by People Work Domains; and Modes of Engagement.

Core Work Roles of the People Professional

Client partnering, as architected into the Tactical People Horizontal Design, contains at least five core People Professional Roles, as depicted in Figure 9.22 (49).

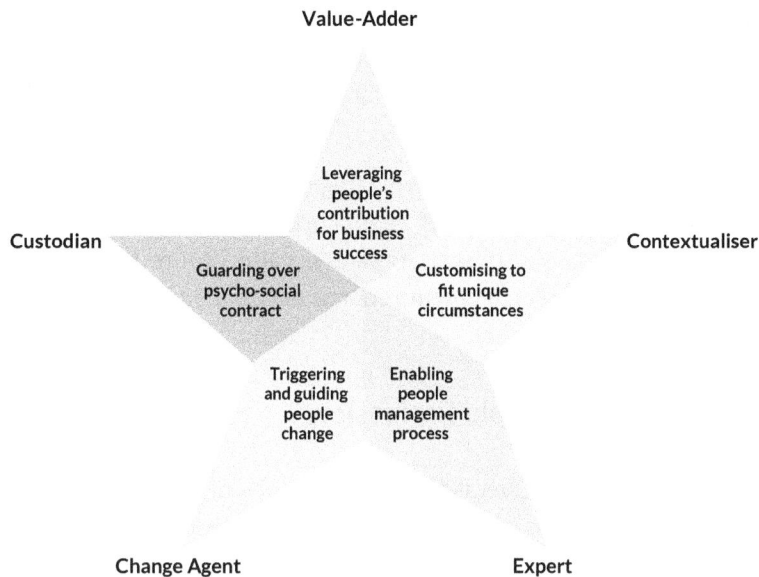

Figure 9.22: Core Client-Partnering Roles of the People Professional

Generic Work Roles of People Professional by People Work Domain

Given the core Client-Partnering roles of the People Professional (see Figure 9.22), the proposed Tactical Horizontal and Vertical Designs of the People Function (see Figures 9.20 and 9.21 respectively) require at least the following Generic People Professional Work Roles by Work Domain, all informed by the Core Client-Partnering Roles as foundation. The LOWs of the Generic Work Roles is a function of what requisite LOW was awarded to the People Function overall, and its respective Work Domains (see Figure 9.21).

At least the following Generic Work Roles can be distinguished. Assuming a LOW4 People Function, the consequential LOW for the roles are given in brackets after each role:

- **People Leadership** (High to Low LOW4) provides overall people direction/philosophy and guidance to people leadership and management within the organisation, and is part of the executive and senior management teams of the organisation (Domains 1 and 2, Figure 9.21).

- **People Generalists** (or Client Executives) (Low LOW4) are positioned as close as possible to clients, providing a one-stop service to clients in defining their people needs, sourcing the appropriate people solutions to satisfy those needs, overseeing the successful embedding of solutions, and ensuring that line management is competent in using those solutions with their accompanying practices, with confidence (Domain 3: Needs, Figure 9.21).

- **People Specialists** (LOW3 and High LOW2) are located in centralised centre(s) of expertise (or excellence), crafting and/or insourcing and implementing the required people solutions and practices, and rendering specialised daily people services to the organisation through the people generalists (Domain 3: Solutions, Figure 9.21).

- **Transactional Processors** (Low LOW3 and down) are situated in a centralised people shared service centre, dealing with the transactional, administrative processing underlying the people solutions and services, the handling of people queries, and the keeping of people records (Domain 3: Enablers, Figure 9.21).

- **People Intelligence** (Low LOW4 and down) collect management information and generate management reports regarding the state of people management in the organisation and people's contribution to the success of the organisation. They also ensure the timeous preparation and submission of statutory people management reports, as required by legislation (Domain 4: People intelligence and reporting, Figure 9.21).

Modes of Engagement of the People Professional

Against the backdrop of the shift in the Overall Engagement Mode of People Professionals (see Table 9.6), four distinct but interdependent Modes of Engagement between People Professionals and their clients – delivered through the above discussed Work Roles – can be distinguished as depicted in Figure 9.23 (50). They populate the Client-centric, Expert-based, Organisational Enabling Design (see Figure 9.21). For the sake of simplicity, only the client-facing People Professional roles, as crafted above, are given in the figure. Note the contextual embeddedness of the Modes of Engagement – these modes have to be designed based on, and lived with high contextual intelligence, to ensure the best contextual fit.

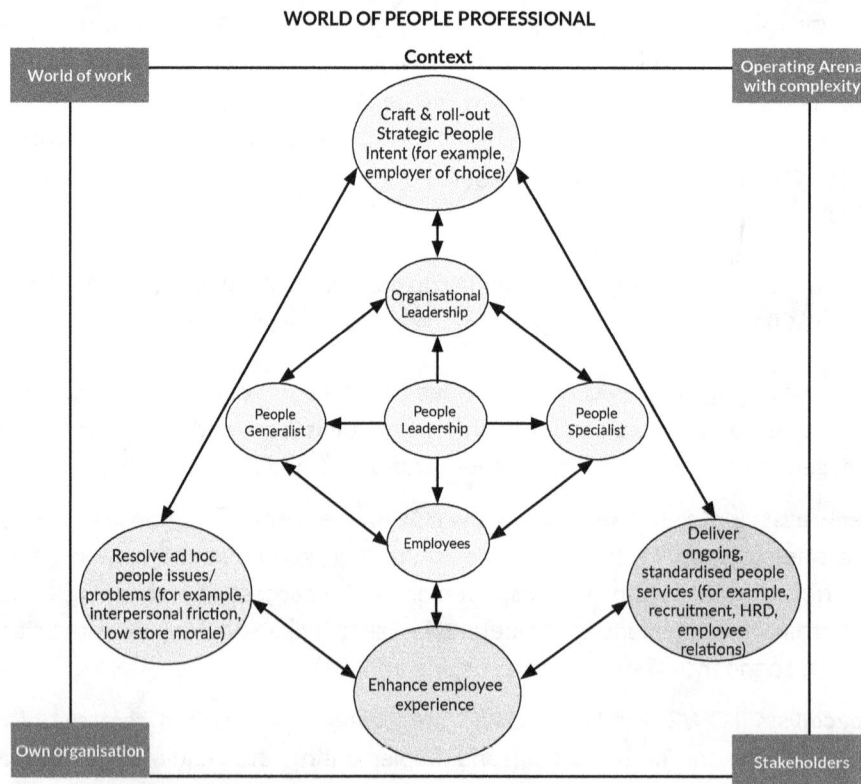

Figure 9.23: Modes of Client Engagement

The four Modes of Client Engagement, as given in Figure 9.23, entail the following:

- *Mode 1:* Craft and roll out the organisation's Strategic People Intent, in alignment with the organisation's Identity.

- *Mode 2:* Deliver standardised, people services associated with the People Value Chain on a daily basis.

- *Mode 3:* Resolve ad hoc, out-of-the-ordinary and unexpected people issues/problems (for example, interpersonal conflict, decreasing morale, increasing people turnover).

- *Mode 4:* Enhance the employee experience.

It is beyond the scope of this chapter to map the work processes associated with each Mode of Engagement. For interest's sake, and to illustrate such a map, the process map of Mode 1: Craft and roll out the Strategic People Intent of organisation, is depicted in Figure 9.24 (51). Where two or more Work Roles are involved, the Work Role taking the lead is given first.

Each Mode of Client Engagement has its own unique critical success factors. In the case of *Mode 1: Craft and roll out Strategic People Intent of Organisation*, typical success factors are strategic focus and synergy, and rolling out the strategic people framework within the window of opportunity (see Figure 9.24). In the case of *Mode 2: Deliver standardised people services*, the typical critical success factors include a clear mapping of processes, overall value chain integration, well-constructed service level agreements (SLAs), and delivery predictability. For *Mode 3: Resolve ad hoc people issues/problems*, the typical factors are the proper scoping of the issue/problem, responsiveness in terms of the perceived urgency of the need, and a well-constructed, pragmatic plan of action. For Mode 4: *Enhance employee experience*, congruence between the talking and walking of the Employee Value Proposition, given that the Proposition is compelling, is a crucial success factor.

MODE 1: CRAFT AND ROLL OUT STRATEGIC PEOPLE INTENT OF ORGANISATION	
Process map	**People Professional Roles involved**
CEO determines overall direction	People Leader, for example, HR Director
Upward selling of looming strategic people challenges/issues by People Leader — Engage with organisation to establish strategic people needs	People Leader/People Generalists
Determine people implications of overall organisational direction/ people needs	People Leader/People Generalists
Discuss within People Leadership and identify required strategic People Intent and initiatives in support of overall organisational direction	People Leadership = People Management Team
Present strategic People Intent and initiatives to organisational leadership, Exco and Board to obtain buy-in and commitment	People Leader
Research people initiatives and develop leading practices, conceptual models	People Specialists
Present leading practices, conceptual model to People Leadership for discussion and sign-off	People Specialists
Present to organisational leadership for approval and agree timelines relative to business agenda	People Leader/People Specialists
Operationalise leading practices, conceptual model, and if necessary customise for different organisational units	People Specialists/People Generalists
Develop integrated strategic project plan (including change navigation) in partnership with stakeholders	People Specialists/People Generalists
Execute flawlessly	People Generalist/People Specialist
Measure value-add	People Generalist/People Specialist
Once implemented, incorporate into ongoing standardised people delivery process	People Specialist
Key rules for success	
• Focused set of strategic people initiatives: Less is more • Involvement of/Consultation with stakeholders throughout process • Proper organisational implementation contracting (to fit into business agenda) • Delivery within strategic window of opportunity	

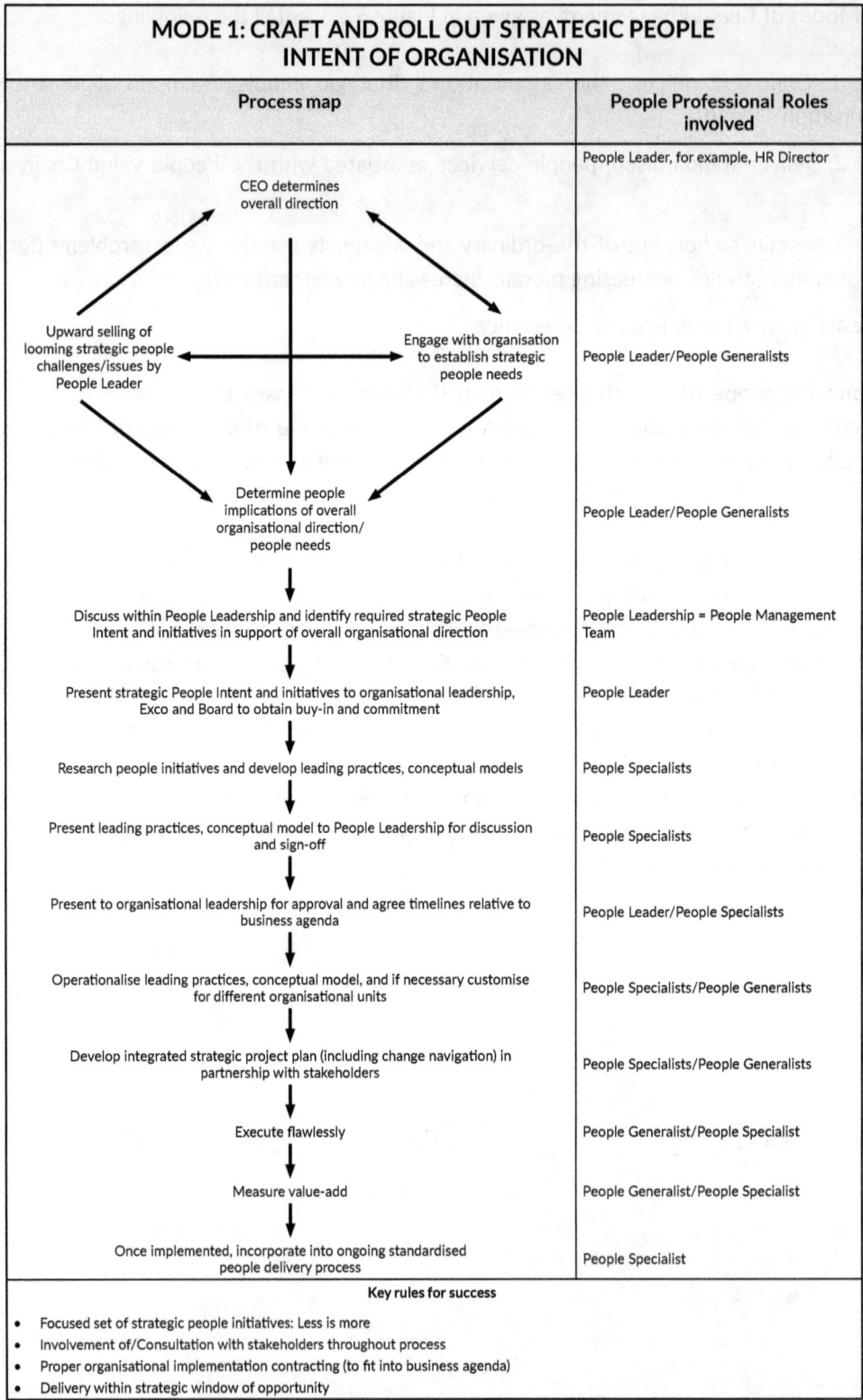

Figure 9.24: Process map of Client Engagement Mode 1: Craft and roll out Strategic People Intent of Organisation

Step B.4: Tactical Lateral Design

At this point in the Tactical Design process, the demarcated People Work Domains have been configured – the *Tactical Horizontal Design*. The requisite LOWs, House Ownership Model, Work Roles and Modes of Client Engagement – *Tactical Vertical Design* – have also been architected. This is the *differentiation process* of the Tactical Design.

The next step is critical, that is the *integration* of the differentiated dimensions of the Tactical People Design. This entails identifying the interdependency between the People Work Domains and Work Roles, and then designing the Integration Mechanisms and Governance necessary to ensure that all of the aforementioned work together synergistically and accountably. That is, the Tactical Lateral Design of the People Function involving putting together the differentiated design pieces. Only two steps in the Tactical Lateral Design process will be discussed here, namely Step B.4.1: Construct an Interdependency Matrix and Step B.4.3: Set up a Governance Model.

Step B.4.1: Construct an WU Interdependency Matrix

To design fit-for-purpose, effective Integration Mechanisms for the People Function, it is vital to understand the *interdependencies* between the design component elements of the Tactical Horizontal and Vertical Designs of the People Function (see Figures 9.20 and 9.21). An Interdependency Matrix thus has to be constructed to map the interdependencies between People Work Domains and Work Roles. This is shown in Table 9.9 which uses Work Roles for illustration. The same type of matrix can be generated for the People Work Domains. It is important here to take account of interdependencies in both directions: from Role A to Role B, and vice versa. The nature of the dependency may differ depending on the specific relationship direction.

Table 9.9: Interdependency Matrix for the crafted People Professional Work Roles

	Client 1 2 3	People Leadership	People Generalist	People Specialist	Transactional Processor	People Intelligence & Reporting
Client	–					
People Leadership		–				
People Generalist			–			
People Expert				–		
Transactional Processor					–	
People Intelligence & Reporting						–

Step B.4.3: Set up the WU Governance Model

With the emerging new order typifying the context in which organisations currently operate (see Figure 2.2), the shift is, generally speaking, towards High Network/High Engagement/High Responsible Governance (see Figure 6.7), based on Consultation, Co-determination and Self-management (see Step A.4.3). Such a governance model can also be adopted for the People Unit, outlining Decision-making Rights and Styles. The outcome is a Decision-making Rights and Style Matrix.

Step B.5: Integrated Tactical Design and Charter

This step is made up of three sub-steps: Step B.5.1: Compile WU Map; Step B.5.2: Draw WU Organogram; and Step B.5.3: Draft WU Charter.

Step B.5.1: Compile WU Map

The outcomes of the Tactical Horizontal, Vertical and Lateral Designs of the People Function now have to be combined into an Integrated Tactical People Design in the form of a visual, organisational map. Put differently, the overall Room Plan has to be drafted for the People Function. This is the culmination and highlight of the Tactical Design Process. Similar to a Room (read WU House Plan), the placement of the Work Domains of the WU relative to one another must occur in accordance with the set Design Criteria and Design Vision, as well as the Basic Delivery Logic chosen for the Function. Where interdependencies exist, the map must show 'Work Domain overlaps'. The design must also show what external support services must be provided at what LOW, to enable the People Function to function effectively.

Based on the proposed Tactical Horizontal, Vertical and Lateral Designs for the People Function, Figure 9.25 gives an Integrated Tactical Design – the complete WU House Plan. This is based on a Front-Back Organisational Design (see Table 9.7) (52) using a partnering delivery logic on the client-facing side of the organisation, with groupings being done in terms of clients and/or markets ('Front' of the Tactical People Design). On the product/service side of the organisation ('Back' of the Tactical People Design), groupings are done in terms of products/services with the support services.

A single comment regarding the proposed Integrated Tactical Design for the People Function in Figure 9.25 is relevant here. The Work Domain called 'People Solutions' is made up of a portfolio of conventional functional People specialisation areas. To further enhance client-centricity, a more radical approach to this Work Domain could be to architect it in terms of the four Modes of Client Engagement: Mode 1: Craft and roll out Strategic People Intent; Mode 2: Deliver standardised people services daily; Mode 3: Resolve ad hoc people issues/problems; and Mode 4: Enhance employee experiences. The respective functional People specialisation areas would then be incorporated into the four Engagement Modes or be 'Sub-Work Domains'. This essentially turns the Tactical Design into a Project/Programme WU Shape (see Table 9.7).

298

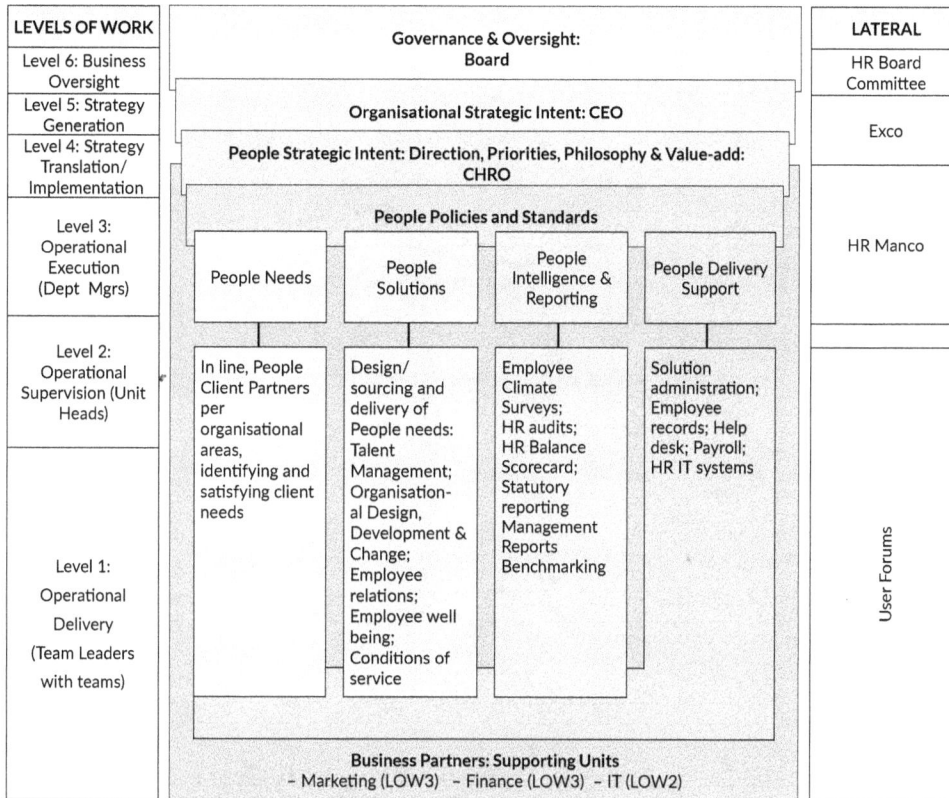

Figure 9.25: Integrated Tactical Design: Front-Back Organisational Shape for People Function: Inside Function perspective

Figure 9.26 provides the same Integrated Tactical Design (as per Figure 9.25) but from a client/organisational perspective (53).

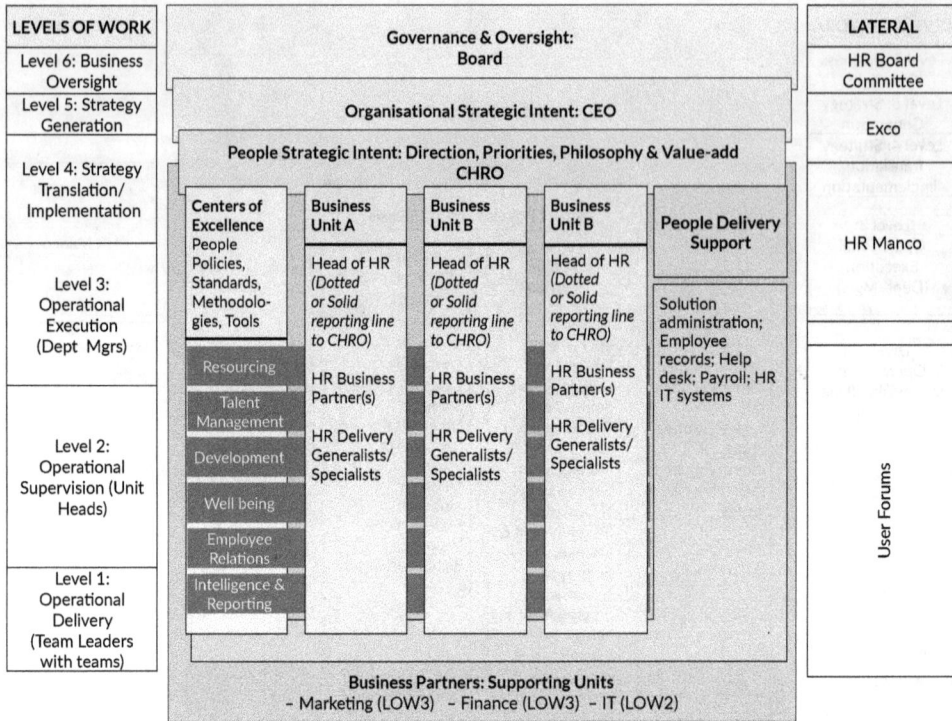

Figure 9.26: Integrated, Tactical Design: Front-Back, Organisational Shape for People Function: Client/organisational perspective

Given the criticality of people in the Knowledge Economy (see Reason 4 for why OD is becoming a mission-critical organisational discipline in Chapter 2), another possible Integrated Tactical Design Option is to (re)design the People Function around critical talent pipelines, each representing a strategic talent value chain, with the People Value Chain components supporting the pipelines in the form of Centres of Excellence. Figure 9.27 depicts this Integrated Tactical Design Map (54).

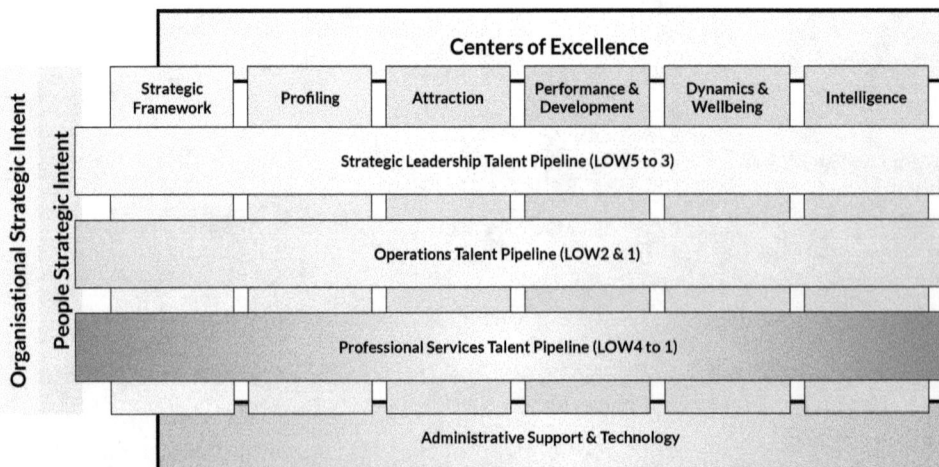

Figure 9.27: Integrated Tactical Design for People Function architected around critical talent pipelines

Step B.5.2: Draw WU Organogram

Only in this step can an organogram of the People Function be drawn, based on the Integrated Tactical Design. This needs to reflect the Basic Delivery Logic informing the Integrated Design Map. Without such a map, architected around a well thought-out Basic Delivery Logic and compiled from the Tactical Horizontal, Vertical and Lateral Designs, the drawing of an organogram becomes an illogical, emotionally charged, whimsical exercise in futility, at the mercy of the wax and wane of political and personal dynamics within the organisation.

Step B.5.3: Draft WU Charter

As already discussed, a concrete expression of the ground rules of the Operating Model – its delivery logic – of the 'To-Be' Organisation can be given in the form of a Work Unit Charter. The box gives a Charter for the People Function designed above.

CHARTER OF PEOPLE FUNCTION

- The *purpose* of the People Function in our organisation (why do we exist, and for whose benefit?) is our secure anchor and fixed reference point against which we judge all of our thinking, decisions and actions: *To bring about and maintain enabling and empowering conditions under which the organisation's people can contribute fully to its continued success by ensuring that the right people are in right numbers at the right time in the right place, not able, willing, wanting, and being allowed to perform with a sense of purpose, thereby giving the organisation a sustainable competitive edge (or value creation) in its chosen markets through its people.*

- We see our *people* as responsible, self-motivated, trustworthy adults who are the only true value unlockers and wealth creators in our organisation, inspiring and driving relentless innovation.

- In pursuit of our purpose, we will work as *Strategic Partners* with our organisational clients, operating within our Function like a *soccer/rugby team*: a group of specialists/generalists working together to attain the overarching goal of organisational success to the benefit of all our stakeholders.

- We will partner with our clients through five key *People Roles*: (i) *People Leadership*, providing overall people direction/philosophy and guidance to our organisation; (ii) decentralised *People Client Executives*, positioned as close as possible to clients and providing one-stop, people solutions to them; (iii) centralised *People Experts*, crafting and/or insourcing people solutions and practices; (iv) centralised *Transactional Processors*, dealing with the transactional, administrative processing required by people solutions/services and handling people queries; and (v) centralised *People Intelligence*, providing strategic information and reporting on the state of people management in our organisation, and our people's contribution to the success of our organisation.

- In partnering with our clients, we will engage with them through four *Engagement Modes:* Mode 1: Craft and roll out the organisation's Strategic People Intent; Mode 2: Deliver ongoing standardised people services daily; Mode 3: Resolve ad hoc, people issues/problems; and Mode 4: Enhance the employee experience.

- Every People Professional at all levels everywhere *collaborate* seamlessly with whoever, whenever and in whatever form across organisational boundaries in delighting our customers, both internal and external, and exceeding their expectations regarding our Purpose as People Function.

- Everyone at any level has the *authority and autonomy* to do whatever it takes to delight our clients and keep our promises to them by challenging, changing and transforming, without any fear, the existing into the better, even if it is different.

Steps 8.6: Ensure Tactical Organisational Alignment to B.10: Do Tactical Design Implementation

Based on the Integrated Tactical Design of the People Function and its Charter, the final steps of the Tactical Design route map can now be executed for the People Unit, from Step 8.6: Tactical Organisational Alignment to Step B.10: Tactical Design Implementation (see Figure 9.1). Of critical importance are the (i) Organisational Alignment of the Tactical Design in and of itself, and (ii) the alignment of the Tactical and Strategic Designs.

During Step B.9, a detailed report on the Tactical Design Solution: People Unit must be produced by the OD Expert. This report will form the basis of implementation. Without proper documentation, the implementation has a high likelihood of derailment given the intensity of personal and organisational dynamics that OD invokes. A typical Tactical Design Solution report template is given in Appendix D: Report Template 4.

Tactical Design Enabling/Support Units: High level Examples of Finance, Information Technology, Corporate University and Academic University Information Services

To illustrate Tactical Design further, high level examples are given of the following Work Units: Finance (55), Information Technology (IT) (56), a Retail Corporate University (57), and a University's Academic Information Services (that is Library) (58). These case studies are drawn from OD consulting assignments by the author (with colleagues in some cases). The only design elements covered in these high level designs are:

- Design Criteria;
- Work Process Map;
- Integrated Tactical Design Map; and
- Organisational Shape.

Case 1: Finance Function

DESIGN CRITERIA
1. Minimise duplication ("the same thing gets done in only one place")
2. Focused competencies/whole pieces of work
3. Clear roles and responsibilities/clear boundaries
4. Cost effective
5. Simple
6. Quick response time
7. Customer focused/"one-stop" customer interface
8. Flat structure
9. Flexible staff deployment: multi-skilling and multi-tasking
10. Quick decision-making
FINANCE WORK PROCESSES

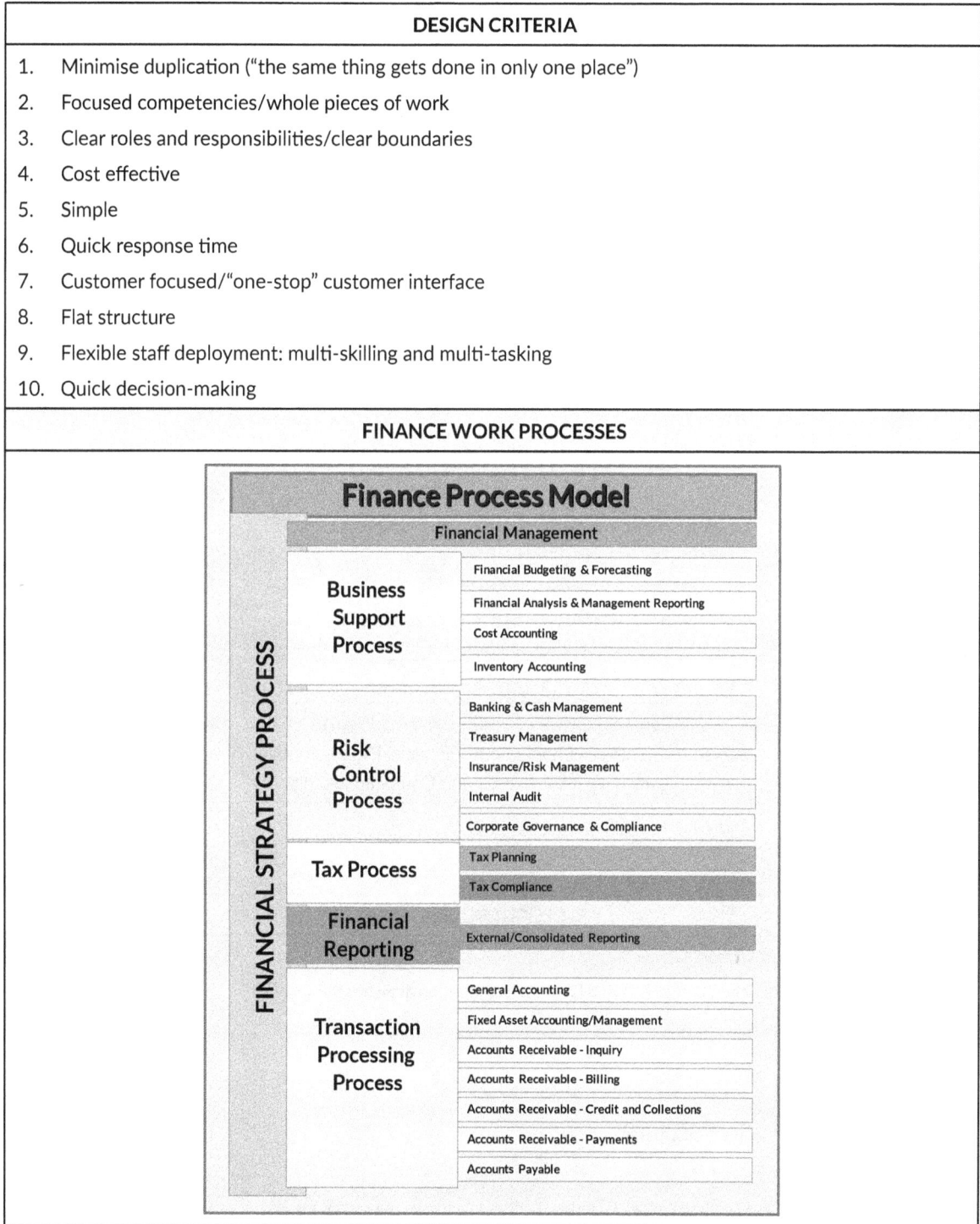

Finance Process Model

FINANCIAL STRATEGY PROCESS

Financial Management

Business Support Process
- Financial Budgeting & Forecasting
- Financial Analysis & Management Reporting
- Cost Accounting
- Inventory Accounting

Risk Control Process
- Banking & Cash Management
- Treasury Management
- Insurance/Risk Management
- Internal Audit
- Corporate Governance & Compliance

Tax Process
- Tax Planning
- Tax Compliance

Financial Reporting
- External/Consolidated Reporting

Transaction Processing Process
- General Accounting
- Fixed Asset Accounting/Management
- Accounts Receivable - Inquiry
- Accounts Receivable - Billing
- Accounts Receivable - Credit and Collections
- Accounts Receivable - Payments
- Accounts Payable

INTEGRATED FINANCE FUNCTION DESIGN MAP

High LOW4	Financial Strategy					
Low LOW4	Financial Policies & Standards					
LOW3	Regional Financial Services	Corporate Financial Services	Investments	Financial Processing	Corporate Governance & Compliance	Internal Audit & Forensic Investigations
	Financial Support	*Professional Services*	*Funds Management*	*Data Capturing & Processing*	*Well-managed Company*	*Assurance*
	• Credit Control • General Ledger (Selected Accounts) • Salary Enquiries • Financial Administration Support	• Financial Accounting (Company Accounts) • Management Accounting (Products/ Services/ Pricing) • Operational Accounting (Debtors & Creditors) • Tax • Budgets • Financial Management Reporting • Insurance • Asset Management	• Revenue Investment & Treasury	• Internal Financial Data Capturing & Processing • External Financial Data Capturing & Processing	• Business Risk Management • Information Security • Compliance (incl. Business Ethics) • Legal • Company Secretariat (incl. Corporate Governance)	• Internal Audit • Forensic Investigations

Functional Support (LOW2)
- IT
- HR
- Facilities Management/Corporate Services

ORGANISATIONAL SHAPE

Front-Back Design: Decentralised Regional Offices (Front) with two Centres of Expertise (Corporate Financial Services, Investments), supported by Delivery Enablement (Financial Processing) and Function Support (Internal Audit and Forensic investigations; Corporate Governance and Compliance)

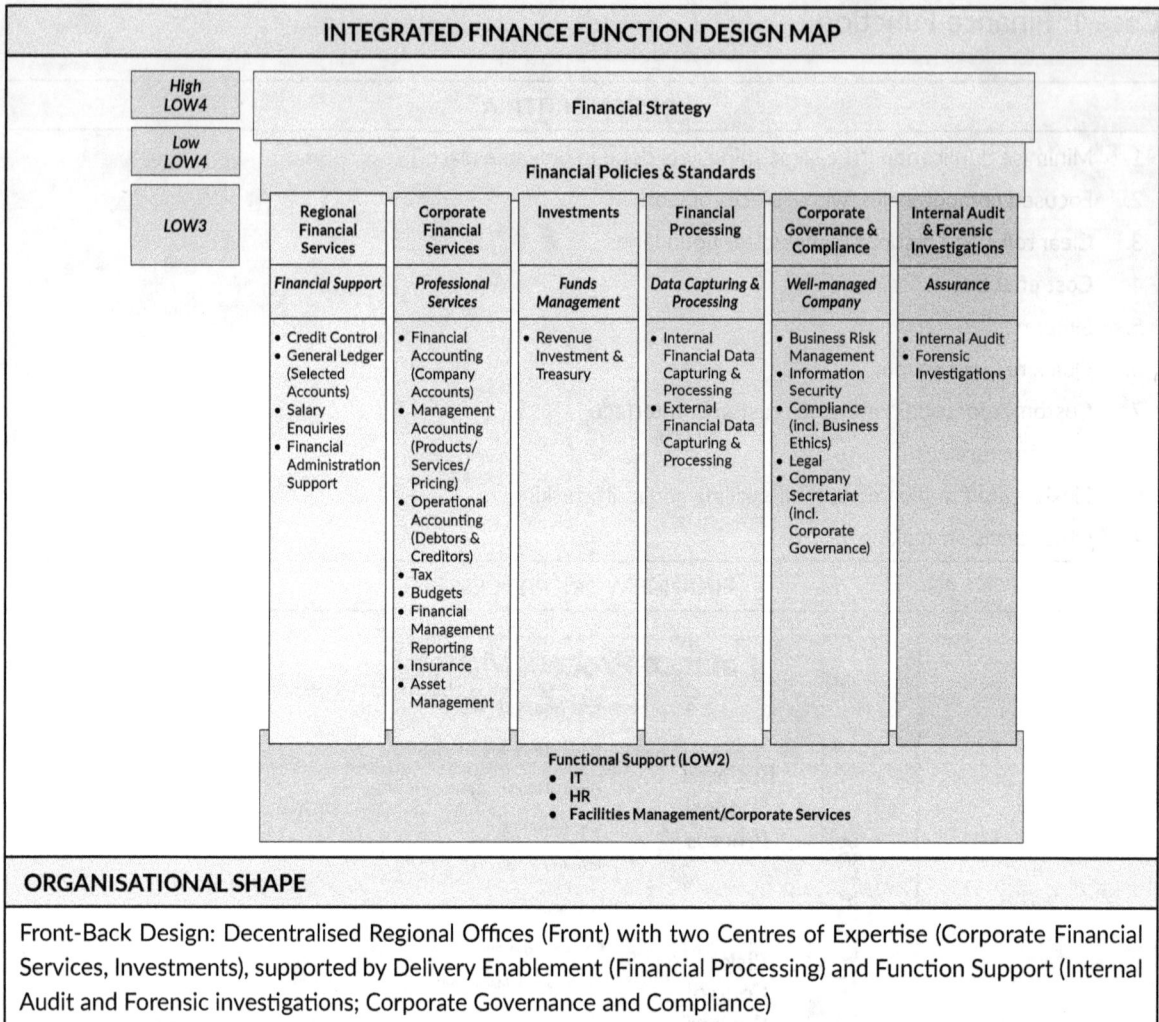

Case 2: IT Function

DESIGN CRITERIA

1. IT Function as a strategic support service
2. Improvement of the interaction between IT and business organisation at a strategic level
3. Ability to serve business needs better
4. Cost efficiency
5. Strategic IT outsourcing approach
6. Consideration of future acquisitions/mergers
7. Retention of critical intellectual knowledge
8. Strategic project execution to remain within IT
9. IT systems to be vital strategic enablers
10. Business must get full use out of existing systems

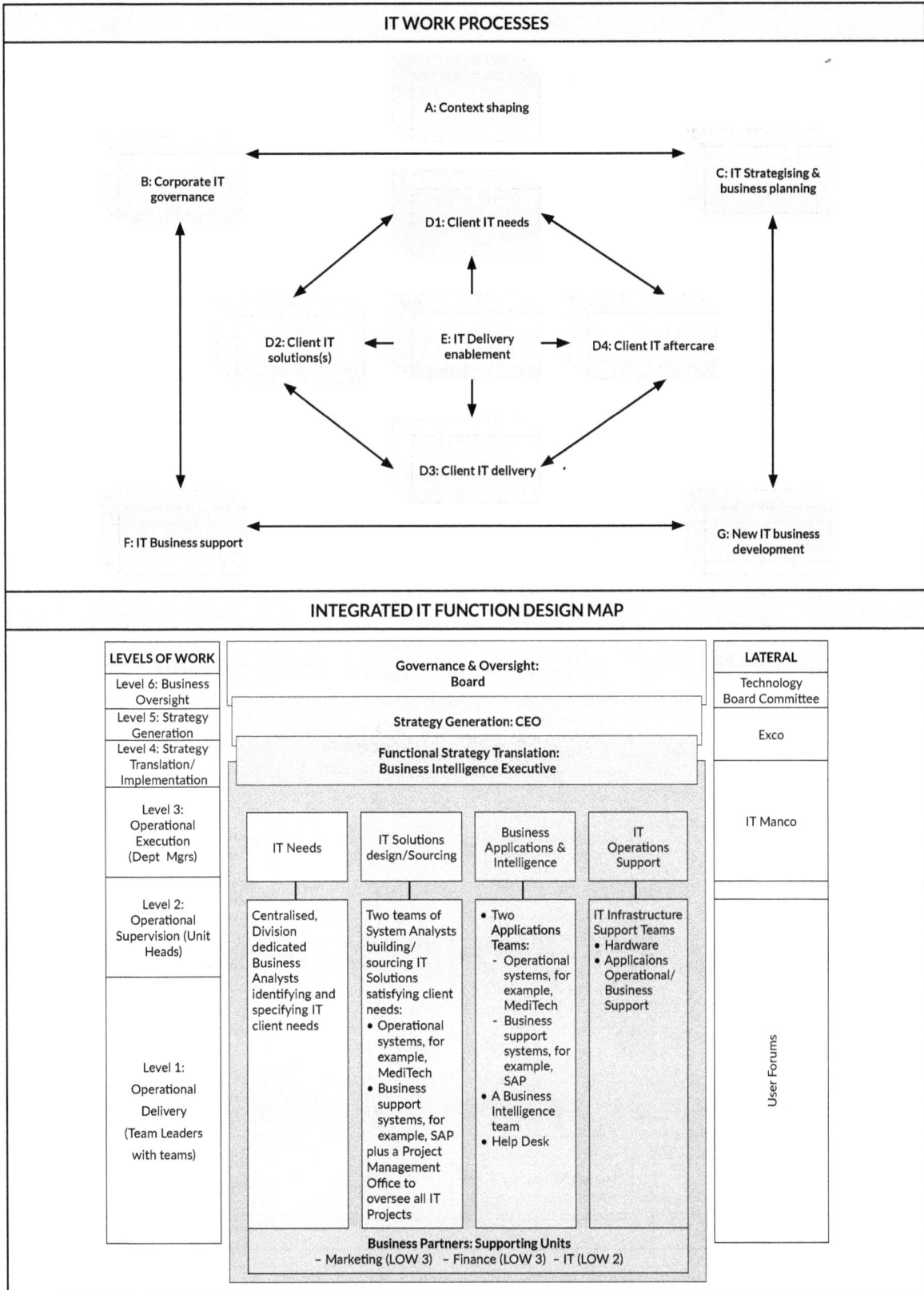

IT WORK PROCESSES

A: Context shaping

B: Corporate IT governance

C: IT Strategising & business planning

D1: Client IT needs

D2: Client IT solutions(s)

E: IT Delivery enablement

D4: Client IT aftercare

D3: Client IT delivery

F: IT Business support

G: New IT business development

INTEGRATED IT FUNCTION DESIGN MAP

LEVELS OF WORK		LATERAL
Level 6: Business Oversight	Governance & Oversight: Board	Technology Board Committee
Level 5: Strategy Generation	Strategy Generation: CEO	Exco
Level 4: Strategy Translation/ Implementation	Functional Strategy Translation: Business Intelligence Executive	
Level 3: Operational Execution (Dept Mgrs)	IT Needs / IT Solutions design/Sourcing / Business Applications & Intelligence / IT Operations Support	IT Manco
Level 2: Operational Supervision (Unit Heads)	Centralised, Division dedicated Business Analysts identifying and specifying IT client needs	Two teams of System Analysts building/ sourcing IT Solutions satisfying client needs: • Operational systems, for example, MediTech • Business support systems, for example, SAP plus a Project Management Office to oversee all IT Projects	• Two Applications Teams: - Operational systems, for example, MediTech - Business support systems, for example, SAP • A Business Intelligence team • Help Desk	IT Infrastructure Support Teams • Hardware • Applicaions Operational/ Business Support	User Forums
Level 1: Operational Delivery (Team Leaders with teams)					

Business Partners: Supporting Units
– Marketing (LOW 3) – Finance (LOW 3) – IT (LOW 2)

ORGANISATIONAL SHAPE
Front-Back Design: Client Service Facing Unit (IT Needs and Solutions) with Delivery Enabling (IT Operations)

Case 3: Retail Corporate University

DESIGN CRITERIA

1. Teamwork, teaming and co-creation of solutions
2. Flexibility – scalability to deal with variable learner numbers
3. Responsiveness – act swiftly upon business needs and deliver satisfactorily against those needs
4. Enable rapid, timeous and accurate information flow for planning and decision-making
5. Learning and Development (L & D) Value Chain interdependencies must be taken into account
6. Flat structure: three levels
7. Competency based, role-centric learning focusing on mission-critical, scarce core competencies
8. Accommodate both centralisation and decentralisation
9. Inclusive – covers L & D for all organisational levels from top to bottom

CORPORATE UNIVERSITY WORK PROCESSES

L& D Direction Setting, Core and Support Processes

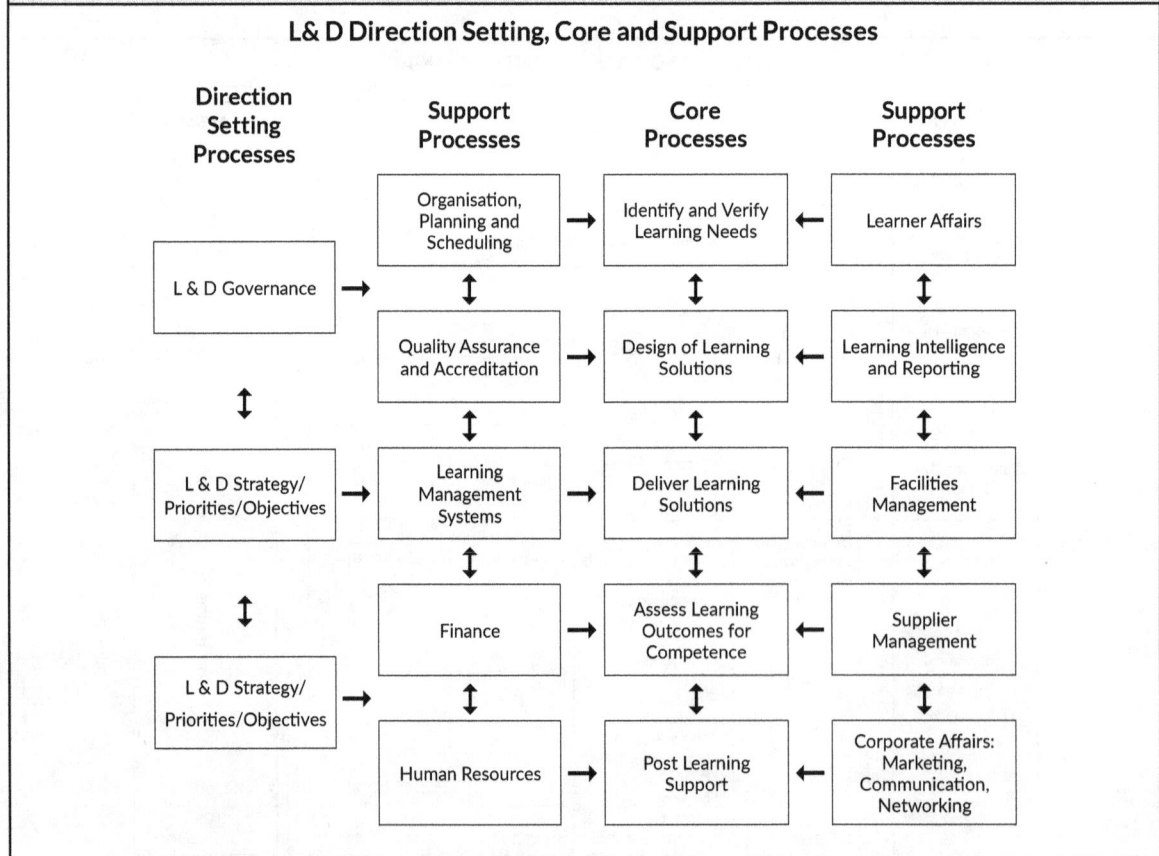

Direction Setting Processes	Support Processes	Core Processes	Support Processes
	Organisation, Planning and Scheduling	Identify and Verify Learning Needs	Learner Affairs
L & D Governance	Quality Assurance and Accreditation	Design of Learning Solutions	Learning Intelligence and Reporting
L & D Strategy/ Priorities/Objectives	Learning Management Systems	Deliver Learning Solutions	Facilities Management
	Finance	Assess Learning Outcomes for Competence	Supplier Management
L & D Strategy/ Priorities/Objectives	Human Resources	Post Learning Support	Corporate Affairs: Marketing, Communication, Networking

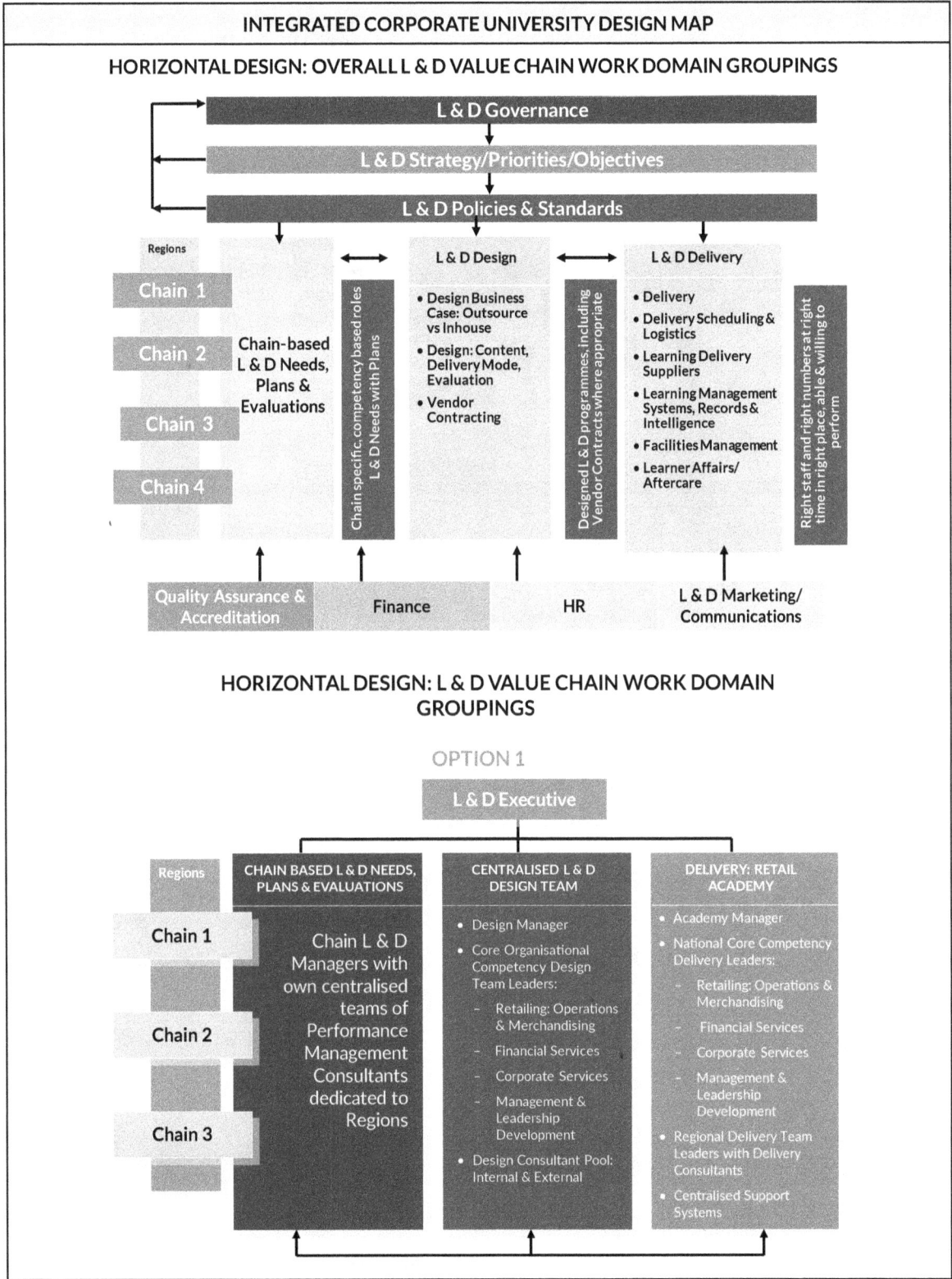

INTEGRATED CORPORATE UNIVERSITY DESIGN MAP

HORIZONTAL DESIGN: OVERALL L & D VALUE CHAIN WORK DOMAIN GROUPINGS

L & D Governance

L & D Strategy/Priorities/Objectives

L & D Policies & Standards

Regions

Chain 1

Chain 2

Chain 3

Chain 4

Chain-based L & D Needs, Plans & Evaluations

Chain specific, competency based roles L & D Needs with Plans

L & D Design

- Design Business Case: Outsource vs Inhouse
- Design: Content, Delivery Mode, Evaluation
- Vendor Contracting

Designed L & D programmes, including Vendor Contracts where appropriate

L & D Delivery

- Delivery
- Delivery Scheduling & Logistics
- Learning Delivery Suppliers
- Learning Management Systems, Records & Intelligence
- Facilities Management
- Learner Affairs/ Aftercare

Right staff and right numbers at right time in right place, able & willing to perform

Quality Assurance & Accreditation

Finance

HR

L & D Marketing/ Communications

HORIZONTAL DESIGN: L & D VALUE CHAIN WORK DOMAIN GROUPINGS

OPTION 1

L & D Executive

Regions	CHAIN BASED L & D NEEDS, PLANS & EVALUATIONS	CENTRALISED L & D DESIGN TEAM	DELIVERY: RETAIL ACADEMY

Chain 1	Chain L & D Managers with own centralised teams of Performance Management Consultants dedicated to Regions	• Design Manager
		• Core Organisational Competency Design Team Leaders:
		  – Retailing: Operations & Merchandising
		  – Financial Services
		  – Corporate Services
		  – Management & Leadership Development
		• Design Consultant Pool: Internal & External
			• Academy Manager
			• National Core Competency Delivery Leaders:
			  – Retailing: Operations & Merchandising
			  – Financial Services
			  – Corporate Services
			  – Management & Leadership Development
			• Regional Delivery Team Leaders with Delivery Consultants
			• Centralised Support Systems

Chain 2			
Chain 3			

HORIZONTAL DESIGN: L & D VALUE CHAIN WORK DOMAIN
OPTION 2

L & D Executive

Regions	CHAIN BASED L & D NEEDS, PLANS & EVALUATIONS	DESIGN & DELIVERY: RETAIL ACADEMY

Chain 1

Chain 2

Chain 3

Chain 4

Chain dedicated L & D Managers with own centralised teams of Performance Management Consultants dedicated to Regions

ACADEMY MANAGER

Manager, L & D Delivery

Manager, L & D Design

Core Competency Design Team Leader	Regional Delivery Team Leader with Delivery Consul-tants	Regional Delivery Team Leader with Delivery Consul-tants	Regional Delivery Team Leader with Delivery Consul-tants
Core Competency Design Team Leader			
Core Competency Design Team Leader			

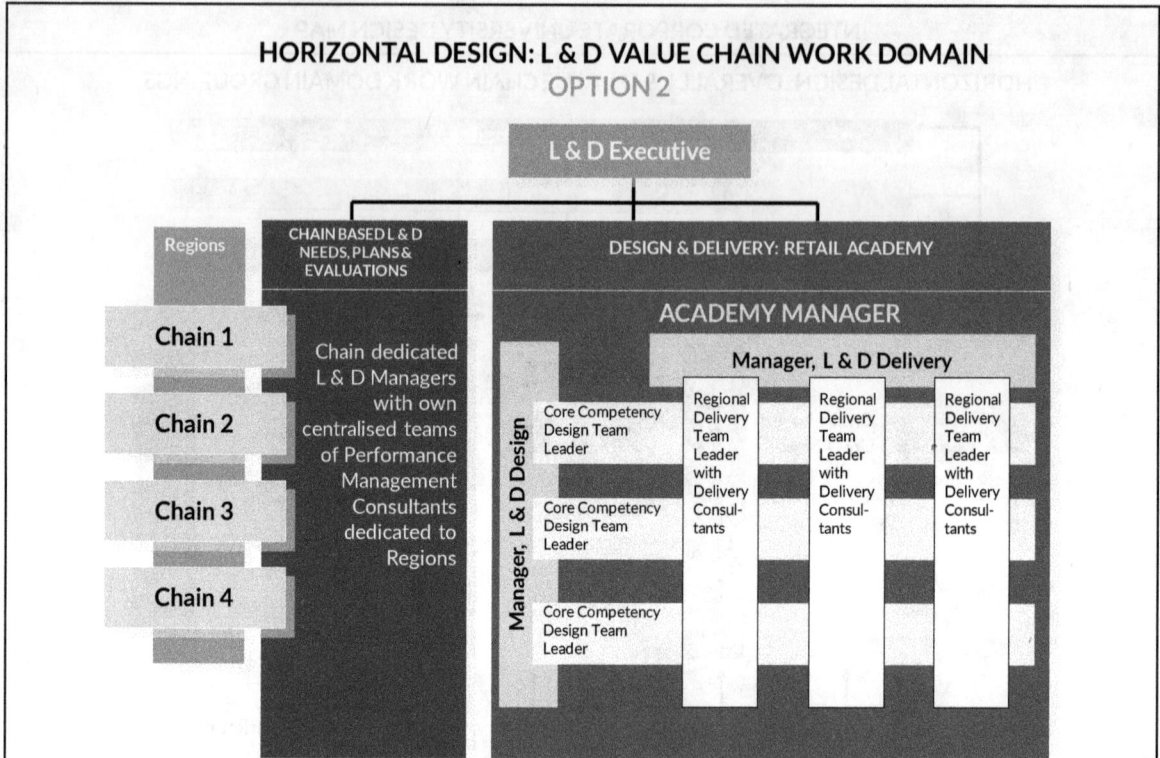

FINAL DESIGN OF COMPETENCY BASED ROLE-CENTRIC RETAIL ACADEMY (RA)
Preferred Option 2 with corporate governance and enabling/support services added

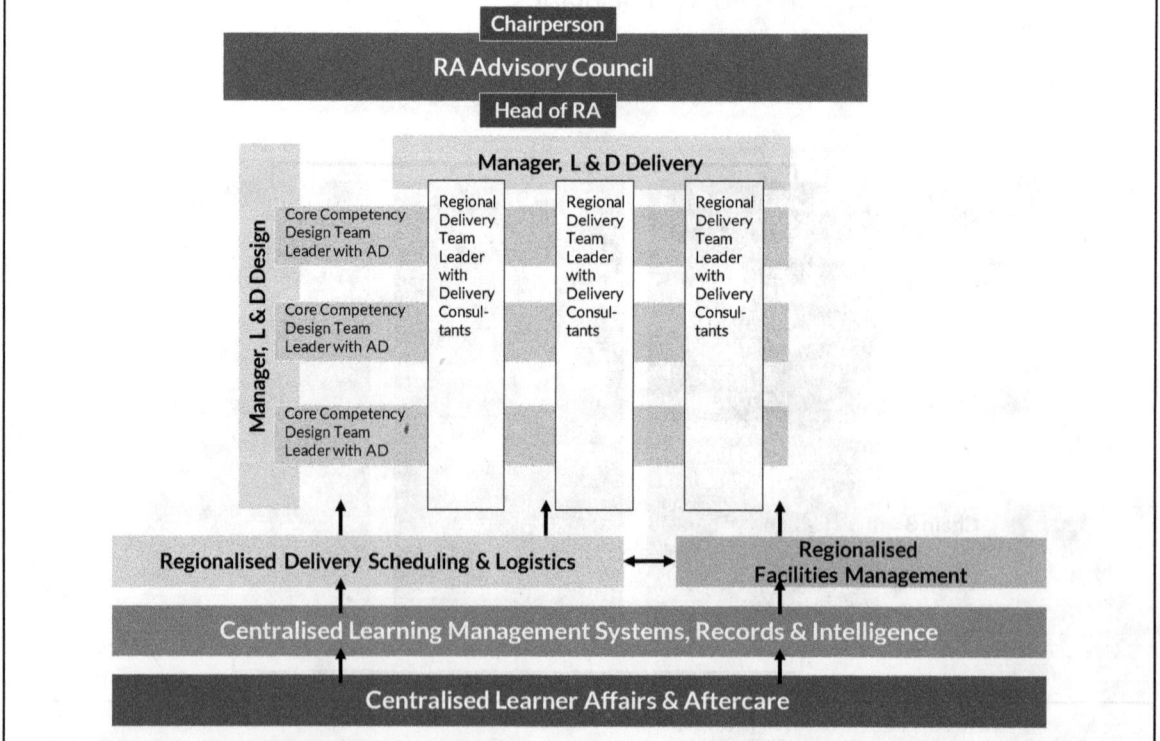

Chairperson

RA Advisory Council

Head of RA

Manager, L & D Delivery

Manager, L & D Design

Core Competency Design Team Leader with AD	Regional Delivery Team Leader with Delivery Consul-tants	Regional Delivery Team Leader with Delivery Consul-tants	Regional Delivery Team Leader with Delivery Consul-tants
Core Competency Design Team Leader with AD			
Core Competency Design Team Leader with AD			

Regionalised Delivery Scheduling & Logistics ⟷ **Regionalised Facilities Management**

Centralised Learning Management Systems, Records & Intelligence

Centralised Learner Affairs & Aftercare

ORGANISATIONAL SHAPE
Option 1: Process based with Chain dedicated L&D Leaders with in-process, centralised design and delivery teams, with lateral National Competency Delivery Leaders and decentralised delivery teams. *Option 2:* Mirror Image with Chain dedicated L&D Leaders and Design by Delivery Teams in matrix. *Final Design:* Preferred Option 2 with corporate governance and enabling/support services added.

Case 4: University's Academic Information Services

DESIGN CRITERIA
• Client centric
• Able to satisfy diverse client needs to be serviced through different delivery channels
• Flexible and adaptable due to ongoing changes in technology and client base
• Pro-activity with regards to changing client needs and technology
• Cost effective
• One-stop-service
• Quick response time/turnaround time
• Minimum duplication
• Clear levels of work with clear roles and responsibilities
• Flat structure
• Innovation driven
• Opportunities for career/professional development
ACADEMIC INFORMATION SERVICES WORK PROCESSES
• Unavailable
INTEGRATED INFORMATION SERVICES DESIGN MAP

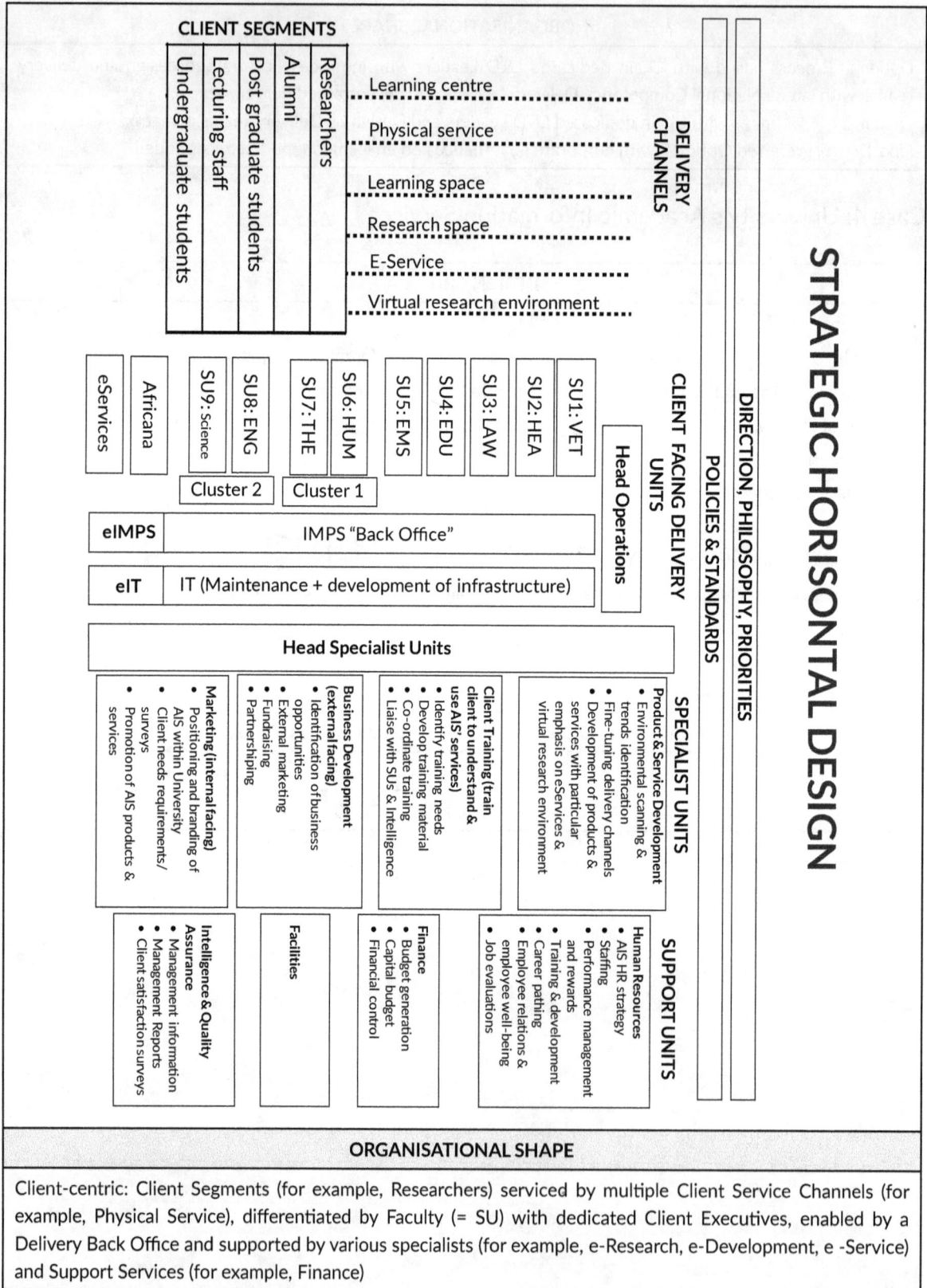

STRATEGIC HORISONTAL DESIGN

CLIENT SEGMENTS

- Researchers
- Alumni
- Post graduate students
- Lecturing staff
- Undergraduate students

DELIVERY CHANNELS

- Learning centre
- Physical service
- Learning space
- Research space
- E-Service
- Virtual research environment

DIRECTION, PHILOSOPHY, PRIORITIES

POLICIES & STANDARDS

CLIENT FACING DELIVERY UNITS

- eServices
- Africana
- SU9: Science
- SU8: ENG
- SU7: THE
- SU6: HUM
- SU5: EMS
- SU4: EDU
- SU3: LAW
- SU2: HEA
- SU1: VET

Cluster 2 | Cluster 1

Head Operations

eIMPS	IMPS "Back Office"
eIT	IT (Maintenance + development of infrastructure)

Head Specialist Units

SPECIALIST UNITS

Product & Service Development
- Environmental scanning & trends identification
- Fine-tuning delivery channels
- Development of products & services with particular emphasis on eServices & virtual research environment

Client Training (train client to understand & use AIS' services)
- Identify training needs
- Develop training material
- Co-ordinate training
- Liaise with SUs & Intelligence

Business Development (external facing)
- Identification of business opportunities
- External marketing
- Fundraising
- Partnershiping

Marketing (internal facing)
- Positioning and branding of AIS within University
- Client needs requirements/surveys
- Promotion of AIS products & services

Intelligence & Quality Assurance
- Management information
- Management Reports
- Client satisfaction surveys

Facilities

Finance
- Budget generation
- Capital budget
- Financial control

SUPPORT UNITS

Human Resources
- AIS HR strategy
- Staffing
- Performance management and rewards
- Training & development
- Career pathing
- Employee relations & employee well-being
- Job evaluations

ORGANISATIONAL SHAPE

Client-centric: Client Segments (for example, Researchers) serviced by multiple Client Service Channels (for example, Physical Service), differentiated by Faculty (= SU) with dedicated Client Executives, enabled by a Delivery Back Office and supported by various specialists (for example, e-Research, e-Development, e -Service) and Support Services (for example, Finance)

Conclusion

This chapter covered the complete Tactical Design process. Typically the process would take up to six to ten weeks per Work Unit to be designed. The ultimate outcome of the process is an Integrated Tactical Design with an implementation Road Map.

The discussion of the Tactical Design in this chapter was based on Design Process Option 1: Expert generated (see Table 4.3). In this option the Client requires the OD Expert to craft a design and submit it to him/her for a decision.

With respect to the other three possible options, the Tactical Design Process will take on the following form:

- **Option 1: Assurance.** The Client has already generated a desired design. The OD Expert merely has to quality assure it independently in an impartial, objective manner against leading OD practice. In this instance, the OD Expert can use the Quality Assurance Questions given at the end of each Tactical Design step to stress test the Client-proposed Tactical Design Solution. Critically important in the case of this option is that the OD Expert does not respond on the spot to the proposed Client solution, but requests at least two full days to work through what is proposed, and then have a work session with the Client to provide well-considered feedback.

- **Option 2: Straw Model.** The OD Expert crafts a 'straw model' design which is workshopped with the relevant key decision makers in the client system for a final decision, followed by a finalisation of the Tactical Design solution. Typically, this workshop – usually one to two day – would take place as an additional step after Step B.5: Integrated Tactical Design. After the workshop, the outstanding steps as outlined above (Steps B.6 to B.10) will be completed.

  The personal experience of the author has shown that one needs to invite the top three levels of leaders of the Work Unit concerned to participate. In LOW language, assuming a requisite LOW4 Work Unit, LOW3 and LOW2 represent the Strategic Translation/Implementation; Operational Execution; and Operational Practice. This will bring balanced, rich perspectives and expertise into the workshops. A programme for a Straw Model design workshop is given in Appendix C: Programme Template 4.

- **Option 3: Co-design.** The OD Expert facilitates an OD co-design process with the relevant stakeholders in the client system, that is Steps B.1 to B.8 are executed through a series of workshops. Critically important is the selection of workshop participants.

  Again, the top three levels of leaders of the Work Unit should participate. An innovative angle to consider is to bring the WU's high potential young leaders as observers into the workshop as a developmental exercise. After all, a number of them will in all probability lead the organisation in the future. A programme of the series of the design workshops with their associated topics is given in Appendix C: Programme Template 5.

Based on a Tactical Design – the Work Unit Room Plan, the Operational Design process – Work Teams and Roles, can now commence as elucidated in the next chapter.

Endnotes

(1) Delivery Enabling and Support Units can be grouped together in terms of the Tactical Design process because the route maps followed are usually highly similar in nature. I will deal with them separately, for reasons that will become apparent later.

(2) Draws heavily on Veldsman (2012).

(3) Davis (2001).

(4) Charan (2005).

(5) Vandewaerde, Voordeckers, Lambrechts & Bammens (2011).

(6) Charan (2005); Conger, Lawler & Finegold (2001); Curseu (2009); Davis (2001); Murphy & McIntyre (2007); Nadler, Behan & Nadler (2006); Payne, Benson & Finegold (2009); Petrovic (2008); Zona & Zattoni (2007).

(7) This feature is encapsulated in the agency theory with regard to the role of Boards. Cf. Vandewaerde, Voordeckers, Lambrechts & Bammens (2011).

(8) Nadler, Behan & Nadler (2006); Vandewaerde, Voordeckers, Lambrechts & Bammens (2011); Zona & Zattoni (2007).

(9) Conger, Lawler & Finegold (2001); McNulty & Pettigrew (1999); Nadler, Behan & Nadler (2006); Payne, Benson & Finegold (2009); Petrovic (2008); Vandewaerde, Voordeckers, Lambrechts & Bammen (2011).

(10) Conger, Lawler & Finegold (2001); Marcus (2008); MacAvoy & Millstein (2003); Murphy & McIntyre (2007); Nadler, Behan & Nadler (2006); Payne, Benson & Finegold (2009); Vandewaerde, Voordeckers, Lambrechts & Bammens (2011); Zona & Zattoni (2007).

(11) Conger, Lawler & Finegold (2001); Marcus (2008); Nadler, Behan & Nadler (2006); Payne, Benson & Finegold (2009); Zona & Zattoni (2007).

(12) Marcus (2008).

(13) Constructed by the author.

(14) Capelle (2014); Veldsman (2012).

(15) Constructed by the author.

(16) Cf. Bain (2008); Nadler, Behan & Nadler (2006); Naidoo (2009).

(17) Bain (2008); Finegold, Benson & Hech (2007); MacAvoy & Millstein (2003); Nadler, Behan & Nadler (2006); Payne, Benson & Finegold (2009); Petrovic (2008); Van Ees, Gabrielsson & Huse (2009).

(18) Constructed by the author.

(19) Constructed by the author.

(20) Drawn from Conger, Lawler & Finegold (2001); Marcus (2008); MacAvoy & Millstein (2003); McNulty & Pettigrew (1999); Murphy & McIntyre (2007); Nadler, Behan & Nadler (2006); Payne, Benson & Finegold (2009); Petrovic (2008); Vandewaerde, Voordeckers, Lambrechts & Bammen (2011); Zona & Zattoni (2007).

(21) Constructed by the author.

(22) Compiled by the author but drawing on the references given under (20).

(23) Compiled by the author.

(24) Compiled by the author.

(25) Veldsman (2016).

(26) Sourced from Veldsman (2012), building on Conger, Lawler & Finegold (2001); Marcus (2008); MacAvoy & Millstein (2003); McNulty & Pettigrew (1999); Murphy & McIntyre (2007); Nadler, Behan & Nadler (2006); Payne, Benson & Finegold (2009); Petrovic (2008); Vandewaerde, Voordeckers, Lambrechts & Bammen (2011); Zona & Zattoni (2007).

(27) Same sources as (26).

(28) Krishnoorthy (2015), GE Vice-President: Executive Development and Chief Learning Officer, questions the value of having a Corporate Centre at all in a VICCAS world, which requires rapid communication, quick decisions and speedy responses. Technology has compressed time, location, costs, and distance. He believes that a corporate HQ is an anachronism in a VICCAS world, where senior leadership acts as gatekeepers, controllers and reviewers with the annual rituals of centralised strategic planning; budgeting creates isolation; and sluggishness and bureaucracy slows down communication and decision-making. A corporate HQ constrains agility, responsiveness and the simplicity of the organisation. Leadership needs to be as close as possible to the centre of action which is where the Client is. In a VICCAS world, senior leadership must rather be the facilitators of action, not the directors and controllers.

(29) Adapted from Bellerby (2017); Collis, Young & Goold (2012); Goold & Campbell (1987); (2002b); (2002c); Goold, Pettifer & Young (2001); Collis, Young & Goold (2007); Collis, Young & Goold (2012); Galbraith (2014); Kates & Galbraith (2007); Kesler & Kates (2011); Roghé, Pidun, Stange & Krühler (2013); Roghé, Toma, Scholz, Schudey & Koike (2017).

(30) Goold & Campbell (1987); (2002b); (2002c) refer to the Corporate Centre as the 'parent' of its Work Units. This is a somewhat unfortunate term, as it implies that Work Units are children in need of parental direction and guidance. According to them, the Corporate Centre must demonstrate "parenting advantage", otherwise there is no justification for its existence.

(31) The design of Operating Units draws heavily on the author's own experience, enriched by ICI Chemical & Polymers Ltd. (1989). See also Goold & Cambell (2002b).

(32) Constructed by the author.

(33) ICI Chemical & Polymers Ltd. (1989) proved a valuable source of these descriptors, especially of Element 6: Work Processes.

(34) Based on the author's experience, drawing on and enriched by socio-technical system design principles (cf. Daniels, Le Blanc & Davis (2014) and Parker, Morgeson & Johns (2017)), as well as Mintzberg (1993); (1997); ICI Chemical & Polymers Ltd. (1989); Mohrman, Cohen & Mohrman (1995); Nadler & Tushman (1988); West (2008).

(35) Sourced from Bals (2017).

(36) Bals (2017).

(37) Bals (2017).

(38) Bals (2017).

(39) Bals (2017).

(40) Bals (2017).

(41) Preference is given to the term 'People Function' over the term 'HRM Function'. The Function is about People and not about a resource.

(42) The discussion draws heavily on Veldsman (2001); (2007a); (2007b); (2008a); (2008b); (2014) and my design of many People Functions over several years, but enriched with insights from Losely, Meissinga & Ulrich (2005); Morton, Newall & Sparks (2001); Sparrow, Hird, Hesketh & Cooper (2010); Ulrich, Brockbank, Younger & Ulrich (2012); Wright, Boudreau, Pace, Sartain, McKinnon & Antoine (2011).

(43) Constructed by the author.

(44) Cf. Pelster & Schartz (2016).

(45) Figure constructed by the author.

(46) Ulrich (1997); Ulrich & Brockbank (2005); Ulrich, Brockbank, Younger & Ulrich (2013); Veldsman (2001); (2007a); (2007b); (2008a); (2008b); (2014).

(47) Constructed by the author.

(48) Thite, Wilkinson & Shah (2012).

(49) These Work Roles are an adaptation and expansion of those which Dave Ulrich and colleagues propose for a Strategic Partnering, People Function (Ulrich, 1997; Ulrich & Brockband, 2005; Ulrich, Brockbank, Younger & Ulrich, 2013).

(50) Constructed by the author.

(51) Source: Author.

(52) Compiled by the author.

(53) Compiled by the author.

(54) Compiled by the author.

(55) Author with Wyand Geldenhuys and Angela McKay.

(56) Author.

(57) Author.

(58) Author with Wyand Geldenhuys. See also Moropa (2010) who was Director of the Academic Information Services at the time of the intervention, and reported on the design intervention.

10

OPERATIONAL ORGANISATIONAL DESIGN

Architecting the Work Teams and Roles of the Organisation

"If you want to walk fast, walk alone.
If you want to walk far, walk together."

(African saying)

"Home is not where we live but where we belong."

(Groucho Marx)

"People should not consider so much what they do, as what they are."

(Meister Eckhart)

The Strategic and Tactical Designs are in place and aligned. The House Plan with its accompanying Rooms have been architected. Aligned, Integrated Strategic and Tactical Design Maps exist. The purpose of this chapter is to address architecting the Operational Design, given the key assumption that fit-for-purpose Strategic and Tactical Designs for the organisation are in place. If they do not exist, rough maps have to be drafted that are relevant to the Operational Design intervention to be initiated.

As was discussed in Chapter 3, Operational Design addresses the design of the specific elements making up Work Units, namely Work Teams and Work Roles (1). Metaphorically, this is architecting the furniture required by and making up the various Rooms in the House. Work Teams and Roles – populated by the right people – operationalise on a daily basis the coal face delivery of the Strategic and Tactical Designs. Operational Design, so to speak, architects the style of living in the House and its Rooms. The vantage point of Operational Design is standing 'Inside Rooms' in order to (re)design the furniture of the Rooms of the House.

It must be understood that Work Teams and Work Roles must be architected all the way from the Board (LOW6) down to Daily Delivery (LOW1) levels. In that sense the term 'Operational' is misleading; it does not refer to 'Operations' as in the lower LOWs but to the design elements – in this case Work Teams and Work Roles – through which the work of the organisation gets done at all organisational levels and in all organisational areas.

A *Work Team* can be defined as a group of persons with complementary knowledge, skills, expertise, and experience, who interact on a regular basis and in an interdependent manner, regarding a given set of different tasks, roles and responsibilities, in order to achieve a shared goal(s) that can only be achieved collectively, not individually (2). A *Work Role* can be defined as an enacted, coherent set of tasks, duties, relationships and conduct for which a person is accountable/responsible within a Work Unit which must be performed to certain performance standards (3).

Operational Design can be triggered by:

- preceding Strategic and/or Tactical (re)Designs which require Operational Design;
- the need to redesign an existing Work Team(s) and/or Work Roles; and
- the need for a greenfield Operational Design: the design of a newly created Work Team(s) and/or Work Role(s).

A full-blown Operational Design covering all the Work Units of a Strategic (re)Design can take up to a year, covering all Work Teams and/or Work Roles. In the case of a single Operational Design – Work Team or Work Role – the time requirement is in the order of four to six weeks.

In the design literature, Operational Design receives a high degree of detailed, independent attention, typically in isolation from Strategic Design *(4)*. There is minimal, if any, cross-referencing to Strategic Design. Operational Design is dominated furthermore by Job Design and Work (System) Design, which focuses virtually exclusively on Work Role Design. In contrast, Team Design has received relatively (far) attention until recently, although this situation is changing. This is ironic if one considers that Work Teams are increasingly being seen as the critical building block of future organisations (see also Figure 6.7 in this regard) *(5)*. In the Job Design and Work (System) Design literature, the virtually exclusive focus is on finding the 'golden' list of job and/or work system characteristics that will be motivating, meaningful, engaging and promote well-being. The discussion of explicit design processes is sorely lacking regarding how to bring such jobs/work systems into being. Put differently, the emphasis is on content, not process.

Also lacking in the literature is the 'stringing together' of Work Teams and Work Roles within Work Units and across the total organisation in order to architect an *integrated, aligned, daily Mode of Working across the organisation*. After all, the organisation forms a dynamic, interconnected, systemic whole: a living, social ecosystem (see Chapter 3). In the literature, the design of a Work Team or Work Role is dealt with predominantly in a stand-alone manner, and not embedded back into the organisation as a living, social ecosystem, made up of a multitude of interacting, reciprocally interdependent Work Teams and Work Roles. Metaphorically, it is like replacing the old kidney of the body with a new one, without, at a minimum, putting it back in the body. Or, at a maximum, putting it back into the body without considering the reciprocal dependencies between all of the organs, *inter alia* the redesigned kidney. A rare exception in this regards is the socio-technical systems approach to be discussed below.

A similar situation exists in practice in my experience. The design of Work Teams and Work Roles are done piecemeal, one-by-one, in a vacuum with no overarching Operational Design Framework (or Philosophy) acting as a reference point. Consequently, no consistent Operational Design Philosophy informs the design of Work Teams or Work Roles across an organisation. The Designs are all over the place in terms of their underlying design philosophy. Thus a heavy premium will be placed in this chapter on the upfront architecting of an Operational Design Framework which must act as an overall reference point when designing specific a Work Team(s) or Work Role(s). In this way, a shared Mode of Working will be ensured in the organisation.

In this chapter I thus aim to bring Work Team and Work Role (that is job) together, as well as the immediate, macro, and more contextual operational design elements, under the rubric of Operational Design, premised on the criticality of an overall Operational Design Framework. Additionally, the Chapter will espouse the mission-critical links between Strategic, Tactical and Operational Design, in this way overcoming the design process silos prevalent in the fragmented OD literature.

The chapter uses the Operational Design route map (introduced in Chapter 4 when addressing the OD life cycle) as its structure. For the sake of convenience, the map is reproduced here again in Figure 10.1. As per the convention followed in this book, the chapter numbering will follow the numbering system used for the design steps in Figure 10.1. May I remind the reader again, that in order to keep the Operational Map given in Figure 10.1 simple, the Change Navigation and Project Management building blocks of the OD process have been left out (see Figure 3.6), but are essential enabling elements of the Design Map.

The following are important to note regarding Figure 10.1:

(i)   The highly iterative nature of Step C.2: Operational Design Framework, made up of the reciprocally interdependent steps:

- C.2A: Operational Design Vision;
- C.2B: Design Autonomy;
- C.2C: Expected People Conduct;
- C.2D: Design Criteria; and
- C.2E: Desired Outcomes.

Collectively these steps generate the Operational Design Framework of the organisation – in particular for its Work Units – in terms of operational delivery. In the terminology used in the design literature, the Operational Design Framework equates to the organisation's Work (System) Design (see Endnote (1)). Steps C.2A and C.2B have to be addressed first in an iterative way in order to set the foundation for Steps C.2C to C.2E. Thereafter, Steps C.2C to C.2E can proceed in any order, given their iterative Design interdependence. The discussion below will proceed from C.2C: Expected People Conduct, through to C.2D: Design Criteria to C.2E: Desired Outcomes.

```
┌─────────────────────────────────┐
│  Step C.1:  Design Givens       │
│       Work Unit Context         │
└─────────────────────────────────┘
                 │
                 ▼
┌─────────────────────────────────┐
│  Step C.2: Operational Design   │
│           Framework             │
└─────────────────────────────────┘
                 │
                 ▼
┌─────────────────────────────────┐
│  Step C.2A: Operational         │
│         Design Vision           │
│  Mechanistic ◄──► Organic       │
└─────────────────────────────────┘
```

Step C.2B: Design Autonomy

```
┌──────────────────────┐              ┌──────────────────────┐
│ Step C.2C: Expected  │ ◄──────────► │ Step C.2D: Design     │
│   People Conduct     │              │      Criteria         │
└──────────────────────┘              └──────────────────────┘
              │                                  │
              ▼                                  ▼
        ┌──────────────────────────────────────┐
        │  Step C.2E: Desired Outcomes          │
        └──────────────────────────────────────┘
                           │
                           ▼
        ┌──────────────────────────────────────┐
        │  Step C.3: Current Design             │
        │     Strengths and Weaknesses          │
        └──────────────────────────────────────┘
```

```
┌──────────────────────┐              ┌──────────────────────┐
│ Step C.4: Work Team  │ ◄──────────► │ Step C.5: Work Role   │
│  Design (per Team)   │              │  Design (per Role)    │
└──────────────────────┘              └──────────────────────┘
         │                                       │
         │      ┌──────────────────────────┐     │
         │      │ Step C.6: Competency     │     │
         │      │      Profiles            │     │
         │      └──────────────────────────┘     │
         ▼                                       ▼
┌─────────────────────────────────────────────────────────┐
│ Step C.7: Evolving phases of increasing Work Team/Work   │
│           Role Autonomy                                  │
└─────────────────────────────────────────────────────────┘
                           │
                           ▼
┌─────────────────────────────────────────────────────────┐
│ Step C.8 Integrated Operational Design                  │
└─────────────────────────────────────────────────────────┘
                           │
                           ▼
┌─────────────────────────────────────────────────────────┐
│ Step C.9: Operational Design Alignment                  │
└─────────────────────────────────────────────────────────┘
                           │
                           ▼
┌─────────────────────────────────────────────────────────┐
│ Step C10: Operational Design Impact Assessment          │
└─────────────────────────────────────────────────────────┘
                           │
                           ▼
┌─────────────────────────────────────────────────────────┐
│ Step C.11: Operational Design Implementation Road Map   │
└─────────────────────────────────────────────────────────┘
                           │
                           ▼
┌─────────────────────────────────────────────────────────┐
│ Step C.12: Operational Design Solution Report           │
└─────────────────────────────────────────────────────────┘
                           │
                           ▼
┌─────────────────────────────────────────────────────────┐
│ Step C.13: Operational Design Implementation            │
└─────────────────────────────────────────────────────────┘
```

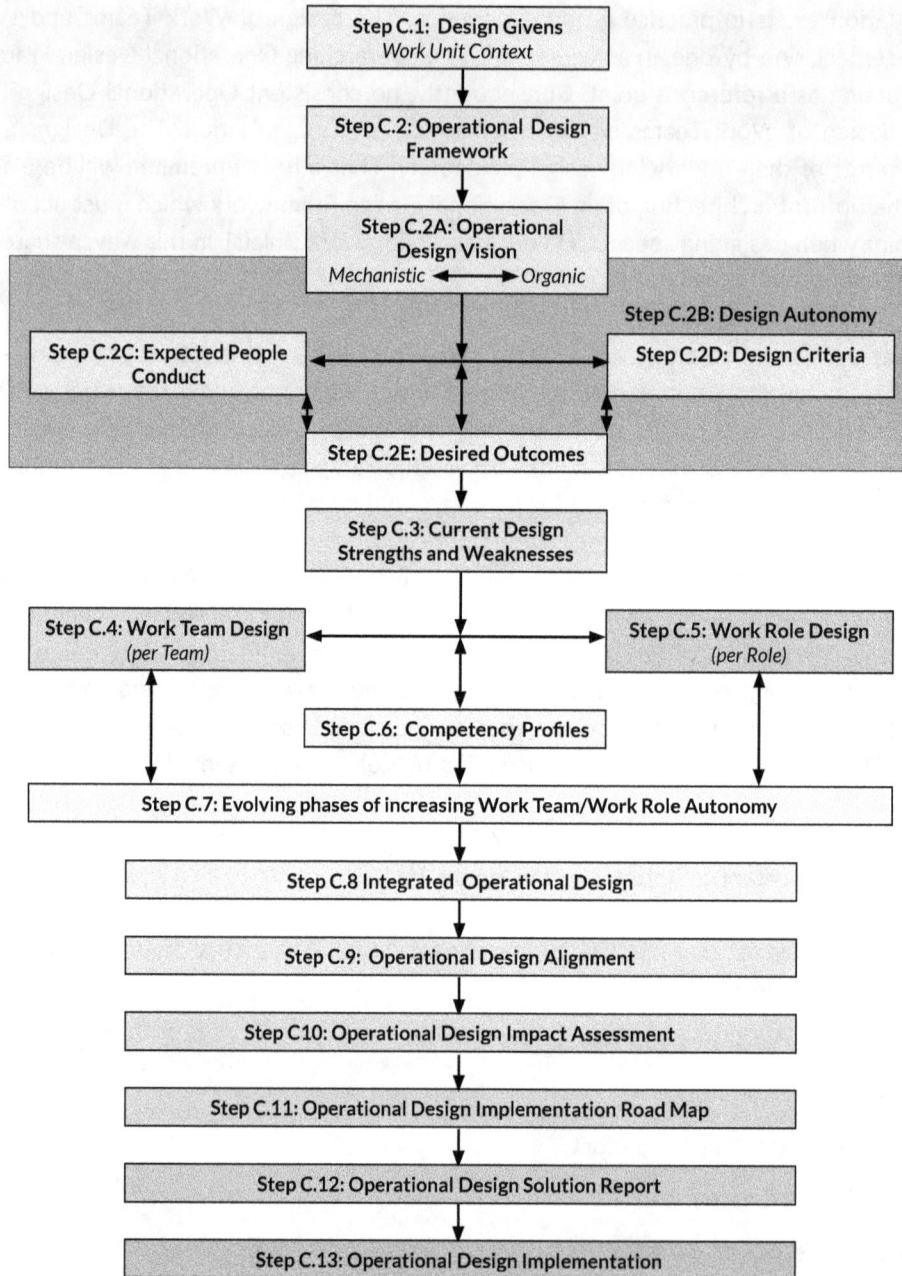

Figure 10.1: Overview of the Operational Design route map

(ii) The interdependency of Steps C.4: Work Team Design and C.5: Work Role Design. Work Roles make up a Work Team, that is, the latter being more macro context. Hence, Work Team Design will be discussed before Work Role Design.

(iii) If a high degree of Design Autonomy (that is Job/Work Crafting) and the evolution of Work Teams and Roles towards greater autonomy (for example, self-managing Work Teams/Work Roles) are architected into the organisation's designs (Steps C.2B: Design Autonomy and C.7: Evolving Phases), it may imply ongoing, real time, in time, redesigning of Work Teams and Roles. Hence, the two-way arrows between Steps C.7: Evolving Phases, C.4: Work Team and C.5: Work. Roles, in turn affecting C.6: Competency Profiles.

(iv) As in the case of Strategic and/or Tactical Design, the Operational Design Process has to be repeated for all Work Units in their totality, resulting from or having been addressed in the preceding Strategic and/or Tactical Design processes.

As the discussion moves through the Operational Design route map – given in Figure 10.1 – towards an overall Operational Design, Design Maps for Work Teams and Work Roles will be progressively built as the discussion unfolds. But first, what follows is a brief orientation to the rich history of Operational Design in order to provide a thinking framework to the unfolding design journey explicated below.

Brief History of Operational Design

How has Operational Design (Job/Work Design) unfolded historically in terms of major milestones? (6)

Scientific Management

The founding father of Operational Design (= Job Design) was F. W. Taylor in the form of Scientific Management (7). His aim was work efficiency through work simplification and standardisation: 'There is one only simple, best way to do a job'. Additionally, splitting Doing (= the manual work) and Thinking (= the mental work) portions of work between workers and management respectively.

Job Enrichment Approach

In reaction to the negative consequences of the work impoverishment resulting from Scientific Management, Hertzberg and colleagues in the late 1950s proposed the Job Enrichment approach, based on their Motivator–Hygiene Theory (also known as the Two-factor Theory). Motivators are intrinsic features of work itself which provide job satisfaction. Hygiene factors are features of the broader work context that are extrinsic to the work, like supervisory and peer relationships and working conditions. If absent, hygiene factors lead to job dissatisfaction, however if present, they do not provide job satisfaction. Motivators if present, cause job satisfaction. If absent, they do not cause job dissatisfaction. Thus, job satisfaction and dissatisfaction have different job causes. 'Job Enrichment' focuses on enhancing the motivators of work. Hence the title of this approach: 'Job Enrichment'.

Socio-technical Systems Approach

Concurrently to the Job Enrichment approach in the USA, the Socio-technical Systems Approach was conceived by Trist, Rice and Bamford from the Tavistock Institute, UK, in the 1950s. Their approach centred around how to attain the optimal fit between the interlocking, technical and social-psychological (= people) systems of the organisation's production system. The aim of the fit is to get the best out of technology and people simultaneously. (Semi-)Autonomous work teams were seen as the appropriate design by which to get this fit right. These are teams who have the freedom (or autonomy) to decide how to organise themselves with respect to the technology they use in order to get the work done (8) *(9)*.

Role Theory

During the 1960s, Katz and Kahn introduced Role Theory in their thinking about organisations. Role Theory highlighted the criticality of Work Roles (similarly defined by them as in the Introduction to this Chapter) in the design and functioning of the organisation. They also introduced the terms 'role conflict', 'role ambiguity' and 'role overload' as key categories designating stressful role dysfunction (10).

Job Characteristics Model

From the 1970s, the job design literature was dominated for more than 30 years by a single conceptual approach to job design, namely the Job Characteristics (JD) Model of Hackman, Lawler and Oldham, drawing also on the Job Enrichment approach (11). Central to this approach to job design is the contention that a set of motivational job characteristics, such as skill variety, task identity, task significance and autonomy, lead to positive, critical psychological states – like meaningfulness – in turn resulting in positive job outcomes, for example job satisfaction, reduced absenteeism, and higher organisational commitment. The level to which these motivating job characteristics have to be present in a job is mediated by the person's need for psychological growth.

Elaborative, Integrative Job/Work Design Approaches

However, the JD Model neglected the wider context in which a job is embedded. In response to this limitation, Elaborative, Integrative Job/Work Design Approaches were proposed from the mid-1980s until the present by the likes of Champion, Cordery, Grant, Humphrey, Morgeson, Parker and Wall. This approach endeavours to overcome the ignorance of the wider context by the JD Theory by including – apart from the motivational component of the JD model – more macro and contextually related work characteristics, like the social context (for example, task interdependence and social support) and the organisational context (for example, work conditions). These additional characteristics are also key in making jobs more motivating and meaningful (12) *(13)*.

Proactive and Pro-social (including Relational) Perspectives

All of the above job design approaches in practice are essentially 'top-down'. Leadership/management and/or an OD Expert architect the job design, which is then prescribed to and imposed on job incumbents. From the late 20th century up to the present, Proactive and Pro-social (including Relational) Perspectives on work design emerged, propagated by the likes of Grant and Parker. The Proactive Perspectives – bottom-up work design – portend that job incumbents must design their jobs themselves. This will cultivate in job incumbents a sense of self-efficacy by being in charge of their own work, leading to energised states such as feelings of enthusiasm and vigour. In this way psychological capital will be built in them, like self-efficacy, optimism, hope and resilience (14).

The Pro-social Perspectives propagate the benefit of socially induced motivation and commitment through being in contact with those who benefit from one's work, that is beneficiaries such as clients, customers and patients. However, in the final instance, top-down (the previously discussed approaches) and bottom-up work designs must be combined to get that the best outcomes all round (15).

Specific examples of Proactive and Pro-social Perspectives are, firstly, Karasek's Job Demands-Control Model. Job Demands include job requirements, work conditions, decision latitude, physical demands, job stress and depression. In short, this Model states that best job design is where job incumbents have sufficient control over Job Demands.

A second example is the Job Demands-Job Resources (JD-R) Model of Demerouti and Bakker. Job Demands refer to the likes of workloads, role overloads, work hours and job security. Job/personal Resources relate to, for example, resources to get the work done, self-esteem, optimism and conservation. The Model posits that employee motivation and well-being are affected by the interaction between Job Demands (negative factors like time pressure or ambiguity that may affect one's well-being) and Job Resources (positive factors that can reduce demands, like peer support or autonomy). The latter must outweigh the former, resulting in 'good' jobs.

What distinguishes the Job Demands-Job Resources Model from the Job Demands-Control Model is the focus of the former on extra work features in addition to control and support (for example, rewards, security) that may serve as resources to counter Job Demands, stimulate growth, and foster achievement. Additionally, the former Model includes the outcomes of engagement (that is absorption, dedication, personal accomplishment and vigour), as well as burnout and strain (like depersonalisation, exhaustion and cynicism).

A third example of these Perspectives, is Wrzesniewski & Dutton's proposed Job Crafting Approach. This approach contends that under conditions like uncertainty and complexity, organisational members must be the active architects of their own jobs, and not merely the passive recipients of what experts propose and introduce as solutions (16). Demerouti and Bakker have placed their Job Demands-Job Resources Model central in their approach to job crafting. For Wrzesniewski and Dutton, job crafting is a specific form of proactive behaviour in which the employee initiates changes in the levels of Job Demands and job resources in order to make their jobs more meaningful, engaging and satisfying (17).

In summary: OD has had a rich history, from its founding in Scientific Management (the early part of the 20th century) to the Job Enrichment and Socio-technical Systems Approaches (both in the 1950s), Role Theory (in the 1960s), the Job Characteristics (JD) Model (from the 1970s onwards), Elaborative, Integrative Job Design Approaches as extensions to the JD Model (mid 1980s until the present), and the Proactive and Pro-social Perspectives (from the late 20th century up to the present). Apart from Scientific Management, elements and principles from all of the above work design approaches will be incorporated to a lesser or greater extent in the Operational Design route map explicated below.

Given the brief historical overview, we are now ready to embark on the Operational Design journey, following the Operational Design route map given in Figure 10.1.

Step C.1: Identify Operational Design Givens

The aim of this step is to identify Work Unit factors that as context will affect the Operational Design, and therefore need to be considered as Operational Design Givens *(18)*. At least four important categories of contextual factors can be distinguished, from which the five most important Design Givens must be extracted:

- The *Basic Work Unit Profile(s) with its Tactical Design(s)*. Is the Work Unit concerned a Corporate Centre; an Operating, Enabling; or Support Unit with its associated specifics: Products/Services; Markets; Clients; Resources and Stakeholders?

- The Work Unit's *Total requisite complexity* = Contextual Complexity x Requisite Work Unit LOW (plus, if relevant, its Home Ownership Model).

- The Work Unit's *Mode of Working*, enabled by a specific *Core Operating Technology and Enablers*. To use a sports metaphor: does the Work Unit require people to work like an athletics, relay, soccer or volleyball team? (This Design Metaphor will be unpacked further under Work Team Design below.) As one moves from an athletics to a volleyball team mode of working, the work interdependency of team members, their degree of multi-tasking and multi-skilling, the need for real time interaction, and the degree of shared goals will increase. All of this is mediated by the Core Operating Technology and Technological Enablers used by the Work Unit, as well as the Technology Enablement Model adopted, for example, the Automated Model (see Figure 5.7).

- *Qualities of the Work Unit Context* – both internally and externally to the Work Unit – that affect, directly and significantly, the effective and efficient functioning of the Unit. Pertinent here is the degree of:
  - predictability: level of certainty;
  - interdependency: the connectedness of variables/elements;
  - complexity: the number of interacting variables/elements to handle;
  - ambiguity (or uncertainty): lack of verified information/knowledge;
  - diversity: the variety in variables/elements to deal with; and
  - stability: the degree and nature of change.

The degree of presence of the above qualities would point to the levels of autonomy that need to be awarded to Work Teams/Work Roles (see the next design step).

The Design Givens provide high level Design Criteria (or at least parameters) for the Operational Design, providing the basis of a contextually aligned, Operational Design Vision with respect to the Work Team(s) and Work Roles of the organisation.

Step C.2: Operational Design Framework

This step consists of five sub-steps: Step C.2A: Operational Design Vision, through to Step C.2E: Design Outcomes (see Figure 10.1). As one proceeds through the five steps, an Operational Design Map will be progressively crafted, finally culminating in an integrated Operational Design Framework.

Step C.2A: Formulate Operational Design Vision

The Operational Design Vision specifies at a high level the overall 'To-Be' Operational Design. Figure 10.2 depicts the range of possible Operational Design Visions relative to the nature of the identified Design Givens in the previous design step.

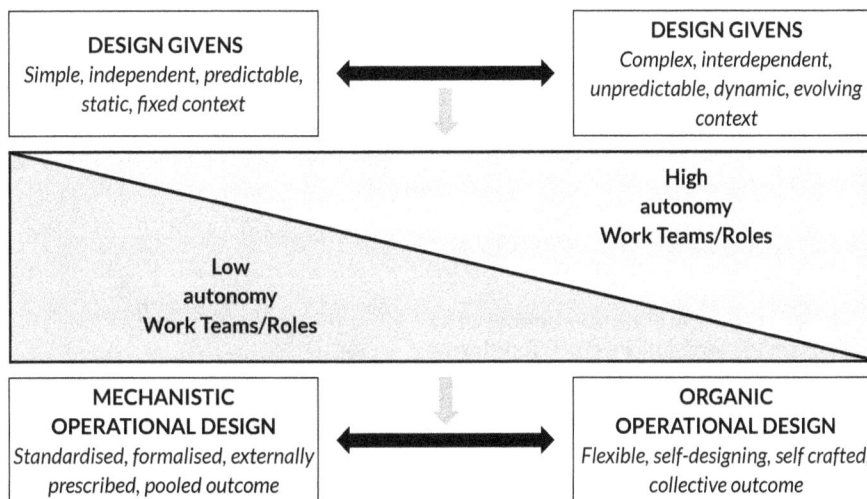

Figure 10.2: From a Mechanistic to an Organic Operational Design relative to the Design Givens

According to Figure 10.2, the required degree of autonomy of Work Teams/Roles – the freedom to take independent decisions and actions – is affected by the degree of autonomy to be built into the Operating Design overall. In turn, this would affect the choice of a fit-for-purpose Operational Design: Mechanistic vs. Organic (19). Based on the necessary Operational Design – Mechanistic vs. Organic – as a function of the Design Givens, an overall Operational Design Vision can be crafted for the Work Unit concerned.

The Design Vision can be concretised in the form of a one pager – 'A day in the life of...' – to make the to-be-design even more real in the minds of everyone by providing a tangible illustration of the delivery logic of the new design in reality. Again, the choice of an appropriate Design Metaphor – illustrative of the new delivery logic – can greatly assist, for example like the sports analogy referred to above of working like a certain type of sports team. As has already been stated, this metaphor is unpacked further under Work Team Design.

Step C.2B: Design Autonomy

Upfront in the design process – in conjunction with Step C.2A – the degree of Design Autonomy that has to be built into the Operational Design must decided on. Design Autonomy, referred to as team/job crafting in the literature (20), entails to what degree Work Team members/Work Role incumbents – in a self-initiated way – will have the right to change the Operational Design by shaping, moulding and redefining it in a (semi-)permanent way. In other words, what freedom do Team members/Role incumbents have to (re)craft the basic Operational Design that is being/has been architected. The more individuals believe they have the power to shape their work in order to personalise and individualise it for themselves, the more likely they will find their work meaningful (21). Team members/Work incumbents have two basic motivations to engage in crafting: either to enhance the positive aspects of their work, and/or to minimise/eliminate negative aspects thereof (22).

The decided-on Design Autonomy infuses all of the later design steps, but especially Step C.2. That is why Step C.2B: Design Autonomy incorporates all of the other C.2 steps (see Figure 10.1). The ultimate aim of Design Autonomy is to obtain the best Design Team/Person fit *(23)*. Figure 10.3 depicts a continuum of Design Autonomy, and the factors determining the appropriate degree of Autonomy (24).

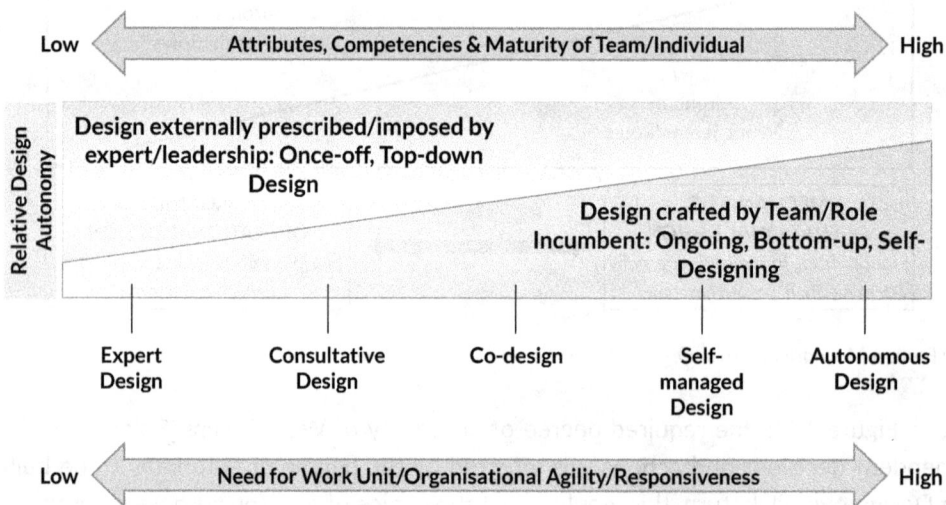

Figure 10.3: Design Autonomy with determining factors

According to Figure 10.3, a range of Design Autonomy permutations exist relative to the weighting of a Once-off, Top-Down Design Process in relation to an Ongoing, Bottom-up, Self-designing Process. This is reflected in a movement from Expert to Autonomous Design, or vice versa. The weighting is a function of the required Work Unit/Organisational Agility/Responsiveness, given the contextual qualities; the Operational Design Vision (discussed above); and the attributes, competencies and maturity of the Team/Individual affected by the Design. It is important to note that at *both* end points of the Autonomy continuum *all* parties are involved. However, their relative involvement in architecting the Operational Design inverses. On the one extreme of Expert Design, the Expert is in the driving seat. On the other extreme, the Team/Role Incumbent(s) takes the lead.

The initiation of the conversation regarding Design Autonomy can be reactive, that is one party responding to the status quo Design Autonomy. Or proactive, that is one party taking the initiative in redefining its position on its preferred, desired Design Autonomy. The current contention is that organisational members must become much more proactive in (re)defining their Design Autonomy by moving more towards Autonomous Design. As one moves from left to right on the continuum in Figure 10.3, the use of Design Thinking in the organisation with a supportive Design Thinking Culture needs to become more pervasive (25).

The critical question is: 'Design Autonomy with respect to what?' Taken the Team/Role Incumbent vantage point, Figure 10.4 illustrates the autonomy variables that have to be considered in constituting the Design Autonomy space (26). This space demarcates decisions regarding to what degree a Team/Role Incumbent(s) has Design Autonomy (27).

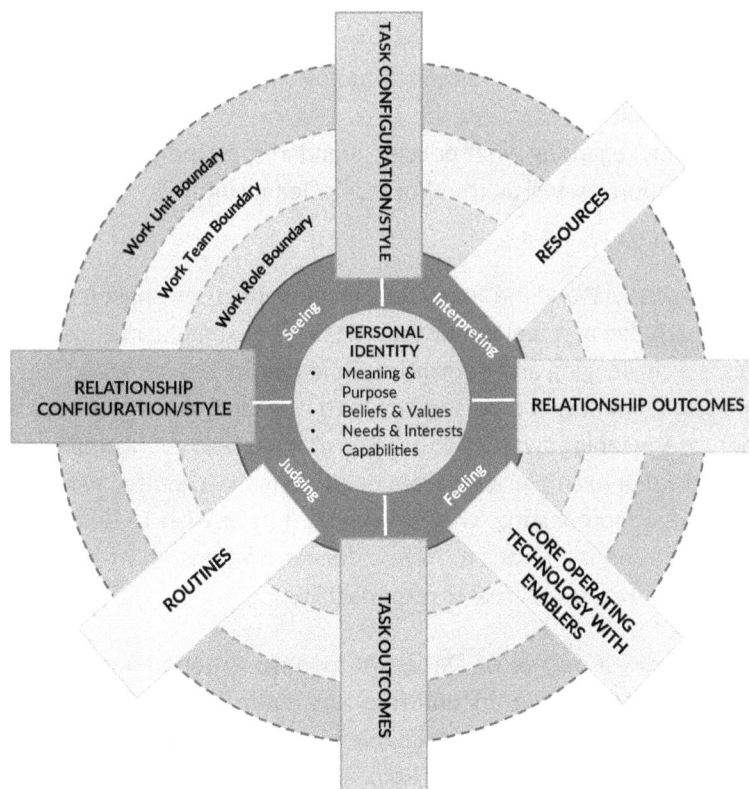

Figure 10.4: Variables defining the Design Autonomy Space

As can be seen from Figure 10.4:

- the first autonomy decision is to establish the *boundary* within which the autonomy can be exercised, that is the 'playing field'. Is the playing field the Work Role, Work Team or Work Unit, where the latter incorporates the preceding every time? For example, if the autonomy boundary is the Work Team, then Work Roles can be redesigned within the Work Team space. If the boundary is the Work Unit, then Work Teams *and* Work Roles can be redesigned. As a boundary changes, the other autonomy factors – Tasks, Relationships, Resources, Core Operating Technology, and Routines – change concurrently.

- the second decision pertains to what *situational elements* Design Autonomy can be exercised:

  o *Task:* (i) Configuration/Style of Tasks to be performed. For example, autonomy regarding work demands, sequencing, priorities, standards, improvement, or mode of delivery. In short, what does the job require and how must it be done?
  (ii) Outcomes. For example, autonomy with respect to what, when, how much, and to what standard?

  o *Relationships:* (i) Configuration/Style of and with stakeholders. For example, autonomy regarding who, with what importance, interacting in what way, and the frequency of interacting?
  (ii) Outcomes. For example, autonomy with respect to what, for whom, when, how much?

  o *Resources:* autonomy regarding what and how many resources, as well as decisions regarding their use?

  o *Core Operating Technology and Enablers:* autonomy with respect to what Technology with what Enablers, and its deployment?

  o *Routines:* autonomy regarding what policies, standards, methodologies and practices, and their degree of codification, as well as the Work Unit/Team culture?

- Personal Design Autonomy regarding:

  o the type of *Experiential World* the Team/Role Incumbent(s) can enact regarding the Design: how to see, interpret, judge and feel about their work. For example, in constituting an Experiential World: 'This is a challenging and demanding Role that makes me grow'.

  o the kind of *Personal Identity* the person wants to have and to shape through the Design: work-wise, the purpose/meaning awarded to it; beliefs/values held about; and need/interests satisfied through the work. For example: 'Our Team needs to make a greater, worthwhile difference that will leave behind a more lasting, worthy legacy'; 'I have wish to deliver something of higher value to my beneficiaries'; 'I want to have a deeper relationship with them', or 'I want to grow more in my Role by taking on greater responsibility'.

To illustrate overall, the highest degree of Design Autonomy: Autonomous Design (see Figure 10.3), exists where Work Team/Work Role Incumbents can craft personally their Task, Relationship, Resources, Core Operating Technology and Enablers, and Resource elements within Work Unit Boundaries in terms of their Work Team/Work Role, and have full Personal Autonomy regarding their Experiences and Personal Identity with respect to the preceding (see Figure 10.4). Essentially, the Work Unit becomes 'independent' from the bigger organisation within its demarcated boundaries. It takes on an intrapreneurial character.

Step C.2C: Expected People Conduct

Based on the Design Vision – reflective of either a relatively Mechanistic or Organic Operational Design – the expected People Conduct, making up the specific behaviours that are commensurate with the Design Vision, must be specified. What is the expected (or desired and required) conduct to be manifested by Team Members and Role Incumbents?

Figure 10.5 depicts a portfolio of possible behaviours which can be used to generate the profile of Expected People Conduct, aligned to the chosen Operational Design Vision (28). The behaviours given in Figure 10.5 are categorised in terms of the expected People Conduct typically associated with a Mechanistic or Organic Operational Design Vision.

MECHANISTIC OPERATIONAL DESIGN VISION	⟷	ORGANIC OPERATIONAL DESIGN VISION
Passive involvement	⟷	Active involvement
Little innovative/creative behaviour	⟷	Frequent innovative/creative behaviour
Individualistic behaviour	⟷	Cooperative, interdependent behaviour
Repetitive predictable behaviour	⟷	Creative innovate behaviour
Short term focus	⟷	Medium/Long term focus
Dependent, externally referenced behaviour	⟷	Independent, internally referenced, behaviour
Low concern for quality	⟷	High concern for high quality
Low risk orientation	⟷	High risk orientation
Concern for activities	⟷	Concern for results
Little accountability/responsibility	⟷	High accountability/responsibility
Inflexible to change	⟷	Flexible to change
Low task orientation	⟷	High task orientation
Low organisational identification	⟷	High organisational identification
Focus on efficiency (= Doing things right)	⟷	Focus on effectiveness (= Doing right things)
Single, simple decisions/actions	⟷	Complex, diverse decisions/actions
Low self control	⟷	High self control
Low initiative	⟷	High initiative
Low self-leadership focus	⟷	Strong self-leadership focus
Individualistic	⟷	Team work
Low tolerance for mistakes	⟷	High tolerance for mistakes

Figure 10.5: Portfolio of possible behaviours to generate a profile of Expected People Conduct commensurate with the adopted Design Vision

Figure 10.6 shows the territory of the Operational Design Map covered up to this point in the discussion of the Operational Design process.

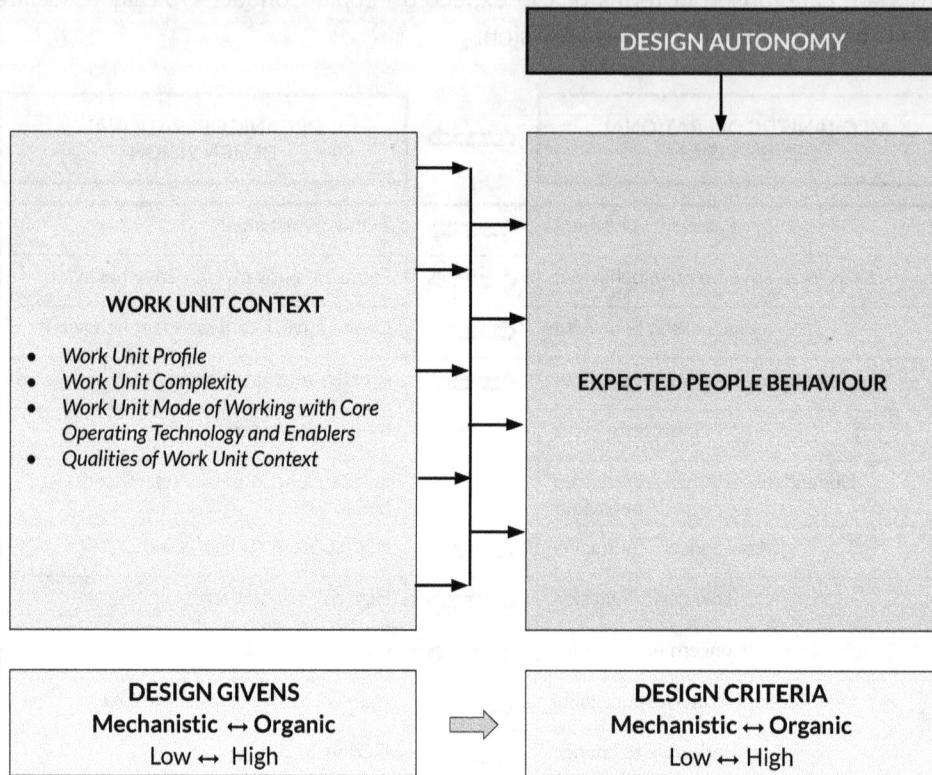

Figure 10.6: Location of Design Givens and Expected People Conduct in the Operational Design Map

Step C.2D: Design Criteria

The objective of this step is to craft Design Criteria for the Operational Design that will enable and support the Expected People Conduct – as manifested in specific behaviours – profiled in the previous step (see Figure 10.5). Given the iterative nature of the sub-steps making up Step C.2 (see Figure 10.1), the inverse route can also be followed: first formulate the Criteria, and then determine the associated Expected People Conduct in the form of specific behaviours.

Five categories of Operational Design Criteria can be distinguished (29) (30):

- Task;

- Capability;

- Immediate Social Setting;

- Macro Organisational Setting; and

- Wider Context.

Figure 10.7 depicts the placement of the Design Categories – with their commensurate Design Criteria – within the Operational Design Map as referenced against, and anchored in, the Expected People Conduct as required by a Mechanistic or Organic Operational Design.

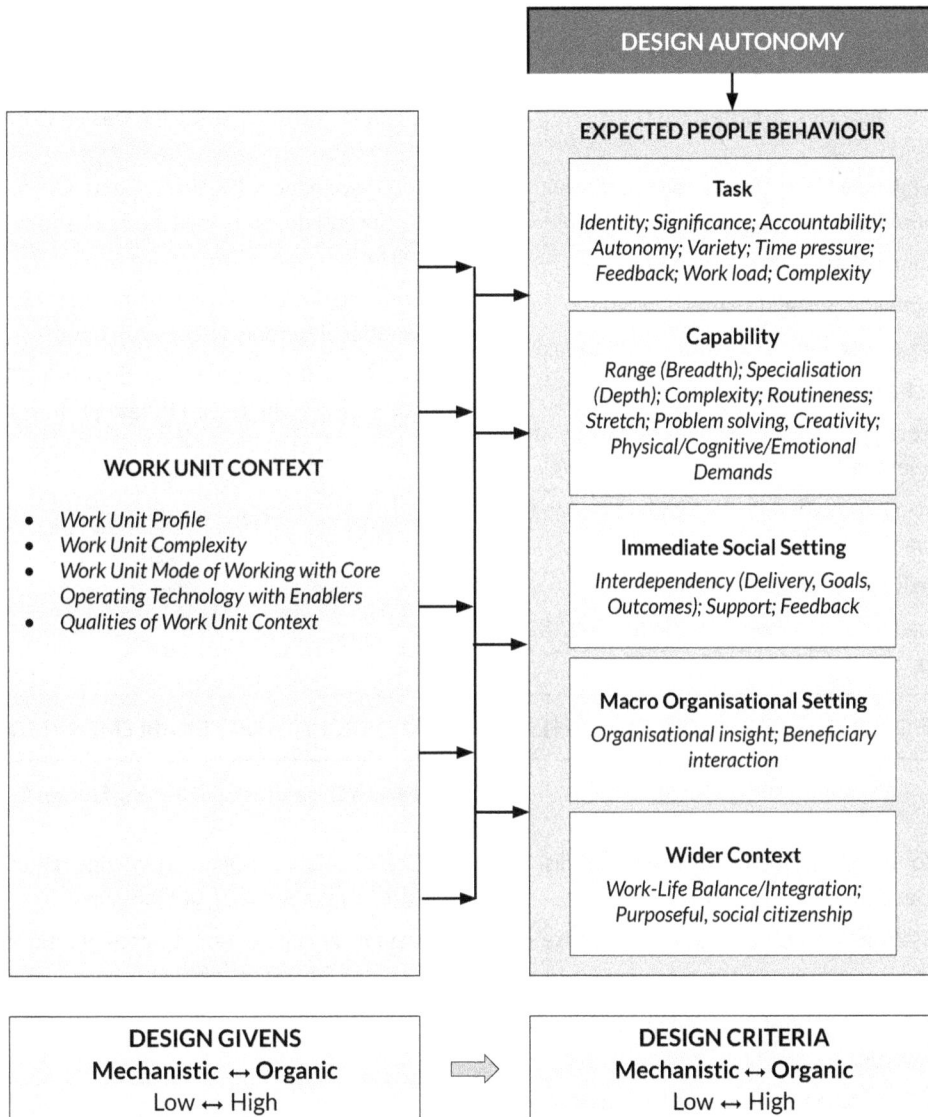

Figure 10.7: Location of Design Categories – with their commensurate Criteria – within the Operational Design Map

Table 10.1 provides descriptions of the specific Operational Design Criteria listed in Figure 10.7. The higher the presence of a given Criterion, the stronger the presence of an Organic Operational Design. Vice versa for a Mechanistic Design when the presence of a criterion is weaker. All of the Criteria, listed by category, have to be referenced against the backdrop of the Core Operating Technology and its Enablers and the Technological Enablement Model used by the Work Unit (see Tables 5.5 and 5.6, and Figure 5.7).

Table 10.1: Descriptions of the Operational Design Criteria per Design Criterion Category

OPERATIONAL DESIGN CRITERIA	
The higher the presence of a Criterion, the more the shift from a Mechanistic Design to an Organic Design	
Task Design Criteria *(31)*	**Immediate Social Setting Design Criteria**
• Identity: Whole piece of work for a particular customer/client • Significance: Value-add of task output • Accountability: Being in charge of a task(s) • Autonomy: Freedom to act with regard to task • Variety: Range of different tasks • Time pressure: Optimum amount of time in which to complete tasks • Feedback: Information needed with regard to task performance • Complexity: Difficulty of tasks • Work load: Volume of work (maximum 80%-85% loading)	• Interdependency (Delivery, Goals, Outcomes): Reciprocal dependency on others and self to perform • Support: Reciprocal Co-worker/Team/Self emotional support to get work done • Feedback: Reciprocal Co-worker/Team/Self information with regard to task performance
CORE OPERATING TECHNOLOGY WITH ENABLERS AND TECHNOLOGY ENABLEMENT MODEL	
Capability Design Criteria	**Macro Organisational Setting Design Criteria**
• Range (or Breadth): Number of different skills/expertise required • Specialisation (or Depth): Degree of expertise • Complexity: Difficulty of skills/expertise • Routineness: Degree of variation in application of skills/expertise • Stretch: Time taken to become a true master of skill/expertise (Ideal: 2 to 3 years) • Problem solving: Level of difficulty • Creativity: Degree of inventiveness • Physical/Cognitive/Emotional Demands: Demand mix and magnitude	• Organisational insight: Knowledge required about wider organisation to get job done • Beneficiary interaction: Degree of interaction with parties who are benefitting from work outcomes
	Wider Context
	• Work-Life Balance/Integration • Purposeful, social citizenship: Making a worthy, lasting difference for the common good

Step C.2E: Design Outcomes

The Expected People Conduct in interaction with the Design Criteria must bring about certain desired Design Outcomes: Immediate and Ultimate. Figure 10.8 gives the positioning of these Outcomes in the Operational Design Map. Once again, one may decide to start with the desired Design Outcomes the Operational Design must bring about, and then design 'backwards' in considering which Design Criteria and Expected People Conduct would give rise to the specified, desired Design Outcomes.

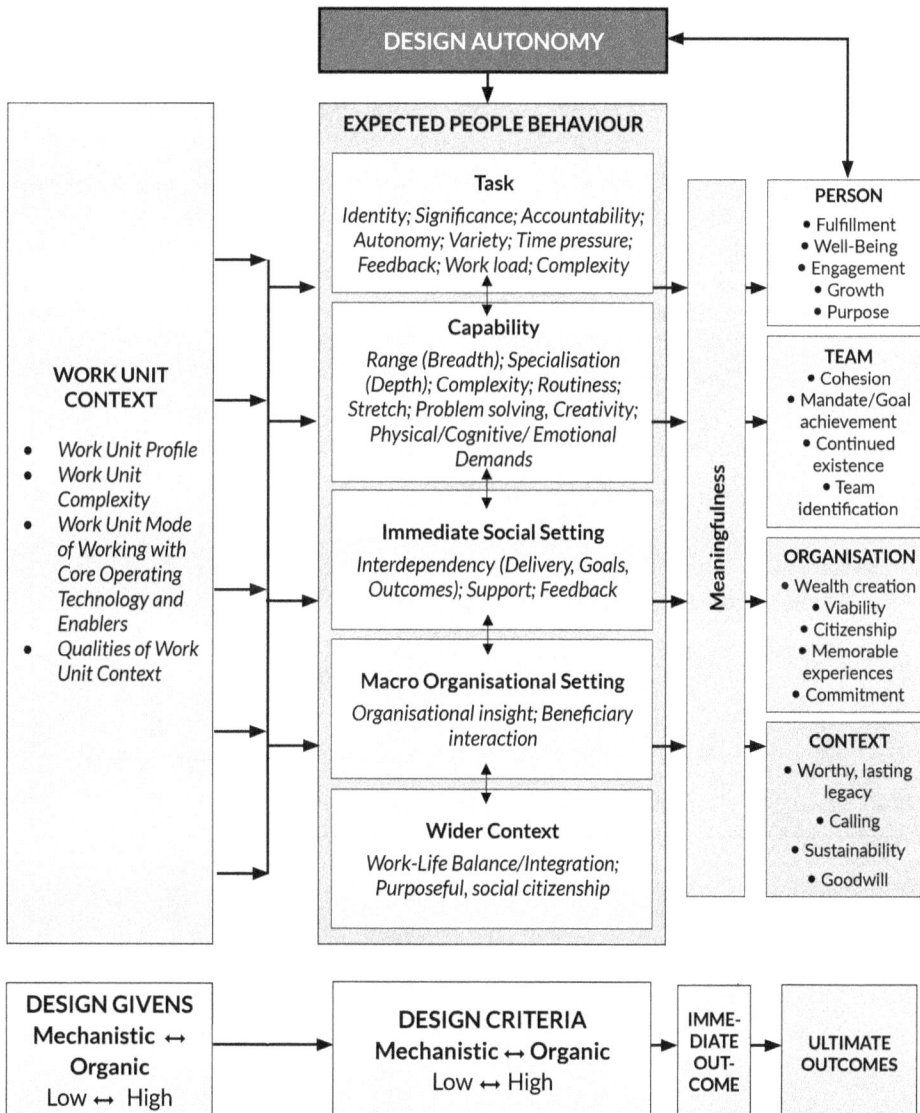

Figure 10.8: Location of Design Outcomes in the Operational Design Map

It has been found that the most critical *Intermediate* Outcome of the Operational Design is the degree of meaningfulness the Operational Design has for the people working in the Work Teams/Work Roles resulting from the Design (32). Meaningfulness pertains to the degree to which people experience their work – and its result/outcome – as being of real significance and worth by: (i) making a *true difference* through the value it delivers to stakeholders; (ii) *binding one* with others in a deep way; (iii) allowing one to *express one's true self*; and (iv) *becoming more of oneself* through one's work. In short, meaningfulness pertains to (i) *Doing well*: work that is good in itself; (ii) *Doing good*: work that is of benefit to others; (iii) *Doing with*: forming authentic relationships with others (33); and (iv) *Doing beyond*: work that serves the greater good. In turn, meaningfulness nurtures greater personal authenticity (34). It has been found that higher meaningfulness is enabled by more Organic Operational Designs (35).

Meaningfulness as an Intermediate Outcome will affect the *Ultimate* Outcomes with respect to the Person, Team, Organisation and Context (36). In general, the higher the meaningfulness as an Intermediate Outcome is – because of an Organic Design – the better the Ultimate Outcomes. Numerous Outcomes are possible. The Outcomes listed in Figure 10.8 appear from a practice point of view to be the more critical ones – 'Less is more' – in terms of a meaningful Design. By way of illustration, the shaded box provides indicators of work engagement – a Person Outcome – given its current pre-eminence as measure of a 'good' Operational Design (37).

WORK ENGAGEMENT INDICATORS

Vigour
- At work, a person feels themselves bursting with energy
- At work, a person feels strong and vigorous

Dedication
- To the person, his/her job is challenging
- The person is enthusiastic about his/her job

Absorption
- When the person is working, he/she forgets everything else around him/her
- The person is completely immersed in his/her work

At this point in the Operational Design process, the elements of an Operational Design Framework (Steps C.2A to A.2E) have been crafted, as depicted in Figure 10.9 *(38)*.

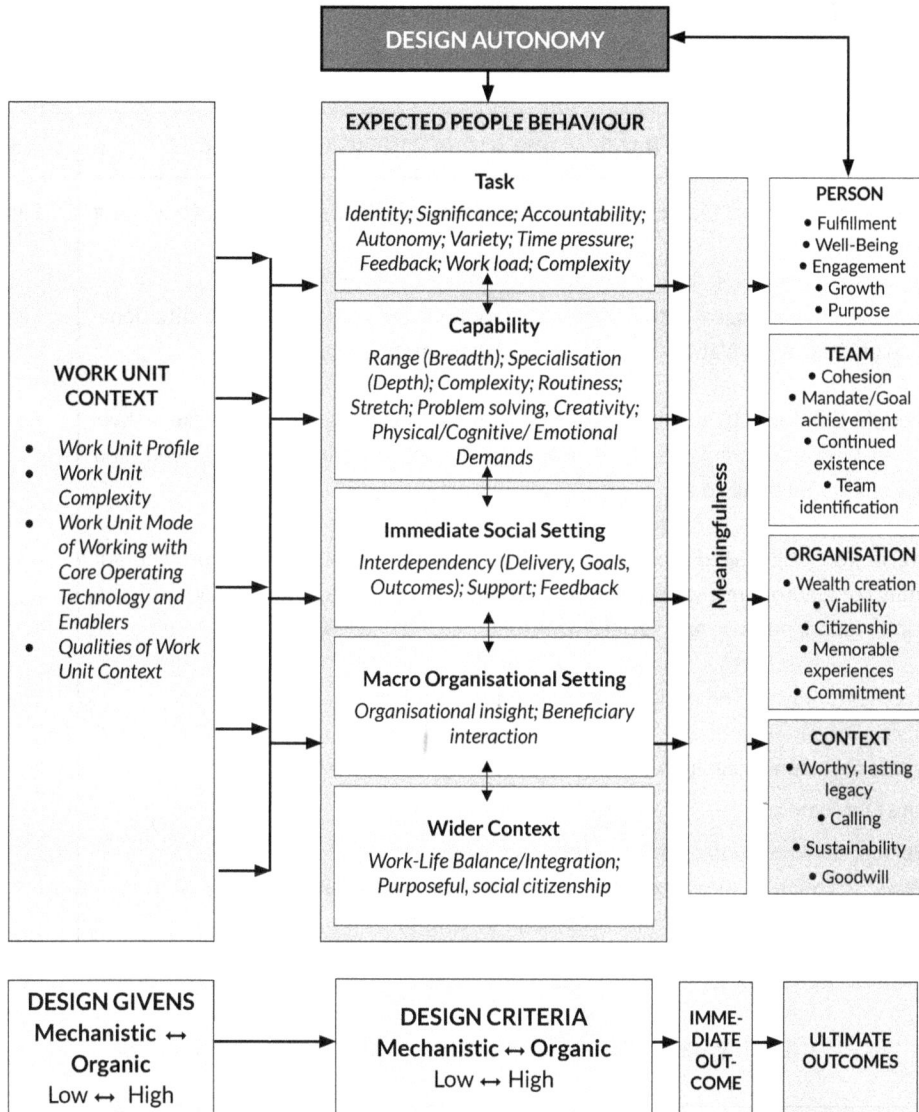

Figure 10.9: Complete Operational Design Framework as part of the Operational Design route map

The individual elements given in Figure 10.9 must be moulded into an integrated Operational Design Framework that will direct and guide the design of the Work Teams and Work Roles in the next design steps. As stated in the introduction above, the Operational Design Framework outlines the day-to-day living in the House and Work Units that are aligned to the Strategic and Tactical Designs. The Framework is applicable to *all* Work Teams/Work Roles architected in order to provide Operational Design consistency. In particular, the generation of fit-for-purpose Design Criteria for specific Work Team and/or Work Role Designs needs to draw heavily on this Framework.

Important to note again, is that the degree of Design Autonomy decided on up front (see Step C.2B) will determine the degree of specificity awarded to all the design elements contained in Figure 10.9. In addition, the Operational Design Framework renders the need to generate Work Team/Work Charters superfluous.

The box gives an example of what such an Operational Design Framework could look like. The source of a Charter element is given in the right-hand column. This column will be left out in the actual Charter.

OPERATIONAL DESIGN FRAMEWORK: A HYPOTHETICAL EXAMPLE	Source
Design Vision. An Operational Design that is flexible, self-designing, self-crafted, generating a collective outcome.	Figure 10.2
Design Autonomy. *Self-managed* within Work Unit boundaries, covering (i) all situational elements such as Tasks and Relationships; and (ii) all Personal variables.	Figure 10.3
Expected People Conduct (10 most Critical Behaviours). The design must invoke active, innovative, self-directed, independent, teaming, long term, quality, results-driven and effectiveness orientated behaviour.	Figure 10.3
Design Criteria (top 10). The design must facilitate, enable, encourage and provide for identity, significance, autonomy, variety, complexity, support, feedback, organisational insight, beneficiary interaction, purpose and social citizenship.	Table 10.1

Design Outcomes (primary). The design must engender the following outcomes:
 	
• **Immediate Outcome:** meaningfulness
• **Ultimate Outcomes:**
    ○ Person: fulfilment, engagement, purpose, well-being
    ○ Team: cohesion, mandate/goal achievement, team identification
    ○ Organisation: wealth creation, citizenship, memorable experiences
    ○ Context: sustainability, goodwill, worthy, lasting legacy
	Figure 10.8

Quality assurance: Operational Design Framework

QUALITY ASSURANCE QUESTIONS *Does the Operational Design Framework meet the following requirements?*	DESIGN STEP	ADDRESSED: YES/NO *(Yes: +; No: x)*
Have the five most important **Operational Design Givens** of the Work Unit been specified?	Step C.1	
Has a clear **Operational Design Vision** been crafted?	Step C.2A	
Has the degree of **Design Autonomy** regarding the Operational Design been clearly defined?	Step C.2B	
Has the **Expected People Conduct** – making up the specific behaviours that are commensurate with the Design Vision – been specified?	Step C.2C	

QUALITY ASSURANCE QUESTIONS *Does the Operational Design Framework meet the following requirements?*	DESIGN STEP	ADDRESSED: YES/NO *(Yes: +; No: x)*
Have the ten prioritised **Operational Design Criteria** commensurate with the Design Vision and Expected People Conduct been identified and defined?	Step C.2D	
Have the desired **Immediate Outcomes** (Meaningfulness) and **Ultimate Outcomes** (Person, Team, Organisation, Context) been specified?	Step C.2E	
Have all of the above been moulded into a coherent, aligned **Operational Design Framework**?	Step C.2 in total	

Step C.3: Current Design – Strengths and Weaknesses

The existing Operational Design's strengths and weaknesses must be assessed against the Operational Design Framework as a reference point. The diagnosis will allow one to build on what is currently good in the existing design, and minimise/eliminate what is bad.

The Operational Design Framework has been architected. Thus the detailed design process can now start with the Work Team Design.

Step C.4: Work Team Design (39)

Work Teams fulfil at least five generic functions in the organisation (40):

- *Interpretive:* creating a shared, social reality for members.
- *Task execution:* doing the work.
- *Social:* providing a sense of belonging.
- *Regulative:* generating and enforcing values and norms that govern member conduct.
- *Agency:* voicing member concerns and acting as a platform of influence.

Figure 10.10 graphically illustrates the building blocks of the Work Team (41) in the form of a Team Landscape, constructed in terms of a Complexity/Chaos Theoretical Lens as framing world view (see Table 3.1). The box following Figure 10.9 provides descriptions of these team building blocks. The arrow in the figure indicates which building block relates to Work Team Design in the Team Landscape.

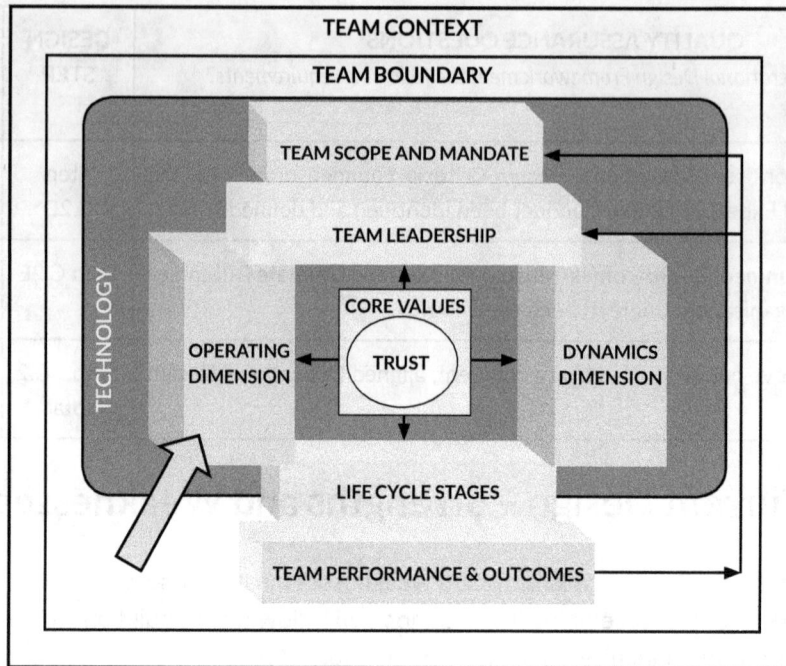

Figure 10.10: Building Blocks of the Work Team

DESCRIPTIONS OF WORK TEAM BUILDING BLOCKS

- All teams are embedded within a certain **context**, for example, the Work Unit and Organisation it belongs to; the relationships with significant others in its setting; stakeholders; and major past events in the history of the team; enabling and supporting Work Unit and Organisational processes and practices around the team.

- A **team boundary**, which demarcates the team's area of accountability and operations, as well as the sphere of influence.

- A **team scope and mandate**, which provides the team with its terms of reference. It spells out the team's reasons for existence, the role it has to play in its Work Unit and Organisation, its required inputs and outputs, and its level of empowerment and autonomy. Simply put: the overall team task.

- The **capacity of the team** to deliver its expected outputs is determined by four elements:
  - The style and quality of **leadership** demonstrated.
  - The appropriateness of its **operating dimension** (= doing the work), as expressed in:
    - its mode of working, that is delivery logic (= formal design); task structuring; and Work Roles with their associated accountability, responsibility, autonomy;
    - composition: member number and required profiles;
    - required competencies and resources within the team, and how they are distributed; and
    - desired culture and climate (including values and norms).
  - The healthiness of its emerging **dynamics dimension** (= working together) in terms of members' interpersonal interactions; critical team processes (for example, information processing, decision-making, problem solving, conflict handling, creative and innovative thinking); interpersonal and group dynamics; informal team roles; actual team culture; and climate.
  - The **technology** used to do the work and deliver on the team scope and mandate.

> - **Life cycle stages**: the team developmental stages of forming, storming, norming and performing.
> - **Team performance and outcomes:** pertaining to both tasks and relationship outcomes, reflecting the degree of overall team effectiveness.
> - **Core values:** pertaining to what is right/wrong; important/unimportant; good/bad.
> - **Trust:** delivering on expectations and promises in consistent and predictable ways over time.

Although the picture in Figure 10.10 appears static, a Work Team is a verb, not a noun (42), especially when viewed from a Complexity/Chaos Theoretical Lens. According to this Lens, a Work Team, forms an interconnected whole of non-linearly, reciprocally influencing, interacting building blocks. Hence, the two arrows and blocks overlapping in Figure 10.10. Everything affects everything else. The relationships between the building blocks – not the building blocks *per se* – are primary.

Dynamically, relationships between the building blocks are characterised by the ongoing resolution of opposing tensions. The resolution of tensions manifests in emergent, self-organising and self-destructing patterns of functioning within the team. The patterns form virtuous or vicious cycles shaping the team dynamics. The cycles are expressive of a limited number of underlying organising rules as the team as an interconnected whole moves through successive states of chaos (tensions are unresolved) and order (the resolution of tensions in the form of a pattern). The nature of a pattern is also affected by the life cycle stage of the team, for example norming or performing.

Figure 10.11 depicts the steps to be followed with respect to a Work Team Design. For the sake of showing the link to what has proceeded before in terms of the Operational Design Process, Step C.2: Operational Design Framework is also shown in the figure, as well as the relative placement of the Team Design Process to that of the Work Role Design Process.

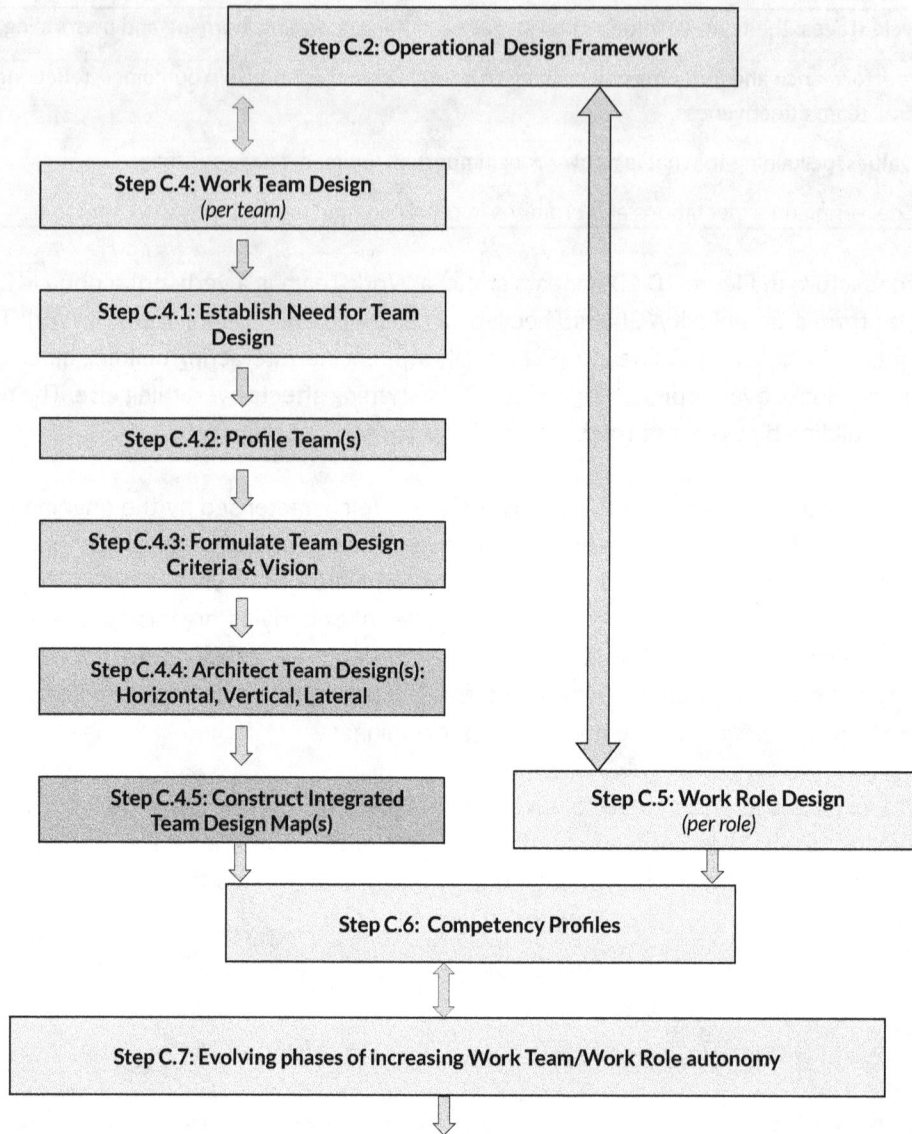

Figure 10.11: Overview of Work Team Design

The box gives two case studies of team-based organisations. In terms of Design Autonomy, the first design is top-down and externally prescribed/imposed. The second design is ongoing, bottom-up and self-designing.

TEAM-BASED ORGANISATIONS
TOP-DOWN, EXTERNALLY PRESCRIBED/IMPOSED: HOLACRACY (43)

Holacracy (from the Greek meaning 'whole') – coined by Arthur Koestler in his 1967 book *The Ghost in the Machine* – is the name for an Organisational Shape proposed by Brian Robertson in 2007, as per his 2015 book entitled *Holacracy: The New Management System for a Rapidly Changing World.*

In this design, the organisation in its entirety is made up of overlapping, agile, self-managing teams (= team as holos but acting together collectively as a wholeness of teams), acting symbiotically, democratically, and in concert together. The aim of the Organisational Shape is to replace hierarchy completely by managing the organisation through a configuration of teams and teaming. No formal chain of command with an associated hierarchy exists. Within teams, highly autonomous team members fulfil multiple roles and/or switch between roles with teams. 'Lower' level Operating Teams are embedded in, and linked to, 'higher' organisational teams (= circles) by team representatives. Team dynamics and operations are laid down in a "Holacracy Constitution", which sets out the design-specific core vocabulary, principles, and practices of the design.

The design is claimed to increase agility, efficiency, transparency, innovation and accountability within an organisation. Paradoxically, holacracy has been criticised for its rigidity because of its prescribed constitution (= laid-down, holographic rules) which demands compliance at all times; the time-consuming process of reaching organisational consensus through teams; and an internal, instead of an external, customer-centric focus.

ONGOING, BOTTOM-UP, SELF-DESIGNING: AMOEBA ORGANISATION (44)

Within a context of intense competition, fast technological change and short/shortening product life cycles, the Japanese firm Kyocera has gone the route of extreme decentralisation. It is comprised of thousands of small customer focused/facing business units of 5 to 50 members. The analogy of its Organisational Shape is that of an amoeba, which is the smallest independent uni-cellular organism in the universe. An amoeba has the innate ability to multiply and change its shape in rapid response to fast changing, turbulent contexts.

The agile business units (= teams) are profit centres which operate independently in serving their clients; determine their own shape (= ambidextrous); innovate as they see fit in terms of opportunity identification and realisation; develop their own way of working with other units; and look beyond their own interest by working for the good of the company as a whole. Units divide, merge and dissolve autonomously as they see fit.

Since the principle is management-by-all, with everyone acting like independent owners/partners of the organisation, formal management has to show high employee consideration/care and treat employees fairly and kindly, in turn engendering high trust and rapport. The organisational culture is entrepreneurial and collaborative, infused by the core values of fairness, integrity, diligence, and philanthropy to all employees. The company motto is: "Respect the divine and love the people."

A common set of strategic goals and objectives exists, based on a commitment to price, quality and timely delivery. An overall plan exists at the organisational level, which is discussed monthly at the amoeba level. There are also formal, daily group meetings that are attended by all Unit members, who discuss matters such as budget, performance, profitability and customers. Inter-amoeba meetings are also held. Simplified support systems exist.

> Total transparency informs everything – both financial and non-financial. A direct line of sight exists from performance through to success and profitability. As a profit centre, the profitability of an amoeba is calculated as its value add divided by hours worked. Employees are shareholders, and share in profits.

Step C.4.1: Establish Need for Work Team Design

The first design consideration is to determine whether a Work Team Design for the Work Unit is required in the first place, in contrast to a Work Role Design. The accompanying shaded box gives the conditions under which the choice for a Work Team Design would be justified (45) (46).

GUIDELINES FOR CHOOSING A WORK TEAM DESIGN

The when and why of teams

- A highly uncertain, turbulent, complex, dynamic and rapidly changing work setting demanding agility, responsiveness and flexibility.

- Organisation-wide challenges beyond a specific organisational function and the hierarchy.

- Complex, unstable tasks accompanied by a rapidly changing, more complex, unstable Core Operating Technology and Enablers.

- Highly interdependent tasks: pooled/reciprocal dependency and a high need for lateral integration and co-ordination.

- Necessity for multiple perspectives/disciplines, requiring cross-functional perspectives.

- Outside-In, client centricity: performance of whole pieces of work for groupings of similar clients/customers.

- High autonomy to, and empowerment of, organisational members.

- Need for continuous, relentless, disruptive innovation.

- Need for ongoing, rapid, real time, shared learning/teaching to keep ahead of revolutionary change.

Step C.4.2: Profile Team

Step C.4.2.1: Determine type of Work Team

The decision has been made that a Team Design is appropriate. Next, the type of team needed has to be profiled. Figure 10.12 depicts four dimensions according to which teams can be differentiated (47). The profile of the team to be designed can be plotted on these dimensions. This profile also provides strong clues as to possible Team Design Criteria.

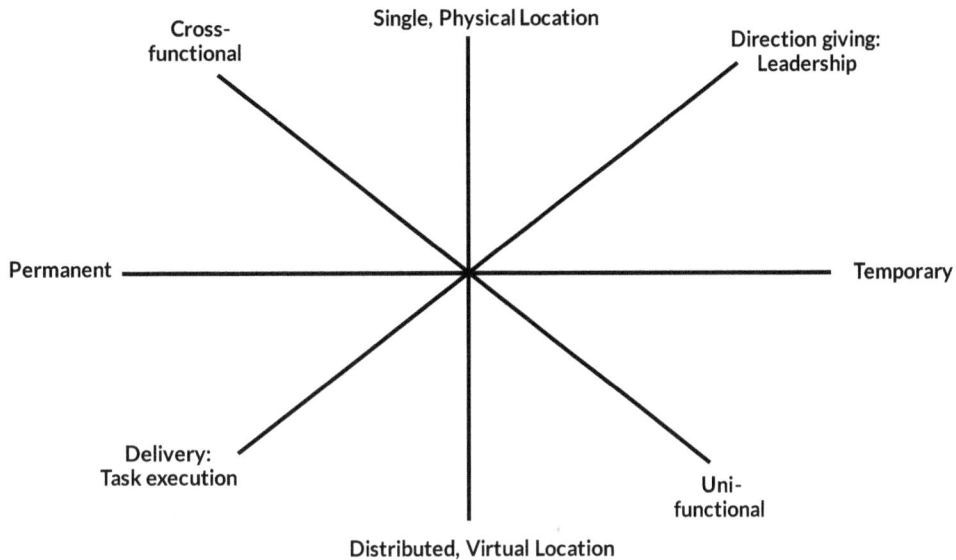

Figure 10.12: Dimensions on which to differentiate Work Teams

All the dimensions given in Figure 10.12 would be relevant to the discussion below, except Temporary Teams, for example, Task Forces, which are not considered below. However, Temporary Teams were listed as a Strategic Lateral Integration Mechanism (see Table 7.5). The Design Givens of a particular type of Work Team must be considered in the design steps to follow. For example, globally distributed teams pose unique, design requirements like different time zones, emotional-social distance, and power distribution across different locations (48). Likewise, top management teams also impose also their own design requirements (49).

Step C.4.2.2: Demarcate Work Team

The objective of this step is to determine the essential nature of a Work Team(s). For each Work Team making up the Work Domains of the Work Unit, this exercise has to be done. Figure 10.13 gives a graphic layout of the design elements of a Work Team that can be used to profile such a Team, with the elements being defined in Table 10.2. The Work Team Profile can be used to uncover the essential content of the Work Team design elements in a systemic, integrated manner. The numbering of the design elements indicates the order in which they must be addressed logically, given the interdependency between the elements, that is the Profile provides the baseline information for the actual design of a Work Team. A Work Team Profile design template is available in Appendix B: Design Template 12.

The similarity of this Profile to that of an Operating Unit is readily apparent (see Figure 9.11 with the descriptors of the design elements given in Table 9.4.) A Work Team, after all, is a 'Mini-Work Unit'. For this reason, the guidelines given there for the creation of distinct, powerful Work Units are also, with some adaptation to Teams, directly applicable to the design of distinct, powerful Work Teams (see the box under Step B.2.1).

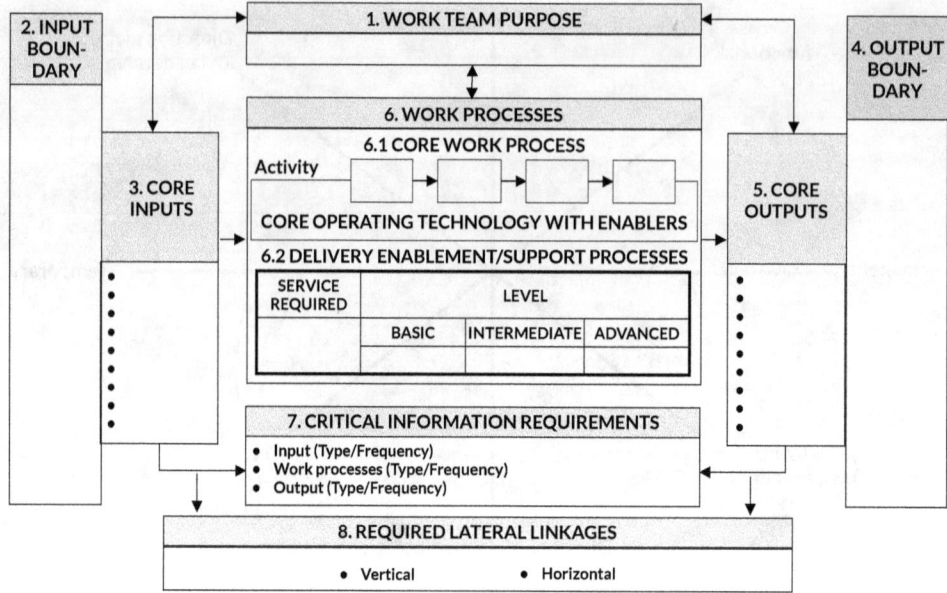

Figure 10.13: Work Team Design Profile

The Work Team Profile given in Figure 10.13 – with the descriptors of the design elements given in Table 10.2 – provide a solid foundation from which to direct and guide the balance of the design process.

Table 10.2: Descriptors of Operational Design: Team elements

TEAM DESIGN ELEMENT	DESCRIPTION
1. Team Purpose	Why does the Work Team exist: the rationale for its existence?
2. Input Boundary	Where does the Work Team's Area of Accountability start on the input side: supplier side?
3. Core Inputs	What inputs does the Work Team receive from its Key Supplier(s) with their requirements to be acceptable, for example, timing, quantity, quality?
4. Output Boundary	Where does the Work Team's Area of Accountability end on the output side: customer side?
5. Core Outputs	What outputs does the Work Team supply to its Key Customer(s) with their requirements to be acceptable, for example, timing, quantity, quality?
6. Work Processes 6.1 Core Work Process, leveraged by Core Operating Technology and Enablers	Work to be done by the Work Team to define, deliver and satisfy customers' needs. Series of interdependent activities required to transform inputs into output(s): a product/service. A true core process runs from a product/service input to the export of the finished product/delivery of the service.

TEAM DESIGN ELEMENT	DESCRIPTION
	Classification of Core Work Process levels:
	• *Key transformations:* Key points at which substantive changes take place in the input. A key transformation represents the reason *why* Work Team activities take place. It embodies the essence of the core work process. It is the point at which in the core work process the value-add is the greatest. A Work Team is often named after the key transformation.
	• *Supplementary transformations:* Significant but not essential changes to the composition of the input.
	• *Ancillary operations:* Peripheral or 'cosmetic' changes to the product/ service in process.
	• *Transportation:* Geographical change only.
	• *Storage:* No change in the product/service.
	As one moves from Storage to Transformation, the degree of change and value-add to the inputs move from minimum to maximum.
	Core Operating Technology and Enablers: Means used to produce the organisation's products/services.
6.2 Delivery Enabling/Support Processes	Series/set of interdependent activities required to enable/support the execution of the core work process of the Work Team.
	Classification of delivery levels of Enabling/Support Processes:
	• *Basic:* Delivery of day-to-day, first line enabling/support activities (for example, ordering of consumables; performance appraisal; band aid repairs; data capturing; recruitment; training).
	• *Intermediate:*
	○ Delivery of focused enabling/support activity advice or expertise.
	○ Operating and maintenance of programmes, procedures, standards and/or courses associated with enabling/support process systems (for example, a specific Information Technology).
	• *Advanced:*
	○ Delivery of enabling/support process systems level advice or advanced expertise with respect to enabling/support activities (for example, major maintenance, leadership assessment).
	○ Design, implementation and termination of overall enabling/ support process systems (for example, capital expansion).
	○ Generation of enabling/support process strategy, priorities and policies.

TEAM DESIGN ELEMENT	DESCRIPTION
	As one moves from Basic to Advanced Enabling/Support work processes, there is: o a decrease in the frequency of the performance of the activities inside the Work Team; and o an increase in the degree of required, in-depth specialisation of the activities that need to be performed. An important design consideration with respect to the Delivery Enabling/Support Processes is at what delivery level these processes must be available on a daily basis within the Work Team – Basic, Intermediate or Advanced – given the requirements of the Core Operating Technology and Enablers used by the Team.
7. Critical Information Requirements	What information does the Work Team require to get the job done? • Input information • Work process information • Output information
8. Required Lateral Linkages	What essential interfaces – horizontal and vertical – are needed to link the Work Team to the Work Unit it belongs to, as well as the rest of the organisation? • Horizontal: other Work Teams, inside and outside the Work Unit • Vertical: reporting links

Step C.4.2.3: Align Work Teams

If the Work Unit is made up of more than one Work Team, they must form an aligned (or coherent) whole along the core value chain. In particular: (i) the purpose and mandates of Work Teams must not overlap, that is they must be distinct; (ii) the Input and Output Boundaries relative to the Work Team Purpose must agree and be unambiguous in order to avoid border disputes; and (iii) the Supplier and Customer handovers (what, when, to what specifications) by Work Teams must be clear.

Step C.4.3: Formulate Team Design Criteria and Vision with Design Metaphor

The *first* Design Criterion to set is the Level of Work (LOW) of the Team to be designed (see Table 7.1). Is this a LOW5, LOW4, LOW3, LOW2 or LOW1 team, and what is its Contextual Complexity (see Table 5.2)? The 'ceiling' Total Complexity of the team will be set by the Total Complexity of the Work Unit = LOWx Contextual Complexity, of which the Team forms part.

The *second* source of Work Team Design Criteria is provided by the Operational Design Framework, whether more Mechanistic or more Organic (see Step C.2), that serves as a reference point for all Work Team/Work Role Designs. As stated above, the Operational Design Framework outlines the day-to-day living in the organisational House with its Rooms.

Thirdly, the need for a Team Design (see shaded box, Step C.4.1) and the characteristics of a high performance/high engagement team also provide a handy complementary source from which further Team Design Criteria can be derived. The accompanying shaded box provides some of the more important characteristics of high performance/high engagement teams (50).

FEATURES OF A HIGH PERFORMANCE/HIGH ENGAGEMENT TEAM

- A good fit with, and understanding of, context.
- A clear, challenging team scope and mandate at the requisite Level of Work, with clearly demarcated boundaries, given the expected role that the team has to play in the Work Unit.
- Appropriately resourced relative to the team scope and mandate.
- A high commitment by team members to the team scope and mandate.
- Well defined, clearly structured individual roles and contributions with clear accountabilities and responsibilities.
- A team delivery mode that is conducive to achieving the team scope and mandate, as well as team intra-dependency.
- Competent, motivated and passionate team members, matched to the team scope, mandate and delivery mode.
- A high understanding and acceptance of team members of each other, that is inclusivity.
- A willingness by team members to support each other, within and outside the team.
- Open and honest communication/information sharing amongst team members.
- A high appreciation for different and opposing opinions and views within the team.
- Sound values, such as fairness, equity and transparency.
- Effective problem solving/trouble shooting by the team.
- Healthy conflict resolution processes within the team.
- The open expression of inner feelings and thoughts by team members.
- Pride in and satisfaction with team performance.
- A high level of trust within the team.

The key consideration in choosing Team Design Criteria is what conditions the Team Design must facilitate, enable, encourage and provide for. For example, the intended Team Design must facilitate, enable, encourage and provide for a good fit with the context; build focused competencies; enhance customer-centricity; and engender ongoing innovation. Additionally, what are the Expected People Behaviour and Design Outcomes the design must bring about as contained in the Operational Design Framework (see Figure 10.8)? Usually up to at least 10 prioritised Criteria need to be selected.

As discussed earlier on with regard to Strategic Design Criteria, short descriptions (or definitions) need to be given of each Criterion to clarify exactly what is meant by them. This will ensure a uniform understanding of the Criteria, and make their use easier when debating the merits and demerits of different design options. For example, the Criterion of client-centricity means a one stop service will be provided to clients. The set of selected, prioritised Design Criteria serves as the ultimate reference point and court of appeal when debating and deciding during the design process which, among several different design options, is the best fit-for-purpose design.

The crafting of a Team Design Vision – A one pager, 'A day in the life of…' – can assist significantly in concretising the 'To-Be' design in the minds of everyone, and provide an even more tangible illustration of the team design in reality. Most helpful is the choice of a Design Metaphor to visualise more concretely the new Mode of Working as reflective of the delivery logic contained in the Team Design Vision.

For example, a *sports metaphor*: Do we want to work like:

- *a team of athletes:* independent specialists making independent contributions, resulting in an additive achievement;

- *a relay team:* the sequential handover of work, requiring cumulative efforts to achieve a shared goal;

- *a soccer/rugby team:* an interdependent set of players, performing together in real time to produce a joint result); or

- *a volleyball team:* an in time, multi-skilled, multi-tasking group of players tackling a piece of work together as it arises in real time.

The accompanying box gives further detail on this sport metaphor (51).

SPORT AS DESIGN METAPHOR
Athletics team
Individual stars, each one performing a particular, specialised task that is for the most part independent of what the other units/team members do, and the results of any of the other units/team members. One member's performance does not affect another member's performance directly, although it will affect the sum total of the unit's/team's performance. The team's performance depends mostly on pooling everyone's individual and independent efforts, so that the overall team performance is simply the sum of its parts: *Pooled interdependency.*
Relay team
Each team member runs his/her part of the race (= doing their piece of work) before handing the baton over to the next team member. One must run one's part of the race to the best of one's ability, and hand over the baton in the right manner at the right time to the next party in the race. The team's overall performance is the sum total of the performance of each individual in his/her leg of the relay, and the quality of hand overs: *Sequential interdependency.*
Soccer team
A group of people carrying out precisely planned actions, with each team member co-ordinating with others according to a prescribed plan in real time. The team depends for success on every person doing closely what has been programmed and practiced for a specific play, so that its efforts end up being perfectly coordinated. If one does not pull his/her weight, then the overall team performance suffers. Overall team performance is the result of a joint team effort: *Reciprocal interdependency.*

SPORT AS DESIGN METAPHOR
Volleyball team Each team member must accommodate all of the other team members as the action evolves in order to deal with a task situation that is in flux and infused by many exceptions. Rapid change is the only constant, demanding real time, in time, responsiveness and agility. While some team members are true stars, they are relatively rare and the exception. There is intense back-and-forth co-ordination among team members who must work closely together in real time on a constant basis. Each team member depends on the others. Usually each team member has more than one skill and has the potential to contribute to the team's performance in diverse ways. Team members must engage in 'mutual adjustment' so that they can take into account what frequently are unexpected events. Overall team performance is the total effort by all in real time: *Reciprocal interdependency.*

Step C.4.4: Architect Team Design: Horizontal, Vertical, Lateral

The Design Criteria and Vision with a Design Metaphor have been set. The objective of this step is to architect the Team Design horizontally, vertically, and laterally.

Step C.4.4.1: Horizontal Team Design

Architect Mode of Working of Work Team

At the crux of the Horizontal Team Work Design is, *firstly*, architecting the Mode of Working of the Work Team in accordance with its set Design Criteria, Vision and Metaphor (incorporating the critical success factors of the Core Operating Technology used by the team). Regarding its chosen Mode of Working, it is critical to understand the structural interdependence required within the Work Team when delivering its work.

The choice of a fit-for-purpose, structural independence is central to Work Team Design (52). Variations in structural interdependence in teams is well illustrated in the sport metaphor of different sports teams given in the box above: from pooled through sequential to reciprocal interdependency. Structural interdependence – whether pooled, sequential or reciprocal – effects three interdependencies regarding the Work Team's Mode of Working, and hence overall team performance (53):

- *Task Interdependence:* how to get the work done.
- *Relationship Interdependence:* how to interact as team members whilst working together.
- *Outcome Interdependence:* team members' relative share in contributing to the team outcome(s) overall.

Figure 10.13 depicts the above discussion graphically.

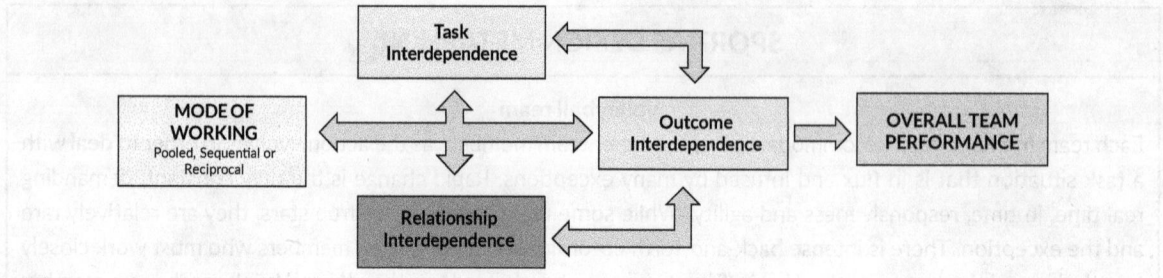

Figure 10.14: Structural Interdependence of Mode of Working determining Task, Relationship and Outcome Interdependencies within the Work Team, affecting overall Team Performance

Table 10.3 provides an application of the different Modes of Working on the Task, Relationship and Outcome Interdependencies within a Work Team, with its effect on Overall Team Performance.

Table 10.3: Different Modes of Working on Task, Relationship and Outcome Interdependencies within the Work Team, with their effect on overall Team Performance

| | | INTERDEPENDENCE | | | OVERALL TEAM PERFORMANCE |
		Task	Relationship	Outcome	
MODE OF WORKING	**Pooled**	Low: Stand-alone, specialised, individually allocated tasks	Low: Quality of relationships has no effect. Mostly interaction for social purposes only	Low: Separate, individual contributions	Sum total of individual performances
	Sequential	Medium: Relatively specialised tasks as part of overall task, performed independently at certain points in the process by individuals, the output of which is handed over to the next person in the process	Medium: Quality of relationship is only critical at handover points in terms of what, when, and at what quality standards	High: Breakdown at any point along the process affects total outcome. In case of a significant breakdown, no real time recovery is possible	Total process performance
	Reciprocal: Dedicated specialists	High: Shared task in which dedicated specialists, also having a common set of general skills, perform in real time through joint pre-planning, co-ordination and practice	High: Overall quality of relationships is critical during the delivery of the total task in real time	High: Outcome is total team effort, although the outcome can be the result of the brilliance of one or two individual team member(s), but supported by other team members	Sum total of combined team and individual performances

		INTERDEPENDENCE			OVERALL TEAM PERFORMANCE
		Task	Relationship	Outcome	
	Reciprocal: Generalists	High: Joint delivery in real time of shared task by generalists through in time, real time planning and co-ordination	High: Quality of relationships is critical during real time, in time joint delivery of shared tasks	High: Outcome is total team effort, depending on generalists co-performing shared task	Joint performance as a team

Identify distinct, mission-critical Work Roles regarding Mode of Working

Secondly, In order to 'anchor' the Work Team Design, distinct mission-critical Work Roles have to be identified and their Core Purpose defined with respect to the Mode of Working of the Work Team. As can be deduced from Table 10.3, structural interdependence directly determines the types of Work Roles that must be architected for the Work Team through which the Team's work will get done. A good example of generic Work Roles are those that were identified in the People Function, Tactical Design in the previous chapter, namely People Leadership; People Generalists (or Client Executives); People Specialists; Transactional Processors; and People Intelligence.

At this point of the design process, the mission-critical Work Roles with regard to the Team's Mode of Working have to be identified. Although the detailed Operational Design of the Work Roles of the Work Domain/Work Team will be covered under Step C.5 (see below), high level Role Profiles can be generated, covering the total scope of the Team's work. These Role Profiles must cover at least the following:

- Core purpose;
- Critical Tasks (= Key Performance Areas); and
- Key Outputs.

A Work Role Profile Template is given in Appendix B: Design Template 3.

Step C.4.4.2: Vertical Team Design

For each identified Work Role, the requisite LOW must be awarded as referenced against the Work Team's Total Complexity.

Step C.4.4.3: Lateral Team Design

Using the identified Work Roles as the basis, the Lateral Team Design requires the following steps (see Strategic Design Step A.4 in Chapter 7) for the Work Team concerned:

- Construct its Interdependency Matrix (in this regard the above Structural Interdependence discussion under Step C.4.4.1, especially Table 10.3, is essential input).

- Decide on appropriate Integration Mechanisms.

- Set up the Governance Model of the Team in terms of Decision-making Rights and Styles.

Step C.4.5: Construct Integrated Team Design Map(s)

Figure 10.13 can be used to construct an Integrated Work Team Design Map(s) with the following adaptations (see Appendix B: Design Template 13):

- Design Element 6: Replace title 'Work Processes' with title 'Horizontal and Vertical Designs'. In this box, graphically depict the Horizontal Tactical Design: Configuration of Work Domains into a Team Shape, and the Vertical Tactical Design: Requisite Levels of Work.

- Design Element 7: Replace title 'Critical Information Requirements' with the title 'Critical Team Intelligence'. In this box, list the critical intelligence the Work Team must have at its disposal at all times. A balanced scorecard can be used to represent this intelligence.

- Design Element 8: Replace title 'Required Lateral Linkages' with title 'Lateral Design'. In this box depict the Lateral Design, specifically the crafted Integration Mechanisms and Team Governance Model.

The quality assurance questions for a Work Team Design are given at the end of this chapter.

Next, the design of Work Roles can be addressed.

Step C.5: Work Role Design

The 'furniture' of a Work Unit may consist of more than one Work Team with its associated Work Roles, or a Work Unit may in its totality equate to a Work Team, and hence only consist of a set of Work Roles. Figure 10.15 depicts the steps to be followed with respect to Work Role Design. Given its pivotal role as overall reference point, Step C.2: Operational Design Framework is again shown in the figure.

If a Work Unit consists of a Work Team(s), then both the left-hand *and* right-hand sides of the Operational Design process given in Figure 10.15 are applicable. The Work Team Design would lead to the identified Work Roles (see Step C.4.4.1 above). If the Work Unit Design equates only to Work Roles, then only the right-hand side of the figure of the Operational Design process is applicable. For the sake of discussing a complete, stand-alone Work Role Design process, it is going to be assumed that the right-hand side of Figure 10.15 of the Operational Design Process is applicable in what follows *(54)*. Metaphorically, the furniture of the Work Unit equates to Work Roles only.

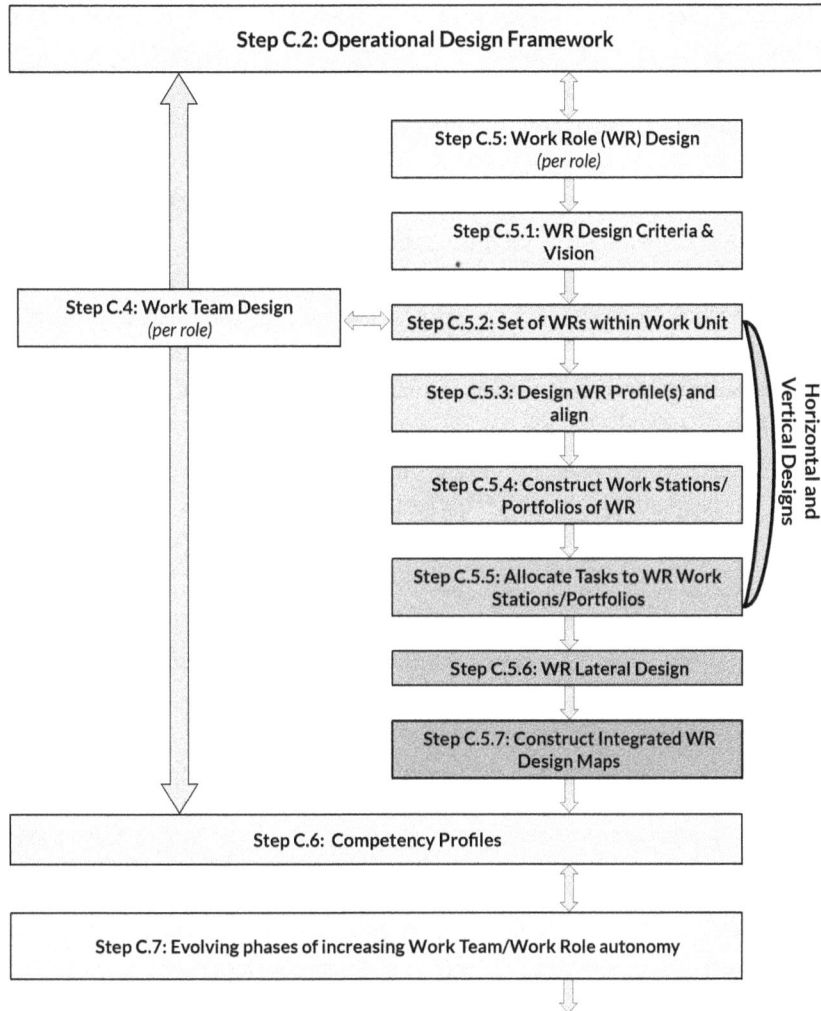

Figure 10.15: Overview of Work Role Design

Step C.5.1: Formulate Work Role Design Criteria and Vision

Similar to Work Team Design, the *first* Design Criterion to set is the Level of Work (LOW) of the Work Role to be designed (see Table 7.1). Is this a LOW5, LOW4, LOW3, LOW2 or LOW1 Work Role in combination with its Contextual Complexity? The 'ceiling' Total Complexity of the Work Role will be set by the LOWx Contextual Complexity = Total Complexity of the Work Unit to which the Work Role belongs.

The *second* source of Work Role Design Criteria is provided by the Operational Design Framework, whether more Mechanistic or Organic (see Step C.2). *Thirdly,* the characteristics of a high performance/ high engagement Work Role provide a handy complementary source from which further Work Role Design Criteria can be derived (see the shaded box entitled 'Work Engagement Indicators', Step C.2E: Design Outcomes).

The Work Unit Design Criteria and Vision, with the consequential Mode of Working selected for the Work Unit (see Step B.2: Tactical Horizontal Design), also play an important role in the selection of Work Role Design Criteria. By way of illustration, using a sport metaphor again: does the Work Unit aspire to work like an athletics, relay, soccer or volleyball team? As one moves from an athletics to a volleyball team mode of working, the interdependency of team members; their degree of multi-tasking and multi-skilling; the need for real time interaction; and the degree of shared goals increases. The selected Design Criteria and Vision must incorporate these features.

The normal conventions laid down for Design Criteria throughout the book apply: up to 10 prioritised Criteria; defining the Criteria; using the Criteria to choose between Work Role design options; and concretising the Criteria through their translation into a Role Design Vision, that is a 'Day in the Life' of performing the Work Role. In addition, finding an appropriate Design Metaphor.

Step C.5.2: Determine the set of Work Roles within the Work Unit

The aim of this design step is to identify the range of Work Roles required by the Work Unit under consideration, given its Mode of Operation, that is the grouping of the Core, Delivery Enabling and Support Processes into Work Roles. The set of Work Roles must cover in its totality all of the work to be performed within the Work Unit as contained in the work processes of the Work Unit.

The shaded box provides guidelines for the designing of distinct, meaningful Work Roles.

GUIDELINES FOR DESIGNING DISTINCT, MEANINGFUL WORK ROLES

A Work Role must:
- be pitched at the requisite Level of Work x Contextual Complexity Level;
- form a whole task that is meaningful and significant;
- have distinct boundaries;
- have not more than five Key Performance Areas and Critical Outcomes respectively;
- have its authority and responsibility matched;
- allow for continued growth and development;
- be pitched at the 'top end' of Role performance, which its incumbent will only be able to achieve after a sustained period of training, development and experience over time (usually only after two to three years); and
- be aligned to the Mode of Working of the Work Unit/Team, as expressed in its set Design Vision and Metaphor.
- as a set of Roles, cover all of the Work Unit's work.

Step C.5.3: Design a Work Role Profile for each Work Role identified, and align to the Operational Design Framework

The objective of this step is to architect a Work Role Profile for each Work Role identified. In other words, design the Work Role in terms of the set Work Role Design Criteria and Vision, aligned to the

Operational Design Framework.

The elements that make up a Work Role, with their descriptions, are given in Table 10.4. This table also provides basis for the template for a Work Role Profile (see Appendix B: Design Template 14).

Table 10.4: Work Role Profile

Element	Description
1. Work Context	Context in which the Work Role is embedded with its Contextual Complexity, the Design Givens (see Step C.1)
2. Core Purpose	Why does the Role exist?
3. Requisite Level of Work	What is the requisite Level of Work of the Role in terms of Total Complexity?
4. Scope of Work with Boundaries	What portion of the Core Work Process is the Role accountable for within what boundaries, that is authorisation levels, physical, safety, legal and ethical and/or time horizon?
5. Key Performance Areas (KPAs)	What are the major areas of delivery?
6. Critical Outcomes	What outputs must be delivered to what specifications?

7. Organisational Location	• Where is the Role located in the organisation as reflected in the organogram:
	
	   o Which Role does this Role report into?
	   o Which Roles report into this Role?
	   o With which Roles at the same level does the Role need to interact, that is peers?

The Work Role Profile (= Work Role Design) forms the ultimate, overall outcome of the Work Role, Operational Design Process. In the box below, an example is given of the Client Executive Role in the Fashion Design Unit of a global retail organisation (55).

ROLE PROFILE	CLIENT EXECUTIVE
1. **Work Context: Operating Arena with its requisite contextual complexity (CC)**	CC4 (out of a possible 5). Overall context: Multi-national retail organisation with locations in multiple countries with high regional/local autonomy and low global integration, operating within a 5 to 10 year time horizon with multiple but related markets/customers/products in a rapidly changing, relatively unpredictable global context. Role specific context: the Work Role forms part of the Fashion Design Unit (FDU) of the organisation, located at Group level.

ROLE PROFILE	CLIENT EXECUTIVE
2. Core Purpose	To provide tactical-operational leadership to the Client Team, aimed at satisfying client fashion needs, in alignment with the FDU's Strategy Intent of satisfying the fashion needs of the Group.
3. Requisite Level of Work	LOW3: Operational Execution. To specify and satisfy, within a roll forward 1 to 2 year time horizon, the fashion needs of clients within the Group as per market/customer and profitability requirements.
4. Scope of Work with boundaries	Client Need Specification and Delivery of the Fashion Design Value Chain (see below).

FASHION DESIGN VALUE CHAIN PROCESS

Client Need Specification → Client Solution Design → Client Delivery

1: Retailer Fashion Need for coming season

2: Strategic Fashion View for coming season (Trend booklet)
- Expected Trends
- Season predictions
- Strategic positioning
- Examples
- Accessories

3: Retailer Brief

4: High level Fashion design/mix for coming season
- Design by Categories
- Volumes
- Pricing

5: Retailer Go ahead

6: Detailed Fashion design/mix for coming season
- Designs by Categories
- Volumes
- Pricing

7: Retailer Approval = Need satisfied

Cycle of two months are repeated three times per year, starting one year ahead of season with 1st cycle most intense

| 5 Key Performance Areas (KPAs) | **KPA1: Craft and roll out a client engagement management plan and budget for the Client Serving Unit (CSU)**

1.1 Keep abreast of and act upon *leading client engagement practices and trends*.
1.2 Formulate and implement a *client recruitment and engagement plan* for the CSU within a two year roll forward time horizon, ensuring that the FDU has at all times a sustainable *client portfolio* of new and existing clients.
1.3 Generate an *annual business client sign-on and engagement plan with budget* for the CSU.
1.4 Engender Client Team *buy into and ownership* of all of the above.

KPA2: Design and implement a Client Serving Delivery Model for the Client Serving Unit

2.1 Craft and roll out an appropriate *Client Serving Delivery Model* for the CSU with clear roles, accountabilities, authorities and responsibilities.
2.2 Identify and install the required client onboarding/serving *policies, standards, processes and procedures*. |

ROLE PROFILE	CLIENT EXECUTIVE
5 Key Performance Areas (KPAs) (Continues)	2.3 Determine and acquire the necessary *systems and resources* for the CSU to function effectively ('doing the right things') and efficiently ('doing things right') in serving its clients. **KPA3: Lead the Client Serving Unit masterfully** 3.1 Build and maintain a *well-functioning, trust-based team*, able to meet its client service commitments timeously. 3.2 Provide *inspiring, ethical, caring and exemplary leadership* to the CSU team. 3.3 Instil in the CSU team a desire to live the *core values and philosophy* of the FDU and the business. 3.4 Seek out training and development opportunities to *continuously grow* the CSU team and self. **KPA4: Build constructive and healthy relationships with the stakeholders of the Client Serving Unit** 4.1 Build and maintain *effective, trust-based, long term relationships with CSU clients* – especially strategic clients – in the business, meeting and exceeding their needs and expectations proactively in the present and going into the future, and maximising business opportunities with them. 4.2 See and position the Unit within the *total Fashion Design Value Chain* of the FDU, particularly ensuring a effective working relationship with the Client Solution Design Team and acting as an effective interface between clients and this Unit. 4.3 Work co-operatively and constructively with *all other parts of the business* in order to synergistically achieve the overall goals of the business.
	KPA5: Monitor and track the performance of the Client Serving Unit 5.1 Set up a CSU *Performance Measurement Model* with necessary metrics and required information/data, with a particular focus on *client satisfaction*. 5.2 Generate regular, timeous CSU *Performance Intelligence and Reports* to monitor and track performance. 5.3 Take the *necessary actions to enhance CSU performance*, if and where necessary.
6. Critical Outcomes	Satisfied clients with the right fashions at the right time in the right locations at the right price, quality and quality, within a two year time horizon, giving them a competitive edge in their chosen markets.
7. Organisational Location	

ROLE PROFILE	CLIENT EXECUTIVE
7.1 Place in Organisational Structure	
7.2 Reports into	Fashion Unit Executive (LOW4: Strategic Development)
7.3 Reportees	Key Account Managers (LOW2: Operational Practices) Client Administrator (LOW1: Operational Delivery)
7.4 Interacts with	Solutions Executive (LOW3: Operational Execution)

Step C.5.4: Construct the Work Stations/Portfolios of the Key Performance Areas of the Work Role

The Key Performance Areas (= Work Role Themes) of a Work Role – Element 5 of the Work Role Profile (see Table 10.4) – can consist of one or more Work Stations/Portfolios. A Work Station/Portfolio is a coherent and congruent set (or grouping) of Tasks which have to be performed by a Role Incumbent with respect to a Key Performance Area (56).

Examples of such Work Stations/Portfolios can be seen in the sample Work Role Profile: Client Executive, given above in the box. One example was extracted and is given in the shaded box below.

KPA2: Design and implement a Client Serving Delivery Model for the Client Serving Unit

2.1   Craft and roll out an appropriate *Client Serving Delivery Model* for the CSU with clear roles, accountabilities, authorities and responsibilities.

2.2   Identify and install the required client onboarding/serving *policies, standards, processes and procedures.*

2.3   Determine and acquire the necessary *systems and resources* for the CSU to function effectively ('doing the right things') and efficiently ('doing things right') in serving its clients.

A Work Station/Portfolio is made up of the following elements as listed in the box.

ELEMENTS OF A WORK STATION/PORTFOLIO	
Element	**Description**
Core Purpose	Why does the Work Station/Portfolio exist?
Task Composition	Tasks making up Work Station/Portfolio (extracted from the total Work Unit Task Matrix) (see below)
Critical Outcomes	What outputs must be delivered to what specifications?

The shaded box provides guidelines for designing distinct, meaningful Work Stations/Portfolios.

GUIDELINES FOR DISTINCT, MEANINGFUL WORK STATIONS/PORTFOLIOS

A Work Station/Portfolio must:

- be a whole piece of work;
- have at least one key transformation centred around a focused competence/competency;
- form a coherent and congruent grouping of tasks that fit together;
- be aligned to the Mode of Working of the Work Unit/Team; and
- the sum total of the Work Stations/Portfolios must cover in total all of the tasks contained in the Task Matrix (see below) of the Work Unit.

Figure 10.16 depicts the above discussion graphically, and shows its relation to the Work Role Design Process flow (see Figure 10.15).

Step C.5.3	Team 1.....Team n Level of Work					
	Work Role 1 Key Performance Areas		Work Role 2 Key Performance Areas		Work Role 3 Key Performance Areas	Work Role n Key Performance Areas
Step C.5.4	Work Portfolio 1	Work Portfolio 2	Work Portfolio 3	Work Portfolio 4	Work Portfolio 5	Work Portfolio 6
Task 1	x					
Task 2	x					
Task 3		x				
Task 4			x			
Task 5		x				
Task 6				x		
Task 7						x
Task 8					x	
Task 9						x
Task n					x	

Step C.4 appears in the header. *Step C.5.5* label appears to the left of the matrix. "Task Matrix" label appears vertically on the right side.

Figure 10.16: Work Role Design in terms of Work Portfolios* with their associated Tasks
Note: Read also 'Work Station'

The shaded box provides guidelines for designing distinct, meaningful Work Stations/Portfolios.

GUIDELINES FOR DESIGNING DISTINCT, MEANINGFUL WORK STATIONS/PORTFOLIOS

A Work Station/Portfolio must:

- be a whole piece of work;
- have at least one key transformation centred around a focused competence/competency;
- form a coherent and congruent grouping of tasks that fit together;
- be aligned to the Mode of Working of the Work Unit/Team; and
- the sum total of the Work Stations/Portfolios must cover in total all of the tasks contained in the Task Matrix of the Work Unit.

Step C.5.5: Allocate Tasks to Work Stations/Portfolios of Work Roles

The Task Matrix of a Work Unit is made up of *all* of the Tasks to be performed within the Work Unit (57), or within the Work Teams making up the Work Unit. Works Stations/Portfolios, and consequently the Key Performance Areas for a specific Work Role, are to be constructed using the Task Matrix as the reference source of *all* of the Tasks to be performed in the Work Unit. All the Work Unit Tasks have to be incorporated into the Work Roles of the Unit. From a design perspective, a Task refers to 'what' needs to be done, not 'how' it is to be done.

At the Work Station/Portfolio level, one of two basic Work Role design approaches can be followed:

- *Approach 1: Work Stations/Portfolios only.* The design approach terminates with the architecting of the Works Stations/Portfolios making up the Key Performance Areas of a Work Role, and do not unpack further the specific Tasks associated with each Works Station/Portfolio (in terms of Figure 10.16, this design approach only includes Step C.5.4).

  The strength of this approach is that because the Work Role Profile is more high level, it does not become so quickly outdated because of changes at the Task-level of the Profile. It also provides the role incumbent with the autonomy to craft the specifics of his Work Role, as and when required. The weaknesses of this approach are that it may not always be clear what specific Tasks are included in a Work Station/Portfolio; the time demands of a Work Station/Portfolio are at best guestimates; and Work Unit Tasks may be missed and thus not allocated.

- *Approach 2: Work Stations/Portfolios with associated Tasks.* The Tasks making up each Work Station/Portfolio are unpacked (in terms of Figure 10.16, Steps C.5.4 and C.5.5). The strength of this approach is that because the Work Role Profile is done in detail, the make-up of a Work Station/Portfolio is very clear task-wise in terms of boundary demarcation, time demands, performance contracting purposes, and training and development requirements.

  In turn, one of two sub-approaches are possible with respect to Approach 2:

  - *Sub-approach 2.1: Top Down* (Step C.5.4 to Step C.5.5, see Figure 10.16). The Tasks per Work Station/Portfolio are unpacked using the relevant Task and Action Dimensions of the Task Matrix (discussed below). The choice of Dimensions is dependent on whether a Mechanistic or Organic Work Role Design is pursued (also discussed below). The strength of this approach is that it is more focused; provides more coherent Work Stations/Portfolios; and is somewhat faster.
  - *Sub-approach 2.2: Bottom Up* (Step C.5.5 to Step C.5.4, see Figure 10.16). One starts with the Task Repertoire of the Work Unit, and then groups Tasks into logical Work Stations/Portfolios across Work Roles. The strength of this approach is that Tasks reflect what needs to be done and dictates the logic of Works Stations/Portfolios. However, it is much more time consuming in arriving at a logical Work Station/Portfolio.

From practical experience, my own preferred approach is Approach 1 (first choice) or Sub-approach 2.1, for the reasons given above.

Step C.5.5.1: Construct the Task Matrix of a Work Unit

A Task Matrix is constructed around a Task Classification Framework. The suggested Task Classification Framework consists of:

- *Operating Tasks:* Action Dimensions (Breadth) x Task Dimensions (Depth); and

- *Leadership Tasks:* Action Dimensions (Breadth) x Task Dimensions (Depth).

Table 10.5 provides a suggested Task Classification Framework in terms of which the Task Matrix of a Work Unit can be structured, with examples of LOW1/LOW2 Tasks *(58)* (59). A complete Task Matrix of a Work Unit must, of course, cover all the LOWs contained in a Work Unit, in separate LOW-based Task Repertoires.

Table 10.5: Task Matrix, populated by LOW1/LOW2 Tasks

			ACTION DIMENSIONS (Breadth of Task Matrix Coverage)				
			Do Executing task at hand	**Conceive and Plan** What is to be achieved by when, by whom, with what, at what costs and returns	**Organise and Co-ordinate** Having the right things at the right time, in the right place with the right people ready for action	**Track and Monitor** Measuring what is being/ has been achieved	**Change** Improving ways in which things get done
OPERATING TASKS	TASK DIMENSIONS *(Depth of Task Matrix Coverage)*	**Inputs from Suppliers**	Acquire stock	Draft stock plan	Generate stock ordering schedule	Exercise stock control	Change stock requirements
			Monitor staffing levels	Determine staffing needs	Organise recruitment drive	Monitor staffing levels	Change staff profile
		Work Processes: Core	Produce products/ service	Do production scheduling	Allocate work and resources	Monitor key process indices	Adjust production process
		Work Processes: Enabling/ Support	Generate reports and take action	Define information needs	Determine appropriate methods of satisfying information needs	Assess utility of reports	Redefine information needs
			Do maintenance	Draft maintenance plan	Roll out maintenance plan	Track roll out of maintenance plan	Change maintenance approach, for example, from planned to preventive

		Output to Clients	Attend customer contact meetings	Set objectives to meet customer requirements	Set up customer contact schedule	Track sales Determine customer satisfaction levels Monitor inventory	Respond to redefined customer requirements
		Context	Assist other teams in organisation	Plan participation in organisation-wide forums	Allocate participants in forums Participate in forums	Monitoring of events in organisation	Suggest changes in forums
		ACTION DIMENSIONS *(Breadth of Task Matrix Coverage)*					
LEADERSHIP TASKS			***Do*** Executing a particular leadership task	***Coach*** Helping/assisting others to perform a leadership tasks	***(Re)Design and Build*** Generating Work Unit systems/procedures through leadership tasks can be executed in a standardised, formalised way	***Link and Mediate*** Liaising with stakeholders and key role players at the Team/Unit organisational context interface	***Envision and Embed Values*** Building and communicating a desired future state, and mobilising team members around that state
	TASK DIMENSIONS ***(Depth of Task Matrix Coverage)***	***Enablement:*** Providing the wherewithal to get the task done Build rapport	Do across organisational collaboration	Design customer interface forums and processes	Coach on liaison roles fulfilled by team members	Do mediation with stakeholder Arbitration Build customer/supplier focus	Do mission and vision, translation and communication Be a role model

361

		Internal Empowerment: Reduction of Task Uncertainty	Set goals Set standards	Build work execution process Build team work systems and procedures	Coach on performance enhancement Facilitate trouble shooting Assist with problem solving Coach on conflict resolution	Acquire required work resources	Define core team task Define world class competitive Criteria
		External Empowerment: Reduction of Contextual Uncertainty	Develop team members	Design manpower planning system	Provide guidance on team development	Provide T & D resources	Set T & D priorities

Using the Task Matrix given in Table 10.5 as a reference, the shaded box provides descriptions of some common terms used regarding Operational Design (read 'Work' or 'Job Design') (60).

COMMON OPERATIONAL DESIGN TERMS USED REGARDING THE TASK MATRIX

- *Job enlargement:* Making a Job (= Work Role) 'bigger' by covering more Tasks that are similar 'horizontally', usually across the Action Category of the Task Matrix Dimension of Breadth. For example, regarding the Core Work Process, not only a single Doing Task, but adding more Doing Tasks as well as Conceiving and Planning Tasks, or Tracking and Monitoring Tasks.

- *Job Enrichment:* Making a Job (= Work Role) 'more demanding' by covering more Tasks 'vertically', usually by adding 'deeper' Operating Tasks (for example, Inputs from Suppliers; Output to Clients) and/or Leadership Tasks (for example, Enablement).

- *Multi-Tasking:* Being able to do more of the same Tasks for similar types of Roles from one Discipline, for example, Operating Tasks, to enable more flexible deployment of a person. In this sense, multi-tasking is similar to Job Enlargement.

- *Multi-skilling:* Being able to do Tasks from different types of Roles from different Disciplines, for example, Operations, Supply Chain, Maintenance, Operating Tasks, to enable the more flexible deployment of a person across Work Domains.

Design Templates for the Task Matrices of Operating and Leadership Tasks respectively are given in Appendix B: Design Templates 15 and 16.

The shaded box provides guidelines regarding populating the Task Matrix with Tasks.

GUIDELINES ON TASKS MAKING UP A TASK MATRIX

- Focus on 'what' not 'how'.
- Stick to a 'high level' 'what'.
- Write in action form, that is 'Order stock'.
- Be short and to the point, but clear and specific, that is 'Do maintenance on machines A, B and C'.
- The Operating Tasks Map must match the scope of the Work Unit as given by its Purpose and boundaries.
- *All* Tasks required by the future desired, *final* state of the Work Unit must be included.
- To keep track of Tasks, a task numbering system can be devised.

Step C.5.5.2: Determine the Time Work Loading of each Task

For *each* Task, its *Frequency* by *Time Unit* (daily/weekly/monthly/yearly) = *Total Time required per year* must be determined. In turn, the Total Time – summated across all Task times – must be determined *per* Work Station/Portfolio, in turn totalled *across* Work Stations/Portfolios, to give the total time required to perform the Work Role as a whole.

In sum total, Work Stations/Portfolios in terms of time must not make up more than between 80%-85% of the total time of a Work Role to allow for unexpected/unplanned work and/or crises, and provide time to try out new/different things.

Quality assurance: Task Matrix

QUALITY ASSURANCE QUESTIONS

OPERATING TASK MATRIX

- Is the focus on Tasks (= what), as opposed to activities (= how)?

- Is the Task Matrix complete across the full range of Action Dimensions – Do; Conceive and Plan; Organise and Co-ordinate; Track and Monitor; Change – in terms of:

  - input tasks to suppliers;
  - core business process tasks;
  - support process tasks; and
  - output tasks to customers.

- Have Tasks been defined relating to policies, procedures and regulatory/compliance requirements for the wider organisational context?

- Have the duration and frequency of each Task been determined?

- Are all the Tasks listed which are relevant to the future, desired Work Unit?

- Do all of the Tasks identified add value?

LEADERSHIP TASK MATRIX

- Have all the Tasks across the full range of the Action Dimensions – Do; Coach; (re)Design and Build; Link and Mediate; Envisions and Embed Values – been covered for:

  o Enablement;
  o Empowerment: Task Uncertainty; and
  o Empowerment: Contextual Uncertainty?

- Has the duration and frequency of Tasks been determined?

- Are the Leadership Tasks aligned to the Mode of Working of the future desired Work Unit/Team?

- Do all of the Tasks identified add value?

Step C.5.5.3: Architect Work Role Designs: Mechanistic to Organic

In terms of Figure 10.2, as the Operational Design Framework (Step C.2) shifts more from a Mechanistic to an Organic Operational Design, the Work Stations/Portfolios of a Work Role move to a greater depth and breadth coverage in terms of both Operating and Leadership Tasks. Simply put, an Organic Work Role covers more of the Task and Action Dimensions – in depth and breadth – given in Table 10.5, as guided by the Operational Design Criteria listed in Table 10.1. Tables 10.5 to 10.8 provide examples of the shift in the construction of Task Matrices from Highly Mechanistic to Fully Organic Work Roles, as reflected in task coverage.

According to Table 10.6, this Work Role solely contains the Doing of Operating Tasks related to the Core Work Process, and represents the 100% Operator Work Role.

Table 10.6: Highly Mechanistic Work Role: 100% Operator Work Role

			ACTION DIMENSIONS *(Breadth of Task Matrix Coverage)*
OPERATING TASKS	**TASK DIMENSIONS** *(Depth of Task Matrix Coverage)*	***Work Processes: Core***	**Do** Executing task at hand

According to Table 10.7, this is the Work Role of the relatively autonomous Operator in which Operating Tasks have been expanded to include a logical, holistic, collection of Tasks, both in terms of:

- Task Dimension (Inputs from Suppliers; Core Work Process; and Output to Customers); and

- Action Dimension (Do, Organise and Co-ordinate; and Track and Monitor).

Table 10.7: Mixed Mechanistic/Organic Work Role: Relatively autonomous Operator

			ACTION DIMENSIONS (Breadth of Task Matrix Coverage)		
			Do Executing task at hand	**Organise and Co-ordinate** Having the right things at the right time, in the right place with the right people ready for action	**Track and Monitor** Measuring what is being/has been achieved
OPERATING TASKS	**TASK DIMENSIONS** *(Depth of Task Matrix Coverage)*	*Inputs from Suppliers*			
		Work Processes: Core			
		Output to Clients			

According to Table 10.8, this is the Work Role of the leadership empowered, self-managing Operator, in which:

- the Operating Tasks include a full set of Tasks containing both the Action and Task Dimensions;
- some Leadership Tasks with respect to the Action Dimension (Do; Link and Mediate) and Task Dimension (Enablement).

Table 10.8: Highly Organic Work Role: Leadership empowered, self-managing Operator

			ACTION DIMENSIONS (Breadth of Task Matrix Coverage)				
			Do Executing task at hand	**Conceive and Plan** What is to be achieved by when, by whom, with what, at what costs and returns	**Organise and Co-ordinate** Having the right things at the right time, in the right place with the right people ready for action	**Track and Monitor** Measuring what is being/ has been achieved	**Change** Improving the way in which things get done
OPERATING TASKS	**TASK DIMENSIONS** *(Depth of Task Matrix Coverage)*	*Inputs from Suppliers*					
		Work Processes: Core					
		Work Processes: Enabling/ Support					
		Output to Clients					
		Context					

			ACTION DIMENSIONS *(Breadth of Task Matrix Coverage)*	
			Do Executing a particular leadership task	**Link and Mediate** Liaising with stakeholders and key role players at the team-/unit -organisational context interface
LEADERSHIP TASKS	*TASK DIMENSIONS (Depth of Task Matrix Coverage)*	*Enablement:* Providing the wherewithal to get the task done		

Fully Organic Work Role: Self-designing/governing – Leaderless Work Unit/Work Team

In this case, the *complete* Task Matrix – as per Table 10.5 – is built into the Work Role by selecting a logical, holistic grouping of tasks across the Matrix as guided by the chosen Design Criteria. The Leadership Tasks are not grouped into separate Leadership Work Role(s), but form an inherent part of the 'Operating' Team Work Roles.

Step C.5.5.4: Compile an expanded view of Work Role Design in terms of Work Stations/Portfolios with their constructed Task Matrices: Task Map of Work Role

Table 10.9 provides an expansion on Figure 10.16 by incorporating the above discussion of the generic Task Matrix. Additionally, consider in its construction different permutations of the Matrix, dependent on how Mechanistic or Organic the Work Role Design is. Table 10.9 provides a handy basis for the template of the Work Role Task Map (see Appendix B: Design Template 17). This map forms an appendix to the complete Work Role Design (see Table 10.4).

Table 10.9: Work Role Task Map per Key Performance Areas

WORK TEAM:				
WORK ROLE:				
	KEY PERFORMANCE AREA 1		**KEY PERFORMANCE AREA....n**	
	Action Dimensions 1 to n	**Task Dimensions 1 to n**	**Action Dimensions 1 to n**	**Task Dimensions 1 to n**
Operating Tasks 1 to n	*By Action Dimension and Operating Task* • Task 1 with time demand • Task 2 with time demand .... • Task n with time demand	*By Action Dimension and Operating Task* • Task 1 with time demand • Task 2 with time demand .... • Task n with time demand	*By Action Dimension and Operating Task* • Task 1 with time demand • Task 2 with time demand .... • Task n with time demand	*By Action Dimension and Operating Task* • Task 1 with time demand • Task 2 with time demand .... • Task n with time demand
Leadership Tasks 1 to n	*By Action Dimension and Operating Task* • Task 1 with time demand • Task 2 with time demand .... • Task n with time demand	*By Action Dimension and Operating Task* • Task 1 with time demand • Task 2 with time demand .... • Task n with time demand	*By Action Dimension and Operating Task* • Task 1 with time demand • Task 2 with time demand .... • Task n with time demand	*By Action Dimension and Operating Task* • Task 1 with time demand • Task 2 with time demand .... • Task n with time demand
TOTAL TIME				

Step C.5.6: Lateral Work Role Design

In the case of a Work Unit populated by only Work Roles, the Lateral Design of the Work Unit in terms of an Interdependency Matrix, Integration Mechanisms, and the Governance Model of the Work Unit have to be architected (for more detail, see Strategic Design Step A.4.2 in Chapter 7). Where Work Roles are embedded in Work Teams, making up the Work Unit, the Lateral Design of the Work Team concerned will be applicable (see Step C.4.4.3 above).

Step C.5.7: Construct Integrated Work Role Design Maps

By Work Role designed, (i) the output from Step C.5.5.4 provides an Integrated Work Role Design Map: Work Role Profiles (with Task Maps appended); and (ii) the output of Step C.5.6 provides the portfolio of Work Roles of the Work Unit – the Lateral Role Design: Integration Mechanisms and Governance Model. Altogether, these outcomes form the basis to construct Integrated Work Role Design Maps for the Work Roles architected.

Step C.6: Generate Competency Profiles

The Work Team(s) and Work Roles have been architected (that is Steps C.4 and C.5, Figure 10.1). Next, the competency profiles for the Work Team(s) and Work Roles have to be determined. Figure 10.17 depicts a suggested Competency Map made up of different Ability Domains. Table 10.10 provides definitions of the Domains with their associated Ability Elements (61).

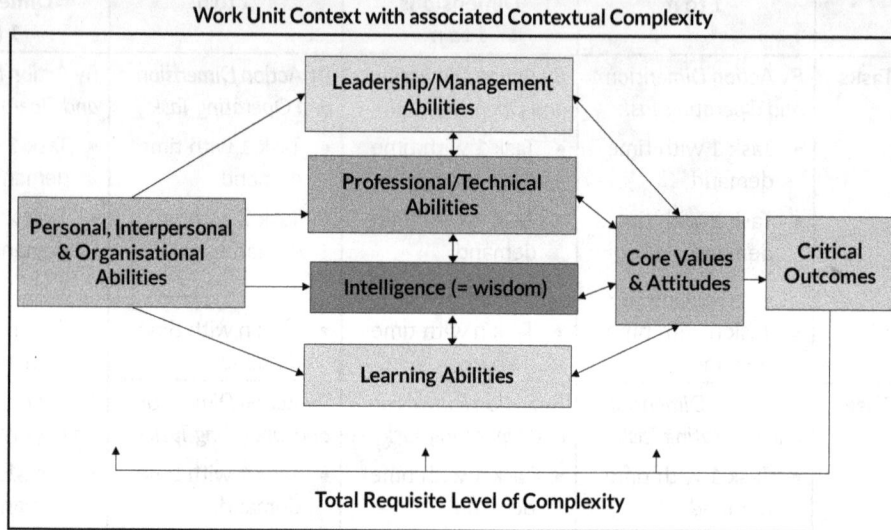

Work Unit Context with associated Contextual Complexity

Figure 10.17: Suggested Competency Map

Table 10.10: Definitions of the Ability Domains with their associated Ability Elements

ABILITY DOMAIN	DEFINITION	ABILITY ELEMENT
Personal, Interpersonal and Organisational Abilities	Ability to manage oneself and one's interpersonal relationships successfully, and function effectively in an organisational setting	**Personal Attributes,** for example, Self-awareness; Integrity; Adaptability/Flexibility/Agility/Responsiveness **Personal Abilities,** for example, Conceptual; Decision-making/Problem solving; Drive **Interpersonal Abilities,** for example, Persuasiveness; Trustworthiness; Empathy; Communication **Organisational Abilities,** for example, Teaming; Cross-functionality; Organisational networking, lobbying and coalition forming; Political savviness; Diversity sensitivity

ABILITY DOMAIN	DEFINITION	ABILITY ELEMENT
Leadership/ Managerial Abilities	Ability to develop and mobilise people around a shared vision and values, and lead people towards actualising the vision and living the values	**Transactional leadership competencies**: ability to enhance, maintain and improve existing – Operational Excellence (How) **Transformational leadership competencies**: ability to change existing into something new and/or bring something new into being – Envisioning (What) **Transcendental leadership abilities**: ability to instill a sense of meaning and purpose – Legacy (Why)
Technical/ Professional Abilities	Ability to apply knowledge, skills, expertise, experience (KSEE) appropriately within the complexity of the setting	**Sector KSEE** **Discipline KSEE** **Role specific KSEE**
Intelligence (= Wisdom)	Ability to know what and how to do things, with whom, at what time and in what way	**Personal and Interpersonal Intelligence (including Emotional Intelligence)** A resilient, well crystallised, authentic Identity: who and what am I; what I stand for; how I relate to and impact others, and how I build genuine relationships with them; what I aspire to; and in what way and with what style I want to realise my aspirations **Systemic Intelligence (including Cognitive Intelligence)** 'Big picture' thinking and insight, in the present and going into the future **Ideation Intelligence (including Spiritual Intelligence)** Able to conceive increasingly more daring and inspiring dreams (= ideas) about different/new futures, purposes, meanings **Action Intelligence** Able to bring about lasting, meaningful change **Contextual Intelligence (including [Trans] Cultural Intelligence)** Able to engage constructively – at the requisite level of complexity – with the Operating Arena, in the present and going into the future

ABILITY DOMAIN	DEFINITION	ABILITY ELEMENT
Learning Abilities	Ability to learn new things and use learning effectively by changing oneself and the setting in which one operates	**Learning the ropes**: the ability to grasp how things work and interrelate **Learning how to perform**: the ability to be streetwise about how to produce results in a given setting **Learning through redesigning**: the ability to change processes and resources in order to reach desired outcomes more efficiently ('Doing things right') **Learning through reframing**: the ability to reflect upon and change values, beliefs, assumptions and norms in order to create new frames of reference (or paradigms) ('Doing the right and/or different things') **Learning about learning**: the ability to gain deeper insight into how one learns personally, how client systems learn, and how to enhance learning processes
Core Values and Attitudes	What is right, important and good	

Based on the above Competency Map (see Figure 10.17), the box below provides an excerpt from the Competency Profile of a Director-General of a National Department within the South African Public Sector (62).

LEVEL OF WORK	DEPARTMENT EQUIVALENT POSITIONS	PERSONAL, INTERPERSONAL, AND ORGANISATIONAL ABILITIES Ability to manage oneself and one's interpersonal relationships successfully, and function effectively in an organisational setting	LEADERSHIP/MANAGERIAL ABILITIES Ability to develop and mobilise people around a shared vision and values, and lead people towards actualising the vision and living the values

5: Strategic Formulation (SF)
Establish and implement a Strategic Intent within a five year time horizon for the Department relative to its mandate, which is able to sustain the Department as a viable, value-generation entity
	Director-General	**Personal Abilities**
		
		• **Conceptual**
		  o Able to think holistically and systemically in a proactive manner with regard to the Department
		  o Able to think critically and out of the box from a long term perspective
			Transcendental Leadership
			
			• Able to lead by giving purpose and meaning to what needs to be done
			• Ensure the Department leaves behind a lasting, worthy legacy

LEVEL OF WORK	DEPARTMENT EQUIVALENT POSITIONS	PERSONAL, INTERPERSONAL, AND ORGANISATIONAL ABILITIES Ability to manage oneself and one's interpersonal relationships successfully, and function effectively in an organisational setting	LEADERSHIP/MANAGERIAL ABILITIES Ability to develop and mobilise people around a shared vision and values, and lead people towards actualising the vision and living the values

5: Strategic Formulation (SF)
Establish and implement a Strategic Intent within a five year time horizon for the Department relative to its mandate, which is able to sustain the Department as a viable, value-generation entity
(Continued)
	Director-General	**Decision-making/Problem solving**
		
		  o Able to search and find relevant information, and assess and use such knowledge gained, to arrive at reasoned departmental decisions in a complex context
		  o Demonstrates a deep institutional memory about the Information and Communication Technology Sector and Department
		  o Able to display sound departmental judgement and decisive decision-making within the relevant windows of opportunity, based on good intelligence
		
		• **Personal Attributes**
		
		  o Act ethically with integrity and consistency
		  o Display creativity, resilience and perseverance
		  o Able to respond quickly and effectively to change whilst maintaining personal and work effectiveness
		  o Able to live with uncertainty and unpredictability, taking calculated risks
		  o Able to achieve results, regardless of circumstances
		
		• **Interpersonal Abilities**
		
		  o Is aware of impact of own behaviours and actions on others and on self
		  o Keeps promises
		  o Able to create a positive impression and command respect
		  o Able to communicate well and actively listen
		  o Display empathy and care for others, treating them with respect and dignity
		  o Able to understand and accommodate other persons' concerns, values, needs and attitudes relative to the Department's direction, challenges and priorities
			Transformational Leadership
			
			• Develop a mission, inspiring vision, and values for the Department within its mandate
			• Mobilise total Department around vision, mission and values
			• Identify necessary strategic initiatives to actualise mission vision, and obtain Department-wide buy-in for these initiatives
			• Model the way in actualising the mission and vision
			• Able to represent the Department at government and industry levels effectively and with authority
			
			Transactional Leadership
			
			• Able to build and sustain a high performance, inclusive organisational culture, and a positive, supportive organisational climate in the Department

LEVEL OF WORK	DEPARTMENT EQUIVALENT POSITIONS	PERSONAL, INTERPERSONAL, AND ORGANISATIONAL ABILITIES Ability to manage oneself and one's interpersonal relationships successfully, and function effectively in an organisational setting	LEADERSHIP/MANAGERIAL ABILITIES Ability to develop and mobilise people around a shared vision and values, and lead people towards actualising the vision and living the values
		o Able to create, on an ongoing basis, opportunities for others to learn, develop, and sustain their well-being • **Organisational Abilities** o Able to work cross-functionally and cross-departmentally with ease o Able to build sound stakeholder relationships, engendering sustainable goodwill for the Department and balancing diverse interests in a fair and equitable manner o Demonstrates strong networking, lobbying, and coalition forming abilities to the benefit of the Department o Able to do effective departmental contextual scanning o Ability to assess and handle multiple departmental demands and shifting priorities in an ever changing context, and adjust personal behaviour accordingly	

A Competency-based Design: The Professional Maturity Growth Curve Design

Knowledge is the fuel of the knowledge economy. As discussed in Chapter 2, 85% plus of the assets in the knowledge economy are intangible. It was argued that 70% of the intangible assets of the knowledge economy are resident in people in the form of their creativity, knowledge, expertise, abilities and experience.

Knowledge generation, dissemination and/or application is the particular province of Professional Specialists, like Engineering, Information and Communication Technology, Legal, Human Resource, Financial, Marketing, Research and Development, and Corporate Affairs Specialists, whether employed by an organisation in an enabling role; being in an outside professional services organisation; or being in private practice. As pre-eminent knowledge workers, these Professional Specialists are at the centre of the knowledge economy. Within the employment relationship, the power has shifted from the employer to these knowledge workers because they are the originators, owners, disseminators, and users of knowledge.

Ongoing personal professional growth – and the recognition of such growth through a higher professional status – is a key driver to continued, enhanced performance by professionals. Key to a true professional is the enhanced ability to handle increasing levels of more complex professional assignments individually, requiring higher levels of professional problem-solving and decision-making in more complex settings, relative to more 'wicked' challenges, issues and problems. This continual professional growth makes a significant contribution to the organisation's/department's continued and enhanced performance and success. Under these circumstances a hierarchical Organisational Design with a fixed number of positions – where upward movement is dependent on resignations, promotions, retirement, death or illness – is demotivating and constraining to the continued growth of professionals.

The Professional Maturity Growth Curve Design is frequently used for organisations/departments that are made up of autonomous professionals who render professional services to clients within and/or outside the organisation (63). Within a job family, the Work Role (= Competence Level) of a person is determined in terms of a professional maturity curve based on the complexity level of work that a person can competently, consistently and predictably handle. The professional maturity growth curve plots – from low to high – the different Professional Work Roles (= levels of competence) of increasing complexity that an individual can perform at on the curve. A person attains a position on the curve based on concrete evidence of his/her demonstrable competence in a Work Role located on the curve.

There are no fixed number of incumbents for a given Work Role on the curve. Once a person has demonstrated his/her competence to perform and contribute at the required level for a next Work Role (= competence) on the curve consistently and predictably, he/she is promoted to that level with its commensurate rewards and benefits. Work Roles are designed and placed on the curve to take an average of three to four years to reach, although a person moves at his/her own rate and may reach a next level more quickly. Figure 10.18 graphically depicts the above discussion.

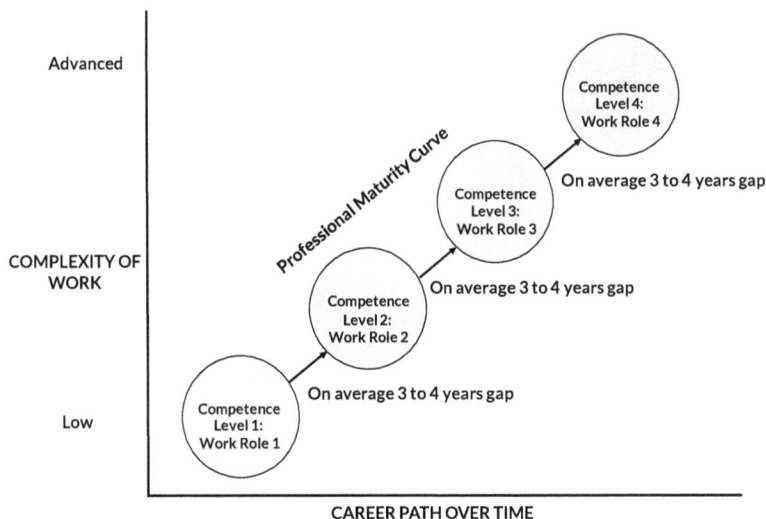

Figure 10.18: Professional Maturity Growth Curve Design

The competency profile of a Work Role on the curve consists of different competency domains which can be made up of, for example, (i) professional/technical competencies based on current and expected future client needs; (ii) client management competencies; (iii) personal, interpersonal and organisational competencies; (iv) business acumen; and (v) leadership/managerial competencies (see also the Competency Map, given in Figure 10.17).

A further strength of the Professional Maturity Growth Curve Design is that of the possibility of a dual career hierarchy. The professional maturity growth curve accommodates an initial, single career professional path up to the point where it splits into two further career paths:

- Path 1: A *leadership/management career path* for those aspiring and able to move into management; and

- Path 2: A *professional path* for those aspiring to become an advanced professional guru.

The dual career hierarchy prevents an outstanding professional – with little ability and/or inclination for leadership/management – from moving into a management role merely to gain more status, responsibility and/or remuneration. Figure 10.19 illustrates this design graphically.

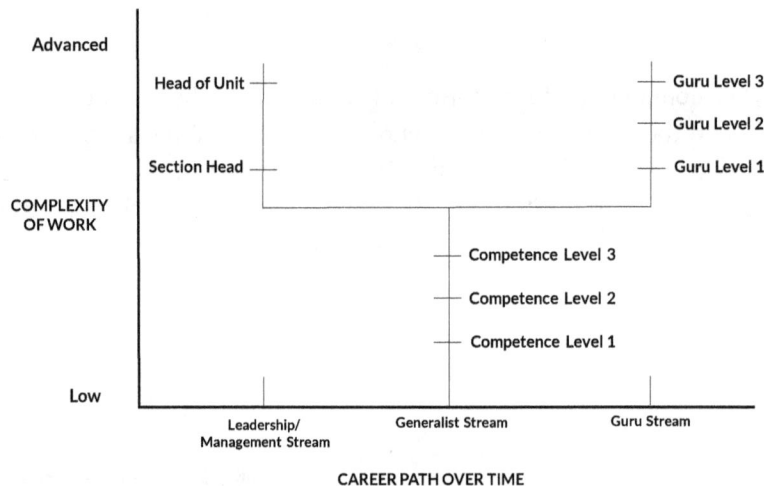

Figure 10.19: Dual Career Hierarchy, Professional Career Growth Curve

Professional support staff could also be placed on a support maturity curve, the top of which could be a bridging para-professional position to put the person on the bottom of the full blown professional curve. Otherwise, the support person would stay and move only on the support curve.

In the shaded box, a case study of a dual career hierarchy design is given for the Legal Department of an organisation (64).

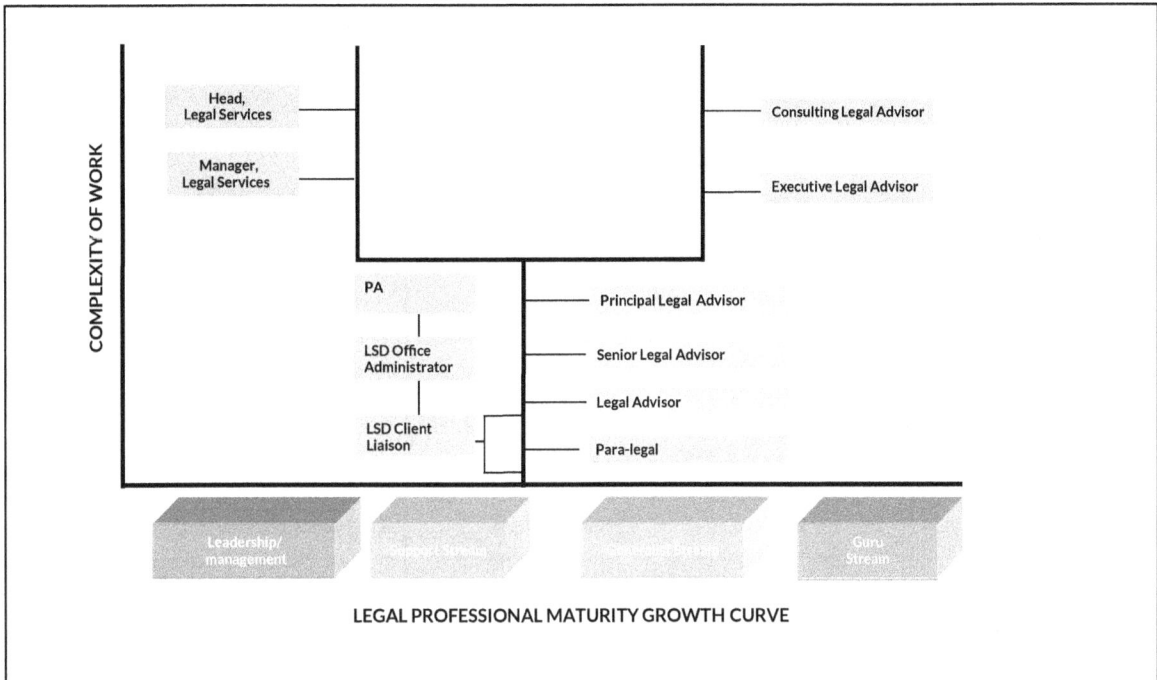

Head,
Legal Services

Manager,
Legal Services

Consulting Legal Advisor

Executive Legal Advisor

PA

LSD Office
Administrator

LSD Client
Liaison

Principal Legal Advisor

Senior Legal Advisor

Legal Advisor

Para-legal

COMPLEXITY OF WORK

Leadership/
management

Guru
Stream

LEGAL PROFESSIONAL MATURITY GROWTH CURVE

For a Professional Maturity Growth Curve Design to be successful, the following enabling processes/ systems must be in place:

- The competency requirements of the organisation/department, now and in the future, must be placed along a growth curve with its staffing model.

- An impartial, objective assessment process to place people on the curve.

- A robust performance contracting and appraisal process as a key lever for a move along the curve.

- Robust personal development plans.

- Ongoing mentoring and coaching processes.

- Well communicated, clear career paths, concurrently providing people with career navigation skills.

- Strong talent planning and growth processes, like ongoing learning and development opportunities.

Table 10.11 gives the applicability, strengths and weaknesses of the Professional Growth Curve Design.

Table 10.11: Applicability, strengths and weaknesses of the Professional Growth Curve Design

ORGANISATIONAL SHAPE: PROFESSIONAL GROWTH CURVE DESIGN	APPLICABILITY	STRENGTHS	WEAKNESSES
Grouping activities along a curve of increasing complexity, requiring higher levels of competence, allowing persons to progress along the curve as and when they provide concrete evidence of their ability to perform at a next level of competence, consistently and predictably	• Need to enhance the ability of professionals to handle increasing levels of more complex assignments, in this way growing professionally and adding more value • Strong inherent drive for personal growth exists • Areas rich in intellectual capital	• Capitalises on personal desire to grow professionally and better oneself • Make existing organisational members more valuable as they progress along curve • Spontaneous maintenance and enrichment of intellectual capital of organisation • Number of people occupying the respective competence levels on curve not limited	• Unrealistic expectations amongst organisational members regarding the rate at which they can progress along the curve • Finding the right balance between technical/professional competencies and personal/interpersonal/ organisational competencies along the professional maturity curve • Unrealistic expectations and demands by organisational members regarding unlimited investment in ongoing learning development and mentoring/ coaching activities • Unfounded, critical questioning of the fairness, objectivity and impartiality of the assessment of the attained/ demonstrated level of competence • Overcrowding at the top of the curve if the competence hurdles are too low, allowing people to get too easily to the top of the curve

The quality assurance questions for a Work Role Design are given at the end of this chapter.

Step C.7: Construct Evolving Phases of increasing Work Team/ Work Role autonomy

The final Operational Design decision is whether to build into the Work Team/Work Role the increasing freedom to take independent action from the leadership/management of a Work Unit/Team. Put differently: will a Work Team/Work Role incumbent have increasing autonomy over the tasks they are responsible for? Will the level of involvement – expressed in autonomy – evolve? In the VICCAS world, increasing levels of agility, responsiveness and flexibility at the coal face where delivery takes place have become critical. For simplicity sake, the focus is in the discussion below, on increasing Work Team autonomy (65). The same principles apply to increasing Work Role autonomy, which is not discussed.

Five levels of autonomy, from the vantage point of involvement by the Work Team and its members, can be distinguished (66):

- **Involvement through Tell/Sell – 0% autonomy to Work Team**

  The Work Unit/Team Leader has complete responsibility for the Work Domain, makes all decisions, and merely informs team members accordingly. The Team acts only when directed.

- **Involvement through Consultation – 25% autonomy to Work Team**

  The Work Unit/Team Leader makes the decisions, but invites comments from team members on those. Or, team members have the opportunity to offer suggestions on matters of concern to them, but the Work Unit/Team Leader retains the discretion to accept or reject such suggestions. The Team only acts after having been consulted on the course of action to take.

- **Involvement through Co-determination – equal levels of autonomy: 50%/50%**

  The Work Unit/Team Leader and team members make decisions jointly on important matters/tasks. The Team only acts once a course of action decision has been agreed on jointly.

- **Involvement through Self-management (= Upward Consultation) – 75% level of autonomy to Work Team**

  The Team has a full say in matters within their Work Domain within laid down policy/procedural guidelines, but consults with the Work Unit/Team Leader on intended decisions/actions. The Work Unit/Team Leader still remains accountable, and the Team acts only after having consulted with all relevant parties.

- **Involvement through Self-government (= Upward Tell/Sell) – 100% autonomy to Work Team**

  The Team has a full say in all respects within their Work Domain, as well as the context of the Domain. The Team is free to make decisions in whatever way it wishes within policy guidelines. The leadership tasks within the Team have been fully taken over by the team. No formal Work Unit/Team Leader Role exists. The team acts, and then informs the relevant parties.

Figure 10.20 illustrates the above discussion.

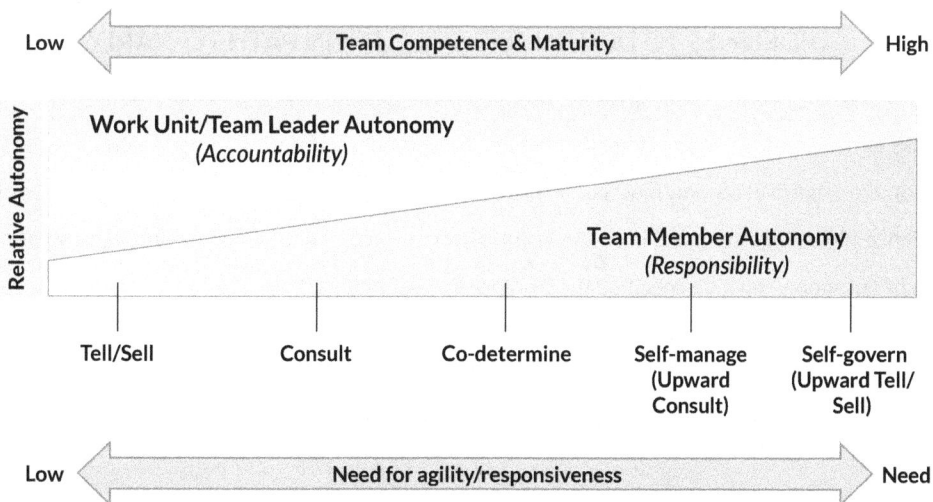

Figure 10.20: Levels of involvement, reflecting the relative degree of autonomy between the Work Unit/Team Leader and Team

Experience has shown that if the evolution of autonomy – operationalised into who is responsible for what tasks – is not deliberately mapped against clear timelines, no to little evolution occurs. The Task Matrix of a Work Unit provides a handy means to plot what Tasks will be awarded greater autonomy. Figure 10.21 depicts a way of mapping the evolution towards greater team autonomy. Appendix B: Design Template 18 can assist in the mapping of an evolutionary path.

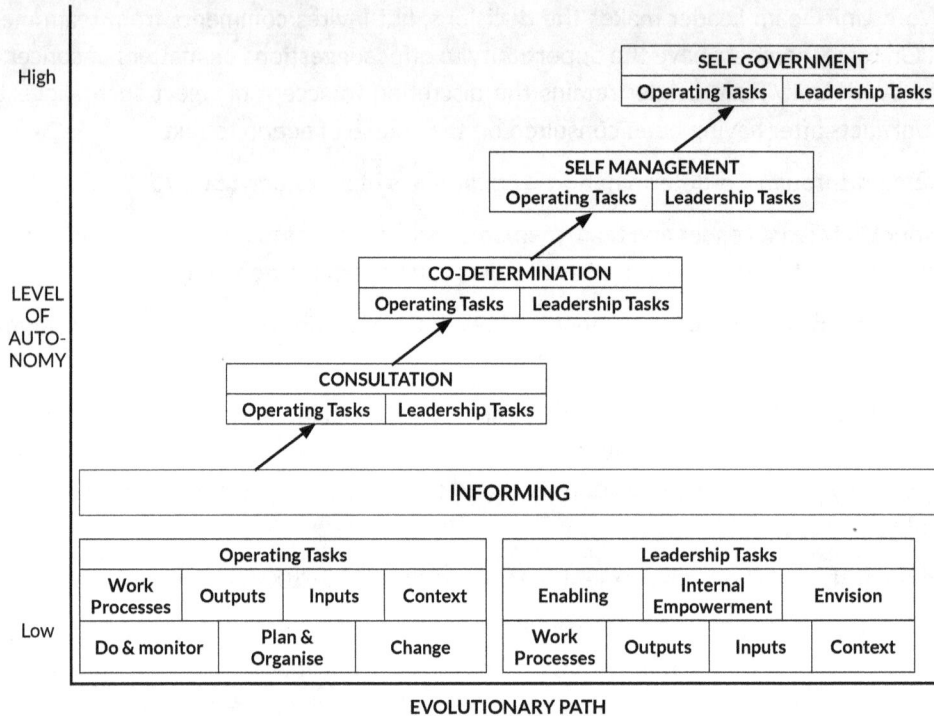

Figure 10.21: Mapping the Evolutionary Path towards greater Team Autonomy

Guidelines to design the evolution path are given in the shaded box.

GUIDELINES TO DESIGN THE EVOLUTION PATH TOWARDS GREATER TEAM AUTONOMY

- All tasks within the Team Work Domain must be covered during the evolutionary path.

- The ultimate stage of autonomy must equal the future desired *final* state of the Work Team's Mode of Working.

- Coherence ("Hanging together") in the levels of autonomy across and within evolutionary stages.

- Levels of autonomy must be specified for *all* Work Roles/Stations/Portfolios.

- Teams usually reach their ultimate stage of autonomy only after three to five years. On average, there are usually four to five stages of autonomy over this period of time.

- The required competencies must be redefined by stage of evolution.

Steps C.8: Map Integrated Operational Design to C.13: Implement Operational Design

Based on the preceding steps, the final steps of the Operational Design can now be executed (see Figure 10.1):

- *Step C.8: Draw the integrated Operational Design Map(s)*
  Integrated Operational Design Maps – drawing the outputs of all of the preceding design steps – can now be created. Templates for drawing these maps are given for Work Teams (Appendix B: Design Template 13) and Work Roles (Appendix B: Temples 14 and 17).

  The shaded box provides some guidelines with respect to the drawing of an integrated Operational Design Map(s).

GUIDELINES WITH RESPECT TO THE DRAWING OF AN INTEGRATED ORGANISATIONAL MAP

- The map must depict the Desired End State relative to the Operational Design Framework.

- If required, Interim Design States may also be architected if the Desired End State is radically different to the current design. Pilot implementations, or implementing minimum viable designs, can also be considered.

- Only at this time can Work Team/Role organograms be drawn for the Operational Design if appropriate.

- *Step C.9: Ensure the Tactical-Operational Design alignment*
  Two types of alignment are necessary:

  (i) *Intra-Alignment:* The building blocks of the Work Unit as a mini-organisation must support and reinforce the Operational Design as contained in its Work Teams and/or Work Roles: Leadership, Culture, People, Resources, Performance and Workplace. For example, if the Work Unit is to be populated by Work Teams, all of the aforementioned building blocks must be 'team friendly'. An important consideration is the level of Design Autonomy built into the design (see Figure 10.3). Different degrees of Design Autonomy require different Personal Attributes, Competencies and Maturity (67).

  (ii) *Inter-alignment:* The alignment between the Operational Design (Work Teams and/or Work Roles) with the Tactical Design (Work Unit) has to be confirmed by comparing them for consistency, especially in terms of the congruence of the respective Design Visions and Criteria relative to the Operational Design Framework. For example, if the Operational Design is highly Organic, the Tactical Design must also be similar.

- *Step C.10: Conduct Operational Design Impact Assessment*
  The gap between the existing and (re)designed Operational Designs must be determined; priorities set in terms of closing them; and the required actions to close them, identified. Appendix B: Design Template 19 can assist in this regard.

- *Step C.11: Generate Operational Design Implementation Road Map*
  An implementation strategy and plan – with a change navigation plan – for the Operational Design must be generated. Templates 8 and 9, Appendix B – though for Strategic Design respectively – can be readily adapted and used for this purpose.

Some guidelines for an implementation of an Operational Design are given in the box.

GUIDELINES FOR AN OPERATIONAL DESIGN IMPLEMENTATION PLAN
As stated before under Strategic Design Implementation, the bias of the author is towards an incremental roll out of a brownfield redesign, and a big bang roll out in the case of a greenfield design.
Brownfield: Operational Redesign

Incremental Implementation Strategy and Plan by Organisational Level (not to be confused with LOWs) of new design.

LAUNCH – First 30-60 days: Reshape organisation and activate Work Teams/Work Roles

- **Action 1:** *Road show/workshop* to finalise redesigned Work Team(s)/Work Roles. (It is assumed that everyone was kept informed/consulted as the Work Team(s)/Work Role(s) was architected. There should not be any surprises at this stage.)
- **Action 2:** Identify, assess and appoint *Work Team members/Work Role incumbents*, if relevant, by respective Design Levels, by cascading down from the highest Design Level implicated, down the organisation.
- **Action 3:** *Go live.* In sequencing the roll out, consider interdependencies carefully. Look for quick wins from the new design.
- **Action 4:** Conduct Team Building Sessions with Work Units with new Work Teams or/and new Work Roles, focusing on the hardware (that is the design with enabling organisational processes) and software (the change journey to date and how the team/role is going to work together as a Team/Work Unit and with other Teams/Roles within the Work Unit). (See Appendix C: Programme Template 1, for a suggested two day programme, to be adapted to an Operational Design roll out.)

MOMENTUM – Months 2-3: Organisational Alignment

- **Action 5:** Do progressive alignments around Work Teams/Work Roles, for example, budgets, performance contracts and personal development plans.
- **Action 6:** (In parallel to Actions 2 to 5): Specify/define changing operational requirements, for example, communication flows, information requirements and authorisation levels.
- **Action 7:** Monitor and track implementation against Design Measurement Model, and take corrective action.

REFINING AND LEARNING – Months 6 to 9 and beyond: Making Design work to its fullest potential

- **Action 8:** Fine tune the design as operating bugs appear. Allow localisation in specific organisational areas in order to address unique circumstances.
- **Action 9:** Learn how to reap the full benefits of the new design.

Greenfield: First time Operational Design
LAUNCH – First 30-60 days

- **Action 1:** Big Bang, cascading from top level down in terms of staffing up the new Work Teams/Work Roles – simultaneously, and in parallel – in the logical sequence of setting up the Work Units/Teams/Roles.

- **Action 2:** Conduct Team Building Sessions with Work Units with new Work Teams or/and new Work Roles, focusing on the hardware (the design with enabling organisational processes) and software (the change journey to date and how the team/role is going to work together as a Team/Work Unit and with other Teams/Roles within the Work Unit). (See Appendix C: Programme Template 1, for a suggested two day programme, to be adapted to an Operational Design roll out.)
- **Action 3:** Monitor and track implementation against Design Measurement Model, and take corrective action

REFINE AND LEARN – Months 3 to 6 and beyond: Making Design work to its fullest potential

- **Action 4:** Fine tune the design as operating bugs appear. Allow localisation in specific organisational areas in order to address unique circumstances.

- **Action 5:** Learn how to reap the full benefits of the new design.

- Step C.12: Draft Operational Design Solution Report
  A detailed report on the Operational Design Solution must be produced by the OD Expert, which will form the basis of implementation. Without proper documentation, the implementation has a high likelihood of derailment given the intensity of personal and organisational dynamics that OD invokes. A typical Operational Design Solution report template is given in Appendix D: Report Template 4.

- Step C.13: Implement Operational Design
  The implementation takes place in which the OD Expert may or may not be involved. The accountability of the Expert stops formally at Step C.12. He/she needs to be contracted anew to advise on/assist with this step.

Quality assurance: Work Team Design

QUALITY ASSURANCE QUESTIONS	DESIGN STEP	ADDRESSED: YES/NO *(Yes: +; No: x)*
WORK CONTEXT • Have the Design Givens of the Context been built into the Work Team Design?	Step C.1	
NEED FOR TEAM DESIGN • Has a clear need for a Team Design been established?	Step C.4.1	

QUALITY ASSURANCE QUESTIONS	DESIGN STEP	ADDRESSED: YES/NO *(Yes: +; No: x)*
PER WORK TEAM, MAKING UP THE OPERATIONAL DESIGN		
TEAM PURPOSE AND REQUISITE COMPLEXITY • Is the reason for the Team's existence been defined to indicate a unique product/service? • Is the scope of work of the Team meaningful, and does it add value to the Work Unit? • Is the key transformation/value-adding process of the Work Team clearly mapped? • Does the Purpose focus on the desired future state of the Work Team, operationally?	Step C.4.2.2	
INPUT AND OUTPUT BOUNDARIES • Are the input and output boundaries distinctly defined to ensure clear ownership of the Team Purpose? • Do the Team boundaries allow the Team to function as a self-contained entity (within cost constraints)? • Can control of variance at source be achieved with the Team boundaries?	Step C.4.2.2	
CORE INPUTS • Have the direct suppliers to the Team been defined correctly? • Have supply quality requirements been indicated clearly? • Are inputs identifiable and measurable?	Step C.4.2.2	
CORE OUTPUTS • Have the immediate customers of the Team been identified right, relative to the team purpose? • Has the product/service to be delivered to customers been clearly defined? • Have the quality, quantity, time and cost requirements of the core outputs been specified clearly?	Step C.4.2.2	
WORK PROCESSES **Core Work Process** • Has the appropriate work process been mapped for achieving the desired outputs with the given inputs? • Are the core work process activities fully listed and mapped? • Have core work activities been properly classified: transformation/transportation/ancillary/storage? • Have the Core Operating Technological requirements been specified? **Delivery Enablement AND Support Work Processes** • Have the necessary delivery enablement/support processes been mapped? • Have the types of in-house delivery enablement and support requirements, with the corresponding level of enablement/support, been identified: Basic, Intermediate, Advanced? • Have the types of external enablement/support requirements been specified?	Step C.4.2.2	

QUALITY ASSURANCE QUESTIONS	DESIGN STEP	ADDRESSED: YES/NO *(Yes: +; No: x)*

CRITICAL INTELLIGENCE REQUIREMENTS
• Has the critical intelligence – with its means of measurement – been determined and crafted for:
   ○ key team inputs?
   ○ key team outputs?
   ○ core team processes?
• Are the measures chosen practical and relevant?
• Does the measured information provide for good intelligence for proactive action?
	Step C.4.2.2	

WORK TEAM ALIGNMENT • Are the Work Teams making up the Work Unit aligned with clear boundaries?	Step C.4.2.3	
MODE OF WORKING: HORIZONTAL DESIGN • Has the way the team need to work, as outlined in the set Work Team Design Criteria and Vision, been designed? • Has the structural interdependence of the Mode of Working been accommodated in the Horizontal Design? • Does the size of the team promote effective teamwork and positive dynamics (between 8-10 members)?	Step C.4.4.1	
WORK ROLES: VERTICAL DESIGN • Have the distinct, mission-critical Work Roles needed by the team – with their requisite LOWs – been identified and profiled?	Step C.4.4.2	
REQUIRED LATERAL LINKAGES AND GOVERNANCE: LATERAL DESIGN • Have vertical linkages and Integration Mechanisms been identified and crafted? • Have horizontal linkages and Integration Mechanisms been identified and crafted? • Is the Work Team Governance Model clearly specified with a clear Decision-making Rights and Style?	Step C.4.2.2 Step C.4.4.3	
COMPETENCY PROFILE • Are the key competencies required by the team fully listed and described? • Do the key competencies match the team's mode of work in terms of skill range, variety, flexibility, interdependence and autonomy? • Are the key competencies relevant to the team purpose? • Do the key competencies reflect realistic, maximum requirements for team performance? • Do the key competencies allow for the continued growth and development of team members?	Step C.6	
EVOLVING PHASES OF INCREASING WORK TEAM AUTONOMY • If applicable, have the stages of evolving team autonomy – with an implementation plan and timetable – been clearly specified? • Have the competencies per stage of evolution been defined?	Step C.7	

QUALITY ASSURANCE QUESTIONS	DESIGN STEP	ADDRESSED: YES/NO *(Yes: +; No: x)*
INTEGRATED TEAM DESIGN • Has the Integrated Team Design Map – also visually depicted – been constructed?	Step C.8	
WORK TEAM OPERATIONAL DESIGN FRAMEWORK • With the Operational Design Framework as a reference point, do all of the above comply, and are they congruent with the set Work Team Design Criteria and Vision? • Does the Work Team Design meet the chosen degree of Design Autonomy?	Steps C.2 and C.4.3 Step C.2B	
TACTICAL-OPERATIONAL DESIGN ALIGNMENT • Has the Intra-Team alignment been confirmed? • Has the Inter-Work Unit alignment been confirmed?	Step C.9	
OPERATIONAL DESIGN IMPACT ASSESSMENT • Has an impact assessment been conducted?	Step C.10	
OPERATIONAL IMPLEMENTATION ROAD MAP • Has an implementation road map been generated?	Step C.11	
DESIGN SOLUTION REPORT • Has a Design Solution Report been generated?	Step C.12	

Quality assurance: Work Role Design

QUALITY ASSURANCE QUESTIONS	DESIGN STEP	ADDRESSED: YES /NO *(Yes: +; No: x)*
WORK CONTEXT • Have the Design Givens of the Context been built into the Work Role Design?	Step C.1	
SET OF WORK ROLES FOR WORK UNIT • Has a full set of Work Roles been identified and designed for the Work Unit, covering all of the work to be done in the Work Unit, assuming a complete Work Unit Task Matrix? • Are the Work Roles distinct, meaningful and value-adding?	Step C.5.2	
PER WORK ROLE		
CORE PURPOSE AND REQUISITE LEVEL OF WORK • Has the purpose of the Work Role been clearly defined? • Does it correspond with the Work Unit's requisite Level of Total Requisite Complexity = LOWx Contextual Complexity?	Step C.5.3	
SCOPE OF WORK WITH BOUNDARIES • Does the Role have a clear scope and boundaries? • Does the scope correspond with the Work Role's requisite Level of Total Requisite Complexity = LOWx Contextual Complexity?	Step C.5.3	

QUALITY ASSURANCE QUESTIONS	DESIGN STEP	ADDRESSED: YES /NO (Yes: +; No: x)
KEY PERFORMANCE AREAS • Do the Key Performance Areas cover the full scope of work of the Work Role? • Are the Key Performance Areas at the requisite Level of Total Requisite Complexity? • Is the Work Role pitched at the top end of performance to make it meaningful and value-adding, requiring an incumbent to take on average two to three years to achieve maximum performance, thus allowing ongoing growth and development?	Step C.5.3	
WORK STATIONS/PORTFOLIOS • Are Work Stations/Portfolios clearly demarcated, distinct and meaningful, representing whole pieces of work? • Do Work Stations/Portfolios represent clear competence foci? • Are the Work Stations/Portfolios coherently aligned to Key Performance Areas as well as the overall purpose and scope of the Work Role? • Have the Operational and Leadership Tasks been allocated to Work Stations/Portfolios in accordance with the Design Criteria, as operationalised in the constructed Task Matrix? • Does the frequency of performance of tasks allow for the retention of competence? • Does the Role carry an achievable work load time-wise in terms of the sum total of Work Station/Portfolio Tasks?	Steps C.5.4 and C.5.5	
CRITICAL OUTCOMES • Are the Critical Outcomes clearly specified? • Are the outcomes aligned with the Work Role's Key Performance Areas?	Step C.5.3	
LATERAL DESIGN • Is the location of the Role in the Work Unit clear? • Are the Role Integration Mechanisms clearly defined and set up? • Is the Work Role Governance Model clearly specified with a clear Decision-making Style and Rights?	Step C.5.6	
COMPETENCY PROFILE • Are the key competencies required by the respective Work Role(s) fully listed and described? • Do the key competencies of the Work Role match the Work Unit's/Team's Mode of Working in terms of Design Criteria and Vision? • Are the key competencies relevant to the purpose and scope of the Work Role? • Do the key competencies allow for continued growth and development by a Work Role incumbent? • If applicable, have the stages of evolving Work Role maturity been clearly specified in the form of a competency growth curve? Have the competency and performance requirements and evidence for each stage, as well as the assessment process, been clearly specified?	Step C.6	

QUALITY ASSURANCE QUESTIONS	DESIGN STEP	ADDRESSED: YES /NO (Yes: +; No: x)
EVOLVING PHASES OF INCREASING WORK ROLE AUTONOMY • If applicable, have the stages of evolving Work Role autonomy – with an implementation plan and timetable – been clearly specified? • Have the competencies per stage of evolution been defined?	Step C.7	
INTEGRATED WORK ROLE DESIGN • Has an Integrated Team Design Map – also visually depicted – been constructed?	Step C.8	
WORK ROLE OPERATIONAL DESIGN FRAMEWORK • With the Operational Design Framework as a reference point, do all of the above comply, and are they congruent with, the set Work Role Design Criteria and Vision? • Does the Work Role Design meet the chosen degree of Design Autonomy?	Steps C.2 and C.5.1 Step C.2B	
TACTICAL-OPERATIONAL DESIGN ALIGNMENT • Has the Intra-Work Role alignment been confirmed? • Has the Inter-Work Role/Team alignment been confirmed?	Step C.9	
OPERATIONAL DESIGN IMPACT ASSESSMENT • Has an impact assessment been conducted?	Step C.10	
OPERATIONAL IMPLEMENTATION ROAD MAP • Has an Implementation Road Map been generated?	Step C.11	
DESIGN SOLUTION REPORT • Has a Design Solution report been generated?	Step C.12	

Conclusion

This chapter covered the complete Operational Design Process. Typically a total Operational Design Process could take up to six weeks per Work Team/Work Role to be designed. The outcomes of the Process would be: (i) an overall Operational Design Framework as the 'way of living' in the House and Rooms of the organisation, used to direct and guide all Operational Design interventions in the organisation as reference point; and (ii) the (re)design of specific Work Teams and Work Roles, aligned to the Strategic and Tactical Designs of the organisation.

The discussion of the Operational Design Process in this chapter was based on Process Option 1: Expert generated (see Table 4.3). In this option, the Client requires the OD Expert to craft a design and submit it to him/her for a decision.

With respect to the other three possible options, the OD process would take on the following forms:

• *Option 1: Assurance:* The Client has already generated a desired Operational Design, that is Work Team/Work Role design. The OD Expert has merely to independently quality assure, in an impartial, objective manner against leading OD practice, the Client's proposed design. In this instance, the OD Expert can use the Quality Assurance Questions throughout the Operational Design Process to stress test the client-proposed OD Solution. Critically important in the case of this option is that the OD Expert does not respond on the spot to the Client's proposed solution, but requests at least two days to work through what is proposed, and then have a work session with the Client to provide well-considered feedback.

- *Option 2: Straw Model:* The OD Expert crafts a 'Straw Model' design, which is workshopped with the relevant key decision makers in the Client system for a final decision, followed by a finalisation of the Operational Design Solution. Typically, this workshop – usually one day – would take place as an additional step after Step C.8: Integrated Operational Organisational Design. After the workshop, the outstanding steps as outlined above, namely Steps C.9 to C.12, will be undertaken.

  The personal experience of the author has shown that one needs to invite the top three levels of leaders of the Work Unit to participate. In LOW language, assuming a requisite LOW4 Work Unit, LOWs 3 to 2 will represent the Strategic Translation/Implementation, Operational Execution and Operational Practices. This will bring balanced, rich perspectives and expertise into the workshops. A programme for the Straw Model Design Workshop is given in Appendix C: Programme Template 6.

- *Option 3: Co-design:* The OD Expert facilitates an OD co-design process with the relevant stakeholders in the client system, that is Steps C.1 to C.11 are executed through a series of workshops. The selection of workshop participants is critically important.

  Again, the top three levels of the Work Unit should participate. An innovative angle to consider is to bring the Work Unit's high potential young leaders in as observers to the workshop as a developmental exercise. After all, a number of them will in all probability lead the organisation in the future. A programme of the series of the design workshops, with their associated topics, is given in Appendix C: Programme Template 7.

At this point, all of the Levels - Strategic (=House Plan), Tactical (=Rooms) and Operational Design (=Furniture) with their respective Dimensions - Horizontal, Vertical and Lateral - have been covered. In order to revert back to a big picture perspective, it is suggested that the reader do a quick, high level review of Chapter 4 in order to re-affirm their understanding of the overall Organisational Design process.

The next chapter deals with imaging the organisation of the future for the future.

Endnotes

(1) On a point of terminology. Typically, in the literature, Operational Design is referred to 'Work Design' or 'Work System Design' (for example, Grant & Parker (2009); Morgeson & Humphrey (2008); Parker (2014); Parker, Morgeson & Johns (2017)), which embraces both Work Team and Work Role Design. Instead of 'Job' like in 'Job Design', the term 'Work Role' will be used in this chapter. This preference is based on the understanding that whereas a 'Job' is a made up of a given set of tasks, a Role refers to the enacted and crafted tasks, responsibilities and conduct by its incumbent – both formally assigned and informally taken up or emergent. In the book's frame of reference, Operational Design entails architecting Work Roles. This thinking is also in line with that of, for example, Grant, Fried & Juillerat (2011); Morgeson & Humphrey (2008); and Parker, Morgeson & Johns (2017).

(2) Cf. Edmondson (2012); ICI Chemical & Polymers Ltd. (1989); Mathieu, Hollenbeck, van Knippenberg & Ilgen (2017); Kriek (2019); Mohrman, Cohen & Mohrman (1995); Mueller, Procter & Buchanan (2000); Ramos (2012); Salas & Fiore (2012); Salas, Shuffler, Thayer, Bedwell & Lazzara (2015); Tafoya (2010); Walton & Hackman (1986); West (1994); (2008).

(3) Bailey, Madden Alfes, Shantz & Soane (2017); Daniels, Le Blanc & Davis (2014); Grant & Parker (2009); Grant, Fried & Juillerat (2011); Hanna (1988); Morgeson & Humphrey (2008); Ramos (2012); Parker, Morgeson & Johns (2017); Parker (2014).

(4) According to Parker, Morgeson & Johns (2017), there were more than 17,000 published articles on job design/work design at the time of their comprehensive review on job design articles in the Journal of Applied Psychology over 100 years.

(5) Cf. Bersin, McDowell, Rahnema & van Durme (2017); Hackman (1987); ICI Chemical & Polymers Ltd. (1989); Lee & Edmondson (2017); McDowell, Agarwal, Miller, Okamoto & Page (2016); Mohrman, Cohen & Mohrman (1995); Mueller, Procter & Buchanan (2000); Schumpter (2016); Schwartz (2016); West (2008). In Deloitte's *Global Human Capital Trends 2016*, Organisational Design came out as the year's most important trend, in particular organisations architected as a network of highly empowered, interconnected, flexible teams (Rigby, Sutherland & Noble, 2018). The same trend was reported in the 2018 Deloitte report, which had more of a focus on teams leading teams, especially executive teams (Agarwal, Bersin, Lahiri, Schwartz & Volini, 2018).

(6) This short trip through the history of work design is based on Ashton (2017); Daniels, Le Blanc & Davis (2014); Grant, Fried & Juilerat (2011); Parker (2014); Morgeson & Humphrey (2008) and Parker, Morgeson & Johns (2017).

(7) Taylor (1911).

(8) See also Katz & Kahn (1978).

(9) In a review of 134 U.S. socio-technical experiments, Pasmore, Francis, Haldeman & Shani (1982) found that this work design approach led to enhanced productivity, quality and satisfaction, and lower costs. However, they noticed that actual changes to technical systems were relatively infrequent. Later reviews of autonomous work teams were similarly positive (for example, Cohen & Bailey, 1997), as were studies of later reincarnations of the concept such as team empowerment (for example, Kirkman & Rosen, 1999). (Quoted by Parker, Morgeson & Johns, 2017).

(10) Katz & Kahn (1978); Parker, Morgeson & Johns (2017).

(11) Hackman & Oldham (1975); (1976); (1980).

(12) Cf. Champion (1988); Champion & Taylor (1985); Champion, Mumford, Morgeson & Nahrgang (2005); Morgeson & Champion (2005); Morgeson et al. (2010); Morgeson & Humphrey (2006); Parker & Wall (1988); Parker, Wall & Cordery (2001).

(13) In Humphrey et al.'s (2007) meta-analysis of studies into Elaborative, Integrative Job Design Approaches, motivational work characteristics explained 34% of the variance in job satisfaction, while social and contextual characteristics explained a further 17% and 4%, respectively (quoted by Parker, 2014). For this reason, the inherent job characteristics as proposed in the JD Model still remain the most important job design component.

(14) Vogt, Hakanen, Brauchli, Jenny & Bauer (2016).

(15) Parker (2014); Parker, Morgeson & Johns (2017); Zhang & Parker (2019).

(16) Grant & Parker (2009).

(17) See, for example, Demerouti & Bakker (2014).

(18) Grant & Parker (2009); Morgeson, Dierdorff & Hmurovic (2010); Parker, Morgeson & Johns (2017); and Parker, Wall & Cordery (2001) also argue that context has an important impact on Operational Design. According to Grant and Parker (2009), the relationship between context and work design can take several possible forms, including (i) contexts that promote more positive work design features (for example, high task identity); (2) contexts that amplify the positive effects of work design on individual outcomes (for example, satisfaction); (3) contexts that multiply the adverse effects of poor work design (for example, very low autonomy); (4) work designs that have compensatory effects in particular "unsupportive" contexts (for example, poor supporting organisational systems); and (5) work designs that convey (mediate) relationships between context and individual outcomes. I will assume that by considering the context carefully upfront, a *contextually* fit-for-purpose Operational Design will be architected. According to Parker (2014), the most consistent contextual moderator of work design is uncertainty. Job enrichment appears to enhance performance most when operational uncertainty is high.

(19) These terms were first introduced by Burns and Stalker, as quoted in Burton, Obel & Håkonsson (2015); Luhman & Cunlife (2013) and Mintzberg (1993); (1997). Morgeson & Champion (2002); Morgeson, Dierdorff & Hmurovic (2010) and Mumford, Morgeson & Nahrgang (2005) refer to mechanistic and motivational work design, whereas Walton & Hackman (1986) distinguish Control vs. Commitment management approaches. See also Hanna (1988).

(20) For example, Berg, Dutton & Wrzesniewski (2013); Demerouti & Bakker (2014); Lysova, Blake, Dik, Duff & Steger (2019); Tims, Bakker & Derks (2015); Wrzesniewski & Dutton (2001) and Wrzesniewski, Berg & Dutton (2010).

(21) Bailey, Madden Alfes, Shantz & Soane (2017); Berg, Dutton & Wrzesniewski (2013); Zhang & Parker (2019).

(22) Zhang & Parker (2019).

(23) The Socio-technical Systems Approach talks about a similar principle entitled 'Minimal Specification', which encompasses doing a minimum, basic design which allows for customisation to fit varying, unique work contexts/circumstances (cf. Daniels, Le Blanc & Davis, 2014).

(24) Constructed by the author, based on insights gained from Berg, Dutton & Wrzesniewski (2013); Bruning & Campion (2018); Demerouti & Bakker (2014); Tims, Bakker, Derks & van Rhenen (2013); Tims, Bakker & Derks (2015); Vogt, Hakanen, Brauchli, Jenny & Bauer (2016); Wrzesniewski & Dutton (2001); Wrzesniewski, Berg & Dutton (2010) and Zhang & Parker (2019).

(25) See Elsbach & Stigliani (2018). Refer also to the overview of Design Thinking, given in Endnote 9, Chapter 2.

(26) Constructed by the author, drawing on the same sources listed under (24).

(27) Parker, Morgeson & Johns (2017) raise the intriguing point of involving beneficiaries and stakeholders in architecting the Operational Design of the organisations they have a stake in. This puts a different angle onto Design Autonomy, which is consistent with the shift of organisations to social enterprises raised in Chapters 2 and 5.

(28) Adapted from Schuler (1992).

(29) These categories, with their associated Criteria (listed in Table 10.2), were sourced from Ashton (2017); Champion (1988); Champion & Taylor (1985); Champion, Mumford, Morgeson & Nahrgang (2005); Clegg (1982); Daniels, Le Blanc & Davis (2014); Grant (2007); Grant & Parker (2009); Grant, Fried & Juilerat (2011); Hackman & Oldham (1975); (1976); (1980); Morgeson, Dierdorff & Murovic (2010); Morgeson & Humphrey (2006); (2008); Moussa, Bright & Varua (2017); Parker (2014); Parker & Ohly (date unknown); Parker, Wall & Cordery (2001); Parker, Morgeson & Johns (2017); Wall (1982) and Zhang & Parker (2019).

(30) As was argued in Chapter 2 where OD was defined, design is a separate exercise to the specific people who are necessary to staff up and operate the design. OD looks at architecting the work to be done within the organisation. Only once the design has been crafted, does the question arise regarding the number and type of people required by the design, and who is available and suitable at present in the organisation to staff up the Design, that is the Person-Work fit (Lysova, Blake, Dik, Duff & Steger, 2019; Zhang & Parker, 2019). For this reason worker characteristics are not seen as part of the design Criteria, in contrast to Morgeson & Humphrey (2008); Parker, Wall & Cordery (2001) and Zhang & Parker (2019), who include these characteristics in their integrative Model of Work Design. However, people requirements will be taken into account under Step C.9 when the Operational Design Alignment is architected.

(31) The JD Model of Hackman and Oldham predominantly includes the Criteria listed in the Task Design Category. In a longitudinal meta-analysis study, Wegman, Hoffman, Carter, Twenge & Guenole (2018) set out to examine changes in the relative importance of the five core job characteristics of the JD Model – task identity, task significance, skill variety, autonomy and feedback from the job – as well as changes in the relationship between job characteristics and job satisfaction over time. On average, workers perceived greater levels of skill variety and autonomy since 1975, and greater interdependence since 1985. There were no increases in task significance, task identity and feedback. In contrast, the results of a supplemental meta-analysis did not support significant changes in the association between the five core job characteristics and satisfaction over time. Thus, although there is some evidence for a change in job characteristics, the findings did not support a change in the value placed on enriched work over time.

(32) Cf. Bailey, Madden Alfes, Shantz & Soane (2017); Berg, Dutton & Wrzesniewski (2013); Champion, Mumford, Morgeson & Nahrgang (2005); Dik, Byrne & Steger (2013); Hackman & Oldham (1975); (1976); (1980); Hansen (2013); Hirschi (2018); Johns (2010); Kahn & Fellows (2013); Lysova, Blake, Dik, Duff & Steger (2019); Morgeson et al. (2010); Morgeson & Humphrey (2006); Mullins (2018); Parker, Wall & Cordery (2001); Ryde & Sofianos (2014); Yeoman & O'Hara (2017).

(33) Lysova, Blake, Dik, Duff & Steger (2019); Ryde & Sofianos (2014).

(34) Pratt, Pradies & Lepisto (2013).

(35) Bailey, Madden Alfes, Shantz & Soane (2017); Lysova, Blake, Dik, Duff & Steger (2019).

(36) Cf. Grant & Parker (2009); Hackman & Oldham (1975); (1976); (1980); Lysova, Blake, Dik, Duff & Steger (2019); Morgeson, Dierdorff & Murovic (2010); Morgeson, Dierdorff & Murovic (2010); Morgeson, Dierdorff & Murovic (2010); Morgeson & Humphrey (2006); Morgeson & Humphrey (2008); Mumford, Morgeson & Nahrgang (2005); Parker (2014); Parker, Wall & Cordery (2001); Parker, Morgeson & Johns (2017); Wall (1982); Yoo, Soebin, Ho, Soe & Yoo (2018).

(37) Adapted from the Utrecht Work Engagement Scale (Schaufeli, Salanova, González-Romá & Bakker (2002); Schaufeli, Bakker & Salanova (2006). See also Kahn & Fellows (2013).

(38) The Model presented in Figure 10.9 is in the direct lineage of the Elaborative, Integrative Job/Work Design Approaches discussed under the brief history of Operational Design.

(39) Based on the author's experience with team design/building, but also drawing on the likes of Costa, Fulmer & Anderson (2018); Gilson, Maynard, Jones Young, Vartiainen & Hakonen (2015); Goodman & Associates (1986); Hackman (1987); Kriek (2019); Mohrman, Cohen & Mohrman (1995); Owen (2017); Ramos (2012); Salas & Fiore (2012); Salas, Shuffler, Thayer, Bedwell & Lazzara (2015); West (1994); (2008).

(40) Walton & Hackman (1986).

(41) Same sources as per (39).

(42) Schumpter (2016).

(43) Bernstein, Bunch, Canner & Lee (2016); Investopedia: https://www.investopedia.com/terms/h/holacracy. asp#ixzz5HkpmtUsr, accessed on 7/6/2018; Laloux (2014); Lee & Edmondson (2017); Thoren (2017); Shumpeter (2014); Stanford (2015); Wikipedia (accessed on 7/6/2018).

(44) Adler & Hiromoto (2012).

(45) Cf. Edmondson (2012); Hackman (1987); McDowell, Agarwal, Miller, Okamoto & Page (2016); Mohrman, Cohen & Mohrman (1995); Parker (2014); Rigby, Sutherland & Noble (2018); West (2008).

(46) A study by Bikfalvi, Jäger & Lay (2014) found that just under two thirds of manufacturers in European countries with more than 20 employees (63.5%) have introduced teamwork. In small companies with fewer than 50 employees, more than half (57.3%) said that they worked in teams. In the larger companies with at least 250 employees, the proportion was shown to be almost three quarters (73.9%).

High-tech companies and medium-tech companies proved to have significantly higher proportions of teamwork adopters than low-tech companies. Product complexity and advanced technology apparently either stimulated, or were best supported by, teamwork. Firms that have introduced new products and services in the last three years introduced teamwork more frequently compared to non-innovators. Companies following a high road strategy – competing by technology, quality or flexibility – were more likely to use teamwork than companies following a low road strategy – competing predominantly by low costs and prices (64.7% compared with 59.7%). This distinction of high road companies corresponded with the result showing that companies with above average exports have implemented teamwork more frequently (66.1% compared with 61.6%).

In summary, the researchers found that six out of ten European manufacturing companies have introduced teamwork, if teamwork is defined in a broad way. Furthermore, diffusion rates varied significantly by country, firm size and, to a lesser extent, sector. R&D expenditure, product complexity, innovation capability, strategy, and to a smaller degree international competition and supply chain position, created significant differences between firms opting for teamwork as an organisational practice in contrast to companies neglecting it.

(47) Constructed by the author. See also Kriek (2019); Mohrman, Cohen & Mohrman (1995); Neeley (2015); Owen (2017); Schumpter (2016); Walton & Hackman (1986); Zaccaro, Marks & DeChurch (2012).

(48) Cf. Neeley (2015).

(49) Guadalupe, Li & Wulf (2013).

(50) Based on the author's experience with Team Design and Team Building, supplemented with Curphy & Hogan (2012); Goodman & Associates (1986); Hackman (1987); Kriek (2019); R. Likert, quoted in Pasmore (1988); Mohrman, Cohen & Mohrman (1995).

(51) Source unknown.

(52) Courtright, Thurgood, Stewart & Pierotti (2015); Mueller, Procter & Buchanan (2000).

(53) Adapted from Courtright, Thurgood, Stewart & Pierotti (2015). See also Poole & Contractor (2012); Zaccaro, Marks & DeChurch (2012).

(54) Becker & Huselid (2010) bemoan the gap that exists between Strategic Human Resource Management (SHRM) and Job Design (JD) (read 'Operational Design: Work Roles'). SHRM must be a source of competitive advantage, and position employees as strategic assets affecting the organisation's performance. Jobs are the means to the end of achieving the organisation's strategic goals. In order to close this gap, they propose Strategic Jobs as the bridge between SHRM and JD. These are jobs that make: (i) a disproportionate contribution to the organisation's performance; (ii) are rare (less than 15% of all jobs); (iii) have a immediate strategic impact by directly affecting the organisation's ability to execute its strategy through its strategic capability; and (iv) have a high incumbent performance variability: the gap between high and low incumbent performance is significant. SHRM must build an inimitable system of practices in the form of strategic, organisational capabilities to enhance performance in the organisation's strategic jobs.

(55) Source: Author.

(56) Also called "Task Clusters" (Morgeson & Champion, 2002) (quoted by Grant, Fried & Juillerat, 2011).

(57) Cf. Burton, Obel & Håkonsson (2015); Cross (1990; Hackman (1987); ICI Chemical & Polymers Ltd. (1989); MacKenzie (1986); Veldsman (1995).

(58) Mumford, Morgeson & Nahrgang (2005) distinguish between Jobs (= Work Roles); Duties (= KPAs); Task Cluster (= Work Portfolios/Work Stations); and Tasks (= Tasks).

(59) For example, ICI Chemical & Polymers Ltd. (1989).

(60) Cf. Mumford, Morgeson & Nahrgang (2005); Parker, Morgeson & Johns (2017); Wall (1982).

(61) Compiled by the author.

(62) Based on a consulting assignment by the author.

(63) Also called Dual Career Path Design (Bussin, 2017d).

(64) Source: Author.

(65) Draws on Bikfalvi, Jäger & Lay (2014); Christos (2017); Lee & Edmondson (2018); Rolfsen & Johansen (2014); Veldsman (1995); Wall (1982).

(66) Christos (2017); Kriek (2019); Rolfsen & Johansen (2014); Veldsman (1995).

(67) Zhang & Parker, 2019).

11

IMAGING THE ORGANISATION
OF THE FUTURE FOR THE FUTURE

Towards a Future-fit Organisational Design

"Imagination will often carry us to worlds that never were. But without it, we go nowhere."

(Carl Sagan)

"You never change things by fighting the existing reality. To change something, make the existing model obsolete."

(Richard Buckminster Fuller)

"The greatest danger in times of turbulence is not the turbulence. It is to act with yesterday's logic."

(Peter Drucker)

We have now covered the comprehensive, integrated route map for designing a fit-for-purpose organisation in totality, having moved seamlessly from Strategic Design through Tactical Design to Operational Design. The next key question to consider is: What would the *future-fit* Organisational Design look like? Would it be able to be fit-for-purpose within the emerging new order?

The purpose of this chapter is to take the bold step into the unknown by imaging the organisation of the future, for the future, in the search for a future-fit Organisational Design *(1)*. This journey of exploration will cover the following topics: *first*, the expected Forces of Change going into the future; *second*, the appropriate Vantage Point from which to view the organisation in the emerging new order; *third*, the Design Criteria and Vision for the future-fit Organisational Design; *fourth*, the general shift in Organisational Design: from the Command-and-Control to the High Network/High Engagement/High Responsible Organisational Shape.

Fifth, the DNA of the High Network/High Engagement/High Responsible Organisational Shape: Specific Design Criteria; *sixth*, forms of teaming making up the future-fit Teaming Organisational Design; *seventh*, the integrated future-fit Teaming Organisational Design: its Horizontal and Vertical Designs; *eighth*, making the future-fit Teaming Organisational Design happen: its Lateral Design; *ninth*, the Organisational Landscape Alignment required by the future-fit Teaming Organisational Design; and *tenth*, an Organisational Charter for the future-fit Teaming Organisational Design.

Where necessary, the exposition in this chapter will tie back to discussions in prior chapters, giving continuity in terms of earlier futuristic thinking regarding fit-for-purpose organisations.

The basic requirement for the future-fit organisation is to be able to operate effectively and efficiently in the world of tomorrow: the design must fit future, contextual demands. Hence, what are the Expected Forces of Change organisations would be exposed to in the future world?

Expected Forces of Change going into the future

Currently a fundamental, radical transformation is occurring at the very being of the world as we know it, representing an emerging new order that is reshaping the world in its totality and essence. This transformation is driven by at least five reciprocally interacting, snowballing Forces of Change that have significant implications for the organisation of the future. These Forces are illustrated in Figure 11.1 *(2)*.

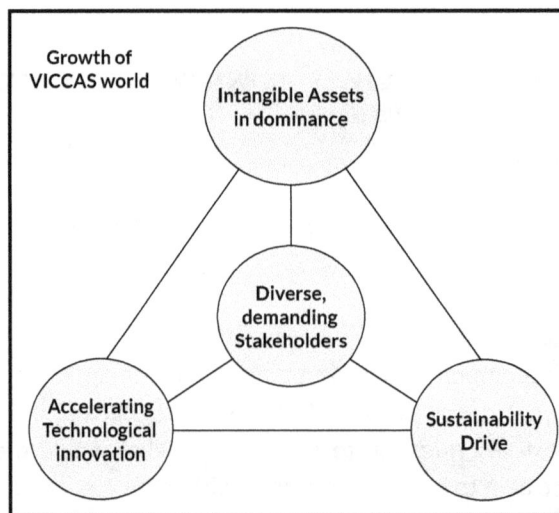

Figure 11.1: Forces for Change shaping the emerging new order

What do these Forces illustrated in Figure 11.1 entail, and what are their implications for organisations that are aspiring to be future-fit?

Force of Change: VICCAS World

Qualitatively, we are facing the rapid 'invasion' everywhere of the VICCAS World of increasing **V**ariety, **I**nterdependency, **C**omplexity, **C**hange, **A**mbiguity, and **S**eamlessness. Increasingly, the world is moving towards Complicated Contexts of Unknown Knowns to Complex Contexts of Unknown Unknowns, and even Chaotic Contexts of Unknowables (3). This qualitative Force is infusing all four of the other Forces because it forms the context in which the other Forces are engulfed by this unstoppable invasion (see Figure 11.1).

This Force will have at least the following future-fit Organisational Design implications. Organisations will have to: (i) work in a boundariless manner because the world is becoming a global village, although regionally enclosed suburbs are emerging: (ii) interconnect and collaborate more closely, both internally and externally, in mobilising the right capabilities through dense networks in order to co-address wicked challenges, issues and problems, as and when they emerge (4). Co-opetition rather than competition is the name of the game: co-operation AND competition (5); (iii) organically and fluidly reconfigure themselves in real time to deal with the unfolding, increasing unknown context; (iv) constantly experiment through rapid iterations with changing offerings; and (v) continually reinventing their conventional ways of doing things.

Force of Change: Technological Innovation

Exponentially accelerating technological innovation, encapsulated in the term 'Fourth Industrial Revolution', is radically transforming the means of conceiving, producing, and delivering products/services. This revolution was depicted in Chapter 5 by the acronym, DIVAS: **D**igitisation; **I**nterconnectivity; **V**irtualisation; **A**utomation; and **S**mart (6). In short, tomorrow's world will be an intelligence-driven, virtualised reality of being present and delivering anything, anywhere, anytime, anyhow for anyone on an ongoing basis through largely automated platforms and decision-making algorithms, with minimum human mediation.

This Force will have at least the following future-fit Organisational Design implications. Organisations will have to: (i) radically re-think their traditional strategic choices regarding their Business/Value models, markets/customers, products/services, means of going to the market, and their footprint in their Operating Arena; and (ii) constantly reinvent their delivery logic in real time, all the time, in order to stay ahead of the game, because the rules of the game are constantly being reinvented. They will have to find new game plans on an ongoing basis.

Force of Change: Intangible Assets

Given the above Forces of the VICCAS world and technological innovation, the dominance of Intangible Assets relative to Tangible Assets will grow even further from the currently estimated 85%. Concurrently, people's share of over 70% of Intangible Assets will become even greater as calls on their unbounded creativity, innovation, expertise, knowledge, skills and experience become even greater. Going into the future, people will become even more predominant value unlockers of the potential contained in the assets of their organisations, by means of which sustainable wealth must be created (7).

This Force will have at least the following future-fit Organisational Design implications. Organisations will have to: (i) consider their employees as *whole* persons coming to work, and architect 'humane' designs that are able to satisfy their basic needs, such as meaning/purpose, fulfilment, efficacy, belonging and existence. In short, they must become people-centric organisations; (ii) accommodate a wider diversity, more inclusively; (iii) craft compelling Employee Value Propositions, infusing their delivery logic into its very being, in this way creating memorable employee experiences; and (iv) give people real shares and stakes in their organisations, psychologically, spiritually, ethically and financially (8).

Force of Change: Stakeholders

Going into the future, organisations will be faced by an ever-extending, increasingly diverse, range of highly activist stakeholders with ever shifting interests, demands and expectations, which are most frequently in conflict, demanding invidious trade-offs. The vast numbers of strident voices of stakeholders will be amplified significantly by the growing, pervasive power of social media, allowing stakeholders' rapid mobilisation around issues, local and global, at anytime, anywhere, anyone (9).

This Force will have at least the following future-fit Organisational Design implications. Organisations will have to: (i) become artful in building and nurturing deep, morally-based relationships with stakeholders, based on core values such as legitimacy, fairness and equity, in this way building social capital; (ii) adopt an Outside-In delivery logic, which enables them to connect meaningfully with stakeholders by bringing their 'voices' into the daily operations of organisations (10); and (iii) create lasting, inimitable, memorable stakeholder experiences.

Force of Change: Sustainability Drive

There will be an increasing thrust – sometimes enforced, formally and/or morally – of the core value orientation of sustainability through stewardship. That is, leaving the world a better place for current and upcoming generations. As discussed before, sustainability can be expressed according to five interdependent Ps: Productivity; Prosperity; People; Peace; and Planet. This requires the ongoing actions of recovery, renewal, restoration and retention of existing value *whilst* delivering value going into the future.

This Force will have at least the following future-fit Organisational Design implications. Organisations will have to: (i) be Purpose-driven citizens with a social consciousness, demonstrating in real terms how they are leaving the world a better place (11). They will have to become multi-purpose social enterprises, leveraging themselves from an uncompromising moral foundation: 'This is what we stand for'; (ii) extend their delivery logic to embrace three interdependent delivery modes (= strands) – technical-social-virtuous – which have to be jointly optimised; (iii) convert their linear core value chain into a circular value chain of zero waste; and (iv) infuse everything they do with sustainability: Consumed/Delivered Value <Replaced Value.

In summary, without any doubt, the future is going to look vastly different. For this reason, organisations have to look different design-wise. There is a rapidly growing, implosive tension between organisations' current ('As Is') and desired ('To-Be') designs, where the former is increasingly becoming future-*unfit*. The future-fit Organisational Design implications flowing from the above-described Forces of Change can be typified in a number of terms, put as verbs. As verbs they are reflective of the hyper-turbulent and hyper-fluid context explicated above: connecting; collaborating; reinventing; reconfiguring; experimenting; purpose/meaning giving; moving Outside-In; memory-creating; sustaining; and proactive futuring.

Imperative of relentless, ongoing, disruptive innovation accompanied by continuous deep learning

The above described emerging new order has invoked the consequential, merciless imperative of relentless, ongoing, disruptive, even destructive, innovation as THE critical strategic renewal success factor for organisations aspiring to remain future-relevant, as well as fit for the 21st century (12). This imperative demands looking at everything – across all domains of the organisation – afresh, from first principles, to see the impossible as possible, find new answers to questions, ask totally new questions, and regarding nothing as untouchable or unchangeable. There are no holy cows or sacred grounds. Everything, but everything, has to be questioned afresh in a zero-based-fashion, such the organisation's Operating Model.

In turn, the relentless, ongoing disruptive innovation has invoked the necessity of continuous deep learning/teaching by all within the organisation – learning, relearning and unlearning – that is faster than the rate of change externally. Organisations have to become learning and teaching entities (13). They will have to fail better in order to succeed faster through iterative, future-referenced, purposeful experimentation (14).

In order to disruptively innovate and constantly learn/teach, organisations have to transform themselves into network organisations comprised of dense, deep, reciprocal teaming and partnering relationships, both inside and outside the organisation (15). This will equip them with the reinventing capacity to thrive in the emerging new order. Networking requires fuzzy, highly porous, continuously redrawn organisational boundaries, allowing for rapid knowledge creation, synthesisation, and dissemination with many partners, paced to and in response to the rate of change (16).

Suggested rules of the emerging new order are given in the shaded box.

RULES OF THE EMERGING NEW ORDER

- Half-time mindset: halving the time every time one interacts with a client.
- Connect everything with everything.
- Grow intangible assets faster than tangible assets.
- Put service into every product, and product into every service.
- Be able to do anything, anytime, any place, anyhow.
- Put your offering online and make it interactive.
- Customise every offer.
- Make sure your offering gets smarter with use, and anticipate your customers' desires.
- Help your customers get smarter every time they use your offer.
- Extract knowledge from every client/vendor exchange.
- Don't grow what you can buy.
- Let the customer price your offering.
- Use it, don't own it. If you do own it, use it up.
- Value what's moving, not what's standing still.

(Stan Davis, Futurist)

Appropriate Vantage Point from which to the view the organisation in the emerging new order

In engaging with the emerging new order, one has to adopt an appropriate, future-fit Vantage Point that will give one a 20/20 vision when looking at and understanding the organisation as an action platform. As was explicated before, implicated in the emerging new order – and the new mindset regarding organisations befitting this order – is the requirement to view the organisation as a contextually embedded, dynamic, interconnected, and systemic whole. The organisation must be seen as a living, self-renewing, social ecosystem (17). This picture of the Organisational Landscape is shown in Figure 11.2 (18). According to this figure, the Design of the organisation is but one building block in the totality of the Organisational Landscape.

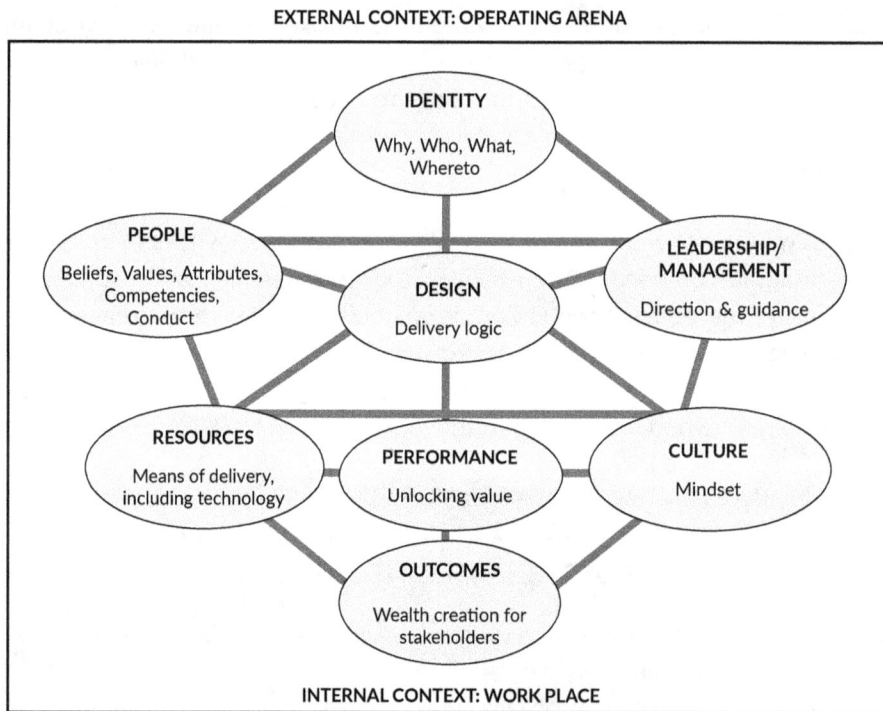

EXTERNAL CONTEXT: OPERATING ARENA

IDENTITY

Why, Who, What, Whereto

PEOPLE

Beliefs, Values, Attributes, Competencies, Conduct

DESIGN

Delivery logic

LEADERSHIP/ MANAGEMENT

Direction & guidance

RESOURCES

Means of delivery, including technology

PERFORMANCE

Unlocking value

CULTURE

Mindset

OUTCOMES

Wealth creation for stakeholders

INTERNAL CONTEXT: WORK PLACE

Figure 11.2: An organisation as a dynamically interconnected, systemic whole

Going into the future, the basic understanding of the organisation and its Design, therefore, cannot be that of a machine made up of independent parts merely interacting linearly, with the aim of maximising the functionality of each part separately in relative isolation from the context. This view of the organisation – representing a mechanistic world – has become inappropriate to the emerging new order as elucidated in the five Forces of Change explicated above.

Rather, the organisation has to be seen as a self-designing, non-linear whole, configuring into patterns. These patterns can form either virtuous or vicious dynamic cycles – expressive of a limited number of underlying organising rules, as they move through successive states of chaos and order in resolving dynamic, opposing tensions, such as control vs. autonomy. Key to the interactions making up patterns are not its constituent components, but the configured relationships between them (19).

Seeing the organisation as a living, social ecosystem implies, first and foremost, that Organisational Design is about configuring and institutionalising a virtuous, dynamic relational pattern of delivery for the organisation, based on a simple set of underlying rules. Critical to architecting a virtuous pattern is ensuring alignment (or congruence) across the total Organisational Landscape between all of its building blocks (see Figure 11.2). High Organisational Alignment has a direct bearing on higher organisational performance and success (20).

Design Criteria and Vision for the future-fit organisation

As already elucidated throughout *Designing Fit-for-Purpose Organisations*, Design Criteria form the DNA of the organisation; its genetic code. Design Criteria give the 'building' specifications for what a fit-for-purpose design for an organisation would look like, in this instance a *future-fit* organisation. Design Criteria state what the design must facilitate, enable, encourage and provide for in order to make the organisation future-fit, such that the design can give the organisation a competitive edge in the emerging new order.

Derived from the discussed future-fit Organisational Design implications of the Forces of Change, it is proposed that the future-fit organisation has to be architected according to a number of suggested Criteria in combination – given in Figure 11.3 – enabling it to thrive sustainably in the emerging new order. The suggested Design Criteria are described and justified in Table 11.1. They are grouped into five categories: Identity; Outcome; Organisational Hardware; Organisational Software; and Sustainability. The Criteria are also tagged according to the delivery mode they represent, indicated respectively in Table 11.1 by the symbols: T: Technical; S: Social; and V: Virtuous (21).

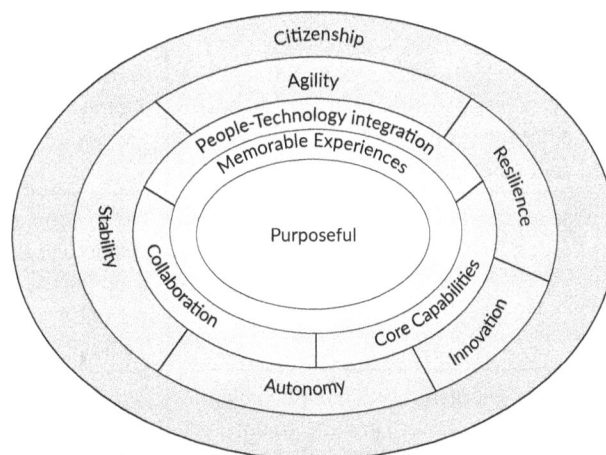

Figure 11.3: Suggested Design Criteria for future-fit organisations

According to Figure 11.3, the Criteria are graphically ordered in the form of embedded circles. Metaphorically, a circle represents undivided completeness in motion, as a turning wheel in a never-ending, open-ended journey towards perfection through time (22). Thus, the 'circularised' Criteria imply that the entrenchment of the Criteria into the very DNA of the future-fit Organisational Design is an ongoing, reflective journey of iterative refinement whilst moving into the unknowable future. The importance of looking at and applying the Criteria as a *reciprocally*, *interdependent set* to bring about a future-fit organisation overall cannot be overstressed.

The relative placement of Criteria in Figure 11.3 is also critical. The circle at the centre of Figure 11.3 contains the specification of 'Purposeful' – central to the organisation's Identity – acting as an all-pervasive, directing and guiding Criterion infusing all of the other Criteria, and consequently also the organisation's delivery logic in its totality. Nurturing 'Memorable Experiences' for all stakeholders – the value to be created by the organisation – serves as a specification of the over arching Outcome, to be delivered by the organisation, the second circle from the centre. However, aligned to – and in resonance with Purpose.

In the third circle are the three 'hardware' specifications for the future-fit organisation, the so-to-speak 'platform' from which the delivery, performance and success of the future-fit organisation must be leveraged – Optimising People-Technology Integration; Building Deep Core Capabilities; and Fostering Collaboration. In the fourth circle from the centre are the 'software' qualities the design must promote – the organisational qualities of Agility, Resilience, Innovation, Autonomy and Stability. In the all-embracing outer circle is the sustainability design specification of true, genuine citizenship.

Table 11.1: Description of, and rationale for, the suggested Design Criteria for future-fit Organisations

FUTURE-FIT CRITERION	DESCRIPTION	RATIONALE
Identity • Purposeful (S) (23) (24)	Why do we exist, and for whose benefit?	Provides a secure, fixed reference point and anchor in the VICCAS world
Outcome • Memorable Experiences (S) (25)	Delighting customers and employees beyond their wildest expectations by making a significant, value-adding difference in their respective worlds on an ongoing basis	Customers and employees are central to the continued, future success of the organisation, demanding an Outside-In approach to its delivery logic
Organisational Hardware • Optimised People-Technology Integration (T) (26)	Means used to get the work done	The exponentially accelerating technological innovation demands a good People-Technology fit in order to capitalise fully on the benefits flowing from this innovation
• Core capabilities (T) (27)	What the organisation must be able to do exceedingly well in order to ensure an ongoing, competitive edge	Without well-developed, core capabilities, the organisation is unable to leverage a viable, robust, competitive edge

FUTURE-FIT CRITERION	DESCRIPTION	RATIONALE
Collaboration (S) (28)	Working with other parties in a networking, partnering way, inside and outside the organisation	The 'unknowability' of the emerging new order requires the collective seeking of answers and solutions to 'wicked' challenges, issues and problems across disciplinary and functional boundaries
Organisational Software (= Qualities) • Agility (S) (29)	Nimbleness to move at speed in a flexible, responsive way relative to the rate of change	'First-to-respond' is a critical competitive edge in the emerging new order
• Resilience (S) (30)	Ability to proactively prepare for and reactively bounce back after setbacks, failures and crises	Ongoing, disruptive innovation and iterative experimentation significantly increase the likelihood of setbacks, failures and crises
• Innovation (T) (31)	Ongoing renewal and reinvention	The imperative of disruptive innovation requires constant real time, in time reinvention
• Autonomy (that is Empowerment; Decentralisation) (S) (32)	Freedom to make decisions, where and when action is required with who-ever	People need the power to respond rapidly to changing circumstances through exercising their own judgement by using their knowledge, skills, expertise, energy and creativity effectively
• Stability (T) (33)	Secured continuity and sameness through time, whilst changing and reconfiguring continuously	The organisation needs the firm discipline of non-negotiable, 'untouchables' to give minimum certainty and predictability in a sea of turbulent change
Sustainability • Citizenship (V) (34)	Serve the greater good by leaving the world a better place for current and upcoming generations through a lasting, worthy legacy	The drive towards the moral imperative of sustainability, increasingly being enforced formally through legislation and regulation, but also by informal pressure by activist stakeholders, whenever and where-ever

Based on the above suggested Design Criteria – given in Figure 11.3 and Table 11.1 – the *Design Vision* for a future-fit organisation could be:

> *A Purpose-driven organisation, creating out-of-this-world, memorable experiences for customers and employees, effectively leveraged from an optimal People-Technology integration, well-entrenched organisational capabilities and deep collaboration, concurrently being infused by the pervasive, delivery qualities of agility, resilience, innovation, autonomy, and stability, whilst acting at all times and under all circumstances as a genuine citizen by serving the greater good.*

What *Design Metaphor* would depict the future-fit organisation adequately? Two possibilities come to mind: a jazz band making music together, or an armada of autonomous ships acting in accordance with an overall, shared destination and action plan.

General shift in Organisational Design: From Command-and-Control to the High Network/High Engagement/High Responsible Organisational Shape

The trend towards a fit-for-purpose Organisational Design in the emerging new order has already been alluded to in Chapter 6 as the move from the Command-and-Control Organisational Shape – the pyramid – to a High Network/High Engagement/High Responsible Organisational Shape – the spider web (35). This move is re-validated when referenced against the above discussed, future-fit Design Criteria and Vision. This move is depicted graphically in Figure 11.4.

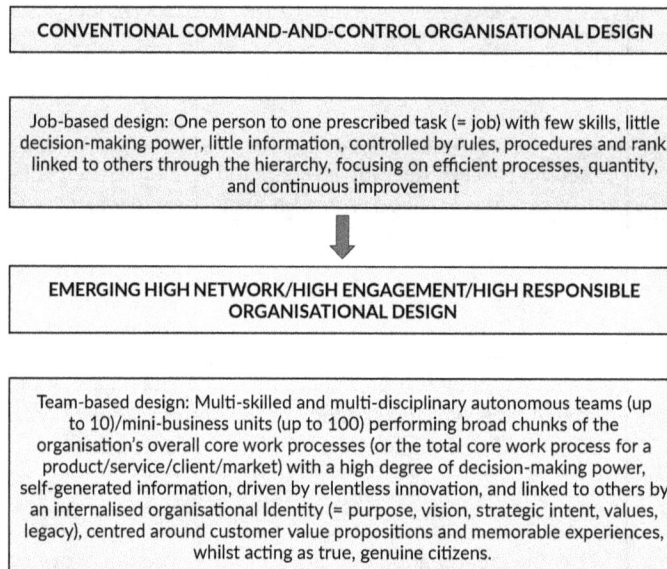

> **CONVENTIONAL COMMAND-AND-CONTROL ORGANISATIONAL DESIGN**
>
> Job-based design: One person to one prescribed task (= job) with few skills, little decision-making power, little information, controlled by rules, procedures and rank, linked to others through the hierarchy, focusing on efficient processes, quantity, and continuous improvement
>
> ⬇
>
> **EMERGING HIGH NETWORK/HIGH ENGAGEMENT/HIGH RESPONSIBLE ORGANISATIONAL DESIGN**
>
> Team-based design: Multi-skilled and multi-disciplinary autonomous teams (up to 10)/mini-business units (up to 100) performing broad chunks of the organisation's overall core work processes (or the total core work process for a product/service/client/market) with a high degree of decision-making power, self-generated information, driven by relentless innovation, and linked to others by an internalised organisational Identity (= purpose, vision, strategic intent, values, legacy), centred around customer value propositions and memorable experiences, whilst acting as true, genuine citizens.

Figure 11.4: Move from a Command-and-Control Organisational Shape to a High Network/High Engagement/High Responsible Organisational Shape

The High Network/High Engagement/High Responsible Organisational Shape described in Figure 11.4 is built around patterns of relationships that reconfigure themselves on an ongoing basis, as and when the context changes, changes in the customer value proposition are introduced, and/or innovation takes place. No static Organisational Shape exists, but rather a transient Shape in a constant state of reconfiguring. Thus it would be more appropriate to see the future-fit organisation not as a noun but as a verb (36).

Furthermore, the High Network/High Engagement/High Responsible Organisational Shape is a multi-teaming system: a relatively tightly coupled, relational network of highly empowered, agile, interconnected teams at all levels in the organisation, from the C-suite down to the operational levels of the organisation. Thus teaming and teams are the key building blocks of future-fit Organisational

Designs (37). Previously in Chapter 10, a team was defined as a group of persons (between 2 and about 10) with complementary knowledge, skills, expertise and experience who, interact on a regular basis and in an interdependent manner, regarding a given set of different tasks, roles and responsibilities, in order to achieve a shared goal(s) that can only be achieved collectively, not individually (38).

Again, given the constant self-designing of teams by themselves in real time, it would be more appropriate to talk about a 'teaming' organisation rather than a team-based organisation because of the constant fluid, organic re-configuration of relational webs and organisational patterns (39). The shift is from the 'I' to 'We'. Relationship Intelligence becomes key: knowing when and where to relate with whom, why and for how long. Even more critical is strong Collective Intelligence. That is, shared intelligence that emerges from collaborative efforts and sharing, by hearing and listening to all of the voices in the organisation and beyond (to be discussed further below) (40).

The case study in the box provides a contrast between the Command-and-Control and High Network/ High Engagement/High Responsible Organisational Shapes (41).

COMMAND-AND-CONTROL VS. HIGH NETWORK/HIGH ENGAGEMENT/ HIGH RESPONSIBLE ORGANISATIONAL SHAPES

CONTEXT

Since the 19th century, each neighbourhood in The Netherlands has had a neighborhood nurse who would make home visits to care for the sick and elderly. With the advent in the 1990s of the Dutch health insurance system, the idea took hold to consolidate the self-employed, autonomous nurses into singular organisations in order to attain economies of scale and more efficient staff utilisation. Soon after their establishment, organisations start to merge, their number dropping from 295 to 86 in just five years.

TRADITIONAL NURSING ORGANISATIONS: COMMAND-AND-CONTROL ORGANISATIONAL SHAPE

The Health Care organisations adopted a functional, bureaucratised design, which included: (i) specialised tasks, such as intake, work allocation, daily planning, and call centres; (ii) time norms for each type of health intervention to ensure accurate planning and drive up efficiencies; (iii) to reduce costs, the different health treatments (= now called products) were tiered by level of expertise required: only more experienced, more expensive nurses delivered the more difficult, more expensive products. Lower paid nurses delivered lower level, cheaper products; (iv) nurses worked to tight time based schedules of patient visits based on the per-determined delivery times for products. Schedules were given to them; (v) to track efficiencies, a sticker with a bar code was placed on the door of each patient's home, and nurses had to scan in the barcode along with the product delivered after each visit. All activities were time-stamped in a central system, monitored and tracked centrally; and (vi) hierarchical levels of Regional Managers and Directors were introduced for closer control and oversight.

OUTCOME OF COMMAND-AND-CONTROL ORGANISATIONAL SHAPE

Patients lost the personal relationship they had with the same nurse who had build up a close relationship with them. Every day (or even several times a day if their situation called for it), a new, unknown face entered their homes. Patients had to continuously retell their medical history to hurried nurses who had products to deliver at standard times against a tight visit schedule. They had no time for listening because they had to meet the standard time, then rush to the next patient.

Patients became objects to whom products were applied. The human connection with patients was lost. The quality of medical care was also compromised as there was no continuity in care. Subtle clues about patient health improvement/deterioration were missed because of the fragmented, hurried delivery by different nurses to the same patient.

Additionally, nurses lost their sense of pursuing a vocation (or calling). Their profession became a mockery of bureaucratic compliance, driven by relentless efficiency; they became mere delivery channels of products against tight schedules. As the organisation grew, there also was an increase in organisational levels to further tighten control and over-inspection.

BUURTSORG: HIGH NETWORK/HIGH ENGAGEMENT/HIGH RESPONSIBLE ORGANISATIONAL SHAPE

Within Buurtsorg, meaning "Neighborhood care" in Dutch, nurses work in fully self-managing, self-organising teams of not more than 10-12, with each team serving around 50 patients in a small, well-defined, allocated neighborhood. A patient always sees the same one or two nurses who treat them, and relate to them as whole persons. The aim is to enable patients to recover their ability to take care of themselves as much as possible, in this way making Buurtsorg redundant whenever possible.

Nurses perform all of the health care tasks within their neighborhood in a multi-tasking, multi-skilling, rotational manner, interacting with all the stakeholders in their neighborhood: doctors, pharmacies and hospitals, in the way they see best. They decide if they need to expand their team or split it if the work load becomes too big.

Teams are leaderless. Leadership tasks are distributed amongst team members. A different nurse is chosen every time to facilitate a team meeting. All decisions are made collectively. A team decides on its own mode of delivery, scheduling, and work rotation. It also handles its own training and assesses its own performance. Teams have to do self-help around the traditional support functions. Or, call for assistance if they do not have the expertise.

No regional middle management exists. Only regional coaches – with no job descriptions – to enable teams to function effectively as fully, self-managing, self-organising teams. Regional coaches support on average 40-50 teams.

A very lean 'head office' exists of 30 people whose sole reason for existence is to support the teams in the field, in total 7,000 people at the time of the case study. The hierarchy is turned upside down: Head Office exists to support delivery in the field.

OUTCOME OF HIGH NETWORK/HIGH ENGAGEMENT/HIGH RESPONSIBLE ORGANISATIONAL SHAPE

Extremely positive outcomes have been achieved by Buurtsorg.

An independent 2009 Ernst and Young study found that Buurtsorg required on average close to 40% fewer hours of care per patient than the other nursing organisations. Patients stayed in care only half as long; healed faster; and many more of them became more independent, looking after themselves. A third less of emergency hospital admissions occurred. If a patient was admitted, the average hospital stay was shorter.

Nurses felt they could truly live their sense of vocation and calling. Absenteeism amongst nurses was 60% lower and turnover 33% less than in the traditional nursing organisations.

Ernst and Young estimated that close on €2 billion per year would be saved if all health care organisations in the Netherlands were designed as Buurtsorg.

DNA of High Network/High Engagement/High Responsible Teaming Organisational Shape: Specific Design Criteria

At least the following conditions – associated with the emerging new order – make teaming crucial, and thus a Teaming Organisational Shape the most appropriate, future-fit Organisational Design (42):

- The *highly uncertain, complex, dynamic context and work setting* – typified by high turbulence and constant, rapid change – requiring agility, flexibility, responsiveness, and resilience.

- The resolution of *organisation-wide challenges* beyond stand-alone, organisational functions and hierarchies.

- The *complexity and 'unknownness' of the challenges, issues and problems* faced, necessitating multiple perspectives/disciplines, demanding cross-functional and multi-disciplinary teaming input.

- Using *customer delight and centricity* as a sustainable competitive edge requiring integrated *organisational* solutions.

- *Ongoing disruptive innovation* with the associated need for continual, rapid, real time learning/ teaching, demanding the mobilisation of the enabling power of team creativity and inquisitiveness.

- The nature of *emerging tasks and/or technology* – complex, unstable, ambiguous and fluid – place them beyond the reach of single individuals.

- The increase in the *structural interdependency of tasks* – reciprocal dependency – necessitating a high need for lateral integration and co-ordination by multiple teaming parties.

- The need for agility, flexibility and responsiveness, requiring awarding high *autonomy* (that is empowerment) to work entities, teams, and organisational members to make decisions where and when actions need to happen.

Thus the need for a Teaming Organisational Shape is undisputable in engaging with the emerging new order. At least the following suggested Design Criteria for *teaming and teams* need to be considered, viewed against the backdrop of the generic Design Criteria for the future-fit organisation (see Figure 11.3 and Table 11.1) (43):

- A clear, robust *Identity* (= Purpose, Vision, Strategic Intent, Core Values, Legacy) attached to a well-defined *Client Value Proposition*, which is reinterpreted and re-invented on an ongoing basis.

- Performance of a *whole task* relative to a Client Value Proposition for a well-defined set of clients.

- *Autonomous* – high self-governance and management regarding its area of accountability, design, task execution, and relationship management with stakeholders.

- Constant, real time *self-designing* with respect to its mode of working with well-demarcated, meaningful and significant work roles.

- *Multi-tasking and multi-skilling.*

- *Smart and intelligent*: in time, real time, self-generated information with absolute transparency in information sharing.

- High *participation* by all at all times.

- High *contextual connectedness* through many rich and deep network connections.

Forms of Teaming making up the Future-fit Teaming Organisation

The constellation of the future-fit teaming organisation is composed of: (i) three interdependent, basic forms of teaming, namely Capability Building, Client Delivery and Delivery Enablement, embedded in three Work Streams (44); and (ii) Forums at different LOWs. Figure 11.5 illustrates this Organisational Shape graphically.

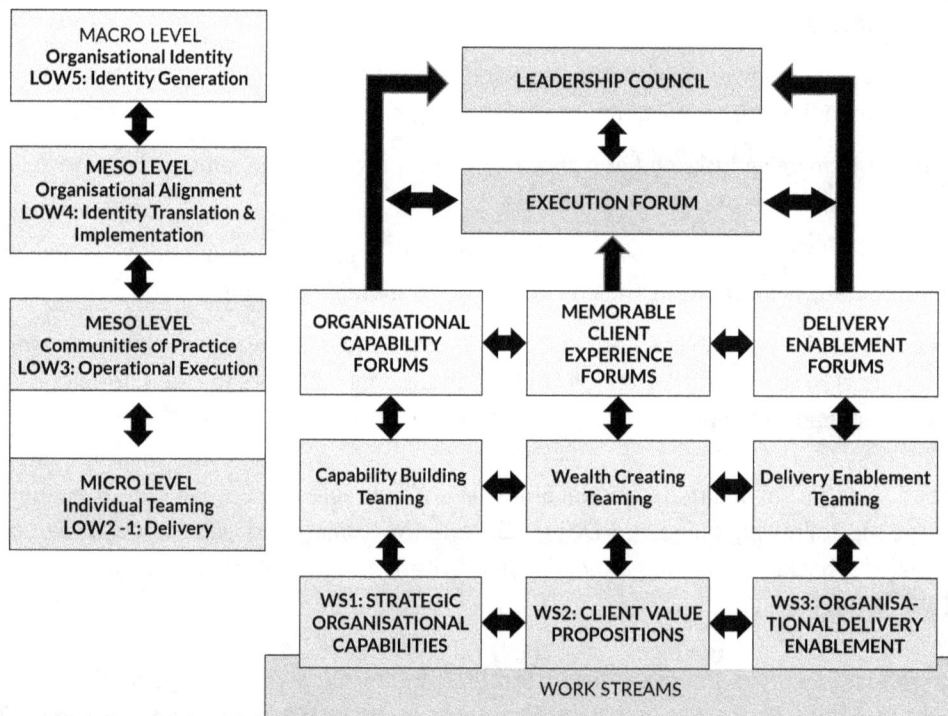

Figure 11.5: Constellation of teamings making up the teaming organisation
Note: WS = Work Stream

Work Streams

In general, the design configuration of a Work Stream is fluid, emerging and reconfiguring in real time, all the time, on an as-needs basis. Work Stream boundaries are highly permeable. However, they are relatively fixed in terms of the Work Stream's mandate – as derived from the organisation's Identity – in order to provide stability to the organisation in terms of reasonably stable mandates to act in their designated theatres of action. Throughout, within and across Work Streams, teaming may be enhanced by virtual platforms where required, given the organisation's footprint. Across, and in particular within, a Work Stream, a high degree of Design Autonomy exists: namely, Autonomous Design – ongoing, bottom-up, self-designing (see Figure 10.3) (45).

According to Figure 11.5, *horizontal* teaming occurs within three Work Streams within the organisation:

- **Work Stream 1: Strategic Organisational Capabilities: Capacity Building Teaming**. The strategic capabilities pertain to the respective Work Domains making up the Client Value Chain: Client Needs, Solutions, Delivery and Aftercare. Cross-functional/multi-disciplinary Teaming within this Work Stream establish, nurture, grow and reinvent the core organisational capabilities informing the Client Value Chain. Teams specialise in one of the Work Domains of the Client Value Chain. These capabilities are strategic because they equip the organisation with the in-depth ability to compete in unique, uninimitable ways. Capability Teams are the store houses of the generic knowledge, skills, expertise, facilities, policies, standards, processes, methodologies, and practices related to a given Work Domain. In short, the organisational memory regarding the respective Capability Work Domains.

  A Capacity Building Team has a deep knowledge, expertise and experience about its Work Domain, which it provides to the teams populating Work Stream 2: Client Value Propositions, which is their client. In essence, teaming in this Work Stream forms the Innovation Hubs of the organisation, because they drive capability innovation with respect to the Client Value Chain by providing the general means that have to be customised to deliver a specific Client Value Chain action within Work Stream 2. Their Work Domain, Client Value Propositions, relate to building inimitable organisational capabilities regarding the organisation's Client Value Chain.

  Capability Teaming also forms the home base of organisational members working as team members within an action area of the Client Value Chain in Work Stream 2. From their home base, organisational members decide which Client Value Proposition Team in Work Stream 2 they want to be involved in. Once they have done 'front line duty', they return to their home base from where to take up a new assignment in Work Stream 2.

- **Work Stream 2: Client Value Propositions: Wealth Creation Teaming**. This Work Stream is made up of sets of cross-functional/multi-disciplinary Wealth Creation Teams, each focusing on different Client Value Propositions. The aim is to deliver memorable client experiences through the Outside-In, integrated execution of the Client Value Chain for a given segment of Clients/Markets, owned by that a specific set of teams. For each specific Client Value Proposition that the organisation aims to deliver on, a set of dedicated Wealth Creation Teams exists for the Proposition that the team owns. Thus multiple sets of Wealth Creation Teams exist in the organisation, delivering in parallel on different Client Value Propositions. Wealth Creation Teams seamlessly integrate the strategic capabilities provided by the Capability Teams from Work Stream 1, relative to their specific Value Propositions. A Value Proposition defines the team's theatre of action in order to give the organisation a competitive edge regarding those clients and markets.

  Whilst the Capability Teams in Work Stream 1 are relatively permanent, a set of Wealth Creation Teams in Work Stream 2 relative to their Client Value Proposition reconfigure constantly and autonomously in real time from an Outside-In (= Client) perspective in their relentless search to enhance the client experience and delight relative to the Client Value Proposition they own and are delivering on. Wealth Creation Teams behave as start-up, entrepreneurial teams, setting out with minimum viable products/services that the team progressively enhances in real time. They are sufficiently multi-skilled to perform their own basic and intermediate delivery enablement and support, doing their own finances, recruitment and procurement, using the platforms provided by the Delivery Enablement Work Stream (see below).

Capability Teams in Work Stream 1 give stability to the organisation, whereas Wealth Creation Teams provide the organisation with agility. Wealth Creation Teams focusing on related Client Value Propositions are grouped together in Business Units (not more than 100 members per Unit) (46).

- **Work Stream 3: Organisational Delivery Enablement: Delivery Enablement Teaming.** This Work Stream consists of separate groupings of Specialist Teams such as Finance, People, Procurement and IT. These teams provide the enabling policies, standards, technology, methodologies and practices – the 'tool box' with respect to their specialist area, typically delivered through projects/programmes – used by the teams in the other two Work Streams to enable their work. These teams acts as catalysts, engendering high performance delivery in the other two Work Streams through the tool boxes they supply. Specialist teams have their own internal Client Value Propositions relative to the other Work Streams who are their clients. The Enablement Teams do not perform the daily specialist activities at a basic or even intermediate level on behalf of the other Work Streams. However, they may provide dedicated partners to Work Stream 1 and 2 units/teams.

  As was elucidated above, the teams in the other Work Streams are multi-tasked and multi-skilled to perform the everyday basic and intermediate specialist activities themselves. However, the 'tool box' they need to perform these activities are provided by the Delivery Enablement Teams who can act in an advisory and coaching role. The common platforms provided by the enablement tool boxes also give stability to the organisation. Agility is resident in Wealth Creation, and to a lesser extent in Capability Work Streams. However, teams use the tool boxes in localised and customised ways that suit them (47).

Levels of Work

According to Figure 11.5, *vertical* Work Streams are structured in terms of three Levels of Work:

- **Micro: Individual teams (LOW2-1).** At this level, daily delivery occurs through teaming within a Work Stream.

- **Meso: Communities of Practices (LOW3).** At this level, all the teams within a Work Stream come together – at the times and with a frequency mutually agreed upon – in shared forums to deliberate *operational execution* in their specific Work Stream, that is they form a Community of Practice which integrates a Work Stream. A Community of Practice's overall mandate is operational delivery and alignment; it sets the direction and guidance for its Work Stream, or portions thereof. It acts as a forum to plan and organise Work Stream activities and abilities overall, and assesses the Work Stream's overall performance. Cross-representation of Work Streams also occur at this level in order to create an integrated implementation thrust across the organisation.

- **Meso: Organisational Alignment (LOW4) – Execution Forum.** This Forum focuses on *organisational delivery alignment* across the three Work Streams of the organisation on an ongoing basis. This is all about reviewing overall organisational performance: 'How well are we doing as an organisation?' (48). The Forum acts as the organisation's overarching Innovation Hub, seeking new/different delivery synergies in delighting clients. The Forum consists of a broad range of representatives from all the three Work Streams, forming a team of teams (49) who attend as and when required. The analogy of the Executive Forum is that of the 'Parliament' of the organisation. In a sense, the Forum replaces the Corporate Centre. It meets on a regular basis, with a relatively set agenda.

- **Macro: Organisational Identity (LOW5) – Leadership Council.** At this level the Leadership Council – consisting of a broad range of representatives from the three Work Streams, acting also as a team of teams – is the conceiver, champion, and custodian of the *Organisation's Identity – its Purpose, Vision, Core Values, Strategy and Legacy – and its appropriate translation into aligned Client Value Propositions* (50). This mandate of the Leadership Council – Identity and Client Value Propositions – is another source of stability in the organisation. The analogy of the Leadership Council is that of a 'Senate' of the organisation, in which nominated representatives from all three of the Work Streams serve as and when required. The Leadership Council is chaired by the CEO/MD, and its membership is needs-driven. Its agenda is mutually agreed upon, as are the frequency and timing of its meetings.

Work Roles

In the future-fit, teaming organisation, Work Roles are embedded in teams; Work Roles belong to teams, not to team members. Even so, Roles are not fixed but are crafted and re-configured on an as-needs basis, relative to the value they create in terms of Client Value Propositions. Few Role titles with fixed Role descriptions exist (51). Based on the work to be done, and as the work unfolds, Work Roles are identified, architected, and terminated, including Leadership Roles. Where the need for fixed Leadership Roles exist, for example, the Leader of a Client Delivery Team, a suitable person would be 'appointed' to the Role for a fixed period, commensurate with the typical time span of its LOW. People are matched to the competencies required by Work Roles, through which they rotate as needed.

The box gives a case study of Spotify as an example of a teaming organisation (52).

CASE STUDY: TEAMING ORGANISATIONAL SHAPE
Context
Spotify is an audio streaming platform launched by Spotify AB on 7 October 2008. It is headquartered in Stockholm, Sweden, and was listed on the New York Stock Exchange in February 2018.
Spotify has access to more than 40 million audio tracks. As at February 2019, it had 207 million monthly active users, including 96 million paying subscribers. Spotify is available in most of Europe, the Americas, Australia, New Zealand, and parts of Africa and Asia. It runs on most modern devices, including Windows, macOS and Linux computers, and iOS, Windows Phone and Android smartphones and tablets. In September 2010, the World Economic Forum (WEF) announced the company as a 2011 Technology Pioneer. In August 2017, Spotify was the most downloaded music app on the iOS platform in the United States.

Forms of teaming

Across geographically dispersed offices and teams, Spotify groups employees into four types of teams:
 	
• *Tribes:* A Tribe acts as an Innovation Incubator. Each consists of between 30 and 200 engineers, with a clear mission, set of principles, and a senior leader.
 	
• Within each Tribe are two smaller groups, called Squads and Chapters:
 	
    o *Squads:* self-organising teams of no more than nine people, connected by a shared mission and led by a product owner who acts as custodian of team priorities; is the lead entrepreneur/product champion; and is well-experienced in delivery. A Squad represents a mini-start-up, facilitating creativity through cross-functional roles. A Squad scrums together – agile team terminology – to pursue joint projects. Operations Teams exist to support Squads to get the work done.
 	
    o *Chapters:* a small 'family' of people with similar competencies and working in a similar competency domain within the same Tribe. A Chapter meets on a regular basis and focuses on personal growth and skills development by sharing personal challenges and finding personal solutions. A Chapter shares the same manager. A Chapter Lead is also part of a Squad to keep him/her in touch with the daily reality in the organisation.
 	
• Bridging Squads and Chapters is a *Guild*, which represents a Community of Practice. It includes all Squads and Chapters working in the same area. It is made up of employees with similar skills and interests, who wish to share their knowledge, expertise and experiences. The Guild's purpose is to organically enable the rapid, seamless sharing of knowledge, expertise and experience in order to open up diverse working experiences, in this way nurturing creativity and success across roles. Guilds are different from the other organisational groupings in that they are voluntary and not restricted to a geographical office. That is, they cut across the whole organisation. In contrast, Squads and Chapters are location specific. A Guild is led by a Guild Co-ordinator who is a competency leader known for his/her technical excellence.

Integrated Future-fit Teaming Organisational Design: Horizontal and Vertical Designs

The Horizontal and Vertical Designs of the Teaming Organisational Shape – its division of work though differentiation – were discussed above. Design-wise, the map of the Integrated Teaming Organisational Design can be plotted next: How do the teaming forms configure into a whole organisation? Figure 11.6 depicts this map.

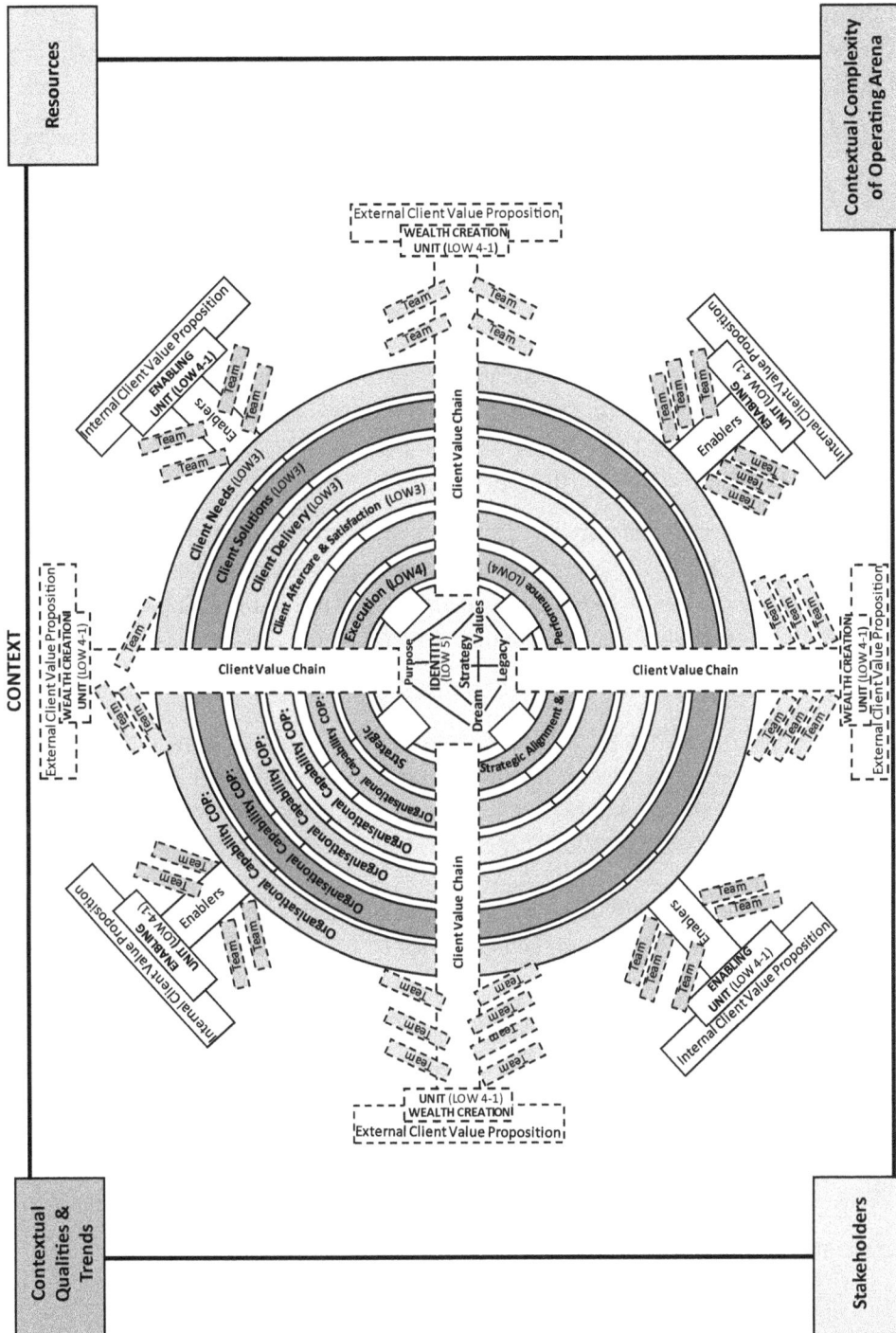

Figure 11.6: Integrated Teaming Organisational Design

According to Figure 11.6, the Integrated Teaming Organisational Design consists of the following:

- The *Context* in which the organisation is embedded (its Operating Arena) made up of Contextual Qualities and Trends; Resources; Stakeholders; and the Contextual Complexity of the organisation's Operating Arena.

- The organisation's *Identity* at the centre of the Design, owned by the Leadership Council.

- Various autonomous *Client Value Chain Units* – each with its unique *External* Client Value Proposition – populated by self-designing Wealth Creation Teams. The Units with their teams reconfigure all of the time, in real time, also through internal and external partnering. Hence the dotted-line boundaries.

- In the circles, moving from the Identity centre outwards, *first*, the Strategic Execution, Alignment and Performance Circle owned by the Execution Forum; *second*, different Core Capability Units split by the respective Work Domains of the Client Value Chain – Client Needs, Client Solutions, Client Delivery, and Client Aftercare and Satisfaction – owned by Communities of Practice. These circles, representing Organisational Capabilities, sit behind the Client Value Chains, demonstrating in this graphic way that the former serves the latter.

- *Delivery Enablement Value Chain Units* – each with their unique *Internal* Client Value Proposition – populated by self-designing, Delivery Enablement Teams. Again, dotted lines are used to graphically illustrate that these Units with their teams reconfigure all of the time. The Units are shown behind the preceding circles to graphically depict that the Units serve the Core Capability and Client Value Chain Units.

The Integrated Teaming Design is a concrete example of the generic Network Organisational Shape – A Contracted Ecosystem: a tightly coupled Network with negotiated movement with formalised, permanent relationships within a fixed set of members, contractually bound to each other for agreed upon, fixed periods of time (see Tables 6.13 and 6.16).

The map of the Integrated Teaming Organisational Design presents a static picture – a snapshot at a single point in time. How does the design create an overall co-ordinated, integrated, synergistic thrust as an organisation: the dynamic picture of the Design as a 'movie' through time? The answer lies in the Lateral Design of the Teaming Organisational Design, enabling the dynamic integration of the organisation.

Making the future-fit Teaming Organisation work: Lateral Design

At the heart of the Lateral Design of the Teaming Organisation are two principles:

- Attaining integration through *real time, dynamic, reconfiguring processes*, not fixed, tangible structural mechanisms such as the hierarchy.

- *Ambidexterity (53):* finding the optimum, real time, dynamic balance between (i) *stability* – the discipline of ensuring continuity and certainty through time: order; *AND (ii)* ongoing, *reinvention, re-configuration and self-designing* – stretching to deal with continual, fast, (radical) change triggered by the imperative of disruptive innovation: chaos (54). The organisation is in a state of dynamic stability (55).

It has been found that organisations that are stable *and* fast at the same time are three times more likely to be high performing than those that are fast but concurrently lack stability (56).

The proposed Lateral Design for the Teaming Organisational Design – as manifested in dynamic, integrating processes that are real time, interdependent and reciprocally interacting – is given in Figure 11.7 (57).

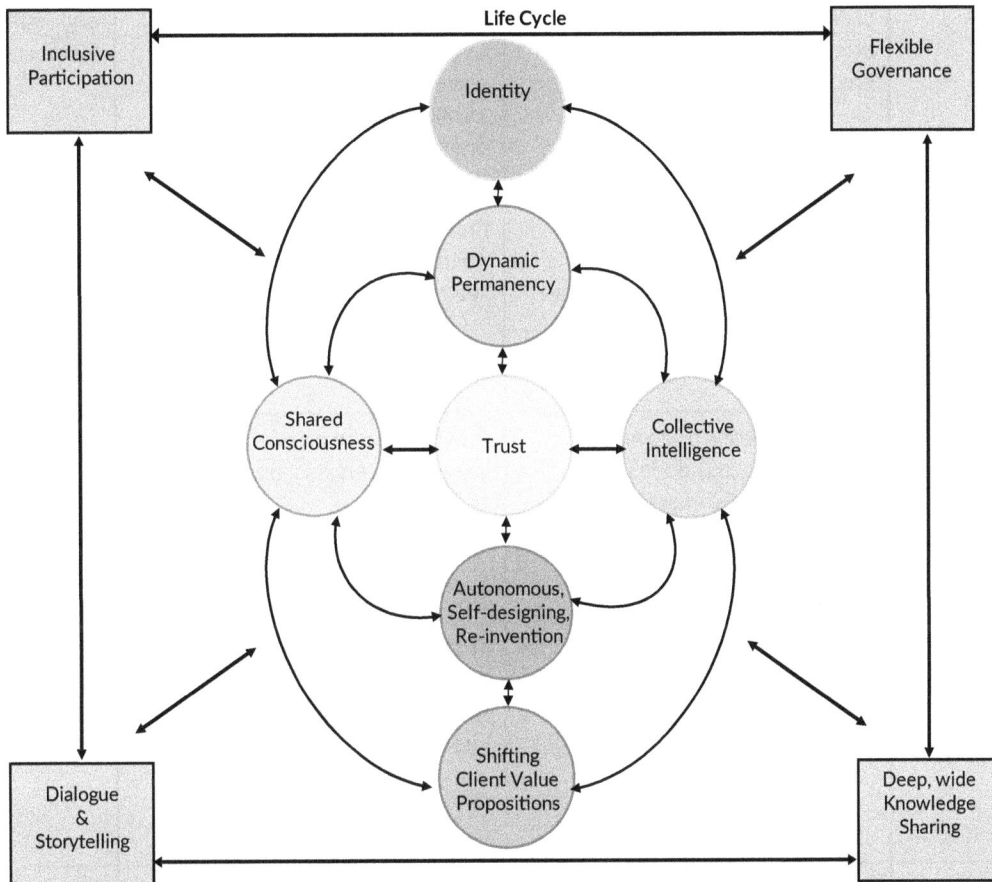

Figure 11.7: Proposed Lateral Design for the Teaming Organisational Design: Dynamically Integrating Processes

Table 11.2 provides an explication of the Integrating Processes given in Figure 11.7 in terms of type, definition, integrating contribution, and custodian of the process. In terms of a Contingency Theoretical Lens (see Table 3.1), each of the processes – individually and severally – will be differentially operationalised in different organisations.

Table 11.2: Overview of the Lateral Design Integrating Processes

INTEGRATING PROCESS	DEFINITION	INTEGRATING CONTRIBUTION	CUSTODIAN OF PROCESS
Stabilising Processes			
Trust (58)	Interacting parties meeting expectations and keeping promises, consistently and predictably	Trust is central to effective, real time integration in the teaming Organisational Design (hence its placement in the centre of Figure 11.7). Without trust, the teaming organisation cannot operate and deliver	All organisational members
Identity (59)	Who and what we are; what we aspire to; what we stand for; and what we want to leave behind as organisation: Purpose, Dream, Strategic Intent, Core Values, Legacy	Provides a secure, fixed reference point and anchor in the turbulent sea of change	Leadership Council
Dynamic Permanency (60)	Ways and means of doing and getting things done in the organisation. For example, organisational policies, standards, routines, and methodologies as enabling means	Provides clarity on how things are done in the organisation	Work Stream 1: Strategic Organisational Capabilities
Shared Consciousness (61)	Common way of understanding the organisation's Operating Arena: its make-up, dynamics and evolution	Enables and empowers organisational members to use the same frame of reference in seeing, interpreting, thinking, deciding and acting on the world, the Organisation's Identity and Client Value Propositions	All organisational members
Collective Intelligence (62)	Wisdom of knowing how, when, what and with whom to do things collaboratively in the organisation	Enables and empowers organisational members to act in flow as a collective: 'Moving as one in making things happen' though joint reflective learning	All organisational members
Change-invoking Processes			
Autonomous, Self-designing, Reinvention (63)	Freedom to innovate at one's own discretion, as and when, in order to stay ahead of the game or change the game	Empowers real time renewal at speed in response to the imperative of disruptive change	Primarily Work Stream 2: Client Value Propositions but also Work Stream 3: Organisational Delivery Enablement

Shifting Client Value Propositions (64)	Creating unimitable, memorable client experiences	Empowers real time renewal with agility in response to shifting client expectations and needs	Work Stream 2: Client Value Propositions
Collaboration Enabling Processes			
Inclusive Participation (65)	Making the voices of everyone heard and listened to everywhere, anytime, anyhow	Mobilise the full stakeholder power contained in their goodwill, access to opportunities and resources, as well as their knowledge, skills, expertise and experience	All organisational members
Flexible Governance (66)	Accountabilities with awarded authority, decision-making rights and styles within the framework of participation	Ongoing, real time contracting of required accountabilities, authority, decision-making rights and styles as a relative function of rapidly changing circumstances	All organisational members
Deep, Wide Knowledge Sharing (67)	The integration, synthesis and codification of the organisational memory in all its forms – tacit knowledge, explicit knowledge and practical wisdom – through the upward spiralling process of converting the former two types of knowledge into the latter type (68)	Without shared knowledge in all its forms, collective, informed action cannot occur to address wicked challenges, issues and problems	All organisational members
Dialogue and Storytelling (69)	Jointly making sense of, giving meaning to, and ascribing purpose to, the reality being acted upon	Without collective dialogue and shared storytelling, the organisational reality enacted on as a collective by organisational members becomes senseless, meaningless and purposeless	All organisational members
Evolutionary Process			
Life Cycle (70)	Teams and teaming go typically through evolutionary phases, for example, forming, storming (not always observed), norming, performing, and transforming or adjourning	If the life cycle evolution of teams to the performing and transformation stages is recognised and deliberately steered, team effectiveness across the organisation, and hence organisational effectiveness, can be enhanced significantly	All teams and teaming

Organisational Landscape Alignments required by the future-fit Teaming Organisational Design

In the final instance, the Teaming Organisational Design is embedded in the Organisational Landscape. The other building blocks making up the Landscape must support and reinforce the Design (see Figure 11.2). The key question is what alignments (or fit) are required in the components making up the Organisational Landscape to bring about alignment?

Table 11.3 provides some of the more critical alignments required to support and reinforce the Teaming Organisational Design.

Table 11.3: Critical Organisational Alignments required to support and reinforce the Teaming Organisational Design

ORGANISATIONAL LANDSCAPE BUILDING BLOCK	CRITICAL ALIGNMENTS: KEY FEATURES
Identity: Strategic Intent and Core Values (71)	Whereas the Purpose, Dream, and Legacy will be kept relatively stable, the following could be reconceived on an ongoing basis: (i) the *Strategic Intent* – how to realise all of the aforementioned – will be evolving; be informed by iterative experimentation; and be crafted by bringing all of the voices into the room, that is high stakeholder involvement; and (ii) the *Core Values* must include at least the following: mutual respect, equality, inclusivity, teaming, fairness, integrity, innovation and client-centricity to be continuously re-interpreted and applied
Leadership/Management (72)	Servanthood/Stewardship (including citizenship) Stance; multi-directional; shared through rotating Roles; 'We' agenda; process-based, for example, making ongoing dialogue and fierce conversations occur; posing questions; enabling and empowering; learning/teaching; coaching and mentoring; visible presence where moments of truth are created in the organisation
Culture (73)	Pioneering/Entrepreneurial; collaboration/partnering; status quo challenging/questioning; co-responsibility; action bias; simplicity; speed; transparency; informed/informing; mistakes are OK; learning/teaching; honest feedback; empowerment
People (including policies and practices) (74)	*People:* Central to success of organisation as value unlockers and wealth creators; whole person perspective: body, mind, soul, spirit; self-motivated, responsible adults; curious; creative; inquisitive; learning attitude; teaming orientation; systemic thinking; risk-taking; flexible; service attitude *People policies/practices:* Employee experience; two-way person/organisation match; personalised treatment; self-help; self-deployment; multi-skilled/multi-tasked; narrow salary differences; self-set salaries with peer calibration for base pay; employability; JIT/life-long learning; competency maturity curve; career pathing; flexible work arrangement; employment security; social responsibility

ORGANISATIONAL LANDSCAPE BUILDING BLOCK	CRITICAL ALIGNMENTS: KEY FEATURES
Resources (75)	Self-designed/governed, team-based organisational processes (for example, information gathering; problem-solving; decision-making; conflict handling); decentralised, flexible resource deployment in real time, all the time (for example, budgets); principle-/rule-guided: "Freedom within a Framework" (76)
Performance (77)	Team-based performance enhancement with ongoing, immediate, multi-directional/ peer performance feedback; assignment/project-based performance appraisal; performance-based team rewards; equal profit share
Outcomes (78)	Integrated, sustainability reporting
Workplace (79)	Teaming-friendly; collaborative; fluid; living room-like spaces; self-decorated; no status markers; open and reflective spaces; smart; safe and healthy

Organisational Charter of the Future-fit Teaming Organisation

The shaded box provides an example of what a possible Organisational Charter – its ground rules – for the Teaming Organisation as future-fit organisation could look like, based on the above discussion *(80)*.

ORGANISATIONAL CHARTER OF A TEAMING ORGANISATION

- The *Purpose* of our organisation – Why do we exist and for whose benefit – is our secure anchor and fixed reference point against which we judge all of our thinking, decisions and actions. Our Purpose is...........

- Guided by our *Client Value Propositions* – derived from our Purpose – we aspire to create unimitable client and employee experiences.

- Our unbounded passion is *disruptive innovation* – fueled by rapid learning – for the sake of delighting our clients to no end and even more.

- We see our *people* as responsible, self-motivated, trustworthy adults who are the true value unlockers and wealth creators in our organisation, driving our relentless innovation.

- In creating these unimitable client and employee experiences, we *collaborate seamlessly* with whoever, whenever, and in whatever form, though genuine teaming and partnering.

- Our collaborative (N=100 members) and teaming (n=8-10) entities are small and personal.

- Everyone has the *authority and autonomy* – at any time and in anyway – to do whatever it takes to delight our customers and keep our promises to them by challenging, changing, and transforming the existing into the better and different without any fear.

- Ultimately we are *socially responsible citizens*, aiming to leave the world a better place for current and upcoming generations through the sustainability actions of recovery, renewal, restoration and retention of existing value, *whilst* delivering value going into the future.

Conclusion

The ultimate fit-for-purpose organisation is one whose design is future-fit. The purpose of this chapter was to imagine the organisation of the future, for the future, Evaluated against a set of future-fit Design Criteria such as Purpose, Memorable Experiences and Agility, it was proposed that a Teaming Organisational Design is the strongest contender for being a future-fit organisation.

This design is a concrete example of the generic Network Organisational Shape – A Contracted Ecosystem. The crux of this design is to be found in autonomous, self-designing teaming in different forms and shapes around never-ending, reinvented Client Value Propositions, moulded into an overall organisational thrust through strong, dynamic integrating processes such as a Shared Consciousness and Collective Intelligence. To reap the full benefits of the Teaming Organisational Design, alignment across the Organisational Landscape is crucial.

What was proposed in this chapter was a future-fit design *solution*. To make this proposed design solution a concrete reality, the design has to be formally architected by putting it through the comprehensive, integrated design route map elucidated in detail in previous chapters.

The next, and final, chapter explicates the critical success factors in turning Organisational Design into a truly mission-critical organisational discipline.

Endnotes

(1) Different terms are used for this future-fit organisation, some of which are: post-modern (Loñar, 2005); self-managing (Lee & Edmondson, 2017); adhocracy (Birkinshaw & Ridderstråle, 2017); networking (Silva & Guerrini, 2018); and teal (Laloux, 2014). Birkinshaw & Ridderstråle (2017) distinguished the evolution of organisations in three stages:

- *Bureaucracy* – the industrial age – co-ordination of activities through standardised rules and procedures leveraged from and through hierarchically arranged individual positions. The Age of Technocrats.
- *Meritocracy* – the information age – co-ordination of activities through mutual adjustment of self-interested parties leveraged from individual expertise, knowledge and expertise. The Age of Experts.
- *Adhocracy* – the current world – the co-ordination of activities occurs around external opportunities, leveraged by passionate, committed, individual action. The Age of Mavericks/Entrepreneurs.

For Laloux (2014), his proposed Teal Organisation is inspired by the next stage of human consciousness.: A Teal Organisation is integrated, integral (= multi-dimensional), autonomous, inclusive, systemic, purpose, and value-driven.

(2) The Forces discussed below have been derived from, and extended into, the future, from the five reasons offered in Chapter 2 for the growing criticality of Organisational Design as mission-critical organisational discipline, except where noted otherwise.

(3) Cf. Kurtz & Snowden (2003); Snowden & Boone (2007).

(4) Cf. Burton & Obel (2018); Covin (2015); Fenton & Pettigrew (2000); Friedman (2016); Hamel (2015); Huber (2011); McChrystal (2015); Pettigrew & Masini (2001); Silva & Guerrini (2018); Worley & Lawler (2010).

(5) Zineldin (2004).

(6) Refer to Step A.1.3: Core Operating Technology with Enablers, Chapter 5.

(7) Covin (2015); Fenton & Pettigrew (2000); Friedman (2016); Garrett-Cox (2016); Hamel (2015); Laloux (2014).

(8) Laloux (2014); Middleton (2019).

(9) Christos (2017); Friedman (2016); Laloux (2014); Rφd & Fridjhon (2016).

(10) Laloux (2014); Lehtimäki (2017).

(11) Refer to Step A.0, Chapter 4.

(12) Christensen & Overdorf (2000); Covin (2015); Friedman (2016); Nonaka, Kodama, Hirose & Kohlbacker (2014); Silva & Guerrini (2018). Clayton M. Christensen and his colleagues introduced the term "Disruptive innovation" in 1995, although the Austrian economist Joseph Schumpeter had already coined the term "Creative destruction" in 1942.

(13) Arets (2019); Birkinshaw & Ridderstråle (2017); Bussin (2017a); Edmondson (2012); Friedman (2016); Hamel (2015); Laloux (2014); Loñar (2005); Martens (2019); McChrystal (2015); Petković, Mirić & Čudanov (2014); Pettigrew & Masini (2001); Silva & Guerrini (2018).

(14) Edmondson (2012).

(15) Petković, Mirić & Čudanov (2014); Ramos (2012); Silva & Guerrini (2018).

(16) Bhalla, Dyrchs & Strack (2017); Friedman (2016); Goold & Cambell (2002b); Loñar (2005); Silva & Guerrini (2018).

(17) Already explicated in Chapter 3.

(18) A replication of Figure 3.2.

(19) Cloete (2019); McChrystal (2015); Laloux (2014); Ramos (2012); Silva & Guerrini (2018).

(20) See Step A.6, Chapter 8.

(21) See Chapter 2: Defining Organisational Design.

(22) Chevalier & Gheerbrandt (1996).

(23) Adler, Hecksher & Prusak (2011); Birkinshaw & Ridderstråle (2017); Covin (2015); Fink (2019); Laloux (2014); Loñar (2005); McChrystal (2015); Middleton (2019); Mullins (2018); Pettigrew & Masini (2001); Ramos (2012); Stodd (2016); Verwey, Du Plessis & Haveman (2017); Worley & Lawler (2010). To note: Larry Fink is Chairperson and CEO of Blackrock, the largest investment company in the world.

(24) The Gartenberg study, which included 500,000 people across 429 firms and involved 917 firm-year observations from 2006 to 2011, found a positive impact on both operating financial performance (return on assets) and forward-looking measures of performance (Tobin's Q and stock returns) when the organisation's Purpose was communicated clearly and consistently by its leadership (quoted by Quinn & Thakor, 2018).

(25) Adler & Hiromoto (2012); Rigby, Sutherland & Noble (2018); Thoren (2017).

(26) Mullins (2018); Stodd (2016). Also see Table 5.7.

(27) Christensen & Overdorf (2000); Fenton & Pettigrew (2000); Goold & Cambell (2002b); Verwey, Du Plessis & Haveman (2017); Pettigrew & Masini (2001); Silva & Guerrini (2018).

(28) Adler, Hecksher & Prusak (2011); Adler & Hiromoto (2012); Covin (2015); Edmondson (2012); Kurtmollaiev, Pedersen, Fjuk & Kvale (2018); Lee & Edmondson (2017); Mullins (2018); Ramos (2012); Rigby, Sutherland & Noble (2018); Roghé, Toma, Scholz, Schudey & Koike (2017); Silva & Guerrini (2018); Stodd (2016); Verwey, Du Plessis & Haveman (2017); Thoren (2017).

(29) Bersin, McDowell, Rahnema & van Durme (2017); Bersin, O'Reilly, Magoulas & Loukides (2019); Bhalla, Dyrchs & Strack (2017); Birkinshaw & Ridderstråle (2017); Bussin (2017a); Cappelli & Tavis (2018); Christos (2017); Gunsberg, Callow, Ryan, Suthers, Baker & Richardson (2018); Hawryszkiewycz (2017); Loñar (2005); Keller & Meaney (2017); Lehtimäki (2017); Martens (2019); McChrystal (2015); Mullins (2018); Thoren (2017); Ramos (2012); Rigby, Sutherland & Noble (2018); Roghé, Toma, Scholz, Schudey & Koike (2017); Stodd (2016); Verwey, Du Plessis & Haveman (2017); Thoren (2017); Worley & Lawler (2010).

(30) Kantur & Eri-Say (2012); McChrystal (2015); Limnios, Mazzarol, Ghadouani & Scilizzi (2014).

(31) Adler & Hiromoto (2012); Covin (2015); Bhalla, Dyrchs & Strack (2017); Fenton & Pettigrew (2000); Foss, Lyngsie & Zahra (2015); Mullins (2018); Nonaka, Kodama, Hirose & Kohlbacker (2014); Quinn & Thakor, 2018); Rigby, Sutherland & Noble (2018); Silva & Guerrini (2018); Stodd (2016); Thoren (2017).

(32) Foss, Lyngsie & Zahra (2015); Goold & Cambell (2002b); Laloux (2014); Lee & Edmondson (2017); Loñar (2005); Middleton (2019); Mullins (2018); Pettigrew & Masini (2001); Ramos (2012); Rigby, Sutherland & Noble (2018); Thoren (2017).

(33) Christos (2017); Fiser & Dostaler (2013); Keller & Meaney (2017); Worley & Lawler (2010).

(34) Middleton (2019).

(35) Covin (2015); Fenton & Pettigrew (2000); Ghosal & Bartlett(1998); Petković, Mirić & Čudanov (2014); Pettigrew & Masini (2001); Ramos (2012); Worley & Lawler (2010); Thoren (2017).

(36) Cloete (2019); Covin (2015); Fenton & Pettigrew (2000); Silva & Guerrini (2018).

(37) Adler & Hiromoto (2012); Bersin, McDowell, Rahnema & van Durme (2017); Bersin, O'Reilly, Magoulas & Loukides (2019); Birkinshaw & Ridderstråle (2017); Gill (2018); Laloux (2014); Lee & Edmondson (2017); Mathieu, Hollenbeck, van Knippenberg & Ilgen (2017); McChrystal (2015); McDowell, Agarwal, Miller, Okamoto & Page (2016); Pelster & Schwartz (2016); Ramos (2012); Rigby, Sutherland & Noble (2018); Rφd & Fridjhon (2016); Thoren (2017).

(38) See the Introduction to Chapter 10.

(39) Edmondson (2012); Mathieu, Hollenbeck, van Knippenberg & Ilgen (2017); Ramos (2012); Rφd & Fridjhon (2016); Silva & Guerrini (2018).

(40) Rφd & Fridjhon (2016).

(41) Laloux (2014).

(42) Refer to the references under (37).

(43) Adler & Hiromoto (2012); Covin (2015); Gill (2018); Laloux (2014); Lee & Edmondson (2017); Loñar (2005); McChrystal (2015); Ramos (2012). See also references under (37).

(44) Rigby, Sutherland & Noble (2018) distinguish customer experience teams (= Client Delivery); business process teams (= Capability Building); technology systems teams (= Delivery Enablement). Laloux (2014) refers to parallel teams, nested teams and a network/web of teams.

(45) See Figures 10.3 and 10.4.

(46) Adler & Hiromoto (2012); Bellerby (2017); Bersin, McDowell, Rahnema & van Durme (2017); Birkinshaw & Ridderstråle (2017); Brickley, Smith & Zimmerman (2003); Christos (2017; Covin (2015); Fenton & Pettigrew (2000); Hawryszkiewycz (2017); Laloux (2014); Lee & Edmondson (2017); McChrystal (2015); Pettigrew & Masini (2001); Ramos (2012); Worley & Lawler (2010).

(47) Laloux (2014).

(48) Birkinshaw & Ridderstråle (2017); Kesler & Kates (2011); Laloux (2014); Lee & Edmondson (2017); Lehtimäki (2017); Loñar (2005); Worley & Lawler (2010).

(49) McChrystal (2015).

(50) Same references as (48).

(51) Laloux (2014); Ramos (2012).

(52) Christos (2017); Spotify (2019).

(53) Also called 'structural ambidexterity' (see Fiset & Dostaler, 2013). Galbraith (2014) talks about the re-configurable organisation.

(54) Birkinshaw & Ridderstråle (2017); Christos (2017); Fiset & Dostaler (2013); Galbraith (2014); Keller & Meaney (2017); Mullins (2018); Nonaka, Kodama, Hirose & Kohlbacker (2014); Silva & Guerrini (2018); Worley & Lawler (2010).

(55) Boynton & Victor (1991).

(56) Keller & Meaney (2017).

(57) Constructed by the author, drawing on insights gained from McChrystal (2015, p. 245).

(58) Adler, Hecksher & Prusak (2011); Kriek (2019); Loñar (2005); McChrystal (2015); Silva & Guerrini (2018).

(59) Birkinshaw & Ridderstråle (2017); Covin (2015); Laloux (2014); Loñar (2005); McChrystal (2015); Middleton (2019); Mullins (2018); Pettigrew & Masini (2001); Ramos (2012); Stodd (2016); Verwey, Du Plessis & Haveman (2017); Worley & Lawler (2010).

(60) Christos (2017); Fiser & Dostaler (2013); Keller & Meaney (2017); Worley & Lawler (2010).

(61) Edmondson (2012); McChrystal (2015); Middleton (2019); Rφd & Fridjhon (2016). Edmondson (2012) uses the equivalent term "Interpretative schemes".

(62) Edmondson (2012); Kriek (2019); Laloux (2014); McChrystal (2015); Rφd & Fridjhon (2016).

(63) Foss, Lyngsie & Zahra (2015); Goold & Cambell (2002b); Kriek (2019); Laloux (2014); Lee & Edmondson (2017); Loñar (2005); Middleton (2019); Mullins (2018); Pettigrew & Masini (2001); Ramos (2012); Rigby, Sutherland & Noble (2018); Silva & Guerrini (2018).

(64) Birkinshaw & Ridderstråle (2017); Hawryszkiewycz (2017); Thoren (2017).

(65) Laloux (2014); Lee & Edmondson (2017); McChrystal (2015); Pettigrew & Masini (2001); Thoren (2017).

(66) Birkinshaw & Ridderstråle (2017); Laloux (2014); Lee & Edmondson (2017); Silva & Guerrini (2018).

(67) McChrystal (2015); Nonaka, Kodama, Hirose & Kohlbacker (2014); Pettigrew & Masini (2001); Silva & Guerrini (2018).

(68) Nonaka, Kodama, Hirose & Kohlbacker (2014).

(69) Cappelli & Tavis (2018); Laloux (2014); Loñar (2005); Mullins (2018); Thoren (2017).

(70) Tuchman (1965) quoted in Curphy & Hogan (2012). See also Kriek (2019); Rφd & Fridjhon (2016) and West (2008).

(71) Strategic Intent: Birkinshaw & Ridderstråle (2017); Laloux (2014); Lehtimäki (2017); Worley & Lawler (2010). Core values: Adler & Hiromoto (2012); Covin (2015); Laloux (2014); McChrystal (2015); Stodd (2016).

(72) Bersin, McDowell, Rahnema & van Durme (2017); Cappelli & Tavis (2018); Christos (2017); Edmondson (2012); Hamel (2015); Laloux (2014); Martens (2019); McChrystal (2015); Rφd & Fridjhon (2016); Worley & Lawler (2010).

(73) Birkinshaw & Ridderstråle (2017); Covin (2015); Gill (2018); Hamel (2015); Laloux (2014); Martens (2019); Rφd & Fridjhon (2016); Tafoya (2010); Worley & Lawler (2010); Thoren (2017).

(74) People: Gill (2018); Martens (2019); Rφd & Fridjhon (2016); Thoren (2017). People policies/practices: Boxall & Macky (2009); Cappelli & Tavis (2018); Gill (2018); Laloux (2014); Lee & Edmondson (2017); Martens (2019); Thoren (2017); Wood & de Menezesb (2011); Worley & Lawler (2010).

(75) Birkinshaw & Ridderstråle (2017); Cappelli & Tavis (2018); Christos (2017); Laloux (2014); Lee & Edmondson (2017); Ranjay (2018); Tafoya (2010).

(76) Ranjay (2018).

(77) Cappelli & Tavis (2018); Gill (2018); Martens (2019); Thoren (2017); Wood & de Menezesb (2011); Worley & Lawler (2010).

(78) Worley & Lawler (2010).

(79) Gill (2018); Laloux (2014); McChrystal (2015); The Economist (2017); Thoren (2017).

(80) Sutherland (2019) generated an *Agile Manifesto* for the Agile Organisation:

- **Individuals and interactions** over *Processes and tools.*

- **Working software** over *Comprehensive documentation.*

- **Customer collaboration** over *Contract negotiation.*

- **Responding to change** over *Following a plan.*

TURNING ORGANISATIONAL DESIGN INTO A TRULY MISSION-CRITICAL ORGANISATIONAL DISCIPLINE

Critical Success Factors

"In theory, there is no difference between theory and practice, except in practice"
(Unknown)

"Real knowledge is to know the extent of one's ignorance."

(Confucius)

"We shall not cease from exploration
And the end of all our exploring
Will be to arrive where we started
And know the place for the first time."

(T.S. Eliot)

The purpose of the OD journey undertaken in *Designing Fit-for-Purpose Organisations* was to enable readers to gain an in-depth insight into Organisational Design as a key leadership task: the Where, Why, Whereto, When, Who, What, and How of design. The book aimed to capacitate readers with the necessary conceptual and action tools to architect complete organisational Operating Models with Fit-for-Purpose Delivery Logics for the emerging new order. It offered a comprehensive, integrated route map for designing – in a comprehensive, dynamic, and integrated fashion – an organisation as a systemic, organic whole, covering the entire organisation (Strategic Design), its Functions (Tactical Design), and its Work Teams and Work Roles (Operational Design).

In our extensive, in-depth journey through the OD Landscape, we have covered:

- the *right set of lenses* (or mental model) to engage with OD as a mission-critical organisational discipline (Chapter 2);

- the *basic vocabulary and language* of OD as the conceptual tools to inform and shape the OD discourse in the organisation (Chapter 3);

- a high level overview of the typical *Life Cycle of OD interventions* (Chapter 4);

- the different *Levels and Dimensions of OD*: Strategic (Chapters 5 to 8); Tactical (Chapter 9); and Operational Levels (Chapter 10), each with their respective Horizontal, Vertical and Lateral Dimensions; and

- imagined the *organisation of the future for the future*, by exploring the Teaming Organisational Shape as the future-fit expression of the High Network/High Engagement/High Responsible Organisational Design (Chapter 11).

The purpose of this chapter – the final chapter in the book – is to discuss what it will take to turn Organisational Design into a truly, mission-critical organisational discipline. More specifically, what are the critical success factors (CSFs) needed to make Organisational Design a value-adding, organisational discipline. And by implication, what are the risks of Organisational Design failing to make this expected contribution? By addressing the CSFs for Organisational Design as an organisational discipline, the chapter also deals with what will keep Organisational Design as an organisational discipline vibrant going into the future, that is keeping it future-fit. In some cases, the term 'OD' will be used below in a shorthand fashion to designate OD as organisational discipline. The context should make it clear in which way OD is used.

The CSFs, and by implication risks, will be discussed sequentially in terms of the Where, Why, Whereto, When, Who, What, and How of Organisational Design as a mission-critical discipline, ending with an OD Maturity Curve. All of the CSFs need to be in place concurrently in order to increase the likelihood of Organisational Design becoming and being a truly mission-critical organisational discipline. Figure 12.1 depicts graphically what will be covered in this chapter.

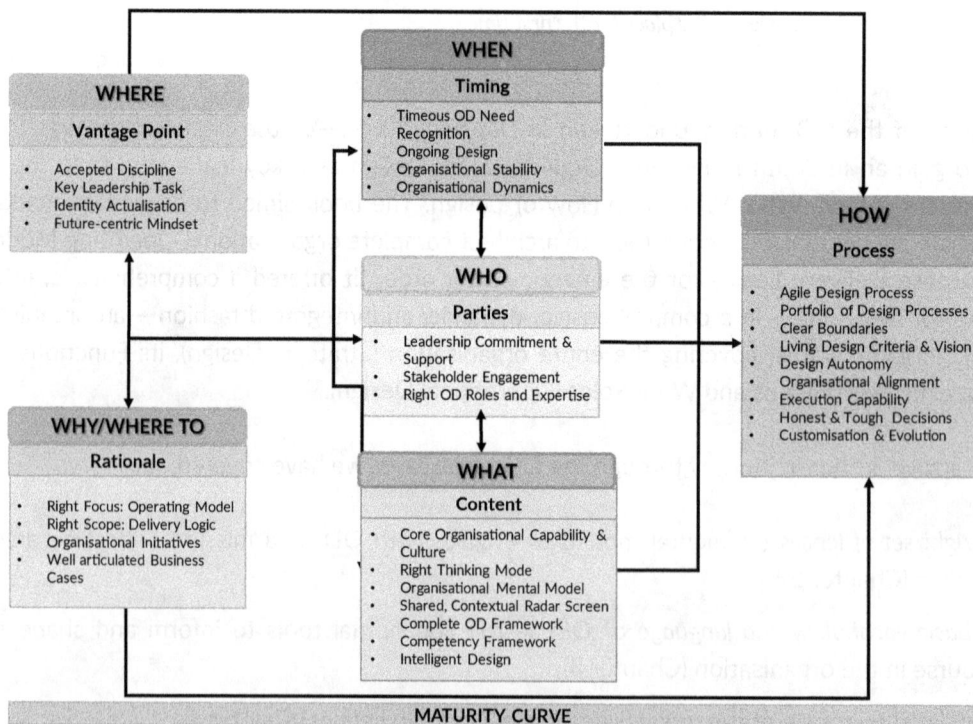

Figure 12.1: Turning Organisational Design into a truly mission-critical organisational discipline: Critical Success Factors

'Where' Critical Success Factors

'Where' CSFs entail adopting the right vantage point with respect to OD as an organisational discipline. Put differently, positioning OD in the right way and place. At least the following 'Where' CSFs can be considered (see Figure 12.1):

- **Acceptance of OD as a formal organisational discipline.** As a departure point, the myths regarding OD have to debunked in order to have a proper view of it (see Chapter 2). OD is a formal organisational discipline with an extensive, evolving body of knowledge with well-established concepts, principles, approaches, processes and lessons learnt (1). OD is not black magic and/or an obtuse art practiced by charlatans in dark, smoke-filled, back rooms, or performed by conniving executives at dinner tables in exclusive restaurants on serviettes over glasses of exceptional wine. However, it must be accepted that OD is both a science and art.

- **OD is a key leadership task.** Leadership of organisations must see OD as a key leadership task of equal standing of, and requiring similar attention to, the other leadership tasks, like the Identity or Business/Value Models (see Figure 2.1) (2). Leadership must view themselves as the primary architects of the delivery logic of their organisations, their Operating Models. Design cannot be treated as a stepchild of the leadership task repertoire, and given no or only cursory attention. Or, reduced to the mere drawing of organograms.

- **Identity Actualisation.** OD is the primary means by which the Identity of the organisation – its Purpose, Vision, Strategic Intent, Core Values, and Legacy – is turned into a concrete reality in order to give the organisation a robust competitive edge though its design. OD gives hands and feet to the organisation's strategic aspirations. This contribution of OD is well argued and widely accepted (3). If it is to make this key contribution, OD must be awarded this key position from the outset. Each and every annual strategic Indaba must end by considering whether the existing design of the organisation – its Operational Model – is aligned to its Identity, and will enable its actualisation, effectively and efficiently, within its set strategic horizon.

- **Future-centric OD mindset.** If OD is to provide the organisation with a competitive edge, leadership has to adopt a future-centric, OD mindset. This mindset uses a Future-into-Present order in which a desired future is first imagined by leadership at the outer boundary of the organisation's strategic horizon, before returning to the Present to translate, *inter alia* the Strategic Intent into a fit-for-purpose design, enabling the actualisation of the chosen desired future. This is not a mindset of starting with the Present, also a Present-referenced design, and then merely extrapolating the existing design into the Future, assuming few or no contextual trend breaks. It is more of the same with regard to the selected chosen Operating Model, perhaps only with incremental, superficial adjustments. Mere extrapolation from the Present into the Future in the emerging new order – articulated in Chapter 11 – will make the organisation a certain victim of the future.

In summary: The right vantage point with respect to OD – its 'Where' CSFs – entails: (i) position OD as a proper, value-adding organisational discipline; (ii) treat it as a key leadership task; (iii) accept that OD gives a competitive edge to the organisation; and (iv) see OD from a future-centric perspective.

'Why' and 'Whereto' Critical Success Factors

The 'Why' and 'Whereto' CSFs encompass adopting the right rationale for doing OD (the 'Why'), framed by the right expectations of what it can deliver (the 'Whereto'). What is the basic motivation for accepting OD as a formal organisational discipline in the organisation, and spending time, energy and resources on it? Also, what benefits can it deliver?

At least the following 'Why' and 'Whereto' CSFs can be considered (see Figure 12.1):

- **Right focus: Operating Model.** The scope of OD is the organisation's Operating Model, its delivery logic. OD cannot deliver more or less, or serve as a substitute for something else, like an inappropriate organisational culture or poor leadership (4). For example, if the Strategic Intent of the organisation is wrong, then the design of the organisation cannot make up for poor strategic thinking. Paradoxically, an effective design with the wrong Strategic Intent will only dig the organisation into a deeper hole because of the design delivery ineffectiveness. The right design staffed with the wrong people will also fail to deliver. Vice versa, the wrong design with competent people will underperform.

- **Right scope: Delivery Logic.** The delivery logic of OD must be scoped appropriately from the outset, and as a result will have the right overall purpose (5). As was elucidated in Chapter 2, going forward, a future-fit delivery logic must be made up of three interdependent modes, forming an indivisible holistic whole, that have to be jointly optimised:

  o *Technical:* the people requirements of the Core Operating Technology and Enablers used by the organisation to satisfy customer needs.
  o *Social:* how the work of the organisation must be done by its people in utilising the Core Operating Technology and Enablers to deliver.
  o *Virtuous:* be value-based and -referenced, delivering in a humane way, with stewardship, for the greater, sustainable good.

- **OD interventions are organisational initiatives.** OD initiatives are *not* People Function initiatives, owned by the Function. Yes, the OD expertise will be primarily resident in the Function which will offer that expertise as a mission-critical organisational capacity (see below). OD interventions themselves are owned by the organisation, even if it is a Tactical Design intervention linked to a specific Function in the organisation. Each and every OD intervention must deliver *organisational* benefits, whether strategically, tactically and/or operationally. This will also ensure that all OD interventions and solutions have the right sponsorship at the right organisational levels.

- **Well-articulated business cases with clear, organisational benefits.** For every intended OD intervention, a solid business case with clearly specified, expected organisational benefits must be formulated, informed by a strong justification. The intention of OD interventions must also always be clearly communicated. The expected organisational benefits of new designs must clearly outweigh the costs of the OD intervention, including both the hard and soft benefits and costs. If the former does not outweigh the latter by a significant margin – I would argue by at least 25%-30% – the OD intervention is not worth the effort, given its hard and soft change impacts on the organisation, such as uncertainty, confusion, and insecurity.

In summary: The adoption of the right rationale for, and right expectations of, OD – its 'Why' and 'Whereto' CSFs – embrace the following: (i) award the right focus and (ii) scope to OD; (iii) pitch all OD interventions as organisationally owned; and (iv) ensure that a solid business case – with well-argued, significant organisational benefits – exists for each OD initiative.

'When' Critical Success Factors

The 'When' CSFs refer to detecting whether an 'As-Is' Design is still fit-for-purpose. That is, recognising – correctly and timeously – when an OD intervention has become *unfit*. Metaphorically put, has the design reached its 'sell-by-date', and if yes: why?

At least the following 'When' CSFs must be considered (see Figure 12.1):

- **Timeous OD need recognition.** The recognition of an OD need within the right window of opportunity is critical. The organisation must install an OD 'Early Warning System' in order to timeously pick up the need for a (re)design (6). First, the organisation must be able to proactively recognise a *Strategic Trigger*. Because the organisation's Identity – especially its Strategic Intent – and its design must be aligned, a significant change in the Strategic Intent would necessitate the need to reconsider an existing OD. For example, replacing Operational Excellence with Customer-centricity as the Strategic Intent. Assuming the current OD is aligned to Operational Excellence, this change in Strategic Intent would make the existing design *unfit*-for-purpose.

  Of course, this assumes that shared agreement on the Identity exists amongst the organisation's leadership. If not, then such agreement must first be reached. Identity forms the departure point and ultimate the reference point for a fit-for-purpose design. In the absence of a well-crystallised Identity, OD will occur in a strategic vacuum and the chances of a fit-for-purpose design will be slim.

  Second, proactively recognising a *Tactical-Operational Trigger*. Although still fit-for-purpose relative to the organisation's Strategic Intent, the design at the tactical-operational level is not consistently delivering on the set Design Criteria and Vision, as well as not realising the expected organisational benefits. Alternatively, tactical-operational requirements have changed and designs have to be adapted accordingly. For example, a shift in a customer expectation(s), like speed of order fulfilment, or the implementation of a new Core Operating Technology or Enabler.

- **Ongoing design.** Apart from the early, proactive detection OD needs, the emerging new order imposes the requirement of ongoing design. The world of tomorrow is infused by ongoing, radical and fundamental change, as well as the imperative for disruptive innovation, and learning faster than the rate of change (7) – discussed under the Forces of Change early in Chapter 11 – make it essential that the organisation – as a whole or in parts – self-designs on an ongoing basis, in real time, all of the time. No longer is OD a once-off event. It has become a continuous, dynamic, iterative, never-ending process, especially with the growing focus on Business by Design resulting from the rise of the experience-based economy (discussed in Chapter 2). Both as a process and an outcome, OD is no longer a noun but has become a verb (8).

- **Relative Organisational Stability.** OD can only proceed if relative stability exists in the organisation to ensure healthy and constructive OD processes, which are able to produce timeous, fit-for-purpose designs. Instability is not conducive to value-adding OD journeys. For example, an Merger/ Acquisition (M&A) is in the offing; a major leadership (re)shuffle is underway or about to happen; critical leadership positions – implicated by the OD intervention – are vacant; a change in ownership of the organisation is expected/has been decided on in the very near future; or the leader of the area to be (re)designed is only acting. If instability exists, the source of the instability must be dealt with first before any value-adding design intervention can proceed.

- **Healthy, Constructive Organisational Dynamics.** Design can only flourish if a well-functioning leadership community/team with healthy dynamics exists in an organisation in general and/or in the to-be-redesigned area. An effective design process and robust design solution needs fierce, zero-based conversations with no protection of holy cows. Only if the former is in place – that is a well-functioning leadership community/team – can the latter occur. Toxic leadership and organisation, or institutionalised destructive, negative organisational politics, will scuttle the likelihood of a fit-for-purpose design being crafted. Under these conditions, design is frequently used to drive political ends, settle political disputes, and pursue personal agendas. Even if one manages 'miraculously' to arrive at the right design solution, the toxicity or destructive political games will corrupt the desired 'To-Be' Design beyond recognition whilst it is being implemented (9).

In summary: the recognition of whether and when an existing design is becoming *unfit* for purpose, its 'When' CSFs, entail (i) having a proactive, early warning system in place; (ii) accepting that ongoing design in real time is now the new normal and par for the course; (iii) relative organisation stability; and (iv) healthy, constructive organisational dynamics, if OD is to reach its full potential as organisational discipline.

'Who' Critical Success Factors

The 'Who' CSFs encompass the parties involved in OD. What parties have, for what reasons, a stake in OD in the organisation? At least the following 'Who' CSFs must be considered (see Figure 12.1):

- **Leadership sponsorship and commitment.** The status of Organisational Design as mission-critical organisational discipline in general, and the contribution by specific OD interventions, must be endorsed by visible, ongoing leadership sponsorship and commitment shared from the 'highest' level across the whole organisation at all times. Leadership must model this support and commitment in concrete ways through their ongoing endorsement – in word and deed – of OD as mission-critical discipline in general, and specific OD interventions. Otherwise, in its intention and practice, OD will have little chance of having any credibility and durability in the organisation (10).

- **Proactive, deep stakeholder engagement.** An overall, organisational stakeholder engagement strategy and plan for OD in general must be crafted proactively. Naturally, the general strategy and plan must be made specific to each particular OD intervention. By having a general stakeholder engagement strategy and plan in place, the organisation will ensure that the right voices are heard at the right time and place in the organisation as and when specific OD interventions are launched. Also, it will facilitate stakeholder buy-into and ownership of OD as a core organisational capability, aimed at ensuring a viable future for the organisation with its obvious, resultant benefits for stakeholders. The exclusion of a key stakeholder, or an inappropriate engagement, could derail OD in general, but even more so a specific OD intervention(s) significantly, if not even completely (11) *(12)*.

- **Necessary OD Roles and Expertise at the requisite complexity level.** The necessary OD roles – positioned at the right organisational level – must be in place to direct, guide and craft fit-for-purpose OD solutions. The OD Expert(s) – whether internal or external – must have the proper *OD expertise* at the *requisite level of design complexity*, as necessitated by the identified, strategic-tactical-operational OD need(s) of the organisation relative to its contextual complexity, now and going into the future. Design needs vary in complexity, and consequently in the required OD expertise. For example, the difference between (re)designing a national vs. a global organisation. Or, a total design vs. an organisational tactical (= functional) design. Or, (re)designing a single product/market organisation vs. a multiple product multi-unit, organisation (13) *(14)*.

In summary: the parties to be engaged in the OD concerned, its 'Who' CSFs, include: (i) having visible, ongoing leadership sponsorship and commitment; (ii) proactively nurturing deep stakeholder engagement; and (iii) ensuring that the necessary OD Roles and Expertise at the requisite complexity levels are in place.

'What' Critical Success Factors

The 'What' CSFs refer to the content of OD – the make-up or 'Google map' of the territory called 'OD' – relative to the organisational design implications of a VICCAS world. It entails the *conceptual* OD tools the organisation must have at its disposal to think about design.

At least the following 'What' CSFs must be considered (see Figure 12.1):

- **OD as core organisational capacity and culture.** If OD is a key leadership task; provides a competitive edge; and has become an ongoing, everyday activity (see above), then it is only logical to take the next step and conclude that OD has become a core organisational capability. This is especially true if the growing trend is considered regarding Outside-In, Design Thinking as a core organisational capability, focusing on architecting memorable experiences for customers and/or employees (15) *(16)*. OD has become one of the crown jewels of the organisation. Therefore it must be strategically built and nurtured with clear ownership within the organisation.

- Furthermore, a recursive relationship exists between Design Thinking – manifested in the use of Design Thinking tools – and institutionalising a congruent Design Thinking Organisational Culture. For this reason, such a culture must be deliberately nurtured by leadership in the organisation *(17)*. Organisational members also must receive the necessary training in Design Thinking *(18)*.

- **Right thinking mode.** OD requires the synchronous balancing of different modes of thinking: (i) Convergent/Synthetic Thinking (= Big Picture thinking) *and* Divergent Thinking (= Analytical, detailed thinking); (ii) Single Loop Thinking (= Problem solving) *and* Double Loop Thinking

(= questioning values, beliefs, assumptions); (iii) Critical, Creative Thinking (= Thinking outside the Box); (iv) Proactive Thinking (= Future-into-the-Present); and (v) an Open Mind with no holy cows or givens. Without the right thinking mode, real risks exist of rehashing the old. Merely putting new wine in old bottles, and/or applying, pre-decided 'CEO bottom drawer' designs.

- **Right mindset regarding the organisation as a phenomenon.** OD must be informed by the appropriate way of thinking about the organisation itself: its ontology. For example, the organisation does not merely equate to an organogram or to the sum total of its separate parts. At present, the mindset that appears the best way to think about organisations is the Complexity view. Figure 3.2 gave an example of such a view of the organisation. Important features of this view of the organisation are: relationships; an integrated whole; patterns, whether virtuous or vicious; and the fusion of opposites: And/Both and dynamic/evolving (see Table 3.2) (19).

- **A shared, contextual, radar screen continuously scanning the context of the organisation – its Operating Arena.** The radar screen must give the 'width' and 'depth' of the organisation's context – in terms of make-up, dynamics, and trends – comprehensively and truthfully, in the present and going into the future. This radar screen is essential because the design process and design solutions must relate to and fit the context in which the organisation is operating. It must be shared amongst the leadership of the organisation so that Design Solutions are conceived. For example: Does everyone in the organisation accept the growing presence of the VICCAS world?

Figure 12. 2 gives an example of such a radar screen in terms of its dimensions. It has to be populated with and activated by shared contextual content (20), like a shared understanding of the emerging new order. Figure 2.2 can be most helpful in this regard.

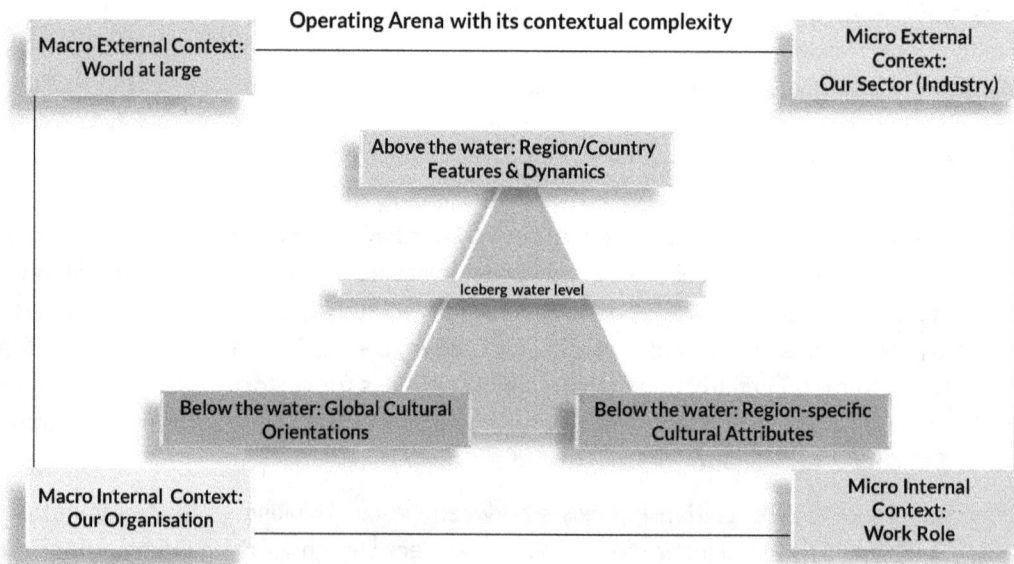

Figure 12.2: Example of a contextual radar screen to be populated by a shared understanding of the emerging new order

- **Complete OD framework.** The organisation must have a common OD vocabulary and language to inform a constructive, shared OD discourse in the organisation. As was elucidated in Chapter 3, a complete OD framework would include all Design Levels – Strategic, Tactical and Operational – and all Design Dimensions with respect to each Design Level – Horizontal, Vertical and Lateral *(21)*. The framework needs to populated with the latest thought leadership regarding OD; updated on an ongoing basis; and enriched with the organisation's own OD lessons learnt.

- **Comprehensive, competency framework**. This framework has to be used to determine the 'hard' and 'soft', visible/tangible and deep/intangible people requirements of design solutions. People make designs work. Thus the right design must be populated with the right people. This necessitates having a comprehensive Competency Model in order to translate the design into a complete set of people competencies, especially deep competencies like mindsets and values. The Competency Landscape given in Figure 10.17 is an example of such a framework.

- **Intelligent design.** A comprehensive Measurement Model must be constructed – preferably in a balanced scorecard format – in order to monitor and track 'intelligently' the design process in real time. A smart design measurement process would be fourfold in its coverage: (i) the design and implementation process: the meeting of the usual project parameters like budget, resource utilisation, and milestones/deadlines; (ii) the degree of adoption by organisational members of the new design as the new normal of working in the organisation; (iii) the realisation of the intended benefits of the design solution; and (iv) the level of change readiness energy in the organisation for design in general, as well as specific design interventions (22). An example of such a measurement model was given in Figure 8.7.

In summary: The 'What' CSFs as conceptual tools – depicting the map of the OD territory – must cover: (i) establishing OD as core organisational capacity, supported by a recursively enabling Design Thinking organisational culture; (ii) adopting the right thinking mode in doing OD, as well as (iii) the right mental model with regard to the organisation, like the Complexity view; (iv) having a shared, contextual radar screen, populated with a shared understanding of the context; (iv) drawing on a complete OD framework, informed by the latest OD thought leadership; (iv) using a comprehensive competency framework to determine the full people requirements of design solutions; and (v) adopting an Intelligent Design Measurement approach.

'How' Critical Success Factors

The 'How' CSFs refer to the process of architecting fit-for-purpose OD solutions the *action tools* of OD: what is essential in the organisation to make OD work?

At least the following 'How' CSFs must be considered (see Figure 12.1):

- **Agile design process.** The design process must allow for many possible, design *process* options: from Assurance through to Co-design (see Table 4.3, for possible options with their applicability) (23). This will make the process adaptable to fit varying circumstances and different process requirements, as well as allowing scope for greater Design Autonomy (see below). The importance of deciding on the appropriate process option cannot be overstressed. This choice can make or break a successful OD intervention. So different horses for different courses, as the saying goes.

- **Complete, integrated Portfolio of Design Processes.** A complete portfolio of clearly mapped, comprehensive, and integrated Design Processes must be available in the organisation. At a minimum, the following route maps are required: the OD intervention life cycle (see Chapter 4); an overall generic OD process (see Figure 3.6, Chapter 3); a Strategic Design Process (see Figure 4.1, Chapter 4); a Tactical Design Process (see Figure 4.2, Chapter 4); and an Operational Design Process (see Figure 4.3, Chapter 4). In the end, all of these processes must be moulded into an aligned, comprehensive, integrated design route map (24) *(25)*. The processes must be updated, improved, and even reinvented continuously with the latest OD thinking, benchmark site visits to other organisations, and own lessons learnt. In addition, new design process collaboration, participation and delivery technologies can be applied to leverage the efficiency and effect of the design process.

- **Clear boundaries around OD interventions.** The scope of OD interventions must be well demarcated: what is in and what is out. Otherwise, a design solution may be over- or under-architected. The boundaries of interventions must always include the full, threefold mode of the delivery logic as outlined in Chapter 2: Technical-Social-Virtuous.

- **Living, aligned Design Criteria and Vision.** Throughout the process of architecting and implementing design solutions, the set Design Criteria and Vision must at all times be kept as a real time, ongoing reference point. This will ensure that the consideration of options; the choice of a fit-for-purpose option; the operationalisation of an option as a solution; and its implementation remain objective, impersonal, impartial and factual (26). If the Design Criteria and Vision are absent or are its criticality underplayed, the likelihood is high that destructive organisational politics such as power plays, the pulling of rank, lobbying, and personal agendas will corrupt or even totally derail the design process. No agreed upon reference point will exist against which appeals can be made in the case of differences of opinion. In terms of organisational alignment, Design Criteria and Visions for specific design interventions must be congruent from the Strategic, through the Tactical, to the Operational Design Levels. Creative means must also be found and used to make the Design Criteria and Vision, informing the 'To-Be' design solution, real before its implementation through, for example, gamification and virtualisation (for example, augmented reality).

- **Balanced Design Autonomy.** Given ongoing OD and the need for agility, an optimum Design Autonomy balance must be found between a Once-off Top Down Design and an Ongoing Bottom-up Design for each Design Solution (see Figure 10.3). Given the emerging new order as explicated in Chapter 2, the weighting has to shift increasingly to at least (i) Co-design for Strategic/Tactical Design; and (ii) Self-managed to Autonomous for Operational Designs in order to be able to respond with agility to the unfolding, emerging context (27). A pre-requisite to this shift is capacitating organisational members with Design Thinking Tools and nurturing a Design Thinking Organisational Culture, in which the use of the tools and organisational culture reinforce each other recursively (28).

- **Organisational Landscape Alignment.** Alignment must be a non-negotiable to significantly enhance the likelihood of the successful, permanent embedding of Design Solutions. First, Design Solutions must be internally aligned. Second, it must be accepted that design makes up one component of the Organisational Landscape (Figure 3.2). Given the reciprocal interdependency of all of these components, the alignment of a Design Solution – a new Organisational Design – with the other components of the Organisational Landscape is critical. Then, and only then, can overall organisational synergy be attained, and will the chosen design be sustainable, being reinforced by the other Organisational Landscape components (29).

- **Execution capability.** It is essential that the crafting and delivery of design solutions are enabled by strong programme management and change navigation to significantly enhance the chances of successful OD interventions. A total organisational redesign – strategic-tactical-operational – can take anything from 12 to 18 months, from architecting a solution to its roll out. In accordance with their scopes, OD interventions must be adequately resourced, including with time, people and funds. Otherwise, the process to craft the best fit-for-purpose design will be compromised from the word 'Go' (30). All of the above must be supported by a thorough risk mitigation plan (31).

- **Brutal honesty and tough decisions.** The strengths and weaknesses of the current design must be assessed with uncompromising honesty – warts and all. No holy cows must be protected. Frequently the right design solutions require being tough minded, making difficult decisions and implementing hard trade-offs (32). Leadership must not shy away from making these decisions or their implementation. However, they must be taken in an ethical manner, resonating with the organisation's core values. The absence of brutal honesty and tough decision-making will rapidly erode the credibility and legitimacy of Organisational Design as a critical organisational discipline.

- **Customisation and evolution of design solutions.** During implementation, freedom must be allowed for the ongoing adjustment and refinement of a signed-off design solution on condition that the set Design Criteria and Vision are adhered to. It is near impossible to take full account in a design solution of all possible local circumstances, variations and eventualities. Design solutions must thus not be overspecified (33). The route of a *minimum viable design* can be followed, especially in the case of high Design Autonomy (see the discussion above).

In summary: the process of architecting fit-for-purpose OD solutions and the action tools – its 'How' CSFs – cover the following: (i) an agile design process with options allowing for adaptability; (ii) a complete integrated Portfolio of Design Processes, enabling the architecting of fully aligned, comprehensive, congruent design solutions; (iii) clear boundaries around OD interventions in order to reduce the likelihood of over- or under-architected solutions, and applying fully the threefold delivery logic modes; (iv) a living, aligned Design Criteria and Vision to ensure that in time wise choices are made with respect to design solution options; (v) finding the optimum balance of Design Autonomy; (vi) ensuring Organisational Landscape alignment to support and reinforce design solutions; (vii) building a deep execution capability to enhance the chances of successful OD interventions, both during design and implementation; (viii) being brutally honest and making tough decisions that are ethically informed by the organisation's values; and (ix) allowing for the customisation and evolution of design solutions to fit unique, local circumstances.

OD Maturity Curve

The maturity of OD as a mission-critical discipline in the organisation evolves, and can be plotted against a Maturity Curve (34). The Stage of OD Maturity on such a Curve can be assessed on two dimensions, determining the nature and quality of the Design Solutions architected and rolled out in an organisation:

- *Integration*: the level at which the solution is pitched to make a difference – the 'Height' of the solution- varying between Low and High.

- *Delivery Logic*: the extensiveness of delivery covered by the solution – the 'Breadth' of the solution- varying between Narrow and Broad.

Figure 12.3 depicts graphically an OD Maturity Curve.

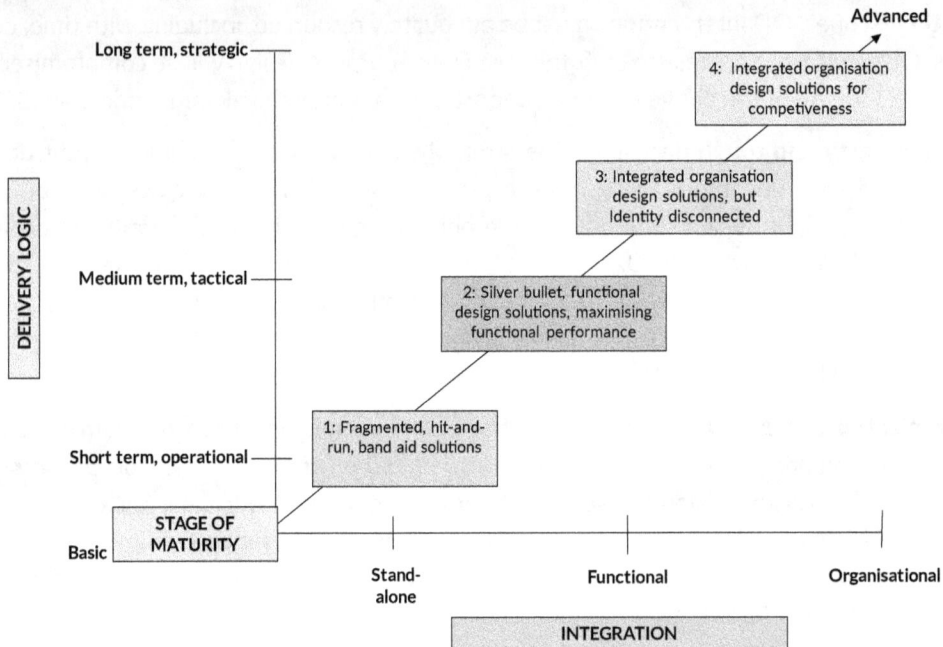

Figure 12.3: OD Maturity Curve

According to Figure 12.3, four Stages of OD Maturity can be distinguished in any organisation:

- *Stage 1: Fragmented, hit-and-run, band aid solutions.* Design solutions – at any organisational level and in any area – are stand-alone (= no integration at all) and address short term, operational delivery problems/issues (= a very restricted delivery logic). The organisation has a design pain that must be quickly fixed. Often these solutions merely entail a redesign of the organisation by redrawing the organogram; constituting a committee/forum to improve inter-departmental co-ordination; or redesigning an existing Work Role/introducing a new Work Role to fill an apparent gap, like a Client Liaison Role or an Interdepartmental Planning Role. The typical leadership talk is: 'Let's do a quick fix to let the pain go away as quickly as possible.'

- *Stage 2: Silver bullet, functional design solutions, maximising functional performance.* Design solutions that equate organisational design to the 'saving' effectiveness of a particular organisational functionality (= intra-integration) focusing on medium term, tactical, delivery logic (= a function restricted delivery logic). This is the 'Burning Platform' situation. For example, redesigning the organisation's Supply Chain, Operations or Information Technology. The typical leadership talk is: 'Addressing the design of this crucial organisational functionality will save the day for our organisation overall.'

- *Stage 3: Integrated Organisation Design solutions, but Identity is disconnected*. These design solutions address organisation-wide design needs (= long term, strategic delivery logic) but are uninformed by the organisation's Identity (= disconnected integration). This is the organisation that suffers from the blind spot of not having the insight that design entails architecting the Operating Model of the organisation. Design is the mission-critical means through which to actualise the organisation's Identity, that is its Purpose, Vision, Strategic Intent, Core Values and Legacy. Put differently, it is the leadership that has not realised that Organisational Design can give their organisation a competitive edge. The typical leadership talk is: 'Let's get our organisation to operate more efficiently by doing things right.'

- *Stage 4: Integrated Organisation Design solutions for competitiveness*. Design solutions are architected for the organisation as an integrated entity (= full integration) and a strategic means to gain and sustain a competitive edge (= long term, strategic delivery logic). The typical leadership talk is: 'Let's get our organisation to operate effectively and efficiently: doing the right things, right.'

Stage 4 represents the stage at which Organisational Design has become a truly mission-critical organisational discipline.

The level of maturity of OD in the organisation is a direct function of the state of the above-discussed CSFs. A higher CSF state will move the OD Maturity level positively. Alternatively, a deterioration in CSFs can lower an organisation's OD maturity. An upward movement will require a deliberate organisational intervention with respect to the portfolio of CSFs discussed above.

A base-line diagnosis of the CSFs is essential to establish the maturity stage an organisation is at. The wise selection of a 'quick win' CSF intervention will expedite a quicker movement up the Maturity Curve. An achieved Maturity Stage is never a fixed given for all time, but fluctuates dynamically over time as the state of CSFs change. It is therefore also recommended that the assessment of the state of CSFs needs to take place formally at least once a year at an organisational level.

Conclusion

The purpose of this chapter – the final chapter in *Designing Fit-for-Purpose Organisations* – was to discuss what it will take to turn Organisational Design into a truly mission-critical organisational discipline. More specifically, what are the critical success factors (CSFs) to make Organisational Design a value-adding organisational discipline, now and going into the future? The CSFs, and by implication risks, were discussed in terms of the Where, Why, Whereto, When, Who, What, and How of Organisational Design as mission-critical organisational disciplines. The configuration of these 'Ws' places an organisation in a certain OD Maturity Curve Stage, reflecting the degree to which OD is truly a mission-critical organisational discipline.

This has brought us to the end of our journey through the OD territory. The purpose of *Designing Fit-for-Purpose Organisations* was to capacitate you as a reader with the necessary insights and tools – conceptual and action – to architect Organisational Operating Models with fit-for-purpose Delivery Logics for the emerging new order.

Hopefully our journey was able to concretely demonstrate the intended, fivefold, unique, important contribution of *Designing Fit-for-Purpose Organisations* promised in Chapter 1, including:

- seamlessly merging the *theory and practice of OD*, giving equal weight to theory and practice through theory-informed OD practice, and inversely, practice-informed OD theory;

- extending OD to include not only the conventional technical and social *delivery modes*, but also to include a virtuous mode, thus reconceiving OD in terms of a triple delivery mode: Technical-Social-Virtuous. In this way, OD will resonate with the rise of the social enterprise and the snowballing sustainability pressure on organisations to be good citizens;

- present – for the first time in a single place – an *overall integrated OD approach and process* made up of all three design levels: Strategic, Tactical and Operational, including for each level the Horizontal, Vertical and Lateral Design Dimensions;

- using a *comprehensive integrated OD route map* as a primary organising framework for *Designing Fit-for-Purpose Organisations*, based on a seamless combination of an in-depth literature review and cutting-edge practice. Currently, such a route map is not available in the literature in a single place; and

- incorporating the *latest contextual trends* – reflective of the emerging new order – affecting the architecting of fit-for-purpose designs, such as the VICCAS world, accelerating technological innovation, stakeholder activism, and sustainability.

In the final instance in our extensive travels through the OD territory, perhaps the ultimate, overarching contribution of *Designing Fit-for-Purpose Organisations* was to demonstrate – undeniably, robustly and concretely – that OD is truly a fully-fledged, mission-critical organisational discipline. It is 'mission-critical' because it is the means through which fit-for-purpose organisations can be designed that are future-ready.

My sincerest hope is that *Designing Fit-for-Purpose Organisations* created the above value for you as a reader. My ardent wish is that you have been capacitated – at least up to a minimum level – to architect designs that will leave the world a better place for all because they are fit-for-purpose, future-wise, and will thus enable organisations to make a lasting, worthy difference for all.

Endnotes

(1) Burton & Obel (2018); Burton, Obel & Håkonsson (2015); Capelle (2014); Fenton & Pettigrew (2000); Huber (2011); Keller & Meaney (2017); Kesler & Kates (2011); MacKenzie (1986); Meyer (2013); Nadler & Tushman (1988); Puranam (2012); Snow, Miles & Miles (2006).

(2) Ambroise, Prim-Allaz, Teyssier & Peillon (2018); Agarwal, Bersin, Lahiri, Schwartz & Volini (2018); Bersin, Geller, Wakefield & Walsh (2016); Bussin (2017a); (2017c); Miles, Snow Fjeldstad, Miles & Lettl (2010); Mosley & Meaney (2017); Teece (2010); Santos, Pache & Birkholz (2015); Stanford (2015); Yeoman & O'Hara (2017).

(3) Ambroise, Prim-Allaz, Teyssier & Peillon (2018); Bellerby (2017); Brickely, Smith & Zimmerman (2003); Burton & Obel (2018); Capelle (2014); Capelle (2017); (2018); Foss, Lyngsie & Zahra (2015); Galbraith, Downey & Kates (2005); Greenwood & Miller (2010); Gruber, De Leon, George & Thompson (2015); Keller & Meaney (2017); Mosley & Meaney (2017); Nadler & Tushman (1988); (1997); Nusem, Wrigley & Matthews (2017); Stanford (2015); Veldsman (2002); Worley & Lawler (2010).

(4) Similar references to (2).

(5) Cf. Bellerby (2017); Burton & Obel (2004); Bussin (2017a); (2017c) (2017d); Capelle (2014); Goold & Campbell (2002b); Kates & Galbraith (2007); MacKenzie (1986); Miles, Snow Fjeldstad, Miles & Lettl (2010); Mintzberg (1993); (1997); Nusem, Wrigley & Matthews (2017); Stanford (2015); Nadler & Tushman (1988).

(6) See Table 4.1, Chapter 4 for examples of OD needs.

(7) Cf. Covin (2015); Fenton & Pettigrew (2000); Huber (2011); McChrystal (2015); Pettigrew & Masini (2001); Worley & Lawler (2010).

(8) Aubry & Lavoie-Tremblay (2018); Bersin, McDowell, Rahnema & van Durme (2017); Dunbar & Starbuck (2006); Galbraith (2002); Hawryszkiewycz (2017).

(9) Brickley, Smith & Zimmerman (2003); Goold & Campbell (2002a); Kates & Galbraith (2007); Kesler & Kates (2011); Keller & Meaney (2017); MacKenzie (1986); Nadler & Tushman (1988); Pearce (2013); Roh, Turkulainen, Whipple & Swink (2017); Stanford (2015).

(10) Kates & Galbraith (2007); Kester & Kates (2011); Laloux (2014); Stanford (2015).

(11) Brophy (2017); Stanford (2015).

(12) This point resonates with Parker, Morgeson & Johns' (2017) view of involving beneficiaries and stakeholders in architecting the Operational Design of the organisations they have a stake in, which was noted in Chapter 11.

(13) Kates & Galbraith (2007); Kesler & Kates (2011); Stanford (2015).

(14) In Deloitte's Global Human Capital Trends (2016) it was found that only 14% of executives believed their companies were ready to effectively redesign their organisations; just 21% felt expert at building a cross-functional, team-based organisation; and only 12% understood the way their people worked together in networks of teams.

(15) Chandler (2018); Elsbach & Stigliani (2018); Gruber, De Leon, George & Thompson (2015); Kolko (2015); Yoo, Boland & Lyytinen (2006).

(16) Nusem, Wrigley & Matthews (2017) describe a non-profit organisation's journey in building organisational design as an organisational capability.

(17) Elsbach & Stigliani (2018) outline the recursive relationship between design thinking tools and a design thinking, organisational culture as follows. *First*, the use of specific design thinking tools (for example, experimentation or prototyping) to help in the development and support of an organisational culture defined by values, norms, or assumptions related to experimentation or openness to failure. These tools are: (i) *Need finding tools* – such as ethnographic interviews and customer journey mapping – contributing to user-centric cultures; (ii) *Idea-generation tools* – such as brainstorming and co-creation/co-design – contributing to cultures of openness to ambiguity, risk taking, and collaboration; and (iii) *Idea-testing tools* – such as rapid prototyping and experimentation – contributing to cultures of openness, experimentation, openness to failure, and design-oriented strategic thinking.

Second, and inversely, organisational cultures influence – both positively and negatively – the effective use of the above design thinking tools. Organic design thinking cultures – defined by values, norms and assumptions, such as collaboration, a free flow of information and experimentation – support the use of specific design thinking tools (that is tools of prototyping, co-creation, and customer journey mapping). In contrast, bureaucratised cultures – defined by control, authority, productivity, quantitative-measured performance, and siloed specialisation – impede the use of these tools.

(18) Kurtmollaiev, Pedersen, Fjuk & Kvale (2018) also regard Design Thinking as a core (dynamic) organisational capability. In a quasi-experimental field study of the effects of Design Thinking training, they found that the training had a positive effect on the managers' sensing and seizing capabilities, which in turn had a positive effect on their transformation capability; team innovation output; and team operational capability. These positive effects were accompanied by a direct negative effect of the training on the operational capabilities of the participants' teams. Although the training participants became inspired to make changes in their teams' operating routines and procedures, these changes were not constructive for the teams of those participants who failed first to strengthen their dynamic Design Thinking capabilities through the training.

(19) Stanford (2015) also stresses the importance of the choice of the right Organisational Model.

(20) Constructed by the author.

(21) As was discussed in Chapter 1, at present the fragmented nature of the Organisational Design literature is a major weakness: strategic, tactical and operational designs are seen and done in silos. *Inter alia*, the intention of *Designing Fit-for-Purpose Organisations* is to overcome this fragmentation through the comprehensive, integrated route map it offers.

(22) Mosley & Meaney (2017); Stanford (2015). Stanford (2015) only refers to benefits realisation.

(23) Mosley & Meaney (2017).

(24) Brophy (2017); MacKenzie (1986).

(25) Currently also missing in the OD literature which *Designing Fit-for-Purpose Organisations* endeavours to overcome.

(26) MacKenzie (1986).

(27) Dunbar & Starbuck (2006); Mosley & Meaney (2017).

(28) Elsbach & Stigliani (2018).

(29) Brophy (2017); Dunbar & Starbuck (2006); Mohrman, Cohen & Mohrman (1995).

(30) Stanford (2015).

(31) Mosley & Meaney (2017).

(32) Brophy (2017); MacKenzie (1986).

(33) Kates & Galbraith (2007); MacKenzie (1986).

(34) Constructed by the author based on his observations of the state of OD organisations over many years.

APPENDICES

Appendix A: Glossary of Key Organisational Design Terms

Autonomy: The freedom to take independent action. How much control/say will a team/person have over its/his/her tasks, decisions and actions?

Brownfield: Redesign.

Change Readiness Energy: The amount of people energy in the organisation available to affect the intended change.

The energy is made up of the sum total of ten variables: need for and desire to change; sponsorship and stakeholder commitment; leadership visibility; vision clarity; benefits of change relative to costs of change; resource availability (time, people, money); confidence in implementation capability; clear route map, roles and contributions; change adopter confidence and competence; recognition and celebration of successes.

Command-and-Control Vision of Organisational Architecture: Job-based design: One person to one prescribed task (= job) with few skills; little decision-making power; little information; controlled by rules, procedures and ranks; linked to others through the hierarchy; focusing on efficient processes, quantity, and continuous improvement.

Control of variance at source: All the activities that have a direct influence on the performance of a Work Unit/Domain must be under its control.

Criteria Design: The specifications that the design must meet. The conditions the design must facilitate, enable, encourage, and provide for.

Crown Jewel: A "mission critical" capability of the organisation. Examples of such jewels are core competencies, key talent, critical resources, key technologies, brand(s), strategic markets/clients and/or products/services.

Decision-making Styles:

- *Tell:* The accountable party makes the decision and instructs those who are responsible for doing the work, to do the work.

- *Consult:* The accountable party asks for input from the responsible parties, considers their input, makes a decision, and instructs them.

- *Co-determine:* The accountable party and responsible parties jointly debate the intended action and make a decision together.

- *Self-manage:* The responsible party (or parties) consults upwards with the accountable party, makes the decision and informs the accountable party accordingly (upward consultation).

- *Self-govern:* The responsible party (or parties) makes the decision and informs the accountable party (upward telling/selling).

Decision Rights:

These Rights are made up of five rights, expressed as **VARII**:

- **V**eto (or Ratify): Go/No Go, such as the approval of or compliance to a policy, standard or practice.
- **A**ccountability: Final decision maker regarding the work process or element thereof who is accountable for the decision/action regarding the work process or element thereof (only one Work Unit/Role).
- **R**esponsible: Who does the work regarding the work process or element thereof, for example policies and standards (can be more than one Work Unit/Role).
- **I**nput (or Consult): Who must provide input to the decision/action before and whilst the work is being done regarding the work process or element thereof.
- **I**nformed: Who must be informed once the decision has been taken regarding a work process or element thereof, and during its implementation.

Delivery Logic: Made up of three interdependent modes (= strands) forming an indivisible, holistic whole (= rope) that have to be jointly optimised:

- *Technical:* People requirements of the Core Operating Technology and Enablers used by the organisation to satisfy customer needs.
- *Social:* How the work of the organisation must be done by its people by utilising the Core Technology to deliver.
- *Virtuous:* Delivering in a humane way, with stewardship, for the greater good. 'Humane' refers to endorsing people's dignity and well-being through the design; 'stewardship' to a leaving the world sustainably a better place for future generations; and 'greater good' to considering the interests/ needs of all stakeholders, and not only the self-serving, parochial interests of the organisation and its shareholders.

Dimensions, Design: Each Design Level contains three Design Dimensions:

- **Horizontal:** The grouping of the flow of work into Work Units/Domains.
- **Vertical:** The allocation of the requisite Levels of Work to respectively the Organisation, Work Units and Work Roles.
- **Lateral:** The Integration Mechanisms and Governance Model to integrate the Horizontal and Vertical Designs.

Design Autonomy *(also referred to as team/job crafting):* To what degree work team members/work role incumbents – in a self-initiated way – have the right to change the Operational Design by shaping, moulding and redefining it in a (semi-) permanent way. In other words, what freedom do team members/

role incumbents have to (re)craft the basic Operational Design that is being/has been architected?

Effectiveness: Doing the right things.

Efficiency: Doing things right.

Greenfield: New design.

High Flexibility/High Involvement organisational architecture: Team-based Design – Highly autonomous, multi-skilled and multi-disciplinary autonomous teams/mini-business units performing broad chunks of the organisation's overall work processes (or total work process) with a high degree of decision-making power, self-generated information, driven by and linked to others by an internalised Organisational Identity, focused on customers and quality, whilst acting as true, genuine citizens.

Interdependency: Five basic types of interdependencies can be distinguished:

- **Pooled:** A work unit/role functions highly independently. Its performance output does not affect another work unit/role. Its performance output is added to the overall output.

- **Sequential:** The performance output of a work unit/role is the input to another unit/role. The one Unit delivers work to another.

- **Reciprocal:** The performance output of one unit/role becomes the input of another unit/role, whose performance output in turn becomes the input to the first unit/role. Mutual interdependency exists between parties to get the work done.

- **Enabling:** One work unit/role provides and maintains the direct means required by another work unit/role to get the work done.

- **Supporting:** One work unit/role provides specialist advice, counselling, knowledge and/or expertise to another work unit/role, enabling it to make the right decisions and take the right action.

Design Levels: Organisation design occurs at the strategic, tactical and operational levels:

- **Strategic Design:** Design of the organisation as a total entity and the essential macro elements making up this entity, e.g, its, Work Units, Corporate Centre, Centres of excellence, and Service Centres ('House').

- **Tactical Design:** Design of different Work Units of the organisation ('Rooms').

- **Operational Design:** Design of Work Teams and Work Roles making up Work Units ('Furniture').

Levels of Work (LOW): The kind of work that must be performed at a requisite level of complexity.

Organisation: Purpose-directed, consciously organised social entity operating within identifiable boundaries embedded within a certain context.

Organisational design (or architecture): Operating Model of the organisation that pertains to the delivery logic required by the organisation (or part thereof, for example, Operations, Finance, People Management) to define, unlock and deliver ongoing value for stakeholders within its context (or

Operating Arena). OD provides a formal map of how the required work of the organisation must be done effectively as demarcated by boundaries of accountability, responsibility and authority: doing the right things in the right place at the right time by the right person with the necessary checks and balances.

Design Process Options:

- **Assurance:** Client has already generated a design, which the OD Expert must quality assure.

- **Expert Generated:** The OD Expert crafts a design and submits the solution to the Client for sign-off.

- **Straw Model:** The OD Expert crafts a straw model design which is workshopped with the relevant key decision-makers in the client system, before being finalised by the Expert.

- **Co-design:** The OD Expert facilitates an OD co-design process with the client system to co-architect a Design Solution.

Work Role: An enacted, coherent set of tasks, duties, relationships, and conduct for which a person is accountable/responsible, within a certain Work Unit, which must be performed to certain performance standards.

Work Role Profile elements:

- Core purpose: Why does the Role exist?

- Key performance areas: What are the major areas of performance (in terms of work stations/ portfolios).

- Outcomes: What must be produced and to what specification?

Organisational Shapes:

1. **Activity based**

   Functional: Groupings around common activities;

   OR

   Process: Groupings in terms of end-to-end core workflow(s);

   OR

   Projects: Groupings based on projects, which in turn are grouped into programmes;

   OR

   Co-operative: Groupings based on membership.

2. **Mirror/Image Matrix**

   Simultaneously vertical and horizontal overlaid groupings. One grouping represents functional areas, while the other grouping represents products/services or clients.

3   Hub and Spoke

Groupings of activities by geographical region.

4.   Portfolio or Divisionally based

Groupings by related products/services, each with its own set of activities (functional or process groupings);

OR

Groupings by related clients/markets, each with its own set of activities (functional or process groupings).

5.   Front/Back

On the client facing side of organisation (the 'Front' of the organisation), groupings in terms of distinct segments of the client and/or markets typically spread over a number of countries. The 'Back' of the organisation is made up of groupings in terms of different products/services, made up of one or more operational entities.

6.   Network

Partnering: : a set of independent organisations, teams and/or individuals who form relationships in a common space in order to jointly unlock value and create wealth for mutual benefit, whether organisationally or publically.

Types of Networks:

- **Contracted Ecosystem:** Formalised, permanent relationships within a fixed set of members, contractually bound to each other for agreed upon, fixed periods of time. Examples include outsourcing, joint ventures and franchising networks.
- **Synergistic Ecosystem:** Informal, temporary relationships within a fixed set of members, bound to each other through a verbal agreement for mutually agreed-upon times. For example, a strategic alliance.
- **Managed Ecosystem:** Formalised, self-organising relationships within a varying set of members for mutually agreed-upon, varying periods of time. Examples include Linux (an open-source software community) and Wikipedia (a free, online encyclopedia).
- **Instantaneous Ecosystem:** Informal, temporary relationships within a set of varying members who join and leave of their own volition at any time it suits them. Examples include leaderless ecosystems such as leaderless revolutions, social movements, and crowdsourcing.

7.   Cluster

Grouping of similar business units into clusters, typically sector/industry based.

8.   Holding

Grouping of similar businesses/companies according to investment portfolio principles.

9.   Hybrid (or Mixed)

Grouping based on a mixture of any of the above Organisational Shapes.

10. **Professional Maturity Curve**

Grouping of activities along a curve of increasing complexity, requiring successive, higher levels of competence, and allowing people to progress along the curve as and when they provide concrete evidence of their ability to perform at the next level of competence, consistently and predictably.

Task: *What* needs to be done, not How it is done.

Task Matrix: All of the tasks to be performed within a Work Unit/Work Team.

Work Team: A group of people with complementary knowledge, skills, expertise and experience, who interact on a regular basis and in an interdependent manner regarding a given set of different tasks, roles and responsibilities, in order to achieve a shared goal(s) that can only be achieved collectively, not individually.

Total Work Requisite Complexity: Requisite LOW of Work Roles x Requisite Contextual Complexity of organisation's operating arena.

Design Vision: A one page description of what the organisation will look like when it is operating in terms of the Design Criteria (a 'day-in-the-life' of the organisation).

Work Processes: The flow of an interdependent set of activities through the organisation, starting with the client need and ending with a satisfied need.

Types of Work Processes:

- **Core Work Process:** A process that creates and delivers value to the client.

- **Delivery Enablement Processes:** Processes that enable the core work process to occur.

- **Support Work Processes:** Processes that enable the organisation to function as an entity.

Works Stations/Portfolios: Coherent and congruent set (or grouping) of tasks which have to be performed by a role incumbent with respect to a Key Performance Area: The 'chunks' of work which are allocated to people.

Work Unit: An area of accountability.

Four types of Work Units:

- **Board:** Unit that plays an independent, oversight governance role over the organisation and its leadership.

- **Corporate Centre** (in the conventional language, the Head Office): Unit that provides direction, guidance and governance to the total organisation.

- **Operating Unit(s):** Unit containing the total core work process – the client delivery process – or a portion thereof.

- **Enabling Unit(s):** Unit containing the support processes that enable delivery by the operating entity/entities. For example, in the case of a manufacturing organisation, the maintenance of production equipment.

- **Support Units:** Units containing the processes that enable the organisation to function as an organisation, for example, Finance, People, IT.

Appendix B: Design Templates

INDEX OF DESIGN TEMPLATES
Design Template 1: OD BUSINESS CASE
Design Template 2: OD READINESS ASSESSMENT
Design Template 3: STRATEGIC DESIGN – WORK ROLE
Design Template 4: STRATEGIC INTEGRATION MECHANISMS
Design Template 5: STRATEGIC DESIGN GOVERNANCE MODEL
Design Template 6: STRATEGIC ORGANISATIONAL ALIGNMENT
Design Template 7: STRATEGIC DESIGN IMPACT ASSESSMENT
Design Template 8: STRATEGIC DESIGN ROLL OUT STRATEGY AND PLAN
Design Template 9: STRATEGIC CHANGE NAVIGATION STRATEGY AND PLAN
Design Template 10: TACTICAL DESIGN – OPERATING WORK UNIT PROFILE
Design Template 11: TACTICAL DESIGN – INTEGRATED OPERATING WORK UNIT MAP
Design Template 12: OPERATIONAL DESIGN – WORK TEAM PROFILE
Design Template 13: OPERATIONAL DESIGN – INTEGRATED WORK TEAM DESIGN MAP
Design Template 14: WORK ROLE PROFILE
Design Template 15: TASK MATRIX: OPERATING TASKS
Design Template 16: TASK MATRIX: LEADERSHIP TASKS
Design Template 17: INTEGRATED WORK ROLE PROFILE
Design Template 18: WORK TEAM/ROLE – EVOLUTION STAGES OF INCREASING AUTONOMY
Design Template 19: OPERATIONAL DESIGN IMPACT ASSESSMENT

DESIGN TEMPLATE 1: OD BUSINESS CASE	
ORGANISATIONAL UNIT:	REQUESTER: POSITION:
REASON(S) FOR OD INTERVENTION	SCOPE OF OD INTERVENTION
EXPECTED DELIVERABLES	EXPECTED VALUE ADD
URGENCY OF OD INTERVENTION (BY WHEN)	CHOSEN DESIGN PROCESS OPTION
GROUND RULES	ANY SPECIAL REQUIREMENTS WITH REGARD TO THE OD PRACTITIONER REQUIRED
BUDGET REQUIRED (If applicable)	
SIGNATURE	DATE
CONTACT DETAILS	

DESIGN TEMPLATE 2: OD READINESS ASSESSMENT									
Readiness element	Low Readiness/ High Risk			Medium Readiness/ Medium Risk			High Readiness/ Low Risk		
	1	2	3	4	5	6	7	8	9
Right sponsorship Motivation for rating:									
Clear need and benefits Motivation for rating:									
Permanently appointed leadership Motivation for rating:									
Agreement on Strategic Intent Motivation for rating:									
Well-functioning leadership team/community Motivation for rating:									
Willingness to allocate the necessary resources (= time, people, money) to the OD intervention Motivation for rating:									
Expected benefits of the new design outweighs the costs of the OD intervention Motivation for rating:									
Necessary OD expertise is available and is at requisite level of complexity as demanded by the OD intervention Motivation for rating:									
OVERALL RATING									
DECISION TO PROCEED OR NOT									
IF "NO", CONDITIONS TO ADDRESS IN ORDER TO ENHANCE READINESS TO PROCEED									

DESIGN TEMPLATE 3: STRATEGIC DESIGN – WORK ROLE	
WORK ROLE TITLE:	
Requisite Level of Work	
Core Purpose	To.........
Critical Tasks (= Key Performance Areas) (Not more than five)	**Start with a verb**
Key Outputs (Not more than five)	

DESIGN TEMPLATE 4: STRATEGIC INTEGRATION MECHANISMS					
Integration Mechanism	Purpose/ Mandate	Work Domain/ Agenda covered	Owner	Participants	Frequency of being invoked

DESIGN TEMPLATE 5: STRATEGIC DESIGN GOVERNANCE MODEL						
LEVEL OF WORK/WORK PROCESS (OR ELEMENT THEREOF)	DECISION-MAKING RIGHTS Relevant Work Unit/Work Role					
	Veto/ Ratify	Accountable	Responsible	Input	Informed	
6 Context shaping						DECISION-MAKING RIGHTS
						DECISION-MAKING STYLE
Corporate Governance						DECISION-MAKING RIGHTS
						DECISION-MAKING STYLE
5 Returns/Yields						DECISION-MAKING RIGHTS
						DECISION-MAKING STYLE
Direction, Objectives, Philosophy						DECISION-MAKING RIGHTS
						DECISION-MAKING STYLE
4 Organisational Policies and Standards (specify which)						DECISION-MAKING RIGHTS
						DECISION-MAKING STYLE
Organisational Systems (specify which)						DECISION-MAKING RIGHTS
						DECISION-MAKING STYLE
4 Work Unit Direction, Objectives, Philosophy, Return/ Yields						DECISION-MAKING RIGHTS
						DECISION-MAKING STYLE
Resourcing						DECISION-MAKING RIGHTS
						DECISION-MAKING STYLE
3 Delivery Work Process						DECISION-MAKING RIGHTS
						DECISION-MAKING STYLE
2 Delivery Standards						DECISION-MAKING RIGHTS
						DECISION-MAKING STYLE
1 Daily Delivery						DECISION-MAKING RIGHTS
						DECISION-MAKING STYLE

DESIGN TEMPLATE 6: STRATEGIC ORGANISATIONAL ALIGNMENT		
ORGANISATIONAL LANDSCAPE BUILDING BLOCK	**ALIGNMENT QUESTION**	**TYPICAL ASPECTS TO CONSIDER**
Leadership alignment	What type(s) of leadership is required by the design?	• Style (for example, Autocratic, Democratic or Participative) • Person centric vs. Task centric • Visionary, Philosophy, Values vs. Goals, Plans, Standards
Culture alignment	What shared way of seeing, interpreting and doing things must exist to reinforce the design?	• Typology 1: Role, Power, Support or Achievement Culture (Harrison, 1972) • Typology 2: Clan, Adhocracy, Hierarchy, Market (Cameron & Quinn, 2006)
People alignment	What is the general profile(s) of the people required to staff up the design?	• Personal attributes • Knowledge, Skills, Expertise • Values and Beliefs • Attitudes and Styles • Conduct
Resources (including policies, standards, systems, practices) alignment	How must resources change to reinforce the design?	• Types • Distribution • Ownership
Performance alignment	How must the Key Performance Areas (KPAs) and Indicators (KPIs) change to reinforce the design?	In terms of an adapted Balanced Scorecard (Kaplan & Norton, 1992): • Financial • Internal Efficiencies • Growth and Innovation • Stakeholder satisfaction/ Goodwill
Workplace	How must the physical workplace be changed to reinforce and support the design?	For example, physical lay-out of working spaces; who sits where; furniture.

DESIGN TEMPLATE 7: STRATEGIC DESIGN IMPACT ASSESSMENT						
CRITICAL DESIGN VARIABLE	CURRENT DESIGN	FUTURE DESIRED DESIGN	ASSESSED GAP TRANSLATED INTO CHANGE NEED	RISK ASSESSMENT 1=High; 2=Medium; 3=Low	IMPLEMEN-TATION PRIORITY 1=High; 2=Medium; 3=Low	REQUIRED ACTIONS TO CLOSE CRITICAL GAPS
Mental Model required by Design Beliefs, Assumptions, Values, Norms, Attitudes						
Design Criteria						
Design Vision with Metaphor						
Horizontal Design						
Vertical Design (including competencies)						
Lateral Design						
Organisational Alignment • Leadership/ • People • Culture • Resources • Performance • Work Place						
Costing (for example, salaries, facilities)						

DESIGN TEMPLATE 8: STRATEGIC DESIGN ROLL OUT STRATEGY AND PLAN

OVERALL ROLL OUT STRATEGY
(Big bang vs. Incremental)

| |
| |

ROLL OUT PLAN

What (In time sequence)	By When	How	Who Accountable/Responsible Parties	Handover Log

ROLL OUT MEASUREMENT MODEL

Design roll out metrics	People adoption metrics	Organisational performance metrics

ROLL OUT STRUCTURE AND PROCESS

| |
| |

TEMPLATE 9: STRATEGIC DESIGN CHANGE NAVIGATION STRATEGY AND PLAN

CHANGE NAVIGATION STRATEGY
(Directive vs. Participative, involved)

CHANGE NAVIGATION ELEMENTS	CHANGE NAVIGATION PHASES WITH INTERVENTIONS				
	Aware	Mobilise	Design	Roll out	Stabilise
Change Leadership & Sponsorship					
Stakeholder Commitment					
Change specific Communication					
Change Team Capability					
Change Adopters' Resilience					
Organisational Alignment					

CHANGE GOVERNANCE

CHANGE NAVIGATION MEASUREMENT: CHANGE READINESS ENERGY	Low	Medium	High
• Understanding/Acceptance of Business Case • Vision Clarity • Perceived benefits of change outweighs costs thereof • Strong, visible leadership/modelling • Stakeholder Buy-in/Commitment • Clear road map with clearly defined contributions • Required skills, knowledge, expertise • Resource availability/confidence in implementation ability • Perceived fairness/legitimacy of change process • Celebration of milestone achievements			

ACTIONS TO ENHANCE CHANGE READINESS ENERGY LEVELS	

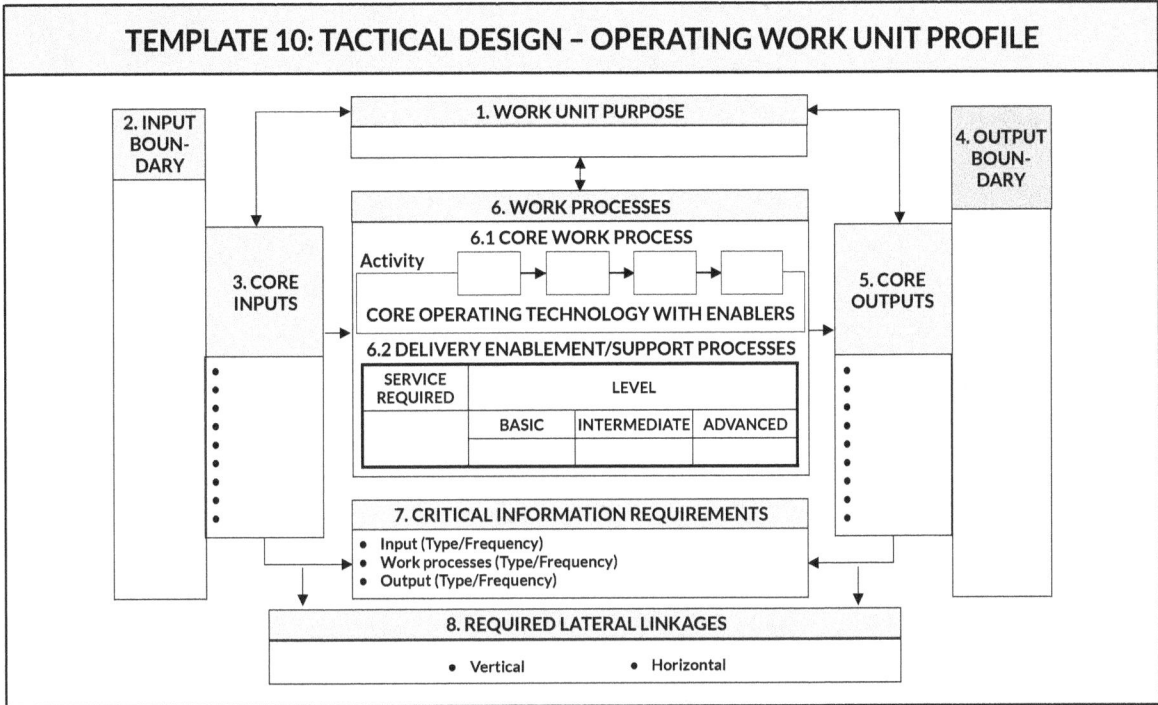

TEMPLATE 10: TACTICAL DESIGN – OPERATING WORK UNIT PROFILE

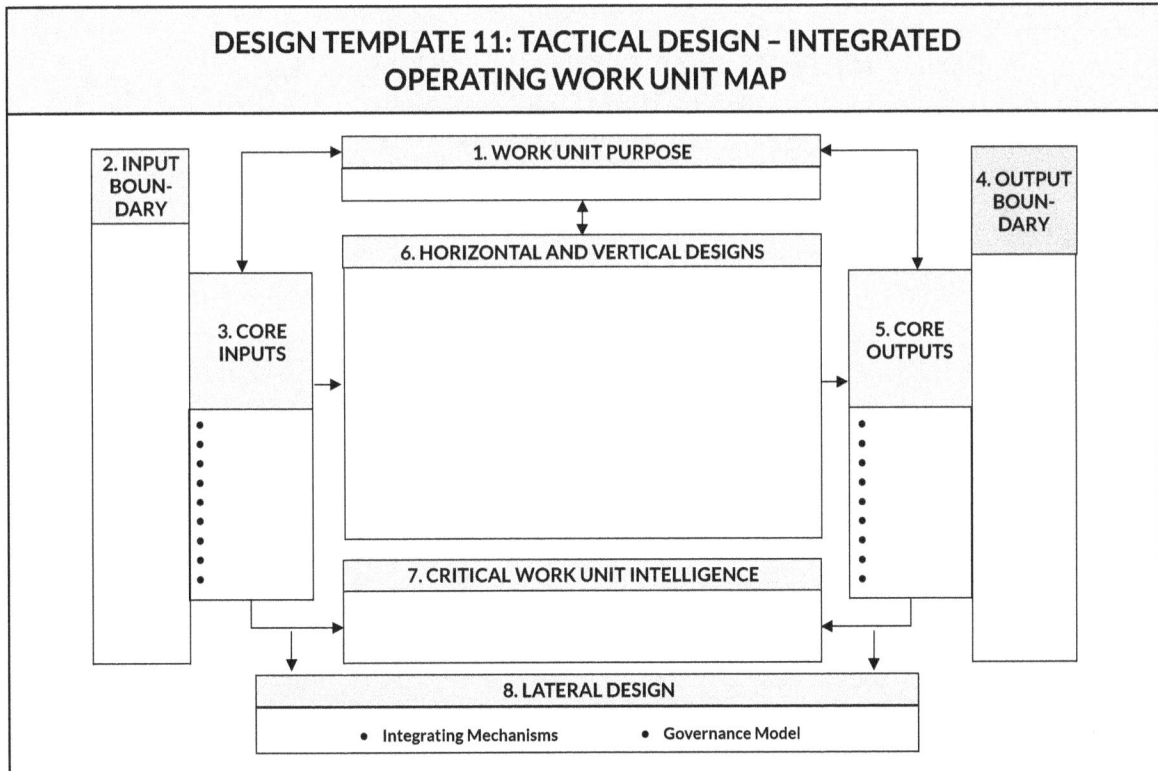

DESIGN TEMPLATE 11: TACTICAL DESIGN – INTEGRATED OPERATING WORK UNIT MAP

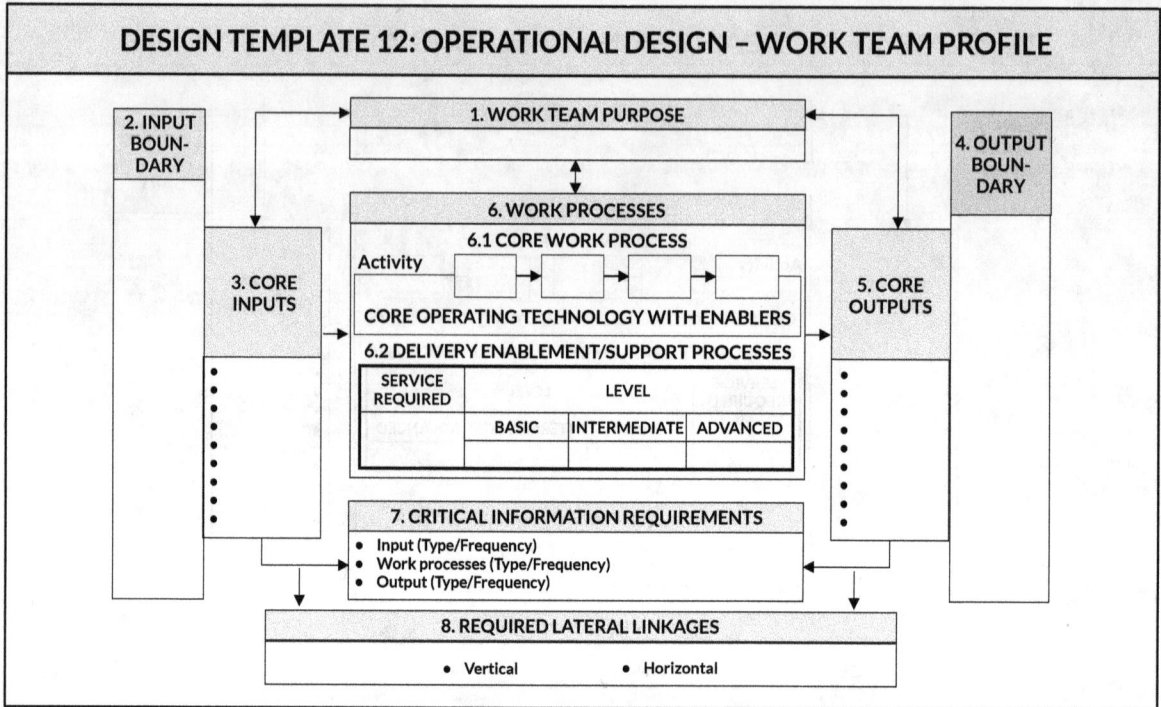

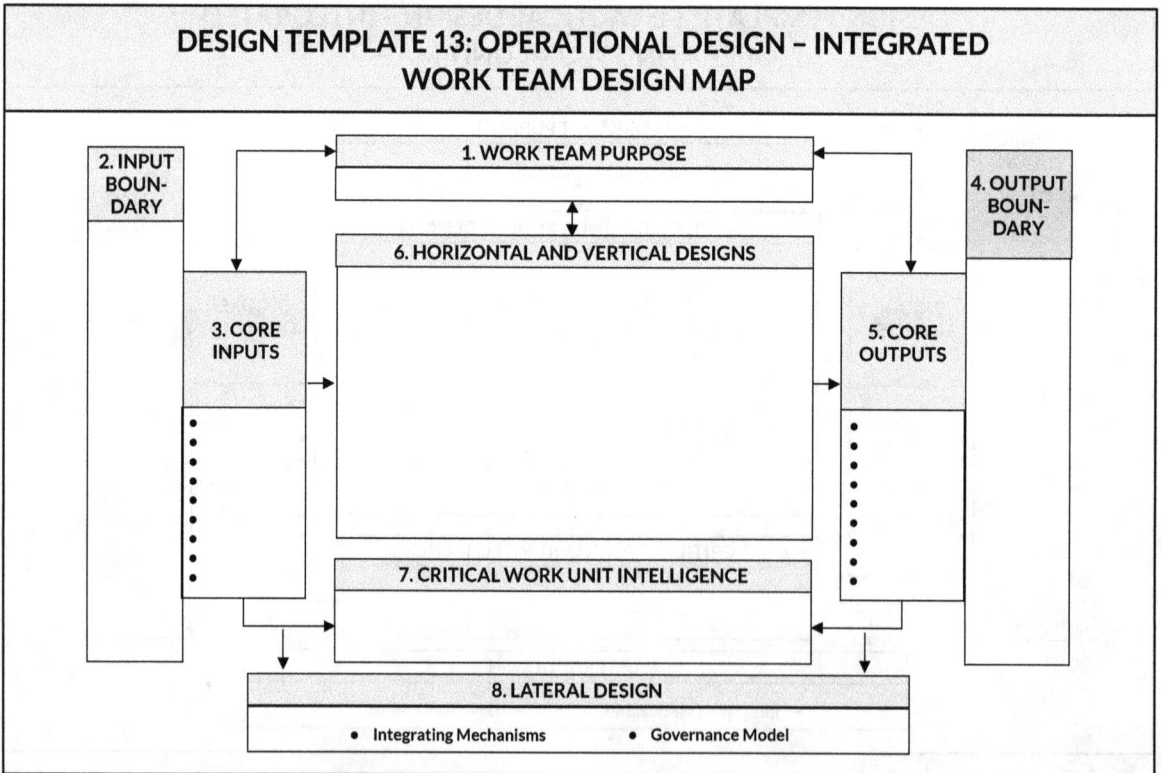

DESIGN TEMPLATE 14: WORK ROLE PROFILE	
WORK ROLE	
Section	**Description**
Work Context	The context in which the work role is embedded with its contextual complexity; the Design Givens.
Core Purpose	Why does the role exist?
Requisite Level Of Work	The requisite level of work in terms of total complexity.
Scope of Work with Boundaries	What portion of the core work process is the role accountable for within which boundaries, that is authorisation levels, physical, safety, legal, ethical and/or time horizon?
Key Performance Areas	What are the major areas of performance (= KPAs)?
Critical Outcomes	What outputs must be delivered to what specifications?
Organisational Location	• Where is the role located in the organisation as reflected in the organogram? o Which role does this report into? o Which roles report into this role? o With which roles at the same level does the role need to interact, that is peers.

DESIGN TEMPLATE 15: TASK MATRIX – OPERATING TASKS				
CATEGORY	**TASK LIST**	**DURATION** **(in hours or** **portion thereof)**	**FREQUENCY OF** **PERFORMANCE** **(over monthly cycle)**	**TOTAL TIME**
A: Input task 1: Plan 2: Organise 3: Do 4: Monitor 5: Change				
B: Work processes **BA: Core process tasks** 1: Plan 2: Organise 3: Do 4: Monitor 5: Change **BB: Enabling/Support** **process tasks**				
C: Output to customers' tasks				
D: Contextual tasks				
TOTAL MONTHLY WORK LOAD (in hours)				

DESIGN TEMPLATE 16: TASK MATRIX – LEADERSHIP TASKS				
CATEGORY	TASK LIST	DURATION (in hours or portion thereof)	FREQUENCY OF PERFORMANCE (over monthly cycle)	TOTAL TIME
A: Enabling tasks 1: Do 2: Coach, facilitate and advise 3: (Re)design and build 4: Link and mediate 5: Envision				
BA: Internal empowerment tasks 1: Do 2: Coach, facilitate and advise 3: (Re)design and build 4: Link and mediate 5: Envision				
BB: External empowerment tasks 1: Do 2: Coach, facilitate and advise 3: (Re)design and build 4: Link and mediate 5: Envision				
TOTAL MONTHLY WORK LOAD (in hours)				

DESIGN TEMPLATE 17: INTEGRATED WORK ROLE PROFILE			
WORK ROLE			
Section	**Description**		
Work Context	The context in which the work role is embedded with its contextual complexity; the Design Givens.		
Core Purpose	Why does the role exist?		
Requisite Level of Work	What is the requisite level of work of the role in terms of total complexity?		
Scope of Work with Boundaries	What portion of the core work process is the role accountable for within what boundaries, that is authorisation levels, physical, safety, legal, ethical and/or time horizon?		
Key Performance Areas	What are the major areas of performance (= KPAs)?		
Critical Outcomes	What outputs must be delivered to what specifications?		
Organisational Location	• Where is the role located in the organisation as reflected in the organogram? o Which role does this report into? o Which roles report into this role? o With which roles at the same level does the role need to interact, that is peers		

Appendix **TASK MAP BY KEY PERFORMANCE AREAS**	**KEY PERFORMANCE AREA 1**		**KEY PERFORMANCE AREA....n**	
	Action Dimensions 1 to n	**Task Dimensions 1 to n**	**Action Dimensions 1 to n**	**Task Dimensions 1 to n**
Operating Tasks 1 to n	• *By Action Dimension and Operating Task* • Task 1 with time demand • Task 2 with time demand .... • Task n with time demand	• *By Action Dimension and Operating Task* • Task 1 with time demand • Task 2 with time demand .... • Task n with time demand	• *By Action Dimension and Operating Task* • Task 1 with time demand • Task 2 with time demand .... • Task n with time demand	• *By Action Dimension and Operating Task* • Task 1 with time demand • Task 2 with time demand .... • Task n with time demand
Leadership Tasks 1 to n	• *By Action Dimension and Operating Task* • Task 1 with time demand • Task 2 with time demand .... • Task n with time demand	• *By Action Dimension and Operating Task* • Task 1 with time demand • Task 2 with time demand .... • Task n with time demand	• *By Action Dimension and Operating Task* • Task 1 with time demand • Task 2 with time demand .... • Task n with time demand	• *By Action Dimension and Operating Task* • Task 1 with time demand • Task 2 with time demand .... • Task n with time demand
TOTAL TIME				

DESIGN TEMPLATE 18: WORK TEAM/ROLE – EVOLUTION STAGES OF INCREASING AUTONOMY										
	STAGE 1 (By when)		STAGE 2 (By when)		STAGE 3 (By when)		STAGE 4 (By when)		STAGE 5 (By when)	
	Operating Tasks	Leadership Tasks	Operating Tasks	Leadership Tasks	Operating Tasks	Leadership Tasks	Operating Tasks	Leadership Tasks	Operating Tasks	Leadership Tasks
Self-government										
Self-management										
Co-determination (Joint problem solving)										
Consultation (Sell)										
Informing (Tell)										

DESIGN TEMPLATE 19: OPERATIONAL DESIGN IMPACT ASSESSMENT						
CRITICAL DESIGN VARIABLES	CURRENT DESIGN	FUTURE DESIRED DESIGN	ASSESSED GAP TRANSLATED INTO CHANGE NEED	RISK ASSESSMENT 1=High; 2=Medium; 3=Low	IMPLEMENTATION PRIORITY 1=High; 2=Medium; 3=Low	REQUIRED ACTIONS TO CLOSE CRITICAL GAPS

• Purpose
• Boundaries: Input and Output
• Core Inputs from Suppliers
• Core Outputs to Customers
• Work Processes
  ○ Core
  ○ Support
• Mode of Working
• Work Teams
• Work Roles with Work Stations/Portfolios/ Roles (including competencies)
• Critical Information Requirements
• Lateral Linkages
• Evolutionary Path						

Lateral Tactical-Operational Alignment						
Strategic and Tactical Design Alignments						
Mental Model: Beliefs, Assumptions, Values, Norms, Attitudes						
Costing						
Design Criteria						
Design Vision						

Appendix C: Programme Templates

INDEX OF PROGRAMME TEMPLATES
Programme Template 1: TEAMING & ALIGNMENT DESIGN WORKSHOP PROGRAMME
Programme Template 2: STRAW MODEL STRATEGIC DESIGN WORKSHOP
Programme Template 3: STRATEGIC CO-DESIGN WORKSHOPS
Programme Template 4: STRAW MODEL, TACTICAL DESIGN WORKSHOP
Programme Template 5: TACTICAL CO-DESIGN WORKSHOPS
Programme Template 6: STRAW MODEL OPERATIONAL DESIGN WORKSHOP
Programme Template 7: OPERATIONAL CO-DESIGN WORKSHOPS

PROGRAMME TEMPLATE 1: TEAMING & ALIGNMENT DESIGN WORKSHOP PROGRAMME		
Day 1		
Time	Subject	Responsible
08h30 – 08h45	Introduction & welcome	Leader of Team

08h45 – 09h15	• Purpose
	   o To share our experiences of the redesign intervention to date
	   o To identify and action unfinished business, as well as lessons learnt
	   o To set the team up for future success
	   o To agree on how we are going to work together as a team
	   o To get to know one another as team members
	• Format: overview of workshop programme as given below
	• Ground rules for workshop (some of these rules could foreshadow team values. Put up, and ask for comment). Suggested rules:
	   o Everyone's opinion counts
	   o Active listening
	   o Equal participation
	   o Play the ball, not the person
	   o One session, not separate discussions
	   o Honest and open
	   o Give recognition
	• Expectations of workshop
	
	Leader of team leaves. Remember to ask him/her to prepare his/her own Sads, Mads, Glads
		Group Facilitator/ Leader of Team

Time	Subject	Responsible
09h15-10h15	<ul><li>The change journey to date:<ul><li>Sads</li><li>Mads</li><li>Glads</li></ul></li><li>Where on change transition cycle</li><li>"Unfinished Business": what still needs attention arising out of the journey to date?</li><li>Open "Parking Lot" flipchart</li><li>Open "Action Planning" flipchart</li></ul>	Group Facilitator
10h15 – 10h30	Tea/Coffee	All
10h30 – 11h00	Leader of team rejoins Feedback to team leader. Team members ask to give feedback. Leader of team to add own Sads, Mads, Glads as feedback occurs and indicate where he/she is on the change transition cycle	Group Facilitator
11h00 – 11h30	Celebrating our past successes	Leader of Team
11h30 – 12h00	Business case for change and future outcome	Leader of Team
12h00 – 13h00	New design, work role profiles, decision-making rights/styles down to appropriate organisational level Team to be given everyone's role profiles and asked to review everything overnight that was covered during the day for discussion the next morning	Leader of Team Group Facilitator
13h00 – 14h00	Lunch	All
14h00 – 14h45	Leader of team's expectations of work team (customised)	Leader of Team
14h45 – 15h00	Tea/Coffee	All
15h00 – 16h00	Mode of working together and team roles:<ul><li>What type of team are we, for example, athletes, relay, soccer or volleyball?</li><li>Once decided what team we are, what are the implications of this type for us working together?</li><li>Team life cycle (= Forming, Storming, Norming, Performing) and what actions to take to move the team along the life cycle</li></ul>	Group Facilitator
16h00 – 17h00	Team values/norms, code of conduct, team members:<ul><li>Our team values</li><li>Team code of conduct</li><li>Getting to know one another. Who are we as individuals, for example, use animals as an analogy. Each team member to describe him/herself as an animal. Make this a fun exercise</li></ul>	Group Facilitator
19h00 for 19h30	Dinner	All

Day 2		
Time	Subject	Responsible
08h30 – 09h15	Revisit new design, work roles and decision-making rights/styles to clarify understanding. What needs to: • stop • start • continue in terms of new design, roles and decision rights/styles?	Group Facilitator
09h15 – 10h30	Organisational line of sight: Identity (Purpose, Core Values, Dream, Strategic Intent, Legacy); Definition of Victors	Leader of Team
10h30 – 10h45	Tea/Coffee	All
10h45 onwards Note: Work in lunch & tea breaks	• Organisational/business planning process and organisational/ business objectives • Revise work role performance objectives and scorecards • Alignment of budgets	Leader of Team
	• Meeting structure, agenda, information flows, reports and reporting lines	Leader of Team

	• Construct roadmap – The way forward (45 minutes)
	• Hand over log
	• Wrap-up (action planning)
	  o Action
	  o Responsible person(s)
	  o Deadline
	  o Status
		Leader of Team
		Leader of Team
		Group Facilitator

	Closure	Leader of Team

PROGRAMME TEMPLATE 2: STRAW MODEL STRATEGIC DESIGN WORKSHOP (1 DAY)

- Need for the Organisational (re)Design

- Scope of OD assignment and deliverables

- Overall ground rules agreed on

- Organisational identity

- Design foundation

    o Organisational Context
    o Work Processes Map
    o Core Operating Technology with Enablers
    o Design Givens
    o Design Criteria and Design Vision with Design Metaphor
    o Existing Design: Strengths and Weaknesses

- Strategic organisational design map reflecting:

    o Horizontal Design
    o Vertical Design
    o Lateral Design

If more than one design option, show each with pros and cons.

- Strategic design charter

- Required organisational alignments

    o Leadership alignment
    o Culture alignment
    o People alignment
    o Resources alignment
    o Performance alignment

- Strategic Design impact assessment: Gaps and risks with critical actions

PROGRAMME TEMPLATE 3: STRATEGIC CO-DESIGN WORKSHOPS

Typically the workshops need to be one to two weeks apart in order to allow for in-between information collection, the write-up of workshop outputs and the maturing of insights. Do not put workshops too far apart or momentum is lost.

Workshop 1
(2-3 days)

Session 1: Orientation

- Welcome, Purpose, Expected Outcome
- Overview of Workshop
- Overview of Strategic Organisational Design route map
- Ground Rules to inform Design Process

Session 2: Critical organisational profile

Session 3: Laying the foundation

- Organisational Context
- Work Processes Map
- Core Operating Technology with Enablers
- Design Givens
- Design Criteria and Design Vision with Design Metaphor
- Existing Design: Strengths and Weaknesses

Workshop 2
(2-3 days)

Session 4: Horizontal Design

- Grouping of work processes into Work Units: Operating, Enabling and Support Entities, Corporate Centre, Board
- Organisational Shape: Configuration of Work Units
- Ownership of Crown Jewels of organisation
- Organisational partnering opportunities

Session 5: Vertical Design

- Requisite Level of Work for the Organisation Overall
- House Ownership Model
- Requisite Level of Work of each Work Unit

Workshop 3
(2-3 days)

Session 5: Vertical Design (continued)

- Mission critical Work Roles: Identification and Profiling

Session 6: Lateral Design

- Interdependency Matrix
- Integrating Mechanisms
- Governance Model: Decision-making Rights and Styles

Session 7: Integrated Strategic Design

Session 8: Strategic Design Charter

Session 9: Organisational Alignment

- Leadership alignment
- Culture alignment
- People alignment
- Resources alignment
- Performance alignment
- Workplace alignment

Workshop 4
(2-3 days)

Session 10: Strategic Design Impact Assessment: Gaps and risks with critical actions

Session 11: Strategic Design Implementation Road Map

- Design Roll out Strategy and Plan
- Change Navigation Strategy and Plan

Road Ahead/Closure

PROGRAMME TEMPLATE 4: STRAW MODEL, TACTICAL DESIGN WORKSHOP (1 DAY)

- Need for the Organisational (re)Design
- Scope of OD assignment and deliverables
- Overall ground rules agreed on
  - Work Unit Profile – Tactical Design Diagnosis
  - Purpose
  - Input and Output Boundaries
  - Core Inputs and Outputs with Suppliers and Customers
  - Work Processes
  - Core Operating Technology with Enablers
  - Critical Information Requirements
  - Required Lateral Linkages
- Design Foundation
  - Work Unit Context
  - Work Processes Map
  - Core Operating Technology with Enablers
  - Design Givens
  - Design Criteria and Design Vision with Design Metaphor
  - Existing Design: Strengths and Weaknesses
- Tactical Organisational Design Map reflecting:
  - Horizontal Design
  - Vertical Design
  - Lateral Design

If more than one design option, show each with pros and cons.

- Tactical Design Charter
- Required Organisational Alignments
  - Leadership alignment
  - Culture alignment
  - People alignment
  - Resources alignment
  - Performance alignment
  - Workplace Alignment
- Tactical Design Impact Assessment: Gaps and risks with critical actions

PROGRAMME TEMPLATE 5: TACTICAL CO-DESIGN WORKSHOPS

Typically the workshops need to be one to two weeks apart in order to allow for in-between information collection, the write-up of workshop outputs and the maturing of insights.

Workshop 1
(2-3 days)

Orientation
- Welcome, Purpose, Expected Outcome
- Overview of Workshop
- Overview of Tactical Design route map

Session 0: Work Unit Profile – Tactical Design Diagnosis
- Purpose
- Input and Output Boundaries
- Core Inputs and Outputs with Suppliers and Customers
- Work Processes
- Core Operating Technology with Enablers
- Critical Information Requirements
- Required Lateral Linkages

Session 1: Laying the foundation
- Work Unit Context
- Work Processes Map
- Core Operating Technology with Enablers
- Design Givens
- Design Criteria and Design Vision with Design Metaphor
- Existing Design: Strengths and Weaknesses

Workshop 2
(2-3 days)

Session 2: Horizontal Design
- Grouping of Work Processes into Work Domains
- Work Unit Shape: Configuration of Work Domains
- Ownership of Crown Jewels of Work Unit
- Work Unit partnering opportunities

Session 3: Vertical Design
- Requisite Level of Work for the Work Unit
- Work Unit Ownership Model
- Requisite Level of Work for each Work Domain

Workshop 3
(2-3 days)

Session 3: Vertical Design (continued)
- Mission critical Work Roles: Identification and Profiling

Session 4: Lateral Design
- Interdependency Matrix
- Integrating Mechanisms
- Governance Model: Decision-making rights and styles

Session 5: Integrated Work Unit Design

Session 6: Work Unit Charter

Session 7: Organisational Alignment
- Leadership alignment
- Culture alignment
- People alignment
- Resources alignment
- Performance alignment
- Workplace alignment

Workshop 4
(2-3 days)

Session 8: Work Unit Design Impact Assessment: Gaps and risks with critical actions

Session 9: Implementation Road Map

- Design Implementation Strategy and Plan with Measurement Model
- Change Navigation Strategy and Plan

Road Ahead/Closure

PROGRAMME TEMPLATE 6: STRAW MODEL OPERATIONAL DESIGN WORKSHOP (1 DAY PER WORK UNIT)

- Need for the Organisational (re)Design
- Scope of OD Assignment and Deliverables
- Overall ground rules agreed on
- Design Givens
- Operational Design Framework: Elements
  - o Operational Design Vision
  - o Expected People Conduct
  - o Design Criteria
  - o Desired Outcomes
  - o Design Autonomy

- Operational Design Framework: Integrated

- Current Operational Design: Strengths and Weaknesses

- Work Team Design
  - o Rationale for a Team Design
  - o Type(s) of Work Team
  - o Design Criteria and Vision
  - o Integrated Work Team Design Map(s)

- Work Role Design
  - o Design Criteria and Vision
  - o Integrated Work Role Design Map(s) with respective Task Matrices

- Required Work Unit Alignments
  - o Leadership alignment
  - o Culture alignment
  - o People alignment
  - o Resources alignment
  - o Performance alignment
  - o Workplace alignment

- Operational Design Impact Assessment: Gaps and risks with critical actions

PROGRAMME TEMPLATE 7: OPERATIONAL CO-DESIGN WORKSHOPS (PER WORK UNIT)

Typically the workshops need to be one to two weeks apart in order to allow for in-between information collection, the write-up of workshop outputs and the maturing of insights. The length of the workshops will be determined by the number of Work Teams/Work Roles to consider.

Important to note: The Task Matrix of each Work Unit must be generated before the Workshops.

Workshop 1
(2-3 days)

Orientation
- Welcome, Purpose, Expected Outcome
- Overview of Workshop
- Overview of Operational Design route map

Session 1: Work Unit Design Givens

Session 2: Operational Design Framework: Elements
- Design Vision
- Expected People Conduct
- Design Criteria
- Desired Outcomes

Session 3: Design Autonomy

Session 4: Integrated Operational Design Framework

Session 5: Current Design: Strengths and Weaknesses

Workshop 2
(2-3 days)

Session 6: Work Team Design
- Need for Team Design
- Profile Work Team(s)
- Design Criteria and Vision with Design Metaphor
- Architect Team Design
    - Horizontal
    - Vertical
    - Lateral
- Integrated Team Design Map(s)

Session 7: Work Role Design
- Work Role Design Criteria and Vision with Design Metaphor
- Set of Work Roles within Work Unit
- Design Work Role Profile(s)
- Construct different Task Matrices per Work Role
- Lateral Design: Interdependency Matrix, Integrating Mechanisms, Governance Model
- Integrated Work Role Design Maps

Workshop 3
(2-3 days)

Session 8: Competency Profiles

Session 9: Integrated Operational Design and alignment with Operational Design Framework

Session 10: Operational Design Alignment (intra-alignment)

- Leadership alignment
- Culture alignment
- People alignment
- Resources alignment
- Performance alignment
- Workplace alignment

Session 11: Strategic-Tactical Alignments (inter-alignments)

- Leadership alignment
- Culture alignment
- People alignment
- Resources alignment
- Performance alignment
- Workplace alignment

Session 12: Strategic Design Impact Assessment: Gaps and risks with critical actions

Session 13: Implementation Road Map
- Design Implementation Strategy and Plan with Measurement Model
- Change Navigation Strategy and Plan

Road Ahead/Closure

APPENDIX D: REPORT TEMPLATES

INDEX OF REPORT TEMPLATES
Report Template 1: STRATEGIC DESIGN SOLUTION
Report Template 2: BOARD DESIGN SOLUTION
Report Template 3: CORPORATE CENTRE DESIGN SOLUTION
Report Template 4: TACTICAL OPERATIONAL, ENABLING OR SUPPORT UNIT DESIGN SOLUTION
Report Template 5: OPERATIONAL DESIGN SOLUTION – WORK TEAMS AND/OR WORK ROLES

REPORT TEMPLATE 1: STRATEGIC DESIGN SOLUTION

- Executive Overview
- Need for the organisational redesign
- Scope of OD assignment and expected deliverables
- Expected benefits/value-add of revised design
- Ground rules agreed on for the redesign intervention
- Overall Strategic Design Framework
  - Organisational contextual factors impacting on the Design
  - Work Process Map
  - Core Operating Technology with Enablers
  - Design Givens
  - Design Criteria and Design Vision with Design Metaphor
  - Strengths and Weaknesses of current Design
- Integrated Strategic Organisational Design Map reflecting:
  - Strategic Horizontal Design
  - Strategic Vertical Design
  - Strategic Lateral Design
- Strategic Design Charter
- Organisational Landscape alignment required
  - Leadership
  - Culture
  - People
  - Resources Performance
  - Workplace
- Strategic Design Impact Assessment
- Strategic Design Implementation Strategy and Plan: Roll out and change navigation

REPORT TEMPLATE 2: BOARD DESIGN SOLUTION

- Executive Overview
- Need for the Board Organisational (re)Design
- Scope of OD assignment and Deliverables
- Ground rules agreed on
- Overall Tactical Design Framework:
  - Right Positioning: Operating Framework
  - Core Operating Technology and Enablers
  - Design Givens
  - Design Criteria and Design Vision
  - Strengths and Weaknesses of existing Board
- Tactical Organisational Design Solution, reflecting:
  - Horizontal Design
    - ❑ Right Work: Scope of work
    - ❑ Right Mode of Operation: committees, boundaries, flow of work
    - ❑ Right Rhythm: Logical annual sequencing of scope of work tasks
  - Vertical Design
    - ❑ Right Roles and Competencies
  - Lateral Design
    - ❑ Right Agenda
    - ❑ Right Questions
    - ❑ Between meetings updating mechanisms
- Integrated Board Design with visual Integrated Tactical Board Map

If more than one design option, each must be shown with its pros and cons

- Required Board Alignment
  - Leadership
  - Culture
  - People and number
  - Climate
  - Interaction patterns
  - Performance and rewards
- Critical gaps between current and proposed Board Designs
- Suggested Implementation Plan

REPORT TEMPLATE 3: CORPORATE CENTRE DESIGN SOLUTION

- Executive Overview
- Need for the Tactical Organisational (re)Design
- Scope of OD assignment and Deliverables
- Ground Rules agreed on
- Positioning, Role and Scope of Corporate Centre
  - o Direction and Control exercised over its Work Units
  - o Role of Corporate Centre
  - o Scope of Work: Work Domains
- Overall Tactical Design Framework for Corporate Centre
  - o Contextual factors impacting on the Design
  - o Work Process Map
  - o Design Givens
  - o Design Criteria and Design Vision
  - o Strengths and Weaknesses of current Design
- Tactical Organisational Design Solution, reflecting:
  - o Horizontal Design
  - o Vertical Design
  - o Lateral Design

 If more than one design option, each must be shown with its pros and cons

- Corporate Centre Charter
- Required Organisational Alignments
  - o Leadership
  - o Culture
  - o People
  - o Resources
  - o Performance
  - o Workplace
- Critical gaps between current and proposed Designs
- Suggested Implementation Plan

REPORT TEMPLATE 4: TACTICAL OPERATIONAL, ENABLING OR SUPPORT UNIT DESIGN SOLUTION

- Executive Overview
- Need for the organisational redesign
- Scope of OD assignment and expected deliverables
- Expected benefits/value-add of revised design
- Ground rules agreed on for the redesign intervention
- Overall Tactical Design Framework
  - Organisational contextual factors impacting on the Design
  - Work Process Map
  - Core Operating Technology with Enablers
  - Design Givens
  - Design Criteria and Design Vision with Design Metaphor
  - Strengths and Weaknesses of current Design
- Integrated Tactical Design Map reflecting:
  - Tactical Horizontal Design
  - Tactical Vertical Design
  - Tactical Lateral Design
- Tactical Design Charter
- Tactical Design Alignment required
  - Leadership/Management
  - Culture
  - People
  - Resources
  - Performance
  - Workplace
- Tactical Design Impact Assessment
- Tactical Implementation Strategy and Plan: Roll out and change navigation

REPORT TEMPLATE 5: OPERATIONAL DESIGN SOLUTION – WORK TEAMS AND/OR WORK ROLES

- Executive Overview
- Need for the Organisational (re)Design
- Scope of OD assignment and deliverables
- Ground rules agreed on
- Design Givens
- Operational Design Framework: Elements
  - Operational Design Vision
  - Expected People Conduct
  - Design Criteria
  - Desired Outcomes
  - Design Autonomy
- Operational Design Framework: Integrated
- Work Team Design(s)
  - Design Criteria
  - Design Vision
  - Integrated Team Design Map(s)
- Work Role Design(s)
  - Design Criteria
  - Design Vision
  - Integrated Work Role Design Map(s) (Task Matrices per Key Performance Areas for a Work Role can be given as Appendices)
- Required Work Unit Alignments
  - Leadership
  - Culture
  - People
  - Resources
  - Performance
  - Workplace
- Critical gaps between current and proposed Designs
- Suggested Implementation Plan

REFERENCES

Aßländer, M.S. (2011). Corporate social responsibility as subsidiary co-responsibility: A macroeconomic perspective. *Journal of Business Ethics*, 99, 115-128.

Adi, I. (2018). Business exists to deliver value to society. *Harvard Business Review*, March/April 2018, 96(2), 82-87.

Adizes, I. (1988). *Corporate lifecycles. How and why corporations grow and die and what to do about it.* Englewood Cliffs: Prentice Hall.

Adler, P., Hecksher, C. & Prusak, L. (2011). Building a collaborative enterprise. *Harvard Business Review*, July-August 2011, 95-101.

Adler, R.W. & Hiromoto, T. (2012). Amoeba management: Lessons from Japan's Kyocera. *Sloan Management Review*, Fall 2012, 83-89.

Agarwal, D., Bersin, J., Lahiri, G., Schwartz, J. & Volini, E. (2018). *The rise of the social enterprise. 2018 Deloitte Global Human Capital Trends.* Place of publication uncited: Deloitte Development LLC.

Aguinis, H. (2011). Organisational responsibility: Doing good and doing well. In S. Zeldeck (Editor-in-Chief). APA *Handbook of Industrial and Organisational Psychology. Vol 3: Maintaining, expanding and contracting the organisation.* Washington: American Psychological Association, 855-879.

Ambroise, L., Prim-Allaz, I., Teyssier, C. & Peillon, S. (2018). The environment-strategy-structure fit and performance of industrial servitized SMEs. *Journal of Service Management*, 29(2), 301-328. https://doi.org/10.1108/JOSM-10-2016-0276

Anand, N. & Daft, R.L. (2007). What is the right Organisational Design? *Organisational Dynamics*, 36, 329-344.

Anderson, L. & Van der Heyden, L. (2017). *Directing digitisation. Guidelines for boards and executives.* Fountainbleau: Insead.

Arets, J. (2019). *Improving organisational performance? Reinvent your L&D business model in changing times.* Paper presented at Organisational Development Conference 2019 on 27 February, Knowres, Sandton, South Africa.

Ashforth, B. E. & Schinoff, B. S. (2016). Identity under construction: How individuals come to define themselves in organizations. *Annual Review of Organizational Psychology and Organizational Behavior*, 3, 111–137.

ASHE Higher Education Report. (2010). *Partnerships and Collaborations in Higher Education*, 36(2). Hoboken: Jossey-Bass.

Ashton, L. (2017). Work design – how to design the job, not too much and not too little. In M. Bussin (Ed.). *Organisation design for Uber times. Structuring organisations in times of radical change.* Johannesburg: KR Publishing, 123-128.

Aubry, M. & Lavoie-Tremblay, M. (2018). Rethinking Organisational Design for managing multiple projects. *International Journal of Project Management*, 36, 12-26.

Autor, D. H. (2015). Why are there still so many jobs? The history and future of workplace automation. *Journal of Economic Perspectives*, 29, 3–30.

Bailey, C., Madden, A., Alfes, K., Shantz, A. & Soane, E. (2017). The mismanaged soul: Existential labor and the erosion of meaningful work. *Human Resource Management Review*, 27, 416–430.

Bain, N. (2008). *The effective director. Building individual and Board success.* London: Institute of Directors.

Bals, L. & Turkulainen, V. (2017). Achieving efficiency and effectiveness in Purchasing and Supply Management: Organization design and outsourcing. *Journal of Purchasing and Supply Management*, 23, 256-267.

Bartleby (2018). Artificial stimulant. *The Economist*, 15 September 2018, 67.

Bateman, M. & Novkovic, S. (2015). Introduction. *Journal of Co-operative Organization and Management*, 3, 1–2.

Becker, B.E. & Huselid, M.A. (2010). Commentary. SHRM and job design: narrowing the divide. *Journal of Organisational Behaviour*, 31, 379-388.

Bellerby, M. (2017). *Organisational designs. From start-up to global. Dynamic designs for growth.* Johannesburg: KR publishing.

Berg, J.M., Dutton, J.E. & Wrzesniewski, A. (2013). Job crafting and meaningful work. In B.J. Dik, Z.S. Byrne & M.F. Steger (Eds.). *Purpose and meaning in the workplace.* Washington: American Psychological Association, 81-104.

Bergh, V. (2017). Tried and tested organisanisation designs and frameworks. In M. Bussin (Ed.). *Organisation design for Uber times. Structuring organisations in times of radical change.* Johannesburg: KR Publishing, 71-87.

Bernstein, E., Bunch, J. Canner, N. & Lee, M. (2016). Beyond the Holocracy hype. *Harvard Business Review*, July-August 2016, 38–49.

Bersin, J., Geller, J. Wakefield, N. & Walsh, B. (Eds.). (2016). *Global Human Capital Trends 2016. The new organisation: Different by design.* London: Deloitte University Press.

Bersin, J., McDowell, T., Rahnema, A. & van Durme, Y. (2017). The organization of the future. In *Rewriting the rules of the digital age. 2017 Deloitte Global Human Capital Trends.* London: Deloitte University Press 18-27.

Bersin, J., O'Reilly, T., Magoulas, R. & Loukides, M. (2019). *Future of the firm.* Sebastopol: O'Reilly Media, Inc.

Bhalla, V., Dyrchs, S. & Strack, R. (2017). Twelve forces that will radically change how organizations work. *The New Way of Working Series*, Boston Consulting Group, 27 March 2017.

Bikfalvi, A., Ja¨ger, A. & Lay, G. (2014). The incidence and diffusion of teamwork in manufacturing – evidences from a Pan-European survey. *Journal of Organizational Change Management*, 27(2), 206-231. DOI 10.1108/JOCM-04-2013-0052

Birchall, J. (2011). *People-centred businesses. Co-operatives, mutual and the idea of membership*. Houndmills: Palgrave MacMillan.

Birken, M. (2000). *Building the integrated company*. Aldershot: Gower.

Birkinshaw, J. & Ridderstråle, J. (2017*). Fast/Forward. Make your company fit for the future*. Stanford: Stanford Business Books.

Boxall, P. & Macky, K. (2009). Research and theory on high-performance work systems: progressing the high involvement stream. *Human Resource Management Journal*, 19(1), 3–23.

Boynton, A.C. & Victor, B. (1991). Beyond flexibility: Building and managing the dynamically stable organisation. *California Management Review*, Fall 1991, 53-66.

Broomes, V. (2013). Enhancing impact of CSR on economic development and livelihoods in developing countries. In K. Haynes, A. Murray and J. Dillard (Eds.). *Corporate social responsibility. A research handbook*. New York: Routledge, 316-333.

Brophy, K. (2017). What is true organizational design. *NZ Business + Management*, September 2017, 11-12.

Brown, T. with Barry Katz (2019). The new blueprint. *Fortune*, March 2019, 41-43.

Brickley, J.A., Smith, C.W. & Zimmerman, J.L. (2003). *Designing organisations to create value. From strategy to structure*. New York: McGraw.

Bruning, P.F. & Campion, M.A. (2018). A role-resource approach-avoidance model of job crafting: a multimethod integration and extension of job crafting theory. *Academy of Management Journal*, 61(2), 499–522. https://doi.org/10.5465/amj.2015.0604

Bugnar, N., Mester, L. & Petrica Dana, M. (2009). Strategic alliances: from success to failure. Annals of the University of Oradea. *Economic Sciences Series*, 18(1), 202-206.

Burton, R.M. & Obel, B. (2004). *Strategic organizational diagnosis and design*. New York: Springer.

Burton R.M., Obel B. & Håkonsson, D. (2015). *Organizational design: a step-by-step approach*. Cambridge: Cambridge University Press.

Burton, R.M. & Obel, B. (2018). The science of organizational design: fit between structure and coordination. *Journal of Organization Design*, 7(5), 1-13. https://doi.org/10.1186/s41469-018-0029-2

Bussin, M. (2017a). Organisation Design versus Organisation Development – The link. In M. Bussin (Ed.). *Organisation design for Uber times. Structuring organisations in times of radical change*. Johannesburg: KR Publishing, 27-38.

Bussin, M. (2017b). Organisation strategy and anticipating the future – It all starts here. In M. Bussin (Ed.). *Organisation design for Uber times. Structuring organisations in times of radical change*. Johannesburg: KR Publishing, 39-54.

Bussin, M. (2017c). Structure follows strategy. In M. Bussin (Ed.). *Organisation design for Uber times. Structuring organisations in times of radical change*. Johannesburg: KR Publishing, 55-66.

Bussin, M. (2017d). Tall or flat structure? In M. Bussin (Ed.). *Organisation design for Uber times. Structuring organisations in times of radical change*. Johannesburg: KR Publishing, 1129-147.

Cabrera, D., Cabrera, L., Powers, E., Solin, J. & Kushner, J. (2018). Applying systems thinking models of organizational design and change in community operational research. *European Journal of Operational Research*, 268, 932-945.

Cameron, K.S. & Quinn, R.E. (2006). *Diagnosing and changing organisational culture*. San Francisco: Jossey-Bass.

Campion, M. A. (1988). Interdisciplinary approaches to job design: A constructive replication with extensions. *Journal of Applied Psychology, 73*, 467–481.

Campion, M. A. & Thayer, P. W. (1985). Development and field evaluation of an interdisciplinary measure of job design. *Journal of Applied Psychology, 70*, 29–43.

Campion, M.A., Mumford, T.V., Morgeson, F.R. & Nahrgang, J.D. (2005). Work redesign: Eight obstacles and opportunities. *Human Resource Management*, 44(4), 367-390.

Campion, M. A., Mumford, T. V., Morgeson, F. P. & Nahrgang, J. D. (2005). Work redesign: Obstacles and opportunities. *Human Resource Management, 44*, 367–390.

Capelle, R.G. (2014). *Optimising organizational design. A proven approach to enhance financial performance, customer satisfaction and employee engagement*. San Francisco: Jossey-Bass.

Capelle, R.G. (2017). Improving organization performance by optimizing organisation design. *People+Strategy*, Spring 2017, 40(2), 26-31.

Cappelli, P. & Tavis, A. (2018). HR goes agile. *Harvard Business Review*, Mar/Apr2018, 96(2), 46-52.

Chandler A.D. (1962). *Strategy and Structure: Chapters in the History of the American Industrial Enterprise*. Cambridge, MA: MIT Press.

Chandler, C. (2018). Business by design. *Fortune*, 1 January 2018, 45-59.

Charan, R. (2005). *Boards that Deliver. Advancing Corporate Governance from Compliance to Competitive Advantage.* San Francisco, Jossey-Bass.

Chevalier, J. & Gheerbrandt, A. (1996). *A dictionary of symbols.* London: Penguin Books.

Christensen, C.M. & Overdorf, M. (2000). Meeting the Challenge of Disruptive Change. *Harvard Business Review*, March–April 2000, 3-12.

Christos, D. (2017). The future requires a new operating model – The virtual organization. In M. Bussin (Ed.). *Organisation design for Uber times. Structuring organisations in times of radical change.* Johannesburg: KR Publishing, 89-122.

Christos, D. & Bussin, M. (2017). Machines, robots and artificial intelligence In M. Bussin (Ed.). *Organisation design for Uber times. Structuring organisations in times of radical change.* Johannesburg: KR Publishing, 11-25.

Clegg, C.W. (1982). Modelling the practice of job design. In J.E. Kelly & C.W. Clegg (Eds.). *Autonomy and control in the workplace.* London: Croom Helm, 105-127.

Cloete, D. (2019). *Applying complexity theory and thinking to Organisational Design.* Paper presented at Organisational Development Conference 2019 on 27 February, Knowres, Sandton, South Africa.

Collis, D. J., Young, D. & Goold, M. (2007). The size, structure and performance of corporate headquarters. *Strategic Management Journal*, 28, 383–405.

Collis, D. J., Young, D. & Goold, M. (2012). The size and composition of corporate headquarters in multinational companies: Empirical evidence. *Journal of International Management*, 18(3), 260–275.

Conger, J.A., Lawler, E.E. & Finegold, D.L. (2001). *Corporate boards: Strategies for Adding Value at the Top.* San Francisco, Jossey-Bass.

Costa, A.C., Fulmer, C. A. & Anderson, N.R (2018). Trust in work teams: An integrative review, multilevel model, and future directions. *Journal of Organisational Behaviour*, 39, 169–184.

Courtright, S.H., Thurgood, G.R., Stewart, G.L. & Pierotti, A.J. (2015). Structural Interdependence in teams: An integrative framework and meta-analysis. *Journal of Applied Psychology.* Advance online publication. http://dx.doi.org/10.1037/apl0000027

Covin, G. (2015). The 21st century corporation. Every aspect of your business is about to change. *Fortune*, 1 November 2015, 39-47.

Cross, M. (1990). *Changing job structures. Techniques for the design of new jobs and organisations.* Oxford: Heinemann Newnes.

Curphy, G. & Hogan, R. (2012). *The Rocket model. Practical advice for building high performance teams.* Tulsa: Hogan Press.

Curseu, P.L. (2006). Emergent states in virtual teams: a complex adaptive systems perspective. *Journal of Information Technology*, 21(4), 1-16.

Czarniawska, B. (2008). *A theory of organising.* Cheltenham: Edward Elgar.

Da Gama, B. (2019). *Engaging today's employees – exploring tactics that work.* 2019 HR Summit: Building an agile workforce. Mercer Africa, 10-11 April 2019, Sandton.

Daniels, K., Le Blanc, P.M. & Davis, M. (2014). The models that made job design. In M.C.W. Peeters, J. de Jonge & T.W. Taris. *An introduction to contemporary Work Psychology.* Chichester: John Wiley and Sons, 63-88.

Davenport, T.H. (2017). The rise of cognitive work (re)design: Applying cognitive tools to knowledge-based work. In J.Kaji (Ed.). Navigating the future of work. *Deloitte Review*, 21, July 2017, 108-125.

Davis, P. (2001). The governance of co-operatives under competitive conditions: Issues, processes and culture. *Corporate Governance: The International Journal of Business in Society*, 1(4), 28 – 39. http://dx.doi.org/10.1108/EUM0000000005975

Davis-Peccoud, J. & Moolman, T. (2015). Invest smartly by redesigning your operating model. *Business Day*, 18 March 2015.

De Guerre, D.W., Se Guin, D., Pace, A., Burkeida, N. (2013). IDEA: A collaborative design process integrating innovation, design, engagement, and action. *Sysems Practice Action Reseach*, 26, 257-279. DOI 10.1007/S11213-012-9250-Z

Delios, A. (2010). How can organisations be competitive but dare to care? *Academy of Management Perspectives*, 24(3), 25-36.

Demerouti, E. & Bakker, A.B. (2014). Job crafting. In M.C. W. Peeters, J. de Jonge and T.W. Taris (Eds.). *An iIntroduction to Contemporary Work Psychology.* London: John Wiley, 414-433.

Dik, B.J., Byrne, Z.S. & Steger, M.F. (2013). Introduction. Towards an integrative science and practice of meaningful work. In B.J. Dik, Z.S. Byrne & M.F. Steger (Eds.). *Purpose and meaning in the workplace.* Washington: American Psychological Association, 3-14.

Donaldson, L. & Joffe, G. (2015). Fit – The key to Organisational Design. *Journal of Organisation Design*, 3(3), 38-45 (2014). DOI: 10.7146/jod.18424

Doz, Y.L. & Hamel, G. (1998). *Alliance advantage. The art of creating value through partnering.* Boston: Harvard Business Press.

Doz, Y. (2018). Why successful companies usually fail. *INSEAD Knowledge*, 4 September 2018 (downloaded 6/9/2018).

Dubb, S. (2016). Community wealth building forms: What they are and how to use them at the local level. *Academy of Management Perspectives, 30*(2), 141–152. http://dx.doi.org/10.5465/amp.2015.0074

Dunbar, R.L.M. & Starbuck, W.H. (2006). Learning to design organisations and learning from designingthem. *Organisation Science,* 17(2), 171-178.

Eckel, P.D. & Hartley, M. (2009). Developing academic strategic alliances: reconciling multiple institutional cultures, policies and practices. *Journal of Higher Education*, 79(6), 613-637.

Edmondson, A.C. (2012). *Teaming. How organisations learn, innovate, and compete in the knowledge economy.* San Francisco: Jossey-Bass.

Eisenhardt, K.M. & Martin, J.A. (2000). Dynamic capabilities: what are they? *Strategic Management Journal, 21*(10-11), 1105-1121.

Elmuti, D., Abebe, M. & Nicolosi, M. (2005). An overview of strategic alliances between universities and corporations. *The Journal of Workplace Learning*, 17(1/2), 115-129.

Elsbach, K.D. & Stigliani, D.I. (2018). Design thinking and organizational culture: A review and framework for future research. *Journal of Management*, 44(6), 2274 –2306. DOI: 10.1177/0149206317744252

Evans-Greenwood, P., Lewis, H. & Guszcza, J. (2017). Reconstructing work: Automation, artificial intelligence, andthe essential role of humans. In J.Kaji (Ed.). Navigating the future of work. *Deloitte Review*, 21, July 2017, 126-145.

Falletta, S. (2008). *Organizational Diagnostic Models. A Review & Synthesis* (Revised). Place of publication not stated: Leadersphere.

Fenton, E.M. & Pettigrew, A.M. (2000). Theoretical perspectives on new forms of organizing. In A.M. Pettigrew & E.M. Fenton (Eds.). *The innovating organisation.* London: Sage, 1-46.

Ferazzi, K. (2014). Managing yourself. Getting virtual teams right. *Harvard Business Review*, December 2014, 120-123.

Finegold, D., Benson, G.S. & Hecht, D. (2007). Corporate boards and company performance: Review of research in light of recent reforms. *Corporate Governance*, 15(5), 865-878.

Fink, L., Chairman and Chief Executive Officer, BlackRock (2019). *Purpose & Profit: Larry Fink's 2019 Letter to CEOs* (of companies in which BlackRock invests on behalf of its clients).

Fiset, J. & Dostaler, I. (2013). Combining old and new tricks: ambidexterity in aerospace design and integration teams. *Team Performance Management*, 19(7/8), 314-330. DOI 10.1108/TPM-10-2012-0031

Fisher, J. & Grant, B. (2012). Beyond corporate social responsibility: Public value and the business of politics. *International Journal of Business and Management*, 7(7), 2-14.

Fisher, L.M. (2005). Ricardo Semler Won't Take Control. *Strategy + Business*, 29 November 2005, 41 (downloaded 30 March 2019).

Fjeldstad, Ø.D., Snow, C.C., Miles, R.E. & Lettl, C. (2012). The architecture of collaboration. *Strategic Management Journal*, 33(6), 734–775. DOI: 10.1002/smj.1968.

Foss, N.J., Lyngsie, J. & Zahra, S.A. (2015). Organizational design correlates of entrepreneurship: The roles of decentralization and formalization for opportunity discovery and realization. *Strategic Organization*, 13(1), 32–60. DOI: 10.1177/1476127014561944

Friedman, T.L. (2016). *Thank you for being late. An optimist's guide to thriving in the age of accelerations.* London: Allen Lane.

Gadman, S. & Cooper, C. (2005). Strategies for collaborating in an interdependent impermanent world. *Leadership and Organisation Development Journal*, 26(1), 23-34.

Galbraith, J.R., Lawler, E.E. & Associates (1993). *Organising for the future. The new logic for managing complex organisations.* San Francisco: Jossey-Bass.

Galbraith, J.R. (1994). *Competing with flexible lateral organisation.* Reading, MA: Addison-Wesley.

Galbraith, J.R. (1997). *Organisational design.* Reading, MA: Addison-Wesley.

Galbraith, J.R. (2000). *Designing the global organisation.* San Francisco: Jossey-Bass.

Galbraith, J.R., Downey, D. & Kates, A. (2005). *Designing dynamic organisations.* New York: Amacon.

Galbraith, J.R. (2006). Matching strategy and structure. In J.V. Gallos (Ed.). *Organisation development.* San Francisco: Jossey-Bass.

Galbraith, J.R. (2008). Organisation design. In T.G. Cummings (Ed.). *Handbook of organisation development.* Los Angeles: Sage.

Galbraith, J.R. (2014). *Designing organisations.* San Francisco: Jossey-Bass.

Garrett-Cox, K. (2016). *Values and the Fourth Industrial Revolution Connecting the Dots Between Value, Values, Profit and Purpose.* White Paper, Global Agenda Council on Values (2014-2016), September 2016. Cologny/Geneva: World Economic Forum.

Garud, R., Kumaraswamy, A. & Sambamurthy, V. (2006). Emergent by design: Performance and transformation at Infosys technologies. *Organisation Science*, 17, 277–286.

Geldenhuys, C.A. & Veldsman, T.H. (2010). A Change Navigation-based, Scenario Planning Process within a Developing World Context from an Afro-centric Leadership Perspective. *SA Journal of Human Resource Management*, 9(1). DOI:10.4102/sajhrm.v9i1.265.

Gharajedaghi, J. (2011). *Systems thinking. Managing chaos and complexity. A platform for designing business architecture.* Amsterdam: Elsevier.

Ghosal, S. & Bartlett, C. (1998). *The individualised corporation.* London: Heinemann.

Gibney, R., Zagenczyk, T. J., Fuller, J. B., Hester, K. & Caner, T. (2011). Exploring organizational obstruction and the expanded model of organizational identification. *Journal of Applied Social Psychology,* 41(5): 1083–1109.

Gill, L. (2018). 10 Components that successfully abolished hierarchy (in 70+ companies). *Blog Corporate Rebels*, 22 March 2018.

Gilles, R. (2015). Bridging global networks of links the key to success. *Business Day*, 25 February 2015.

Gruber, M., De Leon, N., George, G. & Thompson, P. (2015). Managing by design. *Academy of Management*, 58(1), 1-7.

Gilson, L.L., Maynard, M.L., Jones Young, N.C., Vartiainen, M. & Hakonen, M. (2015). Virtual Teams Research: 10 Years, 10 Themes, and 10 Opportunities. *Journal of Management*, 41(5), 1313–1337. DOI: 10.1177/0149206314559946

Gioia, D. A., Patvardhan, S. D., Hamilton, A. L. & Corley, K. G. (2013). Organisational identity formation and change. *The Academy of Management Annals*, 7(1): 123–192. http://dx.doi.org/10.1080/19416520.2013.762225

Goodman, P.S. & Associates (1986). *Designing effective work groups.* San Francisco: Jossey-Bass.

Goold, M. & Campbell, A. (1987). *Strategies and styles. The role of the centre in managing diversified corporations.* Oxford: Blackwell Publishers.

Goold, M. & Campbell, A. (2002a). Do you have a well-designed organization? *Harvard Business Review*, March 2002, 117-124.

Goold, M. & Campbell, A. (2002b). *Designing effective organisations. How to create structured networks.* San Francisco: Jossey-Bass.

Goold, M. & Campbell, A. (2002c). Parenting in complex structures. *Long Range Planning*, 35, 219–243.

Goold, M. & Campbell, A. (2003). Structured networks: Towards the well-designed matrix. *Long Range Planning*, 36, 425–426. DOI:10.1016/S0024-6301(03)00112-2.

Goold, M., Pettifer, D. & Young, D. (2001). Redesigning the Corporate Centre. *European Management Journal*, 19(1), 83–91.

Gottschalk, T.D.M.D. (2014). Capabilities of the new strategic organization. *Journal of Corporate Real Estate*, 16(4), 290 – 298. http://dx.doi.org/10.1108/JCRE-02-2014-0003

Grant, A.M. (2007). Relational job design and the motivation to make a prosocial difference. *Academy of Management Review*, 32(2), 393–417.

Grant, A.M. & Parker, S.K. (2009). Redesigning work design theories: The rise of relational and proactive perspectives. *The Academy of Management Annals*, 3(1), 317–375.

Grant, A.M., Fried, Y. & Juillerat, T. (2011). Work matters: Job design in classic and contemporary perspectives. In S. Zedeck (Ed.). *APA Handbook of Industrial and Organisational Design. Volume 1: Building and developing the organisation.* Washington: American Psychological Association, 417-453.

Greenwood, R. & Miller, D. (2010). Tackling design anew: Getting back to the heart of organisational theory. *Academy of Management Perspectives*, November 2010, 78-88.

Gruber, M., De Leon, N., George, G. & Thompson, P. (2015). Managing by design. *Academy of Management Journal*, 58(1), 1–7. http://dx.doi.org/10.5465/amj.2015.4001.

Guadalupe, M., Li, H. & Wulf, J. (2013). *Who Lives in the C-Suite? Organizational Structure and the Division of Labor in Top Management.* Working Paper 12-059, 18 June 2013. Boston: Harvard Business School.

Gulati, R., Puranam, P. & Tushman, M. (2012). Meta-organization design: rethinking design in interorganizational and community contexts. *Strategic Management Journal*, 33(6), 571-586. DOI: 10.1002/smj.1975.

Gunsberg, D., Callow, B. Ryan, B. Suthers, J. Baker, P.A. & Richardson, J. (2018). Applying an organisational agility maturity model. *Journal of Organizational Change Management*, 31(6), 1315-1343. https://doi.org/10.1108/JOCM-10-2017-0398

Hackman, R. J. (1987). The design of work teams. In J. W. Lorsch (Ed.). *Handbook of Organizational Behavior.* Englewood, NJ: Prentice-Hall, 315-342.

Hackman, J. R. & Oldham, G. R. (1975). Development of the Job Diagnostic Survey. *Journal of Applied Psychology*, 60, 159–170.

Hackman, J. R. & Oldham, G. R. (1976). Motivation through the design of work: Test of a theory. *Organizational Behavior and Human Performance*, 16, 250–279.

Hackman, J. R. & Oldham, G. R. (1980). *Work redesign.* Reading, MA: Addison-Wesley.

Hamel, G. (2015). What really matters now. *London Business School Review*, 1, 32-33.

Hanna, D.P. (1988). *Designing organisations for high performance.* Boston: Addison-Wesley.

Hansen, J-I. (2013). A person-environment fit approach to cultivating meaning. In B.J. Dik, Z.S. Byrne & M.F. Steger (Eds.). *Purpose and meaning in the workplace.* Washington: American Psychological Association, 37-55.

Harbou, R. & Schmidt, J. (2018). Tomorrow's Factories Will Need Better Processes, Not Just Better Robots. *Harvard Business Review,* 11 May 2018, 2-4.

Harari, Y.H. (2018). *21 Lessons for the 21st century.* London: Jonathan Cape.

Harrison, R. (1972). Understanding your organisation's character. *Harvard Business Review,* May-June 1972, 119-128.

Hawken, P. (2010) (revised edition). *The Ecology of Commerce.* New York: Harper Business.

Hawryszkiewycz, I. (2017). *Designing creative organisations. Tools, processes and practice.* Bingley: Emerald.

Hirschi, A. (2018). The Fourth Industrial Revolution: Issues and implications for career research and practice. *The Career Development Quarterly,* 66, 192-204. DOI: 10.1002/CDQ.12142

Holman, P. (2015). Complexity, self-organisation and emergence. In G.R. Bushe & R.J. Marshak (Eds.). *Dialogic organisation development. The theory and practice of transformational change.* Oakland: Berrett-Koehler, 123-149.

Huber, G.P. (2011). Organisations: Theory, design, future. In S. Zedeck (Ed.). *APA Handbook of Industrial and Organisational Design. Volume 1: Building and developing the organisation.* Washington: American Psychological Association, 117-160.

ICI Chemical & Polymers Ltd. (1989). *Work structuring and job design. A manual.* Wilton, Middlesbrough, Cleveland: ICI Chemical & Polymers Ltd.

Inamizu, N., Fukuzawa, M., Fujimoto, T., Shintaku, J. & Suzuki, N. (2014). Group leaders and teamwork in the over-lean production system. *Journal of Organizational Change Management,* 27(2), 188-205. DOI 10.1108/JOCM-08-2012-0122

International Co-operative Alliance. (2018). https://www.ica.coop/en (sourced 5 June 2018).

Jaques, E. (2006). *Requisite Organisation: A Total System for Effective Managerial Organisation and Managerial Leadership for the 21st Century.* Baltimore: Cason Hall & Co. Publishers.

Jaques E. & Clement, S.D. (1994). *Executive Leadership: a practical guide to managing complexity.* Cambridge, MA: Cason-Hall & Co. Publishers.

Jarillo, J.C. (1993). *Strategic Networks. Creating the borderless organisation.* Oxford: Butterworth-Heinemann.

Jemielniak, D. (2014). *Common Knowledge? An Ethnography of Wikipedia.* Stanford: Stanford University Press.

Jevtić, M., Jovanović, M. & Krivokapić, J. (2018). A new approach to measuring the correlation of organisational alignment and performance. *Management: Journal of Sustainable Business and Management Solutions in Emerging Economies,* 23(1), 41-52. DOI: 10.7595/management.fon.2017.0029

Johns, G. (2010). Commentary. Some unintended consequences of job design. *Journal of Organisational Behaviour,* 31, 361-369.

Kahn, W.A. & Fellows, S. (2013). Employee engagement and meaningful work. In B.J. Dik, Z.S. Byrne & M.F. Steger (Eds.). *Purpose and meaning in the workplace.* Washington: American Psychological Association, 105-126.

Kale, P. & Singh, H. (2009). Managing strategic alliances: what do we know now, and where do we go from here? *Academy of Management Perspectives,* 23(3), 45-62.

Kates, A. & Galbraith, J.R. (2007). *Designing your organisation. Using the Star model to solve 5 critical design challenges.* San Francisco: Jossey-Bass.

Kantur, D. & Eri-Say, A. (2012). Organizational resilience: A conceptual integrative framework. *Journal of Management & Organization,* 18(6), 762–773.

Kaplan, R. S. and Norton, D. P. (1992). The balanced scorecard – measures that drive performance. *Harvard Business Review,* January-February 1992, 71-79.

Katz, D. & Kahn, R.L. (1978). *The social psychology of organisations.* New York: John Wiley & Sons.

Keller, S. & Meaney, M. (2017). *Leading organisations: Ten timeless truths.* London: Bloomsbury.

Kesler, G. & Kates, A. (2011). *Leading organisation design.* San Francisco: Jossey-Bass.

Kelliher, C. & Richardson, J. (Eds.). *New ways of organising work.* New York: Routledge.

King, M. (2002). *King Report on Corporate Governance for South Africa (King II)* (2002). Johannesburg, Institute of Directors in Southern Africa.

Kiron, D. (2017). Why your company needs more collaboration. *MIT Sloan Management Review,* 59(1), 16-19.

Kohlbacher, M. & Reijers, H. A. (2013). The effects of process-oriented organizational design on firm performance. *Business Process Management Journal,* 19(2), 245 – 262. http://dx.doi.org/10.1108/14637151311308303

Kolko, J. (2015). Design thinking comes of age. *Harvard Business Review,* September 2015, 66-71.

Kreiner, G. E. & Murphy, C. 2016. OI work. In M. G. Pratt, M. Schultz, B. E. Ashforth & D. Ravashi (Eds.). *The Oxford Handbook of Organisational Identity.* Oxford: Oxford University Press, 219–238.

Kriek, D. (2019). *Team leadership. Theories, tools and techniques.* Johannesburg: Knowres.

Kurtmollaiev, S., Pedersen, P.E., Fjuk, A. & Kvale, K. (2018). Developing managerial dynamic capabilities: A quasi-experimental field study of the effects of design thinking training. *Academy of Management Learning & Education*, 17(2), 184–202. https://doi.org/10.5465/amle.2016.0187

Kurtz, C. & Snowden, D.J. (2003). The new dynamics of strategy: sense-making in a complex and complicated world. *IBM Systems Journal*, 42, 462-483.

Krishnoorthy, R. (2015). The corporate HQ is an anachronism (A post). *Harvard Business Review*, 13 March 2015.

Laloux, F. (2014). *Reinventing organisations. A guide to creating organisations inspired by the next stage of human consciousness.* Brussels: Nelson Parker.

Lankoski, L. & Smith, N.G. (2017). Alternative objective functions for firms. *Organization & Environment*, Special Issue, 1–21. DOI: 10.1177/1086026617722883.

Lawler, E.E., Finegold, D.L., Benson, G.S. & Conger, J.A. (2002). Corporate Boards: Keys to effectiveness. *Organisational Dynamics*, 30(4), 310-324.

Lawler, E.E. & Worley, C.G. (2012). Designing organizations for sustainable effectiveness. *Organizational Dynamics*, 41, 265–270.

Lawler, E.E. & Conger, J.A. (2015). The sustainable effectiveness model: Moving corporations beyond the philanthropy paradigm. *Organizational Dynamics*, 44, 97–103.

Lee, J., Eon, M., Kim, B. & Katerattanakul, P. (2007). Virtual organisation: resource-based view. *International Journal of e-Business Research*, 3(1), 1-17.

Lee, M.Y. & Edmondson, A.C. (2017). Self-managing organisations: Exploring the limits of less-hierarchical organizing. *Research in Organizational Behavior*, January 2018, 37, 35-58.

Lehtimäki, H. (2017). *The strategically networked organization. Leveraging social networks to improve organisational performance.* Bingley: Emerald.

Levin, A.C. (2005). Changing the role of workplace design within the business organization: A model for linking workplace design solutions to business strategies. *Journal of Facilities Management*, 3(4), 299-311.

Leyer, M., Stumpf-Wollersheim, J. & Pisani, F. (2017). The influence of process-oriented Organisational Design on operational performance and innovation: a quantitative analysis in the financial services industry. *International Journal of Production Research*, 55(18), 5259-5270. DOI: 10.1080/00207543.2017.1304667

Lev, B. (2001). *Intangible Assets: Values, Measures and Risks.* Oxford: Oxford University Press.

Lev, B. (2004). Sharpening the Intangibles Edge. *Harvard Business Review*, June 2004, 109-116.

Limnios, E.A.M., Mazzarol, T., Ghadouani, A. & Scilizzi, G.M. (2014). The resilience architecture framework: Four organisational archetypes. *European Management Journal*, 32, 104-116.

Lin, L. (2014). Organizational structure and acculturation in acquisitions: Perspectives of congruence theory and task interdependence. *Journal of Management*, 40(7), 1831–1856. DOI: 10.1177/0149206312442385

Liao, C. (2017). Leadership in virtual teams: A multilevel perspective. *Human Resource Management Review*, 27, 648–659.

Liu, Y., Sarala, R.M., Xing, Y. & Cooper, C.L. (2017). Human side of collaborative partnerships: A microfoundational perspective. *Group & Organization Management*, 42(2), 151–162. DOI: 10.1177/1059601117695138

Loñar, D. (2005). Postmodern organisation and new forms of organisational control. *Ekonomski anali br 165*, April 2005 – June 2005, 105-119.

Losely, M., Meissinger, S & Ulrich, D. (2005). *The future of Human Resources Management.* New Jersey: John Wiley.

Lu, M., Watson-Manheim, M.B., Chudoba, K.M. & Wynn, E. (2006). Virtuality and team performance: understanding the impact of variety of practices. *Journal of Global Information Technology Management*, 9(1), 4-23.

Luhman, J.T. & Cunliffe, A.L. (2013). *Key concepts in organisation theory.* London: Sage.

Ludik, J. (2019). *Will AI and automation help or hinder good people management – practical implications for HR.* HR Directors Conference, 13-14 March 2019, Knowres, Cape Town.

Lysova, E.I, Blake, B.A, , Dik, B.J, Duff, R.D. & Steger, M.F. (2019). Fostering meaningful work in organizations: A multi-level review and integration. *Journal of Vocational Behavior*, 110, 374-389.

MacAvoy, P.W. & Millstein, I.M. (2003). *The recurrent crisis in corporate crisis.* New York: Palgrave Macmillan.

MacKenzie, K.D. (1986). *Organisational design: The organisational audit and analysis technology.* New Jersey: Alex Publishing Company.

MacKey, J. & Sisodia, R. (2013). *Conscious capitalism.* Boston: Harvard Business Review.

Makarius, E.E. & Larson, B. (2017). Changing the perspective of virtual work: Building virtual intelligence at the individual level. *Academy of Management Perspectives*, 31(2), 159–178. https://doi.org/10.5465/amp.2014.0120

Manderscheid, S.V. & Ardichvili, A. (2008). A conceptual model for leadership transition. *Performance Improvement Quarterly*, 20(3-4), 113-129.

March, J. (Ed.). (1965). *Handbook of organisations.* Chicago: Rand-McNally.

Marcus, M. (2008). Board Capability. An Interactions Perspective on Board of Directors and Firm Performance. *International Studies of Management and Organisation*, 38, 98-116.

Mariani, J., Sniderman, B. & Harr, C. (2017). More real than reality: Transforming work through augmented reality. In J.Kaji (Ed.). Navigating the future of work, *Deloitte Review*, 21, July 2017, 146-163.

Marion, R. (2008). Complexity theory for organisations and organisational leadership. In M. Uhl-Bien & R. Marion (Eds.). *Complexity leadership. Part 1: Conceptual foundations.* Place of publication not indicated: Information Age Publishing, 1-15.

Matheson, C. (2009). Understanding the policy process: The work of Henry Mintzberg. *Public Administration Review*, November/December 2009, 1448-1161.

Mathieu, E. (2012). Reflections on the evolution of the multiteam systems concept and a look into the future. In S.J. Zaccaro, M.A Marks & L.A. DeChurch (Eds.). (2012). *Multi-team systems. An organization form for dynamic and complex environments.* New York: Routledge, 511-544.

Mathieu, J.E., Hollenbeck, J.R., van Knippenberg, D. & Ilgen, D.R. (2017). A century of work teams in the Journal of Applied Psychology. *Journal of Applied Psychology*, 102(3), 452–467. http://dx.doi.org/10.1037/apl0000128

Martens, V. (2019). *Agile organisational development – the new kid on the block.* Paper presented at Organisational Development Conference 2019 on 27 February, Knowres, Sandton, South Africa.

Mazzarol, T., Limnios, E.M. & Reboud, S. (2011). *Co-operative enterprise: A unique business model?* Paper presented at Future of Work and Organisations, 25th Annual ANZAM Conference, 7-9 December 2011, Wellington, New Zealand.

McAfee, A. & Brynjolfsson, E. (2017). *Machine. Platform. Crowd. Harnessing our digital future.* New York: W.W. Norton.

McChrystal, S. (with T. Collins, D. Silverman & C. Fussell). (2015). *Team of teams. New rules of engagement for a complex world.* London: Portfolio Penguin.

MacDonald, C. (2018). Book review of "The Sharing Economy: The End of Employment and the Rise of Crowd-Based Capitalism" by Arun Sundararajan. Cambridge, MA: MIT Press, 2016. *Business Ethics Quarterly*, 28(4), 501–505.

McDowell, T., Agarwal, D., Miller, D., Okamoto, T. & Page, T. (2016). Organizational design. The rise of teams. In J. Bersin, J. Geller, N. Wakefield & B. Walsh (Eds.). *Global Human Capital Trends 2016. The new organisation: Different by design.* London: Deloitte University Press, 17-25.

Meyer, A. (2013). Emerging assumptions about organizational design, knowledge and action. *Journal of Organization Design*, 2(3), 16-22. DOI: 10.7146/jod.2.3.15576

Middleton, J. (2019). *Scaling the organisation – UCOOK case study.* Paper presented at Organisational Development Conference 2019 on 27 February, Knowres, Sandton, South Africa.

Miles, R.E. & Snow, C.C. (1995). The network firm: A spherical structure built on a human investment policy. *Organisational Dynamics*, 23(4), 5-18.

Miles, R.E., Snow, C.C., Fjeldstad, Ø.D., Miles, G. & Lettl, C. (2010). Designing organisations to meet 21st-century opportunities and challenges. *Organizational Dynamics*, 39(2), 93-103.

Minichilli, A., Zattoni, A. & Zona, F. (2009). Making Boards effective: An Empirical Examination of Board Task Performance. *British Journal of Management*, 20(1), 55-74.

Mintzberg, H. (1981). Organisation design: fashion or fit? *Harvard Business Review*, January-February 1981, 100-116.

Mintzberg, H. (1993). *Structure in fives: Designing effective organisations.* Englewood Cliffs, NJ: Prentice-Hall.

Mintzberg, H. (1997). *The structuring of organisations. A synthesis of the research.* Englewood Cliffs, NJ: Prentice-Hall.

Miterev, M., Turner, J. R. & Mancini, M. (2017a). The organization design perspective on the project-based organization: a structured review. *International Journal of Managing Projects in Business*, 10(3), 527-549. https://doi.org/10.1108/IJMPB-06-2016-0048.

Miterev, M., Mancini, M. & Turner, J.R. (2017b). Towards a design for the project-based organization. *International Journal of Project Management*, 35(3), 479-491. DOI: 10.1016/j.ijproman.2016.12.007.

Mohrman, S.A., Cohen, S.G. & Mohrman, A.M. (1995). *Designing team-based organisations. New forms of knowledge work.* San Franscico: Jossey-Bass.

Morgeson, F.P. & Champion, M.A. (2002). Minimising tradeoffs when redesigning work: Evidence from a longitudinal quasi-experiment. *Personnel Psychology*, 55, 589-612.

Morgeson, F. P. & Campion, M. A. (2003). Work design. In W. C. Borman, D. R. Ilgen & R. J. Klimoski (Eds.). *Handbook of psychology: Industrial and organizational psychology* (Vol. 12, pp. 423–452). Hoboken, NJ: Wiley.

Morgeson, F.P. & Humphrey, S.E. (2006). The Work Design Questionnaire (WDQ): Developing and Validating a Comprehensive Measure for Assessing Job Design and the Nature of Work. *Journal of Applied Psychology*, 91(6), 1321–1339.

Morgeson, F. P. & Humphrey, S. E. (2008). Job and team design: Toward a more integrative conceptualization of work design. In J. Martocchio (Ed.). *Research in Personnel and Human Resource Management*, 27, 39–91. London: Emerald Group Publishing. http://dx.doi.org/10.1016/S0742-7301(08)27002-7

Morgeson, F. P., Dierdorff, E.C., Murovic, J.L. (2010). Commentary: Work design in situ: Understanding the role of occupational and organizational context. *Journal of Organisational Behavior*, 31, 351–360.

Moropa, R. (2010). Academic libraries in transition: some leadership issues – a viewpoint. *Library Management*, 31(6), 381-390. DOI 10.1108/01435121011066144

Morton, C., Newall, A. & Sparkes, J. (2001). *Leading HR*. London: Chartered Institute of Personnel and Development.

Mosley, C. & Matviuk, S. (2010). Impact of leadership on identifying right organizational designs for turbulent times. *The IUP Journal of Soft Skills*, 4(1&2), 57-67.

Moussa, M., Bright, M. & Varua, M.E. (2017). Investigating knowledge workers' productivity using work design theory. *International Journal of Productivity and Performance Management*, 66(6), 822-834. DOI 10.1108/IJPPM-08-2016-0161

Mueller, F., Procter, S. & Buchanan, D. (2000). Team working in its context(s): antecedents, nature and dimensions. *Human Relations*, 53(11), 1387-1424.

Mulaudzi, R. (2019). *SA stokvels generate R44 bn each year – but members reap little benefit.* https://www.gsb.uct.ac.za/stokvels (Accessed 8 February 2019).

Mullins, N. (2018). *Mercer Global talent trends 2018. Unlocking growth in the human age.* Presentation at SA Board of People Management, 21 June 2018, Midrand.

Murphy, S.A. & McIntyre, M.L. (2007). Board of Director Performance: A Group Dynamics Perspective. *Corporate Governance*, 7(2), 209-224.

Murray, A. (2015). "Uber-nomics". *Fortune.* 1 January 2015.

Nadler, D. & Tushman, M. (1988). *Strategic organizational design. Concepts, tools and processes.* Glenview: Scott, Foresman and Company.

Nadler, D. A. & Tushman, M. L. (1995). Types of organisational change: From incremental improvements to discontinuous transformation. In D. A. Nadler, R. S. Shaw, A. E. Walton & Associates. *Discontinuous change.* San Francisco: Jossey-Bass.

Nadler, D.A. & Tushman, M.L. (1997). *Competing by design.* Oxford: Oxford University Press.

Nadler, D.A., Behan, B.A. & Nadler, M. (2006). *Building Better Boards. A Blueprint for Effective Governance.* San Francisco: Jossey-Bass.

Naidoo, R. (2009). *Corporate governance. As essential guide for South African companies.* Durban: LexisNexis.

Nedopil, C., Steger, U. & Amann (2011). *Managing complexity in organisations.* Houndmills: Palgrave Macmillian.

Neeley, T. (2015). Global teams that work. A framework to bridge social distance. *Harvard Business Review*, October 2015, 74-81.

Nielsen, K.R. (2018). Crowdfunding through a partial organisational lens – the co-dependent organisation. *European Management Journal*, 36, 695-707.

Nicholson, N. (1990). The transition cycle: Causes, outcomes, processes and forms. In S.F. Fisher and G.L. Cooper (Eds.). *On the move: The psychology of change and transition.* Chichester: John Wiley, 83-108.

Nohri, N. & Eccles, R.G. (1992). *Networks and organisations: Structure, Form, and Action.* Boston: Harvard Business Press.

Nonaka, I., Kodamaa, M., Hirose, A. & Kohlbacker, F. (2014). Dynamic fractal organisations for promoting knowledge-based transformation – A new paradigm for organisational theory. *European Management Journal*, 32, 137-146.

Normark, P. (1996). A role for cooperatives in the market economy. *Annals of Public and Cooperative Economics*, 67(3), 429-439.

Novak, B. (2008). Cisco connects the dots: Aligning leaders with a new organisational structure. *Global Business and Organisational Excellence*, 27(5), 22-32.

Novkovic, S. (2008). Defining the co-operative difference. *The Journal of Socio-Economics*, 37, 2168–2177.

Nusem, E., Wrigley, C. & Matthews, J. (2017). Developing design capability in nonprofit organizations. *Design Issues*, Winter, 33(1), 61-75. DOI: 10.1162/DESI_a_00426

Okechukwu, E. (2016). The Fourth Industrial Revolution by Klaus Schwab. *The Transnational Human Rights Review*, (3): http://digitalcommons.osgoode.yorku.ca/thr/vol3/iss1/4

Ørberg Jensen, P.D., Larsen, M.M. & Pedersen, T. (2013). The organizational design of offshoring: Taking stock and moving forward. *Journal of International Management*, 19, 315–323.

Orhan, M.A. (2014). Extending the individual level of virtuality: Implications of task virtuality in virtual and traditional settings. *Administrative Science*, 4, 400–412. DOI:10.3390/admsci4040400

Owen, J. (2017). *Global teams. How the best teams achieve performance*. Harlow, England: Pearson.

Pearce, J.L. (2013). How can we create collaborative design knowledge in politicized contexts? *Journal of Organization Design*, 2(3), 38-40. DOI: 10.7146/jod.2.3.15517

Pless, N. M., Maak, T. & Waldman, D. A. (20120 Different approaches toward doing the right thing: Mapping the responsibility orientations of leaders. *Academy of Management Perspectives*, 26(4), 51-65.

Poole, M.S. & Contractor, N. (2012). Conceptualising the multiteam system as an ecosystem of networked groups. In S.J. Zaccaro, M.A Marks & L.A. DeChurch (Eds.). (2012). *Multi-team systems. An organization form for dynamic and complex environments*. New York: Routledge, 193-224.

Porter, M.E. (1980). *Competitive strategy. Techniques for analysing industries and competitors*. New York: Free Press.

Porter, M.E. (1985). *Competitive advantage*. New York: Free Press.

Prahalad C.K. & Hamel, G. (1990). The core competence of the corporation. *Harvard Business Review*, 68, 3, 79–91.

Pratt, M. G., Schultz, M., Ashforth, B. E. & Ravashi, D. (2016). Introduction: Organisational identity, mapping where we have been, where we are, and where we might go. In M. G. Pratt, M. Schultz, B. E. Ashforth & D. Ravashi (Eds.). *The Oxford Handbook of Organisational Identity*. Oxford: Oxford University Press, 1–18.

Price, J.F. (2013). Strategic distraction. The consequence of neglecting organizational design. *Air & Space Power Journal*, July–August 2013, 129-139.

Puusa, A. Mönkkönen, K. & Varis, A. (2013). Mission lost? Dilemmatic dual nature of co-operatives. *Journal of Co-operative Organization and Management*, 1, 6–14.

Parker, S.P. (2014). Beyond motivation: Job and work design for development, health, ambidexterity, and more. *Annual Review of Psychology*, 65, 661–91. DOI: 10.1146/annurev-psych-010213-115208.

Parker, S.K., Morgeson, F.P. & Johns, G. (2017). One hundred years of work design research: Looking back and looking forward. *Journal of Applied Psychology*, 102(3), 403–420. http://dx.doi.org/10.1037/apl0000106.

Parker, S.K. & Ohly, S. (2008). Designing motivating jobs. In R. Kanfer, G. Chen & R. Pritchard (Eds.). *Work Motivation: Past, Present, and Future*. SIOP Organizational Frontiers Series, 233-318.

Parker, S. & Wall, T. (1998). *Job and work design: Organizing work to promote well-being and effectiveness*. Thousand Oaks, CA: Sage.

Parker, S. K., Wall, T. D. & Cordery, J. L. (2001). Future work design research and practice: Towards an elaborated model of work design. *Journal of Occupational and Organizational Psychology*, 74, 413–440.

Pasmore, W.A. (1988). *Designing effective organisations: The socio-technical systems perspective*. New York: John Wiley & Sons.

Payne, G.T., Benson, G.S. & Finegold, D.L. (2009). Corporate Board Attributes, Team Effectiveness and Financial Performance. *Journal of Management Studies*, 46(4), 704-731.

Perlmutter, H. 1969. The Tortuous Evolution of the Multi-national Corporation. *Columbia Journal of World Business* January/February 1969, 9-18.

Petković, M., Mirić, A.A. & Čudanov, M. (2014). Designing a learning network organization, *Management*, 73, 17-24. DOI: 10.7595/management.f on.2014.0029

Petrovic, J. (2008). Unlocking the role of a board director: A review of the literature. *Management Decision*, 46, 1373-1392.

Pettigrew, A. & Masini, S. (2001). The adoption of innovative forms of organizing in Europe and Japan in the 1990s. In J. Gual & J.E. Ricart (Eds.). *Strategy, organisation and the changing nature of work*. Cheltenham: Edward Elgar, 169-200.

Pratt, M.G., Pradies, C. & Lepisto, D.A. (2013). Doing well, Doing good, and Doing with. Organisational practices for effectively cultivating meaningful work. In B.J. Dik, Z.S. Byrne & M.F. Steger (Eds.). *Purpose and meaning in the workplace*. Washington: American Psychological Association, 173-196.

Preiser, R., Biggs, R., De Vos, A. & Folke, C. (2018). Social-ecological systems as complex adaptive systems: organizing principles for advancing research methods and approaches. *Ecology and Society*, 23(4), 46. https://doi.org/10.5751/ES-10558-230446

Puranam P. (2012). A future for the science of organisation design. *Journal of Organisation Design*, 1(1), 18–19. DOI: 10.7146/jod.6337

Puranam, P., Alexy, O. & Reitzig, M. (2014). What's 'new' about new forms of organising. *Academy of Management Review, 39(2)*, 162-181.

Rajak, D. (2011). *In good company. An anatomy of corporate social responsibility.* Stanford: Stanford University Press.

Ramos, P.P. (2012). *Network models for organisations. The flexible design of 21st-century companies.* Houndmills, Palgrave Macmillan.

Ranjay, G. (2018). Structure that's not stifling. *Harvard Business Review, 96(3)*, 68-79.

Ravashi, D. (2016). Organisational identity, culture, and image. In M. G. Pratt, M. Schultz, B. E. Ashforth & D. Ravashi (Eds.). *The Oxford Handbook of Organisational Identity.* Oxford: Oxford University Press, 65–78.

Reason, P. & Bradbury, H. (Eds). (2002). *Handbook of Action Research: Participative Inquiry and Practice.* Thousand Oaks: Sage.

Reddy, D. (2019). *Case study: How organisations are changing to meet the demands of the Fourth Industrial Revolution.* Paper presented at Organisational Development Conference 2019 on 27 February, Knowres, Sandton, South Africa.

Rezaee, Z. 2009. *Corporate governance and ethics.* New Jersey: John Wiley & Sons.

Rigby, D.K, Sutherland, J. & Noble, A. (2018). Agile at scale. How to go from a few teams to hundreds. *Harvard Business Review*, May-June 2018, 1-10.

Rφd, A. & Fridjhon, M. (2016). *Creating intelligent teams.* Johannesburg: kr publishing.

Roberts, J. (2004). *The modern firm. Organisation design for performance and growth.* Oxford: Oxford University Press.

Roghé, F., Pidun, U., Stange, S. & Krühler, M. (2013). *Designing the corporate center: How to Turn Strategy into Structure.* Boston: Boston Consulting Group.

Roghé, F., Toma, A. Scholz, S. Schudey, A. & Koike, J.K. (2017). Boosting performance through organization design. *The New Way of Working Series.* Boston: Boston Consulting Group.

Roh, J., Turkulainen, V., Whipple, J.M. & Swink, M. (2017). Organizational design change in multinational supply chain organisations. *The International Journal of Logistics Management, 28(4)*, 078-1098. https://doi.org/10.1108/IJLM-06-2016-0146

Rolfsen, M. & Johansen, T.S. (2014). The silent practice: sustainable self-managing teams in a Norwegian context. *Journal of Organizational Change Management, 27(2)*, 175-187. DOI 10.1108/JOCM-08-2012-0124

Rosen, E. (2009). *The culture of collaboration.* San Francisco: Red Ape Publishing.

Rowbottom, R. & Billis, D. (1987). *Organisational design. The Work-level approach.* Aldershot: Gower.

Ryde, R. & Sofianos, L. (2014). *Creating authentic organisations. Bringing meaning and engagement back to work.* London: Kogan Page.

Salas, E. & Fiore, S.M. (2012). Why work teams fail in organisations: Myths and advice. In L.M. Shore, J.A-M. Coyle-Shapiro & L.E. Tetrick. *The employee-organisation relationship. Applications for the 21st century.* New York: Routledge Taylor & Francis, 533-554.

Salas, E., Shuffler, M.L., Thayer, A.L., Bedwell, W.L. & Lazzara, E.H. (2015). Understanding and improving teamwork in organisations: A scientifically based practical guide. *Human Resource Management, 54(4)*, 599–622. DOI:10.1002/hrm.21628

Santos, F., Pache, A. & Birkholz, C. (2015). Making hybrids Work: Aligning business models and organizational design for social enterprises. *California Management Review, 57(3)*, Spring 2015, 36-58. DOI: 10.1525/cmr.2015.57.3.36

Saporito, B. (2015). Making good, plus a profit. *Time*, 23 March 2015.

Schaufeli, W. B., Salanova, M., González-Romá, V. & Bakker, A.B. (2002). The measurement of engagement and burnout: A confirmatory factor analytic approach. *Journal of Happiness Studies, 3(1)*, 71-92.

Schaufeli, W. B., Bakker, A. B. & Salanova, M. (2006). The measurement of work engagement with a short questionnaire. *Educational and Psychological Measurement, 66(4)*, 701-716. 10.1177/0013164405282471.

Schildt, H. (2017). Big data and organizational design – the brave new world of algorithmic management and computer augmented transparency. *Innovation, 19(1)*, 23-30, DOI:10.1080/14479338.2016.1252043.

Schilling, M.A. & Steensma, H.K. (2001). The use of modular organisational forms: An industry-level analysis. *Academy of Management Journal, 44(6)*, 1149-1168.

Schinoff, B. S., Rogers, K. M. & Corley, K. G. (2016). How do we communicate who we are? In M. G. Pratt, M. Schultz, B. E. Ashforth & D. Ravashi (Eds.). *The Oxford Handbook of Organisational Identity.* Oxford: Oxford University Press, 219–238.

Schmidtke, J.M. & Cummings, A. (2017). The effects of virtualness on teamwork behavioral components: The role of shared mental models. *Human Resource Management Review, 27*, 660–677.

Schumpter (2016). Team spirit. *The Economist*, 19 March 2016, 60.

Schumpeter (2014). The holes in holacracy. *The Economist*, 5 July 2014, 59.

Schwab, K. (2016). *Four leadership principles for the Fourth Industrial Revolution.* Davos: World Economic Forum, 11 October 2016. https://www.weforum.org/agenda/2016/10/four-leadership-principles-for-the-fourth-industrial-revolution/. (downloaded 11/06/2018).

Schwarzmüller, T., Brosi, P., Duman, D. & Welpe, I.M. (2018). How does the digital transformation affect organizations? Key themes of change in work design and leadership. *mrev*, 29(2), 114 – 138. DOI: 10.5771/0935-9915-2018-2-114.

Semler, R. (1994). *Maverick! The success story behind the world's most unusual workplace.* London: Arrow.

Semler, R. (1989). Managing without managers. *Harvard Business Review*, September-October 1989 (downloaded 30 March 2019).

Shephard, K., Gray, J.L., Hunt, J.G. & McArthur, S. (2007). *Organisation design, levels of work and human capability*. Ontario: Global design society.

Silva, A.L. & Guerrini, F.M. (2018). Self-organized innovation networks from the perspective of complex systems: A comprehensive conceptual review. *Journal of Organizational Change Management*, 31(5), 962-983. https://doi.org/10.1108/JOCM-10-2016-0210

Skekhar, S. (2006). Understanding the virtuality of virtual organisations. *Leadership & Organisation Development Journal*, 27(6), 465-483.

Skurnik, S. (1999). The role of cooperative entrepreneurship and firms in organising economic activities – Past, Present and Future. *The Finnish Journal of Business Economics*, 1, 103-124.

Smith, C. & Lankosi, L. (2018). Balancing profit and social welfare: Ten ways to do it. *Insead Knowledge*. https://knowlege.insead.educ/responsibility//balancing-profit-and-socail-welfare-ten-ways-to-do-it-9421 (accessed 4 July 2018).

Spear, R. (2000). The co-operative advantage. *Annals of Public and Cooperative Economics*, 71(4), 507-523.

Stanford, N. (2007). *Guide to Organisational Design*. London: The Economist in association with Profile Books.

Sparrow, P., Hird, M., Hesketh, A. & Cooper, C. (2010). *Leading HR*. Houndmills: Palgrave Macmillan.

Snow, C.C., Miles, R.E. & Miles, G. (2006). The configurational approach to organizational design: Four recommended initiative. In R.M. Burton, B. Eriksen, B., D.D. Häkonsson & C.C. Snow (Eds.). *Organisation design. The evolving state-of-the-art*. New York: Springer, 3-18.

Snowden, D.J. & Boone, M.E. (2007). A leaders' framework for decision-making. *Harvard Business Review*, November 2007, 1-8.

Wikipedia. (2019). *Spotify*. https://en.wikipedia.org/wiki/Spotify (downloaded 1/03/2019)

Sparrow, P., Hird, M., Hesketh, A. & Cooper, C. (2010). *Leading HR*. Houndmills: Palgrave Macmillan.

Stacey, R.D., Griffin, D. & Shaw, P. (2000). *Complexity and management. Fad or radical challenge to systems thinking?* London: Routledge.

Stacey, R. (2015). Understanding organisations as complex responsive processes of relating. In G.R. Bushe & R.J. Marshak (Eds.). *Dialogic organisation development. The theory and practice of transformational change*. Oakland: Berrett-Koehler, 151-176.

Stanford, N. (2015). *Guide to organisation design. Creating high-performing and adaptable enterprises.* London: The Economist in association with Profile Books.

Stein, J. (2015). Baby, you can drive my car. And stay in my guest room. And do my errands. And rent my stuff. My wild ride through the new on-demand economy. *Time*, 9 February 2015.

Steinmetz, K. (2016). The way we work. A poll reveals the size of the peer-to-peer revolution. *Time*, 18 January 2016, 34-37.

Stodd, J. (2016). Organisational design for a socially dynamic organization. Special supplement: Digital age learning, *EFMD Business Magazine*, 11(2), www.globalfocusmagazine, 11-14.

Sutcliffe, H. & Allgrove, A-M. (2018). *How do we build an ethical framework for the Fourth Industrial Revolution?* World Economic Forum, 7 November 2018 (downloaded on 12/3/2019).

Sutherland, J. (2012). *The Agile Manifesto, Elaborated*. https://www.scruminc.com/agile-manifesto-elaborated-2/ (downloaded 27 February 2019).

Szilagyi, A.D. & Wallace, M.J. (1983). *Organisational behaviour and performance*. Dallas: Scott, Foresman and Company.

Tafoya, D.W. (2010). *The effective organisation. Practical application of complexity theory and organizational design to maximize performance in the face of emerging markets.* New York: Routledge.

Tannenbaum, R. & Schmidt, W.H. (1958). How to choose a leadership pattern. *Harvard Business Review*, 36, 95-101.

Taylor, F. W. (1911). *The principles of scientific management*. New York: Norton.

Teece, D.J. (2010). Business Models, Business Strategy and Innovation. *Long Range Planning*, 43, 172-194.

The Economist. (2010). *The World Turned upside down. Special Report.* 17 April 2010.

The Economist. (2015). *The future of work. There's an app for that.* 3 January 2015, 15-18.

The Economist. (2016). *Artificial Intelligence. Special Report.* 25 June 2016.

The Economist. (2017). *Sofas and surveillance. The office of tomorrow.* 29 April 2017, 49-50.

The Economist. (2018a). *GrAIt expectations. Special report. AI in business.* 31 March 2018, 1-12.

The Economist. (2018b). *Thinking outside the box. Digitisation will not just transform how goods are moved around the world, but also how the world shops.* 28 April 2018, 20-22.

Thite, M., Wilkinson, A. & Shah, D. (2012). Internationalization and HRM Strategies across Subsidiaries in Multinational Corporations from Emerging Economies – a Conceptual Framework. *Journal of World Business* 47, 251-258.

Thorelli, H.B. (1986). Networks: Between markets and hierarchies. *Strategic Management Journal*, 7(1), 37-51.

Thoren, P-M. (2017). *Agile people: A radical approval for HR Managers.* Sweden: Lioncrest & Johannesburg: Knowledge Resources.

Tims, M., Bakker, A.B., Derks, D. & van Rhenen, W. (2013). Job crafting at the team and individual level: Implications for work engagement and performance. *Group & Organization Management*, 38(4), 427–454. DOI: 10.1177/1059601113492421

Tims, M., Bakker, A.B. & Derks, D. (2015). Examining job crafting from an interpersonal perspective: Is employee job crafting related to the well-being of colleagues? *Applied Psychology: An International Review*, 64(4), 727–753. DOI: 10.1111/apps.12043

Tolchinsky, P.D. & Wenzl, L. (2014). High engagement organization design. *People & Strategy*, 37(1), 34-38.

Ulrich, D. (1997). *Human Resource Champions.* Boston: Harvard Business School Press.

Ulrich, D. & Brockbank, W. (2005). *The HR Value Proposition.* Boston: Harvard Publishing Company.

Ulrich, D., Brockbank, W., Younger, J. & Ulrich, M. (2012). *HR from the outside in. Six competencies for the future for human resources.* New York: McGrawHill.

Ulrich, D., Brockbank, W., Younger, J. & Ulrich, M. (2013). *Global HR competencies.* New York: McGrawHill.

Vandewaerde, M., Voordeckers, W., Lambrechts, F. & Bammens, Y. (2011). The board of directors as a team: getting inside the black box. *Proceedings of the 7th European Conference on management, leadership and governance.* Sophia-Antipolis, France, 6-7 October 2011, 436-442.

Van Eeden, D. (2019). *Creating next generation organisations: Embarking on a journey of transformation Semco-style.* HR Directors Conference, 13-14 March 2019, Knowres, Cape Town.

Van Ees, H. Gabrielsson, J. & Huse, M. (2009). Toward a Behavioral Theory of Boards and Corporate Governance. *Corporate Governance: An International Review*, 17(3), 307-319.

Van Tonder, C. L. (2004). Below-the-surface and powerful: The emerging notion of organization identity. *Organization Development Journal*, 22(2), 68–78.

Veldsman, T.H. (1995). The philosophy behind self-managing work teams. *SA Journal for Industrial Psychology*, 26, 152-160.

Veldsman, T.H. (2001). *To have a future or not? Reinventing People Management to fit a different competitive reality.* Top HR Conference, August 2001, Midrand.

Veldsman, T.H. (2002a). Introduction. Experiencing the heat in the People Effectiveness Arena. Engaging with the forces and counterforces of change. T.H. Veldsman. *Into the people effectiveness arena. Navigating between chaos and order.* Johannesburg: Knowledge Resources, 1-11.

Veldsman, T.H. (2002b). Plastic surgery, Heart transplant or a different DNA code? T.H. Veldsman. *Into the people effectiveness arena. Navigating between chaos and order.* Johannesburg: Knowledge Resources, 100-123.

Veldsman, T.H. (2007a). The People Effectiveness Compass: Holding a Steady Course in Worsening Weather Conditions (Part 1). *Management Today*, 23(8), 58-60.

Veldsman, T.H. (2007b). The People Effectiveness Compass: Holding a Steady Course in Worsening Weather Conditions (Part 2). *Management Today*, 23(9), 58-60.

Veldsman, T.H. (2008a). People Management in the New Order. In Pursuit of Leading World-class Practices (Part 1). *Management Today*, 24(8):56-60.

Veldsman, T.H. (2008b). People Management in the New Order. In Pursuit of Leading World-class Practices (Part 2). *Management Today*, 24(9):60-64.

Veldsman, T.H. (2008c). A typology of organisational change interventions: turning the working horses of organisational change into winners. In C. van Tonder & G Roodt (Eds.). *Organisational Development.* Pretoria: Van Schaik, 193-217.

Veldsman, T.H. (2011). Strategic Talent Partnering between Higher Educational Institutions and Organisations. In I. Boninelli & T. Meyer (Eds.). *Human Capital Trends.* Johannesburg: Knowres Publishing, 83-111.

Veldsman, T.H. (2012a). An Organisation Person-fit Competency Model Appropriate to a Newly Emerging World of Work. In J. Herholdt (Ed.). *Managing performance in organisations.* Johannesburg: Knowledge Resources, 53-76.

Veldsman, T.H. (2012b). The soft underbelly of corporate governance (Part 1): The hardware of board Dynamics. *African Journal of Business Ethics*, 6(1), 56-64.

Veldsman, T.H. (2012c). The soft underbelly of corporate governance (Part 2): The software of board Dynamics. *African Journal of Business Ethics*, 6(1), 65-74.

Veldsman, T.H. (2013). Ten critical features of becoming a high performance/high engagement/high responsibility organisation: the critical key is people effectiveness. *Human Capital Review*, May 2013.

Veldsman, T.H. (2014). Designing HR. In D. van Eden (Ed.). *The Chief Human Resource Officer*. Johannesburg: Knowledge Resources, 313-342.

Veldsman, T.H. (2015a). *Whereto Organisational Design? In search of design Criteria for future-fit organisations?* Proceedings of the 11th European Conference on Management Leadership and Governance (ECMLG), Military Academy, 12-13 November 2015 edited by J.C.D. Rouco. Reading: Academic Conferences and Publishing International Ltd.

Veldsman, T.H. (2015b). The power of the fish is in the water. *African Journal of Business Ethics*, 9(1), 63-83

Veldsman, T.H. (2016a). The world of tomorrow: Leadership challenges, demands and requirements. In T.H. Veldsman and A.J. Johnson. (Eds). *Leadership. Perspectives from the Front Line.* Johannesburg: Knowres, 169-188

Veldsman, T.H. (2016b). The Leader Landscape as a meta-framework. In T.H. Veldsman and A.J. Johnson. (Eds). *Leadership. Perspectives from the Front Line.* Johannesburg: Knowres, 13-30.

Verwey, A., Du Plessis, F. & Haveman, Y. (2017). Global changes and UBER times ahead. In M. Bussin (Ed.). *Organisation design for Uber times. Structuring organisations in times of radical change.* Johannesburg: KR Publishing, 1-9.

Visser, W. (2011). *The age of responsibility. CSR 2.0 and the new DNA of business.* Chichester: John Wiley.

Visscher, K. & Visscher-Voerman, J.I.A. (2010). Organisational design approaches in management consulting. *Management Decision*, 48(5), 713-731.

Vogt, K., Hakanen, J.J. Brauchli, R., Jenny, G.J. & Bauer, G.F. (2016). The consequences of job crafting: a three-wave study. *European Journal of Work and Organizational Psychology*, 25(3), 353–362. http://dx.doi.org/10.1080/1359432X.2015.1072170

Wall, T.D. (1982). Perspectives on job redesign. In J.E. Kelly & C.W. Clegg (Eds.). *Autonomy and control in the workplace.* London: Croom Helm, 1-20.

Walters, D. (2005). Performance planning and control in virtual business structures. *Production Planning & Control*, 16(2), 226-236.

Walton, R.E. & Hackman, J.R. (1986). Groups under contrasting management strategies. In P.S Goodman & Associates. *Designing effective work groups.* San Francisco: Jossey-Bass, 168-201.

Webster, J. & Wong, W.K.P. (2008). Comparing traditional and virtual group forms: identity, communication and trust in naturally occurring project teams. *The International Journal of Human Resource Management*, 19(1), 41-62.

Wegman, L.A., Hoffman, B.J., Carter, N.T., Twenge, J.M. & Guenole, N. (2018). Placing job characteristics in context: Cross-temporal meta-analysis of changes in job characteristics since 1975. *Journal of Management*, 44(1), 352–386. DOI: 10.1177/0149206316654545

Weiss, R. (1990). Losses associated with mobility. In S.F. Fisher and G.L. Cooper (Eds.). *On the move: The psychology of change and transition.* Chichester: John Wiley, 3-12. West, M.A. (1994). *Effective teamwork.* Leicester: BPS Books.

West, M.A. (2008). Effective teams in organisations. In N. Chmiel (Ed.). *An introduction to Work and Organisational Psychology. A European perspective.* Oxford: Blackwell Publishing, 305-328.

Wheatley, M. J. (2010). *Leadership and the new science: Discovering order in a chaotic world.* San Francisco, CA: Berrett-Koehler.

Whitley, R. (2006). Project-based firms: new organisational form or variation on a theme? *Industrial and Corporate Change*, 15(1), 77-99. DOI:10.1093/icc/dtj003.

Wikipedia. (2019) *Semco.* https://en.wikipedia.org/wiki/Ricardo_Semler (downloaded 25 March 2019).

Wikipedia. (2019). *Stokvels.* https://en.wikipedia.org/wiki/Stokvel (accessed on 5 February 2019).

Williams, G., Haarhoff, D. & Fox, P. (2015). *The virtuosa organization.* Johannesburg: Knowres Publishing.

Wood, S. & de Menezesb, L.M. (2011). High involvement management, high-performance work systems and well-being. *The International Journal of Human Resource Management*, 22(7), 1586–1610.

Worley, C.G. & Lawler, E.E. (2010). Agility and organizational design: A diagnostic framework. *Organisational Dynamics*, 39(2), 194-204.

Wright, P.M., Boudreau, J.W., Pace, D.A., Sartain, E.L., McKinnon, P. & Antoine, R.L. (2011). (Eds.). *The Chief HR Officer. Defining the new role of Human Resource Leaders.* San Francisco: Jossey-Bass.

Wrzesniewski, A. & Dutton, J.E. (2001). Crafting a job: Revisioning employees as active crafters of their work. *Academy of Management Review*, 26, 179-2017.

Wrzesniewski, A., Berg, J.M. & Dutton, J.E. (2010). Turn the job you have into the job you want. *Harvard Business Review*, 88, 114-117.

Yeoman, R. & O'Hara, J. (2017). *Meaningfulness and mutuality: Principles for organizational design.* http://www.hrmagazine.co.uk/article-details/meaningfulness-and-mutuality-principles-for-organizational-design. (Downloaded 5 June 2018).

Yoo, Y., Boland, R.J. & Lyytinen, K. (2006). From organisation design to organisation designing. *Organisation Science*, 17(2), 215-229.

Zaccaro, S.J., Marks, M.A. & DeChurch, L.A. (2012). Multi-team systems: An Introduction. In S.J. Zaccaro, M.A Marks & L.A. DeChurch (Eds.). (2012). *Multi-team systems. An organization form for dynamic and complex environments.* New York: Routledge, 3-32.

Zamagni, S. & Zamagni, V. (2010). *Cooperatve enterprise. Facing the challenge of globalisation.* Cheltenham: Edward Elgar.

Zammuto, R. F., Griffith, T. L., Majchrzak, A., Dougherty, D. J. & Faraj, S. (2007). Information technology and the changing fabric of organization. *Organization Science, 18,* 749–762.

Zhang, S. & Fjermestad (2006). Bridging the gap between traditional leadership theories and virtual team leadership. *International Journal of Technology, Policy and Management,* 6(3), 274-291.

Zhang, F. & Parker, S.K. (2019). Reorienting job crafting research: a hierarchical structure of job crafting concepts and integrative review. *Journal of Organisational Behaviour,* 40, 126-146.

Zineldin, M. (2004). Co-opetition: the organisation of the future. *Marketing Intelligence and Planning,* 22(7), 780-789.

Zona, F. & Zattoni, A. (2007). Beyond the Black Box of Demography: Board Processes and Task Effectiveness within Italian firms. *Corporate Governance,* 15(5), 852-864.

INDEX